Early Modern English Drama

A Critical Companion

Edited by

Garrett A. Sullivan, Jr.
The Pennsylvania State University

Patrick Cheney
The Pennsylvania State University

Andrew Hadfield
University of Sussex

New York Oxford
OXFORD UNIVERSITY PRESS
2006

Oxford University Press, Inc., publishes works that further Oxford University's objective of excellence in research, scholarship, and education.

Oxford New York
Auckland Cape Town Dar es Salaam Hong Kong Karachi
Kuala Lumpur Madrid Melbourne Mexico City Nairobi
New Delhi Shanghai Taipei Toronto

With offices in
Argentina Austria Brazil Chile Czech Republic France Greece
Guatemala Hungary Italy Japan Poland Portugal Singapore
South Korea Switzerland Thailand Turkey Ukraine Vietnam

Published by Oxford University Press, Inc.
198 Madison Avenue, New York, New York 10016
http://www.oup.com

Oxford is a registered trademark of Oxford University Press

Library of Congress Cataloging-in-Publication Data

Early modern English drama : a critical companion / edited by Garrett A. Sullivan, Jr.; Patrick Cheney; Andrew Hadfield.
p. cm.
Includes bibliographical references and index.
ISBN 13: 978-0-19-515386-6 (pbk. : alk. paper)
ISBN 0-19-515386-3 (pbk. : alk. paper)
1. English drama—Early modern and Elizabethan, 1500–1600—History and criticism.
2. English drama—17th century—History and criticism. I. Sullivan, Garrett A. II. Cheney, Patrick Gerard, 1949– III. Hadfield, Andrew.

PR653.E17 2006
822'.309—dc22 2004066273

Printed in the United States of America
on acid-free paper

Contents

Preface

The editors intend this volume to serve as a complementary text in a college or university course in Renaissance drama, undergraduate or graduate. Whereas most "companion" texts divide material according to topics, ours begins with a slightly different structural principle: authors and their works. In its broadest contour, we have designed the volume to address this classroom model: students will read plays, typically by known authors (sometimes by more than a single author); and students will benefit from reading informed commentary, geared to their needs and representing important topics of recent critical inquiry. For each work, an authoritative contributor addresses not only a play but also a specific cultural or literary topic, from London to the law, servants to sovereigns, geography to Jews. Through this design, we hope that students will read most of the great plays and authors of the period, at the same time that they acquire familiarity with various topics vital for understanding a special area of investigation.

The Introduction's brief discussion of the conditions of playgoing in early modern England is extended in the next two chapters, which also help to contextualize the rest of the volume. The first chapter (by Wendy Wall) addresses the question of authorship itself, especially the problematic relation between an author's (or authors') writing of a play for the stage and the fact that such a work might eventually find its way into print, with or without the author's (or authors') consent. The environment of dramatic authorship and publication in Elizabethan, Jacobean, and Caroline England differs from that in our time, and students will want to know something about this topic. As such, the overall purpose of this chapter is not to simplify authorship but to complicate it. The second chapter complements the first by looking further into the environment of the stage itself by focusing on theater companies and the conditions of play performance.

The remaining chapters examine as many works that we have space for in a single volume. We have organized this larger set of chapters according to a general chronology of dates for composition, performance, or publication. For twenty-three of the plays, the authors are known. (In the case of *The Revenger's Tragedy*, the play's authorship is contested, whereas *Arden of Faversham* remains anonymous.) One chapter (by Martin Butler) discusses the masque, an intermediary form between plays and the other major form of the period, poetry, in relation to Ben Jonson's *Masque of Blackness.* Three playwrights are featured with four chapters devoted to each because they invented and established the institution of English drama for the centuries to come: Christopher Marlowe, William Shakespeare, and Ben Jonson. Other dramatists who appear in more than a single chapter include Thomas Middleton and John Webster. Henry Medwall, Thomas Kyd, Francis Beaumont, John Fletcher, William Rowley, Elizabeth Cary, and John Ford round out the theatrical cast.

The volume's full cast is not arbitrary, as we include those authors and works most often taught in college and university courses. The recent publication of two anthologies of Renaissance drama, Arthur Kinney's *Blackwell Anthology of Renaissance Drama* and David Bevington et al.'s *English Renaissance Drama: A Norton Anthology,* confirms many of our choices, while identifying primary course texts that our volume well complements. For Marlowe, Shakespeare, and Jonson, teachers and students alike will lament the absence here of such plays as *Dido, Queen of Carthage, The Tempest,* and *Epicoene,* to name just a few obvious omissions (we were not able to commission a chapter on Dekker's *Shoemaker's Holiday*). Yet we had to make choices, in some cases by selecting plays that focused centrally on topics we thought important.

Teachers and students will find opportunity to use the volume in a variety of ways. Most obviously, they may read an individual chapter on a play assigned on a particular class day. But they might also like to *transport* topics from one play to another. Most of the chapters provide "background" or "contextual" material on the designated topic. Yet many of the topics pertain directly to many of the plays. As a result, readers can easily consider the topic taken up in conjunction with one play in relation to another. For instance, readers could transport the topic of "the humoral body" from *Bartholomew Fair* (in Gail Kern Paster's chapter) to any number of plays, such as Shakespeare's *Othello.* Similarly, readers might find the chapter on comedy in *Twelfth Night* (from Robert Maslen's chapter) portable to many other comedies, such as Middleton's *A Chaste Maid in Cheapside.* Moreover, if teachers and students are reading a play not covered in the volume, they may nonetheless find some information relevant to it. Thus, if the class is focusing on Marlowe's *Dido,* readers might take a look at the chapter on Jonson's *Volpone* (by Raphael Lyne) because it focuses on "the classics." Or if the class is reading Jonson's *Epicoene,* they might examine the chapter on Marlowe's *Edward II* (by Alan Stewart) because it focuses on "same-sex relations." There are many such possibilities, and we encourage teachers and students to experiment in ways that might prove fruitful. Even though we have had to make choices, we hope our design affords a comprehensive approach to an expansive and complex field.

To augment our design, we have had contributors include a reading list at the end of each chapter, so that teachers and students can follow up their work through a recommended set of secondary works. A chronology of Renaissance drama precedes the present introduction and is geared to the contents of the volume; at the back, we conclude with a unit providing brief biographies of the authors included.

Acknowledgments

This volume began through conversations with Tony English, our former editor at Oxford University Press in New York. We would like to thank Tony for ushering in the project and for carrying it through its early phases. We would also like to thank Jan Beatty, executive editor at OUP, for her help with later phases, and her assistant editor, Talia Krohn, for serving as liaison.

The Press supplied five anonymous readers' reports on the volume, and we are grateful for the support the readers lent to the project and the helpful criticisms they provided. We hope that the final product is improved because of their work.

The contributors have been, to a person, model citizens in supplying work on time, responding to suggestions, and making changes when asked. It has been a pleasure to work with all of them.

At Penn State, we would like to thank Letitia Montgomery for her help in formatting the twenty-seven essays that make up this volume. We are also grateful to Dustin Stegner, who compiled the thirteen biographies of the dramatists appearing at the end of the volume.

Finally, we would all like to thank our partners and families for their patience and forbearance while we have been at work on this volume, and its companion, *Early Modern English Poetry: A Critical Companion.* Alison, Marie, Debora, Lucy, Patrick, Evan, Maud, and Kelton have all played their parts in helping this work see the light of day, and we are grateful to all of them.

Select Chronology, 1561–1660

1561 *Gorboduc* first acted.

1562 Elizabeth nearly dies of smallpox. Sir John Hawkins begins slave trading in Africa.

1567 Mary Stuart abdicates the throne of Scotland in favor of her son, James VI.

1569–70 Northern Rebellion.

1570 Elizabeth excommunicated by Pope Pius V.

1571 Every cathedral and collegiate church ordered to possess John Foxe's *Acts and Monuments of the Christian Church.*

1572 Duke of Norfolk executed for treason (June 2). Massacre of Saint Bartholomew's Day (August 27).

1575 Progress of Elizabeth I to Kenilworth.

1577–80 Sir Frances Drake circumnavigates the world.

1581 Parliament makes it a treasonable offense to convert anyone to Catholicism.

1582 Duke of Alençon leaves England after failure of marriage negotiations with Elizabeth.

1583 Throckmorton Plot to assassinate Elizabeth exposed.

1584 Lyly, *Campaspe* (?).

1585 Anglo-Dutch Treaty of Alliance.

1585–86 First colony established in Virginia.

1586 Sir Philip Sidney d. after skirmish at Zutphen. Lyly, *Endymion: The Man in the Moon* (?).

1587 Execution of Mary Queen of Scots (February 8).

1587–88 Marlowe, *Tamburlaine The Great, Pts. 1 and 2.*

1588 Defeat of the Spanish Armada.

1589 Kyd, *The Spanish Tragedy;* Marlowe, *The Jew of Malta.*

1589–91 Marprelate Tracts cause a major scandal.

1590 Spenser, *The Faerie Queene,* Bks. 1–3; Anonymous, *Arden of Faversham.*

1592 Marlowe, *Doctor Faustus, Edward II;* Nashe, *Summer's Last Will and Testament.* Theaters close because of plague.

1593 Shakespeare, *Richard III.* Marlowe d.

1594 Shakespeare, *The Taming of the Shrew;* Nashe, *The Unfortunate Traveller.* Admiral's Men and Chamberlain's Men merge. Nine Years War in Ireland begins. Start of series of bad harvests causing shortages and forcing food prices up.

1595 Shakespeare, *A Midsummer Night's Dream, Romeo and Juliet, Richard II.* Raleigh's first voyage to Guiana.

1596 Shakespeare, *The Merchant of Venice;* Spenser, *The Faerie Queene,* Bks. 4–6. Raid on Cadiz.

1597 Shakespeare, *1 Henry IV.*

1598 Jonson, *Every Man in His Humour;* Shakespeare, *2 Henry IV;* Stow, *Survey of London.*

1599 Dekker, *The Shoemaker's Holiday;* Jonson, *Every Man out of His Humour;* Shakespeare, *Henry V, Julius Caesar.* Essex fails to defeat Earl of Tyrone and surprises Elizabeth in her bedchamber.

1600 Heywood, *The Fair Maid of the West, Part One;* Jonson, *Cynthia's Revels;* Marston, *Antonio and Mellida, Antonio's Revenge;* Shakespeare, *Twelfth Night.*

1601 Dekker, *Satiromastix;* Jonson, *Poetaster;* Shakespeare, *Hamlet.* Execution of Earl of Essex (February 25). Irish, Spanish, and papal forces defeated by Lord Mountjoy at the Battle of Kinsale.

1602 Shakespeare, *Othello* (?), *Troilus and Cressida.*

1603 Heywood, *A Woman Killed with Kindness;* Jonson, *Sejanus;* Marston, *The Malcontent;* John Florio's translation of Montaigne's *Essays.* Death of Elizabeth (March 24) and ascension of James I. End of Nine Years War.

1604 Chapman, *Bussy D'Ambois;* Heywood, *If You Know Not Me You Know Nobody, Part One;* Shakespeare, *Measure for Measure;* James I, *Counterblast to Tobacco.* Peace Treaty with Spain.

1605 Shakespeare, *King Lear;* Gunpowder Plot.

1606 Anonymous, *Revenger's Tragedy* (?); Jonson, *Volpone;* Shakespeare, *Macbeth.* Virginia Company formed.

1607 Beaumont, *The Knight of the Burning Pestle;* Shakespeare, *Antony and Cleopatra.* Foundation of Jamestown.

1608 Fletcher, *The Faithful Shepherdess;* Shakespeare, *Timon of Athens.*

1609 Beaumont and Fletcher, *Philaster;* Shakespeare, *Coriolanus, Pericles.*

1610 Shakespeare, *Cymbeline;* Jonson, *The Alchemist.* Galileo observes the moons of Jupiter using the telescope.

1611 Jonson, *Catiline;* Shakespeare, *The Winter's Tale, The Tempest;* Tourneur, *The Atheist's Tragedy.*

1612 Webster, *The White Devil.* Prince Henry d.

1613 Webster, *The Duchess of Malfi;* Middleton, *A Chaste Maid in Cheapside.* Globe Theater burns down.

1614 Jonson, *Bartholomew Fair.* Globe rebuilt. John Rolfe marries Pocahontas.

1616 Jonson publishes his *Works.* Shakespeare d.

1618 Execution of Sir Walter Raleigh (October 29). Thirty Years War begins.

1620 Fletcher, *The Island Princess* (?). Pilgrims establish colonies in Plymouth, Massachusetts.

1621 Dekker, Ford, and Rowley, *The Witch of Edmonton;* Massinger, *A New Way to Pay Old Debts;* Middleton, *Women Beware Women.* Impeachment of Sir Francis Bacon.

1622 Middleton and Rowley, *The Changeling.* Native Americans kill over three hundred Virginian settlers.

1623 Publication of Shakespeare's first folio. Prince Charles and Buckingham travel to Spain to pursue Spanish marriage.

1624 Middleton, *A Game at Chess.*

1625 John Fletcher d. James I d. Ascension of Charles I.

1626 Jonson, *The Staple of News;* Massinger, *The Roman Actor.* Sir Francis Bacon d.

1627 Middleton d.

1628 Duke of Buckingham assassinated.

1629 Ford, *The Broken Heart;* Jonson, *The New Inn.* Charles I dissolves Parliament.

1631 John Donne d. John Dryden b.

1632 Ford, *'Tis Pity She's a Whore;* Massinger, *The City Madam.* Dekker d.? John Locke b.

1633 Ford, *Perkin Warbeck;* Jonson, *Tale of a Tub.* Laud made archbishop of Canterbury. Galileo tried by the Inquisition in Rome.

1634 Milton, *Comus.* Marston d. Webster d.? Ship money levied.

1636 Brome, *The Antipodes.*

1637 Jonson d.

1640 Ford d.? Massinger d. Long Parliament begins; Scots invade northern England.

1641 Shirley, *The Cardinal.* Heywood d. Execution of Thomas Wentworth, earl of Strafford; Laud sent to the Tower of London.

1642 Civil War begins when Charles I raises his standard at Nottingham. Theaters closed.

1648 End of Thirty Years War.

1660 Restoration of Charles I. Theaters reopen.

Introduction

Theatergoing Then and Now

Anyone familiar with theater and film would not be surprised by the suggestion that going to a play on Broadway in New York or in London's West End is a very different experience from going to a movie. Both forms of entertainment make different social and economic demands on their audiences. Whereas many people "dress up" to see a play, few do to attend a film. Tickets to the theater tend to be significantly more expensive than tickets for movies. And whereas patrons of both are exhorted to turn off their mobile phones and stop their conversations once the action begins, making noise during a play is surely the graver breach of etiquette. Simply put, while one can go to the movies for entertainment, the theater tends to be construed as a temple of Culture with a capital C. (Of course, exceptions to this characterization come to mind, but as exceptions.)

As a Cultural site, the theater both establishes and presupposes a particular relationship between audience and actors. In most instances, the audience sits in a darkened hall watching performers on an illuminated stage who both thrive on audience attention and, insofar as they work to create an illusionistic space on that stage, act as if they are addressing only one another. This phenomenon is referred to when we allude to the "fourth wall"—that invisible boundary between the play-world and the world of the audience. The creation of the fourth wall is facilitated by the presence, in many theaters, of a proscenium arch, which both frames the action of the play for the viewer and places her in a space marked off from the space in which that action takes place. In important ways, then, the fourth wall, generated not only through the proscenium arch but also through lighting effects and elements of set design, helps shape the terms of the theatergoer's engagement with the play-world.

Other aspects of theatergoing are also important for shaping those terms. An obvious point: during most performances, audience members are not encouraged to move around or to pass from one part of the theater to another. Both social mores and theater regulations ensure that the theatergoer cannot walk up to the front of the stage mid-soliloquy in order to get a better look at Hamlet. Instead, one is expected to remain in one's assigned seat, with exceptions grudgingly made for urgent dashes to the toilet. Even the range of motion allowed the audience member is restricted—just getting up to stretch your legs, for instance, will lead your neighbors to grumble or hiss. The point is simple: going to the theater demands that not only actors but also playgoers behave (or "perform") in certain ways—ways that are commensurate with the theater's status as Cultural institution.

In early modern London, the commercial theater could not comfortably be called a capital-C Cultural institution. Indeed, its status seems in some ways contradictory. On the one hand, theatrical companies often served as sources of entertainment for the monarch, as was sometimes proudly announced on the title pages of printed plays (a 1600 quarto of Thomas Dekker's *The Shoemaker's Holiday* tells us the play was "acted before the Queenes most excellent Maiestie"). In addition, the companies enjoyed the patronage of aristocrats and royalty, as revealed in their very names: the Lord Admiral's Men, the Queen's Men, and so on. (For more on companies and stages, see chapter 2.) On the other hand, in certain quarters the theaters were routinely denigrated. Civic leaders and puritan opponents of the "idolatrous" drama derided plays as morally corrosive. Moreover, the theaters themselves were assailed as threats to public order. It was claimed that they lured unruly apprentices away from their work, that they competed with the church for their audience, and that pickpockets and prostitutes congregated within the playhouses themselves. Some opponents to the theater made arguments familiar to us today from debates about the effects of media representations of violence, arguing that playgoers later performed at home the kinds of illicit actions they first witnessed on stage. We should be cautious about taking the antitheatricalist view for a normative one in this period. Indeed, the extent to which the theaters operated in the open as stable, well-organized business concerns that drew in a socially diverse clientele could attest to the nonscandalous nature of the theater and theatergoing. What is important to recognize, however, is that the theater was not viewed as a pillar of high culture, but was the subject of controversy.

The student of early modern drama who bears these issues in mind will probably gain a fuller understanding of the nature of the English theater in the Renaissance. This is an exciting time to be studying the work of Shakespeare and his contemporaries, given the wealth of innovative research that has been undertaken in recent years. But it is not just in terms of academic endeavor that our ability to imagine the past has been enhanced: we should also acknowledge the role played by the reconstruction of the Globe Theatre on the south bank of the Thames. The Globe, opened in 1995 after years of campaigning led by American director Sam Wanamaker, was designed with the aim of recapturing a sense of the performance conditions that obtained in the original theater, built in 1599.[1] Just how accurate a reproduction the Globe is remains a subject of some academic controversy (e.g., the location is slightly to the west of the original site owing to the construction of modern buildings, the dimensions may be a little too large, the capacity of fifteen hundred is perhaps too great, and the brightly painted interior is not based on any surviving original design). However, there is little doubt that scholars, actors, and playgoers have gained insights into early modern performance conditions through "the Globe experiment."

In her book on the opening two seasons of the theater, Pauline Kiernan provides a series of acute observations of the experiences of the actors and audiences.[2] One simple but significant discovery was that the stage was nearly always in the shade and that the sun shone onto the galleries. This discovery casts new light (pun intended) on something that scholars have often stressed—that theatergoing was as much an auditory as a visual experience (we are told of playgoers who went to "hear" plays). Given how quickly plays were produced and performed, with the same play seldom staged on consecutive days—the diary of Philip Henslowe, owner of the Rose playhouse, tells us that in September 1594 the Admiral's Men offered fifteen different titles in twenty-seven playing days[3]—companies would not be inclined to invest in spectacular visual effects designed for one play alone. Audiences would have been expected to concentrate on what they heard—despite distractions from those who milled around them in the auditorium—to glean full enjoyment from what was taking place on the stage before them. This suggests what readers of English Renaissance drama have always suspected, that theatergoers were expected to attend to language (rather than spectacle) more closely than we are today.

The experience gained from staging plays at the Globe has confirmed some of the suppositions of theater historians. If the proscenium arch separates the world of the actor from that of the audience, the Globe stage (which extends out into the "pit," is largely dependent upon natural lighting, and is nearly as exposed to the elements as are the "groundlings") allows for an intimacy between the audience and the actors that has been missing in many productions staged throughout the nineteenth and twentieth centuries, often because large, modern theaters militate against such conditions. (Of course, this is not all due to faulty scholarship and bad planning. Architectural considerations have played their part as well. Modern fire and safety regulations would not often permit companies to squash as many people into an enclosed space as was possible in late-sixteenth- and early-seventeenth-century London, a factor that limits the historical veracity of the Globe experiment—and a good thing too, as the original Globe burned down in 1613 when a cannon ball fired during a production of Shakespeare and Fletcher's *Henry VIII* ignited the thatched roof.) The production of *Henry V* that Kiernan describes suggests that under these conditions the audience is likely to become heavily involved in the production and often participate, calling out at times, berating villains, and applauding heroes and heroines enthusiastically. In this setting, then, modern audiences loosely resemble early modern ones; theater historian Andrew Gurr has discussed "the physicality of audience responses" to plays staged in ampitheaters like the Globe (52). The occasional unruliness of early modern audiences might contribute to our understanding of the surviving body of literature that was intensely hostile to the theater, refusing to acknowledge that plays were proper literature and arguing vociferously that the theater was a place that encouraged immoral behavior. Of course, we do not need to agree with such puritanical judgments, which eventually held sway when the theaters were closed in 1642 under the Protectorate. But we should attempt to understand their logic and perhaps shed our reverence for the theater as a temple of sacred art (or Culture). As the "Globe experiment" suggests, attending to the historical conditions of theatrical production and enjoying the theater as an event—as well as a spectacle—can go hand in hand. We hope that this volume contributes both to the reader's sense of historical awareness and to the pleasure gained from engaging with early modern drama.

NOTES

1. It should be stressed that the original Globe was only one type of early modern theater. Andrew Gurr distinguishes between the "amphitheater playhouses" (of which the Globe is a representative) and the "hall playhouses" (*Playgoing in Shakespeare's London,* 3rd ed. [Cambridge: Cambridge UP, 2004]).
2. Pauline Kiernan, *Staging Shakespeare at the New Globe* (Basingstoke: Palgrave, 1999).
3. Roslyn L. Knutson, "The Repertory," *A New History of Early English Drama,* ed. John D. Cox and David Scott Kastan (New York: Columbia UP, 1997) 461–480, esp. 465.

1

Dramatic Authorship and Print

Wendy Wall

I begin with the cinematic image of a grand Renaissance playhouse called the Rose, bustling with actors in doublets and tights rehearsing a play. The financial sponsor is new to the entertainment business. "Who's that?" he asks theater owner Philip Henslowe about one of the actors. Henslowe replies dryly, "No one. He's the author." In this scene from the 1998 Academy Award–winning film *Shakespeare in Love, the* central icon from Western literary culture is humbled, shown to be a mere mortal whose status and power in the playworld are slight.[1]

Is this scenario a strange fiction? Could the author truly be so insignificant? The Stationers' Register (the record of books to be published in the Renaissance) suggests this possibility, for it lists the following typical entry on February 7, 1603: "the book of Troilus and Cressida as it is acted by my lord Chamberlain's Men" (3: 91^{v}). What is astounding to a modern reader is that there is no mention of Shakespeare as author of this play. Instead the entry labels the text according to its status as performance and to the authority of the company staging the event—"as it is acted by my lord Chamberlain's Men." The author's relative unimportance points to a peculiarly early modern understanding of how dramatic texts were produced, imagined, and categorized in this period before copyright, for play texts were created collaboratively and only loosely "owned" by companies rather than individuals. Establishing the authorially sanctioned text or even offering an accurate attribution was hardly a cultural priority. In *A Midsummer Night's Dream* Bottom and his crew's propensity for tinkering with their script seems not to be a comic fiction. Instead of enduring monuments, plays were seen as provisional scripts for performance, subjected to numerous creative forces—annotators, actors, revisers, copyists, censors, compositors, later adapters, and publishers.

Modern readers often approach the magnificent works of Marlowe, Shakespeare, Jonson, Middleton, Beaumont, Fletcher, and others as inherited relics, foundational columns bolstering the canon of English literature. Shakespeare has become a cultural idol whose texts take on an almost sacred status. It's hard for us to imagine such works as created in conditions in which their permanence, their attribution, or their fixity could be treated so casually. Yet, for the most part, playwrights neither spearheaded the publication of their plays nor held a legal claim to the texts they authored. Only about 30 of the 282 plays mentioned by Henslowe were ever published, and these were largely brought forth as the "ephemera of an emerging entertainment industry rather than as valued artifacts of high culture."[2] In order to understand theater during this period, modern readers, it seems, have to unlearn expectations of both text and authorship.

We might ask if Renaissance playtexts even *had* authors. At first glance, such a question seems ludicrous since plays seem patently written by someone. But "author" is a term that designates more than the simple communication of ideas on a page: it indicates a position of status in a culture and a privileged relationship to the text at hand. The author is assumed to have more say over what a text means than the reader or publisher. When David Kastan teasingly asserts that "Shakespeare didn't write the books that bear his name," he doesn't mean that someone else (such as the earl of Oxford) wrote these texts or even that "books" are uniquely the product of publishers (71). Instead he notes that there is little evidence that playwrights routinely worked to make sure that their plays reached book form. Seventeenth-century writers who did oversee the publishing of their works did not yet inhabit the position we now call "author" for the simple reason that this category only later would come to mean an individual writer whose intentions centrally govern the meaning of a work. Early modern plays were instead subject to the "intentions" of co-creators. Rather than setting out to perfect his[3] ideas on paper, a playwright put in motion a whirlwind of activity that necessitated that the text subsequently be "authorized" by various people, events, and institutions. A study of early modern theater and print thus forces modern readers to reconceive the very paradigms that they use to understand texts.

First, a word about the profession of acting. At the end of the sixteenth century, actors had only recently been promoted from the status of vagrants to participate in the burgeoning capitalist industry of theater. In the 1570s the first commercial and permanent playhouses sprung up in the seediest areas of London. Instead of wandering in itinerant troupes, actors and writers began to work for standing companies. Suddenly there was a huge demand for new material and a burst of new plays hit the stage. Using the repertory system, companies produced four to five different plays each week for a relatively heterogeneous audience. The sons of glovers, shoemakers, and bricklayers begin to take on the professions of playwrighting and acting in the highly competitive London theatrical scene. Criticized by religious leaders and civic authorities as a wasteful, immoral, and socially transgressive vocation, theater was not a highbrow or intellectual business.[4]

Most of the playwrights in the period worked freelance, moving from company to company, writing new plays and adding material to existing dramatic works. More than half of the plays in the period were written by more than one author, in the sense that they either began as collaborative productions or showed signs of revisions by other writers.[5] Though plays were generally commissioned by companies, some playwrights, including Shakespeare and Richard Brome, had contractual relationships with companies for a certain number of plays per year.

When writers delivered a script to a company (called the authors' "foul papers" because it was blotted with traces of the writing process), their job essentially ended (Shakespeare was an exception since he was also an actor and part owner in a company). The playhouse scribe then recopied the text to eliminate messy traces of editing; this formed the "fair copy" for the company. A member of the company next annotated the text to create "the book of the play" or "promptbook," which took into account sound effects, props, and stage directions. Without Xerox machines and with only very expensive paper, transcripts were costly to produce. One consequence was that actors were given only their individual parts. As scribes copied parts for actors, the text would inevitably mutate. During rehearsals actors might cut, emend, misremember, or edit the text to suit the performance.[6] Perhaps even a line or two was added here or there to allow an actor to put on a wig or to exit the stage. Hamlet's advice to the comic players—"speak no more than is set down"—might indeed have responded to actors' penchant for improvisation. The bookkeeper may also have added lines for dramatic efficiency or made cuts to allow the play to fit time constraints. The script was then overseen by the master of the revels, a state official in the Lord Chamberlain's department whose job was to license plays for performance and censor seditious material (Edmund Tilney held this job from 1578 to 1610). The text was finally revised to incorporate the master of the revels' changes. By this point, it was truly what scholars have called a "polyvocal" text (Masten 14).

When plays were later revived for performances, playwrights might be hired to "mend" them by adding songs, prologues, scenes, or new characters in order to reflect new theatrical trends or to incorporate topical events. In fact every extant dramatic manuscript from the period shows signs of revision (Rasmussen 441). When taken on tour in the provinces or performed later at court or in London, a play might be cut or otherwise altered to accommodate a new playing space, set of properties, group of actors, type of audience, or milieu. After years of performance, the play might then be sold to a publisher, perhaps to generate a small bit of revenue, promote playgoing as a leisure activity, or include material that couldn't be performed because of the time constraints of the stage. Since bookselling was an extremely risky financial project, companies chose to print only a few plays per year.[7] This means that perhaps as few as one in ten plays were ever published. It's clear, then, that playwrights didn't imagine publication as the sole or primary goal for the scripts they devised; nor was there any legal obligation for a publisher to consult author(s) or locate an "authentic" version of a play. The copy sold to a publisher might be the "foul papers," the "fair copy," the "book of the play," a current version of a revived play copied by the scribe, an obsolete playbook, or perhaps a transcribed manuscript that a player had offered to a friend or patron (Blayney). Twentieth-century editors have hypothesized that actors may have created scripts by "memorial reconstruction," thus generating imperfect and shorter versions of plays acted on stage.[8] Whether this speculation is true or not, it is clear that the playtext sold to the publisher was far removed from the hand of the author.

The text then underwent a further evolution in the print shop, where compositors' varying spelling habits and their practice of not stopping the press to make corrections introduced variables into the text.[9] Despite these extensive alterations, authors largely did not see the transformation of the text into print as a violation of any "rights" that they held. The script was written precisely to be put into a milieu where it *would be* altered, and as such, was "published" when performed. We might say that no single "original" play existed at all, since the text *materialized* in a constantly evolving state.[10]

The absence of an original puts editors today in a quandary, as they wrangle over which early version of a given text to use as the basis for a modern edition or how to authorize one version over another. Even the basic idea of a "date of composition" for a play becomes almost impossible to assign, since the text surfaced in different forms and accreted meanings slowly over time. Two case studies, Christopher Marlowe's *Doctor Faustus* and William Shakespeare's *Hamlet,*[11] allow us to investigate how complicated the results of this mode of theatrical production could be for any given play.

Faustus, Hamlet, and "Troublesome Doubles"[12]

Christopher Marlowe (1564–1593), son of a shoemaker, was educated at Cambridge and became a dramatist for the Lord Admiral's Company. He is known as the author of the two parts of *Tamburlaine the Great* (c.1587), *Doctor Faustus* (c.1588), *The Jew of Malta* (c.1589), and *Edward II* (c.1592). But what it means for Marlowe to *be* an author is a complicated issue. For instance, when an editor undertakes the task of publishing one of Marlowe's most famed texts, *Doctor Faustus,* he or she must begin with the fact that there are two early versions of the play, neither of which is deemed accurate and neither of which is clearly "what Marlowe wrote."[13] Editors start with a standard narrative about the play. It was popular on stage in the mid-1590s. In 1601 publisher Thomas Bell entered *Doctor Faustus* into the Stationers' Register, and it was printed as a quarto (a cheap—and cheaply published—form for ephemeral works) in 1604, just as the play returned to the London stage. In 1602 Henslowe paid William Birde and Samuel Rowley for additions to the play.[14] In 1616 John Wright published a longer quarto edition, which was then reproduced at least six times in the next twenty years (his 1619 edition strikingly advertises the play "with new Additions"). How do we make sense of these two different versions, each of which might have been revised? Although what is commonly known as the A-text (the 1604 quarto) is closest to Marlowe's life span, it is deemed "un-Marlovian" because it is short, truncated, and bereft of particular stage directions. Since it includes commentary on events that happened only after Marlowe's death,[15] it appears to have been revised by a later hand. The B-text (the 1616 quarto) is plagued by seemingly disordered passages, textual problems, and comic scenes that some editors see as unworthy of Marlowe's talents. Were these plays performed independently over the years? Do they reveal Marlowe's shifting intentions over time, published after his death? Or are both spurious renditions corrupted from a text that Marlowe authored which now is lost? Can either of them be said to be "by" Marlowe?

While it might seem commonsensical to attribute the most coherent text to the author, David Bevington and Eric Rasmussen instead argue that the imperfections of the A-text are precisely evidence that this version was set from Marlowe's authorial manuscript, for it looks like an author's draft or foul papers (66–67). The additions that Birde and Rowley made might suggest that the A-text is based on Marlowe's "original" with the B-text a later collaborative revision. But some scholars argue instead that the A-text is a spurious memorial reconstruction by actors in the first place (see Bevington and Rasmussen 62–77). Regardless of which theory is correct, we find that no "original" text exists and that editors readily appeal to the figure of the author to substantiate the authenticity of whichever text is deemed "best." Errors can be a sign that a text *is* or *isn't* authorized.

According to Leah Marcus, the different *Faustus* versions are "updated" stagings, texts that reflect shifts in religious and political issues from the 1590s to the 1610s. Rather than simply choosing which text is "authorized," Marcus suggests, scholars might pay attention to how each of the plays aims for a different effect and makes sense as a whole (40). One is more ceremonial and polished, the other more wildly spectacular. The A-text relies on a stark stage where a character's introspection is emphasized and the abiding hope of a final salvation persists as a theme; the B-text is adorned and allegorical, while expressing a stronger concern with external behaviors and with spiritual decline. Despite such differences, however, each text captures what Marcus sees as a signature feature of Marlowe's writing style, what she dubs the "Marlowe effect" (42); both plays exist "on the same 'ravishing' razor edge between exaltation and transgression" (42). The A-text can be said to be more nationalist and ultra-Protestant, the B-text more internationalist, imperial, and Anglo-Catholic, Marcus argues, but each version shows a magician teetering on the border between daring heroism and frightening transgression within a well-defined set of values (42).

When playwrights and actors altered *Faustus,* then, they might have attempted to preserve the sense of theatrical risk attached specifically to the writing of Marlowe, who was, after all, notorious. There were hints of his involvement in the mysterious affairs of high-ranking government, he spent time in jail for fighting in a duel, he was arrested in connection with an investigation into religious and political treason, and he was rumored to be a spy. Performing a play by Marlowe might whet an audience's expectation for blasphemy or iconoclasm. When revisers retooled the structural elements of the play, they maintained its overarching dynamic. As such, changing texts of *Faustus* might be said to be "authorized" as "Marlowe's" even though they were not modified literally by him, for they cohered around a theatrical style associated with his name (Marcus 65–67).

Shakespeare's *Hamlet* provides a similarly vexed but different textual problem, for it exists in three separate but interrelated versions: the 1603 quarto, the 1604 quarto, and the 1623 folio (an expensive form of publication with larger pages, usually reserved for monumental works and usually bound). Shakespeare (1564–1616), son of a glover, was an active part of the London theatrical scene by 1592 and a share-holding member of the Lord Chamberlain's Men by 1594. Although he averaged an output of two plays per year, he did not oversee the printing of his scripts or arrange to have them immortalized in typographical form.[16] He was not even named on the title pages to any plays published until 1598 when *Love's Labour's Lost* hit the book stalls with the claim that it was "augmented and amended" by Shakespeare, and when the second editions of *Richard II* and *Richard III* included the tag line "by William Shakespeare" after the plot description and attribution to the theater company. These early and somewhat tentative attributions seem designed to deploy authorship in order to generate sales.

"A booke called the Revenge of Hamlett Prince [of] Denmarke as yt was latelie Acted by the Lord Chamberleynee his servants" was entered into the Stationers' Register in July 1602 (3: 212^{r}) and a quarto printed the next year. The title page attributes the play to Shakespeare and boasts that it has been acted in London, Cambridge, and Oxford, among other places. The second quarto, *The tragicall historie of Hamlet, Prince of Denmarke,* appeared in late 1604, again with an attribution to Shakespeare but with information that it was "newly imprinted and enlarged to almost as much againe as it was, according to the true and perfect Coppie." The first quarto (Q1) thus appeals to the prestige of performance, while the second announces itself as a legitimate *written* text. Although subsequent reprintings of *Hamlet* in the 1610s and 1620s simply reproduced quarto 2 (Q2), in 1623 a different version of the play was published as part of the first folio, announced again as based on "True Originall Copies" and authorized by Shakespeare's fellow actors John Heminges and Henry Condell. This version was part of a monumental text put forth by associates close to Shakespeare after the bard's death.

If Shakespeare is the author of *Hamlet,* which text did he write? Did he intend Q2 to supplant Q1, which is deemed by some editors to be a "bad" memorial reconstruction? Is Q2 the "true" text because it restores the play to its inaugural form, as the title page claims (Q1 then being a spurious publication)? Or was Q2 written first (as in the first theory), but then shortened to meet performance needs (Erne)? If this scenario is true, did Shakespeare himself brutally cut the play to create a faster-paced work? Or does Q1 represent instead the early draft of an inexperienced playwright who later expanded his work? Once we sort out the relationship between the two quartos, how are we then to make sense of the folio *Hamlet,* a text published seven years after Shakespeare's death but presented by his close colleagues? Does the folio correct the "good" quarto, and if so, who made the corrections? Or are the folio and each of the quartos imperfect versions of some lost original? In any case, the question of which text was "authorized" by Shakespeare becomes elusive; for all versions, as we have seen, were modified by the censor, promptbook writer, actors, publisher, and compositor.

The first quarto of *Hamlet,* only a bit more than one half the length of the later quarto, has generally been deemed "bad" or "pirated" because it is judged by many editors to be inferior: it is fast-paced, straightforward, and highly theatrical.[17] Scholars document other differences as well. In Q1, "Gertred" is different from the character familiar to modern readers: she assures Hamlet that she is innocent of any part in the conspiracy to murder and, in the famed closet scene, she joins with her son in collusion against her new husband. Q1 Hamlet, for his part, isn't overly introspective, mysterious, or preoccupied with the morbidity of sexuality but is instead a man of action. In general, critics see the first quarto as structured by strong theatrical rhythms, while Q2 appears more meditative, lyrical, complex in its switchback plot turns, and philosophically skeptical (Marcus 138–47). Though the folio is closer to Q2 in general, it offers some points of departure, the most notable being that the folio Hamlet offers self-reproach for his seeming "delay" when he muses on Fortinbras's military quests, a theme that has come to frame interpretations of the play. In the folio as well, as Marcus argues, Hamlet's comments to the players suggest a vision of theater that is more literate and authorial (164–76). Our textual legacies, then, are theatrical, lyrical, and literate versions of *Hamlet,* each incarnation having peculiar features and making sense as a whole.

In practice, editors are reluctant to choose one of these *Hamlet*s over the others, although they almost always privilege the folio or Q2 as the best text. But while arguing for the clear superiority of *one* of the texts, editors tend to conflate all three versions to form a new and modern *Hamlet*—one reauthorized by modern publishing houses such as Norton, Oxford, or Arden. Using the first folio or Q2 as their base text, editors insert passages from the other versions for good measure, along with juicy stage directions and a few passage and word choices from the "spurious" Q1. One of the strange truths of *Hamlet* is that this modern incarnation, the one with which most readers are familiar, certainly represents a form of the play that never was performed on the Renaissance stage. It's simply too long. The abundance of *Hamlet*s thus raises critical questions: did Shakespeare write all three plays (or more, with some now lost) as separate units, each for a particular theatrical situation? Or did the playwright initially produce a vast amount of potential material, a kind of *Hamlet* database that a company might use to shape a particular performance (which Gertrude tonight? they might have asked)?[18] Or did the text simply get updated by the company over time?

It's more than a bit paradoxical that the literary monument we know as *Hamlet* could rest on such shifting textual sands. It's also odd that the masterpiece imagined to solidify Shakespeare's renowned status as *the* author in Western culture emerged from a milieu in which authorial attribution was so unsure. Modern readers are in the predicament of having multiple "originals," an inapplicable concept of "authenticity" and the "literary artifact," and only a faint shadow of the thing that we call "the author." The editor's dream of stripping away the vicissitudes of theater or print in order to locate an original *Hamlet* that might provide unmediated access to Shakespeare remains an elusive fantasy, one hopelessly at odds with what we know about how the theater actually worked.

Emergent Authors

And yet, my account of the missing author is not the whole story, for publication practices and attitudes toward authorship were in the process of changing during the Renaissance. Not all playwrights passively accepted their limited place in the theatrical entertainment business. Ben Jonson emerges as an exceptional figure, important for his energetic attempts to reshape the very concept of dramatic authorship. Jonson had the audacity to publish his own plays, to control their appearance in print, and to use the architectonics of the book to define his writing in literary terms. He actively rewrote his own scripts for publication in the 1616 *Workes of Beniamin Jonson*. Daring to suggest that *plays* were worthy of being designated as "Workes," a title usually reserved for classics, Jonson strikingly sought to distance himself from the protean, hybrid, and collective world of theater and instead to shape a "bibliographic ego"[19] out of his control over dramatic material.

Even before the publication of his *Workes,*[20] Jonson had worried the issue of theatrical authorship. In a preface to his 1605 *Sejanus,* he announced that the book is cleansed of the theatrical contributions of a "second pen" (52) and thus does not represent what audiences had seen on stage (formerly *the* primary advertising strategy for drama).[21] The reader, this text suggests, garners something different from that of the playgoing experience. Similarly the title page to the 1600 quarto of *Every Man out of His Humor* promises the play "as it was first composed by the author B.I. containing more than hath been publikely spoken or acted."[22] Jonson, that is, was retrospectively scripted as sole *author* of these texts; he helped to refashion collaborative performances into authorially governable literary artifacts.[23] Separating the book form from the play's embodiment as theater, he individuated the author and promoted the value of a single authentic text embodying the writer's intentions. His proud announcement of a new position for the writer offers the most critically acclaimed reconceptualization of Renaissance public writing. As Erne argues, publishers in the 1590s paved the way for such authorial assertion by gradually foregrounding authors on title pages (31–77).

Although Jonson was the playwright most actively involved in the printing of his plays, other seventeenth-century writers intervened as well. Chapman, Ford, Massinger, Marston, Middleton, Shirley, and Webster all had a hand in supervising the publication of their works or in checking proofs. When Thomas Heywood apologized for publishing *The Rape of Lucrece*[24] because he feared that it might be seen as a "double sale" (v), or John Marston voiced his concern that speeches in *The Malcontent*[25] translated only poorly into a written document, each writer highlighted the author's involvement in creating a book commodity (4). Some followed Jonson's lead and separated performance from the authorially preferred text. In the 1647 folio collection of Beaumont and Fletcher's works, publisher Humphrey Moseley writes that scenes omitted "with the *Authour's* consent" are now restored (A5^r). Mosely not only implies the author's right to govern performance, but also, in later describing Fletcher's "owne hand" in the process, goes on to paint a picture in which the author's autograph legitimates publication ($A4^v$; see Masten 121–26).[26] Yet the degree to which the author became significant to a printed work often depended on factors that had nothing to do with the author's increasing entitlement or the play's "literary" status— for example, the playwright's relative fame, place in an acting company, personal desire, or class status. These factors nevertheless helped to pave the way conceptually for a legal codification of intellectual property.

The first publication of John Webster's *The Duchess of Malfi*[27] bears witness to the author's increasing prominence in play publication, for it includes a marginal comment, conspicuously placed beside a passage, which reads: "the Author disclaims this Ditty to be his" ($H2^r$). In the introductory matter framing the book, Webster dedicates his "Poem" to Baron Barkeley, as if the play were an object circulating in the patronage system; and he proudly mentions the immortality that poetry traditionally confers on writers and patrons. Three prefatory poems praise the work alternately as a literary monument and as a performance event. In trying to cater to the widest possible readership, the title page to *The Duchess* expresses somewhat contradictory conceptions of the printed playtext: it promises that the tragedy represents what "was Presented priuately, at the Black-Friers; and publiquely at the Globe, By the Kings Maiesties Seruants," but goes on to proclaim that it is "the perfect and exact Coppy, with deuerse *things Printed, that the length of the Play would* not beare in the Presentment." The inclusion of a Latin epigraph from Horace's epistles establishes the text's classical authority, and, as we have seen, marginal commentary demarcates the writer's "property." This document thus reveals what had been popular on stage, but *not quite,* what had been written by the author, but *not quite*. Of what is it an "exact Coppy" if not an authorial original that never made it to audiences? But then why include the "ditty" not the author's and mark it as such? The title page suggests that the buyer should savor a specifically textual version of the work (one situated in literary history), but it also calls upon the success of collective performance to recommend the book.

The Duchess of Malfi was not exceptional. In the first three decades of the seventeenth century, published works begin to categorize plays unevenly as the written product of an author as well as the trace of an event in which the author played a minimal role. While title pages continued to recognize the power of performance and patrons, they also newly emphasized authors. If earlier publications underscored the text's theatricality for readers eager to reexperience a delightful performance, later publications directed readers to think of plays as *written*. While the writer was rarely responsible for this new ascription and while he largely didn't reap monetary rewards from print, the figure of the author did decidedly loom larger in the cultural and publishing landscape of seventeenth-century England.

The case of Jonson has prompted scholars to argue sometimes that writers sought to secure authorial control for the playtext by promoting drama to the elevated status of *poetry*. Yet it isn't quite true that theater was the cause of textual waywardness in the first place. A look at the production and circulation of poems in the Renaissance in fact proves that their textual and authorial situation was much like that of scripts. Although William Caxton set up the first press in England in 1476, a lively manuscript culture continued to thrive alongside print for the next hundred years or more. While poets occasionally handwrote complete books, manuscripts more often circulated on loose papers. Traveling through households, courts, and universities, lyric poems were open to inscription by readers who felt free to amend rhymes, alter lines, and integrate "answer poems" into the original writing. Generated as part of the active social life of educated men, the literary text had unusually unfixed parameters. An author might write several copies of a poem at the request of friends, each slightly different. As these copies circulated, readers might transcribe them with varying degrees of accuracy and place them in new settings that altered the poem's theme, focus, or even the gender of the speaker.[28] Publishers similarly felt free to make revisions or to put any poetic version into print. The result was sometimes the textual mess that modern editors assume to be unique to playscripts: multiple versions with no sure original. Jonson's assertion of authorship was not, then, simply an attempt to endow playwrighting with the credibility held by poets, for Edmund Spenser and others had to expend great labors to refashion poetic authorship as well.[29] Both manuscripts and theatrical scripts adhered to deeply engrained Renaissance protocols in which writing was seen as occasional and dependent on oral culture.

In the electronic age of the twenty-first century, the uniformity and self-identity of the printed book is only beginning to be challenged by cybertexts, forms that confound many of the conventions shaped by print logic: the text becomes less linear and more a web of interrelated units shuffled at the discretion of the reader.[30] In the future, this may change the institution of authorship. But modern readers still unsurprisingly view Renaissance playwrighting through an inherited and firmly ensconced print logic, one that anchors texts to writers. The film *Shakespeare in Love,* in fact, plays out modern fantasies about authorship while revealing their fault lines. Immediately following the opening glimpse of the theater industry with its harsh financial realties and embattled institutional networks, the film takes the viewer into Shakespeare's private bedchamber, where we see him writing. Is this the cherished handwriting of the bard? Is the parchment that he labors to fill those prized "foul papers" that now don't exist but serve as the linchpin for textual theories and editorial wars? With the possible exception of *Sir Thomas More,* in which the ostensibly unique "hand of Shakespeare" is preserved only in collaboration with others, no manuscripts of Shakespeare have survived.

Shakespeare in Love seems to deliver this textual primal scene, unveiling the handwriting of the master as he forges a monumental work at his desk. Yet when the camera zooms in, the viewer discovers that the young novice Will is not, in fact, overcoming a case of writer's block at all. Instead he practices his autograph, succeeding only in spelling "William Shakespeare" repeatedly in variant form. This scene wonderfully caricatures the early modern practices that thwart the ideals of autonomy and authority that Shakespeare's name has come to signify. As Kastan states, "An author writes always and only within specific conditions of possibility, both institutional and imaginative, connecting the individual talent to preexisting modes of thought, linguistic rules, literary conventions, social codes, legal restraints, material practices and commercial conditions of production" (33). Since the author's elusive hand was inscribed so fully within the many shaping forces of Renaissance theater, this modern portrayal of textual authenticity and authorial independence appears an anachronistic phantom haunting our look into the past. Living at a time when the technologies cementing authorship are potentially unsettled by new media, audiences today might find the scene of Shakespeare writing—a solitary mortal with pen firmly in hand—reassuring; for this comforting sight allows us to remake in our own image the complicated scenario of Renaissance theater, authorship, and early print.

NOTES

1. *Shakespeare in Love,* dir. John Madden, writt. Marc Norman and Tom Stoppard, Miramax Home Entertainment, 1998.
2. See David Scott Kastan, *Shakespeare After Theory* (New York: Routledge, 1999) 72. For a different view, see Lukas Erne, *Shakespeare as Literary Dramatist* (Cambridge: Cambridge UP, 2003), who argues that Shakespeare and other playwrights consciously wrote "literary" versions of their plays precisely for a print audience. Erne's thesis remains conjecture since interpretation of his evidence is open to debate.
3. I use the male pronoun deliberately here since there were no publishing female playwrights working with theater companies.
4. See Andrew Gurr, *The Shakespearean Stage 1574–1642,* 3rd ed. (Cambridge: Cambridge UP, 1992) 1–33; and Louis Adrian Montrose, *The Purpose of Playing: Shakespeare and the Cultural Politics of Elizabethan Theatre* (Chicago: U of Chicago P, 1996) 19–40.
5. See Gerald Eades Bentley, *The Profession of Dramatist in Shakespeare's Time 1590–1642* (Princeton: Princeton UP, 1971) 199; and Jeffrey Masten, *Textual Intercourse: Collaboration, Authorship, and Sexualities in Renaissance Drama* (Cambridge: Cambridge UP, 1997) 14–20.
6. See Eric Rasmussen, "The Revision of Scripts," *A New History of Early English Drama,* ed. John D. Cox and David Scott Kastan (New York: Columbia UP, 1997) 441–60.
7. See Peter W. Blayney, "The Publication of Playbooks," *A New History of Early English Drama,* ed. John D. Cox and David Scott Kastan (New York: Columbia UP, 1997) 383–422, esp. 383–89.
8. For recent assessments of the "bad" quarto theory, see Laurie E. Maguire, *Shakespearean Suspect Texts: The "Bad" Quartos and Their Contexts* (Cambridge: Cambridge UP, 1996); and Randall McLeod, "The Marriage of Good and Bad Quartos," *Shakespeare Quarterly* 33 (1982): 421–31.
9. See Margreta de Grazia and Peter Stallybrass, "The Materiality of the Shakespearean Text," *Shakespeare Quarterly* 44 (1993): 255–83, esp. 260.
10. See Stephen Orgel, "The Authentic Shakespeare," *Representations* 21 (1988): 1–25.
11. See William Shakespeare, *The Tragicall Historie of Hamlet Prince of Denmarke* (London, 1603).
12. Marcus uses this phrase approvingly in arguing against composite editions of plays (129). See Leah Marcus, *Unediting the Renaissance: Shakespeare, Marlowe, Milton* (Manchester: Manchester UP, 1992).
13. See Christopher Marlowe, *The Tragicall History of D. Faustus* (London, 1604) or *The Tragicall History of the Life and Death of Doctor Faustus* (London, 1616). These are commonly referred to as the "A-" and "B-" texts.
14. See David Bevington and Eric Rasmussen, *Doctor Faustus A- and B- texts (1604, 1616): Christopher Marlowe and His Collaborator and Revisers* (Manchester: Manchester UP, 1992) 62.
15. See Marcus 39.
16. Erne argues instead that the "literary qualities" of some longer quartos are proof that Shakespeare wrote a version precisely for print publication.
17. See Alfred Pollard, *Shakespeare's Folios and Quartos* (London: Methuen, 1909) 64–88. See Janette Dillon, "Is There a Performance in This Text?," *Shakespeare Quarterly* 45 (1995): 74–86, on the dangers of assuming that a more "theatrical" text transparently shows us what was acted on the Renaissance stage.
18. See Jonathan Goldberg, " 'What? in a Names that which we call a Rose': The Desired Texts of *Romeo and Juliet,*" *Crisis in Editing: Texts of the English Renaissance,* ed. Randall McLeod (New York: AMS P, 1994) 173–201.

19. See Joseph Loewenstein, "The Script in the Marketplace," *Representing the Renaissance,* ed. Stephen Greenblatt (Berkeley: U of California P, 1988) 265–78, esp. 265.
20. See Ben Jonson, *The Workes of Beniamin Ionson* (London, 1616).
21. See Ben Jonson, *Sejanus His Fall,* ed. Philip J. Ayres (Manchester: Manchester UP, 1990).
22. See Ben Jonson, *The Comicall Satyre of Every Man out of His Humor* (London, 1600).
23. See Timothy Murray, *Theatrical Legitimation: Allegories of Genius in Seventeenth Century England and France* (Oxford: Oxford UP, 1987) 39–93.
24. See Thomas Heywood, *The Rape of Lucrece* (1630) (London: Charles Baldwin, 1824).
25. See John Marston, *The Malcontent,* ed. M. L. Wine (Lincoln: U of Nebraska P, 1964).
26. See Francis Beaumont and John Fletcher, *Comedies and Tragedies* (London, 1647).
27. See John Webster, *The Tragedy of the Dutchesse of Malfy* (London, 1623).
28. See Wendy Wall, *The Imprint of Gender: Authorship and Publication in the English Renaissance* (Ithaca: Cornell UP, 1993) 31–57; Arthur Marotti, *Manuscript and Print in the English Renaissance Lyric* (Ithaca: Cornell UP, 1995) 1–73; and Orgel.
29. See Richard Helgerson, *Self-Crowned Laureates: Spenser, Jonson, Milton and the Literary System* (Berkeley: U of California P, 1983); and David Lee Miller, "Authorship, Anonymity, and *The Shepheardes Calendar,*" *Modern Language Quarterly* 40 (1979): 219–36.
30. See Michel Foucault, "What Is an Author?," *Textual Strategies: Perspectives in Post-Structuralist Criticism,* ed. Josue Harari (Ithaca: Cornell UP, 1977) 141–60, for an account of how and when modern views of authorship, what he calls "the author function," shift historically.

READING LIST

Bentley, Gerald Eades. *The Profession of Dramatist in Shakespeare's Time 1590–1642*. Princeton: Princeton UP, 1971.

Blayney, Peter W. "The Publication of Playbooks." *A New History of Early English Drama.* Ed. John D. Cox and David Scott Kastan. New York: Columbia UP, 1997. 383–422.

Erne, Lukas. *Shakespeare as Literary Dramatist.* Cambridge: Cambridge UP, 2003.

Foucault, Michel. "What Is an Author?" *Textual Strategies: Perspectives in Post-Structuralist Criticism.* Ed. Josue Harari. Ithaca: Cornell UP, 1977. 141–60.

Grazia, Margreta de, and Peter Stallybrass. "The Materiality of the Shakespearean Text." *Shakespeare Quarterly* 44 (1993): 255–83.

Kastan, David Scott. *Shakespeare After Theory*. New York: Routledge, 1999.

Loewenstein, Joseph. "The Script in the Marketplace." *Representing the Renaissance.* Ed. Stephen Greenblatt. Berkeley: U of California P, 1988. 265–78.

Maguire, Laurie E. *Shakespearean Suspect Texts: The "Bad" Quartos and Their Contexts.* Cambridge: Cambridge UP, 1996.

Marcus, Leah. *Unediting the Renaissance: Shakespeare, Marlowe, Milton.* New York: Routledge, 1996.

Marotti, Arthur. *Manuscript and Print in the English Renaissance Lyric*. Ithaca: Cornell UP, 1995.

Masten, Jeffrey. *Textual Intercourse: Collaboration, Authorship, and Sexualities in Renaissance Drama*. Cambridge: Cambridge UP, 1997.

Orgel, Stephen. "The Authentic Shakespeare." *Representations* 21 (1988): 1–25.

Rasmussen, Eric. "The Revision of Scripts." *A New History of Early English Drama*. Ed. John D. Cox and David Scott Kastan. New York: Columbia UP, 1997. 441–60.

Wall, Wendy. *The Imprint of Gender: Authorship and Publication in the English Renaissance.* Ithaca: Cornell UP, 1993.

2

Theater Companies and Stages

Roslyn L. Knutson

Theater historians tell the story of playing companies and stages in the early modern period by interpreting documents that have varying degrees of trustworthiness. These documents include the title-page advertisements of printed plays, lawsuits, court records from the Office of the Revels and Office of the Chamber, payments to touring companies made by provincial officials, and individuals' writings such as diaries and letters. The richest single source of information on theatrical commerce is the business diary kept by Philip Henslowe, builder of the Rose playhouse in London in 1587. In this account book, Henslowe recorded performances at the Rose from 1592 to 1597 and payments for playbooks and apparel at the Rose and Fortune from 1597 to 1603. Because there are gaps in the historical record, there is much that we do not know. As a result, opinions differ on significant issues of commerce such as the effectiveness of business models adopted by various companies, the role of the player-turned-entrepreneur, the nature of competition among the companies, and the use of the repertory as a commodity in that competition. In this chapter I suggest a narrative of the playhouse world that illustrates some of the issues and evidence currently being debated. Coupled with the exploration of plays and issues in subsequent chapters, this narrative grounds those plays and their cultural commentary in the early modern world of royal and public spaces in London and the provinces, of investors inside and outside the playhouse world who saw theatrical property as potentially profitable, and of luck mixed with commercial savvy.

The Playhouse World to 1594: Developing a Successful Business Model

Nearly one hundred years separate the performance of *Fulgens and Lucrece* perhaps at court in 1497 from that of *The Jew of Malta* at the Rose playhouse on May 14, 1594. During that time, the business of playing was characterized for the most part by three kinds of companies: those interluders and minstrels who performed at provincial town halls and inns under the sponsorship of a local aristocrat such as Sir Thomas Cornwall in Shropshire; those troupes, including children's companies, who performed at court and in the country under the aegis of the current Tudor monarch, for example, King Edward VI's players and the Children of the Queen's Revels; and those who acquired the patronage of the upper nobility, such as Robert Dudley, earl of Leicester, and William Somerset, earl of Worcester. Significantly for the expansion of theatrical commerce, playing companies in this latter category attracted men with the business acumen to foresee the advantages of a house built exclusively for playing in the London area. These companies, though continuing to tour the provinces and perform at court, gradually realigned their business to include lengthy runs at London playhouses.[1]

The biggest name among the early player-entrepreneurs is James Burbage. In 1576 Burbage persuaded his brother-in-law, John Brayne, to back the construction of a playhouse in Shoreditch called the Theatre. Burbage may have been involved with Brayne in a short-lived earlier venture in 1567, the Red Lion playhouse to the east of London at Mile End.[2] However, it was the Theatre, with its soon-built neighbor, the Curtain, that provided a business model to be copied in 1587 by Philip Henslowe in the construction of the Rose playhouse in Southwark. The model continued to influence entrepreneurs in subsequent years as they built the stages that would define London adult professional theater until the official closure of playhouses in 1642: the Swan in 1595, the Boar's Head in 1598, the Globe in 1599, the Fortune in 1600, the Red Bull in 1605, the Cockpit in 1617, and Salisbury Court in 1630. The Burbage model depended on the availability of playing companies for long engagements, year-round if possible. It needed to develop a steady customer base among Londoners with free afternoons and disposable income. In order to attract playgoers, the companies needed a diverse repertory of plays on popular topics and in fashionable genres. And to build such a repertory, the companies needed playwrights.

In 1583, an event occurred that reasserted an alternative to the Burbage business model of playhouse-plus-company. That event was the creation of the Queen's Men. In 1583 Sir Francis Walsingham, who was Queen Elizabeth's premier minister, prompted Edmund Tilney, who was the queen's master of the revels, to form the new company. Tilney and Walsingham were not inventing a model here; they were refining the long-familiar pattern of companies who "carried the name and influence" of the monarch wherever they performed and thus promoted the impression of a government attentive to the general good.[3] But two features of the Queen's Men were new: (1) the purposeful selection of quality players from existing companies in a kind of "pro draft" and (2) the mission to advertise the political and religious agenda of the queen.[4] This business model depended on extensive touring; the players, dressed in their royal livery on the road, were marked as the queen's privileged spokesmen, acting out the "true story" of nationhood and Protestantism. The Queen's Men were immediately successful. They dominated performances at court, and at provincial stops they often received twice the reward as other companies. Although their schedule included stage runs at public London venues, their raison d'être was to circulate the queen's message among her subjects throughout England. As a function of that mission, the Queen's Men in effect invented the English history play, which championed English heroes and Protestant values.

Given their royal sanction, the Queen's Men should have ruled the playhouse world after 1583, and they did until at least 1588. But their creation did not stifle other theatrical enterprises. In fact, the protection of the crown enabled other companies to deflect harassment from London church and city officials. When challenged, these companies claimed that they too were "the Quenes players,"[5] and that their public performances too were actually rehearsals so that they might be ready when the queen called on them to perform. Arguably, the Queen's Men did not prevail much past 1588 because of factors beyond the control even of the queen and her political will. One such factor was personnel. The Queen's Men lost Richard Tarlton, one of their stars and the premier clown on the English stage, to plague in 1588. And, at about this time, two young men who would become star players, Edward Alleyn and Richard Burbage, joined companies in competition with the Queen's Men.

A second factor was dramatists. In 1587, Christopher Marlowe, a brash young poet from Canterbury who had recently received his master's degree at Cambridge University, came to London and sold plays to the Lord Admiral's Men. In 1592 (if not earlier), a new talent out of Stratford-upon-Avon, William Shakespeare, began selling plays; he sold one to Lord Strange's Men and several more were acquired later that year by the Earl of Pembroke's Men. These companies and others were cultivating an audience among Londoners at the Theatre and Curtain, as well as the Rose, newly built in 1587. Playing day in, day out, month after month at the same public London site, and co-opting the talents of writers otherwise known for nondramatic literature (e.g., Thomas Lodge, prose romance; Thomas Nashe, picaresque fiction; Anthony Munday, political tracts), these companies developed a voracious appetite for theatrical material: perhaps as many as thirty-five plays a year, half of which were new. In contrast, the Queen's Men, who were performing before changing audiences at different towns and venues along their touring circuit, probably got by with a repertory of ten or fifteen plays.

A third factor was the kind of plays being written by dramatists attracted by the burgeoning theatrical marketplace. Marlowe was undoubtedly the break-out figure, with such box-office hits as the two parts of *Tamburlaine, Doctor Faustus,* and *The Jew of Malta,* all sold to the Admiral's Men in the years between 1587 and 1590. Shakespeare started later than Marlowe, appropriating the formula of the English history play patented by the Queen's Men for his serial on the Wars of the Roses, beginning with *1 Henry VI* in 1592. Meanwhile, Thomas Kyd was inventing the English revenge play with *The Spanish Tragedy,* which Shakespeare would copy in *Titus Andronicus*. George Peele and others were copying Marlowe's Tamburlainian model with plays about Mediterranean tyrants such as *The Battle of Alcazar* and *Selimus*. Philip Henslowe's diary of activity at the Rose playhouse documents the commercial opportunity on offer at a London venue in these years. In 1592, for example, Lord Strange's Men played at the Rose from February 19 to June 22. During these months, they performed twenty-four plays, five of which were marked by Henslowe's enigmatic "ne," which seems to indicate a play being marketed as new. Their first "ne" play, "harey the vj" (presumably Shakespeare's *1 Henry VI*), brought in 76s. 8d. as Henslowe's share of the gate receipts;[6] for the rest of the run, *Henry VI* received fifteen performances for an average of nearly 42s. Among the old plays, Marlowe's *The Jew of Malta* and Kyd's *The Spanish Tragedy* had comparably successful runs. *The Jew of Malta* had ten performances for an average return to Henslowe of 43s. 6d.; *The Spanish Tragedy* had thirteen performances for 37s. on average. Strange's Men returned to the Rose in the winter for a month-long run (December 29, 1592–February 1, 1593). They continued ten plays from their spring repertory, adding two new offerings, one of which was Marlowe's *Massacre at Paris*.

Because of gaps in the documentary record and differences in the nature of data, theater historians do not know whether the 1592–93 runs of Strange's Men were exceptional or typical of the companies that performed at other London venues. Nor are Henslowe's receipts (apples) easily comparable to the official rewards of a touring company (oranges), even one as prominent as the Queen's Men.[7] Furthermore, plague returned to London in the late spring of 1592, disrupting playing schedules in London and the provinces into early summer 1594. It might not thus have been obvious to theatrical businessmen whether the Burbage model was generally superior to that of the Queen's Men, but it is obvious to scholars now that the model replicated and refined over the next fifty years was that of a London-based company with a diverse and rapidly changing repertory.

The Playhouse World, 1594–1603: Making Money in the London Market

The plague had subsided by June 1594, and companies scrambled to position themselves for the resumption of playing. Players from Strange's Men and the Admiral's Men, who had toured together in the summer of 1593, separated into two companies, one retaining the patronage of the lord admiral, the other acquiring the patronage of the lord chamberlain. These companies played together briefly in June 1594 at the playhouse at Newington, just to the south of London, but from mid-June they claimed, respectively, the Rose playhouse and the Theatre. Part of the flux that preceded the formation of the Admiral's Men and Chamberlain's Men was the appearance of Sussex's Men at the Rose in January and February 1594 (possibly with some of Pembroke's players in the mix), and the brief April run of Sussex's Men with remnants of the Queen's Men. Perhaps it was this renewed busyness that prompted Francis Langley in the fall of 1594 to build the Swan playhouse. Langley may have attracted a reconstituted Queen's Men to open the Swan in the summer of 1595. Pembroke's Men, now also reconstituted, were playing in the provinces, but by 1597 they were in London at the Swan, where they would perform until plague and arguments with Langley led some of them to incorporate with the Admiral's Men at the Rose.[8] Undeterred by the rocky course of business at the Swan, Langley in 1599 joined a year-old theatrical venture by Oliver Woodliffe called the Boar's Head playhouse just east of St. Bodolph Aldgate, where the Earl of Derby's Men were playing.[9] Also in 1599, the Chamberlain's Men built a new playhouse. The Burbage family, having lost the lease on the property of the Theatre in Shoreditch, dismantled the building (which they owned) and reassembled it as the Globe playhouse on Maid Lane across from Henslowe's Rose. The Admiral's Men built themselves a new playhouse in 1600, the Fortune, north of London in Middlesex. In the same years, the boys' companies reopened after a ten-year hiatus; the Children of Paul's resumed business at the playhouse at St. Paul's in 1599, and the Children of the Chapel opened at the Blackfriars playhouse in 1600.

Theater historians know more about the business of the Admiral's Men at the Rose than any company, 1594–1603, because of Henslowe's diary. We know the titles of the plays performed daily through November 5, 1597, the order of performance, the rhythm of introducing new plays, Henslowe's share of the daily receipts, the breaks taken for holidays such as Lent, financial arrangements with players and dramatists, and starting in November 1597 through 1603 the expenses laid out for playbooks and apparel.[10] Henslowe's records provide the raw data on commercial aspects of the Elizabethan repertory. In addition to counting repertory items and deducing their content and genre, we may interpret the scheduling to reveal certain commercial strategies. One such strategy is the exploitation of popular subjects within a company's own holdings. For example, the Admiral's Men began playing Marlowe's *Doctor Faustus* on September 30, 1594, and in the following months they scheduled it five times in conjunction with a lost magician play, "The Wise Man of West Chester."[11] For another example, the Admiral's Men often scheduled *The Jew of Malta* in proximity to a play Henslowe called

"Mahomett," which undoubtedly exploited similarly prickly views of Mediterranean otherness. In a variation of this principle, the Admiral's Men routinely scheduled two-part plays on consecutive afternoons, as with the pairing of the two parts of *Tamburlaine* in 1594–95. In 1595–96, when this serial was retired, the company scheduled the two-part "Tamar Cham" as a substitute.

Although theater historians know considerably less about the daily business of other companies, what we do know suggests that companies also capitalized on the popular items in each other's repertories. Shakespeare joined the Chamberlain's Men in 1594, bringing his plays with him (presumably); he soon contributed *Romeo and Juliet, A Midsummer Night's Dream,* and *Merchant of Venice* to the company's offerings. In different ways, each play invited playgoers to remember aspects of *The Jew of Malta,* a staple in the repertory of the Admiral's Men. The Chamberlain's Men recalled the *Tamburlaine* plays with Pistol's comic rant in *2 Henry IV,* and they picked up the new fashion in humours plays prompted by the Admiral's *Comedy of Humours* with Shakespeare's *Merry Wives of Windsor* and Ben Jonson's pair, *Every Man in His Humour* and *Every Man out of His Humour*. This competition was not limited to these two companies. If the Queen's Men were indeed playing at the Swan in 1595, and if they had the old Queen's Men's repertory, then the Chamberlain's Men could have offered Shakespeare's *King John* in competition with the Queen's two-part *Troublesome Reign of King John*. An even richer repertorial competition might have occurred if the Queen's Men offered *The Famous Victories of Henry V,* for the Admiral's Men had a new play called "Henry V" in November 1595, and the Chamberlain's Men had one now called *1 Henry IV,* which used narrative bits from the Queen's Men's old play. Various plays on the Wars of the Roses might have referenced one another at the Boar's Head and Globe. Derby's Men, headed by the venerable Robert Browne, probably played the two-part *Edward IV* at the Boar's Head in 1599. Perhaps then or soon after, the Chamberlain's Men might have revived *2* and *3 Henry VI* and *Richard III;* these plays were printed in new editions in 1600 and 1602, respectively, perhaps a sign of their return to the stage.

There is further evidence from the boys' companies of repertorial commerce. There had been organizations of prepubescent players since the reign of Henry VIII, associated with the crown through its chapels and schools. In the 1580s these children's companies staged plays with classical subjects and moral themes at court and at their small indoor playhouses. Closed in 1590 or thereabouts for reasons now lost, the Children of Paul's reopened in 1599 at St. Paul's and the Children of the Chapel in 1600 at the Blackfriars. Both companies had a more commercial edge, competing openly now with the flourishing adult enterprises. To make their repertory more modern and marketable, the Children of Paul's attracted the talents of John Marston, and he opened their season in 1599 with *Antonio and Mellida,* the first part of a revenge play to be completed with *Antonio's Revenge* in 1600. The plays formed a competition across company lines with the Admiral's Men's *The Spanish Tragedy* and the Chamberlain's Men's *Hamlet.* By 1602, the Children of Paul's had *Blurt, Master Constable,* which has a clownish set of policemen similar to Dogberry and his crew in *Much Ado About Nothing*. The Children of the Chapel, bankrolled as they had previously been by Henry Evans, leased the Blackfriars property again in September 1600, this time from Richard Burbage (Richard's father, James, had bought the Blackfriars in 1596, but the Chamberlain's Men did not use it at that time). The Children of the Chapel soon attracted the talents of

Ben Jonson, who had been writing for both the Admiral's and Chamberlain's Men. Jonson provided *Cynthia's Revels* to the boys in 1600–01 and *Poetaster* in 1601. *Poetaster* prompted a commercial sparring among the companies, famously called "The War of the Theaters," when Thomas Dekker provided the Chamberlain's Men with *Satiromastix,* one plot of which makes fun of Jonson's literary pretensions. The Children of Paul's joined the game by playing *Satiromastix* also.

The construction of playhouses in 1598 (Boar's Head), 1599 (Globe), and 1600 (Fortune) illustrate refinements in the Burbage business model. Whereas James Burbage might have built the Theatre in 1576 "on spec," in the sense that he might not have had a resident company in mind, the Burbages definitely had the Chamberlain's Men in mind when they constructed the Globe, as did Philip Henslowe and Edward Alleyn have the Admiral's Men in mind when they built the Fortune. Oliver Woodliffe and Richard Samwell, who built the Boar's Head, were money men, not theater men; they pursued the expansion of their enterprise in 1599 with an understanding that Derby's Men, led by Robert Browne, would be the resident company.[12] Browne invested money as well as professional expertise to the Boar's Head business. Another refinement was the investment of the resident company in the playhouse itself. Burbage had come to own the building of the Theatre largely because he outlasted his brother-in-law, John Brayne, and Brayne's heirs in lawsuits over profits from the playhouse. Burbage's sons in turn inherited the Theatre and the Blackfriars. But when the Globe was built, some of the men who had long owned shares in the company now joined Richard (player) and his brother Cuthbert (company investor) in buying shares in the playhouse; among them were William Shakespeare and John Heminges, who would later join with fellow player Henry Condell in publishing a folio of Shakespeare's plays (1623). At the Fortune, Edward Alleyn and his father-in-law, Philip Henslowe, put up the money for the construction, and they were keenly aware of marketing their new house. They acquired plays with the word "Fortune" in the title. And, in a move to attract their old crowds from the Rose, Edward Alleyn came out of a three-year retirement to introduce new offerings and reprise old favorites. Among those revivals were *The Jew of Malta,* for which the Admiral's Men bought "divers thing*es*" at a cost of £5 10s.; *The Spanish Tragedy,* for which they paid Ben Jonson 40s. plus some part of £10 for new parts; and *Doctor Faustus,* for which Samuel Rowley and William Bird were paid £4 on November 22, 1602, for additions.

The Playhouse World After 1603: Royal Patronage, More Playhouses, and Fewer Companies

Queen Elizabeth died on March 24, 1603, and James VI of Scotland acceded to the throne as King James I. Scattered entries in Henslowe's diary in March and May of 1603 indicate that playing was disrupted, and by summer plague had returned. The companies went on tour, as they had usually done, plague or no. They traveled in 1603, specifically because London civic leaders ordered their playhouses closed, but at some times during every year they traveled out of a deeply ingrained sense that touring was what companies "did," as well as out of an obligation to their patron to represent him in the countryside, both where he had and where he wanted influence (scholars used to believe that companies toured only in financial desperation, but the research from the Records of Early English Drama project has shown that belief to be in error). In October 1603, Edward Alleyn exchanged letters with his wife, who wrote that "All the Companyes be Come hoame & well," but added that "Browne of the Boares head is dead & dyed very pore."[13] The Chamberlain's Men toured also, but now under the patronage of the new king. A royal patent dated May 19, 1603, specified that the company had become the King's Men and authorized them to play at the Globe as well as travel freely in the provinces. The patent names the player-sharers, men familiar from the former Chamberlain's company, including Richard Burbage, William Shakespeare, John Heminges, and Henry Condell. In the winter of 1603, the Admiral's Men at the Fortune acquired the patronage of Prince Henry. Worcester's Men became Queen Anne's Men in 1604; they played at the Boar's Head in 1604, moving to the newly constructed Red Bull in 1606. The Children of the Chapel at Blackfriars became the Children of the Queen's Revels.

For the King's Men, some immediate consequences of their new patronage are suggested by their business with the court in 1603–04, as they awaited the reopening of the London playhouses. Records from the Office of the Chamber show that the King's Men entertained their new patron during the Christmas season at Wilton and Hampton Court, where the king had moved to escape the London plague; the company also received £30 in February 1604 in compensation for the continued closure of the Globe.[14] In August 1604, they attended the king on the occasion of a visit from the Spanish ambassador. By the winter of 1604–05, playing had returned to normal, and the explosion of theatrical activity at court during the holidays illustrates the spirit of festivity that accompanied the cessation of plague. The King's Men gave ten performances, the Prince's Men gave eight, the Children of the Queen's Revels gave two, and Queen Anne's players gave one. The offerings of the King's Men began with *Othello* on the night of All Hallows (November 1); they included *Measure for Measure, Merry Wives of Windsor, Comedy of Errors, Love's Labor's Lost, Henry V,* "The Spanish Maze," *Every Man in His Humour,* and *Every Man out of His Humour* and ended with a second showing of *The Merchant of Venice* on Shove Tuesday (February 12).[15]

Philip Henslowe stopped keeping his diary of theatrical activity at the Rose and Fortune playhouses in 1603. Consequently for evidence on commerce, theater historians have become even more dependent on the publication of plays, official records, and gossip from courtiers and commoners. As it happens, more plays owned by the King's Men survive in print after 1603 than those by the Prince's Men, Queen Anne's Men, or the Children of the Queen's Revels, and more titles of their plays presented at court are recorded. This fact has invited the opinion that the King's Men were more successful than their fellows in the business, and that they appealed to a higher class of playgoer. However, when the evidence of competition is considered from the perspective of commercial strategies, it is possible to argue that little changed in the companies' intra- and cross-repertorial competition. For example, in the years from 1604 to 1607, the Chamberlain's/King's Men acquired at least three revenge plays: *Othello, The Devil's Charter,* and *The Revenger's Tragedy.* As evidence of cross-company competition, Worcester's/Queen Anne's Men at the Boar's Head acquired several plays on the theme of the patient wife and prodigal husband in the years from 1602 to 1605: *How a Man May Choose a Good Wife from a Bad, A Woman Killed with Kindness,* and *The Wise Woman of Hogsden.* The Admiral's/Prince's Men spun the gender roles of the formula in 1604–06 with the two-part *Honest Whore [and Patient Man]*. And the King's Men, having already acquired Shakespeare's *All's Well That Ends Well,* acquired also *The London Prodigal* (1603–04), *The Fair Maid of Bristow* (1603–04), *A Yorkshire Tragedy* (1605–06), and *The Miseries of Enforced Marriage* (1606–07). After 1606, the King's Men imitated the success of the Children of the Queen's Revels in the popular new genre of tragicomedy.

Again in 1608–09, as in 1603–04 and 1592–94, plague returned to London and shut down the playhouses for more than a year. There would be another fierce wave in 1625 before the even more powerful force of religious antitheatricalism shut the playhouses in 1642. When playing resumed, perhaps as late as April 1610, the Children of Paul's had disappeared as a commercial entity. The Children of the Queen's Revels, after some personnel changes, reemerged at the short-lived indoor Whitefriars playhouse. Of particular interest to theatrical commerce at this time, the King's Men acquired the indoor Blackfriars playhouse. James Burbage, father of Richard and Cuthbert and original wheeler-dealer behind the building of the Theatre in Shoreditch, had bought the property of the Blackfriars in 1596. He died before the Chamberlain's Men were relocated there, and Richard, who inherited the property, leased it in September 1600 to Henry Evans to use it for a company of boys as he had before 1590. In 1608, however, he turned the lease back to Burbage, who took it up for the King's Men.

For theater historians, the big commercial question post-1609 has been how the King's Men managed two playhouses, both in the scheduling of playing dates and the assignment of repertory. There appears to be a contemporary witness that the King's Men played at the indoor Blackfriars playhouse in the winter and the outdoor Globe in the summer. In 1699 James Wright published *Historia Histrionica,* in which characters discuss the playhouse world before the start of the Civil War in the 1640s. One of Wright's characters refers to the Blackfriars as a winter house and the Globe as a summer house. Because of this 1699 witness, and because of the higher prices of admission at the indoor houses, one answer to the commercial question has been that the King's Men began to design a repertory specifically for the Blackfriars and its putatively upscale audience. By this theory, part of their plan involved acquiring the talents of Francis Beaumont and John Fletcher, who had teamed up in 1608 after both experienced flops working alone for the Children of the Queen's Revels (Beaumont's was *The Knight of the Burning Pestle,* Fletcher's *The Faithful Shepherdess*). Another part was reacquiring the talents of Ben Jonson, who had recently written *Epicoene* for the Whitefriars company. It is certainly true that Beaumont and Fletcher immediately provided the hit *Philaster,* which the King's Men played at the Globe (according to its 1620 title page) and twice at Court in 1612–13. Fletcher, working alone or in collaboration with other dramatists such as Philip Massinger, produced *The Island Princess* for the King's Men in 1621. Jonson supplied both *The Alchemist* (1610) and *Catiline* (1611) to the King's Men. *The Alchemist* joined *Philaster* and sixteen other plays in performance at court in 1612–13.

But some evidence is at odds with the argument that the company divided its repertory into summer and winter offerings at the Globe and the Blackfriars. Scholars supporting the idea of division have argued that the company made repertorial choices on the basis of novelty and taste: new classy plays were given at Blackfriars, October through April; old "fillers" were given at the Globe, May through September. However, the titles of the King's Men's offerings at court, 1612–13, show a mix of old and new plays, as well as classy and lowbrow ones. A new, undoubtedly classy offering probably in the new genre of tragicomedy was "Cardenio," reputedly in part by Shakespeare and now lost. But others, for example the also-lost "Knot of Fools" and "A Bad Beginning Makes a Good Ending," do not sound like particularly upscale fare. Also, the revivals in the 1612–13 court offerings were decidedly old plays, even if in their own time they were hardly mere fillers: for example, *The Merry Devil of Edmonton, Othello, Much Ado About Nothing, Julius Caesar, 1 Henry IV,* and *The Merry Wives of Windsor.*

Another piece of evidence that questions the old view is that the Globe was open at least in some years in April. Prince Lewis Frederick of Wüttemberg saw *Othello* there in April 1610. Simon Forman, a physician-astrologer and occasional playgoer, saw *Macbeth* at the Globe on April 20, 1611; a play otherwise unknown called "Richard the 2" on April 30; *Cymbeline,* in an undated entry; and the relatively new *The Winter's Tale* on May 15. With evidence that old plays were revived in the winter for the Court and that relatively new plays were performed at the Globe in late spring, it is hard to argue for all that much difference in repertorial offerings at the Blackfriars and Globe. Perhaps the safest course is to use the performance history of *The Duchess of Malfi* as guide. The play was acquired in 1614, and, according to its 1623 title-page advertisement, it was played at the Blackfriars and the Globe. Given that the Globe was immediately rebuilt after it burned in June 1613, it makes sense to assume that the King's Men expected for the future to make full use of their best repertorial material at both of their houses.

Without much evidence on theatrical commerce until Henry Herbert became master of the revels in 1623 and kept record books of court activities, theater historians find it difficult after 1609 to track the success of playing companies other than the King's Men. And by 1625 many of the familiar lines of demarcation among companies were breaking down, as royal patronage ebbed and companies were held together by the sheer willpower of veteran player-managers. The Fortune burned in 1621 and was rebuilt, but it was unable to recapture its previous stature. Lady Elizabeth's Men were at Langley's old Swan playhouse in 1611, if the title page of their play *A Chaste Maid in Cheapside* is to be believed. By 1614, however, they had moved to the multipurpose bear garden and playhouse built by Philip Henslowe (of the Rose) and another investor, Jacob Meade; there they played *Bartholomew Fair* (with some grumbling about the unpleasant location from Jonson). Queen Anne's Men, in part through the energies of their player-manager Christopher Beeston, played at the Red Bull from 1606 to 1617, offering *The White Devil* in 1611. In 1617, Beeston engineered the construction of an indoor house, the Cockpit, perhaps contemplating an imitation of the King's Men's two playhouses. The Cockpit stayed in business, while Beeston spent the next several decades remaking companies out of the remnants of defunct men's and boys' organizations.

Something of the success of early modern English drama as a commercial, literary, and cultural phenomenon is illustrated by the durability of *The Jew of Malta,* whose publication in 1633—perhaps forty-five years after its debut—indicates a still-vital stage life, including performance at court. It had traveled from its original company owners into the possession of companies run by Christopher Beeston. From Henry Herbert's record books, we learn of other plays taken to court in their old age, including *The Alchemist* (January 1, 1623), *Twelfth Night* (February 2, 1623), *Volpone* (December 27, 1624), and *Knight of the Burning Pestle* (February 28, 1636). This last had been acquired by Queen Henrietta's players, who also owned *The Changeling* and *'Tis Pity*

She's a Whore. *The Changeling,* when published in 1653, identified its playing venues as the Cockpit/Phoenix and Salisbury Court playhouses. Unlike the Globe, which was torn down in 1644, the Fortune in 1649, and the Blackfriars in 1655, the buildings of the Red Bull, Cockpit/Phoenix, and Salisbury Court survived the long official closure from 1642 to 1660, at which time Charles II was restored to the throne. But few of the plays and fewer players also survived to restore the former luster of their playhouse world. Samuel Pepys expressed a jaded attitude toward the old drama when he described a performance of *Doctor Faustus* at the Red Bull in 1662 as "so wretchedly & poorly done that we were sick of it." A new sensibility, and a new cadre of playwrights, would determine theatrical commerce for Pepys and his generation of Restoration playgoers.

NOTES

1. For data on touring and provincial performance, see the volumes in the Records of Early English Drama series, for example, *York,* ed. Alexandra F. Johnston and Margaret Rogerson, 2 vols (Toronto: U of Toronto P, 1979). The definitive resources on early modern playing companies and stages are G. E. Bentley, *The Jacobean and Caroline Stage,* 7 vols. (Oxford: Clarendon P, 1941–68); E. K. Chambers, *The Elizabethan Stage,* 4 vols. (Oxford: Clarendon P, 1923); and Andrew Gurr, *The Shakespearian Playing Companies* (Oxford: Clarendon P, 1996). I am much in debt to these sources throughout this chapter.
2. For issues and evidence on the early playhouses, see William Ingram, *The Business of Playing: The Beginnings of the Adult Professional Theater in Elizabethan London* (Ithaca: Cornell UP, 1992).
3. For issues and evidence on the history of the Queen's Men, see Scott McMillin and Sally-Beth MacLean, *The Queen's Men and Their Plays* (Cambridge: Cambridge UP, 1998) 28.
4. McMillin and MacLean 24–36.
5. Chambers 4.302.
6. R. A. Foakes, ed., *Henslowe's Diary,* 2nd ed. (Cambridge: Cambridge UP, 2002) 16; Henslowe's share equaled half the take from the galleries.
7. McMillin and MacLean, collating records from the *Records of Early English Drama* (REED) volumes, find the Queen's Men in 1592–93 at provincial locations such as Faversham, Folkstone, New Romney, Cambridge, Ipswich, Norwich, Saffron Walden, Bristol, Bath, Leicester, Oxford, Coventry, and York (182–83).
8. For issues and evidence on the Swan playhouse, see William Ingram, *A London Life in the Brazen Age: Francis Langley, 1548–1602* (Cambridge: Harvard UP, 1978).
9. For issues and evidence on the Boar's Head playhouse, see Herbert Berry, *The Boar's Head Playhouse* (London: Associated UP, 1986).
10. There are of course errors, inconsistencies, and omissions in Henslowe's records, so this claim is a bit exaggerated.
11. Lost plays are indicated here by quotation marks; plays extant in print are in italics.
12. Berry 33–34. Ingram suggests that a similar partnership of builder and player lay behind the construction of the playhouse at Newington (*Business of Playing* 163–77).
13. Foakes 297.
14. For records of the Office of the Chamber, see David Cook and F. P. Wilson, eds., *Dramatic Records in the Declared Accounts of the Treasurer of the Chamber 1558–1642* (Malone Society *Collections* 6, Oxford: Oxford UP, 1961).
15. For records of the Office of the Revels, see William Streitberger, ed., *Jacobean and Caroline Revels Accounts, 1603–1642* (Malone Society *Collections* 13, Oxford: Oxford UP, 1986).

READING LIST

Bentley, G. E. *The Jacobean and Caroline Stage*. 7 vols. Oxford: Oxford UP, 1941–68.

Berry, Herbert. *The Boar's Head Playhouse*. Illus. C. Walter Hodges. London: Associated UP, 1986.

Cerasano, S. P. "Edward Alleyn: 1566–1626." *Edward Alleyn: Elizabethan Actor, Jacobean Gentleman*. Ed. Aileen Reid and Robert Maniura. London: Dulwich Picture Gallery, 1994.

Chambers, E. K. *The Elizabethan Stage*. 4 vols. Oxford: Clarendon P, 1923.

Cook, David, and F. P. Wilson, eds. *Dramatic Records in the Declared Accounts of the Treasurer of the Chamber 1558–1642*. Malone Society *Collections* 6, Oxford: Oxford UP, 1961.

Gurr, Andrew. *The Shakespeare Company, 1594–1642*. Cambridge: Cambridge UP, 2004.

———. *The Shakespearian Playing Companies*. Oxford: Clarendon P, 1996.

Foakes, R. A. *Henslowe's Diary*. 2nd ed. (1st ed. with R. T. Rickert, 1961). Cambridge: Cambridge UP, 2002.

Ingram, William. *The Business of Playing: The Beginnings of the Adult Professional Theater in Elizabethan London*. Ithaca: Cornell UP, 1992.

———. *A London Life in the Brazen Age: Francis Langley, 1548–1602*. Cambridge: Harvard UP, 1978.

Knutson, Roslyn Lander. *The Repertory of Shakespeare's Company, 1594–1613*. Fayetteville: U of Arkansas P, 1991.

McMillin, Scott, and Sally-Beth MacLean. *The Queen's Men and Their Plays*. Cambridge: Cambridge UP, 1998.

Streitberger, William, ed. *Jacobean and Caroline Revels Accounts, 1603–1642*. Malone Society *Collections* 13, Oxford: Oxford UP, 1986.

3

Fulgens and Lucres and Early Tudor Drama

Greg Walker

This chapter focuses on the drama of the late medieval and early Renaissance periods, the time when the religious mystery cycles and the secular morality plays and interludes held sway. This was the period before the building of the professional theaters (the first of which opened in the suburbs of London in the 1560s), during which rather than people "going to the theater," "theater" in the form of plays performed by touring players or members of the local community "came" to people. This drama was thus essentially localized and was designed to fulfill a range of social functions as well as to entertain. It might instruct and confirm its audiences (and actors) in the principles of their religious faith; criticize moral failings such as greed, pride, lust, or overambition; or protest against social injustices such as poverty or political or economic oppression.[1] Because these plays contained such material and dealt with characters that were often personified sins, virtues, or human attributes such as ignorance or understanding, critics have often dismissed them as crudely didactic, socially and intellectually conservative, and lacking the sophistication of later drama. But this is misleading. Many of the plays were experimental and socially progressive. This chapter considers one such play, Henry Medwall's *Fulgens and Lucres*. As I will suggest, it is both dramatically innovative, playing with its audience's expectations about what constitutes a dramatic performance, and politically sophisticated, dealing with an issue of great sensitivity in an open-ended, accommodating way that neither condemns nor insists upon social change, but allows for a degree of accommodation between social classes. In order to appreciate the distinctive qualities of the play, however, we need to consider it in the context of its original performance. To do so, let us eavesdrop on a curious conversation.

The Dramatic Context: *Fulgens and Lucres* in Performance

It is Christmastide 1491—or thereabouts. And after what one imagines was a very good dinner in the household of Cardinal John Morton, archbishop of Canterbury, a visitor to the hall began loudly and unexpectedly to address the assembled throng regarding their seeming lack of gratitude for the meal that they had just enjoyed. Soon a second man, apparently a household servant, approached him, and they talked about a play that was going to be performed for the entertainment of their patron and his guests. There was initially some confusion, as the first man, our source calls him simply "A," initially thought that the second, let us follow the source and call him "B," was one of the actors, given that, as he said, "Ther is so myche nyce array / Amonge these galandes now aday / That a man shall not lightly / Know a player from a nother man."[2] But, after some discussion of the plot of the play to follow and the intentions of the actors, they stood back to watch the unfolding action attentively. After no more than a couple of minutes, however, A could resist the temptation no longer and declared loudly his intention to approach one of the actors onstage for a job, as he had just announced that he was looking for a servant. This apparent confusion of the play-world with reality evidently horrified B, who warned his fellow,

> [. . .] Pece, let be!
> Be God, thou wyll distroy all the play. (362–63)

But A's response was dismissive. His intrusion, he confidently asserted, would improve the play, not spoil it.

> "Distroy the play," quod a? Nay, nay,
> The play began never till now!
> I wyll be doing, I make God avow,
>
> For there is not in this hondred myle
> A feter bawde [better pimp] than I am one. (363–68)

Such confidence might seem misplaced. But on this occasion A turned out to be right. His intervention did improve the play. For A and B were, of course, themselves actors—or rather, *are* dramatic characters—and their "intervention" in the action initiates the subplot of the innovative play known to modern scholars as *Fulgens and Lucres*. Our "source" is the text of the play, printed by John Rastell (Thomas More's brother-in-law and one of London's most experimental early printers) at some point between 1510 and 1516.

It is worth foregrounding the strangeness of the play's opening in this slightly arch way because it is easy to lose sight of just how dramaturgically sophisticated *Fulgens* is. It is conventional to see "early drama" (by which people usually mean anything before Shakespeare) as a crude form, reliant on simple plots and limited characterization and designed to teach basic religious and moral truths. It is instructive, then, to consider a play such as *Fulgens,* which is so obviously none of these things. *Fulgens* deals with its audience's expectations in an overtly self-referential and playful way. The preliminary exchanges between A and B create the impression that the play flows naturally from the feasting that it accompanies, leaving the audience uncertain whether they are watching actors acting or impatient spectators threatening to spoil the play. Nor are A and B obviously "instructive" figures in any obvious way. They are certainly not morally admirable: they swear, fight, lust after Lucres's female servant, Joan, and generally seek their own financial and social advancement. Yet the play does not overtly condemn them either, using them instead as sources of morally ambiguous comedy and as links between audience and actors in much the way that Shakespeare would use fools such as Feste and Touchstone a century later. All of this is obviously the work of a playwright and acting company so much in command of their chosen medium that they can playfully experiment with its conventions, seemingly confident that their audience will appreciate and enjoy their experimentation.

The teasing complexities of the play, and of A and B's parts in it, do not end there, however. For the names "A" and "B" in the text seem not to have been the given names of characters at all, but flags of convenience indicating two roles that were taken by individuals in Morton's household (and others elsewhere, if the play was later performed by other companies) who would effectively have been "playing" themselves, and bringing their own names with them.[3] Notably the script makes a point of never naming either character, having them refer to each other only as "what calt" ("whatever your name is") and making the noble characters address them vaguely as "thou," "syr," or "he / That I have sought" (1003–04). At one point A even claims to have forgotten his own name and offers to go and ask "som of my company" what it is (1782).

The point about names is not incidental, particularly if it prompts us to reconsider a well-known tale concerning a young and highly precocious servant in Morton's household at about this time, Thomas More. More's son-in-law William Roper's *Lyfe of Sir Thomas More* famously relates how More's interest in drama and talent for mimicry prompted him at times to make impromptu interventions into plays. "Though he was younge of yeares," Roper noted,

> yeat wold he at Christmas tyde sodenly sometimes steppe in among the players and, never studyeng for the matter, make a parte of his owne there presently among them, which made the lookers on more sporte than all the plaiers beside.[4]

Scholars have been reluctant to accept the association of this story with the subplot of *Fulgens,* but this seems unnecessarily severe. Admittedly we have precise dates for neither the first performance of the play in Morton's house nor More's period of service there. But the coincidence seems too strong to ignore, and it seems reasonable to infer that a recollection of a young boy apparently stepping in among the actors during a Christmastide play in the cardinal's great hall and a play written for performance in that hall at roughly the same time, in which a couple of characters seem to step in among the players and make parts of their own (thereby providing more sport for the spectators than the rather dour events of the main plot), might very plausibly refer to the same event. Roper's account may well, therefore, be an only slightly fanciful reconstruction of More's own recollection of having played one of the comic servants, most probably B, who does indeed, as we have seen, promise to improve the play through his involvement.[5] The two roles are thus likely to have been the source of a whole series of in-jokes that we can only begin to guess at from the text alone. (The impact of lines such as A's "This felowe and I be maysterles / And lyve most parte in ydelnes" [398–99] seems predictable, if indeed the two were well-known local characters.) But the idea of two household servants appearing in a play under their own names and, notionally at least, "pretending" to be actors creates fascinating possibilities and tensions in the play on a more general level, raising questions about what exactly is part of the play and what is "real life," who is performing and for whom they are performing.

But there is more to *Fulgens* than simply the possibility that the future lord chancellor of England may have acted in it. It has the distinction of being not only the first secular drama in English to be printed, but also the first for which a known author can be established. The title page of the first edition declared it to have been

> Compyled by mayster Henry Medwall, late chapelayne to ye right reverent fader in god, Johan Morton, cardynall and Archebysshop of Caunterbury.[6]

Henry Medwall was born around September 8, 1461, in Southwark, the borough on the south bank of the Thames, across London Bridge from the city. He attended Eton College and King's College, Cambridge, studying arts and civil law, before finding employment in the service of the future Cardinal Morton, who was then bishop of Ely.

Despite the (possibly erroneous) claim in the printed text that Medwall was "late chaplain" to the archbishop, his work for Morton was primarily legal. As a notary public, he was responsible for drafting and authenticating legal documents and was also keeper of Morton's legal archive. In his spare time he also evidently wrote, and probably also produced, entertainments for his employer's household, for *Fulgens* is not the only play of his to survive. In 1530, John Rastell's son William printed *Nature,* which was also attributed, posthumously, to Medwall's pen.[7]

If we are considering the nature and significance of *Fulgens,* the printed title page is a good place to start, as it suggests a number of interesting things about the play and about its author's and printer's attitudes toward it. First it indicates the affinity that early humanist drama enjoyed with other quasi-dramatic forms such as the dialogue. The edition announces itself in the following terms:

> Here is conteyned a godely interlude of Fulgens, Cenatoure of Rome, Lucres his doughter, Gayus Flaminius & Publius Cornelius, of the disputacyon of nobleness, & is devyded in two partyes, to be played at ii [two] tymes.

The modern convention is, of course, to call the play *Fulgens and Lucres* after the first two characters named here. But this is somewhat awkward, and it has never been made entirely clear why the text should carry the name of the relatively minor character Fulgens (indeed, the name itself is probably a printer's error for Medwall's source's "Fulgeus")[8] alongside that of his daughter, rather than of the central antagonists, Gayus and Cornelius. What Rastell's title page suggests is that he, and perhaps Medwall too, probably thought of the play as *The Disputation of Nobleness,* a title more in keeping with his source, John Tiptoft's *Declamation of Noblesse* (see later), and that the names of the principal characters were provided as supplementary information only. The text is described, we might note, as both an "interlude" (of which more in a moment) and a "disputacyon"—that is, a formal debate, and Rastell's equivocation between the two terms suggests an element of uncertainty on his part about what exactly he was printing and how much appeal it might hold for prospective customers. Previously printers had ignored the rather ephemeral form of drama, choosing instead to print more substantial and respectable genres in prose and verse. So, in printing *Fulgens,* Rastell was taking something of a risk, gambling perhaps on the humanist content of the text attracting some of his regular customers, while he also tried to draw in new buyers who might be interested in reading or staging a play with a substantial social pedigree. Hence his decision to hedge his bets and refer to the book as something his customers would have been familiar with: "a disputation" or dialogue, as well as something that they may have had less contact with: an "interlude" from a distinguished churchman's household.

The term "interlude" has come to refer to an entire genre of early Renaissance moral and political plays performed in the great halls of noble households and other communal spaces and acted by small touring companies or actors drawn from the nobleman's own household. Rastell's use of the term here, along with the other details that he provides on the title page, tells us a good deal about the circumstances of the original production. The play is, we are told, an "interlude [. . .] in two parts, to be played at [two] times." This highlights the intimate association between the play and the household context of holiday feasting and entertainment for which it was written. For the word interlude, or "enterlude" as it was often spelled in the early Tudor period, suggests a play or game (*ludus*) that was brought into the hall between (*inter* or *entre*) the courses of a formal meal. And, as the text itself confirms, the "two times" at which this play was intended to be performed were the two main meals, dinner in the middle of the day and supper in the evening, on a single day, probably during one of the major holidays in the late medieval calendar, Christmas or Eastertide. The action begins with A drawing attention to the festive banquet setting by mischievously asking the spectators,

> A[h], for goddis will
> What mean ye, syrs, to stond so styll?
> Have not ye etyn [eaten] al your fill
> And payd no thinge therefore? (1–4)

Perhaps anticipating the audience's mock indignation at this jibe, he quickly moves on to commend his host's hospitality to all those present before launching into the opening exchanges with his fellow servant B. The first half of the play ends similarly with a reference to dining. The characters commit themselves to meeting again soon, "in the evynyng, aboute suppere" (1360). And, as the second part begins, A enters alone once more to remind the assembled spectators that

> [. . .] my felowys and I were here
> Today, whan ye where at dyner,
> And shewed you a lytyll disport [. . .] (1440–42)

Mention of "A" and "B" returns us to the most innovative feature of the play, as it alone among the early Tudor interludes has something that is legitimate to describe as a fully developed subplot. The main plot is set in ancient Rome and, as the title page suggests, concerns a disputation between two characters, the aristocratic but amoral Publius Cornelius and the virtuous but nonaristocratic Gayus Flamineus. The prize at stake is marriage to the virtuous and beautiful Lucres, daughter to the wealthy senator Fulgens, who has declared that she will marry whichever of them can prove himself the more noble. Publius Cornelius interprets nobility in a social context and argues for the superior lineage of his family, while Gayus interprets it morally and asserts the superiority of his own honor and virtue. In the end Lucres chooses Gayus, as we probably suspected that she might, although not without qualification, as we shall see. Yet the play offers a complex, equivocal exploration of the issues at stake rather than a simple moral that either virtuous poverty or social status is better. Again, Medwall provides sophistication of argument and exposition where we might, if we followed conventional scholarship, have expected didactic simplicity. A and B's courtship of Lucres's maid Joan (referred to in the dramatis personae simply as "Ancilla," a female servant) does not simply offer comic relief from the seriousness of this central "disputation" (although A does at one point refer to the "dyvers toyes" or jests "mengled" with the "matter principall" in order to provide "solace" for those spectators who enjoy "tryfles and japys" [1452–61]). It provides a counterpoint to, and running commentary on, the fortunes of the principal characters. Similarly, their pursuit of Joan offers a rival, more materialistic series of marriage negotiations to set alongside the more idealistic attitudes of Lucres and her father. Indeed, Joan's concerns about the kind of jointure that A and B might offer her probably had more in common with most Tudor marriage negotiations than Lucres's concerns for virtue and honor in a potential spouse.

The Intellectual Context: The Debate About True Nobility

The fact that Medwall felt the need to introduce a subplot should not, however, suggest that he lacked confidence that the central disputation would entertain his audience. On the contrary, the latter concerned an issue of direct importance to both the author and his episcopal employer. The disputation drew upon a prose treatise, the *Contoversia de nobilite* ("The Controversy [or Debate] About Nobility"), written by the Florentine lawyer Buonaccorso da Montemagno in 1428, which was translated into English around 1448 by John Tiptoft, earl of Worcester, and published by England's first printer, William Caxton, as the *Declamation of Noblesse,* in 1481. The central issue at stake in the treatise—"does true nobility consist in aristocratic birth or in personal virtue?"—may seem to modern eyes relatively easy to settle; yet it preoccupied contemporary writers, as, for them, what may appear to us a predominantly moral issue also had profound—and profoundly troubling—social, political, and cultural implications.

The sheer longevity of the debate is a good index of its problematic nature. Its origins were, as with so much of medieval culture, classical. Horace, Cicero, and the Stoics had asserted that nobility resided in personal virtue rather than social status or family wealth,[9] but they were arguing against the prevailing assumptions of Roman society, in which a small number of great families dominated civic politics. The debate was renewed and reinvigorated in the Italian Renaissance. The exiled Florentine Brunetto Latini's *The Books of Treasure* cited Horace in defense of the claim that true nobility was nothing but virtue and good character. Hence, he argued, learned men should be preferred to ignorant aristocrats in appointments to civic offices, as knowledge was the basis of all wisdom, and wisdom brought the only true virtue. Latini's pupil Dante in turn argued in *The Banquet* that those who thought that ancient wealth was the basis of nobility were profoundly mistaken, for "wherever virtue is, there is nobleness."[10]

In England, Geoffrey Chaucer had inserted a defense of the idea that "gentilesse" lay in virtue rather than wealth or lineage into his *Wife of Bath's Tale* when the old faery woman delivered a forthright lecture on the subject to her young, knightly husband:

> [. . .] ye speken of swich gentilesse
> As is descended out of old richesse,
> That therfore sholden ye be gentil men,
> Swich arrogance is nat worth an hen.
> Looke who that is moost vertuous alway,
> Pryvee and apert [in public], and moost entendeth ay [always]
> To do the gentil dedes that he kan;
> Taak hym for the grettest gentil man.[11]

And in the later fifteenth century, there is considerable evidence of a renewed interest in arguments for a nobility of merit at a time when the role and influence of common lawyers and university-educated scholars in government was increasing.[12] The idea became a humanist commonplace because it addressed a real and pressing issue, the status of the educated commoner who had made his way on the strength of his own ambition in a society stratified by birth and lineage and driven by an explicitly aristocratic conception of personal honor from which he was excluded by both birth and profession.

A whole gamut of social and political tensions thus lay behind the "merry tale" told by Richard Pace, the learned secretary to Henry VIII, concerning the nobleman who had announced publicly that if his son could hunt, hawk, and blow a horn, he was educated well enough. In Pace's account it was he himself who delivered the cutting retort that if that were so, the king would need to look to the sons of commoners for his councillors in future.[13]

The issue was still generating heat in 1531, when Sir Thomas Elyot, another royal administrator, but self-taught and himself a country gentleman, argued in his *Boke Named the Governour* that those who "do thinke that nobilitie may in no wyse be but onely where men can avaunte them [boast] of auncient lignage, an ancient robe, or great possessions" were entirely mistaken. If a man is less virtuous than his ancestors, then the contrast between them is a standing reproach to him. If he is *more* virtuous, then he would be foolish to base his claim to nobility on the status of forebears who were less virtuous than he is (Elyot sig. O^{v}).[14] "Thus I conclude that nobilitie is nat after the vulgare opinion of men, but it is only the praise and surname of vertue. Whiche the lenger it contineuth in a name or lignage, the more is the nobilitie extolled and mervailled at" (Elyot $Ovii^{v}$).

It was not so much that these texts mark key moments of profound structural change in society, when new classes of courtier bureaucrats arose to displace old elites and the assumptions that sustained them. Even the briefest glance at the social history of Tudor England reveals that the traditional landed nobility retained its influence long after the publication of *Fulgens* and Elyot's *Governor*.[15] Rather the processes of challenge and accommodation between social classes and groups were a constant feature of life at the apex of late medieval and Renaissance society, part of the structure itself rather than threats from outside. It was in the very nature of the early modern social elite to be in a continual state of flux. New men, and less visibly new women, rose to positions of influence and authority all the time, often founding new dynasties in the process, and old families declined or disappeared, whether through natural wastage (the failure of a line or the inability of an heir to maintain his estate) or political displacement.

Such literary discussions of the nature of true nobility as *Fulgens* contains and the parables of social change which they told, were, consequently a vital part of the political culture. In them we can see reflected both the anxieties of the dominant landed establishment and the aspirations of the emerging meritocracy of scholars, bureaucrats, and men of business who carried on the day-to-day business of government and civil administration. Such texts oiled wheels that might otherwise have ground violently together, paralyzing the political machinery in the process. For, while seeming to argue for radical change, they almost always conclude with a compromise, either explicitly or implicitly suggesting that, while true nobility lay in virtue and good character alone, the ideal individual would combine personal virtue with noble lineage, and so be a nobleman as well as a noble man.[16] Hence Elyot's *Governor* concluded that, unless a man of base estate was so obviously superior to all other candidates that everyone recommended him, the commonwealth's governors should be chosen from among the traditional elites, for "it is of good congruence that they whiche be superiour in condition or haviour shulde have also pre-eminence in adminisatration if they be nat inferiour to other in virtue [. . .] as vertue in a gentylman is commonly mixte with more sufferaunce, more affabilitie, and myldenes than for the more parte it is in a persone rural, or of a very base lynage" (Elyot Bvi^{v}–Bvii).

Such a conclusion has led some critics to take an overtly pessimistic view of the social utility of these humanist texts. Quentin Skinner, for example, citing the passage from Elyot's *Governor* just quoted, concludes that:

> For all their apparent support [. . .] of egalitarian claims [. . .] the northern humanists generally handled the debate about *vera nobilitas* [true nobility] in such a way that any subversive implications of that argument were entirely neutralised [. . .] This stratagem was based on the empirical claim—which at one level was simply a play on words—that while virtue undoubtedly constitutes the only true nobility, it happens that the virtues are always most fully displayed by the traditional ruling classes.[17]

There is a good deal of truth in this, but Elyot's statement does not quite support the use Skinner makes of it. There are crucial qualifications in his proviso that "vertue in a gentylman is *commonly* mixte with more sufferaunce" than it is "for the more part" in baser individuals. The qualifications each carry a due weight. Elyot does not assert that virtue is found exclusively among the governing classes, or that gentlemen always—or even nearly always—possess it, only that when they do they are preferable to men of lower social rank. That is, when traditional assumptions about the social order coincide with more progressive suggestions about individual character and fitness to govern, this situation is preferable to when they do not. This is social conservatism, but of a kind that leaves room for accommodation. The aim was reform, not revolution.

The conclusion that a virtuous man was good but a virtuous nobleman was better was a platitude, but it was an enabling one, precisely because it gave something to each side in the debate. Texts such as *Fulgens* stated the claims of the meritocrats to social respectability and authority, and in satisfyingly celebratory tones, but they also provided sufficient comfort to established interests to secure their compliance in the process of accommodation. Thus the elite classes might absorb the energies of a new generation of scholars and administrators and a new portfolio of useful social ideas, without upsetting the existing hierarchies of patronage and influence. Few really successful lawyers or civil servants, after all, encouraged their sons to follow them into their professions. Rather they invested in land, "set themselves up as gentry," and, if they prospered, established aristocratic dynasties of their own.[18] Hence, Janus-faced, humanist theory accommodated itself to aristocratic practice, painted one way like a lion, the other like a lapdog. What seems hard to deny, however, is that such drama was not wholly or unproblematically conservative. Even at its most didactic, it offered too much stage time and invested too much dramatic energy in the expression of the alternative, countercultural values that it would go on to reject (here those of A and B) for the end result to be wholly or simply reactionary in its effects. Even the most apparently didactic interlude opened a door onto an alternative, imagined, reality that, once ajar, would be hard to close again definitively once the play was over.

Alternatively, some critics have made much of the fact that both Medwall and his patron Morton were themselves "self-made men," *arriviste* commoners who had risen to their present positions through diligent study and their own aptitudes and ambition. Would not such men have favored a work that argued consistently and unambiguously for a nobility of virtue rather than of blood?[19] But, on close examination *Fulgens* proves, like most examples of the tradition, less partisan and more accommodating to both sides of the argument. Given that the author of Medwall's source, John Tiptoft, combined nobility of blood with the kind of scholarly training that endowed him with humanist virtues (he was studying Latin and Greek at the University of Florence when he began work on his translation of Buonaccorso's text), this should not really surprise us. Yet Medwall's play seems even more anxious to appeal to both sides of the argument, and to offend no one, than Tiptoft had been.

Far from offering a straight choice between lineage and honor, *Fulgens* goes out of its way from the outset to tilt the balance so far in favor of Gayus that not even the most die-hard advocate of aristocratic superiority could prefer Cornelius. The latter is a dissolute and vain man who indulges in every excess of the archetypal late medieval overmighty subject. He retains criminals in his service, protecting them from the law, and may even indulge in crimes of violence and extortion himself, if Gayus's claims are correct. And in his own defense he offers not a word about his own merits, resting his case entirely upon the deeds of his ancestors and the fact that, if Lucres chooses him, she will be able to live "in ease and plesaunt idelnesse all her days" (1979). Against this straw man, Gayus's case is a catalogue of conventional virtues. He cites his own noble deeds in defense of the city, his personal piety, and the frugal simplicity of his lifestyle. This said, the future he offers Lucres is not exactly virtuous poverty. Rather he suggests that they might enjoy "moderate richess, / And that sufficient for us both" (2126–27). And more importantly he presents himself to the virtuous maid as "a man accordyng / To youre owne condicions in every thing" (2128–29). So he is in reality no dangerously jumped-up "churl" but a substantial citizen whose pedigree is only slightly less impressive than Cornelius's.

The dangers of a verdict that flies in the face of noble sensibilities are highlighted, and to some extent disarmed in the opening exchanges between A and B. When A, summarizing the plot to follow for B's benefit, announces that the debate will be taken to the Roman Senate, where a decision will finally be offered in favor of the lower-born Gayus, B responds angrily:

> By my fayth, but yf it be even as ye say,
> I wyll advyse them to change that conclusion.
> What? Will they afferme that a chorles [churl's] son
> Sholde be more noble than a gentilman born?
> Nay, beware, for men wyll have therof grete scorn:
> It may not be spoken in no maner of case. (128–33)

Having been forewarned of the "radical" nature of the verdict to come, however, the audience is allowed to soften its indignation when it becomes clear that A has got it wrong: the selection of a husband will not be taken to the Senate at all, but will be decided by Lucres alone, thus reducing it from a matter of state to a purely private decision. And, as she assures her suitors at the outset, her choice must not be seen to have any wider implications.

> [. . .] what so ever sentence I gyve betwyxt you two
> After myne owne fantasie, it shall not extende
> To any other person. I wyll that it be so,
> For why no man ellis hath theryn ado.
> It may not be notyde for a generall precedent. (1857–62)

Even then, when she does finally decide in Gayus's favor she is at pains to make clear to the audience that her choice does not imply any disrespect on her part for Cornelius's lineage or social position:

> And for all that, I wyll not dispise
> The blode of Cornelius: I pray you thinke not so.
> God forbede that ye shulde note me that wyse,
> For truely I shall honoure them where so ever I go,
> And all other that be of lyke blode also.
> But unto the blode I wyll have lytyl respect
> Wher the condicyons be synfull and abject.
>
> I pray you all, syrs, as meny as be here:
> Take not my wordis by a sinistre way. (2189–97)

Finally, when "B" challenges Lucres's decision and suggests the counter case of a gentleman of birth who also has "godely maners to his birth accordyng" (2211), she replies with due deference to traditional wisdom on the subject that,

> Suche one is worthy more lawde and praysyng
> Than many of them that hath their begynnyng
> Of low kynred [kindred/family], ellis God forbede!
> I wyll not afferme the contrary for my hede,
>
> For in that case ther may be no comparyson. (2213–17)

Thus Medwall is at pains to balance intellectual liberalism with social conservatism throughout. By staging the contest between Cornelius and Gayus as a debate, with Lucres acting as judge, he effectively contained aristocratic claims to superiority within a humanist framework: the legal moot or schoolroom disputation. In such a contest the scholar would enjoy a natural advantage, as the weapons employed—eloquence and logic—were ones with which he, rather than his aristocratic opponent, was familiar. Yet, in making the subject of the debate the marriage of Lucres, the only daughter and heiress of the wealthy and noble senator Fulgens, the play also focuses upon questions of lineage, inheritance, and dynastic succession that were of acute concern for aristocratic society, many members of which would have been among Medwall's original audience. The play thus stages a debate that is at heart about both the merits of personal virtue and the means of perpetuating it within established families. The moral, that personal honor was more important than blood alone, was aimed more at the aristocrats in the audience than the scholars. As "B" explicitly claims at the end of the play, it was devised,

> Not onely to make folke myrth and game,
> But that suche as be gentilmen of name
> May be somwhat movyd
> By this example for to eschew
> The wey of vyce and favour vertue;
> For syn is to be reprovyd

More in them, for the[ir] degre
Than in other parsons such as be
Of pour kyn and birth. (2320–27)

Rather than prompting ambitious commoners to aspire to high office, the play encouraged the aristocracy to embrace virtue and so prepare themselves more effectively for public service. The resulting fusion of moral and social distinction would, it was hoped, result in a renovation of established elite society in line with the highest standards of contemporary education and conduct. Again, reform rather than revolution was the intended outcome.

Here too the A and B scenes complement rather than undercut the emphases of the main plot. Their parodic, scatological joust at "farte prycke in cule"—in which each of them hops toward the other tethered in a squatting position, and with a broom handle held between their legs as a lance—parodies the duels of aristocratic honor culture. But the joke is as much on the crassness and folly of the servants who know no better as it is upon the absurdities of the culture it burlesques (especially given that Joan eventually deserts both A and B, leaving them to be discovered, still tethered in this embarrassing position, by Gayus). And, rather than be punished further or condemned for their immorality or folly, A and B remain onstage at the end of the play, ready to merge back into the throng of household servants from which they emerged, once the action is complete. Again, the play offers, as with its central message about true nobility, the opportunity to laugh at others' expense to both the aristocrats and the commoners in the audience, thus fulfilling A's assurance that

It is the mynde and intent
Of me and my company to content
The leste [lowest] that stondyth here. (1472–74)

That Medwall was able to do so with a play that both pushed forward the boundaries of the dramatic medium and established principles of plotting and comic business that still looked fresh a century later says much for the enduring qualities of this particular example of "early drama."

NOTES

1. See Greg Walker, *The Politics of Performance in Early Renaissance Drama* (Cambridge: Cambridge UP, 1998) 209–11, 301–03; Walker, ed. *Medieval Drama: An Anthology* (Oxford: Blackwell, 2000). All line references are to this edition.
2. Walker 308, 53–56.
3. See Meg Twycross, "The Theatricality of Medieval English Plays," *The Cambridge Companion to Medieval English Theatre,* ed. Richard Beadle (Cambridge: Cambridge UP, 1994) 37–84, esp. 79.
4. See William Roper, *The Lyfe of Sir Thomas Moore, Knyghte,* ed. E. V. Hitchcock. Early English Text Society, vol. 197 (Oxford: Oxford UP, 1935) 5.
5. See Alan Nelson, ed. *The Plays of Henry Medwall* (Woodbridge: Boydell and Brewer, 1980) 17.
6. See Walker 304.
7. See Nelson 2–14.

8. See R. J. Mitchell, *John Tiptoft (1427–1470)* (London: Longmans, Green and Co., 1938) 83.
9. See Quentin Skinner, *The Foundations of Modern Political Thought,* 2 vols. (Cambridge: Cambridge UP, 1978) 1:39–40.
10. See Skinner 46.
11. See Geoffrey Chaucer, *The Riverside Chaucer,* 3rd ed., ed. Larry D. Benson (Boston: Houghton Mifflin, 1987) 120, 1109–16.
12. For valuable studies of *Fulgens* in context, see David Bevington, *Tudor Drama and Politics* (Cambridge: Harvard UP, 1968); and Joel B. Altman, *The Tudor Play of Mind* (Berkeley: U of California P, 1978).
13. See John Skelton, *The Complete English Poems,* ed. V. J. Scattergood (Harmondsworth: Penguin, 1983) 473.
14. See Sir Thomas Elyot, *The Boke Named the Governour* (London, 1531).
15. See G. W. Bernard, *Power and Politics in Tudor England* (Aldershot: Ashgate, 2000).
16. Bernard 43.
17. Skinner 238.
18. Bernard 44.
19. John Watkins, "The Allegorical Theatre: Moralities, Interludes and Protestant Drama," *The Cambridge History of Medieval English Literature,* ed. David Wallace. (Cambridge: Cambridge UP, 1999) 767–92, esp. 783–84.

READING LIST

Altman, Joel B. *The Tudor Play of Mind: Rhetorical Inquiry and the Development of Elizabethan Drama.* Berkeley: U of California P, 1978.

Bernard, G. W. *Power and Politics in Tudor England.* Aldershot: Ashgate, 2000.

Bevington, David. *Tudor Drama and Politics: A Critical Approach to Topical Meaning.* Cambridge: Harvard UP, 1968.

Nelson, Alan, ed. *The Plays of Henry Medwall.* Woodbridge: Boydell and Brewer, 1980.

Skinner, Quentin. *The Foundations of Modern Political Thought.* 2 vols. Cambridge: Cambridge UP, 1978.

Twycross, Meg. "The Theatricality of Medieval English Plays." *The Cambridge Companion to Medieval English Theatre.* Ed. Richard Beadle. Cambridge: Cambridge UP, 1994. 37–84.

Walker, Greg. *The Politics of Performance in Early Renaissance Drama.* Cambridge: Cambridge UP, 1998.

———. ed. *Medieval Drama: An Anthology.* Oxford: Blackwell, 2000.

Watkins, John. "The Allegorical Theatre: Moralities, Interludes and Protestant Drama." *The Cambridge History of Medieval English Literature.* Ed. David Wallace. Cambridge: Cambridge UP, 1999. 767–92.

4

Tamburlaine and Renaissance Geography

John Gillies

What is the meaning of Marlowe's *Tamburlaine*? Faced with so bizarre a glorification of barbarism by comic book characters intoning a seemingly endless stream of mouth-filling but mind-numbing blank verse, the student already *au fait* with "Shakespeare our contemporary" is asked to believe that *Tamburlaine* was the enduring hit of the Elizabethan stage. The problem here lies in the word "enduring." Shakespeare's cultural endurance suggests that Elizabethan taste was not so dissimilar from our own, that the distant past is readable in contemporary terms, and thus vitally connected to the present. The phenomenon of *Tamburlaine,* however, suggests just the opposite—that the past is significantly unreadable by the present. It was "another country," where "they do things differently."[1]

The play is strange in various ways. First is the unashamed romancing, heroization, even fetishization, of barbarism. Tamburlaine's presence as such on the Elizabethan stage can be explained in terms of the European legend of the Mongol conqueror, Timur the lame, a legend only recently rehearsed by Elizabethan playwright and pamphleteer George Whetstone.[2] But where Whetstone seems stupefied by Timur—by his genocidal ferocity—Marlowe turns him into a kind of leading man (with a quite unhistorical female romance interest). Marlowe "boosts" his Tamburlaine still higher by surrounding him with a kind of onstage male cheer-squad consisting of his henchmen: Techelles, Usumcasane, and Theridamas. Thus where the traditional tendency of Tudor drama (yet to be definitively evolved by Shakespeare) had been toward dialectical balance—with one excess checkmated by another—Marlowe gives us a willfully lopsided structure in which the illegitimate burgeons into the outrageous and the rise–fall pattern of the medieval tragic tradition morphs into a rise–rise pattern—a kind of structural nonsense. Something other is at stake here, however, than hypertrophy of the heroic. Marlowe does not sentimentalize Timur in the way that would become familiar in the drama of Beaumont and Fletcher or Dryden. The darker parts of Timur's legend—the terroristic idea of himself as the "Wrath of God," the ruthlessness, the complete absence of conventional human sympathy—are not air-brushed away. Marlowe's hero slaughters the innocent and jeers at his defeated enemies. And so far is he from being blamed for this that the audience is invited to join in, or at least comply. What we have then is an eroticized theater of cruelty *avant la lettre*. Finally, and again without basis in the Timur legend, Marlowe sublimates Tamburlaine in terms of an imagery of spatial extensiveness (both geographic and cosmic) that is closely related to a contemporary Elizabethan vision of global empire.[3]

The second major paradox that the play presents us with is the contrast between its immense popularity on the Elizabethan stage and its curiosity status on the modern stage. This in turn makes for a related problem: that of convincingly accounting for the original popularity. Until relatively recently editors and critics have tended to assume that Marlowe simply created a popular taste for "high astounding terms" in opposition to the popular taste for clownage, and partly as a logical consequence of his invention of the blank verse line. While this is plausible to the extent that the prologue boasts of dispensing with "such conceits as clownage keeps in pay," it is much less so in view of an admission by Richard Jones, the printer of the first edition, that he had "(purposely) omitted and left out some fond and frivolous gestures," which had been part of the original performance and evidently parcel of its success with the "vain conceited fondlings" of the audience.[4] What this suggests is a strong symbiosis between the low-cultural clowning from which the printer tried to rescue the play and the high-cultural stateliness at which he aimed the printed version. Such a view finds support in an important recent study of the relationship between text and performance on the Elizabethan stage.[5] For Robert Weimann, Jones's manifesto suggests a substantial level of intervention by the players in devising a popular performance mode in tension with (as much as subservient to) what Jones calls "the eloquence of the author." Most critics agree that notwithstanding Jones's bowdlerizing attentions, some at least of the players' business remains sedimented in the text. This in turn suggests that the play's success in the Elizabethan theater was significantly due to an institutional and popular chemistry with no real modern equivalent. To this may be added the unrepeatable charisma of a great actor (Edward Alleyn), the heady wine of the armada year (1588), and the probability that *Tamburlaine*'s success is at least in part a *succès de scandal,* which by definition is a success of the moment.

To return to the problem of what to make of *Tamburlaine:* evidently the best reading will be one that is true to as many of its contradictory aspects as possible. Such a reading would need to account for the strange conjunction of the barbarous with the heroic, of the monstrous with the sublime, and of the high-cultural with the low-cultural appeal. Again, we will need to account for the coexistence of the ideologically sanctioned (vicarious Elizabethan imperial ambitions) with the ideologically subversive (the outright blasphemies of "that atheist Tamburlaine"). Finally the problem of understanding *Tamburlaine* is to some degree that of recovering its contemporary *frisson,* its audience complicity, a form of bonding to some extent perhaps intuited and forged by the players.

This said, a caveat is in order. While these "paradoxes" are not exactly unknown to critics of *Tamburlaine,* they do tend to be bundled together in unhelpful ways. Thus, the "spatial" dimension is seen to go automatically with the "imperial" dimension and the "sublime" effect. The "high astounding terms" or the specifically verbal poetry is seen to be the domain of "acting" as distinct from "playing." This in turn is understood in terms of an Elizabethan tendency to separate the two along lines suggested by the opposed contemporary pamphlets: "An Excellent Actor" (written in defense of acting as a culturally "high" art, tied to a drama of high literary import) and "A Common Player" (a tract attacking the entire profession in terms of a common perception of players as mere "brokers" or panderers to the crowd) (Weimann 56–62). Even today, the tendency is strong to regard the charisma of Edward Alleyn as a factor of "excellent acting" rather than "common playing," of rhetorical command rather than "gestural"/jesting complicity (i.e., audience address, jeering, gloating, physical mistreatment of captives, etc.).

Briefly, I suggest that a more fruitful reading might work toward untying these bundles. Thus we should be prepared to consider that the spatial and imperial sublime might have actually *required* the subversive (atheism, blasphemy) in order to work its elusive chemistry with the audience. Similarly, the verbal or "poetic" dimension might be seen as requiring not just the stylization of "excellent" acting (critics generally agree that Marlovian acting was perceptibly less "natural" than the Shakespearean acting or "personation" that succeeded it), but the ludic skills (those "frivolous gestures") of the players. This in turn should prepare us to imagine "audience complicity" as operating along the entire performative spectrum, from high to low.

The Space of Conquest

Although never quite thought to be such, the spatial theme of *Tamburlaine* is problematic in its own right. It constitutes one fold of the play's Gordian knot. This is because the spatial theme unfolds in two dimensions—a geographic dimension and a cosmic dimension—that do not entirely coincide. The traditional tendency, however, has been to assume that they do coincide.

Let us, then, treat them separately, beginning with the play's "resounding geography."[6] From the very beginning, the hero's ambition and potency are expressed in an imagery of sheer geographic extent: he will march farther, voyage farther, and conquer more than anyone has ever done. While such boasts—characteristically in the form of speeches packed with exotic sounding place names—have struck readers as geographically incoherent, their detail has been matched with maps in the first true Renaissance atlas: the *Theatrum Orbis Terrarum* (1570) of Abraham Ortelius.[7] This fact allows us a further insight into Marlowe's geographic vision. Not only was it geographically coherent, but it was well up-to-date. This, however, must also mean that it is anachronistic. Marlowe invests his fifteenth-century Mongolian conqueror with a late-sixteenth-century geographic imagination. What this in turn means is that while he does take pains to get the conquests of the historical Timur geographically "right," he nevertheless repositions Tamburlaine in terms of an entirely new understanding of geography: what has been called the "new geography" of the discoveries. We may best express this in Tamburlaine's own words to Zenocrate when refusing her request to refrain from conquering Damascus:

> I will confute those blind geographers
> That make a triple region in the world,
> Excluding regions that I mean to trace,
> And with this pen reduce them to a map,
> Calling the provinces, cities, and towns,
> After my name and thine, Zenocrate.
> Here at Damascus will I make the point
> That shall begin the perpendicular:
> And wouldst thou have me buy thy father's love
> With such a loss? Tell me, Zenocrate. (4.4.73–81)

The "triple region of the world" referred to here is the old geography for which the world consisted entirely of the continents of Europe, Africa, and Asia. Tamburlaine sees himself as "confuting" this world picture, both by "tracing" new regions with "this pen" (his sword) and by "reducing" them to a new cartographic vision. The references are quite deliberate. The "new geography" was new both in the sense of adding unknown continents (America, the antarctic continent) undreamed of by the ancients and in the sense of projecting them in a completely novel way. Whereas the old geography had been inward-looking and simply incurious about what lay beyond, the new geography was outward-looking in the sense of favoring "unknown" continents at least as much as the "known" continents of Europe, Africa, and Asia. (In the prefacing world map to Ortelius's *Theatrum,* America/Antarctica occupies as much space as Europe, Asia, and Africa put together.) Where the old geography had—in its medieval form—been a sacred geography, centered on the holy city of Jerusalem, the new geography was indifferent to religious symbolism and defined entirely by the grid of latitude and longitude. It was equally indifferent to "placiality" in the sense that places hitherto privileged on the old maps by an associated symbolism (such as Colchis, symbolized by a drawing of the golden fleece, or the Red Sea by its invariably red color, or Jerusalem by its centrality) were reduced entirely to spatial coordinates. Ironically, however, by virtue of its very indifference to "place," the new geography (or cartography) was open to political manipulation in a way that the old geography was not. Precisely because no place was privileged by the grid, any place might be given an entirely factitious importance by being made to coincide with key grid coordinates. Thus, Greenwich is keyed to the Greenwich meridian. More notoriously, cartographic lines could be made to respond to political pressure, as in a papal decree of 1493 whereby the Spanish and Portuguese spheres of interest in the Atlantic were divided along a meridian line 100 leagues west of the Cape Verde Islands. When the Portuguese realized that this would deny them any territory in the New World, the decree was renegotiated in the following year as the Treaty of Tordesillas, and the line moved 370 leagues west of the Cape Verde Islands (allowing the Portuguese a claim on Brazil). For Tamburlaine, geographic entities are similarly plastic: they expand or contract or morph in response to his power. Thus, he boasts of keying the new cartography to Damascus.

The manipulability of the new cartography suggests that it was new in an ethical sense as well as in a technological sense. Its sheer extensiveness in relation to the old geography was similarly charged with ethical meaning. The figure of Tamburlaine can be thought of as incarnating the "outward-looking" aspect of the new geography: its romance with the novel, with sheer extent, with exploration and conquest. By Marlowe's time, the ethical difference between the old and the new geographies had come to be epitomized in two opposing legends.[8] In one, a classical legend, Hercules was credited with setting boundaries to the ancient world that forbade further travel or exploration. The most prominent of these were a pair of pillars set up at the Strait of Gibraltar, upon which was engraved the motto: "Non Plus Ultra," or "No Further." Men were forbidden to go further both because of the physical dangers (ocean, monsters) that raged beyond the recognized boundaries of the "inhabited world" and because of the moral danger of transgression. To disrespect these boundaries was to risk becoming as monstrous as the exotic regions themselves. Hence there is a strong tradition in which conquerors of exotic regions were represented as morally suspect. One such was Julius Caesar, whose conquest of exotic worlds (such as Britain) was seen by the poet Lucan as presaging his later invasion of Rome and destruction of the Republic. (It is no accident that Marlowe had translated the first book of Lucan's *Pharsalia* and represented Caesar in superhuman yet monstrous imagery highly suggestive of Tamburlaine.)

The second legend, a legend invented as an emblem of the new geography, represents an inversion of the Herculean ethos. In this account, Columbus's daring in sailing out past the Pillars of Hercules into the Atlantic is celebrated as the key to unthinkably vast geographic domains and wealth. Accordingly Emperor Charles V signaled Spain's overlordship of the New World in a new emblem: a picture of the Pillars of Hercules draped with the motto: "Plus Ultre," or "Ever Further." The significance of the new emblem is not merely geographic (the world is much bigger and more habitable than the ancients ever dreamed) but ethical: the extreme audacity of the explorer and conqueror is positively desirable. Perhaps unsurprisingly one conquistador came up with his own more workaday version of the imperial motto:

Ala espada y el compas
Mas y mas y mas y mas
(By the sword and the compass
More and more and more and more)[9]

In Tamburlaine, then, Marlowe celebrates not just the new geography but also the Spanish imperial ethic of conquest and discovery. Tamburlaine is the Elizabethan stage's version of Cortez or Pizarro or Lope de Aguirre (the conquistador's sword marching in advance of the cartographer's pen).[10] The implication is inescapable in view of the fact that the imperial emblem was being appropriated wholesale by Elizabethan imperial advocates at the very moment of the play. The year of the play's first known performance (1588) was also the year of the victory over the Spanish armada. Increasingly, in the years following the victory (and less obviously for ten years preceding it), Elizabeth is depicted in association with symbols of global empire, all adapted from the Spanish imperial iconography.[11] The same imperial iconography is directly alluded to twice at the ending of each part of *Tamburlaine*. At the end of the first play, Tamburlaine orders his soldiers:

Hang up your weapons on Alcides' post;
For Tamburlaine takes truce with all the world. (5.2.464–65)

If this is not clear enough, the second play ends with Tamburlaine asking for a world map to be brought onto the stage. After tracing upon it the itinerary of his conquests, from Persia through Turkey and the Middle East to Africa and Europe (all of which would have appeared on the right hand side of the Ortelian world map he must have been using), Tamburlaine gestures toward the left part and invites his sons to continue his conquests by annexing the New World (II.5.3.125–60). In view of the fact that Timur's empire had evaporated at his death, and in view of the fact that the audience is being exhorted to endorse an Elizabethan imperial dream in terms of a contemporary world map, one can only imagine them responding enthusiastically to this call.

The second mode of Tamburlaine's spatial expansiveness is cosmic. Thus, Theridamas is assured:

I hold the Fates bound fast in iron chains,
And with my hand turn Fortune's wheel about,
And sooner shall the sun fall from her sphere,
Than Tamburlaine be slain or overcome. (1.2.174–77)

As in the case of the geographic mode, expansiveness is linked to transgressiveness. It is perhaps insufficiently recognized, however, that the transgressiveness of Tamburlaine's cosmic boasts is far more dangerous than that of his geographic boasts. This is partly due to the fact that (for Marlowe at least) there was as yet no "new cosmography" to match the "new geography." Tamburlaine's cosmos is always the old cosmology associated with the name of Ptolemy of Alexandria, in which a stationary earth is represented as encased in roughly nine layers of concentric "spheres," each the circular track of a heavenly body or bodies around the earth: from the sphere of the moon, outward through those of Mercury, Venus, the Sun, Mars, Jupiter, Saturn, the fixed stars, and finally the *primum mobile*—the truly celestial sphere enclosing and animating all the others. Typically, Tamburlaine invokes this traditional cosmic architecture only to usurp it. This is more dangerous than his geographic expansionism not just because there was no ideological counterpart to the new geography in terms of which it might seem legitimate, but because the Ptolemaic cosmos was regularly invoked as a model of the Elizabethan social order. Thus John Case's *Sphaera Civitatis* (Oxford, 1588) is prefaced by a cosmic diagram in which the Queen is literally depicted as the *primum mobile,* controlling the lower spheres and (lowest of all) the earth. In quite the opposite spirit, Tamburlaine glosses the same heavenly architecture as a pretext for usurpation:

> Nature that framed us of four elements,
> Warring within our breasts for regiment,
> Doth teach us all to have aspiring minds:
> Our souls whose faculties can comprehend
> The wondrous architecture of the world:
> And measure every planet's course,
> Still climbing after knowledge infinite,
> And always moving as the restless spheres,
> Wills us to wear ourselves and never rest,
> Until we reach the ripest fruit of all,
> That perfect bliss and sole felicity,
> The sweet fruition of an earthly crown. (2.7.18–29)

Subversive meaning is wrung from the old cosmology by a relentless focus on its creaking joints, just those spots at which the whole structure would shortly begin to crumble before the onset of the "new" heliocentric cosmology of Copernicus, Gilbert, Galileo, and Kepler.[12] The spheres, for example, were not normally imagined as "restless," but as domains of progressively purer being. To speak of them as "restless" was to draw attention to the preternatural (and increasingly implausible) speed with which they were supposed to rotate around the earth in a single day. To the cosmological modernists the idea that all of the fixed stars orbited the fixed earth on a daily basis (as distinct from the earth rotating on its own axis) was simply preposterous.[13] Again, to contemporaries, the idea of the four elements "warring within our breasts for regiment" would have suggested illness rather than an "aspiring mind." The goal of contemporary medicine was to achieve a balance between the elements, rather than a tumult. The idea that nature or the cosmos itself "doth teach us all to have aspiring minds" was virtually blasphemous. Traditionally (as in Cicero's "Dream of Scipio") the virtuous man was exhorted to fix his mind on the serene order of the Ptolemaic heavens in order to wean himself away from grubby earthly concerns.[14] To Tamburlaine, however, the hierarchical cosmos is a ladder for clambering up as high as "we all" can. "Nature" wills us to exert ourselves "and never rest" until we ransack the heavenly order for the ultimate in earthly joys. "The ripest fruit of all" is an outrageous slur on the Book of Genesis.

The paradox of the spatial theme in *Tamburlaine* then is that it pulls in different directions: the geographic theme pulls in the direction of Elizabethan imperialism (a kind of "national service" and thus a good thing) and the cosmic theme in the direction of social insurrection (a national disservice and thus a bad thing). Crucial though it be therefore for any understanding of the play, the spatial theme is not a sufficient explanation of the play's appeal. We will need to supplement it with a review of the play's structure and a rethinking of the "space" of the audience.

Dramatic Structure and the Space of the Audience

The two parts of *Tamburlaine* are structured as a series of encounters between Tamburlaine and his successive antagonists. In part 1, the sequence is from Cosroe to Bajazeth to the Prince of Arabia and the Soldan of Damascus. In part 2, the sequence is less clear. In one sense there is a single foe, personified in Turkish figures such as Orcanes and Callapine (son of Bajazeth). In another sense Tamburlaine faces a series of less overt foes, such as the treachery of Alameda (gaoler to Callapine), "the death of Zenocrate," the cowardice of his son Calyphas, Olympia (the faithful enemy wife who refuses the advances of Tamburlaine's lieutenant, Theridamas), "the family unit" as such (Tamburlaine's own family and Olympia's family), Christ (whom Orcanes takes to have championed him against the faithless Christian, Sigismund), Mahomet, and finally "Death" in the sense of Tamburlaine's own fatal illness. This type of indirect enemy is also present in part 1, in the form of the feminine personifications of that "beauty" (Zenocrate and the virgins of Damascus), which almost dissuades Tamburlaine from his ruthless destruction of Damascus. If one views *Tamburlaine* purely as a rise–rise drama, then the outcome of these encounters is always predictable. In a sense, Tamburlaine always triumphs, even over mortality itself in refusing to absent himself from the final battle with Callapine and in spending his last moments in eager contemplation of the large onstage world map. In another sense, however, the outcome becomes progressively less clear: Tamburlaine is called into question by these encounters and perhaps diminished to the point that his drama implicitly reverts to the rise–fall type after all. Notwithstanding this deep vein of moral "qualification," however, *Tamburlaine* is not an undeclared morality play. What, I suggest, we have instead is a series of calls for audience complicity, a series of progressively more open-ended invitations to "applaud his fortunes as you please" (Prologue, 8). In all of this, it seems to me, the audience is not so much invited to judge Tamburlaine as they are dared to become and remain his "accomplices" as the nature of power becomes progressively clearer and its price steeper. The play is a series of variations on a question to which there is no "right" answer.

The thrust of Marlowe's invitation to complicity is clearer in the first play than the second. The issue of the opening section of part 1 is not so much between subjection and outlawry as between different species of outlaw power. Were Mycetes (the lawful king of Persia) defined as Tamburlaine's antagonist, the issue would still not quite have been between rule and unrule because Tamburlaine is not technically a Persian subject. By describing him as a "Scythian shepherd," Marlowe seizes the idea of the near contemporary Mongolians in the relatively unracialized image of the classical Scythians (who were neither Central Asiatics nor "shepherds," though they were nomads). Either way, Tamburlaine is born an outlaw, a nomad inherently beyond the "sphaera civitatis" or the civilized world imagined by John Case. What is at issue then in the opposition between Tamburlaine and Cosroe (the usurping brother of Myctes) is two versions of naked power. Against Tamburlaine's pure antinomianism (rejection of lawfulness), Cosroe represents something like Macchiavelli's idea of the Prince: namely, the ruler for whom political legitimacy is merely a cloak for power conceived of as "virtù" (or strength), which then becomes essential to the state. Accordingly, Cosroe is a principled manipulator with the state's best interests at heart. While on the one hand glorifying Tamburlaine and keeping faith by promoting him and his followers to "rooms of honour and nobility" (2.3.41), Cosroe also gives Meander (the chief counselor to his defeated rival, Mycetes) "equal place in our affairs" (2.5.14). By so doing, he seeks to make one quantity equivalent to the other. Within the utilitarian mansion of the state, each is intended to occupy a similar "room" (a word suggestively conflating space with office or function).[15] Tamburlaine's valor would thus be emptied out into Meander's treacherous yielding. It is perhaps worth noting the pun on the name "Meander," an eponymously winding river in the Caucasus region:

> The lords and captains of my brother's camp,
> With little slaughter take Meander's course,
> And gladly yield them to my gracious rule. (2.5.26–28)

As opposed to Cosroe's Machiavellian calculus and Meander's sinuous yielding, the power principle represented by Tamburlaine is direct and elemental. It is also non-negotiable in his literal and repeated refusals to ransom captives, to countenance any possibility of mercenary betrayal from within his own ranks ("Not all the gold in India's wealthy arms, / Shall buy the meanest soldier in my train" 1.2.85–86) or to retract a claim or threat. The refusal of any dissimulation or qualification is completely un-Machiavellian. So too is the absolute fidelity with which he rewards absolute loyalty. Tamburlaine's adherents are never pawns, but always absolutely valuable. A keyword to describe this relationship in the Cosroe section of the first play is "friends." Thus Theridamas is won over not just by Tamburlaine's rhetoric or promises of reward but by a kind of mutual erotic attraction. Even before the speech, Techelles remarks, "his deep affections make him passionate" (1.2.164), leaving it slightly unclear whether the reference is to Tamburlaine or Theridamas. In the next thirty lines or so following the speech, the word "friend" is used some five times. Here is the culminating passage:

> These are my friends in whom I more rejoice,
> Than doth the King of Persia in his crown:
> And by the love of Pylades and Orestes,
> Whose statues we adore in Scythia,
> Thyself and them shall never part from me [. . .] (1.2.241–45)

The values of friendship and boundlessness (the refusal of "rooms") take us to the heart of the encounter with Cosroe. Tamburlaine's decision to turn on Cosroe in the very moment of their mutual triumph over Mycetes seems related to the way in which he has just been weighed equally with Meander. Some twenty lines later, Tamburlaine suggestively repeats Cosroe's exit line, "and ride in triumph through Persepolis" (2.5.50), and asks his friends, "is it not passing brave to be a king?" (2.5.53). Theridamas's blasphemous suggestion—"I think the pleasure they enjoy in heaven / Cannot compare with kingly joys on earth" (2.5.59–60)—virtually provokes the audience to respond, with either complicity or outrage. A few lines later the challenge to the audience becomes explicit:

> *Tamburlaine:* Why say Theridamas, wilt thou be a king?
>
> *Theridamas:* Nay, though I praise it, I can live without it.
>
> *Tamburlaine:* What says my other friends, will you be kings?
>
> *Techelles:* Ay, if I could, with all my heart my lord.
>
> *Tamburlaine:* Why that's well said Techelles, so would I
> And so would you my masters, would you not? (2.5.65–70)

The audience is now presented with a direct challenge, and must respond directly in either of two ways, though the incentive to respond positively is strong. Interestingly while Theridamas (the beloved disciple) hangs back, Techelles (the quintessential gang member) goes all the way. The point perhaps is that the invitation to "be a king" is aimed at the audience, not at the elite. And the "implied audience" here is not Shakespeare's "gentles all" or "gentle spectators" but an explicit extension of Tamburlaine's nomad band. The next lines are written in such a way as to accommodate a wide spectrum of response:

> *Usumcasane:* What then my lord?
>
> *Tamburlaine:* Why then Casane shall we wish for ought
> The world affords in greatest novelty,
> And rest attemptless, faint and destitute?
> Methinks we should not. (2.5.71–75)

Evidently the lines will accommodate the positive end of the spectrum (claps, cheers, whistles) but they will also accommodate (i.e., defy, cock a snoot at) the lukewarm or even the downright cool ("Why then Casane shall *we* wish for ought [. . .] Methinks *we* should not"). If Tamburlaine seeks the complicity of the audience with his nomad army, he is equally ready to mock a cool audience for its failure to take up the gauntlet.

This moment, I will suggest, is typical of the Marlovian dramaturgy and the associated audience chemistry in *Tamburlaine*. If the dramaturgy consists of a series of encounters—effectively a structure of repetition—then the audience chemistry can be described in terms of a strategy of surprise. Thus, while audience members find themselves constantly faced with repeated encounters and repeated calls for their complicity, they should also find themselves shocked by the changing content of that complicity. Marching in triumph through Persepolis is one thing. But cheering on the humiliation of Bajazeth or the massacre of the virgins of Damascus is quite another.

The Space of the Nomad

The structure of repetition and surprise can be better grasped in terms of a deeper Marlovian strategy of audience address that I would call "ludic anarchism," a calculated incitement to moral and political heresy that would have been prosecutable anywhere outside of the theater. This is better seen in the light of two quite unrelated theories of what one might call "anarchic bonding": Shaftesbury's notion of "the conspiring virtue" and Deleuze and Guattari's notion of the nomadic group as "war machine."[16]

In his essay *Sensus Communis* of 1709, the philosopher earl of Shaftesbury proposes an apology for the free play of "wit": irreverent and even anarchic verbal humor that may take the form of a cutting ridicule of ideas and people. "The body politic," argues Shaftesbury, is "a kind of remote philosophical object" that fails to compel the robuster human energies (52). It is only in "less parties" or smaller groups that "men may be intimately conversant" and fully alive. Yet because the exercise of wit ("the sprightliest and most active faculties") within the small social sphere characteristically results in friction with the large social sphere (the state), it must seem subversive or conspiratorial to the statesman. This begets a paradox:

> The close sympathy and conspiring virtue is apt to lose itself for want of direction in so wide a field. Nor is the passion anywhere so strongly felt or vigorously exerted as in actual conspiracy or war in which the highest geniuses are often known the forwardest to employ themselves. For the most generous spirits are the most combining. They delight most to move in concert and feel, if I may say, in the strongest manner the force of the confederating charm. (52)

"It is strange," he continues, "that war, which of all things appears the most savage, should be the passion of the most heroic spirits," and that "in war [. . .] the knot of fellowship is closest drawn" (52). This paradox whereby the strongest (if not the highest) human bonds are forged in war is matched by the paradox of "the conspiring virtue," which is precisely that "conspiring" might be a "virtue." (Shaftesbury's use of this word seems open to the Macchiavellian idea of "virtü"—strength or vigor.)

Something very like Shaftesbury's paradox, I suggest, is behind the "anarchic bonding" of Marlowe's *Tamburlaine*. Tamburlaine frames his invitation to the audience to "ride in triumph through Persepolis" as an outrageously Shaftesburian jest:

> "'Twill prove a pretty jest, in faith, my friends
> [. . .]
> Then shalt thou see the Scythian Tamburlaine,
> Make but a jest to win the Persian crown.
> Techelles, take a thousand horse with thee,
> And bid him turn his back to war with us,
> That only made him king to make us sport. (2.5.90, 97–101)

The jest is a lightning rod between stage outlawry and audience outlawry, as the audience members are collectively invited to abandon their own "rooms" of duty and service, eject the master ("before his room be hot"), inherit kingdoms, and (in Macbeth's words) "jump the world to come":

> A god is not so glorious as a king:
> I think the pleasure they enjoy in heaven
> Cannot compare with kingly joys in earth. (2.5.57–60)

At his most outrageous, Tamburlaine is also at his "wittiest," making a travesty of orthodoxy. As we shall see, the wit of this moment is characteristic of all the subsequent "surprises" embedded within the structure of repetition. Characteristically too, Tamburlaine's joke at the expense of the establishment is shared with the audience—but only on Tamburlaine's terms. Thus, in the emblematic scene in which the dying Cosroe asks Tamburlaine why he has betrayed him, the reply is not only framed as yet another inversion of orthodoxy, but framed in the plural: "Nature [. . .] doth teach us all to have aspiring minds" (2.7.18–29). How does one make sense of such an appeal to an Elizabethan audience over the head, that is to say, of the entire political order? At this point, I should like to invoke Deleuze and Guattari's idea of "the war machine."

In Deleuze and Guattari, the state is conceived of as shot through with "nomadic" formations such as gangs or packs that are both parasitic on the body of the state and yet necessary to it in the sense of providing an "alien" (or barbarian) horizon in terms of which to define itself. Unlike the state, which guarantees its stability and permanence by vertical subdivision into a grid of self-replicating institutions (its "rooms"), the "nomad" group is unstructured, roomless, and potentially ephemeral. It does not so much put down roots vertically as spread horizontally through "rhizomes" (haptic, informal links). Where the state is "sedentary," the nomadic group is dynamic—defined by the momentum of the instant. Where the former has a king, the latter has a "chief," a leader who leads through charisma and "friendship" rather than by established law or right. Charisma is thus both overwhelmingly seductive or overpowering and yet ephemeral. It has no guarantee but itself. Both aspects seem important in *Tamburlaine.* Like other European celebrants of the Timur legend, Marlowe seems as fascinated by the ephemerality of Timur's conquests as by the conquests themselves. Brilliantly, he constantly invokes the moment of final dissolution by constantly postponing it throughout two entire plays. The rise–rise pattern is thus predicated on an always imminent collapse, but a collapse (or power vacuum) that is kept perpetually offstage, or for just as long as Tamburlaine's charisma is exercised. What this means is that Tamburlaine's radical incitements to anarchism and his power to extend himself seemingly without cosmographic limit are theatricalized. Thus Tamburlaine's exercise of charisma over his "pack" or "band" is exactly coincident with the actor's exercise of charisma over the "pack" or "band" of the audience. As Tamburlaine's power ends with his death, so that of the actor (originally the charismatic Edward Alleyn) ends with the ending of the performance and the dispersal of the audience.

If Deleuze and Guattari are of use in understanding the logic of charisma in *Tamburlaine,* they are also helpful in approaching the emotional logic of the plays. As we have partly seen, the later moments of "surprise" in the plays tend to be much more emotionally (and morally) difficult than the triumph over Cosroe. When "we" (readers or audience) are invited to join in the fun of mocking (torturing?) Bajazeth and Zabina, or when we are invited to endorse the slaughter of the virgins of Damascus, or when (in part 2) we are invited to applaud Tamburlaine's murder of his own son, our complicity is (so to speak) exploded. How does the audience respond at such moments? Here, I suggest, we would do well to allow for the historical distance between modern and Elizabethan audiences. Where a polite modern audience is likely to disengage with Tamburlaine at such moments and to start counting the human costs of his outlandishness, there seem grounds for supposing that an Elizabethan audience might have experienced the dilemma in a more "tribal" way. Deleuze and Guattari make an interesting distinction between the state and the tribe along emotional lines. Where the state promotes emotional interiority—a disciplined economy of feeling in terms of the key institutions of private and public life—the tribe exteriorizes feeling into "affect":

> [. . .] feelings become uprooted from the interiority of a "subject," to be projected violently outward into a milieu of pure exteriority that lends them an incredible velocity, a catapulting force: love or hate, they are no longer feelings but affects. [. . .] Affects transpierce the body like arrows, they are weapons of war. (356)

The difference is that whereas "feelings" require and "belong to" a subject (the self), "affects" are more anarchic and unstable. If they do acknowledge the self, it is only to assault it. Where "emotion" is governed by the self, affect is typically ungoverned and qualitatively different, wilder and pushed by forces beyond or beneath the self. In modern times the distinction between "feeling" and "affect" has led to two radically different kinds of theater: bourgeois naturalism on the one hand and Artaud's "theater of cruelty" on the other, where "cruelty" is to be understood very much in terms of an overpowering affect. What I am suggesting is that in *Tamburlaine,* Elizabethan theater functions as a Marlovian equivalent of the "theater of cruelty." More precisely perhaps I am suggesting that the plays develop by prizing feeling apart from affect, and then forcing the audience to choose between them. In both plays, the world of the feelings is defined by romantic love (Tamburlaine and Zenocrate), the family (husbands and wives, parents and children), and friendship (Tamburlaine and Theridamas). The world of affect is defined by outlandish ambitions, exultation, savagery, cruelty, and a complete surrender to charisma. This is the world of the tribe or pack or band. This is what I imagine having had a greater appeal for the popular Elizabethan audience, and less appeal for the polite modern audience. Why? Mainly because the family, perhaps the core social institution defining one's feelings, was rather different in early modern times than at present. The early modern family was also a workshop, a going concern, offering surprising equality of status ("room") for servants and children.[17] It was less sentimentally inflected than it has become since the nineteenth century and more about discipline and effort, as attested by a flourishing citizen drama on the evils of prodigal offspring and apprentices and by an outpouring of antitheatrical polemic in which the theater is represented as the antithesis of duty.[18] I do not suggest that the Elizabethan audience simply exulted in Tamburlaine's cruelty—his annihilation of the family—simply that the choice between feeling and affect (cruelty) may have been differently weighted for them than it tends to be for modern audiences.

The most difficult choices between emotion and affect are posed at the climaxes of the two plays. This is precisely because of a doubling or telescoping of the structure of "repetition" at the climaxes. Thus, in the case of the first play, the Bajazeth action is telescoped into the following action centred on Damascus. The point at which this happens is crucial: the attack on Damascus takes place in the context of two long scenes of ritual humiliation of Bajazeth and Zabina. In each of these (4.2, a triumph, and 4.4, a banquet) Bajazeth is brought on in a cage to be debased and humiliated while the next action (the attack on Damascus) gets well under way. What this means is that the Damascus action is registered in terms of the brutal humiliation of Bajazeth. Emblematically speaking, they are different sides of the same combined action.

In this combined action, Zenocrate is the key figure. As the daughter of the Soldan of Damascus and the former fiancée of his ally the prince of Arabia, Zenocrate is torn between the pack dynamic (responsiveness to the charisma of Tamburlaine) and family loyalty. The conflict is first intimated toward the end of act 4, scene 2, the first of the ritual humiliation scenes focused on Bajazeth, when the seige of Damascus is in its first stage with Tamburlaine's army in white. When Tamburlaine explains the symbolism of the three colors, each representing a graded response to an offer of surrender (white betokening mercy, red execution of the commanders only, black slaughter of the entire population), Zenocrate interjects:

> Yet would you have some pity for my sake,
> Because it is my country, and my father's. (4.2.123–24)

But she is met with outright refusal: "Not for the world, Zenocrate" (4.2.125).

What is merely intimated in this scene is fully expressed in the next of the ritual humiliation scenes, act 4, scene 4. Surreally for a banquet scene, Tamburlaine and his group enter "all in scarlet," betokening mercy for the populace of Damascus but not for the governors. To this ostensible symbolism, however, we should add a deeper layer of meaning. "Our bloody colours" would refer to the cruel feeding of this banquet in which the hungry Bajazeth is taunted with scraps of dirty meat from the end of Tamburlaine's sword. The imagery of feeding morphs into the mythology of the cannibal banquet as Zabina likens Tamburlaine to "th'adulterous Thracian king / That fed upon the substance of his child" (4.2.24–25). The reference is to Ovid's story of Tereus, the barbarous king who, in revenge for raping his wife's sister, is fed with the flesh of his own murdered child. While the comparison may seem stretched, it is in fact precise to the extent that Tamburlaine is intent on devouring his own family in that of Zenocrate. To her second plea for home and family (breaking the mood of jollity to which she has been a hearty contributor), Tamburlaine responds with his paean to the new geography ("I will confute those blind geographers [. . .]" 4.4.73–81).

Within this doubled structure of "repetition" the audience is presented with another "surprise": a version of the choice now facing Zenocrate, between the "family" and infinite geographic extension (in the potent image of the "new geography" of the discoveries). If the choice is undoubtedly more agonized than the offer to "ride in triumph through Persepolis," it is no less real for all that. What Marlowe does *not* offer is a version of Shakespearean irony. Tamburlaine is not being undercut here or presented as a Hitlerian figure. Marlowe seriously expects his audience to think the unthinkable and say (with their shouts or cheers) the unsayable. The question is: how far are they willing to go? If Tamburlaine himself shows no sign of blanching just yet, he does when presented with the surrender plea borne in by the virgins of Damascus (act 5, scene 2). As this is presented at the third stage of the color symbolism, when Tamburlaine's army is in black, the logic is that the virgins like the rest of the populace will have to be slaughtered. Tamburlaine's resolution does wobble slightly, but he quickly corrects himself and orders the massacre of the virgins. To be sure, the audience (especially the modern audience) may not see the choice quite in Tamburlaine's terms (that is, as a choice between "beauty" represented by the virgins and Zenocrate and duty represented by his unalterable custom). But they will perhaps notice what this choice signifies for Tamburlaine: a choice between chivalric idealism and global ambition, between personal heroism and the pack imperative. And in these terms, the choice is familiar enough. If Tamburlaine's charisma extorts complete loyalty from the pack, it equally empties him of all privacy, intimacy, or familial loyalty. Tamburlaine becomes a completely exteriorized entity from this point on, emotion becomes affect, the man becomes the tribe, the leader becomes indistinguishable from his charisma. The "surprises" awaiting us in the second play are all of this type: particularly Tamburlaine's murder of his own son Calyphas (a son unfit to be a member of the pack), the suicide of Olympia (the unwilling female captive), the defeat of Callapine (son of Bajazeth), the imminent collapse of Tamburlaine's own dynasty—all can be read as variations on "the death of the family."

So stated, Tamburlaine's choice must seem utterly unappetizing to the modern reader, and the play will appear a morality play despite itself. Speaking as a modern reader, I would have to agree. But we should be cautious of extrapolating our own morality, our tastes, our imperatives, to an early modern audience. They, I feel, would have been quite capable of "applauding" Tamburlaine's most outrageous propositions "as they pleased." To this collection of masters, servants, apprentices, husbands, and wives—all escaping the constriction of their social "rooms" for the brief hour or two of the play, and all perhaps aware (as we are not today) of the theatricalized or ludic character of Tamburlaine's anarchy—the choice may well have seemed as exhilarating as it was unprecedented. I am not suggesting that they *must* have been seduced by Tamburlaine's incitements. Indeed, the possibility that they might strenuously object should have been part of the play's "danger," part of its chemistry and attraction. But the fact that they were nomadically present in the ambiguous "roomless" space of the theater, courted as "friends" rather than treated as subjects, the fact that they were being asked to explore their own powers as a "pack" in the same breath as exploring the "wondrous architecture of the universe," the fact that they knew themselves free then and there (and nowhere else), to be or do anything out of the box or outside the "room"—these were potent charms and living theater.

NOTES

1. This phrase from L. P. Hartley's *The Go Between* is cited in David Lowenthal, *The Past Is a Foreign Country* (Cambridge: Cambridge UP, 1985) xvi.
2. George Whetstone, *The English Myrror* (London, 1586) (Amsterdam: Da Capo P and Theatrum Orbis Terrarum, 1973). For the European Timur legend, see Eric Voegelin, "Macchiavelli's Prince: Background and Formation," *Review of Politics* 13 (1951): 142–68.
3. Roy Strong, *Gloriana: The Portraits of Queen Elizabeth I* (London: Thames and Hudson, 1987).
4. Christopher Marlowe, *Tamburlaine,* ed. J. W. Harper (London: Ernest Benn, 1971) 3.
5. See Robert Weimann, *Author's Pen and Actor's Voice: Playing and Writing in Shakespeare's Theatre* (Cambridge: Cambridge UP, 2000) esp. 56–62.
6. The phrase is Eugene Waith's; see *The Herculean Hero in Marlowe, Shakespeare and Dryden* (London: Chatto & Windus, 1962) 63.
7. See Ethel Seaton, "Marlowe's Map," *Essays and Studies* 10 (1924): 13–25.
8. Earl Rosenthal, "*Plus Ultre, Non Plus Ultra,* and the Columnar Device of the Emperor Charles V," *Journal of the Warburg and Courtauld Institutes* 34 (1971): 204–28.
9. The motto can be found facing the title page of J. H. Elliot, *The Old World and the New, 1492–1650* (Cambridge: Cambridge UP, 1970). "Más alla" is a Spanish vernacular version of "Plus Ultre."
10. For Aguirre, see the film by Werner Herzog, *Aguirre: der Zorn Gottes* (1973). Herzog, whose Aguirre boasts of "producing history as other men produce plays," and whose title translates as "Aguirre: The Wrath of God," appears to have conceived of his mad conquistador through Marlowe's Tamburlaine. See also *The Expedition of Pedro De Ursua & Lope De Aguirre in*

Search of El Dorado and Omagua in 1560–1, tr. William Bollaert, intro. Clements R. Markham (Burt Franklin: New York, 1971).

11. See Frances Yates, *Astraea: The Imperial Theme in the Sixteenth Century* (Harmondsworth: Penguin, 1977); and Roy Strong, *Gloriana: The Portraits of Queen Elizabeth I* (London: Thames & Hudson, 1987).
12. A convenient and still cogent summary of the early modern cosmological revolution can be found in Alexandre Koyré, *From the Closed World to the Infinite Universe* (Baltimore: The Johns Hopkins UP, 1957).
13. Thus, William Gilbert (*De Magnete,* 1600), admitting the apparent oddity of the idea that the earth revolves on its axis every twenty-four hours, points out how "far more extravagant (*insanior*) is the idea of the whirling of the suppositious *primum mobile*" (*De Magnete,* tr. P. Fleury Mottelay [New York: Dover Publications, 1958] 320).
14. For the "Dream of Scipio," see C. W. Keyes., ed. & tr., *Cicero: De Re Publica De Legibus* (London: Heinemann; Cambridge: Harvard UP, 1948) 260–83.
15. The word "room" seems deliberately used in this sense of a socially or naturally ordained space (a kind of cubicle) in opposition to the boundless dimension claimed by Tamburlaine. Thus, Zabina speaks wishfully of swords sticking in Tamburlaine "as in their proper rooms" (5.2.162), and Bajazeth speaks of being "thrown to rooms of black abjection" (5.2.203). One way of reading the plays is as a sustained refusal of the propriety of "proper rooms."
16. Gilles Deleuze and Felix Guattari, *A Thousand Plateaus: Capitalism and Schizophrenia,* tr. Brian Massumi (London: Continuum, 1987) esp. 351–423. Anthony Ashley Cooper, third earl of Shaftesbury, "Sensus Communis, an Essay on the Freedom of Wit and Humour in a Letter to a Friend," *Characteristics of Men, Manners, Opinions, Times,* ed. Lawrence E. Klein (Cambridge: Cambridge UP, 1999) 29–70.
17. For the early modern family, see Peter Laslett, *The World We Have Lost—Further Explored* (London: Routledge, 1992) esp. ch. 1 and 9.
18. For citizen comedy, see Brian Gibbons, *Jacobean City Comedy* (London: Methuen, 1980). For antitheatrical polemic, see Jonas Barish, *The Antitheatrical Prejudice* (Berkeley: U of California P, 1981).

READING LIST

Burton, Jonathan. "Anglo-Ottoman Relations and the Image of the Turk in *Tamburlaine*." *Journal of Medieval and Early Modern Studies* 30 (2000): 125–56.

Dollimore, Jonathan. *Radical Tragedy: Religion, Ideology and Power in the Drama of Shakespeare and His Contemporaries*. 2nd ed. Durham: Duke UP, 1993.

Gillies, John. *Shakespeare and the Geography of Difference*. Cambridge: Cambridge UP, 1994.

Gillies, John, and Virginia Mason Vaughan, eds. *Playing the Globe: Genre and Geography in English Renaissance Drama*. Madison: Fairleigh Dickinson UP, 1998.

Greenblatt, Stephen. *Renaissance Self-Fashioning*. Chicago: U of Chicago P, 1980.

Klein, Bernhard. *Maps and the Writing of Space in Early Modern England and Ireland*. Houndmills, Basingstoke, Hampshire: Palgrave, 2001.

Seaton, Ethel. "Marlowe's Map." *Essays and Studies* 10 (1924): 13–25.

Shepherd, Simon. *Marlowe and the Politics of Elizabethan Theatre*. Brighton: The Harvester P, 1986.

Sullivan, Garrett A., Jr. "Space, Measurement, and Stalking Tamburlaine." *Renaissance Drama* n.s. 28 (1997): 3–27.

Waith, Eugene. *The Herculean Hero in Marlowe, Shakespeare and Dryden*. London: Chatto & Windus, 1962.

Weimann, Robert. *Author's Pen and Actor's Voice: Playing and Writing in Shakespeare's Theater.* Cambridge: Cambridge UP, 2000.

5

The Spanish Tragedy and Revenge

Gregory M. Colón Semenza

Six months after the Columbine High School shootings of April 21, 1999, Carla Hochhalter walked into a pawn shop and, after being handed a .38 caliber pistol from the shop assistant, loaded the weapon (with bullets she had carried into the store) and fired it at her head. She died almost immediately. During the infamous massacre that left fifteen students and teachers dead and twenty-three others seriously injured, Hochhalter's seventeen-year-old daughter had been shot multiple times in the back and chest, leaving her paralyzed from the waist down. Apparently the girl's mother was unable to overcome the feelings of helplessness and despair that have continued to plague so many parents in the wake of the tragic events in Littleton, Colorado.

I can remember quite vividly my own feelings of horror and emptiness upon learning of Hochhalter's suicide, an emotional reaction exacerbated by my aggravated realization that the media seemed deliberately to be downplaying the story. The six-month anniversary of the tragedy was not *supposed* to be depressing, after all. It was *supposed* to be about rebirth, about a small community that had successfully picked up the pieces and moved on. It was *supposed* to be about the students who had returned to the school, about the football team that was undefeated, about the new friendships that had blossomed out of shared trauma. Hochhalter's suicide, and the unending, relentless pain and misery it exposed, threw a wrench into this convenient, resurrectional narrative.

The basic human impulse is always toward comedy. We impose comedic resolutions onto our news coverage, our philosophies and religions, and most of our art because we find too terrifying the idea that the cosmos may be indifferent to our suffering. And, in a sense, precisely what makes us human is our ability to construct narratives that explain our existence in logical and meaningful terms. Carla Hochhalter's story is the one that we do not want to hear. For her there is no happy ending—no evidence of a miraculous uprising out of the ashes. For her there is pain and injustice, and then there is death. That is the end of *her* story.

Thomas Kyd's *The Spanish Tragedy* (c. 1587) is one of English literature's most poignant interrogations of the all too human need for comedic resolution in the face of injustice. The play's central subject—revenge—figures paradoxically as both the primary vehicle by which such a peaceful resolution might be achieved and the major obstacle to human peace and stability.[1] Kyd's masterful handling of this paradox, his ability to demonstrate at once the visceral appeal of revenge and the devastating repercussions of enacting it, accounts for the play's unparalleled success in the Elizabethan period and its enduring respectability in our own. One can reasonably argue that no other play from the English Renaissance—not even Shakespeare's *Hamlet,* which is the offspring of *The Spanish Tragedy*—so convincingly exposes the simultaneously destructive and vital role of revenge in the human imagination and society.

When Hieronimo finally avenges his son's murder in the concluding scene of the play, readers honest with themselves surely must feel something like relief or even satisfaction. But readers also must be willing to confront the moral implications of such an emotional response, since what Kyd makes us desire most is unspeakably horrible: a nightmare circus of human pain and suffering. The featured act presents Hieronimo—knight marshall of Spain (i.e., supreme judge and distributor of justice)—tearing out with his own teeth his mangled, bloody tongue before stabbing himself to death with a penknife. The violence of the scene is gruesome, but those readers tempted to complain about the superfluous excesses of the denouement would be well advised to rethink their positions; the grotesque and spectacular nature of Hieronimo's revenge plot is not so much the problem as it is the central point of *The Spanish Tragedy*.

Aesthetically and scientifically speaking, revenge is a rather beautiful phenomenon. As Simone Weil once noted, "The desire for vengeance is a desire for essential equilibrium,"[2] meaning that a clean act of revenge has at least the illusory ability to erase human mistakes and correct cosmic wrongs. Ethically and practically speaking, revenge is quite ugly precisely because equilibrium *is* illusory—an "imaginary" construct, as Weil recognized (218). Whereas the conclusion of Carla Hochhalter's real-life tragedy simply horrifies us because it lacks any meaningful structure (revenge and, therefore, equilibrium, was not a possibility for Hochhalter because her daughter's assailants had killed themselves), Kyd's fictional tragedy partially satisfies us on account of its momentary achievement of equilibrium. The grotesque violence of the final scene, however, is designed by Kyd to shatter this sense of equilibrium as soon as it is established. The play loudly declares that there is no such thing as a clean act of revenge. And just as Hieronimo is debased by his decision to murder himself and others and thereby to cause more pain, the audience members, who cannot help but identify with him, are debased by the experience of witnessing and being indirectly complicit in the inhuman spectacle that marks the end of the play.

While we share with our Renaissance forebears the same basic yearning for ethical and artistic equilibrium—and the same nauseous repulsion from evidence of human injustice—we are separated from them by our significantly different moral and legal conceptions of revenge and justice. The intolerable fact of human pain has not altered much over the past four hundred years, but our methods for dealing with it certainly have. In what follows, I should like to explore in greater depth the differences between our conception of revenge and that of Kyd's original audience, as well as what historical differences can teach us about both *The Spanish Tragedy* and its place in modern culture.

As might be predicted, religious and secular perceptions of revenge were not always reconcilable in the Renaissance period, and often they tended to clash. By looking briefly at both secular and religious ideas about revenge, we place ourselves in a position to speculate about how the average sixteenth-century audience member might have judged Hieronimo's course of action in *The Spanish Tragedy*. In attempting to come to terms with English attitudes toward private revenge, we must chart the gradual transition over a period of several hundred years from the wergild system of the Anglo-Saxon period to the "appeals" system of the late medieval period to the "indictment" system of the Renaissance.

The wergild system emerges out of the absence of a centralized system of state power. The term derives from the combination of the Old English words *wer* ("man") and *geld* ("payment") and refers to the exact price set upon a person's life, to be paid to the family of the victim by the family of the murderer. The wergild system regards murder as a violation of the rights of an individual or his family, as opposed to a violation of the law or an injury to the state. In no way does it question the right of the offended party to seek compensation for its losses. As Ronald Broude suggests, the wergild system was perceived as absolutely necessary in situations where strong and efficient punitive mechanisms for dealing with crime simply did not exist: "The tradition of self-government was strongest [. . .] in those times, places, and circumstances where no state or similar authority was available to provide redress for wrongs."[3]

By the time Kyd wrote *The Spanish Tragedy,* legal authorities no longer recognized self-government as a legitimate option for dealing with violent crimes. In 1615, Francis Bacon sought to justify the strictness of the laws governing dueling and private revenge in England:

> [W]hen revenge is once extorted out of the Magistrate's hands, contrary to God's ordinance, "mihi vindicta, ego retribuam," and every man shall bear the sword, not to defend but to assail; and private men begin once to presume to give law to themselves, and to right their own wrongs; no man can foresee the danger and inconveniences that may arise and multiply thereupon. [. . .] It may grow from quarrels to bandying [. . .] to trooping, and so to tumult and commotion; from particular persons to dissension of families and alliances; yea to national quarrels.[4]

Although Bacon is careful to mention that God outlaws private revenge, his argument against it is based upon a "slippery slope" appeal, which posits revenge as the potential source of rampant civil disorderliness. Note the flexible and problematic shift of terms throughout the passage, which makes it difficult to determine what the pronoun "it" refers to in the final few clauses: revenge or self-government? As the ambiguity would suggest, the illegality of revenge was by this time so firmly established that one could unhesitatingly describe the crimes of someone like Hieronimo as a direct threat to the law itself. This had not been the case for long.

As the final clause reveals, the Wars of the Roses—those fifteenth-century "national quarrels" that arose from the "dissension" of England's two most powerful families—served as the historical precedent that English lawmakers appropriated in order to condemn and eventually outlaw private revenge. Indeed the slow development of legal restrictions on private revenge stemmed from the Tudor monarchs' attempts to ensure that familial wars such as those fought between the Lancasters and Yorks would never again compromise the stability of the English nation: "The transformations which the Tudor dynasty sought to work upon English socio-legal institutions were motivated by the determination of Henry VII and his successors to secure their power by creating a central government strong enough to counteract the sort of baronial license which had led to the Wars of the Roses" (Broude 47). In short, the need to counteract self-government, which caused devastating "national quarrels," leads to centralized government, which depends in turn upon an effective legal system.

One of Henry VII's first initiatives at the end of the fifteenth century, therefore, was to transform what had formerly been known as the appeals system into what would come to be known as the indictment system.[5] The appeals system was introduced into England by William the Conqueror in the eleventh century, and it replaced the Anglo-Saxon system of the wergild. It allowed family members the right to prosecute the murderers of their loved ones, but it upheld the traditional idea that blood crimes were crimes against individuals or families, not against monarchs or states. As Fredson Bowers notes, "The legal procedure of the appeal, while abolishing the system of the wergild, retained the spirit of the old blood-revenge, for the nearest of kin had to take up the suit against the murderer" (7). The indictment system, on the other hand, reflects Henry VII's transformation of crimes "traditionally regarded as torts (wrongs involving only the offender and victim)" into "felonies (offenses in which the king was concerned)" (45). In a system that classifies murder as a felony, the perpetrators of blood crimes would face the state, not the brother, son, or widow of their victims. As is fairly predictable, the Tudor indictment system was often marred by corruption, but it represented a significant change regarding how revenge was legally classified and prosecuted.

While the Tudor indictment system was more compatible with a Christian tradition stressing the unlawfulness of private revenge under any circumstances, and while its proponents did what they could to emphasize this greater compatibility (consider Bacon's allusion to the Bible), it is important to emphasize that the indictment system was implemented to deal with a civil problem—not a moral or spiritual one. In other words, the indictment system, like the wergild and appeals systems before it (and like all subsequent legal systems in Britain and America), rejects quite explicitly the idea that vengeance is God's alone. The right of the state to enact revenge and, in a sense, to punish murder at all, was typically based upon the injunction in Genesis 9:6 that "Whoso sheddeth man's blood, by man shall his blood be shed." The Old Testament "eye for an eye" mentality is never seriously interrogated, in other words: "Neither Tudor political theory nor Tudor religion rejected the blood-for-blood ethic which was the basis of private, public, and divine vengeance alike" (Broude 50). The question is not so much whether or not violent crimes should be avenged but, rather, how and by whom they should be avenged; whereas in the past the obligation had belonged to members of the victim's family, Renaissance law shifted the responsibility to the government.

How then did Christians contend with the numerous biblical passages avowing the fundamental immorality of vengeance? For instance, the famous refrain of "vindicta mihi" from Romans 12:19 would appear to condemn any sort of revenge carried out by human beings: "Dearly beloved, avenge not yourselves, but rather give place unto wrath: for it is written, Vengeance is mine; I will repay, saith the Lord."[6] Furthermore, Christ's command in Matthew 5:38–39 offers a direct challenge to the lawfulness of the "eye for an eye" mentality: "Ye have heard that it hath been said, An eye for an eye, and a tooth for a tooth: But I say unto you, That ye resist not evil: but whosoever shall smite thee on thy right cheek, turn to him the other also." Rather than simply subordinating the New Testament passages to those Old Testament ones that advocate and even encourage blood revenge, such as Genesis 9:6 or Numbers 35:19 ("The revenger of blood himself shall slay the murderer"), Christians differentiated private (i.e., personal) and public (i.e., governmental) revenge. This distinction allowed Christians to heed the general message of the New Testament ("avenge not *yourselves*"; "*ye* resist not evil") while upholding the Old Testament laws by shifting the burden of revenge onto the state or legal system.

In theory, then, there was little confusion in the sixteenth century regarding the lawfulness of *private* revenge. Illegal in the eyes of both God and the monarch, it must be avoided at all costs; if enacted, the perpetrator of the crime must be punished swiftly and severely.[7] Again in theory, there should be no need for persons to enact private revenge since Tudor legal theory and religion approved of the various public mechanisms set in place to deal with violent crimes and other forms of injustice. The state's ability to discourage and prevent private revenges would depend on its ability to discover and rapidly prosecute criminals.

In practice, this often proved difficult, and here was the rub that caused so much turmoil in Elizabethan England and made plays like *The Spanish Tragedy* so poignant for contemporary audiences. In an age in which England lacked an efficient police system, it would have been difficult to detect crimes while they were unfolding, which would have led, in turn, to a number of legal cases whose outcomes hinged upon largely unverifiable accusations. Such cases are difficult to prove in any age, but to compound the problem the world had not yet given birth to either the advanced legal mechanisms or the technological equipment—finger printing analysis, DNA analysis, videorecorders, lie detectors, and so on—that has made the prosecution of criminals such a *relatively* uncomplicated task in the modern era.

Wherever there is lawlessness or ineffective law, there also is the threat of self-government and the myriad problems that it unleashes. This is no less true today than it was in the Renaissance. The most effective and popular revenge tragedies of our time tend to highlight the need for self-government in several common, almost formulaic scenarios: where law is practically nonexistent, such as the "Wild West" (John Ford's *My Darling Clementine,* 1946); where law enforcement is tyrannical (Clint Eastwood's *Unforgiven,* 1992); where the law applies only to certain members of a society (Joel Schumacher's *A Time to Kill,* 1996); and where the law provides an inadequate punishment for a heinous crime (Todd Field's *In the Bedroom,* 2001). In the Elizabethan period, revenge scenarios were more or less the same; the impulse toward self-government was greater, however, because the legal system was less effective, as we have said, and because the old familial obligations and rights, as defined by the wergild system, were less distant.

Based on this information and the evidence provided by the plays themselves, it is possible for the modern reader to speculate about the state of mind of the typical Renaissance avenger. Spurred to action by the heavy burden of honor and familial obligation, encouraged to pursue compensation for his losses, motivated by the conviction that injustice must not go unpunished, the avenger takes up the sword perfectly aware that he violates God's and the prince's command to "revenge not" himself. The reader of revenge tragedies is all too familiar with the psychological agony such awareness might have caused. Such agony is, in fact, the substance of the most famous lines spoken in *The Spanish Tragedy:*

> *Vindicta mihi*!
> Ay, heaven will be revenged of every ill,
> Nor will they suffer murder unrepaid.
> Then stay, Hieronimo, attend their will,
> For mortal men may not appoint their time.
> *Per scelus semper tutum est sceleribus iter.*
> Strike, and strike home where wrong is offered thee. (3.13.1–7)[8]

The wonderful, rapid oscillation between Hieronimo's faith in a God who will avenge injustice and his susceptibility to the persuasiveness of Seneca's claim that "The safe way for crime is always through crime" demonstrates perfectly the dilemma of the would-be avenger. The near impossibility of negotiating the competing demands of Christian, civil, and personal obligations helps to explain the tormenting ambivalence experienced by the Renaissance avenger, and also the attractiveness of revenge as a dramatic subject for the Elizabethan playwright. Despite the distance between us, we have little difficulty imagining the sense of terror and uncertainty felt by Hamlet or Hieronimo—little difficulty understanding how such emotions might lead one to despair or even madness.

Up to this point I have attempted somewhat paradoxically to describe some of the important historical differences between our world and Kyd's, while reflecting on why we continue to find *The Spanish Tragedy* so compelling four hundred years after its creation. Whereas the specific laws and customs of Renaissance society differed from our own, revenge remains a topic that binds us because the impulse toward self-government emerges precisely out of those moments in which specific laws and customs break down or fail to achieve their intended purposes. In such situations, human beings are faced with the simple fact of injustice and the overwhelming desire for equilibrium. The stories of Carla Hochhalter and Hieronimo are not the same, but they outline a similar psychological predicament.

If it is possible for us to speculate about the mind-set of the typical Renaissance avenger, it is certainly possible for us to speculate about the mind-set of the average Elizabethan viewer of *The Spanish Tragedy*. In fact, few topics have so occupied Kyd scholars as the debate about the likely contemporary response to his dramatic masterpiece. Such scholars have tended to fall into one of two interpretive camps, which are almost diametrically opposed. One group, inspired by the historical research of Lily B. Campbell, argues that the sheer number of documents condemning revenge in the sixteenth century suggests that readers would have perceived Hieronimo as a villain. The other group, led by Fredson Bowers, argues that the strong tradition of secular defenses of revenge, passed down from the wergild system, suggests the likelihood that Renaissance audiences would have identified with and even cheered on the great dramatic avengers.[9] I offer that both groups of readers are essentially correct.

As we have already seen, the arguments both for and against revenge were plentiful in the period, a fact that would have generated intense confusion and inner turmoil for the person faced with the obligation to avenge a family member or loved one. There is no reason to think that an Elizabethan audience would not have been ambivalent about the major moral questions that this play tends to provoke. To argue that Hieronimo's decision to avenge Horatio is *either* appropriate *or* unlawful is to miss the point of his moral predicament, which is that there are equally good reasons for acting and not acting. Bowers tends to ignore this fact by proposing that when Hieronimo "gives up an open revenge in favor of a secret, treacherous device, according to English standards he inevitably becomes a villain" (77). Bowers would have us believe that because English law declares private revenge to be inappropriate, Hieronimo's pursuit of it makes him a villain in the eyes of the average Renaissance playgoer. This seems to me unpersuasive because oversimplified; it assumes that the average playgoer necessarily would have associated the violation of a law—whether judicial, moral, or even Christian—with immorality. On the contrary, human beings in the sixteenth century, as in the modern age, have proven themselves more than willing in times of perceived crisis to justify or rationalize what their cultures deem to be unlawful actions. What Bowers seriously underestimates, in other words, is the complete and consistent willingness of human beings to ignore the ideal standards established by law, philosophy, art, and religion when they believe that their well-being somehow depends upon the rejection of those ideals. One might assume logically that if people are willing to surrender those ideals in real-life situations, they are especially likely to do so within the safe zones of fiction and fantasy. One might even say that great fiction invites the productive exploration of thoughts and feelings that must otherwise be repressed. While I am quite certain that to murder another human being by any act other than self-defense is to commit an immoral, disgusting crime, my knowledge of this fact hardly prevents me from experiencing the pleasure of Lorenzo's violent death in *The Spanish Tragedy*. Nor does the pleasure I take from his brutal murder make me an immoral being.

It does compromise my moral and imaginative integrity, however, and this perhaps is Kyd's most basic lesson. *The Spanish Tragedy* forces viewers to suffer through the same feelings of anguish and moral uncertainty experienced by Hieronimo in order to highlight the dehumanizing power of the revenge impulse. Kyd imposes this moral crisis on his audience by presenting revenge in a deliberately ambiguous manner; throughout the play, he suggests and then provides internal evidence to prove that (1) vengeance is to be enacted by the pagan gods, (2) vengeance is to be enacted by the Christian God, (3) vengeance is to be enacted by the state, and (4) vengeance is to be enacted by individuals.

The frame that opens the play introduces us to the allegorical character called Revenge. Andrea has descended, after death, into a Virgilian underworld where he is to be sentenced to his place in eternity. For reasons that are not wholly clear, Proserpine begs Pluto that she might deliver the sentence, a wish he grants without hesitation. Proserpine then calls upon Revenge to lead Andrea through the land of dreams back into the world of the living, where they will "serve for Chorus" in the play we have come to see (1.1.91). Bowers argued famously in 1940 that "From this point the Ghost and his theme [. . .] are superfluous; and, indeed, need never have been introduced" (68), a general sentiment shared by many readers. I want to suggest, instead, that the theme raises crucial questions about the morality of revenge that condition the manner in which we judge the rest of the play.

To begin with the obvious, Revenge is a figure of the pagan underworld, which is not the same as the Christian heaven or the Christian hell, but has thematic, moral, and atmospheric parallels in both. The figure's moral status, therefore, is at best decidedly ambiguous. Furthermore, Proserpine is not the usual judge of souls in Hades, so her decision to call upon Revenge, like her desire to judge Andrea—seemingly based on a whim—should be interrogated by the audience. Perhaps the first insight such critical reading will yield is that Andrea does not mention revenge prior to this point in the scene, suggesting that the gods actually impose the revenge impulse upon him. When he describes his own death earlier, he mentions no foul play: "For in the late conflict with Portingale / My valour drew me into danger's mouth, / Till life to death made passage through my wounds" (1.1.15–17). Later when Minos describes the same event, he tells us that "by war's fortune [Andrea] lost both love and life" (1.1.40). Based on the fact that Andrea is killed in battle, not in cold blood—a point stressed in the various reports of his death throughout the play—revenge is unjustifiable both morally and legally. Proserpine's "doom" should not be read as the just satisfaction of Andrea's desire for revenge (1.1.79); it should be read as a pass to commit an unlawful act, an invitation to moral depravity. Proserpine has more of the "bad angel" of the morality play tradition in her than has previously been recognized.

If the divine advocacy of revenge in the frame implies that vengeance should be left to God, as the passage in Romans tells us it should, then why is Kyd writing Hades instead of heaven? The problem is further complicated by the implicit presence-in-absence of God in the play. Immediately after Andrea and Revenge assume their place as Chorus, the play introduces explicitly the idea that God alone determines matters of justice. After the general reports to the Spanish king that the Portingals have been defeated and will pay their tribute, the king declares: "Then blest be heaven, and guider of the heavens, / From whose fair influence such justice flows" (1.2.10–11). Notice that the king's decision to bless heaven and God is contingent upon the Spanish victory ("*Then* blest be heaven"), suggesting that God's role as deliverer of justice is not entirely clear or certain. The point is emphasized by the audience's knowledge that matters of judgment are not controlled or influenced by God alone, since the judges of Hades clearly play a role in such affairs. The onstage presence of Hieronimo accents the contradiction since he is knight marshal of Spain, a figure responsible for delivering justice in criminal cases. To whom does the right to judge belong?[10] If the answer is not clear, or if the numerous judges in this play are likely to contradict one another, then is not the very concept of justice seriously undermined?

The seemingly gratuitous subplot involving Alexandro and Villuppo is crucial to Kyd's project because it strengthens the argument that God actually will deliver justice, "feed[ing] into the main plot an expectation that '[. . .] murder cannot be hid.'"[11] After Villuppo falsely accuses Alexandro of treason and murder, the viceroy rashly sentences the innocent man to death. When he is bound to the stake several scenes later, the ambassador enters with news of Balthazar's health, revealing Alexandro's innocence and Villuppo's treachery—a rather subtle version of the deus ex machina. Alexandro had promised Villuppo that his wrongs would be avenged, implying that God would never allow such evil to triumph: "My guiltless death will be avenged on thee, / On thee, Villuppo, that hath maliced thus" (3.1.51–52). And when he is saved and Villuppo's malice finally revealed, Alexandro confirms that justice has been delivered: "Our innocence hath saved / The hopeless life which thou, Villuppo, sought / By thy suggestions to have massacred" (3.1.82–84). While the seemingly miraculous rescue of Alexandro at the last moment *intimates* the existence of a just deity and appears to affirm the validity of St. Paul's claim that vengeance is God's alone, Kyd is sophisticated enough a writer to avoid any explicit mention of God in the scene. He thereby allows the possibility that Alexandro has been saved merely by luck or chance.

Despite the play's deliberately confusing treatment of divine and cosmic justice, one point is painfully obvious in *The Spanish Tragedy:* the public justice systems in place in both Spain and Portugal are inadequate for dealing with the injustice rampant in each society.[12] As the viceroy's near tragic mistake of executing an innocent man makes clear, human beings' very desire for justice often leads to mistakes with rather terrible consequences. Kyd's play argues that—regardless of either God's or the gods' roles in the cosmic scheme of things—the absence of effective *human* justice systems leads to destructive forms of self-government, which, in turn, opens the Pandora's box that Renaissance men such as Bacon most feared.

The argument is underlined by several brilliant details, all of which become apparent while Hieronimo is deliberating on the proper course of revenge. Kyd's first crucial move is to make the Spaniard, Hieronimo, seek legal justice before pursuing revenge, fulfilling a civil obligation consistent with the laws of Elizabethan England: "I will go plain me to my lord the King, / And cry aloud for justice through the court" (3.7.69–70). The fact that the king is deaf to Hieronimo's cries for justice and is so easily fooled by Lorenzo's intervention in Hieronimo's suit highlights the king's failure as a judge; the figurehead of state power and appointed protector of his citizens fails to deliver justice. Lorenzo is not the only facilitator of the king's deafness, though. The fact that Hieronimo is indeed half-lunatic simply proves Lorenzo's accusations that "he be [. . .] helplessly distract," and thereby validates the king's choice not to listen to his cries (3.12.96). Kyd's decision to expose the semi-insanity of a character bearing the title "knight marshall" implies that law and order have been turned completely upside down. But no fact in *The Spanish Tragedy* so loudly proclaims the failure of the public justice system as the decision of Spain's chief magistrate to pursue justice through self-governmental means.

Since we are approaching a conclusion, it probably is worth pointing out that the wheel has come full circle: we have returned to the basic fact of injustice and the human yearning for equilibrium. Hieronimo, devastated by his innocent son's murder and appalled by the apparent lack of justice in the state and cosmos, faces the critical question, which Kyd forces all of us to ask: what is to be done? Though Hieronimo will choose to pursue a course of private revenge, we are skeptical that this is a wise choice. After all, we know of the judges in Hades. We have witnessed Alexandro's miraculous rescue. Yet we too crave justice above all else. Almost despite our intellects, in our hearts we urge on the avenger.

The decision to end *The Spanish Tragedy* with the play within the play constitutes a theatrical tour de force and may be Kyd's greatest gift to the talented dramatists such as Marlowe, Shakespeare, and Jonson, who, though significantly indebted to him, eventually will surpass him. It is the moment where an emergent English art form turns inward and begins to examine its own role in the human struggle for meaning and order. That Hieronimo serves not only as knight marshall but also as master of the revels is no minor matter. Lorenzo's unfortunate request that Hieronimo stage a play recalls the king's earlier demand for a masque, which Hieronimo produces in the play's opening act (1.4.136–73). By emphasizing that Hieronimo is both the writer and director of *Soliman and Perseda,* Kyd suggests that the enactment of revenge itself is no more than another performance: "The plot is laid of dire revenge. / On then, Hieronimo, pursue revenge, / For nothing wants but acting of revenge" (4.3.28–30).

Since Kyd, like Hieronimo, was the author of a revenge play (*The Spanish Tragedy*) and a play called *Soliman and Perseda* (no longer extant), a number of important associations begin to emerge: first, it becomes clear that *The Spanish Tragedy* and the play within it amount to parallel attempts on the parts of their respective authors to locate justice in a seemingly unjust world. The suggestion here is that art, like revenge—but unlike the law or even the gods—is capable of satisfying our desire for essential equilibrium. In a sense, revenge *is* art because it is constructed order.[13] Whereas *Soliman and Perseda* is designed by Hieronimo to correct the injustice of Horatio's murder, *The Spanish Tragedy* seems determined to address our most basic questions and anxieties about injustice. The second important association, then, is between the audience that views *Soliman and Perseda* (the royal families, Don Andrea, and Revenge himself) and us, the audience of *The Spanish Tragedy*.

The power of Kyd's play, in the end, depends on his decision to resist the comedic impulse—to resist giving us the sense of equilibrium we so desire. When Hieronimo announces that he will direct *Soliman and Perseda,* Balthazar implores him to choose a comedy instead ("methinks a comedy were better" [4.1.155]), to which Hieronimo replies: "Fie, comedies are fit for common wits; /[. . .]/ Give me a stately-written tragedy, /[. . .]/ Containing matter, and not common things" (4.1.157–61). And although Andrea will later comment that "These were spectacles to please my soul" (4.5.12), the audience understands that this is a "common" response. The bloody spectacles, after all, serve merely to expose Hieronimo's slide into depravity. Although the deaths of Lorenzo, Balthazar, Pendringano, and Bel-Imperia are acceptable according to the logic of revenge, Isabella's suicide and Hieronimo's shocking murder of the innocent Castile shatter the hope that there can be ethical equilibrium in this world. Hieronimo's bestial lunacy and acts of self-mutilation reinforce the point, suggesting finally that art/revenge can cover up injustice but cannot exorcise it. Like Lear's deafening "howls" after the murder of his most beloved daughter, Hieronimo's self-imposed silence speaks to the general inability of words to articulate the injustice of the cosmos. In a final symbolic act, the playwright kills himself with a pen.

NOTES

1. Though G. K. Hunter has argued that justice—not revenge—"provides the thematic center of the play" (90), I argue in what follows that the two themes are inextricably bound in the Renaissance. See Hunter, "Ironies of Justice in *The Spanish Tragedy,*" *Renaissance Drama* 8 (1965): 89–104.
2. Simone Weil, *Simone Weil: An Anthology,* ed. Siân Miles (London: Virago, 1986) 217.
3. Ronald Broude, "Revenge and Revenge Tragedy in Renaissance England," *Renaissance Quarterly* 28 (1975): 38–58, 43.
4. Thomas Bayly Howell, *A Complete Collection of State Trials from the Earliest Period to the Year 1783,* 5 vols. (London, 1816) 2:1032.
5. For a useful discussion of these legal developments, see Fredson Bowers, *Elizabethan Revenge Tragedy 1587–1642* (Princeton: Princeton UP, 1940) 3–40; Broude 43–52; and Bryce Lyon, *A Constitutional and Legal History of Medieval England* (New York: Harper, 1960) 83–88.
6. Paul's proof came from Deuteronomy 32:35: "To me *belongeth* vengeance, and recompense."
7. As Bowers reminds us, "Blood-revenge [. . .] falls in the same legal category as any other murder with malice aforethought" (11).
8. All quotations of Kyd are from *The Spanish Tragedy,* ed. David Bevington (Manchester: Manchester UP, 1996).
9. Despite their very different readings of Elizabethan attitudes toward revenge, Bowers and Campbell agree that Hieronimo is a villain. Whereas Campbell argues that revenge is always villainous, Bowers argues that Hieronimo becomes villainous "when he consciously gives up

an open revenge in favor of a secret, treacherous device" (77). See also Lily B. Campbell, "Theories of Revenge in Renaissance England," *Modern Philology* 38 (1931): 281–96.

10. The fact that neither Minos, Aeacus, nor Rhadamanth know what to do with Andrea (1.1.32–53) calls further attention to the failures of judgment in the play.
11. Hunter 96.
12. One should not simply assume that the Spanish setting explains the ineffective justice system. While many critics have been tempted to read *The Spanish Tragedy* as a political allegory of Anglo-Hispanic relationships in the Renaissance, Lukas Erne—in one of the best recent studies of the play—warns against this sort of reading, arguing that "the play precisely lacks the anti-Spanish tone that might be expected from a work composed around the time of the Armada" (*Beyond the Spanish Tragedy: A Study of the Works of Thomas Kyd* [Manchester: Manchester UP, 2001] 90).
13. On this notion of revenge as a form of art, see John Kerrigan, *Revenge Tragedy: Aeschylus to Armageddon* (Oxford: Clarendon, 1996) 12–20.

READING LIST

Bate, Jonathan. "The Performance of Revenge: *Titus Andronicus* and *The Spanish Tragedy*." *The Show Within: Dramatic and Other Insets: English Renaissance Drama (1550–1642)*. Ed. François Laroque. Montpellier: Paul Valéry, 1992. 267–83.

Bowers, Fredson. *Elizabethan Revenge Tragedy 1587–1642*. Princeton: Princeton UP, 1940.

Broude, Ronald. "Revenge and Revenge Tragedy in Renaissance England." *Renaissance Quarterly* 28 (1975): 38–58.

Campbell, Lily B. "Theories of Revenge in Renaissance England." *Modern Philology* 38 (1931): 281–96.

Erne, Lukas. *Beyond "The Spanish Tragedy": A Study of the Works of Thomas Kyd*. Manchester: Manchester UP, 2001.

Hallett, Charles A., and Elaine S. Hallett. *The Revenger's Madness: A Study of Revenge Tragedy Motifs*. Lincoln: U of Nebraska P, 1980.

Hunter, G. K. "Ironies of Justice in *The Spanish Tragedy*." *Renaissance Drama* 8 (1965): 89–104.

Jacobs, Henry E. "The Banquet of Blood and the Masque of Death: Social Ritual and Ideology in English Revenge Tragedy." *Renaissance Papers* (1985): 39–50.

Kerrigan, John. *Revenge Tragedy: Aeschylus to Armageddon*. Oxford: Clarendon, 1996.

Levin, Michael Henry. "'*Vindicta mihi!*': Meaning, Morality, and Motivation in *The Spanish Tragedy*." *Studies in English Literature, 1500–1900* 4 (1964): 307–24.

Shapiro, James. "'Tragedies Naturally Performed': Kyd's Representation of Violence." *Staging the Renaissance: Reinterpretations of Elizabethan and Jacobean Drama*. Ed. David Scott Kastan and Peter Stallybrass. New York: Routledge, 1991. 99–113.

Simkin, Stevie, ed. *Revenge Tragedy: Contemporary Critical Essays*. New York: Palgrave, 2001.

Watson, Robert N. "*Religio Vindicis:* Substitution and Immortality in *The Spanish Tragedy*." *The Rest Is Silence: Death as Annihilation in the English Renaissance*. Berkeley: U of California P, 1994. 55–73.

6

Turks and Jews in *The Jew of Malta*

Daniel Vitkus

Christopher Marlowe's *The Jew of Malta* features as its title character a Jewish merchant, Barabas, whose name and identity derive from a deeply rooted anti-Semitic tradition in western European culture. This tradition was carried forward in the London theater, and on the Elizabethan stage, the actor playing the role of Barabas would have donned a red wig and an artificial, oversized nose to appear in the guise of the conventional stage Jew. (In *A Search for Money*[1] [1609] William Rowley describes a usurer wearing "an old moth-eaten cap buttoned under his chinne: his visage (or vizard) like the artificiall Jewe of Maltaes nose.")[2] In the playhouses of London, Barabas was only one of a long line of Jewish merchants that includes Gerontus in Robert Wilson's *Three Ladies of London* (c. 1581), Shylock in Shakespeare's *Merchant of Venice* (1596), and Benwash in Daborne's *A Christian Turned Turk* (1612), as well as the title character of a lost play by Thomas Dekker called *Josef, the Jew of Venice* (performed by the Admiral's Men, c. 1593). Barabas himself refers to this anti-Semitic tradition in the list of crimes of which he boasts to Ithamore:

> Sometimes I go about and poison wells;
> [. . .] Being young I studied physic, and began
> To practice first upon the Italian;
> There I enriched the priests with burials,
> And always kept the sexton's arms in ure
> With digging graves and ringing dead men's knells:
> And after that I was an engineer,
> And in the wars 'twixt France and Germany,
> Under pretence of helping Charles the Fifth,
> Slew friend and enemy with my strategems.
> Then after that I was an usurer,
> And with extorting, cozening, forfeiting,
> And tricks belonging unto brokery,
> I filled the jails with bankrouts in a year [. . .] (2.3.179–95)

This list of dirty deeds is not a "serious" confession. Rather, it is bombastic and ironical. Barabas's catalogue of wickedness forms part of a comic boasting contest during which he and Ithamore attempt to outdo each other with outrageous tales of villainy. This use of black humor subjects the traditional anti-Semitic stereotyping to an irony that undermines the usual demonizing function of the stereotype. Or to put it another way, the stereotype of the Jewish moneylender and poisoner is a role that Barabas irreverently appropriates but then exceeds. The play's representation of Jewish identity is founded upon traditional Christian images of Jews as treacherous, misbelieving Christ-killers and hoarding usurers, but in the character of Barabas, Marlowe does not merely reproduce a neo-medieval bad guy. Barabas is in many ways a strikingly modern figure. He embodies a new force that was reshaping English society—emergent capitalism in its international manifestation.

In order to make Marlowe's Maltese drama more comprehensible, this chapter will provide readers of the play with a range of contextualizing information that should help them to grasp the historically specific meaning of the text. Marlowe's play is a document attesting to the disruptive but exhilarating power that internationalized capitalism brought to bear on the culture of London. The impact of foreign, and specifically Mediterranean, trade on English theater can easily be underestimated because of the fallacious assumption that information coming from abroad came slowly and feebly back to the metropolitan center. The historical reality is that of an increasingly decentered and absorptive English culture, and of a theater obsessed with the assortment of cultures and commodities that existed beyond English shores. In an effort to convey that sense of the London theater's pan-cultural curiosity, this chapter will discuss a variety of issues that pertain to the theatrical, mercantile exoticism of *The Jew of Malta,* including Anglo-Mediterranean trade, relations between Jews and Muslims, the Turkish invasion of Malta in 1565, and English anxieties about Turkish power, Jewish wealth, and multiethnic mixture.

Inspired by the transgressive thrill that accompanied international capitalism's moment of cultural emergence, Barabas takes the stage. Marlowe's Jew articulates a powerful sense of commercial variety, mobile exoticism, and outward-venturing desire at the play's outset. His verbal energy and black humor make Barabas a dynamic, appealing character, and a large part of his appeal is his association with international commerce and its potential to produce vast wealth. The play's first scene introduces Barabas as a cosmopolitan merchant whose far-flung commercial activities are dispersed throughout the Mediterranean. He deals in many different commodities from many lands, but in the end his goal is to concentrate as much wealth as possible within the smallest possible space. His opening soliloquy expresses this centripetal power, located at the center of a spatial and economic system that draws upon widely dispersed commercial activities but brings it all back home to the possessive individual:

> And thus methinks should men of judgement frame
> Their means of traffic from the vulgar trade,
> And as their wealth increaseth, so inclose
> Infinite riches in a little room. (1.1.34–38)

For Marlowe's audience, this success in accumulating, concentrating, and hoarding wealth was new and exciting but also problematic. Barabas, gloating at his good fortune, asks,

> Who hateth me but for my happiness?
> Or who is honoured now but for his wealth?
> Rather had I a Jew be hated thus,
> Than pitied in a Christian poverty. (1.1.111–14)

These lines imply that Christians are forced to live in "poverty" because their religion places ethical constraints (of charity, mercy, thrift, etc.) on economic life. Jews, Barabas insinuates, are able to act more freely to pursue profits through the charging of high interest rates and other financial practices that Christians are taught to condemn and avoid. At the same time, Barabas hints that Christians pursue honor through wealth, not piety (and the play goes on to demonstrate this). Marlowe and his contemporaries were quite familiar with sermons, economic tracts, and moral treatises in which rich Christian merchants were censured for their "Jew-like" practices of usury and sharp dealing. Marlowe's Barabas is not a radically alien figure, not simply "the Jew." He is a character who also exemplifies the activities and attitudes of the ambitious Christian merchants of Elizabethan England, men who pursued profit ruthlessly, participating in a violent international commerce that could turn spectacular profits for those who were willing and able to trade with Jewish merchants in a Muslim-controlled marketplace.

Marlowe places his overreaching anti-hero, Barabas, in Malta, at the crossroads of the maritime Mediterranean, in a zone where Christian and Muslim powers overlapped. Having suffered the unjust confiscation of his wealth at the hands of Malta's Christian rulers, Barabas turns toward alliances with "Turkish" characters, first with the slave Ithamore and later with the Ottoman prince, Selim-Calymath. Changing sides and playing Christians off against Muslims, Barabas is loyal to no one but himself. His negotiations with both Maltese Christians and Turkish Muslims demonstrate the adaptability and flexibility adopted by Jewish communities in the Mediterranean, where Jews lived on both sides of the Christian–Muslim divide and sometimes moved back and forth.

Surviving records show that *The Jew of Malta* was one of the most popular plays performed on the London stage in the late sixteenth century. The play appealed to an audience that was fascinated by the contemporary Mediterranean context, where the Hapsburg and Ottoman superpowers vied for imperial control over trade revenue and territory, and where English merchants did business in distant ports, encountering merchant go-betweens like Barabas. It was both the exoticism and the profitability of the Mediterranean maritime trade that made it an exciting topic for the London stage. During the late Elizabethan period, there was a growing sense of international commerce as a daring enterprise carried out heroically in dangerously exotic regions where piracy, slavery, fraud, and violence were normal practices with which to be reckoned.

By 1589 or 1590, when *The Jew of Malta* was being written by Marlowe, the English nation had initiated an era of increasing contact with foreign lands, mediated by trade, and England was consequently beginning to experience a new economic and cultural openness. This was a process of socioeconomic transformation that particularly affected London, the site of the playhouses for which Marlowe's plays were written. From the beginning of the English Reformation, in 1534, until the 1570s, English subjects were largely preoccupied with domestic issues that arose from internal, religious tensions. While these domestic concerns took priority, international trade between England and the Mediterranean fell into the hands of foreigners, mainly Italian merchants from Genoa and Venice who controlled the transportation of goods by sea between London and the Mediterranean. But when the Venetians became distracted by the war with Turkey that began in 1570, English merchants took this opportunity to reenter the Mediterranean. Soon, in 1579, the English were granted special trade capitulations by the Ottoman government, in preferential terms nearly the same as those already given to the French. This commerce prospered and expanded rapidly. The Turkey Company, an early joint-stock operation, was incorporated by the queen in 1581, and in 1592 it merged with the Venice Company to form the Levant Company. By 1594, an English traveler to the Ottoman entrepot of Aleppo thought it unnecessary to describe the local situation and conditions of commerce there "because [Aleppo] is so well knowen to most of our nation."[3]

In England, the adoption of new systems of credit, debt, currency exchange, and financial speculation were often criticized by English writers as contaminating, foreign importations—specifically, as Jewish or Italianate practices that threatened to corrupt or ruin honest English Protestants and domestic tradesmen. Because of these changing financial circumstances, the meaning of the word "usury" changed. It no longer referred only to the charging of high interest rates on loans. Now a "usurer" was one who practiced any of a variety of new ways of making money without producing a needed commodity or offering a legitimate service. Thomas Beard, in his *Theatre of Gods Judgements* (1595), invokes this broader definition of usury:

> Usurie consisteth not onely in lending and borrowing, but in buying and selling also, and all unjust and craftie bargaining, yea and it is a kind of Usurie to detaine through too much covetousnesse those commodities from the people which concerne the publicke good, and to hoord them up for their private gaine, till some scarcitie or want arise, and this also hath evermore ben most sharply punished [. . .][4]

Marlowe's Barabas is a representation of this new, capitalist speculator; he is not limited to the role of the old, medieval moneylender.

The new economic methods employed by London investors were linked to the latest developments in international trade—in fact, English merchants had learned these methods by following the example of continental bankers and entrepreneurs. The connection between foreign influence and unethical economic dealings was often invoked in English texts that sought to defend English virtue and purity against the influence of Machiavellian merchants from abroad. This malign foreign influence is embodied by the stage "Machevill" who introduces *The Jew of Malta* and its title character to the audience in the prologue. This Italianate Machevill advocates a self-interested, calculating, godless method for the gaining and maintaining of power and wealth. He comes to "present the tragedy of a Jew, / Who smiles to see how full his bags are crammed, / Which money was not got without my means" (30–32).

Barabas is the central figure of the play, a figure who stands in a city on an island in the midst of the Mediterranean, pulling the strings of a wide-ranging network of financial activity that reaches out across the seas and continents. Though the control of Malta may change hands from Muslims to Christians and back again, he remains a persistent presence, slipping back even from death to re-inhabit the city. The other non-Christian menace in *The Jew of Malta* is not Jewish but Turkish. In contrast to Barabas's infiltrating presence within the urban space of Malta, the Turks are an external force that threatens Malta from without. Barabas's evil is intramural, domestic, adaptive, secretive, and economic—he kills by putting poison in one's food, by trickery, or by laying traps; the Turkish menace comes in the form of an invasion that takes place after warning is given to the Maltese leaders—it is an overwhelming force that works its imperial way by means of open, military violence.

Ottoman power frames the action of the play. By the end of the first scene, the news is brought to Barabas by other Maltese Jews that "A fleet of warlike galleys [. . .] Are come from Turkey" (1.1.145–46), and in the following scene a group of Turkish "bashaws" led by the sultan's son, Selim-Calymath, meet with the Knights of Malta to demand the repayment of ten years' tribute. When the Maltese beg for a month's time to collect the huge sum, the respite is granted. Later, in act 3, scene 5, the sultan's messenger returns to collect the overdue tribute. When the Maltese governor, Ferneze, refuses to pay, the Turkish Bashaw responds with this threat:

> Well, Governor, since thou hast broke the league
> By flat denial of the promised tribute,
> [. . .] Selim-Calymath shall come himself,
> And with brass bullets batter down your towers,
> And turn proud Malta to a wilderness
> For these intolerable wrongs of yours. (3.5.19–26)

Marlowe's dramatization of Turkish power drew upon the contemporary sense that the Ottoman empire was continually expanding at the expense of Christian rulers. The sixteenth century was a period during which the Turks had accomplished a program of territorial expansion through military aggression. Belgrade fell in 1521, Rhodes in 1522, Buda in 1529, and Cyprus in 1571. The Turkish threat to Christendom was felt and acknowledged even in England. In 1575, in the dedication to his translation of Curione's *Sarracenicae Historiae,* Thomas Newton wrote: "They [the Saracens and Turks] were indeede at the first very far from our Clyme & Region, and therefore the lesse to be feared, but now they are even at our doores and ready to come into our Houses [. . .]."[5]

One thing that European Christians feared about the Ottoman empire was the Islamic polity's absorptive capacity. Many early modern Christians were converting to Islam, but it was extremely rare to find a Muslim who had converted to Christianity. This fear of "turning Turk" was justified by the great numbers of Christian mariners who became "renegadoes," joining the "Turkish" corsairs in North African ports like Algiers and Tunis and enjoying the privileges of citizenship in those communities. In England, the phenomena of captivity and slavery were represented in a wide range of captivity narratives that described the experiences of men who were enslaved in Muslim areas and then managed to escape or obtain a ransom payment.

Malta was the location of a well-known slave market, and this setting is dramatized in act 2, scene 3, of *The Jew of Malta,* in which Barabas arrives to do some shopping in "the market-place" (2.3.1) where "Every one's price is written on his back,/And so much must they yield or not be sold" (2.3.3–4). There, Barabas purchases Ithamore, a slave who says he was "born in Thrace, brought up in Arabia" (131). His origins indicate that he was already enslaved somewhere in the Arab world before his ship was captured by a Spanish vessel. Ithamore is part of the human cargo that arrives at Malta in a ship commanded by the Spanish vice-admiral, Martin Del Bosco. After dropping anchor at Malta, Del Bosco meets with Ferneze and explains his purpose there:

> Our fraught is Grecians, Turks, and Afric Moors,
> For late upon the coast of Corsica,
> Because we vailed not to the Turkish fleet,
> Their creeping galleys had us in the chase:
> But suddenly the wind began to rise,
> And then we luffed and tacked, and fought at ease:
> Some have we fired, and many have we sunk;
> But one amongst the rest became our prize:
> The captain's slain, the rest remain our slaves,
> Of whom we would make sale in Malta here. (2.2.9–18)

Once Del Bosco learns from the governor about the Turkish tribute, he offers the support of Spain if Ferneze will refuse to pay the Turks when they return to collect their money. The knights agree and the Spanish are allowed to sell their slaves, but Del Bosco never returns to aid the Maltese against the Ottoman invasion. None of this is historically accurate in its details—Malta was never party to a "tributary league" (2.3.23) with the sultan. Nonetheless, when Selim-Calymath and the Turkish fleet invade Malta, Marlowe's audience was reminded of the fact that Malta had recently been the target of Turkish imperial aggression. In 1565, the island was assaulted by a massive Ottoman army, and the three-month siege that followed became famous throughout Europe when the outnumbered defenders of Malta achieved a heroic victory against all odds.

In Marlowe's day, Malta was ruled by a military-religious order called the Knights of St. John of Jerusalem. Founded during the Crusades, the knights left the Holy Land when Christian rulers were driven out in 1291. They went first to Cyprus and then established their order on the island of Rhodes, where they became a kind of aristocratic foreign legion of militant Christians and monks, many of whom came to operate as pirates in the Mediterranean, preying primarily on Muslim vessels. The knights created a formidable cluster of fortresses at Rhodes, but despite the strength their defenses, they were compelled in 1522 to surrender Rhodes when it was attacked and invested by a large, well-supplied Turkish force. Following this setback, Charles V, the Hapsburg monarch, donated Malta to the knights as their new base, and after 1530 they operated out of Malta. Provoked, not by a refusal to pay a Turkish tribute, but by the persistent aggression of the Maltese Knights of St. John against Ottoman ports and shipping, the Ottoman sultan, Suleiman I, ordered a large-scale amphibious assault, which began in May 1565. Though they were outnumbered three to one by the Turkish invaders and suffered tremendous losses, the defenders of Malta succeeded in repulsing the Ottoman armies. Of the force of about thirty thousand invaders, at least two-thirds died during the three-month summer siege, while the Knights of Malta and their soldiers suffered perhaps seven thousand dead. The news that Malta had withstood this attack spread throughout Europe and was celebrated with bell-ringing and prayers of thanksgiving. In England during the siege, one English diocese had promulgated "a form to be used in common prayer" that asked God

> To repress the rage and violence of Infidels, who by all tyranny and cruelty labour utterly to root out not only true Religion, but also the name and very memory of Christ our only Saviour, and all christianity; and if they should prevail against the Isle of Malta, it is uncertain what further peril might follow to the rest of Christendom.[6]

When news of the Christians' victory reached England, the archbishop of Canterbury ordered another form of prayer to be read "through the whole Realm," expressing thanks for the defeat of the Ottomans at Malta.[7] According to James R. Siemon, "the repulsed siege of Malta was not only known as a Christian victory over Islam, but it was also the subject of contemporary rumors about financial complicity between the Jews and the Turks, who were said to have joined forces because the aggressive raids of Malta's Knights had turned it into an infamous market for enslaved captives."[8] This is just one example of how Western European Christians believed that there was a conspiratorial alliance between Turks and Jews against Christians.

During the early modern period, Jews and Muslims were represented and understood in similar ways by the Christians of Europe. In part, the association of the two religious groups derived from a common history of expulsion and forced conversion to Christianity shared by Jews and Moors. In 1492, Iberian Jews who refused to convert to Christianity were expelled. Those who did accept baptism and remain came to be called "Marranos." Iberian Muslims were also forced to convert, and when they remained in Spain they were known as "Moriscos." Eventually, both of these groups were accused of feigning their Christian faith while continuing to practice their original religion in secret. An additional point of similarity was that both Jewish and Muslim men were circumcised, a practice not used by early modern Christians. And finally, both Jews and Muslims practiced an iconoclastic form of monotheism. Barabas's expression of solidarity with Ithamore confirms the Christian perception of Jewish–Muslim affiliation. After they join in boasting about how they treacherously killed or tormented Christians, Barabas says to Ithamore, "make account of me / As of thy fellow; we are villains both:/ Both circumcised, we hate Christians both" (2.3.216–17). The alliance forged between Barabas and Ithamore is darkly emblematic of the genuine cooperation that existed between Jews and Muslims in the eastern Mediterranean.

The Ottoman empire appealed to Jewish refugees because of its religious tolerance, its cultural pluralism, its multicultural society, as well as the commercial opportunities it offered. In late sixteenth-century Constantinople, Jews were the third largest ethnic group, after the Turks and Greeks, and throughout the empire they came to play a very important role in international trade. One historian of early modern Jewry, Bernard Dov Cooperman, declares,

> There can be no doubt that Jews were prominent and active participants in the new Ottoman commercial economy generally, and in the trade between East and West in particular. [. . .] Ottoman expansion [. . .] brought certain new factors into play which served to encourage the Jewish participation in commerce. [. . .] Jews also benefited from the renewed religious bifurcation of the Mediterranean into warring Christian and Muslim worlds. [. . .] this division gave at least some advantage to the religiously "neutral" Jews who could pass between the two worlds with relative ease and who were able to find communities of their co-religionists almost wherever they went.[9]

Marlowe's Barabas embodies this economic mobility and adaptability, though in a demonized form. Barabas's lack of concern for the Turkish threat to Malta's Christian rulers indicates the prevailing belief that Jewish disloyalty or conspiracy could undermine Christian authorities. When the other Jews inform Barabas of the impending Ottoman threat to Malta, he comments in an aside, "let 'em combat, conquer, and kill all, / So they spare me, my daughter, and my wealth" (1.1.151–52).

By placing a permanent community of resident Jews on Malta in his play, Marlowe was representing the centrality of the Jewish community in Mediterranean commerce, but he was not accurately depicting the contemporaneous situation in Malta itself, where there were no free Jews in permanent residence at the time. While Marlowe's play presents a Jewish merchant who purchases and deals in slaves in the Maltese market, in fact it was Jewish travelers who were frequently abducted and sold in that same market. In 1567, many Jews, fleeing to the Levant to avoid the persecutions instigated by Pope Pius V, fell into the hands of the Maltese corsairs. According to a sixteenth-century Hebrew chronicle, "Many of the victims sunk like lead in the depths of the sea before the fury of the attack. Many others were imprisoned in the Maltese dungeons at this time of desolation."[10]

Of course, Jews did not make up the majority of those enslaved in Christian areas like Malta—most of those taken captive were Muslims (like Marlowe's Ithamore). A Morisco writer, Ahmad bin Qasim, reported that in the first decade of the seventeenth century, 5,500 Muslims were being held captive in Venice and Malta alone,[11] and thousands more were held in other areas. Muslims and Jews rowed side by side as galley slaves in Christian ships throughout the Mediterranean, from Gibraltar to Venice. Barabas's relations with both the top and the bottom of the Islamic social hierarchy can be better understood in the context of the mercantile Mediterranean, with its buying and selling of human commodities, its mixing of different faiths at every level of society, and its economy of ransom and tribute.

When the Turks, with the help of Barabas, defeat the Maltese and capture the town, Selim-Calymath keeps his promise to install Barabas as governor. At this point in the play, the text emphasizes that the "captive Christians" (5.2.1) will be enslaved. Selim-Calymath tells Ferneze and the knights, "Ay, villains, you must yield, and under Turkish yokes/Shall groaning bear the burden of our ire" (5.2.7–8). This alliance between Barabas and Selim-Calymath is modeled on a famous alliance that existed at the time between a powerful Jew named Joseph Nasi and the Ottoman sultan, Selim II. This is not to say that Barabas is to be directly identified with Nasi. Marlowe's Jew is a composite figure, representing the new breed of capitalists whose wealth brought them political power—*and* the Jewish merchant who comes to exercise political power because of his position as a mobile, knowledgeable go-between. It will be worthwhile to describe here the career of Joseph Nasi, not only because Barabas is a partial version of him, but also because that story tells us a lot about how Turks, Christians, and Jews interacted at the highest level of the socioeconomic hierarchy in the late-sixteenth-century Mediterranean.

Born in 1520 into an affluent family of Portuguese Marranos or "New Christians," Joseph Nasi emigrated to the Ottoman capital in 1554, where he openly converted to Judaism under the protection of Turkish sovereignty. From his arrival until his death in 1574, Nasi achieved a remarkable amount of power and influence at the Turkish court, eventually becoming one of the greatest statesmen and advisors to the sultan Selim II (reigned 1566–74). Nasi's mansion in Constantinople was a palace, and his business activities as a moneylender, tax farmer, and international dealer in various commodities (especially wine) brought him tremendous wealth. His household and entourage became a focal point of political influence, and he developed a considerable intelligence network of his own. His agents across Europe and the Mediterranean region helped him gather vital economic, political, and military information which he then retailed at the Ottoman court.

Before the death of Suleiman I in 1566, Nasi had successfully ingratiated himself with Selim, the son and heir of the sultan. When Selim II came to the throne, he immediately appointed Nasi as feudal lord and duke of the Aegean island of Naxos and the surrounding archipelago. The new sultan also granted Nasi a number of lucrative commercial privileges, including the custom farm on all wine shipped through the Bosphorus, as well as other financial grants and personal support for Nasi's business interests. As a trusted favorite and key source of information about matters abroad, Nasi wielded a huge personal influence on Turkish foreign policy. For example, according to his biographer, "As a result of his great trade with Poland, Nasi was able [. . .] to negotiate with that country almost as though he were a territorial potentate."[12]

Nasi's assumption of the duchy of Naxos provides a model for Marlowe's depiction of a Jewish governor given reign over an island, like Malta, that was the target of Turkish aggression. Because of the close personal ties that developed between Nasi and Selim, and because Nasi was extremely well informed in the affairs of international trade and diplomacy, he became a trusted councillor, though a foe of the grand vizier Sokolli. Nasi, like the admiral Piali Pasha, supported an anti-French, anti-Venetian policy, while Sokolli favored a continuance of the long-standing alliance with France and accommodation with Venice.

Nasi played a key role, however, in the sultan's decision, made in late 1569, to declare war on Venice and attack Cyprus, which was a Venetian possession. It was widely rumored at the time that Selim had promised to make Nasi "king of Cyprus," should the island fall to his invasion force. Nasi's support for a policy of aggression toward Venice was motivated by a long-standing grudge. Twenty years earlier, Nasi's wife and his mother-in-law, Dona Gracia Nasi, were humiliated by the Venetian authorities when they stopped in Venice en route to their new home in Turkey. Now it was time for revenge: Nasi argued in the imperial council for an all-out effort to take Cyprus, and the sultan was persuaded. In May 1570 an Ottoman fleet carrying an army of fifty thousand was launched. Cyprus was attacked, and after it was occupied by an Ottoman army, it was formally ceded by Venice to the sultan on March 7, 1573, when a peace treaty was signed. Soon after, Selim II began to settle both Jews and Turks in Cyprus.

Nasi never received the overlordship of Cyprus, but he certainly became associated with the island's conquest, and he was henceforth known throughout the Mediterranean and beyond as one of the most influential councillors to the most powerful ruler in the region, the Ottoman sultan. In 1573 the Venetian ambassador to Constantinople referred to Nasi as "the head of all his nation," but the duke of Naxos was not the only powerful Jew at the Ottoman court. Nasi merely provides the most spectacular example of Jewish power-broking in the Mediterranean during the early modern era. There were many other Jews who held positions of wealth and influence within the many-branched economic matrix of the Ottoman empire. Other powerful Jews include Alvaro Mendes (aka Solomon Abenaish) who arrived in Turkey in 1585. Like Nasi, he played a key role in Turkish foreign policy-making and like Nasi he was rewarded for his service to the Sultan with a feudal possession of his own (in his case, the duchy of Myteline, another of the Greek isles). Other examples could be mentioned here, but let it suffice to say that there were many important Jews working for the Turkish state, forming a political elite that helped to maintain what one prominent historian, Avigdor Levy, has called "the Ottoman-Jewish symbiosis."[13]

Some of the most prominent Jews in the Ottoman empire had connections in Christian Europe as well. In *The Jew of Malta,* Barabas defines the international Jewish community as a network of rich and powerful merchants that extends beyond Malta to various parts of Europe:

> They say we are a scattered nation:
> I cannot tell, but we have scrambled up
> More wealth by far than those that brag of faith.
> There's Kirriah Jairim, the great Jew of Greece,
> Obed in Bairseth, Nones in Portugal,
> Myself in Malta, some in Italy,
> Many in France, and wealthy every one. (1.1.120–26)

Marlowe's own interest in foreign lands and politics, and his contact with international networks of Jesuits and other groups, would have undoubtedly placed him in a position of familiarity with Ottoman politics. After all, he traveled on the Continent at the time that Elizabeth I was working to forge an alliance with the Ottoman sultan and was plotting together with him against their common enemy, Hapsburg Spain. International diplomacy, commerce, and intelligence comprised an entangled system that connected English agents like Marlowe to a broad web of information that reached to the Mediterranean and beyond. Marlowe's experience as an "intelligencer" working for the Elizabethan spy network under Walsingham, and specifically his experience on the Continent, would have made him aware of the activities of powerful Jews at the Ottoman court and on the Continent.

Though there are no specific references in *The Jew of Malta* to Nasi, the story of Joseph Nasi's career reveals many of the elements of Jewish–Muslim relations in a Mediterranean context of conflict with Roman Catholic powers like Spain or Venice. These same elements are represented by Marlowe in the character of Barabas, a figure bearing many similarities to Joseph Nasi. Like Nasi, Barabas is appointed as the governor of an island conquered by the Turks; like Nasi, he has a vast trade network that deals in various commodities, including "the wines of Greece" (1.1.5). Both Nasi and Barabas are connected to a commercial network of Jewish merchants, a system that functions in a transnational economy spread out across the map, from London to Constantinople to Krakow. Barabas uses bits of Spanish in his dialogue, perhaps alluding to the Iberian origins of famous Marrano Jews like Nasi or Mendes. Most importantly, Barabas is looked upon favorably by an Ottoman prince called "Selim," who gives him an island to govern. And beyond these specific similarities, all the tale of Joseph Nasi told over reveals an environment in which turncoats act as go-betweens, strategically concealing their true identity and motives as part of a struggle for power, money, and influence in which the enforcement of tribute, the enslavement of captives, the use of fraud and force, and the holding of powerful people for ransom all obtain. This is the Machiavellian economy that we witness in Marlowe's play. All these practices were used by Christians, Jews, and Muslims alike in the early modern Mediterranean.

By the end of the play, the Christians' religious pronouncements are exposed as empty, hypocritical rhetoric. The final lines, spoken by Ferneze, ask that "due praise be given/Neither to fate nor fortune, but to heaven" (5.5.122–23), but this formulaic sentiment is undermined by the governor's unprincipled actions. Ferneze outfoxes the fox, Barabas, and breaks his vows in order to betray and murder Barabas, thereby regaining control of Malta and taking Selim-Calymath as a hostage. In Marlowe's play, all are driven by the same motive that brings the Turks to collect their tribute—what the Turkish bashaw calls "The wind that bloweth all the world besides, / Desire of gold" (3.5.3–4). And in this world dominated by Machiavellian merchants, all are subject to being sold. In the play's final scene, Barabas determines that in such an environment, he must adopt a strategy of flexibility in his relations with Muslims and Christians:

> Thus, loving neither, will I live with both,
> Making a profit of my policy;
> And he from whom my most advantage comes
> Shall be my friend.
> This is the life we Jews are used to lead,
> And reason, too, for Christians do the like. (5.2.111–16)

Barabas dies cursing them both: "Damned Christian dogs, and Turkish infidels" (5.5.85). Meanwhile, English Christians, including the queen herself, were eagerly making a profit of their policy by forging friendly ties with the "infidel" Turks. *The Jew of Malta* represents Jews, Turks, and Roman Catholic Christians in the Mediterranean context, but its critique of greed and religious hypocrisy also points back home to "Jewish" or "Turkish" merchants and policy-makers in Protestant England who put profit before religious principles.

NOTES

1. See William Rowley, *A Search for Money* (London, 1609) 12.
2. Cited by N. W. Bawcutt in his introduction to Christopher Marlowe, *The Jew of Malta,* ed. N. W. Bawcutt (Manchester: Manchester UP, 1978) 2.
3. Cited in D. M. Palliser, *The Age of Elizabeth: England Under the later Tudors, 1547–1603* (New York: Longman, 1983) 290.
4. Thomas Beard, *The Theatre of Gods Judgements or, a Collection of Histories out of Sacred, Ecclesiasticall, and Prophane Authours Concerning the Admirable Iudgements of God vpon the Transgressours of His Commandements* (London, 1597) 413.
5. Augustine Curio [Curione], *A Notable History of the Saracens,* trans. Thomas Newton (London, 1575) sig. A3^{v}.
6. William Keatinge Clay, ed., *Liturgical Services of the Reign of Queen Elizabeth: Liturgies and Occasional Forms of Prayer Set Forth in the Reign of Queen Elizabeth* (Cambridge: Cambridge UP, 1847) 519.
7. Clay 527.
8. Christopher Marlowe, *The Jew of Malta,* 2nd ed., ed. James R. Siemon (New York: Norton, 1994) xii.
9. Bernard Dov Cooperman, "Venetian Policy Towards Levantine Jews in Its Broader Italian Context," *Gli Ebrei e Venezia* (Milano: Edizioni di Comunita, 1987) 68–69.
10. See Cecil Roth, "The Jews of Malta," *Transactions of the Jewish Historical Society of England* 12 (1928–31): 187–251, esp. 215.
11. Cited in Nabil Matar, "Introduction," *Piracy, Slavery, and Redemption: Barbary Captivity Narratives from Early Modern England,* ed. Daniel Vitkus (New York: Columbia UP, 2001) 10.
12. Cecil Roth, *The House of Nasi: The Duke of Naxos* (Philadelphia: Jewish Pub Soc of America, 1948) 55.
13. See Avigdor Levy, *The Jews of the Ottoman Empire* (Princeton: Darwin P, 1994).

READING LIST

Bartels, Emily. *Spectacles of Strangeness: Imperialism, Alienation, and Marlowe.* Philadelphia: U of Pennsylvania P, 1993.

Bawcutt, N. W. "Machiavelli and Marlowe's *Jew of Malta.*" *Renaissance Drama* n.s. 3 (1970): 3–49.

Berek, Peter. "The Jew as Renaissance Man." *Renaissance Quarterly* 51.1 (1998): 128–62.

Bevington, David M. *From Mankind to Marlowe: Growth of Structure in the Popular Drama of Tudor England.* Cambridge: Harvard UP, 1962.

Bradford, Ernle. *The Great Seige* [of Malta]. London: Hodder and Stoughton, 1961.

Chew, Samuel. *The Crescent and the Rose: Islam and England During the Renaissance.* 1937. New York: Octagon Books, 1965.

Hunter, G. K. "The Theology of Marlowe's *The Jew of Malta.*" *Journal of the Warburg and Courtauld Institutes* 27 (1964): 211–40.

Imber, Colin. *The Ottoman Empire 1300–1650: The Structure of Power.* New York: Palgrave Macmillan, 2002.

Patrides, C. A. "'The Bloody and Cruell Turke': The Background of a Renaissance Commonplace." *Studies in the Renaissance* 10 (1963): 126–35.

Shapiro, James. *Shakespeare and the Jews.* New York: Columbia UP, 1996.

Vitkus, Daniel. *Turning Turk: English Theater and the Multicultural Mediterranean, 1570–1630.* New York: Palgrave, 2003.

7

Arden of Faversham and the Early Modern Household

Garrett A. Sullivan, Jr.

This chapter suggests that to understand fully the murder of Thomas Arden in the anonymous *Arden of Faversham,* one has to consider it in relation to the structure and imperatives of the early modern household. Arguably the most striking thing about that murder is just how many people participate in it.[1] Alice, Mosby, Greene, Michael, Clarke, Black Will, and Shakebag are all involved either in the killing itself or in one of the failed attempts that precede it; others, including Bradshaw and Susan, are implicated in the death.[2] Each character is given his or her motive for murder, but the importance of their collective involvement is less psychological than emblematic: Arden is murdered by a group of his dependents and subordinates; some of the killers are drawn from his own household while others have economic dealings with Arden and his wife, Alice. In the logic of this play, the violence done to Arden has much to do with his performance of the role of head of the household.

In twenty-first century America, we are used to the idea that the household represents a private realm largely set off from (if influenced by) the public sphere. In the early modern period, however, these two arenas were understood as overlapping and interanimating. Most importantly, the household was seen as both crucial and structurally similar to the commonwealth. In the words of Robert Cleaver, "A Householde is as it were a little common wealth, by the good gouernment wherof, Gods glorie may be aduaunced, the common wealth which standeth of seuerall families, benefited, and al that liue in that familie may receiue much comfort and commoditie."[3] Good government of the household had a series of interrelated effects: it ensured the well-being of the family, it advanced the glory of God, and it preserved the health of the social whole. In this formulation, the commonwealth is not sealed off from the household. Instead, the "little common wealth" of the household is a building block of the state, which is itself a commonwealth comprised of "seuerall families."

But what precisely is a commonwealth? As the historian Keith Wrightson, in discussion of Edmund Dudley's *The Tree of Commonwealth,* puts it,

> The term "commonwealth" or "commonweal" [. . .] meant both the common good, or common interest, and the social and political structures responsible for achieving that condition of public welfare. [. . .] Its health was to be ensured by the collective endeavours of a plurality of social groups acting under the guidance of the king as the fountain of justice, arbiter of conflict and guarantor of good order. [. . .] [I]f each performed its proper duties, the realm would be welded into a prosperous and harmonious whole in which all would share proportionately in the fruits of commonwealth.[4]

The household was crucial to the maintenance of such prosperity and harmony. As Cleaver suggests, the household was a commonwealth in miniature, and, crucially, it was the head of the household who served as "fountain of justice, arbiter of conflict and guarantor of good order"—as, that is, the household's prince. In the vast majority of cases, this prince was male—and he was always so in the literature prescribing household behavior. William Whately refers to household order as follows: "But what shall it auaile to maintaine a familie, without gouernment; or how can it bee gouerned but by them [i.e., husband and wife]? so that they must also bee good rulers at home, and ioyne in guiding the houshold: the man as Gods immediat officer, and the King in his family: the woman as the Deputie subordinate, and associate to him, but not altogether equall; and both in their order must gouerne."[5] Crucially, the husband is aided in his efforts by his wife, who "ioyne[s him] in guiding the houshold." However, she does so from a position of subordinance, not equality. Neither household nor commonwealth is a society of equals. Maintaining order requires that everyone keep to his or her proper place—and one of the jobs of the head of the household was to ensure that this was so.

As "king in his family," the head of the early modern household often ruled more subjects than merely those bound to him by blood or marriage. Servants and apprentices were staple members of many English households—certainly those of affluent landowners like Thomas Arden (see Burnett in this volume). Moreover, they were understood as "full members of their master's 'family'—a word which contemporaries used to describe the entire household, rather than to refer only to relatives by blood or marriage in the modern sense" (Wrightson 33). The family, then, was often more than a nucleated group connected by kinship bonds. At the same time, the head of the household's responsibilities extended to all of the members of his "family," including both children and servants.

The role of the wife is worth pausing over. As we have seen, she is both mistress of the household and subordinate to her husband. This dual status is often stressed in prescriptive literature of the period. For example, William Gouge underscores the functional equality of husband and wife: they "are the chiefest in a familie, all vnder them single persons: they gouernours of all the rest in the house. Therefore most meet it is, that they should first know their dutie, and learne to practise it, that so they may be an example to all the rest. If they faile in their dutie one to another, they giue occasion to all the rest vnder them to be carelesse, and negligent in theirs."[6] At the same time, the wife is understood as being doubly subjected to her husband, both because of her duty and because of her intrinsic inferiority (both of which obviously undergird the patriarchal structure of the household) (Gouge 26–27). For Gouge, the duty and inferiority of the wife, like that of any subordinate, inform one another: "The *Voluntary* subiection, is that dutifull respect which inferiours carry towards those whom God hath set ouer them: whereby they manifest a willingnesse to yeeld to that order which God hath established. Because God hath placed them vnder their superiours, they will in all duty manifest that subiection which their place requireth" (27). The wife's twin duties are to rule over those in the family subordinate to her and to be ruled by her husband; the husband's duty is to exercise his authority over all those in his household with care and wisdom.[7] These are offices upon which, for a wide range of early modern writers, the entire social order depends. The commonwealth is comprised of numerous households, and its integrity requires that order be maintained within each and every one of them.

The functional equality of wife and husband is readily evident within early modern literature and culture. As Susan Amussen shows in her analysis of manuals for householders, "Wives were joined with their husbands in the management and supervision of the household. The household manuals expected women to make an important economic contribution to the household: they emphasized the wife's role in provisioning the household, and the importance of her thrift."[8] As this statement suggests, there was a gendered division of labor within early modern households, but there was also what Wrightson notes as a certain flexibility of social action:

> The role of the wife within the household economies of the sixteenth century, then, was complex and varied. It extended beyond immediate domestic tasks to include a variety of self-provisioning activities, the supervision of servants, assisting her husband in farmwork or trade, wage-earning in or out of the domestic environment, and independent engagement in small business. The mix would have varied with the circumstances of particular households, but throughout society the central characteristic of the gender division of labour was the flexibility and adaptability of the female role. (48)

At the aristocratic level, what are known as "the Lisle letters" document the activities of Lady Lisle, which extend into various arenas that might somewhat misleadingly seem to be intrinsically "male." Most interesting for this chapter is her involvement in issues pertaining to the management of land; she receives information regarding the payment of rents and the behavior of tenants.[9] All of these examples suggest that the early modern household is not separated from but is fully imbricated in a world of economic practice—indeed, the household is the single most important unit of economic production in this period—and that women were expected to contribute to the productivity of that household.

If there is functional equality between husband and wife, however, we must also not lose sight of the wife's subjection to the "king" of the family. Her subjection is expressed through the legal process known as coverture. At the time of her marriage, the new wife is understood as being legally subsumed into her husband, becoming what was known as a *feme covert*. The wife's property becomes her husband's, and "husband and wife become one legal agent—the husband. [. . .]"[10] Such a legal status finds its analogue in period descriptions of husband and wife as one being, with the wife metaphorized as the body itself—unruly, passion-driven—and the husband as the head—seat of reason and self-regulation.[11] It is not difficult to imagine that an individual wife might bristle at the contradictions of her position: mistress of the household but subject to, even recalcitrant part of, her husband. When the order of the household was contested, however, domestic matters were starkly revealed as a "public" affair.

Feminist critical work on *Arden of Faversham* by scholars such as Catherine Belsey, Frances Dolan, and Julie Schutzman has drawn our attention to the problems posed for the social order by women, like Alice Arden, who failed to adhere to their twin duties.[12] One solution to such problems entailed the performance of public shaming rituals—rituals in which both husband and wife could be objects of ridicule:

> [H]eads of households who were incapable of maintaining order within their homes could expect to have their lack of authority publicly displayed. Charivari or "rough music" rituals served to humiliate both a transgressive wife and her weak husband with next-door neighbors

> performing as parodic surrogates for the offending couple. [. . .] In cases of actual adultery, an unsuspecting husband could venture out of doors to find his status emblematized by a set of horns conspicuously placed outside his house by "concerned" neighbors. In this way, a husband whose authority had been flaunted or evaded became as much an object of his community's surveillance and discipline as his transgressing wife. (Schutzman 298)

The crucial points are that "private" transgressions are understood as "public" affairs and that the wife's actions bespeak, among other things, a failure of household rule on the part of the husband.

Of course, that the wife not only represents a possible threat to household order but is also a primary maintainer of that order is tacit in much of the foregoing. Her status as figure of household rule would come most obviously into focus on the event of her husband's absence. Again, functional equality: the wife was expected to take care of the household when her husband was away. The question of the wife's reliability in that role seemed crucial to Sir Walter Raleigh, who advised his son to marry a woman who would "have care of [his] estate and exercise herself therein."[13] What we see in *Arden of Faversham,* of course, is a wife who does not take such care; in advance of the murder of Arden, Alice tells Mosby he is both present master of her heart and future "master of the house."[14] She also pledges to transfer Arden's wealth, which should be used "to make [Arden and her] children rich," to her lover (1.220–23, esp. 221). Like Lady Lisle, Alice engages in matters pertaining to Arden's estates; her enlisting of Greene in the murder plot is an outgrowth of their discussion of Arden's property (Greene tells her, "Your husband doth me wrong / To wring me from the little land I have" [1.470–71]). We witness a household order that breaks down in a way that is understood as having dire effects for the commonwealth as a whole. Moreover, the play places Alice's transgressive desires within the context of a patriarchal social order in which the head of the household does not adequately perform his role. As Dolan puts it, the play "can be seen as an extended cuckold joke. Like such jokes, and like popular shaming rituals such as the charivari, the play holds the cuckolded husband responsible for his wife's adultery and insubordination" (36). The "king" of the family does not live up to the responsibilities of his position.

Of course it is not Arden's neglect alone that is at issue; early modern culture did not understand negligent husbands as being the only ones at fault when it came to the transgressive actions of their wives, especially in the case of murder. Dolan has underscored the significance of Alice's crime. Alice is guilty not merely of spouse murder, but of "petty treason"—a crime the logic of which depends upon the aforementioned analogy of head of household and monarch (21–31). Put simply, Alice is understood as a traitor for slaying her husband, the king of the family. Servants, too, could be charged with petty treason should they kill their masters. Such a legal logic again reveals the importance of household order in early modern England, as well as anxiety about the potential breakdown of that order. Arguably, it is this anxiety that animated the inclusion of the story of Arden's murder, which took place in 1551, in some of the most important historical texts of the sixteenth century, including Raphael Holinshed's famous *Chronicles of England, Scotland, and Ireland* (a major source for many of Shakespeare's plays). What might seem a "private" matter of domestic unruliness was understood by sixteenth-century historians as one of enough "public" significance to form part of the broader historical record; events that occurred in the household were assumed to impinge upon and have implications for those performed in the commonwealth.

There is an additional reason for the inclusion of Arden's story in Holinshed, however. In both play and historical record, Arden is represented as an acquisitive buyer of land who is abusive of the tenantry. While he appears more rapacious in Holinshed than he does in the play, Arden nevertheless merits the curse of one of his former tenants, Reede, from whom he has taken his small portion of land:

> That plot of ground which thou detains from me [. . .]
> Be ruinous and fatal unto thee!
> Either there be butchered by thy dearest friends,
> Or else be brought for men to wonder at,
> Or thou or thine miscarry in that place,
> Or there run mad and end thy cursed days. (13.32–38)

This moment is a highly charged one in that it locates Arden's actions within an ongoing cultural struggle over the nature and meaning of land. As many critics have noted, Arden (in both the play and in history) is recognizably one of those "new men" who has come to prominence through, among other things, the acquisition of landed wealth. His marriage to Alice, who is higher born than Arden, also helps bring Arden access to various powerful figures of his time; we discover at the very beginning of the play that Arden has been granted land by the duke of Somerset, the lord protector of the young King Edward VI. The transmission of lands might seem innocuous enough, but it must be remembered that in the sixteenth century land was central to an increasingly embattled moral economy predicated upon stable landlord–tenant relations. Just as the head of the household should function as benign patriarch for those in his "family," so should the landlord treat his tenants. To be landowner, then, was from this viewpoint to adopt a social role whose significance becomes obvious, say, in the performance of hospitality to guests, tenants, and beggars. The landlord is a locus of beneficence, and the maintenance of the social order depends upon his acting as a source of enlightened authority. From the perspective of this worldview, the very selling of land can be problematic—land is treated as a mere commodity, rather than a locus of social stability—and Arden's greedy acquisition of property marks him as someone whose self-interest is socially disruptive. Similarly, his frequent absences from home suggest he fails to attend to the social responsibilities that fall upon the worthy landowner.

Pressure was increasingly placed on this moral economy, however. Starting at least with the growing sale of lands enabled by Henry VIII's expropriation of the monasteries, property came gradually but increasingly to be seen as an unproblematically commodified form. By the second half of the seventeenth century, its status as such hardly registered as problematic at all. What is worth stressing, though, is that it is the perspective of the moral economy that *Arden of Faversham* adopts, for Arden is represented as one who mismanages both his house and his estate. Moreover, house and estate should be understood as being finally interpenetrating and inseparable, with actions performed in one arena impacting those in the other. This interpenetrability is communicated by the very trajectory of Arden's body: after Arden is killed in his own house, his corpse is carried to "that plot of ground / Which he by force and violence held from Reede" (Epilogue 10–11). Moreover, "that plot" is marked by his corpse—"in the grass his body's print was seen / Two years and more after the deed was done" (Epilogue 12–13)—in a way that further unites the management of the house (site of the murderous "deed") with that of the estate (of which the plot is a portion). The two worlds overlap, and the violence committed against Arden reads as symbolically continuous with the violence he commits—both attest to his (admittedly different) failures of government.

The interpenetration of estate and household is suggested at the very beginning of the play. Within the first fifteen lines of the play, the "letters patents" that ensure Arden's control of his landed property are juxtaposed with the love letters "that pass 'twixt Mosby and [Arden's] wife" (1.4, 15). This juxtaposition is telling, suggesting as it does the interpenetration of Arden's management of his estates and his relationship with his wife (Sullivan 48–49). More broadly, it is land and household management that are functionally inseparable, again complicating any attempt that we might make to distribute them into clearly demarcated "public" and "private" spheres.

If Arden abuses his tenants—not only Reede, but Greene—he in turn is threatened by his servants. One of the murderers is Michael, Arden's trusted servant, who proves willing to kill his master in exchange for the hand in marriage of Susan, Mosby's sister. Interestingly, while Arden is portrayed as a rapacious landlord, it is not his cruelty that is at issue here for Michael: as Michael puts it at one moment when he hesitates over his projected crime, "My master's kindness pleads to me for [his] life / With just demand" (4.62–63). Instead, his desire for Susan motivates him. What is important to recognize, though, is that Arden's "kindness" is coincident with his neglect. Faced with evidence of his wife's adultery with Mosby, Arden travels to London with his best friend, Franklin (sc. 1); upon realizing Michael's love for Susan, he threatens to dismiss her from the household (sc. 3), but never does so; after being confronted by a public display of Alice's affection for Mosby (they kiss and walk arm in arm), Arden invites Mosby home for dinner (sc. 13). Again and again, Arden does not attend to threats to himself that emerge from within his own household.

It is worth considering further the dinner scene, during which, after many attempts on his life, Arden is finally murdered. Shortly after witnessing the two lovers display their affection for one another, Arden offers hospitality to the one man who poses the greatest threat to the integrity of his household. Alice cunningly feigns dislike for Mosby, thereby prompting Arden to defend him. In an ironic reversal, Alice is seemingly "enforced" to offer Mosby hospitality:

> *Arden:* Alice, bid him welcome; he and I are friends.
>
> *Alice:* You may enforce me to it if you will,
> But I had rather die than bid him welcome. (14.179–81)

In the end, however, Mosby makes himself so much at home that, after the murder and at Alice's request, he "sit[s him] in [her] husband's seat" (14.287). This is a symbolically significant action, one the emblematizes the complete usurpation of the place of the head of household by one to whom Arden has foolishly offered hospitality—foolishly because Arden recognizes from the outset of the play the threat that Mosby poses to the integrity of his family (e.g., 1.1–43). When it comes to managing household affairs, Arden vacillates between, on the one hand, neglect and absenteeism (as in his trip to London) and, on the other, misplaced trust in his subordinates and guests. His "inferiours" turn against Arden; his death involves both members of his household and his tenantry, and it bridges the worlds of family and estate in a way that underscores their interpenetrability.

While Arden is a failure as head of household, *Arden of Faversham* hardly endorses his murder. Neither does it suggest that, in planting himself in Arden's seat, Mosby serves as a fit replacement for Alice's husband. Instead, the play makes plain that while Arden's negligence is reprehensible, the usurpation of the place of the "king of the family" by his wife's lover is far worse. What we witness after the murder is a complete breakdown of order and of hierarchy, wonderfully encapsulated in an aside of Michael's, uttered immediately after Alice bids Mosby to sit in Arden's chair: "Susan, shall thou and I wait on them? / Or, and thou say'st the word, let us sit down too" (14.288–89). Just as Mosby literally takes Arden's place, the servants are poised to sit down with their betters, to locate themselves in a position of equality with them. As we have seen, the social structure of early modern England is based on hierarchy and difference. Michael's is a scandalous suggestion, concrete evidence of the socially corrosive effects of Arden's murder. The effects of this act of "petty treason" threaten the social order as a whole.

William Whately describes in *The Bride-Bush* a central aspect of a husband's duties as follows:

> [H]e must keepe his authority, and maintaine himselfe in that place, wherein his Maker hath set him. Nature hath framed the lineaments of his body to superiority, & set the print of gouernment in his face, which is more sterne, lesse delicate then the womans. He must not suffer this order of nature to be inuerted. The Lord in his Word cals him the head; hee must not stand lower than the shoulders; if he doe, that is a deformed family. (18–19)

This logic is essentially the one that we see expressed in *Arden of Faversham's* depiction of a decaying household and a "deformed family." It is, of course, a misogynist logic, built as it is upon the stated inferiority of women. In concluding this chapter, however, I want briefly to say more about the way in which the character of Alice troubles this logic. Put simply, it is hard to understand Alice as "inferior," at least dramatically.[15] *Arden of Faversham* is largely Alice's play; she is the most compelling character, and the one with the most complexly rendered interior life. In important ways, she is also more than Arden's equal at every turn. Alice resists the kinds of social imperatives expressed in the accounts of household life that we've touched upon throughout this chapter—and, obviously, it is this murderous resistance that makes her such a threat to the order of both household and commonwealth. Her character emerges out of the cultural dynamic that Dolan identifies in her important study of texts focused on "dangerous familiars": it is through their transgressive violation of social and moral laws that womens' subjectivities are formed. Relations of coverture break down; the wife appears as something more and other than an extension of the husband into whom she has been "subsumed" (20–58). One could modify this point: it is through her refusal of the role offered to her by ideologies of marriage and household order that Alice's character is articulated. The violation of household order goes hand in hand with this representation of female subjectivity.[16]

This is not to suggest that for women in actual early modern households the equation between transgression and subjectivity necessarily obtained. In addition, prescriptive accounts of how households *should* work offer little evidence of how they *actually* did. That being said, such accounts do provide a useful lens through which to examine what is not social history but dramatic representation. This chapter has tried to suggest that crucial aspects of this representation are only fully legible when read in conjunction with an analysis of both the history and the ideology of household and family life. From the perspective of that analysis, we see that the "deformation" of Thomas Arden's family is the result not only of the murderous actions of his wife, servants, and tenants, but also of Arden's own failures as husband, landlord, and "little king."

NOTES

1. This chapter draws upon Garrett A. Sullivan, Jr., *The Drama of Landscape: Land, Property, and Social Relations on the Early Modern Stage* (Stanford: Stanford UP, 1998) esp. 31–56.
2. Bradshaw seems to have been unfairly implicated, however. Also, it is Mosby, Alice, and Shakebag who actually deal the blows that kill Arden.
3. Robert Cleaver, *A Godlie Forme of Hovseholde Government* (London, 1598) 13.
4. Keith Wrightson, *Earthly Necessities: Economic Lives in Early Modern Britain* (New Haven: Yale UP, 2000) 27.
5. William Whately, *A Bride-Bush, or a Wedding Sermon* (London, 1617) 16.
6. William Gouge, *Of Domesticall Duties: Eight Treatises* (London, 1622) 21.
7. "This gouernment of a familie is not very common in the world, for it is not a thing that men can stumble on by chance, but *wisdome* must leade vs vnto it" (Cleaver 13).
8. Susan Amussen, *An Ordered Society: Gender and Class in Early Modern England* (Oxford: Basil Blackwell, 1988) 41.
9. *The Lisle Letters,* ed. Muriel St. Clare Byrne, selected and arranged Bridget Boland, abridged version (Chicago: U of Chicago P, 1983) 131–32.
10. Frances E. Dolan, *Dangerous Familiars: Representations of Domestic Crime in England, 1550–1700* (Ithaca: Cornell UP, 1994) 27.
11. For example, Gouge 31 has husbands as "the head of their wiues."
12. Catherine Belsey, *The Subject of Tragedy* (London: Routledge, 1993); Julie R. Schutzman, "Alice Arden's Freedom and the Suspended Moment of *Arden of Faversham,*" *Studies in English Literature* 36 (1996): 289–314; Dolan.
13. Sir Walter Raleigh, "Instructions to his Son and to Posterity," *Advice to a Son,* ed. Louis B. Wright (Ithaca: Cornell UP, 1962) 21–22.
14. Anonymous, *Arden of Faversham,* ed. Martin White (London: Ernest Benn, Ltd., 1982) 1.640. The play is divided into scenes, not acts.
15. The fact that Alice could be understood as needing to be controlled by her husband suggests another kind of "inferiority," however.
16. As critics since Belsey have noticed, the irony of Alice's situation is that she seeks not independence, but to be "re-subsumed" in marriage with Mosby. Alice's violation of the order of Arden's household does not imply that she imagines an alternative structure to it.

READING LIST

Amussen, Susan. *An Ordered Society: Gender and Class in Early Modern England.* Oxford: Basil Blackwell, 1988.

Belsey, Catherine. *The Subject of Tragedy.* London: Routledge, 1993.

Comensoli, Viviana. *"Household Business": Domestic Plays of Early Modern England.* Toronto: U of Toronto P, 1996.

Dolan, Frances E. *Dangerous Familiars: Representations of Domestic Crime in England, 1550–1700*. Ithaca: Cornell UP, 1994.

Helgerson, Richard. *Adulterous Alliances: Home, State, and History in Early Modern European Drama and Painting*. Chicago: U of Chicago P, 2000.

Neill, Michael. *Putting History to the Question: Power, Politics, and Society in English Renaissance Drama*. New York: Columbia UP, 2000.

Orlin, Lena Cowen. *Private Matters and Public Culture in Post-Reformation England*. Ithaca: Cornell UP, 1994.

Schutzman, Julie R. "Alice Arden's Freedom and the Suspended Moment of *Arden of Faversham*." *Studies in English Literature* 36 (1996): 289–314.

Sullivan, Garrett A., Jr. *The Drama of Landscape: Land, Property, and Social Relations on the Early Modern Stage*. Stanford: Stanford UP, 1998.

Whigham, Frank. *Seizures of the Will in Early Modern Drama*. Cambridge: Cambridge UP, 1996.

Wrightson, Keith. *Earthly Necessities: Economic Lives in Early Modern Britain*. New Haven: Yale UP, 2000.

8

Edward II and Male Same-Sex Desire

Alan Stewart

A decade ago, I taught Christopher Marlowe's play *Edward II* for the first time to a group of London undergraduates.[1] The discussion ended up focusing on the question of the king's sexuality and the nature of the relationship with his favorite, Piers Gaveston, and the class concluded that this was in essence a "gay play," although they were not so certain what that might mean. At the end of the seminar, a woman student in her late sixties said that she'd found the class very illuminating: "My ex-husband was in a university production of *Edward II* years ago, and you're right, virtually everybody in that production was gay. Including, as it turned out, my ex-husband."

By the time I taught that class, in the early 1990s, *Edward II* had become *the* English Renaissance play about male homosexuality.[2] In achieving this honor, it had the distinct advantage of having been written by Christopher Marlowe, whose literary output regularly toyed with homoerotic themes and whose biography hinted at his own homosexuality. Evidence given shortly after his death by one Richard Baines was designed to incriminate the poet-playwright: Marlowe, Baines claimed, had been known to quip that "all they that love not Tobacco & Boies were fooles" and, more dangerously, that Christ was the "bedfellow" of John the Evangelist and "that he used him as the sinners of Sodoma."[3] Given the controversy over his sexuality, his apparent spying intrigues, and his death in a barroom brawl at a young age, Marlowe was ripe for modern appropriation as a countercultural figure with outspoken views—and so it was no surprise when in 1991 British film director Derek Jarman took *Edward II* and presented it as a passionately and explicitly pro-queer piece of agitprop, deeming it as "a film of a gay love affair" and dedicating it to "the repeal of all anti-gay laws."[4] By the end of the twentieth century, *Edward II* had become usefully canonical, inserted into play anthologies to facilitate discussion in university classrooms of male homosexuality in the Renaissance, just as *Othello* is used to analyze race and racism and *The Merchant of Venice* to explore Judaism and anti-Semitism.

Edward II in the Twentieth Century

And yet this was not always the case. To appreciate this, we only need look at the production history of the play over the past century.[5] After its initial London performances during the reigns of Elizabeth and James, *Edward II* did not return to the British stage until as late as August 1903, when William Poel and the Elizabethan Stage Society revived the play at the New Theatre in Oxford, starring Harley Granville-Barker as the king. Scarcely eighteen months later in spring 1905, Frank Benson's Shakespearean Company played a version at Stratford-upon-Avon, starring Benson himself. It is clear from contemporary reviews, however, that performance of *Edward II* posed problems for its early-twentieth-century directors, which they attempted to solve by either diminishing or completely occluding certain aspects of the drama.

The most notable challenge was posed by the play's ending, where both Poel and Benson felt obliged to abridge the text at the moment of Edward's murder by Lightborn. From the playscript as originally published in 1594, it is not immediately clear what is happening in this scene. Lightborn orders Matrevis and Gurney to "See that in the next room I have a fire, / And get me a spit, and let it be red hot," in addition to "A table and a featherbed" (5.5.29–30, 33). Glynne Wickham notes that, in a remarkably prop-free play, this is a scene heavy in props: "A bed, table, and brazier are required for the King's murder."[6] Later Lightborn tells the king to "Lie on this bed and rest yourself a while," at which moment Edward sees "my tragedy written in thy brows" (5.5.71, 73). When the king asks him to "forbear thy bloody hand" (5.5.74), Lightborn protests that "These hands were never stained with innocent blood, / Nor shall they now be tainted with a king's" (5.5.80–81). Later, when Edward has failed to sleep, Lightborn tells his associates to "Run for the table" (5.5.109) and orders them to "lay the table down, and stamp on it, / But not too hard, lest that you bruise his body" (5.5.111–12). Then Matrevis notes that "I fear me that this cry will raise the town" (5.5.113), referring presumably to Edward's final screams of agony.

While Marlowe gives only these tantalizing hints at what is happening, his medieval sources, various chronicles, are more explicit: Ranulph Higden's *Polychronicon* says that Edward died "by a red hot poker being thrust up into his bowels,"[7] while according to Swynbroke, the king was pressed down, suffocated by some large pillows, and then killed with a red-hot plumber's iron being applied through a horn up into the bowels to burn his internal organs.[8] The play's most immediate source, Raphael Holinshed's *Chronicles,* adds the detail of the king being held down "with heauie feather beddes, (or a table as some write)" and the heartrending effect of the assault: "His crie did moue many within the castell and towne of Berkley to compassion, plainly hearing him vtter a wailefull noyse, as the tormentors were about to murther him, so that dyuerse being awakened therwith (as they themselues confessed) prayed heartily to God to receyue his soule, when they vnderstoode by his crie what the matter ment."[9] A theatrical representation of this murder would make sense of the required stage properties, and of Lightborn's cruel but literally true promise that his hands will not be stained by Edward's blood.

By reading Marlowe's play together with its sources, it is therefore possible to piece together the horrible details of Edward's murder. But in the early years of the twentieth century, this scene was not to be tolerated on stage. The *Times* reviewer wrote approvingly of Poel's production that "The terrible close to the death scene was rightly curtailed," but lamented the abridgement led to new problems: "it must be regretted that Edward's last words were omitted." *The Leamington Courier* said of Benson's staging that "The death scene, revolting as we know it to have been in detail was, thanks to the skill of the dramatist and actors, robbed of its horrors" (Geckle 78–80).

So what was it about this scene that so scandalized directors and critics? One might expect it to be the sheer onstage brutality of the murder, but some of the perceived horror was at the specific nature of the death: through anal penetration, with its hints at male buggery. And indeed, it was the suggestion of Edward's homosexuality that fascinated and horrified early-twentieth-century commentators, both of the play and its historical basis.

In January 1910, Chalfont Robinson contributed an article to the *American Journal of Insanity,* the content of which might be guessed by its title: "Was King Edward II a Degenerate?" More sympathetic historians dismissed the charges of homosexuality: T. F. Tout opined that "Of the graver charges, which have taken classic shape in Marlowe's powerful but unhistorical tragedy, there is no more evidence than the gossip of several prejudiced chroniclers."[10] Literary critics tacitly avoided the issue by tending to discuss the play as a chronicle play or a history play—Muriel Bradbrook opined that it was "merely a history"[11]—and to leave well alone the more problematic aspects of Edward's personal life.

An alternative approach, however, was suggested by Lauren J. Mills, who in a 1934 article argued that *Edward II* should be understood as a "friendship play," placing it in the context of the literature of Tudor England's obsession with the classical figure of *amicitia,* the idealized friendship between two men that was a staple discussion in the sixteenth-century grammar schoolroom, debated at length in the works of Roman writers such as Cicero. Noting that Edward refers to Gaveston as his "friend" ten times, Mills proffered a new way of reading Edward's vexed relationships: "There existed, then, in sixteenth-century literature, the idea that, when the claims of friendship clash with those of love, friendship should be given precedence. It is that view which clarifies the relationship of Edward and Isabella." Thus, while giving a central place to Edward's relationship with Gaveston, Mills divested it of any sexual component.[12] Mills was followed by critics such as Paul H. Kocher, who noted that Marlowe's Gaveston is "still the overbearing minion [. . .] but mixed confusedly, and humanly, with his selfishness is a real devotion to Edward. Marlowe has dignified the whole relationship between the two men with many traits taken from classical friendship theory." But Kocher, writing in 1946, was able also to point to the way Marlowe's "old individualism [. . .] colors the friendships of Edward with a forbidden passion of homosexuality" with the play's "physical endearments go[ing] far beyond those customary between Elizabethan friends" in other literary works of friendship.[13]

It was only with Tony Robertson's 1958 production for the Cambridge University Marlowe Society, starring Derek Jacobi, that the erotic nature of Edward and Gaveston's relationship was brought center downstage. Harold Hobson, writing in *The Sunday Times,* praised the play's treatment of "unnatural love," a topic he usually found "very boring":

> It is astonishing to anyone like me, who has been wearied to death by *Cat on a Hot Tin Roof* and *Quaint Honour* and *Tea and Sympathy,* to find how theatrically exciting the condemnable relationship between two young men like Gaveston and Edward can be when the playwright accepts it as a simple dramatic fact, like the love of Antony and Cleopatra, and not as a matter for argument, dissimulation or moralising. The hurt neglect of Edward's repulsed queen, the scorn of Mortimer for an ill-born fancy boy, the enmity of the churchmen all become living forces. And every now and then there falls a line that makes the soul shiver with its beauty. (qtd. in Geckle 81–82)

Robertson's production later played in London, with "just about everyone [among the reviewers] mentioning the homosexual relationship of the king with his minions" (Geckle 82).

As productions of the play forced audiences to deal with Edward's homosexuality, literary critics began to pay attention. In 1955, Irving Ribner was still able to hail *Edward II* as "the drama with which the Elizabethan history play attains maturity and some degree of aesthetic greatness" while insisting nonsensically that "there can be no doubt that Marlowe shares the abhorrence of the barons for Piers Gaveston."[14] But by 1964, Leonora Lee Brodwin, hailing the play as "Marlowe's technical masterpiece," lamented the "hesitance of most critics to consider seriously the love theme in *Edward II*."[15] She suggested that "as Marlowe does not present the abnormality of Edward's love as a crucial problem, nor should we" (140). Whereas as in his early plays Marlowe "had identified a masculine surrender to love with effeminacy" (147), in the fruits of his final period he "brought the subject of homosexuality into everything he wrote"—Neptune's attempt to seduce Leander in *Hero and Leander*, Jupiter "dandling" Ganymede on his knee in the opening scene of *Dido Queen of Carthage*, and of course Edward's love for Gaveston. "Although he had earlier portrayed the horror of effeminacy, when Marlowe finally turned to homosexual love as a dramatic subject, it was not such terrors of personal discovery which he dramatized but its open and frank acceptance. Homosexuality had so far ceased to be a problem for Marlowe that it is impossible to distinguish its manifestations from heterosexual love" (148–49). Brodwin even goes so far as to argue that

> As long as the object of love is a woman, Marlowe's heroes find their love degrading and even damning, a distraction rather than fulfillment. Love as a total spiritual fulfillment [. . .] seems to have become fully possible only because of some apparent personal conversion, either actual or purely imaginative, which Marlowe made to homosexual love and which provided such a release of his sympathies that he could feel empathy with all expressions of love [. . .] we can now discern in *Edward II* not only the culmination of Marlowe's art but of his tragic vision as well. (154–55)

When Tony Robertson revisited the play in 1969, in a hugely successful production for the Prospect Theatre Company starring Ian McKellen, the sexual elements of the play were played to the hilt: returning to the details of Edward's murder in Holinshed, Robertson this time "brought the mattress in"; Edward and Gaveston were seen "kissing quite overtly on the stage"; Lightborn was shown, according to one reviewer, "voluptuously submitting his credentials as a virtuoso assassin, and implanting a tender kiss on Edward's lips before enacting the most sickening murder in British drama with a realism I have never before seen attempted." In interview, Robertson spoke of how he was trying to show a "parallel" between the Edward-Lightborn encounter and Edward's relationship with Gaveston, playing with what he saw as the king's masochistic tendencies (Geckle 92–95). The Gaveston/Lightborn analogy gripped the imagination of directors: productions by the Royal Lyceum Company at the 1978 Edinburgh Festival, the Bristol Old Vic in 1980, and the Compass Theatre Company in 1984 all had the actor portraying Gaveston double as Lightborn (Geckle 100).

By the time of John Housman's 1975 production for The Acting Company in New York City, Edward's homosexuality was accepted as the key to the play, and its interpretation pursued pruriently, according to Brendan Gill of the *New Yorker*, who complained that the company "took full advantage of the contemporary appetite for sexual revelation; it pursued with relish every clue that the text provided in respect to Edward's irregular personal life." Sylviane Gold in the *New York Post* balked at Norman Stow's portrayal of the king as "a flagrantly effeminate slave of passion." "Whatever kingly qualities Edward has," she continued "and the poor man doesn't have many—were lost behind the posturings of a drag queen" (Geckle 99–100).

From the 1980s onward, it became increasingly possible to discuss Renaissance same-sex desire openly in academic contexts, thanks largely to the groundbreaking work of historian Alan Bray and the influence of queer theorist Eve Kosofsky Sedgwick, who pioneered the concept of the "homosocial," allowing critics to describe a continuum of relations between men, both erotic and nonerotic. A rush of sophisticated literary criticism on Marlowe emerged from the likes of Jonathan Goldberg, Bruce Smith, Gregory Bredbeck, and Laurie Shannon.[16] But for a later generation of gay artists trying to work with the play as a piece to be performed, *Edward II* was deeply flawed. When Derek Jarman came to film what he saw as a gay love story, he was forced—like the play's early-twentieth-century directors, but for different reasons—to tamper with the play's ending. In Jarman's published screenplay of *Edward II,* the king is not impaled on a red-hot poker; instead, he cuts short Edward's speech of foreboding:

> These looks of thine can harbour nought but death;
> I see my tragedy written in thy brows.
> Yet stay a while: forbear thy bloody hand,
> And let me see the stroke before it comes. (5.5.72–75)

Then, according to the script, "Suddenly and unexpectedly Lightborn takes the poker and throws it into the water. He comes over to Edward and kneels and kisses him." The play then ends with lines imported from the first scene of act 5:

> Continue ever, thou celestial sun;
> Let never silent night possess this clime.
> Stand still you watches of the element;
> All times and seasons, rest you at a stay,
> That Edward may be still fair England's King. (5.1.64–68)

To his assistants, Jarman declared that with this "happy ending" "Marlowe is lucky to have us: we have rescued the play!"[17] But the extent of Jarman's revisions is betrayed by the fact that in the original text, these lines come, pathetically, after Edward has just given up his crown, when the audience knows that Edward—or at least *this* Edward—can no more be fair England's king.

The theatrical and critical fortunes of *Edward II* during the twentieth century can be seen to respond to and reflect the changing reception of homosexuality—from its long-standing position as "unspeakable" vice to crime to psychiatric disorder through the postwar impetus for legal reform, the freedoms of 1970s gay liberation, and the deliberately oppositional queer politics of the 1990s. Even this brief survey shows that *Edward II* is a play that speaks directly—and sometimes confusingly—to contemporary agendas, but what might it mean to examine the play through the nexus of meanings available to its first audience in late Elizabethan London?

Edward II in Its Own Time

Of course, it is impossible to examine the play purely "in its own time" because even at its composition and first performance it was dealing with materials from the past—from the reign of the controversial King Edward II (1307–1327), which came to an end via abdication, and eventually murder, possibly at the hands of the accomplices of his estranged queen, Isabella. Marlowe's historical materials came down from the medieval chronicles through to Raphael Holinshed's *Chronicles,* editions of which had appeared in 1577 and 1587.[18] As critics have long recognized, Marlowe was highly selective in what he took from the chronicles. Out went much to do with warfare in Scotland, Ireland, and Edward's journey to France, private wars—indeed "all quarrels between Edward and the nobles on grounds other than his maintenance of lewd favourites."[19]

Instead, as Lauren Mills argues, Marlowe brings forward the Mortimer-Isabella plot, invents a quarrel between Gaveston and Isabella, and of course focuses on the relationship with Edward and Gaveston. For this last, there was considerable evidence in the chronicles. Ranulph Higden wrote that Edward "was ardently in love with one of his friends, whom he exalted, enriched, advanced, and honoured extravagantly. From this cause came shame to the lover, hatred to the beloved, scandal to the people, and harm to the kingdom."[20] As the author of the *Vita Edwardi Secundi* exclaims, "Indeed I do not remember to have heard that one man so loved another. Jonathan cherished David, Achilles loved Patroclus. But we do not read that they were immoderate. Our king, however, was incapable of moderate favour, and on account of Piers was said to forget himself, and so Piers was accounted a sorcerer."[21] The *Chronicle of Melsa* more bluntly stated that "Indeed this Edward delighted excessively in the vice of sodomy [in vita sodomitico nimium delectabat] and seemed to lack fortune and grace through his entire life."[22] In his survey of these materials, historian John Boswell concludes that "Although there is no way to assess how the populace in general felt about their gay monarch, there can be no doubt that his erotic preferences were widely known and generally regarded as the cause of his downfall."[23]

Marlowe's immediate inspiration, however, was the account of Edward's reign in Holinshed's *Chronicles,* and the playwright's particular additions can be most clearly seen through an examination of his use of that source. In Holinshed's elaboration, Gaveston is presented as a seducer "through whose company & societie hee [Edward] was suddainely so corrupted, that he burst out into most heinous vice." Abandoning the advice of his nobles, and taking "small heede vnto *th*e good gouernemen*t* of *th*e co*m*mon wealth," Edward "gaue himself to wantonness, passing hys time in voluptuous pleasure, & riotous excesse." Gaveston facilitated this wantonness, "furnish[ing] hys court with co*m*panies of Jesters, ruffia*n*s, flattering parasites, musitions, and other vile and naughty ribaulds, *tha*t the K*ing* might spend both dais & nights in iesting, playing, banqueting, & in such other filthy & dishonourable exercises."[24]

In Marlowe's play, Holinshed's hints of the corrupting power of entertainment—jesters, musicians, jesting, playing—are memorably developed as in the first scene Gaveston lays out his plan to seduce the king:

> I must have wanton poets, pleasant wits,
> Musicians that, with touching of a string
> May draw the pliant King which way I please.
> Music and poetry is his delight;
> Therefore I'll have Italian masques by night,
> Sweet speeches, comedies, and pleasing shows;
> And in the day, when he shall walk abroad,

Like sylvan nymphs my pages shall be clad;
My men, like satyrs grazing on the laws,
Shall with their goat-feet dance an antic hay.
Sometimes a lovely boy in Dian's shape,
With hair that gilds the water as it glides,
Crownets of pearl about his naked arms,
And in his sportful hands an olive tree
To hide those parts which men delight to see,
Shall bathe him in a spring; and there, hard by,
One like Actaeon, peeping through the grove,
Shall by the angry goddess be transformed,
And running in the likeness of a hart
By yelping hounds pulled down and seem to die.
Such things as these best please his majesty,
My lord. (1.1.50–71)

Here the entertainments of Holinshed's account are made explicitly theatrical in the form of music, poetry, Italian masques, sweet speeches, pleasing shows, cross-dressing boys, and the representation of Actaeon. But they also convey a gender-unspecific but undeniable eroticism: Edward will be drawn by a "lovely boy," apparently objectified very much as a woman "in Dian's shape," but covering "those parts which men delight to see"—are these the female "parts" of Dian, or the male "parts" of the lovely boy that appeal so much to men? The story of Actaeon is even less definite in its application: is Actaeon Gaveston or Edward, both of whom will in time be "pulled down" by the "yelping hounds," the barons, and not only "seem to die" but indeed die?[25] In presenting Gaveston's (strictly unnecessary) plan for seduction in this way, Marlowe highlights the thoroughgoing eroticism of the relationship between these men. The play begins with Piers Gaveston reading the words of his "Sweet prince" (1.1.6), King Edward II, commanding him to "come [. . .] / And share the kingdom with thy dearest friend" (1.1.1–2). Edward deliberately piles honors on Gaveston, directly opposing the barons who detest the man they see as a baseborn Frenchman, declaring "I will have Gaveston [. . .] / I'll bandy with the barons and the earls, / And either die or live with Gaveston" (1.1.95, 136–37). Their relationship is one of ostentatious public affection, which notably goes beyond the decorum expected between a king and his inferior. Edward's favor is vouchsafed by public displays of affection: "arm in arm, the King and he doth march; / [. . .] leaning on the shoulder of the King, / He nods, and scorns, and smiles at those that pass" (1.2.20, 23–24). He initially welcomes Gaveston by saying

Kiss not my hand;
Embrace me, Gaveston, as I do thee.
Why shouldst thou kneel? Knowest thou not who I am?
Thy friend, thy self, another Gaveston.
Not Hylas was more mourned of Hercules
Than thou hast been of me since thy exile. (1.1.139–44)

Here (as Lauren Mills detected) Edward draws on the rhetoric of an idealized classical male friendship. The concept of *amicitia* was well known to any boy educated within the sixteenth-century English grammar school curriculum, as Marlowe had been. Promulgated by such key classroom authors as Cicero, *amicitia* described a relationship between two virtuous men, often forged during their youth, in which the men shared everything: bed, board, and book.[26] The intense relationship was such that the men became one: to quote another sixteenth-century English proponent, Nicholas Grimald, "Behold thy friend, and of thy self the pattern see: / One soull, a wonder shall it seem, in bodies twain to bee."[27] Here, drawing on that rhetoric, Edward casts himself as "Thy friend, thy self, another Gaveston"; he refers to classical myths demonstrating friendship: Hylas was kidnapped by nymphs while aboard the *Argos,* occasioning acute grief in his friend Hercules. The king's relationship with Gaveston is recognized as such by the elder Mortimer, when he advises his nephew to cease his attacks on Edward:

> Leave now to oppose thyself against the King.
> Thou seest by nature he is mild and calm,
> And seeing his mind so dotes on Gaveston,
> Let him without controlment have his will. (1.4.386–89)

He locates the relationship between the two men in a tradition of great mythological and classical male friendships:

> The mightiest kings have had their minions:
> Great Alexander loved Hephestion,
> The conquering Hercules for Hylas wept,
> And for Patroclus stern Achilles drooped.
> And not kings only, but the wisest men:
> The Roman Tully loved Octavius,
> Grave Socrates, wild Alcibiades.
> Then let his grace, whose youth is flexible,
> And promiseth as much as we can wish,
> Freely enjoy that vain, light-headed earl,
> For riper years will wean him from such toys. (1.4.390–400)

This is the same tradition in which Edward places himself and Gaveston, and Mortimer's discussion would seem to indicate that it should not be taken too seriously in political terms—this is just a passing phase.[28] But Gaveston does not resort to this rhetoric: significantly, in the opening lines of the play, he compares himself to Leander, who died swimming the Hellespont, tacitly casting Edward as Leander's lover, the female Hero. In time, indeed, Edward also figures their relationship as one between a man and a woman, comparing himself to a lover to Danäe:

> Thy absence made me droop and pine away;
> For, as the lovers of fair Danäe,
> When she was locked up in a brazen tower,
> Desired her more and waxed outrageous,
> So did it sure with me. [. . .] (2.2.52–56)

And when the barons meet Gaveston for their final encounter, they insult him in terms that move easily from general corruption to specifically female seduction: "Thou proud disturber of thy country's peace / Corrupter of thy King, cause of these broils, / Base flatterer. [. . .]" (2.5.9–11),

> Monster of men,
> That, like the Greekish strumpet, trained to arms
> And bloody wars so many valiant knights (2.5.14–16).

Now Gaveston is Helen of Troy, a female "strumpet" who leads to the destruction of a nation. It might be argued that, by portraying a supposedly male *amicitia* in terms of (excessive) heterosexual desire, Marlowe is pointing to its limits. Similarly, whereas the classical definition of proper *amicitia* insists it must be a bond between two good, virtuous men, Gaveston is constantly described as ambitious, proud, and evil: by his enemies Coventry, Lancaster, Warwick and the Mortimers, he is deemed "wicked" (1.1.176), "Accursèd," a "villain" (1.2.4, 11), "hateful" (1.4.33), "your minion Gaveston" (2.2.148), an "Ignoble vassal" (1.4.16) with "upstart pride" (1.4.41), "the slave" (1.2.25), "that peevish Frenchman" (1.2.7), "swoll'n with venom of ambitious pride" (1.2.31), "That sly inveigling Frenchman" (1.2.57), "that vile torpedo [flat-fish with a numbing influence]" (1.4.223), "a plague" (1.4.270), "a night-grown mushroom" (1.4.284), a "base [. . .] groom" (1.4.291), and "that base peasant" (1.4.7) who has "bewitched" the king (1.2.55). In a lengthy speech to his uncle the younger Mortimer explains what makes him "impatient" about Gaveston:

> Uncle, his wanton humour grieves not me,
> But this I scorn, that one so basely born
> Should by his sovereign's favour grow so pert
> And riot it with the treasure of the realm.
> While soldiers mutiny for want of pay,
> He wears a lord's revenue on his back,
> And, Midas-like, he jets it in the court
> With base outlandish cullions at his heels,
> Whose proud fantastic liveries make such show
> As if that Proteus, god of shapes, appeared.
> I have not seen a dapper jack so brisk;
> He wears a short Italian hooded cloak,
> Larded with pearl, and in his Tuscan cap
> A jewel of more value than the crown.
> Whiles other walk below, the King and he
> From out a window laugh at such as we,
> And flout our train and jest at our attire.
> Uncle, 'tis this that makes me impatient. (1.4.401–18)

Here Mortimer elaborates on the unacceptable features of Gaveston: alleged base birth (although this is historically without justification) and the concomitant rise to power, and suspicious foreignness, which is conveyed through ostentatiously un-English and specifically Italian costume and behavior—a notion that underscores and comments on Gaveston's plan to seduce the king with Italian masques (1.1.54). Most recent analyses of Renaissance homosexuality have shown how strong and indeed erotic friendships between men could coexist peaceably with those men's marriages to women—and indeed, Edward is shown in the play facilitating a good marriage for Gaveston. But in Marlowe's account, Edward's friendship with Gaveston is—against the grain—represented as being in direct opposition to his marriage to Isabella. In this, Marlowe may again be mirroring the medieval chroniclers: the *Westminster Chronicle* described the relationship between Edward and Gaveston an "illicit and sinful union which led to the rejection of the sweet embraces of his wife" while another source had it "that the King loved an evil, male sorcerer more than he did his wife, a most handsome lady and very beautiful woman."[29] In the play, Isabella laments to Mortimer that

now my lord the King regards me not
But dotes upon the love of Gaveston.
He claps his cheeks and hangs about his neck,
Smiles in his face and whispers in his ears,
And when I come, he frowns, as who should say
"Go whither thou wilt, seeing I have Gaveston." (1.2.49–54)

Edward deliberately places Gaveston beside him on the throne, in the space that should be Isabella's. When Gaveston and Isabella meet, they confront each other in a stylized way that points up their analogous roles in relation to the king:

Isabella: Villain, 'tis thou that robb'st me of my lord.
Gaveston: Madam, 'tis you that rob me of my lord. (1.4.160–61)

Isabella bewails the loss of her husband by recourse to the myth of Jupiter, who abandoned his wife Juno in favor of Ganymede, the boy whom he had seized in the form of an eagle (a dilemma staged by Marlowe in the opening scene of *Dido Queen of Carthage*):

Like frantic Juno will I fill the earth
With ghastly murmur of my sighs and cries,
For never doted Jove on Ganymede
So much as he on cursèd Gaveston. (1.4.178–81)

Ultimately, Isabella is forced to argue for Gaveston's recall in order to repair her relations with Edward. In return he promises "A second marriage 'twixt thyself and me" as a reward (1.4.334), but even this does not work out, as the queen tells Mortimer:

These hands are tired with haling of my lord
From Gaveston, from wicked Gaveston,
And all in vain, for when I speak him fair,
He turns away and smiles upon his minion. (2.4.26–29)

The king does not attempt to deny the barons' accusations: "Were he a peasant," he declares, "being my minion, / I'll make the proudest of you stoop to him" (1.4.30–31). When challenged by the younger Mortimer as to "Why should you love him whom the world hates so?"(1.4.76), Edward responds, "Because he loves me more than all the world" (1.4.77). To Edward, he is "sweet Gaveston" (1.4.108, 306), "sweet friend" (1.4.112, 140). When forced to sign Gaveston's banishment, Edward weeps, prompting the elder Mortimer to observe that "The King is lovesick for his minion" (1.4.86), a term that Isabella also employs contemptuously, complaining later of "how passionate he is / And still his mind runs on his minion" (2.2.3–4, also 1.4.310). Edward makes love for Gaveston the measure of proper love for him—"They love me not that hate my Gaveston" (2.2.37)—and pledges his support for Gaveston in terms that undermine his kingliness:

> Ere my sweet Gaveston shall part from me,
> This isle shall fleet upon the ocean
> And wander to the unfrequented Inde. (1.4.48–50)

When, under pressure, he offers to divide up honors between his barons and earls, he finishes by declaring,

> If this content you not,
> Make several kingdoms of this monarchy,
> And share it equally amongst you all,
> So I may have some nook or corner left
> To frolic with my dearest Gaveston. (1.4.69–73)

Gaveston, of course, is dead by the beginning of act 3, leaving the play with most of its running time still to go. It could be argued that to focus so heavily on Edward's relationship with Gaveston is to misrepresent the play—after all, doesn't Edward embark on a similar relationship with Spencer (the historical Hugh le Despencer) almost immediately? And yet, as several critics have observed, Spencer is a strangely wan character after Gaveston—and Marlowe makes nothing of the fact that one major chronicler, Jean Froissart, records that Hugh had committed "sodomy" with the king; that he, rather than Gaveston, was the impetus for Edward's abandonment of his queen; and that le Despenser's execution had involved the severing of his genitals "because he was a heretic and a sodomite [pour ce qu'il étoit hérite et sodomite]."[30] Instead, although many (historical) years pass between Gaveston's death and that of the king, the play makes it clear that Edward's fall and eventual demise are inexorably linked to his relationship with Gaveston. First the barons make the connection: the younger Mortimer links the country's financial distress with the seductions of the favorite:

> The idle triumphs, masques, lascivious shows,
> And prodigal gifts bestowed on Gaveston
> Have drawn thy treasure dry and made thee weak,
> The murmuring commons overstretched hath. (2.2.156–59)

Even the loyal Kent eventually asserts that

> My lord, I see your love to Gaveston
> Will be the ruin of the realm and you. (2.2.207–08)

In time, too, the king makes the same connection. "O Gaveston," he laments after he has subjected to the humiliation of being shaved with puddle water,

> it is for thee that I am wronged;
> For me, both thou and both the Spencers died,
> And for your sakes a thousand wrongs I'll take.
> The Spencers' ghosts, wherever they remain,
> Wish well to mine; then, tush, for them I'll die. (5.3.41–45)

And of course that death, as the turn-of-the-century directors and critics knew as well as Derek Jarman eighty years later, can be seen to operate as a figurative but brutal verdict on Edward's relationship with Gaveston: the sodomite king dies, in agony, sodomized by a red-hot poker. As Eugene M. Waith argues,"the way in which the King is presumably held down at the last," a detail "which has not been emphasized" by critics, "is particularly appropriate to the design of the play": "Appalling as the entire scene is (no Elizabethan stage-horror exceeds this), it is the perfect culmination of the main movement of the play."[31] Waith's account is itself brutal—and for a queer director such as Jarman such an act could never be the "perfect culmination" for a "gay love affair." And even if, within a certain moral and legal order, such a death were a "perfect culmination" to "the design of the play," fitting poetic justice, Marlowe does not allow us to feel any satisfaction. Instead, as Charles Lamb wrote in *Specimens of English Dramatic Poets* almost two centuries ago, it is a scene that "moves pity and terror beyond any scene, ancient or modern, with which I am acquainted" (qtd. in Geckle 42–43).

The range of reactions of *Edward II* over the centuries—and indeed over the last few years—demonstrates convincingly that in his exploration of the dynamics of same-sex desire, Marlowe cannot be pinned down to a single opinion of his subject matter. Even working within a historical schema that insists that Edward must die, Marlowe signally fails to be either moralistic or didactic: instead his play refuses to allow a simplistic verdict on Edward's love for Gaveston, forcing each audience to confront its own preconceived notions about kingship, friendship, and desire.

NOTES

1. All references to Marlowe's works are to the Everyman edition: *The Complete Plays,* ed. Mark Thornton Burnett (London: J.M. Dent, 1999).
2. It should be emphasized that this discussion is limited to male homosexuality: the modern yoking of "lesbian and gay" studies does not necessarily correspond to any early modern analogizing of desire between men and desire between women. For recent, groundbreaking work on early modern lesbianism, see Kathryn Schwarz, *Tough Love: Amazon Encounters in the English Renaissance* (Durham: Duke UP, 2000); Harriette Andreadis, *Sappho in Early Modern England: Female Same-Sex Literary Erotics, 1550–1714* (Chicago: U of Chicago P, 2001); and especially Valerie Traub, *The Renaissance of Lesbianism in Early Modern England* (Cambridge: Cambridge UP, 2002).
3. See Jonathan Goldberg, "Sodomy and Society: The Case of Christopher Marlowe," *Southwest Review* 69 (1984): 371–78 at 371, 374.
4. Derek Jarman, *Queer Edward II* (London: British Film Institute, 1991) unnumbered page.
5. For a production history, see George L. Geckle, *Tamburlaine and Edward II: Text and Performance* (Basingstoke: Macmillan, 1988) 78–101.
6. Glynne Wickham, "*Exeunt to the Cave:* Notes on the Staging of Marlowe's Plays," *Tulane Drama Review* 8 (1964): 184–94, esp. 192. It may be that only a spit is required, since the brazier is described as "in the next room."
7. Ranulph of Higden, *Polychronicon,* ed. C. Babington and Joseph Rawson Lumby, 8 vols. (London, 1864–86) 8:324.
8. Galfredus le Baker de Swynebroke, *Chronicon,* ed. Edward Maunde Thompson (Oxford, 1889) 33.

9. Raphael Holinshed, *The Firste [Laste] Volume of the Chronicles of England, Scotlande, and Irelande* (London, 1577) sig. Gg.vj.[r] (p. 883).
10. T. F. Tout, *The Place of Edward II in English History* (Manchester: U of Manchester P, 1936).
11. M. C. Bradbrook, "*The Jew of Malta* and *Edward II*," *Themes and Conventions of Elizabethan Tragedy* (Cambridge: Cambridge UP, 1935), rpt. in *Marlowe: A Collection of Critical Essays*, ed. Clifford Leech (Englewood Cliffs: Prentice-Hall, 1964) 120–27, esp. 124.
12. L. J. Mills, "The Meaning of *Edward II*," *Modern Philology* 32 (1934–35): 11–31, esp. 23.
13. Paul H. Kocher, *Christopher Marlowe: A Study of His Thought, Learning, and Character* (Chapel Hill: U of North Carolina P, 1946) 203, 205, and 205 n. 43.
14. Irving Ribner, "Marlowe's *Edward II* and the Tudor History Play," *ELH* 22 (1955): 243–53, esp. 244, 252.
15. Leonora Leet Brodwin, "*Edward II*: Marlowe's Culminating Treatment of Love," *ELH* 31 (1964): 139–55, esp. 139.
16. Alan Bray, *Homosexuality in Renaissance England* (London: Gay Men's P, 1982); Eve Kosofsky Sedgwick, *Between Men: English Literature and Male Homosocial Desire* (New York: Columbia UP, 1985) and *Epistemology of the Closet* (Berkeley: U of California P, 1990); Goldberg; Bruce R. Smith, *Homosexual Desire in Shakespeare's England: A Cultural Poetics* (Chicago: U of Chicago P, 1991) 209–33; Gregory W. Bredbeck, *Sodomy and Interpretation: From Marlowe to Milton* (Ithaca: Cornell UP, 1991); Laurie Shannon, *Sovereign Amity: Figures of Friendship in Shakespearean Contexts* (Chicago: U of Chicago P, 2002) ch. 5. See also Lawrence Normand, '"What Passions Call You These?"': *Edward II* and James VI," *Christopher Marlowe and English Renaissance Culture*, ed. Darryll Grantley and Peter Roberts (Aldershot: Scolar P, 1998) 172–97.
17. Jarman 162.
18. On the historical Edward and Gaveston, see Harold Hutchison, *Edward II: The Pliant King* (London: Eyre and Spottiswoode, 1971); Charles Wood, "Personality, Politics, and Constitutional Progress: The Lessons of Edward II," *Studia Gratiana* 15 (1972): 521–36; Caroline Bingham, *Life and Times of Edward II* (London: Weidenfeld and Nicolson, 1973); G. P. Cuttino and T. W. Lyman, "Where Is Edward II?," *Speculum* 53 (1978): 522–44; John Boswell, *Christianity, Social Tolerance, and Homosexuality: Gay People in Western Europe from the Beginning of the Christian Era to the Fourteenth Century* (Chicago: U of Chicago P, 1980) 298–300; J. S. Hamilton, *Piers Gaveston Earl of Cornwall 1307–1312: Politics and Patronage in the Reign of Edward II* (Detroit: Wayne State UP, and London: Harvester, 1988); Paul Doherty, *Isabella and the Strange Death of Edward II* (London: Constable, 2003).
19. See the summary in L. J. Mills, "The Meaning of Edward II," *Modern Philology* 32 (1934–35): 11–31, esp. 12–13.
20. *Polychronicon Ranulphi Higdeni* 8:298.
21. N. Denholm Young, trans. & ed., *Vita Edwardi Secundi Monachi cuiusdam Malmesberiensis/ The Life of Edward the Second by the So-called Monk of Malmesbury* (London: Thomas Nelson, 1957) 14, 15.
22. Thomas of Burton, *Chronica monasterii de Melsa, a fundatione usque ad annum 1396*, ed. Edward A. Bond, 3 vols. (London, 1866–68) 2:355.
23. Boswell 299–300.
24. Holinshed 1577: 2: 847 [E.iij.[r] i.e. Ee.iiij.[r]].
25. In *Wisedome of the Ancients*, Francis Bacon explains the story of Actaeon as symbolizing the dangers faced by a master from his servants—which might suggest Edward as Actaeon—although he sees that master's vulnerability as lying in his intimacy with his prince—which might suggest Gaveston as Actaeon. See Bacon, *The Wisedome of the Ancients*, trans. Arthur Gorges (London, 1619) C2[v]–C3[r].

26. On *amicitia* in Tudor England, see the standard survey by Lauren J. Mills, *One Soul in Bodies Twain: Friendship in Tudor and Stuart Literature* (Bloomington: The Principia P, 1937); and more recently Alan Bray, "Homosexuality and the Signs of Male Friendship in Elizabethan England," *History Workshop* 29 (1990): 1–19; Lorna Hutson, *The Usurer's Daughter: Male Friendship and Fictions of Women in Sixteenth-Century England* (London: Routledge, 1994); Alan Stewart, *Close Readers: Humanism and Sodomy in Early Modern England* (Princeton: Princeton UP, 1997), ch. 4; Shannon; Alan Bray, *The Friend* (Chicago: U of Chicago P, 2003).
27. Grimald, qtd. in Mills, "Meaning" 17.
28. However, Richard Rowland has argued that "each relationship is capable of a less idealized interpretation" (*Edward II,* ed. Rowland [Oxford: Clarendon P, 1994] 100, n. on line 392). In some accounts of the first-named pair, such as John Lyly's recent *Campaspe* (1586), Hephestion is a model adviser to a self-indulgent Alexander; but in Plutarch's account, Hephestion is an unpopular favorite, deeply resented by Alexander's Macedonian people. The beautiful boy Hylas, on board the *Argos,* was kidnapped by nymphs when the ship laid anchor to pick up water, to Hercules's great grief—but Hylas could represent an image of false love just as easily as an image of devoted friendship. As Shakespeare's *Troilus and Cressida* clearly shows, Patroclus was not necessarily a good influence on Achilles; dismissed by Thersites as a "masculine whore" (5.1.7), Patroclus was often said to have led to Achilles being "unmanned." In Plato's *Symoposium,* Alcibiades speaks freely of his attempts to seduce Socrates; and in Plutarch, the youth's "wildness" is blamed in part for Socrates's downfall as a corrupter of youth.
29. Qtd. in Doherty 37.
30. Jean Froissart, *Chroniques,* book 1, in *Collection des chroniques nationales françaises,* ed. J. A. Buchon (Paris, 1824) 11:52.
31. Eugene M. Waith, "Edward II: The Shadow of Action," *Tulane Drama Review* 8 (1964): 59–76, esp. 75.

READING LIST

Bray, Alan. *Homosexuality in Renaissance England.* London: Gay Men's P, 1982.

———. "Homosexuality and the Signs of Male Friendship in Elizabethan England." *History Workshop* 29 (1990): 1–19.

Bredbeck, Gregory W. *Sodomy and Interpretation: From Marlowe to Milton.* Ithaca: Cornell UP, 1991.

Geckle, George L. *"Tamburlaine" and "Edward II": Text and Performance.* Basingstoke: Macmillan, 1988.

Goldberg, Jonathan. "Sodomy and Society: The Case of Christopher Marlowe." *Southwest Review* 69 (1984): 371–78.

Hutson, Lorna. *The Usurer's Daughter: Male Friendship and Fictions of Women in Sixteenth-Century England.* London: Routledge, 1994.

Shannon, Laurie. *Sovereign Amity: Figures of Friendship in Shakespearean Contexts.* Chicago: U of Chicago P, 2002.

Smith, Bruce R. *Homosexual Desire in Shakespeare's England: A Cultural Poetics.* Chicago: U of Chicago P, 1991.

Stewart, Alan. *Close Readers: Humanism and Sodomy in Early Modern England.* Princeton: Princeton UP, 1997.

9

Dr. Faustus and Reformation Theology

Kristen Poole

In the final scene of *Doctor Faustus,* a group of scholars gathers in the street to discuss the terrible events of the previous night. Blood-curdling cries were heard coming from Faustus's house, which was glowing as if on fire. Faustus's concerned friends and colleagues quickly discover the aftermath of the horror, as they encounter his limbs strewn upon the ground. "The devils whom Faustus served have torn him thus," one of the scholars rightly surmises (5.3.8).[1] (Faustus had, of course, made a pact with the devil, selling his soul for seemingly infinite powers and a guarantee of twenty-four more years on earth.) This final scene is brief, comprised of a mere nineteen lines, but it enacts a sudden and powerful change in perspective. Immediately prior to the scholars' entrance on the stage, the audience had witnessed the cause of the shrieks and flames. Thunder rang through the theater, a posse of devils took the stage, and the miserable Doctor was dragged off to his death, desperately screaming to the last,

> O, mercy, heaven, look not so fierce on me!
> Adders and serpents, let me breathe a while!
> Ugly hell, gape not. Come not, Lucifer!
> I'll burn my books. O, Mephistopheles! (5.2.182–85)

The scholars' subsequent report of these events quickly translates them from terrors experienced firsthand into yesterday's news.

In their plans for Faustus's funeral, the scholars continue to render the intimate drama of his death into an occasion for public edification. The sight of his severed limbs, a moment that would be climactic in another play, is here reduced to dénouement and moral emblem. The Second Scholar bluntly remarks,

> Well, gentlemen, though Faustus's end be such
> As every Christian heart laments to think on,
> Yet [. . .]
> We'll give his mangled limbs due burial;
> And all the students, clothed in mourning black,
> Shall wait upon his heavy funeral. (5.3.13–19)

Faustus's end, as psychologically complicated and tortured as it was, will be condensed into a moral allegory, and the audience for this revised drama will be a captive one of black-clad students. The reference to clothing may seem oddly trivial in the final two lines of the play, but it serves here as a stark distinction to Faustus's earlier exclamation that with his newfound powers he will "fill the public schools with silk, / Wherewith the students shall be bravely clad" (1.1.89–90). We can imagine that in the rowdy atmosphere of the early modern theater the promise of silken finery might have raised a cheer from the substantial student contingent in the audience. Indeed, Faustus's altruistic promise seems oddly out of place in his otherwise narcissistic fantasy of power, suggesting that it is inserted precisely for the purposes of provoking a sympathetic response from the generally impoverished student population. But if the attraction of silk seduced some students into sympathy with the be-deviled Faustus, the Second Scholar's somber re-clothing of the students, and the declaration of universal and compulsive attendance at Faustus's funeral, deftly puts them back in their proper obedient place. Just as the scholars' report of Faustus's death seems to throw cold water on one of the most emotionally and dramatically packed moments of the English stage, so too their words attempt to reign in the imaginations of students who might have envisioned themselves, decked in silken finery, flying through the skies with the magnificent Faustus. These final lines seem to signal an end to theatrical fantasy and the beginning of an occasion for moral contemplation.

The scholars' final appearance on the stage thus subtly transforms the space of the theater into the space of the lecture hall. The transition is not as abrupt as it might seem—*Doctor Faustus* itself revolves around university life. The setting is self-consciously and insistently the university city of Wittenburg, and the central props are the books from which various characters read. The play is about learning and the learned. What, then, are we to learn from this play? In the Epilogue, the Chorus exhorts us to "regard [Faustus's] hellish fall" (4) as a deterrent from practicing the black arts. Fair enough, but it is highly doubtful that many in the audience seriously required a warning against engaging in necromancy or signing contracts with the devil. Like a teacher sidestepping a difficult question, the Second Scholar's and the Chorus's imputed attempts to set up Faustus as a type of moral lesson do not address what, to many Elizabethan spectators, would have been the most important and troubling issues raised by the play: where will you go when you die? And what will determine how you get there? Rather than simply telling us to stay away from dangerous books, *Doctor Faustus* dramatizes some of the pressing theological issues of the day. But if, as the scholars at the end of the play would like, *Doctor Faustus* offers a moral, it is hardly a clear one. In fact, as the play takes us into the murky realm of Elizabethan theology, the moral might be that one can't find a moral—a frustrating and fearful message that expresses the religious confusion of the day.

During his own time as a student at Cambridge, Christopher Marlowe would undoubtedly have been exposed to debates over free will and predestination. It is quite likely that he attended, and almost certain that he knew of, the notorious university debates on the subject.[2] As a master's degree student, Marlowe received extensive training in theology, and this learning is reflected in *Doctor Faustus*. The play lies at a cultural and theological nexus, where residual modes of Catholicism intersected and competed with emerging concepts of Protestantism. At stake here is no less than the role of human free will in God's cosmos. Are the actions of human beings self-directed? And if human beings possess agency, or the willful control of their actions, can this agency affect salvation and a person's fate in the afterlife? The initial line of the Epilogue, again, seems to provide us with something of a pat answer: "Cut is the branch that might have grown full straight." The subjunctive "might" here implies that Faustus could have chosen a pious life; his downfall is the consequence of his own free will. Adding to this idea is the passive construction ("the branch is cut") that distances and exonerates God from the action of ending Faustus's life. But Faustus's understanding of God, an understanding that he shared with many of his contemporaries, does not seem to allow for the choice implicit in the subjunctive "might"; instead, Faustus's God is all-mighty, a God of power who has already cast the die—it is Faustus who seems to be in the passive position, utterly incapable of determining his fate.

In order to better understand these contradictory impulses in *Doctor Faustus,* let us step back and look at the converging theologies of late-sixteenth-century England. For English men and women living in the Middle Ages, questions about the afterlife would have been easy enough to answer. The medieval church set forth an eschatological system that was, however complex in its various representations, quite simple in its basic structure. Essentially, human sin and redemption were calculated in accounting-like terms. On one side of the spiritual balance sheet were a person's transgressions. These ranged from the in-born sins common to all fallen human beings to daily peccadilloes and sins of omission to serious intentional crimes. On the other side of the balance sheet were good works. These included acts of piety and charity. At the end of one's days, divine forces reckoned the difference between the two, and the discrepancy determined how long one would have to stay in purgatory before advancing to heaven.

According to medieval theology, nearly everyone went to purgatory upon their death; only saints could proceed directly to heaven, and only the truly evil would go straight to hell. In purgatory, individuals were purged of their residual sin (that is, the difference between the two sides of the balance sheet, assuming that people nearly always ran a deficit, with more sin than good works). This process of purgation was enacted through physical torment, with all of the tortures that today we commonly associate with the idea of hell. In order to mitigate this period of purgatorial torture, a person could enlist the help of others. Prayers for one's soul would reduce the purgatorial sentence. Rich people could donate large sums of money to monasteries on the condition that the monks would say a certain number of prayers for the donor's soul; poorer people could join prayer guilds, a form of voluntary co-op in which the living said prayers for the souls of the dead on the assumption that subsequent generations would do the same for them. It was even possible to bank prayers and good works through a system called supererogation: if someone had more prayers or acts of charity than were necessary to mitigate his period in purgatory, the surplus could be used for others. Eventually, the church started marketing this surplus by selling indulgences, certificates that absolved a certain amount of sin. The selling of indulgences led to the accusations of ecclesiastical corruption that sparked the long process known as the Reformation.

The theology of the Reformation marked a radical departure from this medieval system, in which the afterlife was subject to human agency and free will. The starting point of the Reformation is generally taken to be the moment in 1517 when a young monk named Martin Luther nailed his famous Ninety-Five Theses to the church door in Wittenburg. In this document Luther protested many of the corruptions he perceived in the church and especially challenged its exploitation of the purgatorial system. Luther advanced the revolutionary claim that human beings are not saved through good works, but rather by faith alone. It was God's grace, and the individual's faith in that grace, that guaranteed entrance into heaven. This declaration rocked the foundations of the church, which were built on an elaborate earthly hierarchy and spiritual network. Not only did the doctrine of *sola fide* ("faith alone") eliminate the idea of the balance sheet, but it transformed the relationship between the individual and God: no longer was that relationship to be mediated by priests or the intercession of saints. Instead, every individual was called upon to have a direct and personal relationship with God.

The Western Christian church thus split in two. Roman Catholics remained within the traditional church and maintained their allegiance to the pope; Protestants formed alternative churches and repudiated the authority of the pope and his clergy. On the Continent, the Reformation would lead to wars and horrific massacres, as Catholic and Protestant regions clashed. In England, the Reformation would also lead to bloodshed, although on a smaller scale, as hundreds of martyrs were burned at the stake. The English Reformation can be seen as a two-pronged movement, with changes taking place both at the level of the government and at the level of the laity. There has been a great deal of discussion amongst historians as to whether the English Reformation took place from the top down or from the bottom up—whether it was driven by official decrees or popular action. In the end it was the combination of these forces, sometimes working together and sometimes at odds, that produced the changes in the English church.

Let's begin at the top. We might consider the official beginning of the English Reformation to be King Henry VIII's break with Rome in 1534. The impetus for this move was not, however, Henry's heartfelt Lutheran convictions—he had even written against Luther's ideas. Rather, Henry's decision to break his allegiance to the pope was the result of his love life and its ensuing political complications. Married to Catharine of Aragon, who had borne him no living sons, and in love with Anne Boleyn, Henry requested a papal sanction for a divorce from Catharine in order to marry Anne. After the pope repeatedly refused this request, the king simply declared that the English church no longer acknowledged the authority of the pope and that he, Henry, was now the English church's spiritual head. (And as head of the church he promptly married Anne, who soon lost hers after she disappointed Henry by bearing him a daughter instead of the son he so desired.) At this point the English "Reformation" was one in name only; Henry's religious views were conservative, and the church's day-to-day services and theology remained largely unchanged. But at Henry's death in 1547, his ardently Protestant son, Edward VI (the nine-year-old child of wife number three, Jane Seymour), assumed the throne and promoted a genuine theological transformation. Then at Edward's death in 1553, Henry's ardently Catholic daughter Mary (child of wife number one, Catharine of Aragon) assumed the throne, declared England once again a papal nation, and began burning outspoken Protestants (earning herself the nickname of "Bloody Mary"). And at Mary's death in 1558, Henry's Protestant daughter Elizabeth (child of wife number two, Anne Boleyn) assumed the throne and returned England to Protestantism.

This royal see-sawing on matters ecclesiastical did not go unnoticed by the populace. Thanks to a cultural fascination with their national history, English men and women at the end of the sixteenth century were often aware that in recent memory their country had been Catholic, then Protestant, then Catholic, then Protestant. Throughout these changes, the official doctrine on the afterlife—arguably the central doctrine of the church and that with which parishioners would be most concerned—kept shifting. The doctrine of purgatory, for example, was in, then out, then in, then out again. Given the fickle nature of the national religion, in which official teachings on the very nature of God were subject to reversal and revision with every new regime, it is not surprising that individuals looked less and less to their political leaders for spiritual guidance. By the time of Queen Elizabeth, the English embraced an impressive range of religious opinions, from radical Protestant ideas to entrenched Catholic loyalties. While one could test the patience of even the tolerant Elizabeth by aggressively advocating extreme unorthodox beliefs, on the whole the Elizabethan religious culture was quite elastic and accommodated this diversity of belief. This religious diversity was spurred by the growing (Protestant) sense that religious opinions were a matter of personal responsibility, and this idea fuelled a tremendous outpouring of religious publications. To a degree that might seem strange to us today, sixteenth-century men and women were avid consumers of religious literature, devouring short pamphlets as well as ponderous theological tomes.

In the end, the theological ideas that ultimately came to dominate late-sixteenth-century religious life were not Lutheran, but Calvinist. Jean Calvin, a reformer who lived in Geneva, is most known for his theology based on double predestination (often simply called predestination). This was not a new idea, having been a tacit part of church doctrine for centuries, but Calvin brought the concept to the fore and worked through its spiritual consequences, which could be at once exhilarating and terrifying. According to predestinarian theology, God determined at the creation of the world that there would be a certain number of human beings who would receive his grace and ultimately dwell in heaven, and a certain number who would be damned and ultimately condemned to hell. The decision as to who was elect and who was reprobate (as the two categories were known) had already been made, and there was nothing human beings could do to alter these designations.

This theological system is the antithesis of a system relying on purgatory, good works, and prayer. Under a purgatorial system, as we have seen, human beings have a great deal of control over their afterlife. Under a system of double predestination, by contrast, human beings have virtually none. Free will, the idea of human agency, and the balance sheet are no longer factors in God's judgment. Modern commentators have found the idea of predestination "depressing,"[3] but that is not necessarily how it was viewed in the sixteenth century. Reading Calvin's magnus opus, entitled *The Institutes of the Christian Religion* (which, unlike many of the theological treatises of the day, is written in an intimate, colloquial style), was clearly a life-altering experience for many. Although this text emphasizes the awesome and terrible majesty of God, it also provides an exhilarating liberation for those who feel they are among the elect. Had the theology been perceived as purely depressing, it is doubtful that it would have captivated the hearts and minds of so many.

The fervor of Calvin's theology was tempered, however, in its practical application in the parish. Clergymen faced two primary difficulties in the dissemination of the doctrine on a local level. First, there is the argument that, if election and reprobation have already been determined, what is the point of leading a moral life? In principle, it seems that the elect could engage in all sorts of debauchery and still be assured of salvation. The answer to this objection is that the elect would not, perforce, engage in debauchery, but would naturally lead a pious life; the wanton libertine must therefore be among the reprobate. Second, there is the fundamental question, how do I know if I am among the elect? This is the issue that caused the most spiritual anguish for parishioners and the most pastoral difficulties for clergy. According to Calvin, the answer is that only God knows for certain the identity of the elect, although a heartfelt faith is a pretty good indication of election. However, in a small passage in the *Institutes,* Calvin warns that there is such a thing as false or temporary faith.[4] This is a type of faith that God gives to the reprobate just to give them a taste of what they're missing. Thus, even the most devout and pious of ministers, convinced of his genuine and heartfelt faith, could in reality be a reprobate just like the drunken libertine.

These two questions threatened to plunge parishioners into a state of moral anarchy or spiritual despair. Thus Calvin's successor in Geneva, Theodore Beza, reintroduced the idea of good works, and it is Beza's adaptation of Calvin's theology that made its way into England. The English dissemination of (Beza's) Calvinism was accomplished in large part through the works of the best-selling author William Perkins. With catchy titles such as *A Treatise tending vnto a declaration whether a man be in the estate of damnation or in the estate of grace: and if he be in the first, how he may in time come out of it: if in the second, how he maie discerne it* (1589) and *A Case of Conscience, the Greatest that ever was: how a man may know whether he be the childe of God, or no* (1592), Perkins's books provided personal guidance for scrutinizing one's state of grace. Unfortunately, Perkins often tied himself in forensic knots when he tried to clarify the doctrine of temporary faith, and his works probably created even more public anxiety about the utterly inscrutable nature of election. Like Beza and unlike Calvin, Perkins ultimately turned to the idea of good works and personal introspection (which fostered the practice of journal writing) as a means of ascertaining one's state of grace.

We return, then, to a religious culture that was concerned with tabulation and good works. This is not to come full circle: the dominant theology at the end of the sixteenth century was strikingly different from that at its beginning. Belief in predestination precluded any actual human influence on the afterlife, and doing good works or keeping diaries was simply a way to gather clues about what had already been written in God's book. But this emphasis on introspection and good works supplied the resemblance of human agency in eschatological matters. Furthermore, the distinction between good works that were performed as a natural consequence of being elect and good works performed in order to assure salvation could be a fine one that was lost on a significant part of the population. There is no doubt that Protestant ministers marshaled an extensive campaign to re-educate the laity through sermons or that there was an enormous quantity of religious literature that was purchased by a public concerned about its afterlife. But, people being what they are, (lengthy) sermons may not have been universally comprehended, and (long) books bought with good intentions may not have been entirely read. While only the extremely ignorant or antisocial could have been completely unaware of the widespread discussion about predestination, only the extremely zealous or dedicated would have been entirely learned in its doctrine. For the majority of the populace, the theological distinctions surrounding the efficacy of good works may well have been fuzzy, and popular religious thought may well have been a muddied combination of new and old.

Elizabethan theology was, then, a messy affair. The Reformation was neither a sudden, effective campaign of unambiguous changes nor a steady progression toward a clear end of transformation. Rather, for much of the sixteenth century the English lurched forward and backward, right to left, in uneven and unsteady paces. Moreover, the disjunction between the doctrine of the top, that promulgated by the bishops du jour, and the doctrine of the bottom, those beliefs and practices maintained by the laity, created at any given point theological confusion and contradiction. The belief in purgatory, for example, long outlived its official demise. And good works, introduced into Calvin's theology by later divines trying to mitigate the anxieties of parishioners, might look to many like the good works that were earlier prescribed for saving one's soul. Because of the great variety of learned theological opinions, and the wide latitude of popular doctrinal understanding, there is really not such a thing as "Elizabethan religious thought."

It is in this regard that Christopher Marlowe's *Doctor Faustus* might be considered a quintessential Elizabethan play. Like the culture that produced it, the theology of *Doctor Faustus* is messy, ambiguous, and often contradictory. The play seems to vacillate between a theology based on free will and God's forgiveness and a theology based on Calvin's conception of double predestination. Alone in his study, Faustus is confronted with opposing angels, and their exchange in many ways epitomizes the dilemma of the play:

> *Faustus:* Contrition, prayer, repentance—what of these?
> *Good Angel:* O, they are means to bring thee unto heaven.
> *Bad Angel:* Rather illusions, fruits of lunacy,
> That make them foolish that do use them most. (2.1.16–19)

Are human beings agents in their salvation, or is the notion that people can affect their afterlife an "illusion" and "lunacy"? The play's answer is a frustrating "yes"—to both questions.

The fact that Faustus converses with a Good Angel and a Bad Angel is itself a symptom of the play's complicated relationship between old and new. Just as the medieval belief in purgatory continued well into the period of the English Renaissance, so too this play represents an interpenetration of residual and emergent genres and characters. The angels are a holdover from the allegorical medieval genre known as the morality play. One of the best known is *Everyman,* in which the central character Everyman encounters Death, who informs him that God wants to see his book of accounts. Desperate and unprepared, Everyman unsuccessfully seeks help from those people and abilities on which he had relied in life (friends, relations, knowledge, beauty, strength, etc.) until he is finally aided by his Good Works. Here medieval theology is boiled down to its simplest elements for the edification and entertainment of a predominantly illiterate audience.

Faustus, however, hardly represents the medieval Everyman: instead, he is the epitome of the Renaissance Man. This figure is often self-made (having raised himself from lower social origins) and possess a wide-ranging expertise in areas of learning, from science to the arts. Doctor Faustus, we learn from the opening of the play, has mastered philosophy, medicine, law, and theology. Indeed, his descent into the black arts at first seems to be the product of his intellectual ennui, as he searches for new challenges and intellectual heights. His summoning of the devils is driven in part by his burning desire for more knowledge, and he uses his magical abilities in the potentially admirable quest "to find the secrets of astronomy" and "to prove cosmography" (Chorus, act 3), both driving ambitions of the sixteenth century. Instead of an Everyman, the generalized representative of humanity, we have in Faustus a highly individualized, complex, and modern character, one whom in many respects epitomizes the ideals of his age. The interaction of this man with the allegorical angels thus presents an encounter that is not only anachronistic, but one that intersplices characters from wildly divergent genres, as if a cowboy from a John Wayne western wandered into a James Bond spy thriller. The result of this generic intermingling is a world that is morally ambiguous, as both the old and the new, the angels and Faustus, seem alternately—or simultaneously—to be the subject of valorization and critique.

Theological contradictions also follow these generic complications. As Faustus begins to flirt with magic, he is drawn toward the idea that he could command spirits to "resolve [him] of all ambiguities" (1.1.79), but the doctrinal ambiguities only continue to expand over the course of the play. On the one hand, we are presented with the idea that repentance is a choice that is open to Faustus. Mephistopheles says that the devils fly to a person when "he is in danger to be damned" (1.3.48), and Faustus speaks of "surrender[ing] up to him his soul" (1.3.88). These comments suggest that man's damnation is not a foregone conclusion and that Faustus has control over his own soul. On the other hand, Faustus reasons that "we must sin, / And so consequently die. / Ay, we must die an everlasting death. / What doctrine call you this? *Che serà, serà,* / What will be, shall be" (1.1.44–48), arguably a rather flip summation of predestinarian doctrine, with its emphasis on "must."[5] This "must" returns when Faustus proclaims, "Now, Faustus, must thou needs be damned? / Canst thou not be saved? / What boots it then to think of God or heaven?" (2.1.1–3).

These doctrinal contradictions pervade the play. Purgatory, for example, seems to still exist within the play's theological system. When Faustus becomes invisible and plays tricks on the pope, the Archbishop explains, "I think it be some ghost crept out of purgatory" (3.2.79–80), at which point the pope commands the monks to say a prayer for the dead in order to appease the ghost. The pope, however, is presented as the butt of the joke here, and his authority is thus called into question; his response could be designed to evoke laughter from a Protestant audience that might view purgatory as a papist superstition. At the end of his life, Faustus himself desperately hopes for and then rejects a form of purgatorial compromise:

> O, if my soul must suffer for my sin,
> Impose some end to my incessant pain.
> Let Faustus live in hell a thousand years,
> A hundred thousand, and at last be saved.
> No end is limited to damnèd souls. (5.2.162–66)

The question of repentance, in particular, is presented in a way that seems almost designed to torment audiences with half-answered questions. Here, for example, is a critical exchange between Faustus and the angels:

> *Faustus:* If heaven was made for man, 'twas made for me.
> I will renounce this magic and repent.
>
> [*Enter the two angels*]
>
> *Good Angel:* Faustus, repent! Yet, God will pity thee.
>
> *Bad Angel:* Thou art a spirit. God cannot pity thee.

> *Faustus:* Who buzzeth in mine ears I am a spirit?
> Be I a devil, yet God may pity me;
> Yea, God will pity me if I repent.
> *Bad Angel:* Ay, but Faustus never shall repent.
> [*Exeunt (angels)*]
> *Faustus:* My heart is hardened; I cannot repent.
> Scarce can I name salvation, faith, or heaven. (2.3.10–21)

The "may" in "God may pity me" opens up a theological space that Faustus had earlier closed off with his "musts." But the prospect offered by "may" is again shut down by the "cannots." What does it mean that "God cannot pity thee"? If this means that God is unable to forgive Faustus, what does this do to the notion of an omnipotent God? What is God unable to do, and why doesn't he transcend even his own laws? If the "cannot" means that God is unwilling to accept Faustus's repentance, what does this do to the idea of a forgiving God? For the Christian, the choices presented here are equally disturbing: either God is not all-powerful, or he is hard-hearted. Similarly, Faustus's contention that he "cannot repent" due to his own hard-heartedness raises significant questions. Is he unable to repent because of his own weakness and failings? Or does the passive construction infer that another force has hardened his heart, and therefore prevented him from repenting?

Such theological dilemmas are further complicated by Faustus's own personality. From the very beginning of the play, Faustus has the unattractive habit of blaming others for his actions, often positioning himself as a passive entity. For his failings and temptations, he blames Aristotle ("Sweet *Analytics,* 'tis thou hast ravished me!" [1.1.6]), the devils ("wicked Mephistopheles, [. . .] thou hast deprived me of those joys" [2.3.2–3]), the stars ("You stars that reigned at my nativity, / Whose influence hath allotted death and hell" [5.2.81–82]), and, in the end, even his parents ("Curst be the parents that engendered me!" [5.2.105]). He repeatedly views himself as a victim of the world and his actions as the consequences of outside forces ("I would weep, but the devil draws in my tears" [5.2.27–28]). Perhaps this is the portrait of a man living in a Calvinist universe, where his destiny is beyond his control, or perhaps this is the image of a whiny narcissist, someone who refuses to accept responsibility for his actions. Perhaps he is the product of a Calvinist system, or perhaps the theological system of the play is skewed and distorted by his personal failings. If Faustus is the lens through which we see divinity, it is a clouded one indeed.

Ultimately, it is not merely Faustus's personality that is called into question, but God's—if divinity can be said to have "personality." Faustus's vision of God is that of a wrathful judge; near his end, he exclaims in terror, "see where God / Stretcheth out his arm and bends his ireful brows!" (5.2.74–75). Yet, if we follow the predestinarian bent of Faustus's understanding of God, this is a wrathful judge who has already judged, one who condemns those whom he himself has damned. Faustus's understanding of the divine is not so far from the Calvinist understanding of God. The medieval God, the God of Everyman, is remote and inaccessible, but perhaps more comprehensible. He determines salvation according to a set of established principles and procedures, and these blanket all of humanity; not only does this God inform people of the rules, but he applies them evenly and consistently. The Calvinist God, by contrast, requires a direct, unmediated relationship with the individual, but this relationship is potentially more terrifying.

This God is utterly numinous, working in mysterious and random ways; it is not for human beings to understand the idiosyncratic, perhaps arbitrary reasons why one person is elect and another has been damned. The rational, reasoning Renaissance Man was thus governed by an irrational and inscrutable God. This was one of the paradoxes of the age, and one of the many paradoxes of *Doctor Faustus*.

But God is not the only judge in this play. The Prologue holds: "To patient judgements we appeal our plaud [i.e., applause]." The line is a conventional feature of the dramatic prologue, which entreats the audience to judge the quality of the play it is about to see and often begs the audience for patience and forgiveness if the play has faults. The burden to judge in this case, however, is heavy. Just as Faustus finds himself torn between the urge to repent and a conviction of his own damnation, or between older and newer theologies, so too an early modern audience would find its relationship to Faustus fraught with uncomfortable ambiguities. For all of his failings, Faustus does have his good points. He has an intellectual curiosity that many might consider admirable, he is clearly well liked by his concerned friends, and he has an engaging sense of humor. In many of the pranks that he pulls, we are invited to laugh along with him, and are thus drawn into his company. Furthermore, the play creates an intimacy between Faustus and audience. Many of the scenes revolve around Faustus alone in his study or alone with his demons—we are privy to his musings, his frustrations, his spiritual wrestling, and his anguished sense of despair.

And yet, for all of the dramatic intimacy, we are asked to judge this man, not only in terms of the success of the play but in terms of his eschatological status. What are we to do? Again, we run headlong into a quandary that revolves around competing and contradictory theological notions. On the one hand, it seems hardhearted on our part to wish eternal damnation upon Faustus, or to have satisfaction in his horrific end as he is dragged off to hell. To show him mercy and kindness, such as that shown to him by the sympathetic Old Man, seems to be the right thing to do. In fact, such an act of kindness might even be considered as a good work on our part, thus either helping our own salvation or giving evidence of our own election. On the other hand, one of the major points of debate in the late sixteenth century was whether or not the elect should have any dealings at all with the reprobate, whether the sheep should congregate with the goats. Argumentative battles were waged over the proper constitution of the earthly "visible church," with some maintaining that this church must by practical necessity be comprised of both the elect and the damned, and others contending that it was the responsibility of the elect to winnow out the damned, lest the church be polluted by their presence. Many people were starting to separate from the central church on the grounds that they should not worship side by side with the reprobate. In this context, mercy to the damned could be construed as an invitation to corruption, and hardheartedness could be considered the righteous act of the militant Christian.

Arguably, though, through the vicissitudes of performance the play comes down harder on God than it does on the audience. The critic Alan Sinfield has written about how "the predestinarian and free-will readings of *Faustus* [. . .] obstruct, entangle, and choke each other."[6] Consequently, the play does not offer the audience a clear moral compass, and a reasoned response is easily swept aside by the emotional reaction to witnessing intense human suffering (even if we know we are "merely" watching an actor play a part on the stage). As Sinfield writes, "It is one thing to argue in principle that the reprobate are destined for everlasting torment, but when Faustus is shown wriggling on the pin and panic-stricken in his last hour, members of an audience may think again. If this is what happened, for some at least, then there are two traps in the play. One is set by God for Dr. Faustus; the other is set by Marlowe, for God" (237). The dramatic enactment of damnation may have rendered public the private anxieties that arise from reading Perkins. It may also have provoked, and tacitly and temporarily licensed, the anger of an audience facing a new and inscrutable God. If, in the mysteries of a predestinarian world, even the most pious member of the audience could be among the reprobate, then Faustus could be an Everyman after all, commanding the audience's sympathies and self-identification. It should be remembered that at the turn of the seventeenth century this play was a phenomenal success.

Doctor Faustus has continued to capture the modern imagination. Among literary critics, this play has been hotly contested. For several decades, critics were divided between those who saw the play as "reflect[ing] Christian doctrine as presented in Scripture and Tradition,"[7] citing "the powerful and consistent Christian outlook of the play,"[8] and those who saw the play as anti-Christian.[9] The strident division between these orthodox and heterodox views in part reflects the conflicted biography of Christopher Marlowe himself, a man who began his brief adulthood as a theology student and ended it a notorious figure accused of atheism. But in large part this critical division was informed by an understanding of the English Reformation as a unified and near universal movement. Recent historical research, however, has revealed the fallacy of the idea of a clear religious tradition in the Elizabethan era. Marlowe and his Doctor Faustus were not alone in their conflicted relationships to free will, predestination, and, ultimately, God—they shared these feelings of confusion and frustration with many in the audience.

NOTES

1. See David Bevington and Eric Ramussen, eds., Christopher Marlowe, *Tamburlaine, Parts I and II, Doctor Faustus, A- and B-Texts, The Jew of Malta, Edward II* (Oxford: Clarendon P, 1995). *Doctor Faustus* exists in two versions, known as the A-text and the B-text; I am citing from the B-text.
2. See Gerald M. Pinciss, *Forbidden Matters: Religion in the Drama of Shakespeare and His Contemporaries* (Newark: U of Delaware P and London: Associate UP, 2000) 28; and Constance Brown Kuriyama, *Christopher Marlowe: A Renaissance Life* (Ithaca: Cornell UP, 2002) 56.
3. See Pauline Honderich, "John Calvin and Doctor Faustus," *The Modern Language Review* 68.1 (1973): 1–13, esp. 4.
4. See Calvin, *Institutes of the Christian Religion,* ed. John T. Battles, trans. Ford Lewis Battles, The Library of Christian Classics, 2 vols. (Philadelphia: Westminster P, 1960) 2: 555–58. I am drawing my discussion of temporary faith from R. T. Kendall, *Calvin and English Calvinism to 1649* (Oxford: Oxford UP, 1979) 21–28; the following discussion of Beza and English Calvinism is also indebted to Kendall, ch. 2, 4, and 5.
5. As many scholars have noted, Faustus's reasoning depends upon distorted or aborted quotations from Scripture; see Joseph Westlund, "The Orthodox Framework of Marlowe's *Faustus,*" *Studies in English Literature, 1500–1900* 3 (1963): 193–94.

6. See Alan Sinfield, *Faultlines: Cultural Materialism and the Politics of Dissident Reading* (Berkeley: U of California P, 1992) 236.
7. See Margaret Ann O'Brien, "Christian Belief in *Doctor Faustus,*" *ELH* 37 (1970): 1–11, esp. 2.
8. See Westlund 191–205, esp. 191.
9. See both Paul H. Kocher, *Christopher Marlowe: A Study of His Thought, Learning, and Character* (Chapel Hill: U of North Carolina P, 1946) 104; and Harry Levin, *The Overreacher: A Study of Christopher Marlowe* (Cambridge: Harvard UP, 1952) 132.

READING LIST

Davidson, Nicholas. "Christopher Marlowe and Atheism." *Christopher Marlowe and English Renaissance Culture.* Ed. Darryll Grantley and Peter Roberts. Hants: Scolar, 1996.

Dickens, A. G. *The English Reformation,* 2nd ed. University Park: The Pennsylvania State UP, 1989.

Dollimore, Jonathan. *Radical Tragedy: Religion, Ideology and Power in the Drama of Shakespeare and His Contemporaries.* Chicago: U of Chicago P, 1986.

Greenblatt, Stephen. *Renaissance Self-Fashioning from More to Shakespeare.* Chicago: The U of Chicago P, 1980.

Haigh, Christopher. *English Reformations: Religion, Politics, and Society Under the Tudors.* Oxford: Clarendon P, 1993.

Hattaway, Michael. "The Theology of Marlowe's *Doctor Faustus.*" *Renaissance Drama* n.s. 3 (1970): 51–78.

Kuriyama, Constance Brown. *Christopher Marlowe: A Renaissance Life.* Ithaca: Cornell UP, 2002.

Lindberg, Carter. *The European Reformations.* Oxford: Blackwell, 1996.

McGrath, Alister E. *Reformation Thought: An Introduction.* 2nd ed. Oxford: Blackwell, 1993.

Ornstein, Robert. "Marlowe and God: The Tragic Theology of *Dr. Faustus.*" *PMLA* 83 (1968): 1378–85.

Riggs, David. "Marlowe's Quarrel with God." *Critical Essays on Christopher Marlowe.* Ed. Emily C. Bartels. New York: G.K. Hall and Co. and London: Prentice Hall International, 1997.

Sinfield, Alan. *Faultlines: Cultural Materialism and the Politics of Dissident Reading.* Berkeley: U of California P, 1992.

10

Henry V and the Tudor Monarchy

Constance Jordan

In early modern Europe, monarchy or the rule of a single person was widely conceded to be the best form of government, certainly superior to aristocracy or the rule of a few (the basis of the Venetian republic) and to democracy or the rule of many. English thinkers generally endorsed this opinion, although their treatises on government were often heavy with words of caution. Because it gave so much power to a single person, they argued, monarchy was uniquely shadowed by the specter of its perversion, tyranny, in which the interests of the ruler prevailed over the people he was supposed to preserve and protect. Different kinds of law were declared essential in providing a basis for social order: natural law or reason, which guaranteed the right of self-defense; divine law, which was supposed to inform the most fundamental social relations; and positive law, fashioned from statute and customary practice.

English subjects understood the workings of monarchy through different media: chronicle histories such as Edward Hall's *The Union of the Two Noble and Illustre Famelies of Lancastre & York* (1548) and, especially, Raphael Holinshed's *Chronicles of England, Scotland, and Ireland* (1577, 1587) gave literate men and women some knowledge of how the monarchy had developed from its earliest periods and how the countervailing powers invested in Parliament and the common law courts had come into being. This information was supplemented by various informal and unofficial sources on contemporary affairs of state: tavern gossip, sermons on Sundays and feast days, and occasional verses on celebrated or sensational subjects printed on single sheets or "broadsides." Thus topics of immediate moment appeared comprehensible by comparison with those of the past; in turn, history was understood in terms of the issues of the day.

For citizens of London, a cherished source of information was the public theater. It represented both the stuff of human comedy and matters of high seriousness drawn from the annals of English and Roman history; its spaces gave audiences a place in which to congregate and exchange news. Located across the Thames in Southwark and in a district known as "the liberties," these theaters were largely exempt from oversight by the burgesses of London; this freedom obviously enhanced their appeal as forums for debate. The particular *timeliness* of the Elizabethan stage, its way of dramatizing public issues for popular consumption, is illustrated by such plays as the anonymously authored *First Part of the Reign of King Richard the Second; or, Thomas of Woodstock* (1591–95), Christopher Marlowe's *Edward II* (1594), and most memorably by Shakespeare's English history plays. Holinshed's chronicles were Shakespeare's primary source, rich with images upon which he could project his understanding of Tudor government, its scope, and such limitations as fate and the common law had imposed upon it. By alluding directly and in figures of speech to the nature of the commonwealth and its body politic, Shakespeare's dramatic representations of moments in history show the role of the monarchy in creating a powerful nation-state that, by the end of Elizabeth's reign, saw itself as rivaling those of Spain and France.

In the sequence of the plays known as the first and second tetralogy, *Henry V* represents a point of culmination. Although the reign of the actual king occurred in the middle of the historical sequence represented in the chronicles, Shakespeare's Harry realizes the terms of a monarchic magnificence present only by suggestion in *1, 2,* and *3 Henry VI; Richard III; Richard II;* and *1* and *2 Henry IV*. The setting of *Henry V* is war—not civil war but a war of conquest. The difference between these kinds of conflict is telling: unlike his father, who was plagued with sedition in England, Harry seeks to subdue and possess France. And again unlike his father, who secured the throne by seeking his feudal rights and, eventually, usurping the throne, Harry is represented as secure in his own kingdom. What he desires is a grander achievement: to gain sovereignty over a foreign power, first by appearing to have a just claim to that power and second by appearing to press that claim in a just manner. He achieves his goals, of course, but not without irony. Shakespeare concludes *Henry V* by observing that the kingdoms Harry ruled his son, Henry VI, would lose: "Whose state so many had the managing, / That they lost France and made his England bleed."[1]

In 1599, however, the date at which *Henry V* was staged, the English people could ignore the warning implicit in the final words of the play and see English imperialism as not only possible but also plausible. Their contest with Spain for control of the Mediterranean and the Atlantic as well as for possessions in the New World was proving auspicious. Men like Sir Walter Raleigh and Richard Hakluyt extolled the wealth to be gained by adventuring west. English arguments for expansion reproved the Spanish for using the Indians barbarically; by contrast, they based their claims for rights of possession in "Virginia" on the superior civilization of English Protestantism. Decrying what they saw as Indian nomadism, they thought they had a natural law right to colonize a wasteland. Victory over the peoples who resisted such conquest seemed assured; the subjugation of Ireland, although achieved only in part, was thought to illustrate a special English destiny. Audiences enjoying *Henry V* could appreciate why Shakespeare could call their queen "our gracious Empress" and celebrate the victory of her "General" (in fact, the earl of Essex) who was returning to London with the Irish "rebellion broached on his sword" (5.Ch.30–33). Given the reasons for linking the monarchy with empire during the last years of Elizabeth's rule, Shakespeare's Harry appears to confirm the expectations of the times.

But the magnificence of Harry's rule is also diminished by its Machiavellian aspect. His justice often resembles a reason of state, and his decisions seem to reflect willful desire rather than rational assessment. The Chorus opens the play by commanding the audience to do the work of imaginative reconstruction, to take the action on stage as the sum of figures whose significance is both an extension and an augmentation of what is literally audible and visible to them: "Since a crooked figure may / Attest in little place a million [. . .] let us ciphers to this great account / On your imaginary forces work" (1.Pro.15–18; see also 3.1–3, 25). But the figure, like Harry's magnificence, implies suspicion. By act 4, the audience is asked to "[mind] true things by what their mock'ries be" (4.54)—words implying that historiography is never without bias.

Harry and the Tudor Monarchy

Shakespeare's Harry inhabits two worlds. His figure in outline is derived from reports of his reign, 1413–22, in the chronicle histories of Holinshed and Hall; his character is essentially Elizabethan and reflects Shakespeare's understanding of monarchy, hedged as it was not only by the presumption of a kind of divinity but also by limits to its exercise of power. By the sixteenth century, the common law was recognized as having produced a body of legal doctrine that acted as an "ancient constitution": its most salient feature was its treatment of the monarch's will in relation to law. While the Roman emperor Justinian had claimed that the monarch's will or pleasure was law—*quod placuit principi legis habet vigorem*—the English lawyer Bracton, arguing a point that would eventually define the constitution for England's subjects, asserted that because the law had made the king, it was by virtue of the law that he reigned: he was not only its embodiment but was also limited by it.[2] Sir John Fortescue reiterated Bracton's provisions in his *De Laudibus Legum Angliae* (1471; later translated as *A learned commendation of the politique lawes of England*), distinguishing between the monarchy in France, where the prince's will made law, and the monarchy in England, where the prince's will was required to be consonant with the law already made: "The king of England cannot alter nor change the lawes of his royalme at his pleasure [. . .] Wherefore his people do frankeley and freely enjoye and occupye theire own goods being ruled by such lawes as they themselfes desyer."[3] In practice, however, the power of the English monarch as well as of magistrates and officials generally was almost limitless. Held to be "of God"—see Romans 13:1–2—obedience to these powers was absolutely required. Overturning Fortescue's doctrine, William Tyndale's popular treatise, *The obedience of a Chrysten man* (1528), stated: "the king is in this worlde without law and maie at his lust do ryght or wrong and shal geve accomptes but to god only."[4] Allowance was made for the subject's devotion to God, which required obedience to the Word before any laws made by men, but how that Word was to be understood admitted a wide interpretation. Much depended on whether it was agreed that subjects could resist misgovernment or had merely to suffer it as a consequence of their own presumed sinfulness.

These theories of rule and their relation to the monarch's will and its commitment to law were tested by the actual conditions that Elizabeth's subjects experienced in the 1580s and 1590s. The queen's exercise of power depended on securing the obedience of all her subjects; she needed the arms of the nobility, the loyalty of the yeomanry, the support of the burgesses, and the unequivocal blessing of the clergy. She required very considerable sums of money, which she had to raise by taxation of various kinds as well as by the appropriation of private estates. The pressure of these dependencies on the queen's rule is felt allusively in the course of *Henry V*, chiefly by the play's recourse to figures denoting a national unity, often sensed as more virtual than real. While Harry celebrates his kinship with his heroic soldiers, his "brothers" (4. Chorus 34, 4.3.60–63), their distinctive humors, tied to rank and status, and their regional pride, expressed in diction and symbol, challenge these figures of fraternity. Shakespeare's repeated punning throughout the play on the word "crown" as king, head, and coin illustrates a tension within Harry's body politic. As head of state, a Tudor monarch was supported by all the members of this body, each of which might be designated as a limb or organ. In reality, of course, every one of the king's subjects had his own head or "crown," vulnerable to accident at any time. In war, heads rolled; those that remained attached to bodies were valued at different rates: nobles were eligible for ransom, common soldiers were not.

The Idea of War

In *Henry V* the issues that had divided the kingdom in the earlier plays of the tetralogy are represented as settled. With the important exception of the Earl of Cambridge's treason, which he undertakes in support of the earl of March, a descendent of Edward III, Harry (unlike his father and his cousin, Richard II) does not contend with laws and customs that limited his authority and power. His character is rather tested by conquest and by the only law that obtained in such a conflict, the law of nations or the *ius gentium*. The action of the play largely turns on whether Harry is a good king, one who acts to promote the interests of his subjects. Is his war with France "just," and will it benefit his people?

There was significant agreement on the conditions of a just war. It had to be waged in self-defense or for revenge of injuries. The reason of self-defense was rarely questioned. By contrast, what constituted an injury was less clear. Treatises roughly contemporary with the reign of Henry V, like Christine de Pisan's *The book of fayttes of armes and of chyvalrye* (1489), argues a point relevant to Harry's claim: theft or the unlawful appropriation of a sovereign territory is a just reason to wage war.[5] Only if his claim is just, and the guilty party refuses to relinquish stolen property, may a monarch go to war; in such cases, the blame for waging war and the destruction it causes is on the guilty party. Shakespeare's contemporary Stephen Gosson, in his *The Trumpet of War* (1598), emphasizes the causative force of an act that "dishonors" (and so injures) a prince: "if the fame and honour of a Prince be hurt, or disgrace and indignitie offered to his embassadours, warre may lawfully be waged to revenge it."[6] William Segar, in his *Honor Military and Civil* (1602), alludes to the possibility of an arbitrated settlement as a first option before combat. Citing Cicero, he states: "discord and dissention among men is ended either by persuasion or force: the one proper to men, and other to bruite beasts: and where the first can not prevaile, the other may be excused."[7] He insists, however, that war is a last resort: "Reasonably therefore are those warres to be taken in hand, where injurie can not be otherwise repulsed, nor peace by other meane preserved" (Segar 4).

But many treatises on war (however just) dwelt on its horrors. The Protestant Heinrich Bullinger, whose sermons were translated and published as *Fiftie Godlie and Learned Sermons* in 1587, argued that even a just war is "a thing most full of perill. [. . .] By warre both scarcitie of everie thing, and derth doe arise. For high wayes are stopped, corne uppon the grounde is troden downe and marred, whole villages burnt, provision goeth to wracke, handicrafts are unoccupied, merchandise doe ceasse, and all do perish both rich and poore."[8] Like Bullinger, Cardinal Allen argued that even a just or "vindicative" war created "injury" on all sides.[9] And like Pierre Boiastuau, whose *A Treatise of Peace and Warre* (purportedly by a Chelidonius Tigurinus) was translated and published in 1571, many writers extolled the benefits of peace. "Peace I say giveth being and strengthe to all things [. . .] for by hir aide the lande is tilled, the fieldes made flourishing and greene, the beasts feede quietly [. . .] the common wealth flourisheth [. . .]

cities and townes be peopled, & the world is multiplied."[10] Such celebrations could suggest that although a monarch might have a right to wage war, he might not be right to exercise that right.

Shakespeare's Harry justifies war against the French by claiming that he has been disinherited; as the son of John of Gaunt, the fourth son of Edward III, he represents himself as the rightful king of France. His claims accord with those in much historical record: the *Gesta Henrici Quinti,* composed 1416–17 by a clergyman who was an eyewitness of the king's French campaign, complains of the French "injury" (*lesio*) to the English king caused by her "perpetual disinheritance" (*exheredacione perpetua*) of his property in France—that is, to the whole kingdom.[11] *The First English Life of King Henry the Fifth* (1513), written by an anonymous author known as the translator of Tito Livio's *Vita Henrici Quinti,* rehearses a similar claim: the king's title to France was "just" and the kingdom was "injuriously withoulden from him by the French king."[12] These claims are outlined again in Holinshed—Canterbury states that the "whole realm of France by undoubted title [appertains] to the king as to the lawfull and onelie heire of Edward the Third"—and in Hall, who has Canterbury say that "fraudulent Frenchmen defraude and take away your ryght and title to the realme of France."[13] We should notice, however, that neither Hall nor Holinshed *endorsed* Henry's claim, perhaps because they knew it to be questionable. For Henry V's claim to France *was* questionable, and Shakespeare conveys that fact in two ways.

As the play opens, the audience must realize that Harry has already asserted his right to France, a fact that makes the clergy's rationale for supporting it—which Harry repeatedly requests in the next scene—appear superfluous. Moreover, not only has Harry made a decision before the audience sees he has any justification for doing so, but the clergy who informs Harry of his rights has an interest in getting him to believe that justice is on his side. Before meeting with Harry, Canterbury reveals that because the Commons "bill" designed to subsidized the war will be met by a counter "offer [. . .] upon our spiritual convocation" (1.1.76–77), it will lose its purpose and be dismissed. As the bill would have confiscated church land, it is clearly in the clergy's interest to suppress it, even at the expense of coming up with its own "offer." Like Harry's willful decision to make war on France before asking whether he is right to do so, the clergy's conniving darkens the English claim to France. As the chronicler Hall observes, the clergy, afraid of being dispossessed by the terms of the bill, decided "to replenish the kynges brayne with some pleasante study [so] that he should nether phantasy nor regard the serious peticion of the importunate commons" (Hall 50). This "pleasante study" is to be on the conquest of France, a project whose interest could not but distract the king from the needs of the commons. Following the clergy's lead without further debate, Shakespeare's Harry tells the French ambassadors that he intends "To venge me as I may, and to put forth / My rightful hand in a well-hallowed cause" (1.2.292–94); and Exeter, his ambassador to King Charles, later gives France one last chance to recognize that Harry's claim is neither "sinister," nor "awkward," "Picked from the worm-holes of long vanished days," but "truly demonstrative" (2.4.85–89).

By act 2, audiences who had followed the earlier history plays might well have recognized that if the French crown had descended through the female line in the past, as Canterbury asserted, it should now be inherited by the closest living descendent of Edward III, Anne Mortimer, the daughter of Edmund, the earl of March, and Philippa, and the granddaughter of Lionel, duke of Clarence, Edward's third son, and not by Henry V, son of John of Gaunt, Edward's fourth son. Anne had married Richard, earl of Cambridge; as Holinshed reports, it was for her rights and those of their son, Richard Plantagenet, duke of York (and father of the future Richard III) that the earl of Cambridge committed treason. Explaining his treason, Shakespeare's earl of Cambridge denies he sought French "gold," although he admits that gold served as a "motive (or feint) / The sooner to effect what I intended" (2.2.151–52)—an allusion to the cause of the Mortimers, who, because there was no bar to female succession, could claim to be lawful heirs (rather than usurpers, trading in money) to the French throne. Shakespeare echoes testimony in Holinshed.[14] As Shakespeare presents them, the terms justifying Harry's conquest of France suggest that he may long for a throne that is not rightfully his.

The Conduct of War

Medieval commentators distinguished between the *ius ad bellum,* or the right to go to war, and the *ius in bello,* or the right way to fight a war. As we have seen, *Henry V* dramatizes the first of these rights but dubiously. The idea that his war may be a kind of masking charade is conveyed throughout the play by characters who demean him and his cause: Corporals Bardolph and Pistol, who have followed him from the Boar's Head tavern in *1* and *2 Henry IV,* and Corporal Nim, whose name is slang for thief. The Chorus's celebration of "youth on fire" at the eve of Harry's invasion is followed by the farcical combat in which Pistol, Nim, and Bardolph draw and sheath swords in an empty display of wounded pride (2.1). As a group, they gesture toward the grander theme of act 2, the actual treason of Cambridge, who, as Harry says, only "seems" to have been honest, and in that seeming has enacted "another fall of man" (2.2.134–39). That the Boar's Head characters will not survive the play is suggested early in act 1 in the reported death of Falstaff, for which the Hostess blames Harry: "The King has killed his heart" (2.1.79). It is true that Harry's presence has energized all the Boar's Head characters in *1* and *2 Henry IV,* but the need for him to maintain his sovereign status requires his distance from them in *Henry V*. Read for a second meaning, however, the Hostess's belief that Harry killed Falstaff's heart can imply that in doing so he killed his own. We need to assess whether Harry shows he has any heart in the remainder of the play.

Shakespeare designs Harry's relations with two other groups of soldiers to convey a cohesion within their ranks that relieves, to some extent, differences of region and class. The fraternity Harry celebrates with his men on the eve of Agincourt—they are a "band of brothers" (4.3.60)—also defines the conditions of his monarchy. One group represents the constitutive parts of the British Isles: Fluellen represents the Welsh; Gower, the English; Jamy, the Scots; and MacMorris, the Irish; and the other the "ungentle" military: the yeomen Bates and Williams, distinguished by their difference from the loyal knight Sir Thomas Erpingham.

A British identity is vigorously proposed and also subtly questioned by the Welsh Captain Fluellen. His reliance on the "laws of war" appears to be his way of maintaining a *ius in bello,* but in practice it is misleading—he misjudges Pistol, thinking his service "gallant"—and in theory wrongheaded—he compares Harry's career to that of "Alexander the Pig" (i.e., Great). Although in purely dramatic terms Fluellen's error is merely a matter of regional accent, as "b's" go to "p's" in Welsh, it casts yet another shadow on Harry's conquest in France, which seems grandly imperialistic by association with those of the Greek emperor, who once great is now merely piggish. Gower mends a division that develops between Fluellen and Pistol over the propriety of wearing a leek in order to assert his Welsh heritage. Calling Pistol no more than a "A bawd, a cutpurse [. . .] that now and then goes to the wars, to grace himself at his return into London under the form of a soldier" (3.6.59, 63–65; see 5.1.78–80), Gower evokes the British identity that has eluded Fluellen's tongue. He tells Pistol to expect a "Welsh correction": "You thought, because he [Fluellen] could not speak English in the native garb, he could not therefore handle an English cudgel. You find it otherwise" (5.1.67–70). Gower holds his group together by tenuous bonds that threaten to dissolve in moments of stress. As I have suggested, the theme of a British empire was to be a favorite of James I, and in that sense, Gower illustrates a future hope.

Harry's yeomen soldiers, Bates and Williams, bring into focus the densest issues of the play: the relations between the monarch and his soldiers in war. This is illustrated in a sourceless episode that portrays Harry, in disguise, visiting his soldiers the night before Agincourt. Probably anticipating death on the morrow, the yeoman soldier Bates comforts himself in the knowledge that if the king's cause is unjust, he who fights for it is exonerated as his "obedience to the King wipes the crime of it out of us" (4.1.125–27). He does not admit that a soldier who regards the king's cause as unjust can refuse an order, and, in any case, both he and his companion Williams agree that a soldier is not empowered to know the moral status of the cause for which he fights. Williams continues by reflecting not on the obedience of soldiers but on a king's responsibility in pursuing war: "if the cause be not good, the King himself hath a heavy reckoning to make, when all those legs and arms and heads chopped off in a battle shall join together at the latter day, and cry all, 'We died at such a place'—some swearing, some crying for a surgeon, some upon their wives left poor behind them, some upon the debts they owe, some upon their children rawly left." In effect, Williams refers to the king's responsibility for the earthly welfare of his subjects and the obligation he has not to waste his men, impoverish their families, and ruin the body politic. He then considers a different aspect of his situation: "I am afeard there are few die well that die in a battle, for how can they charitably dispose of anything, when blood is their argument? Now, if these men do not die well, it will be a black matter for the king that led them to it—who to disobey were against all proportion of subjection" (4.1.128–38). In other words, dying in war is one thing, dying "well" in war, that is, in a state of grace, is another. War leaves no time to prepare for death, and because a superior's command brooks no denial, is it he who is responsible for a subject's damnation?

Harry answers Williams's second point, but avoids the first: "Every subject's duty is the King's but every subject's soul is his own. Therefore should every soldier in the wars do as every sick man in his bed: wash every mote out of his conscience. And dying so, death is to him an advantage" (4.1.164–67). Because Harry does not answer Williams fully, their argument comes to rest not on the king's imperative but on his responsibility to protect his soldiers and preserve the body politic of which they are all a part. The play does not, I think, resolve the argument; rather, it shapes its terms as problematic.

It is not so much that Harry insists on absolute obedience in war, a position that was almost universally conceded, as that he slights Williams's very human concerns. His response is in keeping with his majesty; although disguised as a commoner, he must play the part of a king and protect himself from claims that he neglects his subjects. But the moving soliloquy that immediately follows this episode reveals how conscious Harry is of his own humanity and of how much of it he must forgo in being a king. By reflecting on his neglect of "heartsease," Harry recalls the Hostess's assertion that in repudiating Falstaff and becoming a king indeed, at one with the chief justice of England (*2 Henry IV* 5.5.42–45), he has killed his heart:

> [. . .] What infinite heartsease
> Must kings neglect that private men enjoy?
> And what have kings that privates have not too,
> Save ceremony, save general ceremony?
> [. . .] O be sick great greatness,
> And bid thy ceremony give thee cure. (4.1.218–21, 233–34)

Harry's "great greatness," apparently sick in the knowledge of its real vulnerability, makes him acknowledge what the audience has been aware of all along: "the fault / My father made in compassing the crown" (4.1.275–76).

Like this soliloquy, the sequel to Harry's encounter with Bates and Williams shows something of his heart. By having Fluellen wear the glove that would have caused Williams to strike him, Harry both prevents and graciously accepts Williams's apology for his disrespect: "You appeared to me but as a common man," Williams explains (4.8.46–47). But Harry's gift to Williams, a glove full of "crowns" (4.8.53), is patronizing and by rejecting it Williams testifies to the dignity he can give the common man whom Harry, despite his strategically feigned fraternity, cannot but regard as "common" and for hire.

Actions gesturing toward a British unity, to be comprehended both regionally and in relation to class, are matched by scenes in which English traitors and scoundrels are excised from the burgeoning corporation that is Harry's army and an emblem of his whole people. These purgative moments share an ironic dimension. As we have seen, Cambridge's treason questions actual laws of inheritance. A less portentous incident is also revealing. Conforming to the provisions of *ius in bello* (Gosson, C^{v}; Allen A5), Harry orders Bardolph's execution for his theft of French property: "we would have all such offenders so cut off" (3.6.98). Were it not that Shakespeare's sources have Bardolph steal a "pix" (a small box containing the host; *Gesta* 69; Bullough 4. 389; Hall 64), the audience might conclude that in putting Bardolph to death, Harry's heart is in the right place. But Shakespeare's Bardolph steals a "pax," a crucifix but also the "peace." The pun recalls the status of Harry's claims to France and suggests that his common soldier may be miming his own grander and more dangerous actions. After act 3, Nim does not appear again on stage, but Pistol acts the scoundrel to the end, vowing to return to England a bawd and cutpurse. As unjust war resembled theft, a just war had to be honest. Pistol will act out the subversive element in Harry's war even after it is over.

The Waging of Peace

It is one of the important ironies pervading *Henry V* that Harry's conquest of France ends in the destruction of that country. The words of the defeated French voice the strongest apologies for peace and the sharpest critique of the very concept of a *ius ad bellum*. King Charles's passivity in the face of the first English threats is born of experience. He recalls "the bloody strain" of the Black Prince, the defeat of the French at Crécy, and how the English "mangle the work of nature and deface / The patterns that by God and by French fathers / Had twenty years been made" (2.4.51, 60–62). Assuming injury and theft, the English remind the French that by failing to make restitution, they become responsible for the war that Harry will actually wage. English threats multiply: their dauphin's soul will be "sore changed for wasteful vengeance / That shall fly" from Harry's "gunstones," a curse that shall descend to generations: "Ay some are yet ungotten and unborn / That shall have cause to curse the Dauphin's scorn" (1.2.282, 287–88). Harry before the seige of Harfleur emphasizes the harms that will come to generations: "fresh fair virgins" and "flowering infants" will not survive the coming battle (3.3.91). And during the course of combat, the French will ask for Harry's ransom twice (as if he were their prisoner; 3.6, 4.3), a request that allows him to repeat his determination to fight by telling the French again of the waste they are bringing on themselves. Rotting English corpses will become weapons to plague them in the future (4.3.101–08).

These threats find another register, less violent but no less lethal, in Princess Katharine's English lesson. She learns to name her body parts, thus appearing to rehearse in figures the dismemberment of the French body politic, for which she stands as Charles's heir.[15] The vulgarity inherent in this translation of the royal body into English limbs and features is apparent at the lesson's end, as Katharine observes: "De foot et de cown [. . .] ils sont les mots [. . .] de son [. . .] impudique" (3.4.47–48; French equivalents are "foutre," to fuck; and "con," cunt). Katharine's English lesson is a preface to her courtship, when she "cannot tell" what she thinks about a marriage to an enemy of France but in default of reason defers to her father's wish (5.2.107, 169, 184, 197, 229, 231). She tacitly acknowledges that her courtship has followed rather than preceded Harry's negotiations for her hand. The contrast between a triumphant English barbarism, transformed to a charming naiveté at the moment of Harry's wooing, and a helpless French civility, confined to an alien tongue, is parodied in Pistol's sadly comic encounter with M. le Fer. As the "Boy" observes, Pistol's voice (like Harry's?) is "full" but his "heart" is empty (4.4.60).

These threats are factored into the wages of peace brokered by Burgundy in act 5. His wish is to transform a ruined France so that it once again becomes "this best garden of the world." Burgundy pleads for the restoration of peace, the return of prosperity and the life of the people, lamenting that during war "our vineyards, fallows, meads, and hedges / Defective in their natures grow to wildness [. . .] / our children [. . .] grow like savages" (5.2.54–59), imagery that distills the essence of contemporary complaints of peace. But Harry can offer peace only in transactional terms—in exchange for Katharine, for France. In that sense, the play reverts to the imagery with which it opened. It is indeed a drama in which "ciphers," and crooked ciphers at that, convey complex and sometimes contradictory meanings. Harry offers no occasion for bargaining, demur, delay, nor does Burgundy ask for such a debate. Having already contracted for Katharine and France, Harry cannot effectively be refused; France has no choice but to cede herself to him.

True, Shakespeare closes his cycle of English history plays by reflecting on not England's triumph but her defeat (Epilogue.11–12). There is a sense, however, in which *Henry V* is ineluctably positive in its outlook. Harry's heroism, tinged with brutality, conceived in cunning, is never in doubt. Nor is the prospect of a British imperial rule, shadowed in Harry's conquest of France, much dimmed by suggestions of what that rule might cost. Thus *Henry V* could be said to point in two directions. The first is back to Elizabeth, who, nearing the end of her reign, emphasized her care for her subjects at home: "Though God hath raised me high, yet this I count the glory of my crown: that I have reigned with your loves,"[16] a profession of devotion that gave her vision of England in Ireland and "Virginia" a human dimension. The second is forward to James, who never warmed to his role as sovereign but whose commitment to a British empire in the New World became fully manifest in the first two decades of the next century.

NOTES

1. *The Norton Shakespeare,* ed. Stephen Greenblatt, Walter Cohen, Jean E. Howard, and Katharine Eisaman Maus (New York: Norton, 1997) 5.Epilogue.11–12. I regret that Andrew Hadfield's excellent *Shakespeare and Renaissance Politics* (London: Arden, 2004) appeared too late for me to consult. Readers will find its chapter on the histories very useful.
2. F. W. Maitland, *The Constitutional History of England* (Cambridge: Cambridge UP, 1908) 103–04.
3. Sir John Fortescue, *A Learned Commendation of the Politique Lawes of England,* trans. Robert Mulcaster (London, 1573) f. 25b.
4. William Tyndale, *The Obedience of a Chrysten Man and How Cristen Rulers Ought to Governe* (London, 1561) F[xxxv].
5. Christine de Pisan, *The Book of Fayttes of Armes and of Chyvalrye,* 1489 (London: Early English Text Society, 1932) 11–13.
6. Stephen Gosson, *The Trumpet of Warre* (London, 1598) B7, B7[v].
7. William Segar, *Honor Military and Civil* (London, 1602) 3.
8. Heinrich Bullinger, *Fiftie Godlie and Learned Sermons,* trans. H. I. (London, 1587) 208.
9. William Cardinal Allen, *The Copie of a Letter Written by M. Doctor Allen Concerning the Yeelding up of the Citie of Daventrie* (Antwerp, 1587) 6–7.
10. Tigurinus Chelidonius, *A Treatise of Peace and Warre,* trans. from the Latin by Pierre Boaistuau and from the French by James Chillester (London, 1571) 156.
11. *Gesta Henrici Quinti. The Deeds of Henry the Fifth,* 1416–1417, trans. Frank Taylor and John S. Rostell (Oxford: Clarendon P, 1975) 15.
12. *The First English Life of King Henry the Fifthe,* ed. Charles Lethbridge Kingsford (Oxford: Clarendon P, 1911) 26.
13. Holinshed, in *Narrative and Dramatic Sources of Shakespeare,* ed. Geoffrey Bullough, 8 vols. (London: Routledge; and New York: Columbia UP, 1975) 4. 378; Hall, in *The Union of the Two Noble and Illustre Famelies of Lancastre & York* (London, 1548).
14. The succession question is complicated. As it is framed in *Henry V,* it obviously relates to the French throne, but it also implicitly refers to the English throne. Historical record shows that Richard, the earl of Cambridge, was married to Philippa's daughter, Anne

Mortimer, the great-granddaughter of Edward III, the granddaughter of Lionel, the third son of Edward; hence the earl's claim (overt in Holinshed and implied in *Henry V*) that Anne Mortimer should accede to the *French* throne, which could pass through a female. Holinshed also states, and Shakespeare records (*1 Henry IV,* 1.3.143–44), that Richard II had named as his successor Edmund Mortimer, the earl of March and the brother of Philippa (see, for further clarification, *1 Henry IV,* 1.3.79, n. 3). The *English* throne was therefore also, at least presumptively, in play. Holinshed specifies the motives of the earl of Cambridge, later alluded to by Shakespeare's character: Cambridge had "the *intent* to exalt to the crowne his brother in law Edmund [Mortimer] earle of March as heire to Lionell duke of Clarence; after the death of which earle of March, for diverse secret impediments, not able to have issue, the earle of Cambridge was sure that the crowne should come to him by his wife, and to his children of hir begotten." His confession, that he acted for money, was to protect the earl of March and his own family: "which he did in deed: for his sonne Richard duke of Yorke not privilie but openlie claimed the crowne. [. . .]" (Bullough 4.385, my emphasis). Shakespeare's Henry IV refers to his accession to the throne by "crook'd ways" (*2 Henry IV,* 4.3.311–13); Henry V continues to reflect on them (4.1.275–76).

15. The dauphin is not listed among the French dead (4.8.85–95), but neither does he appear in Burgundy's entourage in act 5. Katharine therefore serves as Shakespeare's representative heir to the French kingdom.
16. *Collected Works,* ed. Leah Marcus, Janelle Mueller, and Mary Beth Rose (Chicago: U of Chicago P, 2000) 337.

READING LIST

Altman, Joel. "'Vile Participation': The Amplification of Violence in the Theater of Henry V." *Shakespeare Quarterly* 42 (1991): 1–32.

Baker, David J. *Between Nations: Shakespeare, Spenser, Marvell and the Question of Britain.* Stanford: Stanford UP, 1997.

Baker, David J., and Willy Maley, eds. *British Identities and English Renaissance Literature.* Cambridge: Cambridge UP, 2002.

Greenblatt, Stephen. "Invisible Bullets: Renaissance Authority and Its Subversion, *Henry IV and Henry V.*" *Political Shakespeare: New Essays in Cultural Materialism.* Ed. Jonathan Dollimore and Alan Sinfield. Manchester: Manchester UP, 1985. 18–47.

Grene, Nicholas. *Shakespeare's Serial History Plays.* Cambridge: Cambridge UP, 2002.

Hadfield, Andrew D. *Shakespeare and Renaissance Politics.* London: Arden, 2004.

Hattaway, Michael, ed. *Cambridge Companion to Shakespeare's History Plays.* Cambridge: Cambridge UP, 2002.

Highley, Christopher. *Shakespeare, Spenser, and the Crisis in Ireland.* Cambridge: Cambridge UP, 1997.

Hodgdon, Barbara. *The End Crowns All: Closure and Contradiction in Shakespeare's Histories.* Princeton: Princeton UP, 1991.

Holderness, Graham. *Shakespeare's History.* New York: St. Martin's P, 1982.

Howard, Jean, and Phyllis Rackin. *Engendering a Nation: A Feminist Account of Shakespeare's English Histories.* London: Routledge, 1997.

Iser, Wolfgang. *Staging Politics: The Lasting Impact of Shakespeare's Histories.* Trans. David Henry Nelson. New York: Columbia UP, 1993.

Kelly, Henry Ansgar. *Divine Providence in the England of Shakespeare's Histories.* Cambridge: Harvard UP, 1970.

Knapp, Jeffrey. *Shakespeare's Tribe: Church, Nation, and Theater in Renaissance England.* Chicago: U of Chicago P, 2002.

Leggatt, Alexander. *Shakespeare's Political Drama: The History Plays and the Roman Plays.* London: Routledge, 1989.

Maley, Willy. *Nation, State, and Empire in English Renaissance Literature: Shakespeare to Milton.* New York: Palgrave Macmillan, 2003.

Meron, Theodor. *Henry's Wars and Shakespeare's Laws.* Oxford: Clarendon P, 1993.

Neill, Michael. *Putting History to the Question.* New York: Columbia UP, 2000.

Patterson, Annabel. "Back by Popular Demand: The Two Versions of Henry V." *Shakespeare and the Popular Voice.* London: Basil Blackwell, 1989. 71–92.

Quint, David. "Alexander the Pig: Shakespeare on History and Poetry." *Boundary* 2 10 (1982): 49–63.

Rackin, Phyllis. *Stages of History: Shakespeare's English Chronicles.* Ithaca: Cornell UP, 1990.

Ribner, Irving. *The English History Play in the Age of Shakespeare.* New York: Barnes and Noble, 1965.

11

Hamlet and Humanism

Neil Rhodes

We have become familiar with the idea that we are living in a "postmodern" world. More recently we have also been offered a vision of a posthuman future in which human beings can be controlled by computer chip implants. Whether or not the arrival of the cyborg signals the end of the human, our present vantage point at the start of the twenty-first century certainly makes it easier to see that humanism has a history. It is a history that begins in the late fifteenth and sixteenth centuries, the period that is also described as early modern. Humanism is a defining element of modernity in its early phase, just as postmodernity may equally be understood in terms of the eclipse of humanism. But this chapter will not be concerned with the postmodern or posthuman. I mention them because I think it will be easier to understand what we mean by humanism if we recognize that it is not something natural or inevitable, but a phenomenon that can be associated with a particular historical era, that of the modern. This era may now be drawing to a close, or may already have done so. If we want to locate its origins, the literary text that provides us with the best focal point is *Hamlet,* produced around the year 1600. This most celebrated work by the most celebrated of all writers owes its status in part to its being a blueprint both for humanism and for modernity. I shall explain how it does so in a moment, but first we need to tackle the term "humanism" itself.

There are conventional academic apologies for attempting to define large and elusive concepts. I think we can take for granted that what follows involves a good deal of simplification and move on to say that the main source of confusion about the term "humanism," at least for the student of English, is that it tends to refer to two rather different things. The first, which is usually called "Renaissance humanism" or "Tudor humanism," refers to an intellectual and cultural movement specific to the early modern period. It derives from the *studia humanitatis,* the redesigned and reinvigorated arts syllabus that spread from Italian universities to the rest of Europe during the fifteenth century. The term survives in modern usage as the "arts and humanities." The second version of humanism emerged in the late nineteenth century, when the term was used to describe a purely secular philosophy of man. Dispensing with God, in this philosophy the human being becomes the ultimate point of reference and source of meaning. It is this second kind of humanism that came under attack in the late twentieth century, though not from a religious point of view, where it was labeled as "liberal humanism" or "essentialist humanism" (Dollimore 189–95, 249–58). These terms (the second in particular) refer to the belief that there is a universal human essence that exists apart from the contingencies of history and ideology. There are in fact connections between these two versions of humanism, as I hope to make clear in the rest of this chapter, but it is as well to remember at the start that they can and often do refer to different things.

The words "humanism" and "humanist" were rarely used in sixteenth-century England, but the cultural movement they later came to describe was enormously significant for the literary revival toward the end of the century. Identifying Renaissance humanism with the *studia humanitatis* is a way of pinpointing it, but this would be to give it a very narrow definition. For our purposes it is better to see it in much broader terms as having an impact in three main areas: religious thinking, literature, and education. Taking these three areas together, and they certainly overlap, we can construct the outlines of Renaissance humanism.

The central figure for humanism in England is Erasmus, who made a huge contribution in each of these areas. He was in fact a Dutchman who never bothered to learn English (early modern intellectuals tended to communicate in Latin), but he made several visits to England in the early decades of the sixteenth century and was a friend of Sir Thomas More, author of *Utopia.* His own book, *Praise of Folly,* written in 1509, puns on More's name in its Latin title, *Encomium Moriae.* It is a teasing work that makes it difficult for the reader to get a secure vantage point because Folly is presented as both the subject and the author of the oration. But some of the satire on contemporary examples of stupidity can be taken straight, and this gives us a useful insight into the humanist view of the religious life. The object of the humanists' attack here, and Erasmus's in particular, is the medieval scholastic philosophy that had resulted in an absurdly pedantic approach to Christian doctrine. The sort of questions the schoolmen liked to pose, Folly says, were along these lines: "Could God assume the shape of a woman, of the devil, of an ass, of a pumkin, or a piece of flint? Suppose him transformed to a pumkin, how could he have preached, performed miracles, been crucified?" And she continues, with heavy sarcasm, "Paul could display faith; but when he said, 'Faith is the substance of things hoped for, the evidence of things not seen,' that was a very unacademic definition" (Adams 57, 58).[1] The point of this is to show that theology had become abstract, reductively academic, and, above all, completely remote from the life of human beings. What humanism advocated instead was a radical, theological shift in attitudes to the moral life of the individual. The humanists wanted to restore to people the right of moral self-determination by going back to the teaching of the New Testament—the Sermon on the Mount and the writing of St. Paul were especially important for Erasmus. They believed that man could aspire to moral perfection and that the power to lead a good life lay within the human being. In short, humanists wanted abstract theological dogma to be replaced by the teaching of Christ himself and by the belief in man's innate capacity to choose between good and evil. It should be stressed, though, that while humanism desired religious reform it should not be confused with the Reformation, which was already on the horizon. Erasmus and More remained Catholics; indeed, More died for his faith.

The most obvious way of getting at the truth of Christ's teaching was to concentrate on the words themselves. Since St. Paul didn't write in corrupt, late medieval Latin it was important to go back to the original Greek of the New Testament, and with this in mind Erasmus published the first edition of a New Testament in Greek in 1516. The study of Greek was in fact something of an innovation at the time. It wasn't taught in the universities and most of the texts in that language were simply forgotten, lying around gathering dust in continental libraries. The single most important event for the revival of

Greek was the rediscovery of Plato in Florence in the later fifteenth century. Works such as Ficino's commentary on Plato's *Symposium,* with its insistence on the spiritual potential of human love, helped to create a Neoplatonic movement in the period that influenced quite a lot of Elizabethan poetry, including Spenser, Donne, and Shakespeare's *Sonnets.* Donne's poem "The Ecstacy" is one example. Needless to say, the schoolmen thought that the study of Greek was subversive, even heretical. That kind of optimistic belief in human love as a means of achieving spiritual perfection would surely undermine their advocacy of the supreme power of the church.

The case of Greek shows how the desire for a religious revival is linked to the revival of classical literature, the second of my three areas of humanist activity. This aspect of humanism obviously has a wider application since it more or less accounts for the term "Renaissance" as the alternative descriptor of the early modern period. The word means a "rebirth" of classical learning and classical cultural ideals. However, Greek was a very advanced subject in sixteenth-century England. When Ben Jonson referred rather condescendingly to Shakespeare's "small Latin and less Greek" in the elegy that appeared at the beginning of the First Folio, he was almost certainly underestimating (especially by our own measure of these accomplishments), but he did put the subjects in the right order. For most people in the period the experience of this aspect of humanism meant a much wider and deeper exposure to Latin literary texts than had previously been on offer. This was due partly to the recent invention of printing, and Erasmus was certainly a great exploiter of the new technology, but it was also a result of ideals as well as material practice. Renaissance humanists believed that literary study developed what the Romans called *humanitas.* This could indicate humanity or human nature in general terms, but also education, culture, and refinement: "civility" would be one way of summing it up. The importance of *humanitas* is associated especially with the Roman orator Cicero, who argued for the civilizing effects of eloquence and literature. He first uses the word in the *Pro Archia,* where he writes: "let the name of the poet, gentlemen, which no barbarian race has ever treated with disrespect, be a sacred name among you [. . .] shall we, then, who have been brought up to all that is best, remain unmoved by the voice of a poet" (Berry 116–17).[2] Cicero was at the center of Renaissance humanism as a literary movement. As the supreme exponent of the power of eloquence from the classical world, he became the ultimate model for writers and speechmakers, so much so that some people regarded his influence as excessive. Shakespeare prudently gives him little more than a walk-on part in *Julius Caesar;* Jonson, showing off his classicism, gave him scrolls of blank verse oratory in *Catiline* and the play was booed off the stage.

This belief in the power of eloquence and the importance of mastering Latin through a study of classical literary texts was at the heart of the humanist educational program in sixteenth-century England. Latin is still called Humanity in some older British universities today. This third element of humanism—education—is the one with the most obvious relevance to Shakespeare since the kind of school syllabus it inspired emphasized writing and speaking skills, models for drama. Erasmus wrote a number of textbooks that were widely used in English schools, including *De Copia,* which aimed to develop facility and abundance in expression, and the *Adagia,* an enormous collection of proverbial wisdom that could be worked into different kinds of discourse. Hamlet's "sea of troubles" is actually a phrase from a Latin translation of a Greek play that

Erasmus collected in the *Adagia*. Shakespeare refashions it to make Hamlet ponder the possibility of actually taking up arms against this sea. With these resources sixteenth-century schoolboys learned the principles of *imitatio* (ideally, the *assimilation* of classical literature rather than a merely mechanical imitation of it), as well as those of *copia*. At the same time they would probably have had some experience of drama. Richard Mulcaster, headmaster of Merchant Taylors' School in Westminster, who educated Spenser, Lodge, and Kyd, was a great believer in the school play as an aid to eloquence. Nearly all such exercises would have been in Latin, but Latin was a transferable skill. Kyd's *The Spanish Tragedy,* a pioneering work of the Elizabethan theater, is one illustration of the way in which a Latin-based education could produce vernacular dramatic eloquence. What's more, Kyd may also have been the author of the lost version of *Hamlet,* which Shakespeare would certainly have known and aimed to improve upon.

This, then, is a brief account of Renaissance humanism. How does it relate to the more modern version of humanism and also to the concept of modernity itself? In the first place, modern humanism emphasizes the importance of the individual and in that respect represents an important strand in the Western cultural tradition. Along with this emphasis goes the belief that as individuals we have the freedom to make our own life choices and the responsibility to make our own moral decisions; the belief, also, that as individuals we have certain rights; and the belief, last, in what we might call the authenticity of subjective experience: "I" am important and what I think and feel constitutes my own identity. This set of assumptions is summed up by contemporary literary theory in its critique of humanism as a belief in the autonomous human subject (Dollimore 153–58, 249–53). It is not difficult to see how these assumptions might derive from the shift in emphasis toward the centrality of the individual and the importance of moral self-determination that characterizes sixteenth-century thinking about the religious life. Erasmus, for example, had written a short essay on the freedom of the will in 1524. This philosophical position was supported by the literary and educational aspects of humanism. A much wider range of imaginative experience for the individual was opened up through the dissemination of classical literature and also, as a result, of new literature in the vernacular. At the same time, the importance attached to rhetoric in the Tudor educational curriculum developed not just facility in self-expression, but also the sense of selfhood that came from an understanding of eloquence as an instrument of persuasive power (Rhodes 24–41). All this is underpinned by the principle of *humanitas,* the belief that the arts and humanities, as we would call them now, are an essential part of the civilizing process.

There are, of course, a great many ways of defining what we mean by "modernity." We might, for example, want to point to the scientific revolution that gets under way around the same time as *Hamlet*. But if we understand the modern as referring to the era that lasted from the end of the middle ages to some point in the twentieth century then we would have to conclude that, while science has gone from strength to strength, the set of assumptions that characterizes humanism in both its early modern and later modern forms has been largely fractured. That is why humanism is central to understanding the concept of the modern. It represents a way of thinking that links ideas about the individual and the inner self with an optimistic belief in the civilizing process. This is something that has a beginning and, probably, an end.

Hamlet is not so much the beginning as the end of the beginning. First performed in or about 1600 it stands on the cusp of the sixteenth and seventeenth centuries and also at the midpoint of Shakespeare's own writing career. It is the play that has been recognized, historically and internationally, as certainly his most distinctive and probably his greatest achievement. One reason it enjoys what is perhaps an unparalleled status in Western literature is that it provides a distillation of the key ideas associated with both humanism and modernity. It offers a blueprint of modern conceptions of the self. But as it does so it brings one aspect of humanism into conflict with the other, which is why we can think of it as representing the end of the beginning. *Hamlet* is a humanist work that also offers a critique of humanism.

The two most significant features of the play are, first, that it is a revenge tragedy and, second, that it is peculiarly dominated by the central consciousness of the hero. The second is usually regarded as much more important than the first, but the fact that Shakespeare bases the first of his major tragedies on a revenge story is highly suggestive. The revenge play is an action drama where the hero is driven by the imperatives of duty and the ruthless logic of vengeance to commit some terrible atrocity in payment for the crimes that have been committed against his family or loved ones. One of the grim adages that sixteenth-century humanists extracted from Seneca, the only surviving Roman writer of tragedy, was the maxim, "You cannot say you have avenged a crime unless you better it." This was the standard model that Shakespeare's audiences would have been expecting his hero to follow. They would have had other expectations too: the lost Hamlet play, performed about ten years earlier, had a ghost in it that cried "miserably [. . .] *Hamlet, revenge,*" and it was described by another contemporary as a typical example of debased "English" Seneca, full of "tragical speeches." It was evidently crude stuff and something of a joke, at least among the more sophisticated theatergoers of the day. So it was extraordinarily daring of Shakespeare to use the Hamlet story for an utterly serious and very different kind of drama. What he does is to turn the basic revenge motif inside out. Instead of acting, Hamlet reflects on the rights and wrongs of action. Instead of writing his name in blood, as it were, he reads, thinks, and philosophizes. This is a character who regards the whole process of revenge as a primitive and barbaric ritual that is offensive to his more refined sensibilities. In fact, he seems to be in the wrong play altogether.

One reason why Hamlet fails to do anything at all for much of the play is the fact that he is a student, a notoriously disabling condition. "To be or not to be" was actually an intellectual exercise set at Edinburgh University in the early seventeenth century, so his most famous soliloquy has an academic flavor in its recipe for inertia. But while Hamlet's student status might reasonably account for his preference for thoughtful reflection over violence, it also gives us a clue to his literary taste. When a group of traveling players arrives at Elsinore, Hamlet asks them to do a special performance for him of one of his favorite speeches: "the play, I remember, pleased not the million. 'Twas caviare to the general. But it was [. . .] an excellent play, well digested in the scenes, set down with as much modesty as cunning" (2.2.439–43). Hamlet's point is that the play was too refined for the common taste, and he also wants to make sure that it is performed with suitable restraint and decorum: "Speak the speech, I pray you, as I pronounced it to you—trippingly on the tongue [. . .] do not saw the air too much with your hand, thus, but use all gently" (3.2.1–5). When we finally get to hear the play that

Hamlet so much admires, it turns out to be in a formal, neoclassical, and rather stilted academic style—exactly the sort of style, in fact, that would appeal to a humanist-educated student. So one aspect of Hamlet's humanism reveals itself as a form of cultural elitism. Not only does he reject an uncomplicated dedication to the revenge ethic as uncivilized, but he also prefers "high art" over the crude action drama of the popular stage represented by, among other things, the more violent and bombastic kind of revenge play itself.

A great deal of the first three acts of *Hamlet* is dominated by these plays within the play. What this suggests is that questions to do with the theater, with rhetoric, and with the nature of representation in general are central to Shakespeare's concerns in his own play. They are also very much Hamlet's concerns. It is this theme that provides us with the link between the literary and educational aspects of Hamlet's humanism and the aspect of humanism that emphasizes the importance of individuality and selfhood. Hamlet's theatrical tastes set him apart from the masses, it is true, but another side of this character is suspicious of the theater altogether. This comes over right at the start in his first substantial speech. His mother tells him that his father's death is a "common" event and then asks, "Why seems it so particular with thee?" Hamlet replies by latching on to the word "seems" and says, angrily, that it isn't the

> forms, moods, shows of grief
> That can denote me truly. These indeed "seem,"
> For they are actions that a man might play;
> But I have that within which passeth show—
> These but the trappings and the suits of woe. (1.2.82–86)

The public display and formal insincerities of the court do, of course, provide a context for this protest, but his disgust with "seeming" goes further than that. What Hamlet does is contrast the outward profession of sorrow, of the kind that an actor might simulate, with an inner integrity. His position here is very like Cordelia's when she refuses to copy the "glib and oily art" of her sisters by showing off her love for her father in an elaborate public statement. Her refusal to speak on that occasion, another court scene at the start of a tragedy, is an attempt to protect an inward truth that would be compromised and degraded by the merely rhetorical utterance of it. Like Hamlet she wants to make a distinction between the formal representation of a thing and the thing itself, which possesses the authenticity of subjective experience. The idea that personal identity is constituted by an adherence to an inviolable, inward truth, which is implied by both Cordelia and Hamlet, but particularly by Hamlet, is a hallmark of modern concepts of selfhood.[3] It is also at the center of that version of humanism that survives in the modern understanding of the term. But at the same time it brings the literary and educational aspects of Renaissance humanism, in which drama and rhetoric are important, into conflict with its more modern version. The more modern version derives from Renaissance thinking about the religious life in relation to the individual and ends up as a secular philosophy of man. *Hamlet* represents a pivotal moment in that transition.

Claudius takes up Gertude's line and replies to Hamlet's protest with the rather obtuse remark that it reveals "an understanding simple and unschooled" on the grounds that "death of fathers" is a "common theme." The "theme" was an academic exercise, and this one was commoner than "To be or not to be," so Claudius is saying that Hamlet must beundereducated because he doesn't seem to be aware of that. And again we can see a conflict acted out in this play, and in Hamlet's mind, between an academic humanism and the version of humanism that emphasizes the authenticity of the inner self. Hamlet *does* have an academic mind, but he also rejects the staler academic expressions in the search for greater intellectual honesty. This is what leads him to reject the feigned emotion of the Player's Hecuba speech in act 2, scene 2. We don't know whether Shakespeare was deliberately parodying another play here—the old Hamlet play, for example—but what is clear is that the style is intended to be distinctively theatrical. What is also clear is that it is *not true,* hence Hamlet's reaction after the Players leave. He uses the insincere display as a means of self-chastisement and as a catalyst for action, but the play within the play has another function. If the play within the play is only a play, then by implication Shakespeare's play, in which it appears, is real. Shakespeare is trying to affirm the truth of his own art by pointing to the discrepancies between his play and the faked eloquence of the Players, and also to the differences between his play and crude revenge drama. And, significantly, it is at the end of the Hecuba soliloquy that Hamlet formulates his plan of using a play as a vehicle for discovering the truth: he will stage a reenactment of his father's murder in fictional disguise in the hopes of stripping away Claudius's public facade and exposing his hidden self. Claudius wants to evade exposure by dismissing death of fathers as a common theme, but Hamlet wants his own play to prise out the inner man: "The play's the thing, / Wherein I'll catch the conscience of the King" (2.2. 606–707).

The question of theatrical representation and truth is not a side issue. It is intimately related to—indeed, inseparable from—the dominating consciousness of Hamlet in the play. The character who reveals his inner self to us does not reveal that self to the other characters in the play. There is in Hamlet a radical disjunction between self and the world, or between the inner self and the self that the world requires him to project. There is a sense in Hamlet that inward truth will be spoiled by a world that he perceives as deceitful and corrupt. So at the core of the play, as well as the conflict between rhetoric and the theater on the one hand and truth and conscience on the other, is a division between action and contemplation. While filial duty urges Hamlet to act, there is a conflicting reluctance in him to be sullied by the grossness of action. "To be or not to be" raises again the issue of "self-slaughter" he contemplates in his first soliloquy, but its alternatives are also those which the critic A. P. Rossiter described as being-in-the-self and being-in-the-world (171–88). Hamlet winds up with the reflection

> Thus conscience does make cowards of us all,
> And thus the native hue of resolution
> Is sicklied o'er withe pale cast of thought,
> And enterprises of great pitch and moment
> With this regard their currents turn awry,
> And lose the name of action. (3.1.85–90)

"Conscience," the inner truth that has to be protected from the world, is the factor that inhibits action. The soliloquy opens with the words "To be" and closes with the word "action," and the problem that Hamlet silently voices is that for him action may indeed only be "acting"—histrionic, theatrical, insincere, untrue. This is the sense of the word that Hamlet intends when he says, "These are actions that a man might play," and that sense is also present in the part of rhetoric known as *actio,* which covered delivery and performance. "Action" in these senses can therefore be seen as the opposite of the idea of conscience as inner being that Hamlet wants to target in Claudius. The modern term "consciousness" did not exist in Shakespeare's day. Instead, he seems to be extending the meaning of "conscience" in that direction by associating it with the humanist concept of selfhood as something constituted by a sense of inward truth.

"To be or not to be" is the most famous of Hamlet's soliloquies, but it is only one of four. The importance of soliloquy is perhaps the most characteristic feature of the play as a whole and the simplest illustration of the point that *Hamlet* is peculiarly dominated by the central consciousness of the hero. There are really two kinds of soliloquy evident on the Elizabethan stage. One is the kind of highly theatrical speech in which a character almost steps out of himself or herself in order to address the audience. The other is the kind that shows the character in an even more self-absorbed state and tries to represent unspoken thought processes. It is this second kind that we get in *Hamlet.* It would be possible to see these four soliloquies (one in each act, though some editions relegate the fourth to an appendix) as representing the progress of the play itself. They certainly represent vital moments in the progress of Hamlet's fluctuating emotions,[4] but it is also important to key these into what happens in the plot. The first, "O that this too too solid flesh" (1.2.129–59), comes immediately after the first court scene and before Hamlet has seen the ghost. Burdened with a sense of disgust at his mother's remarriage, at this point he completely recoils from action and vows to remain silent. "O, what a rogue and peasant slave am I!" (2.2.552–607) comes after he has seen the ghost and decided to feign madness. This further withdrawal from the world is accompanied by a desperate lashing of himself into action. "To be or not to be" (3.1.58–90) seems to be poised between the rejection of action in the first soliloquy and the commitment to action in the second. It is followed by his rejection of Ophelia and Claudius's announcement that he's going to pack Hamlet off to England. "How all occasions do inform against me" (4.4.922–56)[5] is prompted by Hamlet's sighting of Fortinbras's army. Adopting Fortinbras as a role model, he begins to lose his inhibitions about action. The self is being reintegrated with the world. In the fifth act the time for meditation has passed, and yet the problems of "being" and "acting" are never really solved. Hamlet becomes not the agent of revenge but its instrument and then its victim. He does not act; he only reacts. In the end, his killing of Claudius is not an act of vengeance for the death of his father but impulsive retribution for the death of his mother.

We need to key these soliloquies into the plot because there is always a danger in *Hamlet* that the hero's consciousness will seem to float free from its moorings. Yet it is this point that underlines just how innovative and radical Shakespeare was in creating a new kind of a character and a new sense of selfhood that we can think of both as distinctively humanist and distinctively modern.[6] For a play that is so suspicious of acting it may seem perverse to end by quoting an actor, but it is actors rather than critics who have the task of representing the characters that Shakespeare devised to a modern audience. Nominating Shakespeare as her greatest Briton in a BBC television program broadcast in 2002, Fiona Shaw produced this very direct account of Hamlet in terms that a posthumanist or antihumanist critic might describe as those of "essentialist humanism":

> [Shakespeare] does not write about the historical figure, he writes about the human being. [Hamlet] is Everyman, he is all of us [. . .] He makes us understand our thoughts and our feelings, and what could be more useful in our lives than that [. . .] Thought makes us wise and feeling makes us human [. . .] Nobody has been able to map our emotional DNA so accurately.[7]

From the standpoint of much modern criticism this represents a rather naive understanding of the nature of dramatic characterization. But it does sum up, in the language of ordinary speech, a good deal of what is meant by humanism. It also shows, perhaps, that there is still some life left in the concept yet.

NOTES

1. Erasmus, *The Praise of Folly and Other Writings,* trans. & ed. Robert M. Adams (New York: W. W. Norton, 1989).
2. Cicero, *Defence Speeches,* trans. D. H. Berry (Oxford: Oxford UP, 2000). See also Mike Pincombe, *Elizabethan Humanism: Literature and Learning in the Later Sixteenth Century* (Harlow: Longman, 2001), for this and for Cicero and Elizabethan humanism more generally.
3. On early modern ideas of "inwardness," see Katharine Eisaman Maus, *Inwardness and Theater in the English Renaissance* (Chicago: U of Chicago P, 1995); on *Hamlet* specifically, 1–6.
4. For an outstanding analysis of the play in these terms, see Philip Fisher, "Thinking About Killing: Hamlet and the Paths Among the Passions," *Raritan* 11 (1991): 43–77.
5. Line references to this speech are to *The Norton Shakespeare,* ed. Stephen Greenblatt et al. (New York: W. W. Norton, 1997); other references are to *The Complete Works,* ed. Stanley Wells and Gary Taylor (Oxford: Clarendon P, 1998).
6. The best account of selfhood in *Hamlet* is by John Lee (*Shakespeare's "Hamlet" and the Controversies of Self* [Oxford: Clarendon P, 2000]), who challenges the antihumanist position of Jonathan Dollimore and others.
7. Fiona Shaw, *Great Britons: Shakespeare.* BBC 2, 8 Nov. 2002.

READING LIST

Booth, Stephen. "On the Value of Hamlet." *Reinterpretations of Elizabethan Drama*. Ed. Norman Rabkin. New York: Columbia UP, 1969. 137–77.

Bradley, A. C. *Shakespearean Tragedy*. 3rd ed. Basingstoke: Macmillan, 1992.

Davies, Tony. *Humanism*. London: Routledge, 1997.

Dollimore, Jonathan. *Radical Tragedy: Religion, Ideology and Power in the Drama of Shakespeare and His Contemporaries*. 2nd ed. Hemel Hempstead: Harvester Wheatsheaf, 1989.

Fisher, Philip. "Thinking About Killing: Hamlet and the Paths Among the Passions." *Raritan* 11 (1991): 43–77.

Lee, John. *Shakespeare's "Hamlet" and the Controversies of Self.* Oxford: Clarendon P, 2000.

Levin, Harry. *The Question of "Hamlet."* New York: Oxford UP, 1959.

Maus, Katharine Eisaman. *Inwardness and Theater in the English Renaissance*. Chicago: U of Chicago P, 1995.

Neill, Michael. *Issues of Death: Mortality and Identity in English Renaissance Tragedy*. Oxford: Clarendon P, 1997.

Pincombe, Mike. *Elizabethan Humanism: Literature and Learning in the Later Sixteenth Century*. Harlow: Longman, 2001.

Rhodes, Neil. *The Power of Eloquence and English Renaissance Literature*. Hemel Hempstead: Harvester Wheatsheaf, 1992.

Rossiter, A. P. *Angel with Horns: Fifteen Lectures on Shakespeare*. Ed. Graham Storey. London: Longman, 1989.

12

Twelfth Night, Gender, and Comedy

R. W. Maslen

Shakespeare's *Twelfth Night*[1] dedicates itself to discovering the sheer strangeness of attitudes to gender and sexuality in the early modern period. Many of these attitudes seem odd to us now, but Shakespeare seems to go out of his way to suggest that theater audiences in his own time should have found them equally puzzling. Characters in the play wander round in astonishment, bemused by the contradictions in the rules that are supposed to govern relationships between men and women or between persons of the same sex. Everyone is doubtful of the identities of others, doubtful of her own identity, doubtful of the path she should take in order to recover her self-assurance, and sure of only one thing: that she is in a state of heightened sexual arousal. The term "madness" haunts the play, but where this word usually connotes behavior or a state of mind that fails to conform with the social expectations of a dominant culture, in Shakespeare's imaginary city of Illyria the condition is so prevalent that it suggests a world that has lost its balance altogether, deprived of any agreed technique for measuring its conflicting cultural values.

In this comedy, women are mistaken for men, men mistaken for women disguised as men, and definitions of manhood and womanhood themselves called into question. Confusions over identity have been the staple fare of comedy since classical times, when the plays of Plautus and Terence were improbably crowded with twins, doppelgängers, and lost family members (Plautus's comedy *Menaechmi,* in particular, has obvious affinities with *Twelfth Night*). Sixteenth-century Italian comedies by Ariosto and others took up the theme of confusion where the classical comedy-writers left off. But it was in Elizabethan England, and especially in Shakespearean comedy, that comic confusion really began to focus on issues of gender. No body of dramatic work before or since Shakespeare's has lent itself to a more thorough investigation of the uncertainties that surround cultural constructions of masculinity, femininity, and erotic attraction of all kinds. This is one reason why his comedies continue to hold the stage today, in another age when gender and sexuality have come under obsessive scrutiny.

It's hardly surprising that Shakespeare took gender as the subject of his comedies, since comedy itself was linked with sexual and social transgression in the early modern period. With the construction of the first purpose-built playhouses in London during the 1570s, polemical attacks on the theater—which had occurred sporadically since ancient times—reached unprecedented levels; and these attacks repeatedly characterized comedy as a seed-bed for sexual depravity, capable of feminizing men, turning women into voracious sexual predators, and precipitating the breakdown of the entire social hierarchy in the process.[2] As the antitheatrical polemicist Stephen Gosson puts it, "The grounde worke of Commedies, is love, cosenedge, flatterie, bawderie, [and] slye conveighance of whordome."[3] The devil let them loose in London, says Gosson, as a follow-up to the "wanton Italian bookes" with which he planned to corrupt the plain minds of ordinary English people (Kinney 153). Like these books, comedies assail their recipients with an overwhelming excess of sensory stimuli: "straunge consortes of melody, to tickle the eare; costly apparel, to flatter the sight; effeminate gesture, to ravish the sence; and wanton speache, to whet desire to inordinate lust" (Kinney 89). And the efficacy of this method of corruption is evident from the behavior of playhouse audiences, which constitutes a "right Comedie" in itself (Kinney 92): "such wanton gestures, such bawdie speaches, such laughing and fleering, such kissing and bussing, such clipping and culling, Suche winckinge and glancinge of wanton eyes, and the like [. . .] as is wonderfull to beholde."[4] Language like this, in which playhouses become brothels and comedies degenerate into orgies, occurs repeatedly in sermons, tracts, and official documents throughout Shakespeare's lifetime, and may well have cast its shadow over his comic explorations of relations between the sexes, helping to render them as complex and troubling as they are witty. Putting pen to paper to write a comedy was to stir up a hornet's nest of controversial connections in Elizabethan England; indeed, from one point of view, it was to make a pact with the devil himself. And the most controversial connections of all related to gender.

Twelfth Night isn't directly based on a "wanton Italian booke," as many of Shakespeare's comedies are. Its plot comes from a short story, "Apolonius and Silla" (1581), by the English writer Barnaby Rich—though the story derives ultimately from *Gl'ingannati,* one of the "baudie Comedies in [. . .] Italian" that Gosson tells us have been "throughly ransackt to furnish the Playe houses in London" (Kinney 169). But whatever its sources, *Twelfth Night* certainly demonstrates Shakespeare's intense awareness of the anticomic sentiment prevalent among some Londoners. When the heroine Viola disguises herself as a boy and attracts the amorous attentions of a noblewoman, she remarks, using a misogynistic vocabulary that might have been drawn from one of the antitheatrical pamphlets: "Disguise, I see thou art a wickedness / Wherein the pregnant enemy does much" (2.2.25–26). Later she bandies words with Feste the clown and goes on to meditate on the tact required by a professional comedian like Feste if he is to avoid getting into trouble for his witticisms: "He must observe their mood on whom he jests, / The quality of persons, and the time [. . .] This is a practice / As full of labor as a wise man's art" (3.1.55–59). And in the final act of the play both jesting and disguise turn sour. The victim of a practical joke in which the disguised Feste takes part, a would-be lover and social climber called Malvolio, finds himself in prison, suspected of being possessed by "the pregnant enemy"—that is, the devil—and accused of heresy. In an age when doctors prescribed whipping as a treatment for madness, and when heresy was punishable by burning, a prank with an outcome like this was more painful than amusing. Malvolio's fate may have invoked in the audience's minds the link between theater and devilry that had been consolidated by polemicists like Gosson, whose texts were associated with the radical Protestant movement known as Puritanism. Malvolio himself is described as "a kind of puritan" (2.3.125), and his punishment could be seen as comedy's symbolic revenge on its enemies. But the revenge serves also to confirm the polemicists' view that playing with the fire of sexual passions, as Feste and his fellow pranksters do, may have profoundly serious consequences, for the players as well as their victims.

All the same, without some bending of the social and literary conventions that governed gender there could have been no comedies in Shakespeare's time—and certainly no romantic comedies. Contemporary custom dictated that the only virtues women could manifest were passive ones such as sexual self-restraint and verbal and behavioral submissiveness. Women below a certain class who failed to manifest these qualities were given cruel labels—shrew, quean, drab, scold, whore—and ruthlessly punished, with such aggressive forms of torture and public humiliation as the bridle and the ducking stool. At the same time, England had been ruled by women since 1553, and submissiveness was hardly a quality suited to a ruler. Moreover, self-restraint and submissiveness were hardly the most scintillating ingredients out of which to build a good story, let alone a drama. If a woman is supposed to be passive and tongue-tied, what becomes of the processes of courtship that are fundamental to romance? Nobody wanted silent women in a story or a play; even Ben Jonson's comedy *Epicene, or The Silent Woman* has a boy as its heroine, who is only masquerading as the mute wife of the title. So dramatists had to find ingenious ways of having women speak without making them look immodest.

Disguise was an obvious technique: in stories as well as plays women are always donning male disguises to pursue the men they fancy. Barnaby Rich's "Apolonius and Silla" is one such story; and Viola forms part of a line of young girls disguised as boys who populate Shakespeare's plays, from Julia in *The Two Gentlemen of Verona* to Innogen in *Cymbeline*. But in *Twelfth Night* there are also two women who don't feel the need to dress up as men in order to be articulate or active. One is the Countess Olivia, an Elizabeth figure who insists on getting what she wants regardless of custom and who freely exploits all the verbal resources available to women of the ruling classes. The other is Olivia's waiting woman Maria, who represents a third class of active and articulate women: the female trickster, whose exploits were celebrated in the so-called jest-books or collections of comic anecdotes that remained hugely popular from the beginning of the sixteenth century until the time of the modern novel. Maria's wit is of the kind described by John Lyly in his proto-novel *Euphues and His England* (1580): "It is wit that allureth, when every word shall have his weight, when nothing shall proceed but it shall either savour of a sharp conceit or a secret conclusion."[5] Olivia's kinsman Sir Toby Belch clearly agrees with Lyly, since he marries Maria for her wit at the end of the play.

The trio of articulate women who dominate *Twelfth Night* transform the conventional Elizabethan ideal of a woman—Penelope the wife of Odysseus, Virginia the murdered virgin, Patient Griselda, and the rest—into an elusive fantasy that is freely exploited by women for their own ends. Olivia, for instance, plays the part of a chaste, noncommunicative woman in her efforts to avoid the unwelcome attentions of Orsino, duke of Illyria. Since she has sworn, we learn, to marry no man "above her degree, neither in estate, years, nor wit" (1.3.90–91), she chooses to pose as a virginal recluse at the beginning of the play, mourning the death of her brother in solitude for seven years—time enough, one would have thought, to deter even an obsessive admirer like the duke. Viola, too, invokes the ideal chaste and silent woman, after she has disguised herself as the boy Cesario. Cesario enters the service of Duke Orsino, then falls in love with him; and at one point the disguised page tells his master the story of a wordless woman, as a means of hinting at the nature of his own love for the duke. Cesario had a sister, he explains, who fell in love, but who followed the prescriptions of contemporary conduct manuals that enjoined absolute modesty on women:

> She never told her love,
> But let concealment, like a worm i'th'bud,
> Feed on her damask cheek. She pined in thought,
> And with a green and yellow melancholy
> She sat like patience on a monument,
> Smiling at grief. (2.4.109–14)

The "history" or story of this girl, Cesario explains, is nothing but a "blank" (2.4.109). She was constrained, by the restrictive nature of the ideal she imitated, to waste away to nothing without taking part in any kind of narrative. Olivia and Viola, by contrast, are perfectly aware that the ideal is only one of the many fantasies that throng the play. Their confidence that time will resolve their difficulties—Olivia's imposition of a deadline on her mourning, Viola's famous observation, when she learns that Olivia loves her, that "time [. . .] must untangle this, not I" (2.2.38)—may perhaps spring from the fact that they have written themselves into a very different kind of narrative than the blank history of Cesario's sister. Elizabethan fiction—on the page or on the stage—was rich in alternative plots involving women, and most women in Shakespeare's comedies are thoroughly familiar with these plots, choosing between them at will as occasion demands.

The men in this play have their own fantastic versions of the ideal woman, and she too has little in common with the "real" women of flesh and blood we see on stage. (The exception is Sir Toby, who has little patience for the ideal invoked by his niece Olivia and who frankly admires the boldness and wit of her maid, Maria.) The greatest fantasist of them all is the most powerful figure in the play, Duke Orsino. In the first scene, Orsino imagines Olivia's grief as a guarantee of her devotion to him at some fancied future time when she will accept him as her lover:

> O, she that hath a heart of that fine frame
> To pay this debt of love but to a brother,
> How will she love when the rich golden shaft
> Hath killed the flock of all affections else
> That live in her—when liver, brain, and heart,
> These sovereign thrones, are all supplied, and filled,
> Her sweet perfections with one self king! (1.1.32–38)

Clearly the duke has no interest in Olivia's actual thoughts and feelings; his celebrated opening speech is all about his own experience of desire, and Olivia is not even mentioned in it. Instead he is obsessed with a vision of the absolute monarchic power he will wield over the countess when he has won her "liver, brain, and heart," transforming her into an animate receptacle for his own image. In this he resembles Olivia's steward Malvolio, whose fantasies of marrying his mistress focus exclusively on the pleasure he will take in ruling her household while Olivia lies asleep in postcoital exhaustion (2.5.39ff.). The heterosexual fantasies of Shakespeare's men consistently consign women to marginality; so we should hardly be surprised that it's a woman, Viola—disguised as the boy Cesario and sent by Orsino to woo Olivia for him—who delivers the most convincing courtship speech in the play. Asked by Olivia what he would do if he were her lover, Cesario replies that he would set up camp at her gate and fix the world's attention on her by repeatedly calling her name (1.5.237–35). This famous picture of determined wooing may be just another far-fetched fantasy, but at least it's one with *both* Olivia *and* her suitor at the heart of it.

Orsino's view of women, by contrast, is both generalized and inconsistent. In conversation with Cesario, he begins by saying that men are more fickle than women ("Our fancies are more giddy and unfirm, / More longing, wavering, sooner lost and worn, / Than women's are," 2.4.32–34) and ends by claiming precisely the opposite—that women are incapable of loving with equal force to men:

> There is no woman's sides
> Can bide the beating of so strong a passion
> As love doth give my heart; no woman's heart
> So big to hold so much. They lack retention.
> Alas, their love may be called appetite,
> No motion of the liver, but the palate,
> That suffer surfeit, cloyment, and revolt.
> But mine is all as hungry as the sea,
> And can digest as much. Make no compare
> Between that love a woman can bear me
> And that I owe a woman. (2.4.91–101)

Orsino has clearly based this view of women on himself—in other words, it serves only to confirm his narcissism. He started the play, after all, by describing his own love as an "appetite" capable of devouring endless quantities (of sex or of women? He doesn't say which) without being satisfied (1.1.1–15). In that opening speech, his appetite suffers "cloyment, and revolt" after he has listened to romantic music for too long; and this sense of "cloyment" anticipates, one presumes, the devaluation Olivia would suffer in his eyes if once she gave him unrestricted access to her body. Orsino's view of women suggests, in fact, that there is little hope of his achieving a satisfactory long-term relationship with any woman at all. It's in response to his fantastic account of women's inability to love that Viola/Cesario tells him the story of his/her imaginary sister who sat "like Patience on a monument / Smiling at grief." The sister's selflessness is as extreme as Orsino's self-obsession, and her immobility anticipates the likely outcome of any encounter between conventional male and female versions of femininity. Clearly, interaction between the genders depends on the discovery of a third way, to which the boy/girl Viola/Cesario offers a beguiling key.

In the meantime, however, Viola has the unpleasant experience of learning firsthand about men's fantasies of ideal manhood. Throughout Shakespeare's works men define their masculinity through violence, as they often seem to have done in the streets of Elizabethan London (few men did not carry a weapon, and many had no compunction about using these weapons on the slightest provocation).[6] One need only think of Shakespeare's three plays with lovers in their titles—*Romeo and Juliet, Troilus and Cressida, Antony and Cleopatra*—to see how this association of masculinity with violence can damage men's relationships with women. In *Twelfth Night,* as in these three plays, aggressive manliness is the subject of sometimes painful parody. One of Olivia's would-be suitors, Sir Andrew Aguecheek, is the comic antithesis of a man's man: as

Maria points out, "he's a great quarreller, and but that he hath the gift of a coward to allay the gust he hath in quarrelling, 'tis thought among the prudent he would quickly have the gift of a grave" (1.3.25–27). One of the pranks planned by Sir Toby Belch is to expose Sir Andrew's lack of manhood by pitting him in battle against an equally "unmanly" foe, the boy Cesario, whom Sir Toby identifies as failing to conform with the ideal of aggressive masculinity. This prank, like the trick played on Malvolio, turns sour when Sir Andrew confronts first the "Notable pirate" Antonio (5.1.63) and later Viola's brother Sebastian, both of whom are thoroughly "manly" in their willingness to dish out violence. As a result, Sir Andrew and Sir Toby end the play with broken heads. But before this, Cesario/Viola discovers the terrifying pressure exerted on young men by their elders, either to comply with the masculine ideal themselves or else to serve as the guarantor of its embodiment in other men. On being told of Sir Andrew's determination to fight with him, Cesario says: "I have heard of some kind of men that put quarrels purposely on others, to taste their valour. Belike this is a man of that quirk" (3.4.216–18). Sir Toby insists this is not the case, and that Sir Andrew has a genuine grievance against him; but the knight then belies his own words by telling Cesario to strip his phallic sword "quite naked" (3.4.223). Clearly, the abortive combat Sir Toby sets up between the unmanly man Sir Andrew and the womanly boy Cesario is no more than an elaborate comparison of penises. And his own eager participation in the fight that *does* break out—though neither Sir Andrew nor Cesario is involved in it—confirms that the real point of the competition is to prove Sir Toby's own superior manhood rather than to derogate from theirs.

Besides a willingness to resort to violence, the male ideal of masculinity includes an unwavering loyalty to male friends. In *Twelfth Night,* as in many of Shakespeare's plays, this loyalty between men seems inextricably linked with male aggression. Antonio shows his love for Sebastian by twice putting his own life at risk: first following him into Illyria despite the fact that he has "many enemies in Orsino's court" (2.1.39); then substituting himself for the boy in a sword-fight, just as Mercutio substitutes himself for Romeo, with fatal consequences, in Shakespeare's early tragedy. It would seem that loyalty to other men is as much a test of manliness as the intensity of one's passion for combat. When Antonio thinks Sebastian has betrayed him, he stops calling him "sir" and "young gentleman" (3.4.277) and brands him instead an "idol" (3.4.330), an "empty trunk" (3.4.335), a "thing" (5.1.83), a source of "witchcraft" (5.1.70)—terms that strip Sebastian of his gender. Conversely, Sir Andrew's lack of manliness fully justifies Sir Toby in the contempt he shows for his friendship—or so the bibulous knight believes. When Fabian observes to Sir Toby that Andrew is "a dear manikin to you," Sir Toby replies that "I have been dear to him, lad, some two thousand strong or so," converting friendship into exploitation with a flippant pun (3.2.45–47). Sir Toby dupes Sir Andrew of his cash as freely as he tricks him into exposing his cowardice; and in the final act he annuls their friendship with a single vitriolic outburst: "Will *you* help—an ass-head, and a coxcomb, and a knave; a thin-faced knave, a gull?" (5.1.198–99). By virtue of his physical and intellectual frailty, Sir Andrew is a manikin—a little man or a puppet—to be played with and discarded at will by "manly" men like Sir Toby. Male relationships with men, it would seem, are as fragile and fraught with fantasies as are male relationships with women.

Nevertheless, at its best, friendship with other men seems to be the most open, intimate, and reciprocal form of relationship available to men in *Twelfth Night.* Antonio's love for Sebastian is as selfless as the love of Cesario's imaginary sister for an unknown man, and a good deal more active. And in her male disguise as Cesario, Viola gets closer to Orsino than she could ever have done as a woman. After only three days together Orsino is able to tell his new servant, "Thou know'st no less but all. I have unclasped / To thee the book even of my secret soul" (1.4.12–13). This free disclosure of secrets demonstrates that despite their social disparity, in Orsino's eyes Cesario has become what Elizabethan manuals on male friendship describe as a "second self," "another I," a kind of twin of the duke's, as closely bound to him as Viola is to her twin brother. That Orsino sees Cesario in this way is confirmed by his willingness to employ the boy as his substitute in the courtship of Olivia. The mutuality of their affection reveals itself most strikingly in the final act, when Cesario gets the chance to sacrifice his life for his master just as Antonio sacrificed his safety for Sebastian's. On learning that Olivia has fallen in love with Cesario, Orsino promptly resorts to the usual male solution of violence: "I'll sacrifice the lamb that I do love," he declares (5.1.126)—that is, he will kill Cesario to spite Olivia. And the boy at once professes himself willing to die "a thousand deaths" to satisfy Orsino (5.1.129). This is the high point of his/her relationship with the duke. No woman but Viola in Shakespeare's plays gets such an opportunity to achieve, as a man, the ultimate consummation of an Elizabethan man's love for another man, which is to lay down his life for his friend. And no other character, male or female, goes to her death more "jocund, apt, and willingly" than she does here (5.1.128), following him off stage as eagerly as if to a marriage bed.

In Elizabethan culture there was theoretically no place for an erotic relationship between men. The sin of sodomy—which encompassed a range of forbidden sexual activities, among them the penetration of an underaged boy by an older man[7]—was punishable by death, like heresy. Yet there is ample evidence that many of these activities went on, undeterred by the draconian measures taken against them. The boy Cesario's declaration of his willingness to die for Orsino is on one level a public announcement of his willingness to sleep with him: for the Elizabethans, the verb "to die" could also mean "to achieve orgasm." But in Shakespeare's Illyria, unlike Elizabethan London, his wish may legitimately be granted because, of course, Cesario is a woman in disguise. His situation as neither man nor woman, but a hybrid "monster" composed of both (2.2.32), exempts him from the restrictions imposed on men and women, either by law or by the ideal forms of behavior expected of either sex.

The advantages of Cesario/Viola's double gender become obvious soon after Orsino threatens to kill him. Olivia intervenes to save the boy's life, announcing that she has married him (in fact she has married Viola's brother Sebastian), which places him under the protection of Illyrian law. At once the duke turns on Cesario with a verbal attack that seems hardly less vicious than his earlier threat to murder him: "O thou dissembling cub" (5.1.160). But dissembling is not really the issue here; it is distrust. Orsino thinks that the boy has betrayed his trust in him, thus compromising their bond of mutual friendship, which like marriage may be described as "A contract of eternal bond of love" (5.1.152). The misunderstanding is resolved when Sebastian turns up and Cesario/Viola reveals her "true" sex, thus finally unclasping to Orsino the "book" of her "secret soul." At this point the duke discovers that Viola has been dissembling not her love for him but her gender; and *this* kind of deceit he seems to find wholly admirable. He marries her, he says, for "your service done [. . .] So much against the mettle of your sex" (5.1.310–11)—as if it's her ability *not* to be the ideal passive woman he has so far imagined for himself that most delights him about her. In token of this delight, he continues to call her "Cesario" long after he has learned her identity (5.1.372–73), thus preserving our sense of their relationship as a love affair between men as well as between man and woman. And it's in male clothing that Viola leaves the stage with Orsino to begin married life at the end of the play. Her clothes seem to promise that their marriage will be an egalitarian one, based not on mastery and control—as are men's fantasies about women—but on mutual confidence and respect, like the Elizabethan ideal of same-sex friendship. When Orsino discharges Cesario from his service ("Your master quits you"), he installs Viola as "Your master's mistress," his "fancy's queen"—phrases that may be taken to imply that authority will be shared more or less equally between them after marriage (5.1.310–14, 375). ("Master" and "mistress" are terms used throughout the play for men and women in positions of authority: Feste, for instance, tells Viola "I would be sorry, sir, but the fool should be as oft with your master as with my mistress," 3.1.34–35.) In view of the ideals of femininity that have prevailed up to this point, it's hard to imagine Orsino saying these things with such conviction to a woman dressed in ordinary clothes.

The phrase "Your master's mistress" recalls the most explicitly homoerotic poem written by Shakespeare, Sonnet 20. The poem celebrates the beauty of a boy loved by the sonneteer, whose face combines the best qualities conventionally assigned to both sexes: "A woman's face with nature's own hand painted, / Hast thou, the master-mistress of my passion." This suggests, among other things, that Shakespeare could imagine a space where the "masculine" and the "feminine" are fused, and that for him the mind and body of an adolescent boy could constitute such a space. Oscar Wilde supposed that the boy addressed in Shakespeare's sonnets could have been an actor,[8] and there's something profoundly satisfying about the supposition. Boy actors represented a way out of an artistic dilemma created by Elizabethan views on women. Since women were not allowed to perform on the public stage, boys took the female roles in plays. And in doing so they drew attention to the possibility that gender itself might be a matter of performance. As the antitheatrical polemicists pointed out, men could be, or could become, effeminate, and the boy actor's craft showed just how easy it was to accomplish this particular form of gender-bending. Shakespeare's "master-mistress" in the sonnets, and Viola/Cesario in *Twelfth Night,* are bodies in transit through time, altering as they move and attracting men and women alike. In them fantasies of maleness and femaleness intersect and mingle, making possible all sorts of relationships—sexual and nonsexual—that were not officially sanctioned within Elizabethan culture. Hence the polemicists' profound unease about the effect of comedy on its audiences. Hence, too, Wilde's vision of the sonnets as commemorating a boy who gave life to Shakespeare's lines on stage: a vision that itself gave life to new ways of thinking about literature and sexuality in the twentieth century, though not before Wilde himself had been destroyed by late Victorian homophobia.

It is Duke Orsino who first comments on the fusion of gender attributes in Cesario, the page who is also both a woman and a boy actor:

> For they shall yet belie thy happy years
> That say thou art a man. Diana's lip
> Is not more smooth and rubious; thy small pipe
> Is as the maiden's organ, shrill and sound,
> And all is semblative a woman's part. (1.4.29–33)

Malvolio notices it, too, when he says that Cesario stands at a cusp between two stages of male development: "Not yet old enough for a man, nor young enough for a boy [. . .]

'tis with him in standing water, between boy and man [. . .] one would think his mother's milk were scarce out of him" (1.5.139–44). As Malvolio observes, a boy is closer to his mother than most grown men are. And at the end of the play this particular boy is revealed to be a woman, whose performance as the opposite gender has fooled everyone she met in the course of the action. What Viola's achievement as an actor suggests—however improbably—is that nobody need be fixed or trapped in a single mode of being. The comedy begins in stalemate, with Olivia and Orsino locked in the behavior prescribed by their culture for lovers of their class and gender, and with no immediate prospect of escape from their entrapment. When Viola first resolves to enter Orsino's service she plans to present herself to him as a eunuch (1.2.52)—a boy whose sexual development has been artificially arrested by castration, a suitable servant for a man in a state of terminal sexual frustration. But Orsino's and Malvolio's descriptions of Cesario indicate their recognition that he is no eunuch, but an adolescent in the process of growing to sexual maturity, whose mere presence serves as an awakening call to desire for the transfixed characters in the play. Neither male nor female, neither man nor boy, and in the end neither servant nor master, he is a kind of riddle, a pun or double entendre in human form, testifying to the power of comedy as a means of disrupting settled notions and complicating illusory certainties.

The play as a whole is a paean to change, as its full title suggests. The phrase *Twelfth Night* pays homage to a crucial moment of transition in the Elizabethan calendar: the last day of the Christmas festivities, when the celebrations are at their most hilarious as they draw to a close, and when anyone can be "What You Will." *Twelfth Night* extends this moment of transition over many days, and Viola is its presiding spirit, embodying the transitions that are always in process in the human body and mind. At various points in the play, the changes undergone by Viola and her companions look set to be terrible ones, bringing entrapment and death instead of the new life promised by Viola's youth. Melancholy intervenes on many occasions, especially in the songs of the aging clown Feste, which testify to the sorrow that terminates so many transactions between men and women and to the onset of old age and death as the necessary counterweight for the onset of sexual maturity. Even the end of the play is suffused with melancholy, as Malvolio runs off threatening revenge "on the whole pack of you" (5.1.365) and Feste sings his final song alone on stage. But the action as a whole takes place in what Orsino calls a "golden time" (5.1.369)—a time of hope and laughter, like the festival of Christmas. And it's a continuation of this golden time that's predicted in the final scene, when three sets of male/female couples prepare to make a "solemn combination [. . .] Of our dear souls" (5.1.370–71). The play's unsettling emphasis on time, change, and confusion ensures that these final weddings are by no means a return to the "normality" of Elizabethan England, as critics have often described them. Instead, the play makes it possible to believe that there is no such thing as a stable normality where gender is concerned, either in Elizabethan times or in our own.

NOTES

1. All quotations from the play are taken from *The Norton Shakespeare,* ed. Stephen Greenblatt et al. (New York: Norton, 1997).
2. For an account of Elizabethan attacks on the theater, see Jonas A. Barish, *The Antitheatrical Prejudice* (Berkeley: U of California P, 1981). The principal attacks and defenses of the

theater are reproduced in E. K. Chambers, *The Elizabethan Stage*, 4 vols. (Oxford: Clarendon P, 1923) esp. vol. 4, Appendix C ("Documents of Criticism") 184ff., and Appendix D ("Documents of Control") 259ff.

3. See Arthur F. Kinney, ed., *Markets of Bawdrie: The Dramatic Criticism of Stephen Gosson* (Salzburg: Universität Salzburg, 1974) 160.
4. Philip Stubbes, *The Anatomie of Abuses* (1583, reprinted 1595), cited in Chambers 4.223.
5. See John Lyly, *Euphues: The Anatomy of Wit* and *Euphues and His England*, ed. Leah Scragg (Manchester: Manchester UP, 2003) 207.
6. See William Harrison, *The Description of England*, ed. Georges Edelen (New York: Dover Publications, 1994) 237–38.
7. See Bruce R. Smith, *Shakespeare and Masculinity* (Oxford: Oxford UP, 2000) 122–26.
8. See Oscar Wilde, "The Portrait of Mr. W.H.," *The Works of Oscar Wilde*, ed. G. F. Maine (London: Magpie Books, 1992) 1089–112.

READING LIST

Barber, C. L. *Shakespeare's Festive Comedy: A Study of Dramatic Form and Its Relation to Social Custom*. Princeton: Princeton UP, 1959.

Bray, Alan. *Homosexuality in Shakespeare's England*. 2nd ed. New York: Columbia UP, 1995.

Howard, Jean E. "Power and Eros: Cross-dressing in Dramatic Representation and Theatrical Practice." *The Stage and Social Struggle in Early Modern England*. London: Routledge, 1994. 93–128.

Jardine, Lisa. *Still Harping on Daughters: Women and Drama in the Age of Shakespeare*. Hemel Hempstead: Harvester Wheatsheaf, 1989.

Leggatt, Alexander, ed. *The Cambridge Companion to Shakespearean Comedy*. Cambridge: Cambridge UP, 2002.

Levine, Laura. *Men in Women's Clothing: Anti-Theatricality, 1579–1642*. Cambridge: Cambridge UP, 1994.

Neely, Carol Thomas. "Lovesickness, Gender, and Subjectivity: *Twelfth Night* and *As You Like It*." *A Feminist Companion to Shakespeare*. Ed. Dympna Callaghan. Oxford: Blackwell, 2000. 276–98.

Orgel, Stephen. *Impersonations: The Performance of Gender in Shakespeare's England*. Cambridge: Cambridge UP, 1996.

Shapiro, Michael. *Gender in Play on the Shakespearean Stage*. Ann Arbor: U of Michigan P, 1994.

Traub, Valerie. *Desire and Anxiety: Circulations of Sexuality in Shakespearean Drama*. London: Routledge, 1992.

13

Othello and the Moor

Emily C. Bartels

When Shakespeare's *Othello* first appeared in 1604, it was one of the few times a Moor had ever been featured as a central character on the Renaissance stage. George Peele drew initial attention to this new subject in the late 1580s in *The Battle of Alcazar* (c. 1588–89), which dramatizes the historical conflict between two Moors over the Moroccan throne. Between Peele's play and Shakespeare's, no more than a half dozen other representations of the Moor would emerge—including Shakespeare's own depiction of the "incarnate devil" (5.1.40) Aaron in *Titus Andronicus* (1593–94). Yet even within the context of these plays, whose Moors were often notoriously, sometimes jubilantly, bad, *Othello* is unique in presenting a Moor as a complex tragic hero on a par with European figures such as Hamlet, Macbeth, and King Lear.

At the time, and for centuries after, Othello's part would be performed by a white actor. But the character's racial and ethnic identity is registered continually in the script by Venetians who insistently address him as "the Moor." Moreover, that difference was probably signaled further on the stage by a makeup, "the oil of hell," mixed from charred cork and oil, that darkened his skin.[1] In any case, the focus on a Moor as a leading character was no doubt distinctive in 1604—as distinctive as it was when a black actor, Paul Robeson, played the role for the first time before London audiences in 1930 and Broadway audiences in 1943.[2] Robeson's performance boldly challenged the racial segregation supported by mainstream British and American theaters and, according to reviewers, created "such an Othello as may never be found again" (Vaughan 189)—one who, like the Othello of 1604, had never been found before.

If *Othello*'s presentation of the Moor was as remarkable in the seventeenth century as the casting of a black actor was in the twentieth, however, the nature of Shakespeare's innovation was significantly different from Robeson's. For *Othello* emerged before New World slavery had imposed its legacy on evolving race relations and before England would come to read African subjects categorically in the literal and figurative terms of black and white. To be sure, during this period "blackness" was becoming an incriminating sign of racial difference. In Shakespeare's play, for instance, Iago is intent on distinguishing the Moor as malignantly "black" (1.1.88), and both Roderigo and Brabanzio build on his terms. Even the duke, who supports Othello, suggests that the Moor is "far more fair than black" (1.3.289), endorsing blackness as the opposite of what is virtuous and "fair." Yet, as the duke's own comments also imply, Othello himself does not fit a predictable mold. In a move as striking as Robeson's, Shakespeare portrays the Moor as a multidimensional subject who can be neither so clearly segregated out from European society nor so absolutely colored in. In bringing out Othello, Shakespeare brings out the complexities and contradictions within England's vision of the Moor.

Renaissance Africas

To understand what it meant for Renaissance spectators to see a Moor commanding center stage, we need first to understand the cultural geographies that defined Africa during this period. In the nineteenth century, English imperialists would begin to represent the African continent as a "dark" and unified whole, in order to justify English attempts to bring that "darkness" into the light and presumed enlightenment of Europe. In the Renaissance, however, Africa was understood rather as a set of discrete domains, linked to distinctive kinds of people, sometimes more mythic than real. For example, Libya was known for sexually promiscuous "Garamantes," who "contract no matrimonie" and have no "respect to chastity."[3] Ethiopia became proverbially important for "Ethiops" who could not be "washed white," for a Christian emperor ("Prester John") who had been rumored to be living there since the twelfth century (!), for "people without heads, called Blemines, having their eyes and mouth in their breast," and for Anthropophagi, who "are accustomed to eat mans flesh" (Hakluyt 6:168–70). Egypt was famed for being an exotic seat of classical civilization and appeared elusive and alluring, like Shakespeare's Cleopatra, the sexy "serpent of old Nile" (*Ant.* 1.5.26).

These kinds of fantastic figures appeared within fictional and nonfictional accounts of Africa, so much that by Shakespeare's day, they had become exotic set pieces, and almost cliché. When Othello recounts "the story of [his] life" (1.3.128), he invokes these sorts of images, setting his past within a vast and barren terrain peopled by cannibals, "Anthropophagi," and "men whose heads / Do grow beneath their shoulders" (1.3.143–44). Importantly, however, in Shakespeare's play and culture, this landscape is a product of narrative, a sensational story fragmenting Africa into monsters and marvels and not an attempt at ethnography. The response that Othello himself prescribes for such a tale is awe and wonder: he reports that Desdemona, his model audience, "swore in faith 'twas strange, t'was passing strange; / 'Twas pitiful, 'twas wondrous pitiful" (1.3.159–60).

These fantastic representations point primarily to sub-Saharan regions that the English had yet to explore. Yet not all of Africa was "strange" or "wondrous." During Shakespeare's era, England was engaging in firsthand contact with other parts and peoples of Africa, whose representation was therefore more pertinent and "real." Starting in the 1550s, English venturers launched a series of voyages down the west African coast, looking for new trades with the natives ("Negroes") there and for a new route to the East, fabled for extraordinary stores of wealth. Throughout these decades too, England carried on an established trade in North Africa, in Morocco (or "Barbary"), the territory of the Moors. Historical accounts of English contact with these Africas make an important distinction between the two domains, pivoting on the assumption that while west Africa and its Negroes are predominantly "savage," North Africa and its Moors are contrastingly "civilized."

In travel accounts, the land of the Negroes on the western coast appears remote—hard, often dangerous to reach, tainted by disease, unpredictable, unfamiliar, and unyielding in its resources. The English would eventually target its inhabitants for New World slavery (as the Spanish already did). While this future could not have been fully anticipated, early representations tend to depict west Africans in ways that do pave the way for justifications of slavery. In them, Negroes become primitive subjects, isolated from community, custom, and established codes of conduct as well as from contact and communication with the larger world. Religiously, Negroes are likely to be condemned as "infidels." Racially, they are emphasized, in name and image, as characteristically "black," the darkness of their skin taken for a transparent sign of an innate moral darkness.

In contrast, North Africa, especially Morocco, was as an important hub of Mediterranean commerce, providing a gateway both to African trades and to the lucrative East. Queen Elizabeth carried on extensive negotiations for dates, sugar, saltpeter (the raw material of gun powder), and other goods with Morocco. Accordingly, in contemporary representations, Moors stand out as "civilized," if sometimes crafty, heads of state, bargaining with English agents over goods, exchanging letters with the English queen, allowing venturers safe passage through North African domains, and forming alliances and antagonisms with other European nations. While representations of Negroes stress the blackness of that subject, representations of Moors, who might be "tawny," "black," or various shades between, do not always highlight color. More often, Moors are depicted as Muslims, an identity that had both negative and positive connotations. In popular discourse, Muslims were usually incriminated as "infidels." In diplomatic letters to Moroccan rulers, Queen Elizabeth underscores the similarities between Protestant and Islamic faiths—particularly their shared belief in a single God and in a prophet and their antipathy for idolatry.

Tellingly, the most popular book on Africa circulating in England and in English in 1600, and across Europe in a number of languages long before, was *The History and Description of Africa,* written by a Moor, "Leo Africanus" (Al-Hassan Ibn Mohammed Al-Wezâz Al-Fâsi). Africanus had gone to Rome and converted to Catholicism under the aegis of Pope Leo X, but he draws significantly on Islamic authorities and on his own Muslim past to tell Africa's story. John Pory, the English translator of the *History,* anticipates that his readers might find "a More," "a Mahumetan," "unwoorthy to be regarded," and "unfit to undertake such an enterprise."[4] But Pory also praises Africanus for being "extraordinarily learned," not only in "Grammar, Poetrie, Rhetorick, Philosophie, Historie," and other arts and sciences, but also in "all the wisedom [. . .] of the Arabians and Mores" (5). Pory further credits Africanus's Muslim background for giving him leverage in depicting and surviving his travels in Africa. "Had he not at the first beene a More and a Mahumetan in religion," Pory writes, "and most skilfull in the languages and customes of the Arabians and Africans [. . .] I marvell how ever he should have escaped so manie thousands of imminent dangers" (6).

Shakespeare likely modeled his characterization of Othello on the historical Africanus, a sign of the "real" Moor's cultural prominence. The play does not make clear whether or not Othello is, like Africanus, a converted Muslim; Othello obviously knows the rhetoric of Christianity, but he claims no allegiance to any religious faith. Still, although he declares that he can speak "little of this great world" (1.3.86) beyond the battlefield, like Africanus he brings his travels eloquently into Europe as a powerfully seductive tale. Poised uniquely between Europe and Africa, he provides imaginative access to a rich geographical and historical terrain.

Indeed, throughout the play, Othello displays the wide-ranging cultural vision that the Renaissance might expect of the centrally positioned Moor. He not only narrates a past of "battles, sieges, [and] fortunes" across the vast caves, empty deserts, huge mountains, and jagged cliffs of an Africanesque landscape (1.3.129) but also claims that the love token, the handkerchief, he has given to his new wife, Desdemona, was given to his mother by an Egyptian "charmer" (3.4.55). Taking stock of his tragedy at the play's end, he imagines himself as a "base Indian" or, in another version of the text, "Judean" (5.4.356), and as "a malignant and a turbaned Turk" (5.2.362), and he scripts his tears as the "medicinable gum" of "Arabian trees" (5.2.359–60). And, of course, at the beginning of the play, Othello marries a Venetian wife. If *Othello* is any indication, when Shakespeare and England look to the Moor, they look to a subject who—like Leo Africanus—was likely to be connected across the globe.

The Moor in Europe

One subtitle of Shakespeare's play names Othello "the Moor of Venice," and throughout the play the Moor is deeply embedded within Venetian society. Othello may have come to Venice in the role of a mercenary soldier, hired to defend Venice and its colonies against the Turks or other imperialist aggressors. When the play opens, however, he has not been fighting for nine months; instead, he has remained in Venice, engaging Desdemona and her father, Brabanzio, with stories of his ventures, courting and—just before the play begins—eloping with that "fair" Venetian maid (1.1.123). From the beginning until the end of his story, Othello is evaluated in terms of what would or would not "be believed in Venice" (4.1.237)—not in Africa. But what does it mean for the Moor to be "of Venice"? What is at stake for English audiences and for this English play?

Although there were probably no Moors residing permanently in England during Shakespeare's lifetime, they were nonetheless not strangers to the English. English agents lived for extended periods in Morocco to mediate the trade between England and North Africa. In addition, during the Renaissance, Moorish ambassadors made a number of prominent state visits to London. The English could also have encountered Moors across the European continent. Moors had long been subjects of Spain and, as *Othello* suggests, were integrated within other parts of Europe and the Mediterranean. It is perhaps no wonder, then, that Moors were the African subjects who preoccupied Renaissance playwrights at a historical moment when England was seeking ways to make a name for itself through all the world. Notably, the Renaissance plays featuring Moors center either on Europeans who find their fortunes in North Africa or on Moors who live in Europe. In them, instead of being an exotic outsider, the Moor is more often a controversial insider within Euro-Mediterranean domains.

If Moors served as useful liaisons between England, Europe, and non-European domains beyond, their presence across Europe also raised questions about the stability of cultural boundaries and the purity of cultural identity. In Spain, these kinds of questions were coming to a head just when *Othello* emerged. Until the end of the fifteenth century, Moors had been so fully integrated into Spanish society that it was impossible to separate the history of the Moors from the history of Spain.[5] But as the Spanish Inquisition became intent on policing and promoting the purity of the Catholic state and as Spanish imperialists became invested in publicizing Spain's national supremacy, Spanish authorities began to treat the Muslim presence as a source of crisis. Moors were first ostracized as "infidels," their religious practices outlawed; then, they were forced to convert to Christianity, to assimilate into Christian society as "Moriscos" or "little Moors."[6] Yet that conversion could not guarantee belief; it could only legislate the *performance* of belief. The possibility that Moors were simply "passing" as Christians raised the unsettling possibility that other Christians were merely passing too (Root 127). Hence, to erase the very visible reminder of the inscrutable invisibility of faith, the Moriscos were first condemned as Christian "heretics" and, starting in 1609, were officially expelled from Spain (Root 129).

Shakespeare may or may not have seen this expulsion coming in 1604, though it was clearly long in the making. But *Othello* is provocatively dotted with Spanish resonances, especially in the names "Roderigo" and "Iago," which calls up "Sant-Iago, the patron saint of Spain."[7] And the play does emphasize that the Moor within Europe is in a uniquely vulnerable position, that his place within the host society is finally not his own. When we first see Othello, he is being called to court doubly, for conflicting purposes. On the one hand, the Senate and the duke "require" Othello's "haste-post-haste appearance / Even on the instant" (1.2.37–38) to enlist his military leadership against the Turks, who are advancing on Cyprus. On the other, Brabanzio demands that Othello answer charges that he has seduced Desdemona with witchcraft. While the Senate would send the Moor to Cyprus, the irate father would have him confined to prison. Yet these two agendas are not entirely different. In both cases, Othello's movements are being urgently monitored, his autonomy compromised. The Senate has sent "three several quests / To search [Othello] out" (1.2.46–47), and when we first see him, a fourth approaches. Meanwhile, Brabanzio is accompanied by officers who can "subdue" the Moor "at his peril" (1.2.82). Othello himself declares that he "must be found" (1.2.30)—as if he understands that to be "of Venice" is to be ever subject to its terms. When he steps aside for a moment en route, to "spend but a word here in the house" with, we assume, his new wife, he takes only ("but") a word for himself (1.2.48).

For the Moor more than for other subjects, to be *found* in Venice is potentially to be *found out*—to be called not only to duty but also to question. To be sure, in the highest reaches of court, the Senate and the duke embrace the Moor as a "valiant" general (1.3.48). Even after Othello murders Desdemona, Lodovico, a representative of the Venetian court, remembers Othello as one "that was once so good" and condemns Iago—and not the Moor—as a "cursed slave" (5.2.297–98). Yet within the margins of society, Othello is repeatedly slandered by alienated figures who have been displaced from power or prominence—Iago, the ensign, from a post as Othello's lieutenant; Roderigo, the nobleman, from a chance as Desdemona's suitor; and Brabanzio, the senator, from involvement in a crucial meeting of the Senate. Together, they attempt to transform the Moor into an alien Other, projecting their disenfranchised status onto him, each for his own self-interested end. Iago declares Othello a "devil," an "old black ram" currently "tupping" Brabanzio's "white ewe" (1.1.92, 89–90). Roderigo asserts that Desdemona has fallen into "the gross clasps of a lascivious Moor," and expresses outrage that she would tie "her duty, beauty, wit, and fortunes"—which he himself desires—"in an extravagant and wheeling stranger" (1.1.125, 134–35). And Brabanzio, startled that his own daughter would "run from her guardage" under him to the Moor's "sooty bosom" (1.2.71), takes his problem to the court, where he accuses the "foul thief" Othello (1.2.63) of seducing her with witchcraft.

The duke and the Senate hope the charges will prove to be no more than the "thin habits and poor likelihoods / Of modern seeming" (1.2.108–09)—at least in part because Venice needs desperately to deploy the Moor against the Turks. The duke, in fact, offers to let Brabanzio throw "the bloody book of law" at "whoe'er he be" that "hath thus beguiled" Desdemona (1.3.65–68), until Brabanzio discloses Othello as the offender. We will never know how the court would have responded were its territories not threatened by the Turks, since Venice's relation to the Moor is defined by that contingency. All we know is that, under these circumstances, the Senate and duke are willing to overlook social transgressions they would otherwise condemn. Still, although the state's political need for the Moor seems to trump the social protests of its own alienated citizens, Brabanzio's allegations are enough to interrupt urgent state business and to require that Othello clear his name. Thus, even with the Turkish threat building in the offing, Othello's seduction of his Venetian wife comes under public scrutiny—in a way that Roderigo's hope to have her or Cassio's desire to watch Othello "make love's quick pants in Desdemona's arms" (2.1.81) does not.

In the end, then, Shakespeare's Moor of Venice stands in a potentially precarious position within a society that itself has many factions. For the Moor to be embraced by the state provides no guarantee that he will be embraced by all Venetians, just as for him to be rejected by certain Venetians provides no guarantee that he will be rejected by the state. Othello is confident that the "services" he has "done the signory / Shall out-tongue [Brabanzio's] complaints" (1.2.18–19), and he is almost ready to divulge what he has kept in check, that he takes his "life and being / From men of royal siege" (1.2.21–22). Even so, it is the Moor—and not Venice's own underhanded citizens—who must answer the "special officers of the night" (1.1.183) and explain his "own part" when, or whenever, the court so orders (1.3.74).

The Domestic Parallel: Women and Moors

In act 2, Shakespeare takes away the political cushion that ensures the Moor's place in Venice. Although Turkish forces held Cyprus at the time the play was written and so posed an impending threat in the Mediterranean, in the play the Turks are destroyed by a storm at sea before they—and Othello—ever reach Cyprus. In revising history thus, Shakespeare turns our attention from the political to the domestic, leaving the Moor in Cyprus without an "occupation" (3.3.362). Othello's position there is defined instead by a Venetian wife and a Venetian Vice, who wants to see the Moor "damned in a fair wife," as (Iago suggests) Cassio "almost" is (1.1.20). This shift highlights the difference between the Moor's *political* position within Europe and his *social* place. It is one thing, the play suggests, to embrace the Moor as a military or economic ally, providing global access or defense, and another to accept him as an integrated citizen, intermingling socially and sexually with Europeans. At the heart of the derogations against the Moor is the marital bond that transforms the hired outsider (if he has been a mercenary soldier) into a legal insider. If Othello's position as a military leader gives him important leverage and license within the high circles of the Venetian court, his marriage to Desdemona, in contrast, makes him vulnerable to attack, especially from figures on the outs, looking for some way—some scapegoat—to advance their own positions or to enact their private revenge.

It is no small point that, instead of simply derogating the Moor for being a Moor, a foreigner, a cultural Other, or a black man, the master manipulator Iago works by indirection and first targets Othello's wife. That is, in order to coerce the "valiant" Othello into behavior that "would not be believed in Venice," to turn him into a Moor like Aaron, who "will have his soul black like his face" (*Tit.* 3.1.204), Iago chooses to tarnish Desdemona's reputation and turn the "honest" (i.e., "chaste") wife into a "whore" (3.3.230; 4.2.165). While he can then use her defamed image to prejudice the Moor against her, the reverse is not true: Desdemona sees Othello as her "kind lord" (5.2.133) until she takes her last breath. Given Iago's predatory shrewdness, what is provocatively suggested by his modus operandi is that slandering a woman is finally easier, potentially more persuasive and effective, than slandering a Moor. The play, in fact, establishes a crucial parallel between the Moor and the woman, each of whom can be made credibly suspect.[8]

Shakespeare, in fact, bends his source to put Desdemona in a compromising position, as a daughter who eloped, and so to emphasize that the regulation and demonization of daughters—and not just of Moors—is at stake here. The Othello story comes from a sixteenth-century Italian collection, *Hecatommithi,* by Giraldi Cinthio. There, "Disdemona" "consented to marry" "the Moor," although her parents "strove all they could to induce her to take another husband."[9] Even so, there is no indication that the marriage was secret or problematic. Cinthio stresses rather the temporary happy ending: the couple live in "harmony and peace" until the Moor is "dispatched" to Cyprus and faces the unhappy possibility of leaving Disdemona behind. In Shakespeare, however, Desdemona elopes with Othello and hence is called to question thereby for disobedience.

In Shakespeare's Venice—as in Renaissance England, where women were taught to be "chaste, silent, and obedient"—disobeying a father is at least as serious a problem as marrying a Moor. We know what happens when Shakespeare's Juliet (already secretly married to Romeo) refuses her father's request that she marry Paris: Lord Capulet warns that if she does not, she can "hang, beg, starve, die in the streets" and he will "ne'er acknowledge" her (*Rom.* 3.5.192–93). Desdemona clearly realizes the danger of such filial disobedience and, in order to exonerate herself before the court, insists that she has done her "duty," "preferring" her new husband over her father, just as her mother did (1.3.185–86) and just as Renaissance women of a certain age (somewhere between sixteen and twenty-five) were supposed to do. Strategically, however, she glosses over the facts that (we assume) do not follow her mother's precedent and that (she anticipates) have made her marriage questionable: that she *eloped* and with a *Moor.*

Tellingly, her father objects to both. As we have seen, Brabanzio castigates Othello as the source of seduction, corruption, and theft and presents Desdemona, accordingly, as the victim—"a maiden never bold," bewitched against her will by "what she feared to look on" (1.3.94, 98). Alternately, though, Brabanzio also condemns his daughter for "deceiv[ing] [him] / Past thought" (1.1.166–67) and committing an unconscionable "treason of the blood" (1.1.170). Because of her, he cautions fathers to "trust not your daughters' minds" (1.1.171) and warns Othello to "look to her," since "she has deceived her father, and may thee" (1.3.291–92). If Brabanzio "loved" Othello, "oft invited" (1.3.127) him to his house (as Othello claims) even while admittedly anticipating in dream that his daughter and the Moor might run off together, we can only wonder whether the father's disenchantment with the Moor came before or after Desdemona's elopement and whether the elopement was the effect or the cause. Either way, Desdemona stands beside Othello under the shadow of social rebuke, the targeted Venetian beside the targeted Moor, similarly subject to suspicion, scrutiny, and judgment.

That shadow also hangs over Desdemona's position as wife and contributes to the distrust and jealousy Iago will pour into Othello's thoughts. Conceptually, if not actually, in the Renaissance marriage was the thing that could put the female voice and body "into circumscription and confine" (1.2.27), the woman's obedience transferred, with her dowry, from father to husband. Yet symbolically, marriage was also the thing that unleashed desire or "appetite," with the supposedly sexually inactive, virginal daughter becoming a sexually active, though sexually faithful ("chaste") wife. Accompanying that release was a fear that, once set loose, the female sexual body could not be restrained. Notice how ready Othello is to understand "that we can call these delicate creatures ours / And not their appetites" as the "curse of marriage" (3.3.272–73); how quickly he leaps from suspecting that his own wife has committed adultery with one man (Cassio) to imagining a hypothetical scenario of all his soldiers, "the general camp," "tast[ing] her sweet body" (3.3.350–51); and how intently he believes that "she must die, else she'll betray more men" (5.2.6).

Othello presents his own desire, in contrast, as utterly controlled. He supports Desdemona's request to go to Cyprus only, he says, "to be free and bounteous to her mind" and explicitly not "to please the palate of [his] appetite" (1.3.264, 261). With absolute confidence, he assures the court that the "light-winged toys / Of feathered Cupid" will not "taint" his military "business" (1.3.266–67, 268). It may be that the Moor protests too much—that he is defending himself against being stereotyped as a "lascivious Moor" or is revealing his own discomfort with desire. But if the play is opening a window into Othello's peculiar psyche, helping us understand why the Moor is particularly susceptible to Iago's lies, in the process it also scripts him into the patriarchal mainstream. In his eyes and in Venice's, while regulating *male* desire seems possible and plausible, regulating *female* desire does not. After all, although Emilia is tragically loyal to Iago (stealing the handkerchief that will falsely incriminate Desdemona), even she imagines that she might cuckold her husband "for all the whole world" (4.3.73).

In telling Desdemona's story and recording Iago's lies, Shakespeare critiques the *suspicion* of female wantonness (not female wantonness itself) as a destructive social force that leaves no safe space for the expression of female desire. In act 3, Desdemona chides Othello for treating her request that he meet with Cassio as a "boon," a favor, and then warns him: "when I have a suit, / Wherein I mean to touch your love indeed, / It shall be full of poise and difficult weight, / And fearful to be granted" (3.3.77, 81–84). Significantly, Iago's nefarious suggestions stick in Othello's mind after this exchange in a way that they have not before. For Desdemona to speak desire is for her to feed the fear of female sexuality that genders Venice and makes her as vulnerable as the Moor.

It is, of course, Othello who learns to distrust her, who, with Iago's prodding, voices suspicions that Venice might otherwise repress. Yet while Iago is invested in destroying the *literal* connection between the Moor and his "fair" wife, Shakespeare is interested in exploring the *metaphoric* connection—in looking at the Moor not primarily as a political subject, defined by Venice's imperialist aggression and defense, but as a domestic subject, whose simultaneous embrace and alienation within Venice parallel that of his wife. In the end, the story of the Moor *is* the story of Venice. His uneasy and uneven integration into Venice provides a template for understanding the place of his Venetian wife. To read Othello's story through Desdemona, hers through him, is to see that social fear, discrimination, and regulation do not fall exclusively along axes of black and white, Venetian and Moor. Within Venice itself, social standing is constantly up for grabs, with gender proving as precarious a differentiation as culture, ethnicity, or race. And if the Moor can be scripted as the alien within, that distinction proves him like, rather than unlike, Venice's women.

Creating Closure: Discrimination, Blackness, and Race

While slandering Desdemona, Iago simultaneously attempts to blacken Othello's image of himself, using race against the Moor in the same way that he uses sexuality against the Moor's wife. As a result, the more Othello doubts Desdemona's chastity, the more he speaks of himself as "black." Yet reading racial difference in this play is not as simple as Iago would have us—and Othello—believe. Tellingly, since the seventeenth century, critics and directors have struggled over how to depict Othello, whether as African or Arabian, "black" or "tawny." Witness the choices documented in the last fifty some years of film. In a 1952 film noir, Orson Welles played an Orientalized Othello, turbaned like an Arabian, his skin color lightened or darkened by strategic lighting to match his changing his moral demeanor. In 1964, Sir Laurence Olivier performed the part in black makeup and transformed the Moor into a colonized, Christianized West Indian. In 1995, Laurence Fishburne portrayed Othello as a continental African, his skin indelibly tatooed with the exotic signs of his culture. And in the 1997 film *O,* Mekhi Phifer turned Othello into Odin James, a black American basketball player headed to the NBA, situated in an elite white preparatory school in the South.

Some of these representational choices do stretch Shakespeare's play beyond the historical and geographical reach available to the Renaissance, by engaging a New World future that was not fully in place. Still, each derives partly from the Moor within the text, who associates himself with Egypt, Arabia, the East and Middle East, Europe, and Africa *and* declares his face "begrimed and black" (3.3.392). Together these representations underscore the difficulty of fitting the Renaissance Moor into a single image of "race." If the play brings a number of cultural markers to bear on the Moor's characterization, why then is Othello ultimately ready to understand himself as "black"? If blackness distinguished west Africa's Negroes from north Africa's Moors, how did Moors get meshed into a generic category of black subjects? Given the Moors' integration within cultures across the globe, how did England draw the line on difference?

At the same time that England attempted to extend its cross-cultural outreach and establish its prominence in the world, its efforts were marked by a contradictory impulse to reaffirm its own cultural boundaries and, literally and figuratively, to separate black from white. This kind of color-coding was relatively new as a strategy for marking race.

During the Renaissance, the idea of a "race" was remarkably varied and could indicate links of family, lineage, species, and humanity, as well as internal disposition. Instead of functioning primarily to mark distinctions *between* cultures, it as frequently denoted particular groups within a single culture or populations common to all cultures. Shakespeare, for example, makes reference to the "whole race of mankind" (*Tim.* 4.1.39–40), the "happy race of kings" (*R3* 5.5.106), the "lawful race" of a Roman family (*Ant.* 3.13.107), the "sensual race" of a character's passions (*MM* 2.4.160), and the "wanton herd / Or race of youthful and unhandled colts" (*MV* 5.1.71–72). Moreover, since the Crusades, religion had been the key determinant of racial identity—with Christian Europe defining itself relentlessly against the "infidel," Muslim, or Jew.

Because these designations relied on largely invisible features, they were therefore unstable, uncertain, and often indecipherable (as we have seen in the case of Spain). In contrast, skin color provided a clearer way to separate the European from the non-European, the Venetian from the Moor. Perhaps consequently, during this period the English became especially preoccupied with understanding the origins and implications of "black" skin, and they began to use a discourse of blackness to distill and clarify the Anglo-African divide. For a nation interested in suggesting the superiority of white Europeans in a culturally mixed-up world, the denotation of "blackness" provided invaluable "ocular proof" of difference (3.3.365) and had as its advantage a long-established association with evil.

In the decade before *Othello* was written, Queen Elizabeth herself participated in collapsing the Moor into an incriminating category of blackness, even as she was forging important trade relations with Morocco's rulers. In a series of proclamations, she ordered that certain "blackamoors" be deported from England as part of a prisoner exchange with Spain. Yet in at least one case, the subjects in question were not Moors at all but actually west African Negroes, captured from Spanish colonies in the New World. From what we can tell, they were living in England as servants, and their masters were reluctant to give them up (probably because to replace them with English workers would cost more). In coaxing the involved Englishmen to support deportation, Elizabeth represented the targeted subjects as "blackamoors," a term that was never consistently applied to any particular African culture, but that obviously invoked the Moor, and as "Negars and Blackamoors."[10] Whatever this misnomer did to further her cause against the Negroes, the confusion of Moor with Negro produced a new category of "blacks," which the queen then scripted further as the "infidel." While Moors were not the object of these measures, they became, with Negroes, the subject—the *black* subject.

It was arguably because Moors were able to move seamlessly between European and non-European domains that they were drawn into England's attempts to color-code cultural difference. In *Othello,* Iago works to reduce Othello's suggestive reach, as both a figure and a maker of figures, by shifting the Moor's focus, and ours, from cultures to color. He works, that is, to detach Othello's identity from the worldliness that defies classification and to attach it rather to a blackness that all too clearly signals evil. Iago presents himself as someone who knows (as the Moor, he implies, does not) about Venice's "country disposition" (3.3.205), and he reminds Othello that in marrying a Moor, Desdemona unnaturally dismissed suitors "of her own clime, complexion, and degree" (3.3.235). With Iago influencing him thus, Othello begins to imagine that Desdemona is "gone" (3.3.271) because he himself is "black, / And [has] not those soft parts of conversation that chamberers have" (3.3.268–69). No longer sure that he can charm his way around Venetian society, with the "soft parts of conversation" he has exhibited before, Othello sees and critiques himself rather as "black." We, however, see more. In *Othello,* to depict the Moor as a black subject is not to *describe* him objectively; it is, rather, to *circumscribe* him subjectively, for self-serving ends.

Thus, like the Moors of Shakespeare's time, Othello is caught between a discourse that displays his familiarity with a number of cultures and discrimination that colors him in as predictably "black." In bringing the figure of the Moor to center stage, Shakespeare is clearly interested in what drives the dynamic interplay between the two. At the end of the play, Othello asks Lodovico to "speak of me as I am" (5.2.351). And in the end, what makes this play particularly fascinating, its theatrical possibilities rich, its story timeless, and its hero similar to Hamlet, Macbeth, and Lear, is that it refuses to nail Othello categorically down, forcing us rather to take him on and in his own terms. However much the discourse of gender may approximate his vulnerability, and however much the discourse of race may blacken his self-image, in *Othello* as in Renaissance culture, the Moor's uniqueness hinges on the fact that, instead of being easy to read, characterize, classify, and contain, he is intriguingly *not.*

NOTES

1. See Dympna Callaghan, *Shakespeare Without Women: Representing Gender and Race on the Renaissance Stage* (New York: Routledge, 2000) 78.
2. See Virginia Mason Vaughan, *"Othello": A Contextual History* (Cambridge: Cambridge UP, 1994) 181–82.
3. See Richard Hakluyt, *The Principal Navigation, Voyages, Traffiques & Discoveries of the English Nation.* 12 vols. (Glasgow: James Maclehose and Sons, 1903–05); quote vol. 6, p. 168.
4. See John Pory, "To the Reader," *The History and Description of Africa,* by Al-Hassan Ibn-Mohammed Al-Wezâz Al-Fâsi, ed. Robert Brown (New York, 1846) 4.
5. See Barbara Fuchs, "Virtual Spaniards: The Moriscos and the Fictions of Spanish Identity," *Journal of Spanish Cultural Studies* 2 (2001): 13–26.
6. See Deborah Root, "Speaking Christian: Orthodoxy and Difference in Sixteenth-Century Spain," *Representations* 23 (1988): 118–34, esp. 119–23.
7. See Eric Griffin, "Unsainting James: Or, *Othello* and the "Spanish Spirits" of Shakespeare's Globe," *Representations* 62 (1998): 58–99, esp. 68.
8. See Karen Newman, "'And Wash the Ethiop White': Femininity and the Monstrous in *Othello,*" *Critical Essays on Shakespeare's "Othello,"* ed. Anthony Gerard Barthelemy (New York: G. K. Hall, 1994): 124–43.
9. See Alvin Kernan, ed., *The Tragedy of Othello, the Moor of Venice* (New York: New American Library, 1963) 171–86, esp. 172.
10. See Eldred D. Jones, *The Elizabethan Image of Africa* (Charlottesville: U of Virginia P, 1971) 20.

READING LIST

Bartels, Emily C. "Imperialist Beginnings: Richard Hakluyt and the Construction of Africa." *Criticism* 34 (1992): 517–37.

———. "Making More of the Moor: Aaron, Othello, and Renaissance Refashionings of Race." *Shakespeare Quarterly* 41 (1990): 433–54.

Barthelemy, Anthony Gerard, ed. *Critical Essays on Shakespeare's "Othello."* New York: G. K. Hall, 1994.

Burton, Jonathan. "'A Most Wily Bird': Leo Africanus, *Othello* and the Trafficking in Difference." *Post-colonial Shakespeares.* Ed. Ania Loomba and Martin Orkin. London: Routledge. 43–63.

Cohen, Walter. "The Undiscovered Country: Shakespeare and Mercantile Geography." *Marxist Shakespeares.* Ed. Jean E. Howard and Scott Cutler Shershow. London: Routledge, 2001. 128–58.

Greenblatt, Stephen. *Renaissance Self-fashioning from More to Shakespeare.* Chicago: U of Chicago P, 1980. 222–54.

Hall, Kim F. *Things of Darkness: Economies of Race and Gender in Early Modern England.* Ithaca: Cornell UP, 1995.

Hendricks, Margo, and Patricia Parker, eds. *Women, "Race," and Writing in the Early Modern Period.* London: Routledge, 1994.

Little, Arthur L., Jr. *Shakespeare Jungle Fever: National-Imperial Re-visions of Race, Rape, and Sacrifice.* Stanford: Stanford UP, 2000. 68–101.

Matar, Nabil. *Turks, Moors, and Englishmen in the Age of Discovery.* New York: Columbia UP, 1999.

Neill, Michael, "'Mulattos,' 'Blacks,' and 'Indian Moors': *Othello* and Early Modern Constructions of Human Difference." *Shakespeare Quarterly* 49 (1998): 361–74.

Orlin, Lena Cowen, ed. *New Casebooks "Othello": Contemporary Critical Essays.* Houndmills: Palgrave, 2003.

Stolcke, Verena. "Invaded Women: Gender, Race, and Class in the Formation of Colonial Society." In Hendricks and Parker. 272–86.

Wayne, Valerie. "Historical Differences: Misogyny and *Othello*." *The Matter of Difference: Materialist Feminist Criticism of Shakespeare.* Ed. Valerie Wayne. Ithaca: Cornell UP, 1991. 153–79.

14

The Masque of Blackness and Stuart Court Culture

Martin Butler

Ben Jonson's *Masque of Blackness* is sometimes thought of as the seminal Stuart masque, but it was only the latest—albeit the most important—of six festival shows presented to the court during the first two years of James I's reign. Two masques were staged during the 1604–05 Christmas season: *Blackness,* danced in the Banqueting House on Twelfth Night 1605, and *Hymenaeus and the Four Seasons,* a wedding masque staged in the Hall at Whitehall by the earl of Pembroke for the marriage of his brother Philip Herbert, the king's English favorite, on December 27. The previous Christmas, which was kept at Hampton Court, there were no less than three masques. The first, on New Year's Day 1604, was a masque of Indian and Chinese knights sponsored by the duke of Lennox; then on Twelfth Night came a "masquerade" of Scotsmen, who danced a "matachin" or sword dance;[1] and on January 8 the court saw Samuel Daniel's *The Vision of the Twelve Goddesses,* in which Queen Anne herself led the masquers. Earlier still, at Winchester in October 1603, the queen and her women had presented "a gallant mask" to Prince Henry, to much tutting from gossips who felt that "the ladies about the court had gotten such ill names that it was grown a scandalous place, and the Queen herself was much fallen from her former greatness and reputation." Although little is known about this, technically it was the first Stuart masque.[2] And beside these six events, during the same period the royal family saw theatrical presentations as they traveled around their new kingdom: the *Entertainment at Althorp,* staged in June 1603 by Sir Robert Spencer as the queen and Prince Henry passed through Northamptonshire; the London welcome for the king, queen, and prince in March 1604, written by Dekker, Jonson, and Middleton; and the private show presented to the king and queen at Highgate in May 1604 by the earl of Salisbury. Amongst all these ceremonials, *The Masque of Blackness* was a landmark occasion. It was the first masque by Ben Jonson and Inigo Jones—both central figures in the future history of court culture—and the first for which any identifiable music survives. But as the narrative of these seasons suggests, the festival culture of Stuart Whitehall was a complex business, created by a diverse body of artists and patrons, and serving many social and political ends. Even artists of the caliber of Jonson and Jones were only individual players, albeit weighty ones, in the joint enterprise of celebrating and proclaiming Stuart kingship.

Masques were the most collaborative of forms, and the various meanings of *The Masque of Blackness* cannot be understood without extensive knowledge of the web of social customs, political expectations, and artistic patronage that determined masquing practice. The arrival of the Stuarts at Whitehall in 1603 had been the signal for radical transformations in the face of the court and its festivals. Elizabeth had often seen ad hoc entertainments in the countryside as she went on summer progresses, and she leavened

Christmas with plays and occasional "feats of activity" by visiting troupes of actors. James, though, would inhabit a festival culture of far greater state and cost. After the financial shock of the first Stuart Christmas, the Privy Council remonstrated with him to remember Elizabeth's parsimony and avoid making masques a habit,[3] but they quickly became a customary part of court life. Over the next twenty years the court saw more than eighty entertainments, large and small. Twelfth Night became the high point of the calendar, on which a grand masque was usually performed, with shows, music, and dancing that lasted into the early hours, and which was funded by the king or queen. Occasionally masques were staged on New Year's Day or Shrovetide: in the next reign King Charles commonly presented a masque of men on Twelfth Night and Henrietta Maria replied with a masque of ladies on Shrove Tuesday. Important weddings, like those of the earls of Essex (1606) and Somerset (1613), were celebrated with masques and sometimes tilts or chivalric exercises: the advantage of such ceremonials was that the families or friends paid the bill. More important were great state occasions, such as the visit of the king of Denmark (1606), the investiture of the prince of Wales (1610), and the marriage of Princess Elizabeth (1613), which gave occasion for extended festival sequences. Prince Henry's investiture was celebrated by a masque (*Tethys' Festival*), a civic welcome, a chivalric tournament, and parliamentary ceremonials that had been specially invented for the occasion.[4] In addition, more traditional kinds of events continued to flourish. For all James's incompetence with a lance, tilts were held annually on Accession Day down to 1624: these usually lacked the theatrical pageantry of Elizabethan tournaments, but Henry tilted enthusiastically, and lavish celebrations were mounted for Prince Charles's first tilt in 1620. To this was added the day-to-day ceremonial of court life: the receptions and dismissals of ambassadors, the Garter feasts on St. George's Day, the exchanging of New Year's gifts, touching for the King's Evil, banquets, christenings, bear-baitings, and the like. For all that James and Charles have been seen as more remote monarchs than the Tudors, they lived out their lives in the full glare of publicity.

What had changed was a new estimate of the usefulness of ceremonial in projecting the wealth and power of the court. Masques were expensive, but they made a statement, and they did so before audiences that combined a cross-section of England's social elites—the aristocrats and gentlemen who constituted the "political nation"—with invited guests from the community of foreign diplomats and agents residing in London. The diplomats were notoriously punctilious about the honor shown to them, and preparations for every masque were consumed by negotiations about invitations and seating, and a perennial fog of complaint over precedence. Ridiculous though this now seems, it testifies to a shared perception that the political stakes in the performances were high. The invitations to ambassadors could be read for signs of friendship or enmity, and many of the masques' fables carried symbolic messages about the English position on overseas affairs—particularly the marriage masques for Princess Elizabeth, and texts such as Jonson's *News from the New World* (1620) and *Neptune's Triumph for the Return of Albion* (1624; unperformed), written during a decade when there was a serious chance of England being drawn into a European war. At the beginning of the reign, masques celebrated the shift from Elizabethan warmongering to James's new posture of friendship with Spain. *The Masque of Blackness* was used to honor the Spanish ambassador, who was seated by the king and invited to dance publicly with Queen Anne.

No less central was the impression of magnificence and sophistication that masques conveyed to the international community as a whole. The models for Stuart festivity were the great competitor courts, Paris and Madrid, or the smaller Italian city-states such as Florence, which had long-established traditions of festival performance, and where the idea was instilled that theatrical display was a mark of dynastic splendor, the state's artistic accomplishment manifesting its civility and power. A year after *The Masque of Blackness* was performed, James tore down the temporary wooden Banqueting House bequeathed by Elizabeth and replaced it with a permanent stone hall more suitable for the ceremonials of the new dynasty; and when in 1619 this burned down, he rebuilt it again, as the magnificent Palladian structure that remains in Whitehall today. Moreover, the architect, Inigo Jones, made two visits to Italy and systematically incorporated Italian festival designs into his masque sketches: for example, scenes in *Chloridia* (1631), *Albion's Triumph* (1632), and *Britannia Triumphans* (1638) were based on prints of designs by the Florentine architect Giulio Parigi. The masques were thus one means by which the Stuarts drew attention to themselves as monarchs with whom to be reckoned. Masques validated their rule in European terms and made it visible in the international iconography of kingship.

For domestic audiences, masques were occasions that affirmed their place in the great social pyramid over which the king presided and which the hierarchical arrangement of the masquing space presented in miniature. Spectators attending the Banqueting House were joining a class ritual that staged their ties of obligation to the crown while validating their identity as members of the community from which they took their social and psychological bearings. With all the material ostentation that masques involved—such as the expectation that spectators should deck themselves with jewelry and finery so that they contributed to the evening's conspicuous display of prodigality—there must have been a strong sense of participation in a horizontal peer group, and a nice awareness of the vertical discriminations that structured the court. Unsurprisingly, access to the limited seating in the halls was hotly contested and was policed by court officials who sometimes enforced the line between ins and outs with brute force.

For the performers themselves, who were usually aristocrats or high-status gentry who had offices at Whitehall or intimate ties to it, this issue was even more defining. Masque fables were typically couched as expressions of devotion to the king, so that performances symbolically encoded the dependence of masquer on monarch; and since the dancing floor offered limitless opportunities for displaying physical prowess under the royal gaze, masquers might literally dance themselves into favor. This was famously the case in Jonson's *Pleasure Reconciled to Virtue* (1618), when the marquis of Buckingham saved an evening during which the king had started to drift into boredom by cutting capers so athletic that they resurrected his interest and led to renewed expressions of affection for him. More generally, when masques were written for presentation to the prince (rather than for princes themselves to dance), they often thematized the reciprocal bond between master and servant. So Jonson's *Mercury Vindicated from the Alchemists at Court* (1615) turns on a contrast between the monsters that the impoverished alchemists produce, with a bastardized "art" (6, 17) that they boast can rival nature, and the perfect "creatures" (206) who are bred by the king's sunlike power.[5] Not only was this was a suitable theme for the first occasion on which Buckingham danced, but all the masquers must have felt implicated in it. The performance played out the ties of brotherhood and amity amongst the king's servants, while giving expression to the underlying competition between them.

The masques were ideally attuned to articulating the internationalist and pacific ideology of the Jacobean state. James was an ambitious, outward-looking, and modernizing monarch, who understood that joint possession of the English and Scottish crowns made him a force with whom to be reckoned. His desire for union of the realms was not just a vanity project but a response to the new British identity that Stuart succession created, in which the whole island's dignity, history, and prestige were contained. Although in the short term constitutional union was wrecked by antagonisms between the nations, the idea of British identity, and the prosperity and stability which it promised, became deeply ingrained: as we shall see, in *The Masque of Blackness* it was the central ideological motif. At the same time, James was keen to promote peace overseas and to bind together a continent riven by religious and dynastic rivalries. Although a firm Protestant, he never allowed himself to appear a saintly champion of the faith, like Elizabeth; rather, he wanted to counteract religious disagreements by fostering alliances that were indifferent to theology. He wedded his daughter to a Protestant German prince, but much of the reign was spent cultivating friendship with Spain and pursuing a Spanish marriage for Prince Charles that would cement European peace by bridging the confessional divide. Peace with Spain was good for trade, and it kept England out of wars she could not afford; moreover, the Habsburg monarchies were models for the kind of dignified kingship that James admired, in which social order went hand in hand with respect for sovereignty. Unsurprisingly, his masques tended to reflect these ideological preferences and used a visual language that was classicizing and imperial rather than nationalistic and sectarian. They represented James as a peaceful but powerful prince who was physically and symbolically the very embodiment of British identity, and who (in later years) was the one stable point in an increasingly vexed Europe. Masques like *Time Vindicated* (1623), with its crowd of ignorant antimasquers trying to interfere in public affairs, disparaged the excesses of popular enthusiasm in favor of firm, far-seeing kingship. They also promoted attitudes of deference and obedience toward the crown. The structural contrast between the serene dancing of the aristocratic main masquers and the amusing but unruly intrusions of the socially inferior antimasquers displayed what the values of good government should be. James's kingship was legitimized in terms of its wisdom, competence, and, above all, social control.

James's other distinguishing characteristic, immediately apparent in 1603–04, was his status as patriarch of a large family. Elizabeth's sovereignty had been enshrined in a brittle and emasculating cult of virginity, but James was a virile male whose authority expressed itself as fatherhood, domestically in the court and symbolically in the nation. His culture repeatedly put his body on show, emphasizing his masculine power and sexual productivity: as political father he commanded the lives of his subjects, while biologically his progeny meant that the succession was at last assured. In the speeches presented at his formal entry in London, he was hymned as a conquering Augustus, irresistibly penetrating his city and receiving testimonials of burning desire; in *Hymenaei* (1606), the marriage masque for the earl of Essex, the songs acknowledged the "better blisses" of king and queen, who had "proved the strict embrace / Of Union, with chaste kisses, / And seen it flow so in your happy race." Such erotic emphases were even stronger in the next reign, in masques like *Love's Triumph Through Callipolis* (1631) or

Coelum Britannicum (1634), which played out the ongoing romance between Charles and Henrietta Maria, typically depicting Charles as an idealized knight dispatching monsters for love of his queen. The idea that Caroline Neoplatonism was a bloodless affair is highly misleading. Rather, the royal couple's happy sexual union was the very center of their political cult.

A further unintended consequence of Stuart fertility was that the court was no longer a single entity, but a complex of interlocking households, each with its own personnel, finances, and iconography. Once the queen consort (in 1603) and crown prince (in 1610) had acquired their own establishments, the production of court culture became disseminated across a diverse field, and since individual members of the royal family often had views about politics or religion that differed from the king's, the possibility arose that court festival might accommodate dissenting voices. Anne and Henrietta Maria were Catholics, liked to appear in festivals surrounded by their Catholic ladies, and were more directly involved in the production of court theater than were their husbands. Their masques often promoted a competing focus of power to the kings', providing space for feminocentric performances that unsettled Stuart culture's masculinist emphases. As for Prince Henry, this forward youth was an enthusiast for more aggressive policies than his father's and was sympathetic to Protestant alliances on religious grounds. His festivals often had a chivalric aspect that advertised their impatience with James's pacifism: notably, in *Oberon* (1611), Henry masqued as a fairy prince leading out his heroic followers from the caves where they had been hidden from the world. His dances did loyal homage to his father, but one imagines that to James this display of youthful enthusiasm and self-will must have seemed less than deferential.[6]

Ben Jonson's masques have often been seen as paradigmatic for court festival as a whole, so much so that Stephen Orgel's seminal book on the subject was called, simply, *The Jonsonian Masque*. Certainly Jonson's three dozen masques are the single most sustained contribution to Whitehall's culture, and the most inventive. But the idea that Jonson achieved proprietorial control over his masques does not reflect the reality of their performances. Jonson could assert his authority in print, but in practice he was only one of a team of artists responsible for the multimedia events that masques were. Although the printed texts preserve the most enduring record, on the evening the words occupied a relatively small portion of the time and were sometimes cut or adjusted to fit—or were simply inaudible. The bulk of the occasion was given over to dance and song, and no less spectacular was the contribution made by the architect, who was responsible for the stunning costumes and visual effects.

Moreover, powerful though Jonson's example was, he was only one of a dozen poets who wrote for Whitehall, each of whom had their own ideas about the nature of masquing and its representation of kingship. The acutest contrast is with Samuel Daniel, whose two masques took a more distanced attitude to the court than did Jonson's. For all its celebration, Daniel's *Vision of the Twelve Goddesses* was cautious and detached. Presented by a Sybil, who introduced and explained the action, it was less a factual statement of what the court was than a dream of what it might become. Daniel carefully called the masquers dressed as goddesses "the *figure* of those blessings," and did not simply underwrite royal power but offered a conditional image of possible glory. By contrast, *The Masque of Blackness* presented sovereignty as endowed with almost miraculous force, and later Jonsonian masques tended to display and endorse the magic of kingship. In their printed texts Jonson and Daniel sniped at each other, and although their antagonism arose from competition for the same commissions, it also suggests they understood the masque poet's task differently. So too masques by Campion, Chapman, Shirley, and Carew built on but also altered Jonson's model.

It is also important to realize that the "Jonsonian" masque changed over time. What we tend to take for the typical form is the dyad of antimasque and masque, classically embodied in *Oberon* or *The Masque of Queens* (1609). This presents a contrast between the grotesque or unruly antimasquers (satyrs in *Oberon,* witches in *Queens*), who were played by professional actors and whose presence disrupted the decorum of the court occasion, and the gracious aristocrats who danced elegantly but silently in the main masque, then joined in social dancing (the revels) with members of the audience. The distinction between antimasque and masque was radical and absolute: the arrival of the main masquers defeated the antimasquers at a stroke, silencing them and displacing them from the dancing floor, and it was usually reinforced by a scene change that dramatically transformed the place from (say) a horrid hell to the palace of Fame. But this neatly economical structure was dominant only for a brief time, circa 1609–16. Earlier masques, such as *Blackness,* lacked a tight dialectic, being loosely ordered as quests or processions, in which the masquers arrived in the performing space as if at the end of a long journey, offering gifts or gestures of homage. This structure was less contestatory: its performers tended to be described as "antemasquers" rather than "antimasquers." Similarly, later masques varied the Jonsonian dyad into more elaborate arrangements. In some, the clear opposition between antimasque and masque was eroded, allowing the antimasquers to be partially accommodated within the main masque. It eventually became customary to have three major scene changes, so that the evening was divided into four units, while masques in the French style treated the antimasques as balletic "entries," and multiplied the number of entries exponentially. In the 1630s, masques were typically constructed as "triumphs," in which Charles headed a parade of conquering heroes. And further differences are apparent if one considers the masques as musical structures, between those designed as speeches and song, and semi-operatic festivals that were through-composed or used recitative, such as *The Vision of Delight* (1617).

Many of these distinctions were due to technical factors. Particularly, the simple dyad arose from Inigo Jones's use of the *machina versatilis* or turning machine, a scenic system that effected changes by flipping scenery around on its vertical axis, so that a new design was suddenly revealed. At the central moment of *The Masque of Queens,* loud music sounded, the witches who had occupied the antimasque disappeared, and "the whole face of the scene altered, scarce suffering the memory of such a thing." But more elaborate effects were possible once Jones adopted the *scena ductilis* or tractable scene, a system of parallel flats stacked one behind another in grooves that allowed the wings as well as the center to be changed, and the changes to be repeated several times over. Masque resources were further enlarged by the development of the fly-gallery, which accounts for the impressive action on the upper stage in Caroline masques. Additionally, the form of the masques responded to changing social and economic pressures as the court's circumstances altered over time. The most significant factor was whether the monarch chose to perform or not. Charles and Henrietta Maria liked to dance in their own festivals, so their masques were always theatrical displays of royalty, but James never danced, so he occupied the role of chief spectator, and his masques were more like symbolic conversations or negotiations between king and subjects. Other formal shifts can be traced to the presence of Queen Anne, Prince Henry, or great courtiers like Buckingham (as each successively became leading figures in festival patronage) or to the availability or shortage of funds at particular moments. Masques presented to the court from social groups outside also had distinctive components. When lawyers from the Inns of Court brought masques to Whitehall, they sometimes processed from the city in costume, thus reaching a double audience, the court itself and the citizens for whom the street parade was the real festival.

These formal considerations bear directly onto *The Masque of Blackness,* which is often regarded as structurally defective because it lacked the transformation between antimasque and masque that is commonly assumed to be essential for the form. This masque depicted the arrival at Whitehall of a group of "blackamoors": twelve Ethiopian nymphs in exotic costume and with faces and limbs darkened, played by the queen and her ladies, who paid homage to James's throne and presented him with fans inscribed with mystical hieroglyphics. They were brought in by their father, Niger, who, in conversation with Oceanus, god of the ocean, explained that a dream had led them to Britain, which promised that here they might achieve their desire of changing their black complexions into fair. James was hailed as the sovereign power that could do this deed, since his sovereignty was a sunlike force that would bleach them into whiteness:

> [His] beams shine day and night, and are of force
> To blanch an Ethiop and revive a corse.
> His light sciential is, and, past mere nature,
> Can salve the rude defects of every creature. (254–57)

"Blanching an Ethiop" was a proverbial phrase for doing the impossible: James's redemption of the nymphs' blackness by shining benevolently on them symbolized the miracle of his sovereignty. Or so it would have done, had the predicted change immediately taken place. The nymphs remained black-skinned at the end of the masque and were told to wait for a year, bathing themselves in the ocean's foam, so that when they returned the following Christmas they would indeed be white (in fact the companion piece, *The Masque of Beauty,* remained unwritten until 1608, since the 1606 and 1607 seasons were occupied with festivals not sponsored by the queen). In many interpretations, this absence of transformation is taken as an "immaturity" in the masque (Orgel, *Masque* 128) or, worse, as a deliberate irresolution or denial of closure, a sign that the masque was covertly at odds with the praise of monarchy that publicly it offered. However, such deductions are anachronistic, for *The Masque of Blackness* was not organized like the dialectical entertainments of later years, in which negative antimasque converted into glorious masque. It was, rather, shaped as a ceremonious procession or quest, inducting the masquers as visitors from another world, and culminating with an act of gift-giving rather than transformation: formally, it was complete and integrated as it stood. Moreover, the masque did not need a physical metamorphosis to make its political point. As we shall see, its magic was already implicit in the mysterious body of the king.

Critical discussion has rightly focused on the queen's body: this was, after all, what contemporaries remembered most about the occasion. *Blackness* was Anne's second Christmas masque, by which she claimed a greater stake in creating court culture than her husband. James did not commission masques himself, but occupied the role of principal spectator; by contrast, Anne mounted six masques in eight years, and Jonson's text emphasizes that she was *Blackness*'s moving spirit, and chose the subject herself. By putting her body on stage, Anne (who was pregnant at the time) flaunted conventions of feminine modesty and risked censure, all the more so that her African role reversed conventional canons of beauty, and her costume was highly revealing, leaving her arms and shins bare. In a letter, the courtier Dudley Carleton expressed his distaste for this "loathsome sight":[7]

> Their apparel was rich, but too light and courtesan-like for such great ones. Instead of vizards, their faces and arms up to the elbows were painted black, which was disguise sufficient, for they were hard to be known; but it became them nothing so well as their red and white, and you cannot imagine a more ugly sight than a troop of lean-cheeked moors.

Perhaps such disguises were less shocking to Scottish eyes, for Scotland's festival culture had an established tradition of "African" masquing.[8] However, Anne offended against gender norms as well, seeming "courtesan-like" in apparel and upsetting Carleton with the contamination that her cosmetics threatened in the social dancing. When it came to the general revels (he wrote), she danced with the Spanish ambassador, and he "forgot not to kiss her hand, though there was danger it would have left a mark on his lips." Part of the power of Anne's performance was its straying into potentially problematic areas, and the vigor with which it embraced the alien, bringing the exotic into disturbingly close relationship with the domestic. Carleton certainly felt that her show had polluted the court by intruding physical difference so forcefully into the evening's elegant compliments.

However, appropriation of the exotic was not unique to Anne. Encounters with the Other were germane to masques, which made their political meanings by policing the borders between us and them, normal and monstrous, the strange and the familiar. Masques worked by staging the monarch's ability to assert his power in the face of forces that contested it or were antithetical to it; and through their dismissal of outsiders, they instilled in performers and audience a collective sense of kinship, affirming a corporate identity by marking lines of separation from those who were denied access to their community. Representatives of the exotic were thus intrinsic to the legitimation of monarch and court: masques constantly invoked racial, cultural, or social differences to underwrite whatever values Whitehall took for normative. The exotic was particularly visible in the early Jacobean festivals, for the Ethiopians were not the only strange visitors who came to congratulate James. The Indian and Chinese knights and the twelve goddesses had arrived the previous year, while the queen of Sheba—perhaps also depicted as an African woman?—turned up at Hatfield to greet Anne's brother, King Christian, in 1606. The earliest examples of such figures were probably the Patagonian giants, played by men on stilts, who met James on his progress southward from Edinburgh in 1603.[9] On a simple level, these remarkable encounters dramatized the condition of Jacobean Whitehall in the months after the accession, as it was indeed besieged by strangers come from overseas to pay their respects. More importantly, the need to surround James with the exotic reflected the moment of historical transition that surrounded early Jacobean masquing, the fact that this was both a new reign and a new dynasty, and that the succession made a radical break that changed the nature of the state. It was necessary for early Stuart masques not just to celebrate a

Scottish king's arrival in England, but to manage the invention of a new national identity, Great Britain.

"Britain" was the magic word that solved the Ethiopians' problems. They were depicted as discontented with their blackness, which they traced to their country's "intemperate fires" (175), their beauty having been scorched by the "fervent'st love" (143) and "heedless flames" (162) of their sun. But the dream told them

That they a land must forthwith seek
Whose termination, of the Greek,
Sounds *tania;* where bright Sol, that heat
Their bloods, doth never rise or set,
But in his journey passeth by,
And leaves that climate of the sky
To comfort of a greater light,
Who forms all beauty with his sight. (188–95)

In quest of this riddle, they had unsuccessfully visited Mauritania, Lusitania, and Aquitania, but on arrival at Albion's shore, they discovered a new name, Britannia, and the less violent sun that was associated with it:

Their beauties shall be scorched no more;
This sun is temperate, and refines
All things on which his radiance shines. (263–65)

"Britannia" was indeed a brand new name, for James had assumed the title "King of Great Britain" by proclamation on October 20, only eleven weeks before the masque. It was, though, highly controversial. James had proposed to his first parliament (March–June 1604) to rename England and Scotland as Britain, and plans for more substantive union would be put to the 1607 parliament. But what he hoped would be a natural development encountered fierce resistance, for each nation was anxious about absorption by the other and about the consequences of union for law, government, and religion. The 1604 parliament spent three days discussing the name, and eventually rejected it on the grounds that it might prejudice the state by invalidating the statutes and constitution: as Sir Edwin Sandys put it, "By what laws shall this Britain be governed?" Over the summer dozens of tracts were written debating the larger issues, but the question of the name was preempted by the October proclamation. It was all the more remarkable, then, that Jonson's masque put the name at its very center:

Britannia, which the triple world admires,
This isle hath now recovered for her name [. . .]
With that great name Britannia, this blessed isle
Hath won her ancient dignity and style,
A world divided from the world, and tried
The abstract of it in his general pride. (241–42, 246–49)

The echo of the proclamation was intentional: for example, "style" was the technical legal term for a royal title, and so appeared in the proclamation, as did the Virgilian tag about Britain being "a little world within itself." But while Jonson made it sound as if James's wish to be king of Britain had been universally acclaimed, it was in fact highly contentious. The masque deliberately, even provocatively, flew in the face of current events.

Britain was crucial in another way too, for the ladies' transformation depended on the temperateness of the British climate. This was a motif that Jonson inherited from William Camden, his schoolmaster, friend, and the author of the monumental Latin volume *Britannia* (1586). Although written under Elizabeth, *Britannia* was a foundational text for the seventeenth-century invention of Britain. A chorographical history of Britain county by county, based on critically sifted sources and up-to-date archaeology, it was the most authoritative and scholarly account of the country to date, and it opened with a discussion of the earliest inhabitants and the meaning of the name Britain. From archaeological evidence, Camden argued that the island was originally called Brit or Brith, which meant "blue(-colored)" and referred to the natives' custom of painting their bodies, and he discussed the peculiarity that this name had a termination, "-tania," which meant "region" in Greek but was found in only three other countries, Mauritania, Lusitania, and Aquitania. Clearly, Jonson developed the riddle and the itinerary of his wandering Ethiopians from this discussion. And he further found in Camden extracts from classical texts hymning Britain as the temperate land par excellence, in particular the anonymous *Panegyric to Constantine* (fourth century CE), with its fulsome praise of the British climate:[10]

> nature endowed thee with all the blessed gifts of air and soil; wherein there is neither excessive cold of winter, nor extreme heat of summer; wherein there is so great plenty of grain, that it serveth sufficiently both for bread and drink: wherein the forests are without savage beasts, and the ground void of noisome serpents [. . .] and verily (that which for the use of our life we much esteemed), the days there are very long, and the nights never want some light, whiles those utmost plains by the seaside cast and raise no shadows on high, and the aspect both of sky and stars passeth beyond the bound of the night, yea the very sun itself, which unto us seemeth for to set, appeareth there, only to pass along and go aside.

Jonson's printed text cites the *Panegyric to Constantine* in a footnote to the riddle: his rather opaque formulation concerning the British sun, that "doth never rise or set, / But in his journey passeth by / And leaves that climate of the sky / To comfort of a greater light" (191–94), is evidently an attempt to echo the final words of this source, as quoted by Camden. Camden thus provided Jonson not only with the crucial detail of Britain's "temperate air" but also with a symbolic and specific connection between Britain's new name and its temperate climate. The promise that the scorched women could be redeemed in Britain was not an amusing fantasy devised for an evening's entertainment. Rather, it endorsed the new national character as analyzed by the country's leading authority on the subject.

The Masque of Blackness, then, staged a political and ideological miracle: it put into crisis customary distinctions between black and white, near and far, in order to acclaim James's kingship as the marvelous embodiment of a new order, and it did so in direct reaction to the acute criticisms into which the James's plans had run. In this it echoed the tracts in favor of union which, in contrast to the parliamentary criticism, saw the name Britain as creating a kind of political magic, mysteriously incorporating into one two entities that previously had been separate. Hence the pollution threatened by the visiting Ethiopians and the discomfort created by their presence testified ultimately to the British monarch's compelling ability, at this critical juncture, to establish radical new relationships of difference and identity. In recognizing that James's "sciential" light would rectify the effects of their "heedless" sun, the Ethiopians sanctioned his kingship, and they endorsed it with their gestures, offering him homage and gifts. Of course, there was a lesson for James, too, as his legitimation enshrined an ideology of temperance. The fable constrained him by identifying British sovereignty with moral, intellectual, and political moderation. And equally clearly this device was inherently unstable, for it put the queen and her ladies into competition with the king. The effectiveness of James's legitimation was directly proportionate to the anxiety created by their transgressive and disruptive performance. But it was the ethos of *The Masque of Blackness* to embrace trauma, to root James's kingship in the shock of the new, and present it as an imperial power born from a moment of revolutionary change and violent discontinuity. In this regard, it anticipated Jonson's other panegyrics in expressing sovereignty in terms of an overwhelming and irresistible force and took up a considerably more radical position than festival texts prepared by his competitor poets. Nonetheless, the challenging and awe-inspiring devices of the form as a whole meant that all masques were, to a greater or lesser extent, helping to shape and extend the symbolic legitimation of Stuart power. From our historical distance they may seem like elegant dances of compliments that had little relevance to the great events of the time, but contemporaries participating in them must have felt they traded in issues of identity and nationhood that were absolutely foundational to the new state.

NOTES

1. E. K. Chambers, *The Elizabethan Stage,* 4 vols. (Oxford: Clarendon P, 1923) 3:280.
2. Chambers, 1:171; Lady Anne Clifford, *The Diaries of Lady Anne Clifford,* ed. D. J. H. Clifford (Stroud: Allan Sutton, 1990) 27.
3. Historical Manuscripts Commission, Hatfield MSS, 16.388–89.
4. Pauline Croft, "The Parliamentary Installation of Henry, Prince of Wales," *Historical Research* 65 (1992): 177–93.
5. All quotations from Jonson are taken from C. H. Herford, P. Simpson, and E. Simpson, eds., *Ben Jonson,* 11 vols. (Oxford: Clarendon P, 1925–53). Spelling has been modernized.
6. See M. Butler, "Courtly Negotiations," *The Politics of the Stuart Court Masque,* ed. David Bevington and Peter Holbrook (Cambridge: Cambridge UP, 1998) 29–32.
7. Herford, Simpson, and Simpson 10:448.
8. Clare McManus, *Women on the Renaissance Stage* (Manchester: Manchester UP, 2002) 74–76, 82–84.
9. J. Nichols, *The Progresses, Processions and Magnificent Festivities of King James I,* 4 vols. (London, 1828) 1:94.
10. William Camden, *Britannia,* trans. P. Holland (London, 1610) 3.

READING LIST

Aasand, Hardin. "To Blanch an Ethiop and Revive a Corse: Queen Anne and *The Masque of Blackness.*" *Studies in English Literature, 1500–1900* 32 (1992): 271–85.

Andrea, Bernadette. "Black Skin, the Queen's Masques: Africanist Ambivalence and Feminine Author(ity) in the Masques of *Blackness* and *Beauty.*" *English Literary Renaissance* 29 (1999): 246–81.

Bevington, David, and Peter Holbrook, eds. *The Politics of the Stuart Court Masque*. Cambridge: Cambridge UP, 1998.

Butler, Martin. "The Invention of Britain and the Early Stuart Masque." *The Stuart Court and Europe: Essays in Politics and Political Culture.* Ed. Malcolm Smuts. Cambridge: Cambridge UP, 1996. 65–85.

Floyd-Wilson, Mary. "Temperature, Temperance, and Racial Difference in Ben Jonson's *The Masque of Blackness*." *English Literary Renaissance* 28 (1998): 193–209.

Goldberg, Jonathan. *James I and the Politics of Literature*. Baltimore: Johns Hopkins UP, 1983.

Gordon, D. J. *The Renaissance Imagination*. Ed. Stephen Orgel. Berkeley: U of California P, 1975.

Hall, Kim F. *Things of Darkness: Economies of Race and Gender in Early Modern England*. Ithaca: Cornell UP, 1995.

McManus, Clare. *Women on the Renaissance Stage: Anna of Denmark and Female Masquing in the Stuart Court*. Manchester: Manchester UP, 2002.

Orgel, Stephen. *The Illusion of Power*. Berkeley: U of California P, 1975.

———. *The Jonsonian Masque*. Cambridge: Harvard UP, 1965.

Orgel, Stephen, and Roy Strong. *Inigo Jones: The Theater of the Stuart Court*. 2 vols. London: Sotheby Parke Bernet Publications Ltd., and Berkeley: U of California P, 1973.

Peacock, John. *The Stage Designs of Inigo Jones: The European Context*. Cambridge: Cambridge UP, 1995.

Siddiqi, Yumna. "Dark Incontinents: The Discourses of Race and Gender in Three Renaissance Masques." *Renaissance Drama* n.s. 23 (1992): 271–85.

Strong, Roy. *Splendor at Court*. London: Weidenfeld and Nicolson, 1973. Revised as *Art and Power: Renaissance Festivals 1450–1650*. Woodbridge: Boydell, 1984.

Walls, Peter. *Music in the English Courtly Masque*. Oxford: Clarendon Press, 1999.

15

Death and *The Revenger's Tragedy*

Michael Neill

What is our life? a play of passion,
Our mirth the music of division,
Our mothers' wombs the tiring houses be,
Where we are dressed for this short comedy;
Heaven the judicious sharp spectator is,
That sits and marks still who doth act amiss;
Our graves, that hide us from the searching sun,
Are like drawn curtains when the play is done.
Thus march we playing to our latest rest,
Only we die in earnest, there's no jest.

SIR WALTER RALEIGH, "THE LIFE OF MAN"

A good revenge is a form of practical joke.

JOHN KERRIGAN, *REVENGE TRAGEDY*

In his wry reflections on "The Life of Man," Sir Walter Raleigh, elaborating a popular Senecan trope, compares human existence to "a play of passion." What Raleigh meant by that expression was not, as we might anachronistically suppose, a religious drama of Christian sacrifice, but a secular representation of transgression and retribution, ending in death: a species of tragedy, therefore—albeit one exposed to the relentless gaze of a divine audience whose aesthetic discrimination he punningly identifies with judicial inquisition and the "sharp" edge of punishment. Yet for all its tragic outline, Raleigh's "play of passion" is drama of a peculiarly hybrid sort, one that he can disdainfully refer to as a "short comedy"—even if its laughter forms an ominous music whose "division," though ostensibly an ornamental descant (*OED* n. 7a), hints at discord, strife, separation, and bereavement (*OED* n. 1b, 4). After all, in a world of ridiculous "play" where everything seems done in histrionic "jest," the greatest joke is that death turns out to be no joke at all. Raleigh might almost have had in mind the farcical "descant" performed by Pedringano in *The Spanish Tragedy,* where the hapless tool-villain, described by his hangman as "the merriest piece of man's flesh that e'er groaned at my door" (3.6.80–81), jokes his way into the noose, whilst the Page (silently gesturing at the empty box supposed to contain Pedringano's pardon) points up the grim comedy: "I cannot choose but smile to think how the villain will flout the gallows, scorn the audience, and descant on the hangman [. . .] Is't not a scurvy jest that a man should jest himself to death" (3.5.15–16).[1]

From Marlowe's *Jew of Malta* (c. 1591) and Shakespeare's *Titus Andronicus* (c. 1592) to Middleton's *Women Beware Women* (c. 1521), English Renaissance tragedy is full of characters who, like unwitting victims of some macabre practical joke, are made to jest themselves to death in one fashion or another. But no play seems better calculated to excite the deadly mirth of Raleigh's passion play than the anonymous *Revenger's Tragedy* (1606)[2]—a work whose generic contradictions have led critics to identify it as "tragic burlesque," "black farce," or "tragical satire" (Gibbons x–xxvii). Early in the play, in a speech that resonates throughout the ensuing action, the Younger Son is warned by his malevolent step-brother, Lussurioso, "Oh do not jest thy doom [. . .] play not with thy death" (1.2.49–53). "My fault being sport," comes the response, "let me but die in jest" (66). The theatricality implicit in "jest," "play," and "sport" echoes that in Raleigh's poem; and toward the end, the tragedy's self-consciously histrionic hero, Vindice, envisages the accomplishment of his revenge as the climax of a performance acted for the aesthetic satisfaction of the same judgmentally "sharp spectator" that Raleigh envisaged: "No power is angry when the lustful die: / When thunder claps, heaven likes the tragedy" (5.3.47–48). Fuelling heaven's pleasure in the tragic spectacle, Vindice's exuberant humor implies, is the ironic wit with which it has been contrived; and, as in Raleigh's poem, the irony is wickedly reflexive, for the last trick of Vindice's busy invention will serve to encompass his own end—as he himself acknowledges, relishing even the joke that the joker himself is about to die in earnest: "'Tis time to die when we are ourselves our foes" (5.3.122).

One need not, of course, conclude that Vindice's inventor was acquainted with the Raleigh poem. It is rather that both works draw on the same tradition of thinking and feeling about death—a tradition that found its most intense expression in the great Dance of Death cycles that, whether in the form of wall-paintings in churches, graveyards, and palaces or in numerous popular woodcuts and engravings, haunted the imagination of late medieval and Renaissance Europe.[3] The *Danse Macabre*—as the motif came to be known, after its first great exemplar, painted on the cemetery wall at Les Innocents in Paris in 1434–35—represented Death as a sardonic leveler whose capering avatars summon the representatives of every rank in society, from pope to pauper, to surrender themselves to the embrace of death. Of course the primary purpose of such images, like other forms of *vanitas* and *contemptus mundi* moralizing, was to induce pious meditation on the ephemerality of life and the insubstantial nature of worldly success. Such reflection was after all essential to the Christian *ars moriendi,* not least because it alone could protect one against the horror of sudden death—the *mors improvisa* or *repentina* so abhorred by the medieval imagination.[4] Thus in the verses that accompanied the original *Danse Macabre,* when the Sergeant finds himself in the grip of an arrest even more remorseless than his own, he counsels his fellow mortals that failure to master the art of dying will lead to panic and despair:

> Eche man is loth to deie ferr or neer
> That hath nat lernyd [for] deie afforn.[5]

But, despite the religious function signaled by the location of its earliest representations on the walls of cloisters and churchyards, the significance of the Dance could not be contained within this orthodox framework: in particular, the gleeful mockery to which Death the Leveler exposed his loftiest victims easily lent itself to the purposes of a social satire whose thrust was as much secular as pious. The satiric aspect of the motif becomes especially apparent in the surviving verse dialogues that once glossed the parade of images in the great murals: the grim Summoner takes a sardonic relish in the terror and humiliation he inflicts upon the great, even as he offers a kind of solace to the cripple and the blindman, or comes to rescue the weary peasant from his toil. Moreover the very arrangement of the Dance, as it moves from pope and emperor to peasant and pauper, embodies a darkly parodic commentary upon worldly pomp and pride: like the elaborately ranked processions that accompanied all kinds of public ceremonial in early modern Europe, the Dance of Death displayed the hierarchy of worldly distinction in the careful ordering of its participants; but, with the summons of its nearly identical cadavers, it simultaneously announced the cancellation of such order, since (as the Fool observes in verses accompanying the Paris *Danse*) "*Tous mors sont d'un estat commun* [all the dead belong to the same estate]."[6]

In a world much preoccupied by the minutiae of rank, the shockingly *common* condition of the grave, its stripping away of all the signs of authority, status, and wealth, became a standard topos of satiric moralizing. It forms the theme of Hamlet's famous meditations in the Elsinore graveyard, where the prince tricks out the nameless and indistinguishable skulls uncovered by the gravediggers with a series of arbitrarily chosen identities: these, he conjectures—as though in mockingly disordered recollection of the Dance's parade of estates—might (or might as well) be the skulls of Cain, a politician, a courtier, a lawyer, "a great buyer of land," or even of Alexander and "Imperious Caesar." One skull alone is credited with a secure individuality by the First Clown—"This same skull, sir, was Yorick's skull, the King's jester" (*Hamlet* 5.1.174–75)[7]—but only for the jester to be assimilated with Death himself, that "antic" figure of dreadful sameness (*R2,* 3.2.162), who assumes the Jester's guise as an instrument for ferocious ridicule of worldly pomp and display: "Now get you to my lady's chamber and tell her, let her paint an inch thick, to this favour she must come. Make her laugh at that" (5.1.186–89). In *The Revenger's Tragedy* Vindice performs a similarly eldritch transformation upon the skull of his dead mistress:

> Here might a scornful and ambitious woman
> Look through and through herself; see, ladies, with false forms
> You deceive men but cannot deceive worms. (3.5.89–97)

In such tropes the irreducible anonymity of bone reduces all identity to a kind of mask or cosmetic deception—one that death instantly undoes: so in act 3, scene 6 it is as if the Younger Brother's newly severed head had already acquired something of the enigmatic blankness of a skull, since Ambitioso and Supervacuo are absurdly unable to distinguish it from that of Lussurioso, whose head they purposed to "mock off" (3.6.83).

In the *Danse Macabre* itself, the utter indistinction of death was given particularly shocking expression in the shameful nakedness of its leering cadavers. For a society governed by the nice distinctions of what social historians have called the "vestimentary system," this was perhaps the most powerful way of representing the extremity of death's assault upon rank and identity. Thus the bishop in the Basel *Totentanz,* whose gorgeous attire expresses the loftiness of his rank and calling, finds himself in the clutches of an obscenely naked corpse who drags him away to join "the shapeless ones" (*die Ungeschaffnen*) in the absolute undifferentiation of death (Neill 71). In a similar fashion, Thomas Newton's verses on the death of Queen Elizabeth imagine the "greedy worms" who feast upon her corpse as mocking the nakedness that reduces her royal person to obscure nullity:

> For what's her body now, whereon such care
> Was still bestow'd in all humility?
> Where are her robes? Is not her body bare,
> Respectless in the earth's obscurity?[8]

The horror of mortal nakedness revealed in such passages can help us to understand the conspicuous imaginative role allotted to clothing and undress in *The Revenger's Tragedy*.

In the world of this play, where corruption is epitomized by the sartorial extravagance of a court whose women "Walk with a hundred acres on their backs" (2.1.213), flesh itself is imagined as a kind of fabric or costume, and bone as the extremity of nakedness. Flesh is the "costly three-piled" velvet that once "apparelled" the bare bone of Gloriana (1.1.31, 46)—the mistress whose name recalls the mythic splendors of the dead Queen Elizabeth's court. The stripping away of Gloriana's fleshly identity to expose the "shell of Death" beneath the skin transforms her into an instrument of practical satire, Vindice's "terror to fat folks," whose "ragged imperfections" expose the essential truth beneath the "silk and silver" ostentation of a rotten court (1.1.15, 45, 18, 52). When its lustful denizens "are up and dressed and their mask on," Vindice declares, none can perceive their true nature, "save that eternal eye / That sees through flesh and all" (1.3.67–69); but Vindice makes himself the agent of that penetrating stare; and, as if in one of those admonitory engravings where a woman gazes in a looking glass only to a see a death's head leering back at her, he flourishes Gloriana's skull as a satiric mirror of courtly pride and luxury:

> Does the silkworm expend her yellow labours
> For thee? For thee does she undo herself.
> [. . .]
> Does every proud and self-affecting dame
> Camphor her face for this, and grieve her maker
> In sinful baths of milk, when many an infant starves
> For her superfluous outside—all for this? (3.1.71–86)

The extravagant climax of Vindice's sartorial jests is reached in the macabre puppeteering of act 3, scene 5, in which the skull, its features adorned with a "dreadful vizard" (48) of corrosive cosmetics, is *"dressed up in tires"* (42 s.d.) to become the duke's deadly new concubine. "'Tis common to be common," moralizes Hippolito as he awaits the arrival of the duke's latest conquest (38); but this "bony lady" (120) proves to be a creature whose "common" sexual availability is only a "mask" (113) for the more sinister commonness that, in Vindice's fevered imagination, inspires her promiscuous choice of partners:

> Have I not fitted the old surfeiter
> With a quaint piece of beauty? Age and bare bone
> Are e'er allied in action. Here's an eye
> Able to tempt a great man—to serve God;

A pretty hanging lip, that has forgot now to dissemble.
Methinks this mouth should make a swearer tremble,
A drunkard clasp his teeth, and not undo'em.
[. . .]
It were fine methinks
To have thee seen at revels, forgetful feasts
And unclean brothels; sure 'twould fright the sinner
And make him a good coward, put a reveller
Out of his antic amble
And cloy an epicure with empty dishes. (3.5.52–94)

This reinvention of the chaste Gloriana as a denizen of "unclean brothels" links the play to another aspect of the *Danse Macabre*—the grotesque eroticization of death that characterizes its perverse raptures. Since Death always assumes a conventionally masculine role in the Dance, each of his reluctant dancing partners, whatever their sex, is forced to assume a feminine posture of bashful resistance; and the inclusion of Adam and Eve at the beginning of the sequence in some versions (including both the *Totentanz* of Basel and Holbein's famous woodcuts) encourages a reading in which death is identified as the punishment for a sexually imagined Fall. This seems to be the meaning contained, for example, in an engraving from Augsburg by the brothers Ridinger, in which nine women are led by their skeletal partners in a dance around a coffin in which two skeletons, presumably representing the First Couple, lie in fast embrace (Neill 75). The sexual suggestiveness of Death's overtures is especially conspicuous in the Basel *Tod,* where the obscene nakedness of the skipping cadavers (emphasized in several cases by visual puns that appear to endow them with exaggerated male genitalia) transforms the mortal summons into a sexual invitation (Neill 54–58, 75–77).

Inevitably, of course, the erotic suggestiveness of Death's embrace is most conspicuous when his chosen partner is a young woman and he himself assumes the role of gallant wooer. In such episodes it is as though the familiar idea of orgasm as a "little death" is turned on its head, transforming the moment of death into a terrible parody of sexual climax. Thus in the fifteenth-century *Danse Macabre of Women,* Death seizes the Prostitute with a promise to hold her tight; the Newlywed complains "It is not sweetness I feel but fury"; and Death urges the Bride

Let's go take off our clothes;
There's no more work for you
You will come to be in another place.
You shouldn't get too excited.

"Death," she protests, "why do you lust / For me, why take me so quickly."[9] Particularly explicit in its erotic suggestiveness is Thomas Hill's ballad *The Doleful Dance, and Song of Death,* in which Death's summons takes the form of a grotesque quibbling on a familiar euphemism for copulation:

Can you dance *The shaking of the sheets*?—
A dance that everyone must do—
Can you trim it up with dainty sweets,
And every thing as 'longs thereto?

Make ready then your winding sheet,
And see how you can bestir your feet,
For Death is the man that all must meet.
[. . .]
For I can quickly cool you all,
How hot or stout so e'er you be.[10]

It is surely his awareness of this tradition that encourages Vindice at the opening of *The Revenger's Tragedy* to transform Gloriana's skull from a conventional *memento mori* to an erotically charged instrument of death. Of course the image of a young man confronting a skull, brought to such startling life in *Hamlet*'s graveyard scene, was a favorite moral device of Renaissance painters and engravers. It derived from the common practice of keeping an actual skull in one's study as an aid to meditation on the brevity of life and the vanity of worldly goods: this is what Vindice has in mind when he introduces his mistress's skull as "my study's ornament" (1.1.15). But the whole point of such meditational props lay in their absolute anonymity: the young gallant in Frans Hals's *Young Man with a Skull* (National Portrait Gallery of Great Britain), whose fashionable attire proclaims his confident individuality, will soon be no different from the blank bone—the skull whose sightless gaze confronts the viewer in turn with the same discomforting reminder. The difference in Vindice's case is that his is not just *any* skull, but one with a particular history—that of the dead Gloriana, murdered by the old duke because she would not yield to his lust. This skull is therefore both a *memento mori* and a different kind of memorial: like the "handkerchief besmeared with [his son's] blood" that Hieronimo hoards away (*Spanish Tragedy* 2.4.113), or the corpse of his murdered father preserved by the hero of Chettle's *Hoffman,* it is a revenger's token, material proof of a crime that authority has sought to erase from public memory (Neill 243–51). But for Vindice it is also charged with a strange and destructive kind of eroticism:

Thou sallow picture of my poisoned love [. . .]
Once the bright face of my betrothed lady,
When life and beauty naturally filled out
These ragged imperfections [. . .] then 'twas a face
So far beyond the artificial shine
Of any woman's bought complexion
That the uprightest man—if such there be,
That sin but seven times a day—broke custom
And made up eight with looking after her.
Oh she was able to ha'made a usurer's son
Melt all his patrimony in a kiss. (1.1.14–27)

The necrophile excitement that metamorphoses Gloriana's skull into an object of erotic desire recalls the overheated intensity of the language that subjects her murderer, the lecherous duke, to an opposite transformation, through which a grotesquely sexualized version of the *Danse Macabre* is imagined as taking place within the cadaverous body of "his withered Grace" (1.2.96):

Oh that marrowless age
Would stuff the hollow bones with damned desires,

And stead of heat kindle infernal fires
Within the spendthrift veins of a dry duke,
A parched and juiceless luxur. (5–9)

In this extraordinarily compacted image, sterile Age is figured as performing a sexual assault upon the skeletal person of Death, thereby restoring a feverish travesty of amorous "heat" to the duke's emasculated person. According to Galenic medical theory, marrow, blood, and semen were different forms of a single fungible substance;[11] and in Vindice's figure syphilis—described in Shakespeare's *Venus and Adonis* as the "marrow-eating sickness" that breeds "disorder" by excessive "heating of the blood" (741)—is what has rendered Age impotent; yet, by some bizarre sexual deformation, rapacious Age contrives to replenish the "hollow bones" of its emaciated partner with wicked desires that take the place of marrow, substituting the hellfire of syphilitic pain for the heat of natural appetite.

Even at this early point in the play, Vindice—like other satyr-satirists in the Jacobean mold—seems weirdly excited by the very vices he decries; and his unnatural relish of the obscene spectacle he imagines is registered in the clustered liquids and sibilants of "juiceless luxur" that orally enact the very opposite of the dessication they pretend to describe. Small wonder, then, given the weird arousal induced by his contemplation of the skull, that Vindice will enjoy such spectacular success in the guise of a pander—first to his own sister, and then to the bony lady herself. When he wittily redefines this role as that of "A bone setter [. . .] One that sets bones together" (1.3.43–45), he identifies himself in the vocabulary of the *Danse Macabre* as at once a kind of Grim Physician and the Bawd of Death. The sinister double entendre in his jest becomes fully apparent only in act 3, scene 5, when Vindice prepares to introduce the duke to his deathly paramour with the sardonic reflection that "Age and bare bone / Are e'er allied in action" (3.5.54). "Action" here simultaneously quibbles on the theatrical "acting" of his puppet-play with the skull and on "action" as a bawdy term for sexual activity (Williams 25). It initiates a train of morbidly erotic puns through which Vindice points up the diabolical wit of his device. He goes on to laud this "country lady" with her "grave look" as "a quaint piece of beauty" (132, 135, 53), playing on the bawdy meanings of *piece* (Williams 234) and *quaint*—including the homonym that was still current as an archaic form of *cunt* (*OED* n[1]). The skull's quaintness consists not simply in the fashionable elegance of its attire (*OED* a. 4b), nor in the terrible strangeness concealed by its familiar appearance (*OED* a. 7), but in the skill with which it has been masked, in the cunning and ingenuity with which it has been made to serve the plotting of revenge (*OED* a. 1–3), and in the fastidiously virginal primness (*OED* a. 10) with which the white bone (belying the erotic glamour of its outward appearance) will preserve the chastity of its (imaginary) *quaint*. Here indeed (to revert to the play's insistent association of sex with gluttonous eating) is an "empty dish" designed to "cloy an epicure." The precise function of the skull, Vindice reminds us, will be to act not simply as the *memento mori* of "forgetful feasts" (3.5.90), but to strip away the very mask of flesh by which Age is superficially distinguished from Death—to unite bone with bone:

This very skull
Whose mistress the duke poisoned with this drug,
The mortal curse of the earth, shall be revenged
In the like strain and kiss his lips to death. (3.5.101–04)

"Those that did eat are eaten," gloats Vindice, as the poison devours lips, teeth, and tongue (161), marking the point at which literal and erotic death become one and the same—in much the way that the Younger Son envisaged in his punishment for rape: "I must die. Her beauty was ordained to be my scaffold [. . .] I die for that which every woman loves" (1.2.63–64; 3.4.77); or as Spurio suggested when he first kissed his stepmother: "Oh one incestuous kiss picks open hell" (1.2.173)—where *hell,* the place of everlasting death, stands for the female genitalia (Williams 56). "Next to a skull," Vindice has said of the duke, "though more unsound than one, / Each face he meets he strongly dotes upon" (1.1.88–89): now the old man kisses the skull itself, the corrosive poison on its lips mimicking the ravages of the venereal diseases borne by its "unsound" sisters. Vindice, carefully underlining the ironic symmetry of his revenge, is at pains to remind his victim that this "dreadful vizard [. . .] is the skull / Of Gloriana whom thou poisonedst last [. . .] The very ragged bone / Has been sufficiently revenged" (148–53).

So far at least, there is an almost perfect consonance between the revenger's design and the morbid couplings of the Dance of Death on which his puppet-show is based. However, the device involves a concealed irony that significantly destabilizes Vindice's control over the meaning of his own theatrical tableau. For in the Dance, despite its coloring of morbid eroticism, the deathly dancing-partner is always imagined as the sinister double of his victim—a *comes* (companion) or *Gefehrt* (fellow-traveler)—who has accompanied his designated victim from the moment of conception (Harrison 54; Neill 74–75, 84–85). From this perspective, the alliance of Age and Bare Bone looks less like a triumph of revenge's artful irony than a fulfillment of the immanent destiny proclaimed by the patterns of macabre art—so that the Bony Lady is revealed as nothing less than the Old Man's mortal Other, the Death within him animated by the monstrous, self-consuming lust that fills his sapless veins with hell-fire.

Once the painted skull is seen in this way, its "grave look" (135) becomes an admonitory mirror not simply for the other intended victims of the revenger's witty malice, but for Vindice himself; and in the scenes that follow, as though mimicking the chainlike sequence of the *Danse Macabre,* the duke's own corpse will take the place of Gloriana's relic to become the embodiment of Vindice's secret sharer, his own mortal *Gefehrt.* The effect of uncanny doubling that so exquisitely anticipates his self-undoing end was first hinted at when, in order to gain the confidence of the duke's heir, Lussurioso, Vindice assumed the disguise of "Piato," reveling in the comedy of self-duplication that makes it seem "As if another man had been sent whole / Into the world" (1.3.2–3):

> I'll quickly turn into another. (1.1.132)
>
> What, brother, am I far enough from myself? (1.3.1)

"Piato" having fallen into disfavor, the protagonist is subsequently forced to turn into himself again (4.2.32), though the "Vindice" who now seeks Lussurioso's patronage is characterized by a rustic vocal disguise (4.2.26, 43) that identifies him as yet another *alter ego*—"a *double* slave" in more senses than Lussurioso imagines (4.2.184–85). As Vindice marvels at his own self-multiplication—"All this is I!" (4.2.131), "I'm in doubt whether I'm myself / Or no! (4.4.24–25), "I think man's happiest when he forgets himself" (4.4.86)—his new "discontented" self is ordered to eliminate "Piato"; and his wry response ("I'll doom him [. . .] I'm hired to kill myself" [4.2.176, 203]) echoes

Hippolito's sardonic reflection on their patron's unwitting collaboration in his own destruction: "How strangely does himself work to undo him" (4.2.62). The famously extravagant episode in which the protagonist, having disguised the duke's corpse as "Piato," subjects it to mockery and abuse, carries this uncanny process to a black-farcical extreme in which Vindice symbolically acts out his impending self-annihilation:

> That's a good lay, for I must kill myself ! [*points to corpse*] Brother that's I: that sits for me: do you mark it. And I must stand ready here to make away myself yonder; I must sit to be killed, and stand to kill myself—I could vary it not so little as thrice over again, 'tas some eight returns like Michaelmas Term. (5.1.3–8)

What Vindice imagines here, punning on *return* as legal writ and on *turning* and *re-turning* as the figures of a dance (*OED re-turn* v. 2), resembles a one-man Dance of Death, in which he performs the part of his own Grim Summoner—the fellow-traveler who has accompanied him from birth, awaiting his moment. In the wake of this pantomime of multiple self-murderings, Vindice's furtive revelation of identity to the dying Lussurioso, "'twas Vindice murdered thee [. . .] And I am he!" (5.3.79–81)—his equivalent of the prince of Denmark's defiant "This is I, Hamlet the Dane" (*Ham.,* 5.2.257–58)—may seem to register an absurdly misplaced confidence: Vindice, "Piato," and "Vindice," he has been all of these; but, as Hippolito warned ("Brother we lose ourselves" [4.2.199]), this extravagant performer has become so lost in the labyrinth of his own devisings that his final self-undoing seems almost a formality.

A favorite Renaissance motto—found, for example, on the supposed portrait of Marlowe held by Corpus Christi College, Cambridge, and paraphrased in Shakespeare's Sonnet 73—draws attention to the paradoxical way in which death feeds off the very energies that fuel life itself: *quod me nutrit, me detruit.* Vindice's successive guises as the malcontent Piato and as Hippolito's "discontented brother" (4.2.37)—by recalling his own father's death from "discontent, the nobleman's consumption" (1.1.126)—epitomize the way in which the revenger is consumed by the very passion that animates him. It is as if in the duke's cadaver, dressed up in "Piato's" clothes and painted like the Bony Lady herself (23), Vindice were confronted with the image of his own Death; and his boisterous mime of self-murder, wickedly (but unwittingly) anticipates the reflexive ironies of the final scene. There the revenger, overwhelmed by delight at the ingenuity of his own contrivances (5.2.98–100), yet recognizing that he has become his own most lethal enemy, jests himself to death: "'Twas somewhat wittily carried / Though we say it [. . .] This murder might have slept in tongueless brass / But for ourselves, and the world died an ass" (99, 112–16).

The witty plotting of which Vindice boasts has been perfectly exhibited, of course, in the elaborate doublings of the "masque of revengers" that triggers the play's apocalyptic firestorm of revenge. The ironic symmetry that assigns each victim his own murderer, together with the chainlike sequence of ensuing deaths, clearly recalls the pairings of the *Danse Macabre: "The revengers dance. At the end [they] steal out their swords and these four kill the four at the table"* (5.3.42 s.d). The patterning is further emphasized when the masquers' exit is immediately followed by the entry of *"the other masque of intended murderers,"* consisting of four more indistinguishably masked dancers who, in a bizarre replay of the vicious game with the old duke's corpse, find their designated victims already dead. Capitalizing brilliantly on Supervacuo's motto for the masque, with its echo of the bony lady as "death's vizard"—"'Tis murder's best face, when a vizard's on!" (5.1.178)—Trevor Nunn's 1966 production for the RSC dressed its masquers as death-figures from the *Danse Macabre*. This theatrical masterstroke defined the moment at which, as each princeling stabbed his rival in a frenzy of undifferentiated ambition, the frantic striving for worldly eminence was unmasked as itself the vehicle of Death's terminal indistinction.

For all its histrionic extravagance, the satiric holocaust enacted at the end of *The Revenger's Tragedy* had a clear significance, reflecting in an extreme form the pervasive early modern anxiety about death's power to undo the hierarchical fabric of social order. Nowhere, perhaps, was that anxiety more powerfully registered than in the extraordinary elaboration of funeral pomps and monumental art so characteristic of the period (Neill 38–42). The prominence given to funeral rites and tomb-properties in a striking number of English Renaissance tragedies is a testament to this preoccupation; and the scanting of such rites at the end of *The Revenger's Tragedy,* marked by Antonio's curt order to "bear up / Those tragic bodies" (5.3.129–30), is equally significant. Like the characters' cynical attitude toward the secular pride of "sepulchres [for] mighty emperors' bones" (5.1.141) and the "flattering false insculption" of tombs (1.2.13), it expresses the play's profoundly ambiguous response to the leveling power of death. When Antonio discovers the violated body of his wife to the assembled lords in act 1, scene 4, this "precedent for wives" (6) is displayed like a figure from some elaborate Renaissance tomb, a "fair [. . .] monument" (68) whose posture draws attention to the Lucrece-like perfection of her inward chastity:

> A prayer book the pillow to her cheek;
> This was her rich confection, and another
> Placed in her right hand with a leaf tucked up,
> Pointing to these words:
> *Melius virtute mori, quam per dedecus vivere.* (1.4.14–18)

Her sworn revengers promise a wealthy funeral and "a tomb of pearl" (70–71) for one who knows that it is better to die virtuously than to live with shame. But in this play death allows no space for such pious memorials. *The Revenger's Tragedy* proves instead to be written in that black ink of infamy whose power of disgrace and oblivion inspires such indignation in the old duke. This is the ink

> Which envious spirits will dip their pens into
> After our death, and blot us in our tombs.
> For that which would seem treason in our lives
> Is laughter when we're dead. (1.2.5–8)

The laughter that the old man already hears is the same sardonic mirth that Vindice will invite in the jigging couplet with which he pronounces his own earnest-jesting epitaph: "I'faith we're well—our mother turned, our sister true, / We die after a nest of dukes. Adieu (5.3.125–26)."

The cocky defiance of Vindice's farewell is characteristic of the way in which this play responds to the pretensions of worldly power on the one hand and to the levelling violence of death on the other. It contemplates a world given over to secular values, in which power and appetite, unchecked by supernatural sanctions, seem to be contained only by the same self-consuming dynamic that is announced by the tragical satire of

Troilus and Cressida (c. 1602), where the "universal wolf" of appetite, "doubly seconded with will and power, / Must make perforce an universal prey, / And last eat up himself" (*Tro.* 1.3.121–24). In its cynical treatment of worldly greatness, moroever, *The Revenger's Tragedy* has much in common with other satiric tragedies like John Webster's *The Duchess of Malfi* (1612–14). In that play the villain-hero Bosola moralizes, in the guise of a tomb-maker, upon the fashionable ostentation with which great men vainly seek to overcome the levelling power of death:

> Princes' images on their tombs
> Do not lie, as they were wont, seeming to pray
> Up to heaven, but with their hands under their cheeks,
> As if they died of the toothache. They are not carved
> With their eyes fixed upon the stars, but as
> Their minds were wholly bent upon the world,
> The self-same way they seem to turn their faces. (*Malfi* 4.2.156–62)[12]

The consequence of such folly is that princes are doomed, like the pyramids that symbolize their monumental vanity, to "end in a little point, a kind of nothing" (*Malfi* 5.5.79). In *The Revenger's Tragedy,* all the pompous eloquence of monumental art is similarly reduced to the nullity of Vindice's "tongueless brass" (5.3.115), while the poetry of epitaph is even more contemptuously degraded to the gleeful bathos of Spurio's "Old dad dead" (5.1.111). Webster's tragedy, however, manages to wring a grim solace from its final spectacle of ruin: even if the "wretched eminent things" whose corpses litter the stage "Leave no more fame behind 'em than should one / Fall in a frost, and leave his print in snow," the "integrity of life" celebrated in Delio's closing couplet claims a triumph for the duchess's quiet heroism, "Which nobly beyond death shall crown the end" (5.5.120–21). *The Revenger's Tragedy,* by contrast, will have no truck with stoic consolation of this sort: Vindice's pleasure in dying "after a nest of Dukes" matches Bosola's "glory" in the annihilation of his princely masters; but though Vindice's revenge may have begun as a quest for justice, its satisfactions prove in the end to be aesthetic rather than moral. Vindice's pleasure in the sheer ingenuity of his own wit seems perfectly attuned to the play's deeply skeptical sense of how the universe itself is ordered. Whereas the cold indifference of the stars in Webster's tragedy (4.1.100) hints at a world from which God's grace has been withdrawn, the chain of brutally ironic coincidence in *The Revenger's Tragedy* suggests the activity of a supernatural power that intervenes only too busily in human affairs. The nature of its authority, however, is scarcely calculated to command awe; for the comical patness with which the thunder responds to Vindice's cue (4.2.197–98) suggests that heaven is simply the greatest practical joker of all—one whose applause expresses its relish for the same gleefully murderous aesthetic by which Vindice himself is possessed.

The word that best expresses that glee is the same one that registers Vindice's delight in the cunning artifice of his deathly puppet show: "quaint." It is for the even "quainter fallacy" involved in his disguise as a bizarrely exaggerated version of himself that Vindice so relishes performing the part of the rustic "Vindice," Hippolito's "discontented brother" (4.2.5, 38); and his only regret at the ingenuity of his scheme for killing off his Piato-self is that it cheats him of the opportunity to make revenge punningly "familiar" with Lussurioso by showing him "how quaintly" the old duke died, before killing him "over his father's breast" (5.1.16–19). Quaintness of this kind is precisely what Vindice celebrates in the last theatrical twist of his revenge—"'Twas somewhat wittily carried"; but to the play's original audience "quaint," of course, will have suggested something more than mere wit, ingenuity, or elegance of design, for it also carried the more sinister sense of "strange, unfamiliar, odd," reflecting both the uncanniness of Vindice's dizzying self-multiplication and the uneasy sense of self-estrangement with which it afflicts both him and Hippolito:

> Brother we lose ourselves. (4.1.199)
>
> Oh I'm in doubt
> Whether I'm myself or no. (4.4.24–5)
>
> joy's a subtle elf,
> I think man's happiest when he forgets himself. (4.4.85–86)
>
> 'Tis time to die when we are ourselves our foes. (5.3.112)

In act 4, scene 1, as Hippolito anticipates the success of his brother's anti-disguise in his "own shape," he muses on the eerie fashion in which Lussurioso's actions seem designed to play into their hands: "How strangely does himself work to undo him" (4.2.60–61). The shaft is aimed at their final prey, but Hippolito might as well be speaking a motto for Vindice, for himself, or indeed for all the self-undoing silkworms of this pernicious court. As they "march [. . .] playing to [their] latest rest," each in turn becomes the unwitting victim of a malicious wit that offers up their play of passion for the savage mirth of its sharp spectators.

NOTES

1. Cited from Katherine Eisaman Maus, ed., *Four Revenge Tragedies* (Oxford: Oxford UP, 1995).
2. The authorship of this play is hotly disputed. Unreliably attributed to Cyril Tourneur in a playlist by Edward Archer (1656), it has more recently been attributed (by MacD. P. Jackson and others) on internal grounds to Thomas Middleton, but this attribution is resisted by a number of scholars, including the play's latest editor—see Brian Gibbons, ed., *The Revenger's Tragedy,* 2nd ed. (London: A&C Black, 1991).
3. See Michael Neill, *Issues of Death: Mortality and Identity in English Renaissance Tragedy* (Oxford: Clarendon P, 1997) 51–81.
4. See Philippe Ariès, *The Hour of Our Death,* trans. Helen Weaver (London: Allen Lane, 1981) 118–23.
5. Cited from the Lansdowne version of Lydgate's translation in John Lydgate, *The Dance of Death,* ed. Florence Warren (London: Early English Text Society, 1931) stanza lii, 51.
6. Cited from Edward F. Chaney, ed., *La Danse Macabrée des Charniers des Saints Innocents à Paris* (Manchester: Manchester UP, 1945) 43.
7. Cited from the Arden edition, ed. Harold Jenkins (London: Methuen, 1982).
8. Thomas Newton, *Atropon Delion: or, the Death of Delia* (1603), *The Progresses and Public Processions of Queen Elizabeth,* 3 vols., ed. John Nichols (London, 1823) 639.
9. Cited from Anne Tukey Harrison, ed., *The Danse Macabre of Women* (Kent, OH: Kent State UP, 1994) 102, 122.

10. Qtd. from *The Roxburghe Ballads,* 9 vols. (Hertford, 1871–99) 3.184–86.
11. See also Gordon Williams, *A Glossary of Shakespeare's Sexual Language* (London: Athlone, 1997) 44, 203.
12. Cited from the Revels edition, ed. John Russell Brown (London: Methuen, 1964).

READING LIST

Belsey, Catherine. *Shakespeare and the Loss of Eden.* London: Macmillan, 1999.

Coddon, Karin S. "'For Show or Useless Property': Necrophilia and *The Revenger's Tragedy.*" *ELH* 61 (1994): 71–88.

Dollimore, Jonathan. *Radical Tragedy: Religion, Ideology, and Power in the Drama of Shakespeare and His Contemporaries.* Brighton: Harvester, 1984.

Engel, William. *Mapping Mortality: The Persistence of Memory and Melancholy in Early Modern England.* Amherst: U of Massachussets UP, 1995.

Frye, Roland Mushat. *The Renaissance Hamlet.* Princeton: Princeton UP, 1984.

Greenblatt, Stephen. *Hamlet in Purgatory.* Princeton: Princeton UP, 2001.

Kerrigan, John. *Revenge Tragedy: Aeschylus to Armageddon.* Oxford: Oxford UP, 1996.

Llewellyn, Nigel. *The Art of Death: Visual Culture in the English Death Ritual.* London: Reaktion Books, 1991.

Marshall, Peter. *Beliefs and the Dead in Reformation England.* Oxford: Oxford UP, 2002.

Schoenbaum, Samuel. "*The Revenger's Tragedy:* Jacobean Dance of Death." *Modern Language Quarterly* 15 (1954): 201–07.

Simkin, Stevie, ed. *Revenge Tragedy.* New Casebooks. Basingstoke: Palgrave, 2001.

Spinrad, Phoebe. *The Summons of Death on the Renaissance Stage.* Columbus: Ohio State UP, 1987.

16

Volpone and the Classics

Raphael Lyne

In act 3, scene 8 of Ben Jonson's *Volpone*, Mosca and his master confront probable disaster. Bonario has discovered their plots and rescued Celia, and it seems as if the game is up. Nevertheless, Mosca manages some rueful humor:

> *Volpone:* What shall we do?
> *Mosca:* I know not; if my heart
> Could expiate the mischance, I'd pluck it out.
> Will you be pleased to hang me? or cut my throat?
> And I'll requite you, sir. Let's die like Romans,
> Since we have liv'd, like Grecians. (3.8.11–15)[1]

This contrast between Grecians and Romans is based on a superficial interpretation of classical culture. In Mosca's mind the Greeks were hedonists, dedicated as he has been to pleasure and wealth, while the Romans are identified with the philosophy of the Stoics—austere, constant, and preferring suicide to an undignified compromise. Even before setting up this opposition Mosca undermines the notion of the noble Roman suicide. The offer to "requite" a hanging or a throat-cutting is polite but comically impossible. Jonson depicts a character displaying a very common Renaissance habit of thought: Mosca looks to the classics, as so many did, for examples of attitudes and behavior. In *Volpone,* however, characters' interpretations of the Greeks and the Romans are travesties of the upright, serious attention Jonson himself pays to them. These characters read wrongly, and their wrong readings are part of the moral texture of the play.

In the sixteenth and seventeenth centuries engagement with classical literature was a fundamental part of the literary process. It was natural, almost automatic, for writers to imitate Roman and Greek writers. Indeed, one of the most influential modern commentators on classical imitation in the Renaissance has argued that we should treat many instances of imitation as unremarkable aspects of writing—the fact that an English text is doing things with a classical text need not have any significance at all.[2] The Greeks and Romans had set the standards that English writers worked with and against, but they were not thought of as "classics"—the term was not used at the time—rather, they were literature itself. In the educational system Latin (much more than Greek) was the language of academic seriousness and of genuine eloquence. The energetic humanist theorists of education, despite having many arguments amongst themselves, agreed on the connections between the study of classical literature, thought, and history and the intellectual and practical development of individuals and nations. Jonson was one who had taken this to heart: the prefaces to his plays are full of the conviction that there is real benefit to be gained from good reading.[3] Educated writers, then, could have an intimate relationship with the language and its literature, being effectively bilingual in important aspects of their lives. Study at school often featured translations back and forth between Latin and English, so the act of exchanging between them was enshrined in the curriculum.[4] This must have been a complex mental world, in which writers had conflicting allegiances toward the language in which they were brought up and in which they communicated daily and toward the language in which they distinguished themselves and gained recognition at school, at university, and in key careers. In some writers one can identify tensions and conflicts that result: this can emerge as an apprehension, or an avoidance, of the cultural and historical gap between the Latin texts and the English texts deriving from them.[5]

Those committed to the classics found some important reassurances that they were right to try to cross the gap. Classical writers, such as Aristotle in his *Poetics,* and Horace in his *Ars Poetica,* which Jonson himself translated, advocated secure and reasoned standards for the conduct and decorum of literature. As the inventors of such standards, they offered a double justification for later writers' allegiance. John Mulryan helpfully defines that allegiance as "classicism": "a literary and philosophical system that asserts and celebrates the existence of a series of timeless, unvarying principles of conduct and thought," and also "an acknowledgement that those principles are embodied in the writings of ancient Greece and Rome, which should be taken as models."[6] One manifestation of such classicism, which is an important subtext of *Volpone,* is an attempt to regulate reading. The implication, in Jonson, usually aims outward toward the audiences and readers that he strove, often unsuccessfully, to mold to a sympathetic set of tastes and interests. Within his works it is offered in more than one place as an explicit form of advice, a kind of reading list, that aims to foster structured benefits from people's reading.

One example comes in Jonson's early play *Poetaster*. The main plot of the play sees Demetrius and Crispinus, the two poetasters (false poets), attack and defame the moral figure of the poet Horace. (This plot is a thinly veiled replay of Jonson's rivalry with Marston and Dekker.) When the poetasters are revealed and convicted, the presiding epic poet Virgil prescribes a purgative cure for Demetrius and Crispinus. First they must vomit up their harsh and unworthy words—this is a dramatic tour de force—and then they must follow a wholesome literary diet:

> 'Tis necessary therefore he observe
> A strict and wholesome diet. [*To Crispinus.*] Look you take
> Each morning of old Cato's principles
> A good draught next your heart. That walk upon
> Till it be well digested, then come home
> And taste a piece of Terence: suck this phrase
> Instead of licorice, and at any hand
> Shun Plautus and old Ennius: they are meats
> Too harsh for a weak stomach. Use to read
> (But not without a tutor) the best Greeks,
> As Orpheus, Musaeus, Pindarus,
> Hesiod, Callimachus and Theocrite,
> High Homer, but beware of Lycophron,
> He is too dark and dangerous a dish. (5.3.523–36)[7]

Virgil makes a selection of Latin and Greek writers. The extended culinary metaphor makes him shun certain writers for being "harsh," "dark," and "dangerous." Since little of Lycophron's poetry has survived from the third century BCE, he seems merely a convenient target in contrast to more unimpeachable figures (including the mythical Orpheus). Plautus and Ennius (writers of comic drama and epic, respectively) are more tangible cases, both more archaic and (by the standards of Augustan Rome) stylistically rougher than the philosopher Cato or the dramatist Terence (or Virgil himself). While in *Volpone* the fault is to be too modern, it is also possible to be too archaic. The important thing is an appropriate regulation of reading to avoid the dangers evident in dark, dangerous corners of any literature. In Jonson's own voice, in his collection of sage advice *Timber, or Discoveries,* he extends this tone toward English writing:

> And as it is fit to read the best authors to youth first, so let them be of the openest and clearest, as Livy before Sallust, Sidney before Donne. And beware of letting them taste Gower or Chaucer at first, lest falling too much in love with antiquity, and not apprehending the weight, they grow rough and barren in language only. When their judgements are firm and out of danger, let them read both the old and the new; but no less take heed that their new flowers and sweetness do not as much corrupt as other's dryness and squalor, if they choose not carefully. Spenser, in affecting the ancients, writ no language; yet I would have him read for his matter; but as Virgil read Ennius. (568–69)

Again the emphasis is on sensible doses of a digestible diet in which excessive antiquity is a problem—in *Volpone* Jonson reproves the opposite fault. Elsewhere in *Timber, or Discoveries* he continues to struggle with the relationship of past and present literature. He gives a long list of English orators who are Cicero's equal in wit, high praise indeed, but adds the proviso that "Now things daily fall" (545–46). He discusses Virgil and Lucretius (author of an epic poem of natural philosophy, *De Rerum Natura*) using archaic forms on rare occasions, but asserts that English "Chaucerismes," stylistic touches borrowed from the medieval poet, need to be "expung'd and banish'd" (572). This is largely what he lambasts Edmund Spenser for in the earlier cited passage. Jonson always proposes a regulated exposure to literature of the past; he casts himself as an authoritative arbiter.

Even within this culture in which interaction with the classics was a fundamental part of writing, Jonson stands out. R. V. Young does not exaggerate when he says that "with the exception of John Milton, there is no English poet more learned than Ben Jonson, and none who makes learning such an integral part of his literary work" (qtd. in Harp and Stewart 43). Learning, indeed, was vital to his identity and something he sought to impress upon, as much as share with, his audiences and readers. Don E. Wayne describes it as "part of a calculated strategy of self-assertion"[8]—hinting at the passion, even aggression, of Jonson's self-justification. His father, a clergyman, died before his birth, and his mother was remarried to a bricklayer. Before his theatrical career developed Jonson reluctantly worked for his step-father, something he never lived down, thanks to the taunts of his rivals and his own evident sensitivity. He had attended Westminster School thanks to an unknown patron, and was taught there by the brilliant scholar, antiquarian, and educator William Camden, whom he revered—but left at sixteen and did not attend university.[9] Nevertheless Jonson's scholarship continued and grew, and learning was a way of transcending his origins. Scholars have worked out the contents of Jonson's library and identified many of his books that survive today: the range of reading is remarkable, as is the level of the effort and scholarship in his annotations.[10]

Jonson's learning is reflected in his works, which show the varied and meticulously processed influence of the classics. He was also familiar with Lodovico Castelvetro's *Poetice d'Aristotele* (1570) and Giambattista Cinthio Giraldi's *Discorsi* (1554), key neoclassical texts in which Renaissance writers translated the general advice of Aristotle and Horace into much more specific advice that determined modern practice.[11] These share Jonson's rigor and anticipate his attempts to establish concrete principles. Jonson, however, certainly did not stop at these filtered and reprocessed versions of classical ideas. His was a very direct encounter with an unusual intensity—as can be measured in the sharp comment of Dryden:

> He was deeply conversant in the Ancients, both Greek and Latine, and he borrow'd boldly from them [. . .] But he has done his Robberies so openly, that one may see he fears not to be taxed by any Law. He invades Authours like a Monarch, and what would be theft in other Poets, is onely victory in him.[12]

Dryden thought very deeply about such issues, as an imitator and translator himself, and as a critic of the classical tradition and its relationship, and challenge, to English literature. His vocabulary stays just this side of derogatory, as Dryden genuinely marvels at Jonson's ability to work very closely with classical texts, while always transforming them and claiming their material as his own. There can be a fine line between plagiarism and imitation: Jonson is clearly on one side, but many have felt that there is a curious boldness in his willingness to reuse material.

Other works of Jonson's show their classicism more obviously than *Volpone*. His poems, especially the *Epigrams,* are often very closely modeled on Latin and Greek sources. His masques are full of mythological material, the product of copious study. All Jonson's plays for the public stage can be traced back to classical origins to a greater or lesser extent, but it is his three plays actually set in ancient Rome that stand out. *Poetaster* is a story pieced together from facts and fictions about famous Roman poets and their fictional antagonists. It includes lengthy translations from Ovid, Horace, and Virgil, the three central characters, and is itself based upon judgments about poetic standards. The dignified humility of Horace and the transcendent genius of Virgil win out against the shallow poetasters and even against the reckless talent of Ovid. *Catiline* is a history play about the conspiracy of Catiline and Cicero's heroic resistance; it too includes direct translation from Latin literature, as passages from Cicero's *In Catilinam* oration are appropriated wholesale. The third Roman play, *Sejanus,* is a different kind of history. Based on Tacitus, the historian of the decadent empire, it depicts endemic corruption and moral bankruptcy instead of the noble principles of Cicero. However, a non-Roman play such as *Volpone* can show distinctly classical interests too. Indeed, Anne Barton argues that *Volpone* was actually "generated" by Sejanus: "it inherits its darkness from imperial Rome."[13] The corruption and decadence are situated in a lighter Venetian setting, but they recall the anxious and dangerous world of the earlier play.

Elements of *Volpone* derive from numerous classical sources, some specific, some more general, all processed into the structure of the play. The story of an old man who fools those hunting his legacy is found in Latin and Greek satirical sources: Petronius's *Satyricon,* in the story of Eumolus at Croton, and Lucian's *Pluto and*

Mercury.[14] It is also featured closely in Jonson's favorite author, Horace, most explicitly in Satire 2.5, where the epic hero Ulysses is given far from epic advice by the prophet Tiresias: the trick to getting rich, he says, is to befriend the elderly and worm a way into their wills. This classical foreshadowing does nothing to limit the modernity of the play's setting, Venice. A trading republic and a source of fascination for the English, it is the epitome of contemporary fashion, a seething hub for the newest ideas. In the play fashionability is a sign of moral weakness; specifically, it is one of many forms of failure to find a decorous balance between the new and the old. This has a literary dimension in that one manifestation of a slavish attention to the latest thing is misjudgment of the literary canon. This comes to the surface at numerous points in the play.

The farcical story of Sir Politic and Lady Would-be features both a misguided obsession with novel trends and a revealing misunderstanding of the value of classical examples. As travelers, they have a responsibility to their origins, and to the places they visit, which should guide them toward a balanced appreciation of both. Readers are like travelers when they encounter new and old texts: especially within a classicism like Jonson's the emphasis naturally falls on the need to remember ancient standards. However, as is seen in the reading lists of *Poetaster* and *Timber, or Discoveries,* there is also a need to avoid immersion in archaism. Nobody in *Volpone* runs this risk. Lady Would-be is typical in her preference for the latest things:

Sir, a word with you.
I would be loath to contest publicly
With any gentlewoman; or to seem
Froward, or violent (as *The Courtier* says),
It comes too near rusticity in a lady,
Which I would shun, by all means. (4.2.32–37)

She cites the third book of Castiglione's courtly manual *Il Cortegiano* (translated into English by Thomas Hoby in 1561 as *The Courtyer*) as a guide to behavior. Her aim is to be urban at all costs—a value that contrasts with those of Jonson's poems in *The Forrest* and with his favorite classical sources (such as Horace). Lady Would-be's degraded obsession with fashionable books and things is shared by her husband. In the preceding scene he fails to impress Peregrine with some flashy reading and Venetian insider's dialect. Much earlier in the play he expounds shallow reasons for their travels:

Sir, to a wise man, all the world's his soil.
It is not Italy, nor France, nor Europe,
That must bound me, if my fates call me forth.
Yet, I protest, it is no salt desire
Of seeing countries, shifting a religion,
Nor any disaffection to the state
Where I was bred, and unto which I owe
My dearest plots, hath brought me out; much less
That idle, antique, stale, grey-headed project
Of knowing men's minds and manners, with Ulysses;
But a peculiar humor of my wife's,
Laid for this height of Venice, to observe,
To quote, to learn the language, and so forth. (2.1.1–13)

The proverbial first line is as profound as he gets. His disclaimers are curious—in what sense is "shifting a religion" merely a "salt" (wanton) desire? Jonson, after all, converted to Catholicism in prison himself in 1598; this and the subsequent reconciliation with the Anglican church were heavy matters (Riggs 51, 126–34). The possibility of political exile (itself associated with recent religious controversies) is denied in curious terms—the affectionate memory of his "dearest plots" remains obscure. When the actual reason for traveling is finally voiced—this "peculiar humor" of his wife—it is purely bathetic, apparently lacking any vestige even of presumed substance. The most interesting lines undertake a vehement attack on Ulysses, with an echo of the very first lines of Homer's epic *The Odyssey* (Ulysses is the Latin name for Odysseus), where the minds and manners of those encountered on voyage are recalled (the lines are translated in Horace's *Ars Poetica,* lines 201–02 in Jonson's English version). But Ulysses/Odysseus, of course, does not set out with this goal in mind, and the goal itself seems rather substantial. Sir Politic has drastically failed to understand, or to value, the Homeric example, and this reveals a sharper seriousness behind his absurd and laughable actions. He is a vivid travesty of a contemporary phenomenon, the educational traveler;[15] he also makes himself vulnerable to, and deserving of, the deceit of others.

Later in the play his wife reveals her own failure to value classical literature suitably. In her case the crucial error is not to recognize that not all classical authorities are equal. As well as being foolishly fashionable, Lady Would-be is pretentious as she aspires to the noblest feminine pastimes:

> I have, a little, studied physic; but, now,
> I'm all for music: save, i' the forenoons,
> An hour or two for painting. I would have
> A lady, indeed, to have all letters and arts,
> Be able to discourse, to write, to paint,
> But principal (as Plato holds) your music
> (And, so does wise Pythagoras, I take it)
> Is your true rapture; when there is concent
> In face, in voice, and clothes; and is, indeed,
> Our sex's chiefest ornament. (3.4.67–76)

Amid the pretention she reveals her superficiality by introducing the irrelevant details of "face" and "clothes" to the "concent" (harmony) of music. She backs up her enthusiastic twittering with a double authority from the classical world. Plato and Pythagoras are two Greek philosophers and they both do, indeed, say things about music. Lady Would-be appropriates them to justify her latest fad but also reveals her ignorance by ironing out the gradients and textures within the classical corpus. Not all philosophers are of equal weight. Plato, who discusses music in his *Republic,* is an enormously influential and respected philosopher. Pythagoras, whose works do not survive but whose opinions are echoed by others (Plutarch, for example), is not of the same weight. Some of his opinions, such as those connecting music and cosmology in heavenly harmony, and his mathematical precepts, retained respect. But he is also the philosopher of metempsychosis, the transmigration of souls, an opinion that Renaissance readers would most likely have encountered in burlesque or ironic form. Donne's poem "The Progress of the

Soul" is a complex example, an unfinished poem whose goal remains inscrutable, but it is hard to believe Donne took the doctrine seriously per se. (It is, however, possible that the debased versions of metempsychosis found in *Volpone* could be Jonson's response to the intellectually irresponsible side of Donne's poem.) There are considerably older burlesque versions: Lucian's in *The Dream;* Diogenes Laertius's in *De Philosophorum Vitis,* and Erasmus's in *Praise of Folly.*[16] Volpone, who is getting tired of Lady Would-be and no doubt fears a demonstration, retorts that according to one poet "as old in time as Plato, and as knowing," "your highest female grace is silence" (77–78).[17] This causes her some consternation as she expects to be an expert on female graces. "Which o' your poets?" she asks, "Petrarch? Or Tasso? Or Dante? Guerrini? Ariosto? Aretine? Cieco di Hadria? I have read them all" (79–81). Even when she has a clue that this is an ancient poet she cannot see past the modern world—her list is all Italian, stretching back only a few centuries, and containing all the names with which a pretentious traveler should be *au fait.*

All this testifies to the lack of proper reverence for the classics, and the lack of individual responsibility in dealing with them, which are endemic in Venice. This error can be summed up in terms of the classical duality of profit and pleasure, two complimentary features of good literature. The most famous exposition of this comes in Horace's *Ars Poetica,* translated of course by Jonson:

> But he hath every suffrage, can apply
> Sweet mix'd with sowre, to his Reader, so
> As doctrine, and delight together go. (514–16)

The notion that a poem should seek to delight as well as to teach ("sweet" and "sowre," "doctrine" and "delight") was enormously flexible and useful to those who defended poetry, but it could also be used to require seriousness when literature strayed toward excessive entertainment. Katharine Eisaman Maus recognizes the importance of the profit/pleasure duality. For her it runs throughout Jonson's plays at a number of levels:

> The Horatian artist seeks simultaneously to please and to instruct his audience, to gratify a sometimes undiscriminating public while maintaining his own artistic standards; he finds it virtually impossible to realise all his ambitions in any one poem or play. Compromise is inevitable. Yet in play after play Jonson, embodying in his protagonists his own artistic dilemmas, insists upon the provisional character of even his most brilliant compromises, and qualifies them with an awareness of impractical but attractive alternatives.[18]

The variation on this theme in *Volpone* includes some clear judgments, and some less clear. The play itself aspires to profitability and pleasurability, as its "Epistle Dedicatory" indicates,[19] but the characters within fall short of what any author would desire of interpreters. This is a world where reading and thinking are oriented toward pleasure and not profit.

There is a kind of profit that is relevant, but not the moral form envisaged by Horace and Jonson and others. Instead, the laws of the marketplace subdue many things to them. Volpone's performance as a quack doctor, and his wooing of Celia, both involve rich rhetorical performances in which classical materials are cynically pieced together for base personal gain. While he acts the mountebank in order to see Celia, going through the motions of gulling the crowd along the way, Nano sings a song that plays fast and loose with the great authorities of Greek medicine:

> Had old Hippocrates, or Galen,
> (That to their books put medicines all in)
> But known this secret, they had never
> (Of which they will be guilty ever)
> Been murderers of so much paper,
> Or wasted many a hurtless taper. (2.2.107–12)

Hippocrates was a physician of the fifth century BCE, Galen of the second century BCE, and both were enormously influential in developing the theories of medicine, based on the body's humors, that dominated until the sixteenth century. The contempt for their efforts voiced here parallels that for Ulysses in Sir Politic Would-be's discussion of travelers' motives—and it is scandalous in both cases. During his sales pitch for the youth-giving powder Volpone weaves a story that, in terms of the right appreciation of the relationship between modernity and the classics, is also shameful:

> It is the powder, that made Venus a goddess—given her by Apollo—that kept her perpetually young, cleared her wrinkles, firmed her gums, filled her skin, colored her hair; from her, derived to Helen, and at the sack of Troy, unfortunately, lost; till now, in this our age, it was as happily recovered by a studious antiquary out of some ruins of Asia, who sent a moiety of it to the court of France—but much sophisticated—wherewith the ladies there now color their hair. (2.2.206–13)

He aggrandizes his powder not only by linking it with Venus but also by emphasizing that it has benefited yet more from the up-to-date sophistication of the French court—an idea that is anathema within the terms of Jonsonian classicism. In Volpone's advertisement modernity brings value, but it is clear that the underlying path, from classical divinity to the superficial adornments of courtly ladies, betrays the superficiality of the Venetian worldview. Volpone models culture as a kind of Pythagorean metempsychosis, with an essence, like a soul, passing from body to body: a burlesque version, of course, in which the bodies in question become less and less worthy, but the transferred essence gains value (though not true value).

The idea of metempsychosis has other appearances in the play, and it plays a number of roles. It serves as an allegory of decadence, which the characters embrace. It also serves as a measure of taste: the Venetians are seduced by Pythagorean philosophy and the poetry of Ovid. In book 15 of the *Metamorphoses* Ovid depicts the philosopher expounding his theory; it acts partly as a summation of the theme of change in the poem, but it does so only partially and with plenty of irony. Ovid was the favorite poet of the 1590s, and Jonson's *Poetaster* is at least partly a corrective to what Jonson saw as a misguided preference for a morally irresponsible writer. In *Volpone,* written a few years after the Ovidian heyday, a taste for Ovid works as a sign of wrong reading within the structure of classical learning with which Jonson underpins his work. Volpone looks to Ovid when he plots how he and Celia will spend their time as lovers:

> My eunuch sing, my fool make up the antic.
> Whilst, we, in changed shapes, act Ovid's tales,
> Thou, like Europe now, and I like Jove,

Then I like Mars, and thou like Erycine,
So of the rest, till we have quite run through
And wearied all the fables of the gods.
Then will I have thee in more modern forms,
Attired like some sprightly dame of France,
Brave Tuscan lady, or proud Spanish beauty;
Sometimes, unto the Persian Sophy's wife;
Or the Grand Signior's mistress; and, for change,
To one of our most artful courtesans,
Or some quick Negro, or cold Russian;
And I will meet thee in as many shapes;
Where we may, so, transfuse our wandering souls
Out at our lips, and score up sums of pleasure. (3.7.220–35)

"Ovid's tales" are those of the *Metamorphoses.* "Europe" is Europa, raped by Jupiter in the shape of a bull. "Erycine" is a name for the goddess Venus, adulterous lover of Mars. In the original spelling, "antique," there is no distinction between "antic," meaning fun and frolics, and "antique," meaning ancient. Volpone cannot express any distinction between these two, which is his first mistake. His second is the casual way in which he imagines wearying of what the classical world has to offer and turning to "more modern," and more exotic, forms. The Ovidian beginning is capped by a Pythagorean end, as he figures their erotic role-playing as a form of metempsychosis. To a small extent this is an example of imagination, but it is, within the classicism of this play, a profound failure of imagination: pleasure is measured in "sums."

In the play's second scene Volpone's servants put on an Ovidian-Pythagorean entertainment based around a process of transmigration. Volpone is amused by the show, even though it does not even pretend to be good:

Now, room for fresh gamesters, who do will you to know,
    They do bring you neither play, nor university show;
And therefore do entreat you, that whatsoever they rehearse,
    May not fare a whit the worse, for the false pace of the verse.
If you wonder at this, you will wonder more ere we pass,
    For know, here is enclosed the Soul of Pythagoras,
That juggler divine, as hereafter shall follow. (1.2.01–07)

This is not false modesty and it trivializes something that already tends toward a lack of seriousness. The soul is now in Androgyno, after a long line of other bodies: whores, philosophers, kings, knights, beggars, and animals. The first appearance of metempsychosis in the play is vacuous, but it does have ramifications. The entertainment value of the subsequent actions of Mosca and Volpone is qualified by their own susceptibility to inane shows.

Jonson presents right and wrong choices, places where people could have chosen better. In the face of the modern world's failures to understand and value things correctly, he asserts standards. This is an end in itself in relation to classical learning, which was so important to Jonson and his time. It also serves as an indictment of modernity as a principle and as an indictment of the comic world of the play. However, Jonson is too subtle a writer to limit his exploration to a clearly categorical harangue. There are significant complications that arise from an implicit uncertainty and insecurity about the right ways to handle sources, and whether the play truly does incorporate its materials into a whole that provides both profit and pleasure. The lack of moral censure for the bad, and reward for the good, at the end of the play is of course the most important aspect of this. There is also a more specific example of problematic classicism in the song that Volpone sings to Celia:

> Come, my Celia, let us prove,
> While we can, the sports of love;
> Time will not be ours for ever,
> He, at length, our good will sever;
> Spend not then his gifts in vain.
> Suns that set may rise again:
> But if once we lose this light,
> 'Tis with us perpetual night.
> Why should we defer our joys?
> Fame and rumour are but toys. (3.7.166–74)

This is a close translation of the fifth poem of Catullus, a poet who combines frank eroticism with more weighty content, and who does not have so clear an immoral reputation as Ovid. Celia is appalled by this poem's advice that the only true moral failure is to get caught. However, the poem somewhat transcends its context, largely because of its origin—within a long tradition of erotic entreaties that Catullus wittily revives. This would be a sharp enough challenge to simple models of how classical decorum might work, but the poem appears elsewhere in Jonson's work, as the fifth poem in his collection *The Forrest* (289). The interactions between the various poems there are very complex. The song to Celia is an example of profane love that stands in comparison with the sacred love of the later poems, but the collection's miscellaneous content allows more complex connections. No poem in *The Forrest* is inherently trivial or immoral. So there are hints of instability even in the sources of Jonson's stability, and he does not duck these problems even in *Volpone,* a play in which sound appreciation of the classical tradition is a moral issue. The presence of the Catullan poem in the play (especially when we consider its inclusion elsewhere) is an implicit recognition of the problems of allegiance to the classics: Greek and Latin writers provide a complex inheritance and do not always fall clearly in line with or against decorum and morality.

These classical elements are not isolated: they are aspects of central themes. For Jonson learning and the literature of the Greeks and Romans were fundamental parts of any world picture. His classicism did provide a note of solace and constancy in a changing world, and this provides conviction behind the standards he proposes. However, as the Venetian attitudes demonstrate, he could feel beleaguered and alone in asserting those standards. This manifests itself in the connection between the classicism of *Volpone* and the play's ominous notes. Ian Donaldson sees a remarkable combination of comic entertainment and an ever-present sense of time and mortality: "Jonson's striking and unusual achievement in *Volpone* is his placing of the agreeably amoral activities of Mosca and Volpone within this chillingly long perspective of time. Few comedies suggest so powerfully the yielding of the forces of 'quickness' to the fact of death" (134). The place of the classics in *Volpone* interacts with important contemporary theories of reading Latin and Greek writers, and it enables Jonson to set out a charged moral agenda for reading and acting. However, its sharpest edge comes in relation to what Donaldson identifies as the dialogue between present pleasure and approaching endings. The Venetians and their visitors take pleasure without profit, but they also take pleasure without noticing the ticking of the clock. The classics act partly as an antidote, a source of timeless value that can transcend the immediate marketplaces of the play, but there is deep-rooted doubt that such characters can really re-embrace the things they have abandoned in their pursuit of the present.

NOTES

1. Unless otherwise stated, Jonson quotations are taken from *Ben Jonson,* ed. Ian Donaldson (Oxford: Oxford UP, 1985).
2. See George W. Pigman, "Versions of Imitation in the Renaissance," *Renaissance Quarterly* 33 (1981): 1–32.
3. Joseph Loewenstein puts him in the context of seventeenth-century humanism in "Humanism and Seventeenth-Century English Literature," *The Cambridge Companion to Renaissance Humanism,* ed. Jill Kraye (Cambridge: Cambridge UP, 1996) 269–93, esp. 269–71, 278–82.
4. See Rebecca W. Bushnell, *A Culture of Teaching: Early Modern Humanism in Theory and Practice* (Ithaca: Cornell UP, 1996), and M. L. Clarke, *Classical Education in England* (Cambridge: Cambridge UP, 1959).
5. See Thomas M. Greene, *The Light in Troy: Imitation and Discovery in Renaissance Poetry* (New Haven: Yale UP, 1982).
6. See Richard Harp and Stanley Stewart, ed., *The Cambridge Companion to Ben Jonson* (Cambridge: Cambridge UP, 2000) 163.
7. Jonson, *Poetaster,* ed. Tom Cain (Manchester: Manchester UP, 1995).
8. See Don E. Wayne, "Mediation and Contestation: English Classicism from Sidney to Jonson," *Criticism* 25 (1983): 211–37, esp. 217.
9. See David Riggs, *Ben Jonson: A Life* (Cambridge: Harvard UP, 1989) 11–17.
10. See David McPherson, "Ben Jonson's Library and Marginalia: An Annotated Catalogue," *Studies in Philology* 71 (1974): 1–106.
11. See David Farley-Hills, "Jonson and the Neo-Classical Rules in *Sejanus* and *Volpone,*" *Review of English Studies* n.s. 46 (1995): 153–73.
12. See D. H. Craig, ed., *Ben Jonson: The Critical Heritage 1599–1798* (London: Routledge, 1990) 253.
13. See Anne Barton, *Ben Jonson, Dramatist* (Cambridge: Cambridge UP, 1984) 105.
14. See Douglas Duncan, *Ben Jonson and the Lucianic Tradition* (Cambridge: Cambridge UP, 1979) 144–64.
15. See Sara Warneke, *Images of the Educational Traveler in Early Modern England* (Leiden: E.J. Brill, 1995).
16. See Brian Parker, ed., *Volpone, or The Fox,* Revels ed. (Manchester: Manchester UP, 1999) app. B.
17. The poet is the Greek tragedian Sophocles, in his *Ajax,* l. 293, in *Sophocles,* ed. David Grene and Richmond Lattimore, *Complete Greek Tragedies,* vol. 2 (Chicago: U of Chicago P, 1969).
18. See Katharine Eisaman Maus, *Ben Jonson and the Roman Frame of Mind* (Princeton: Princeton UP, 1984) 76; and on the laws of poetry, see also Richard Dutton, *Ben Jonson: Authority: Criticism* (Houndmills: Macmillan, 1996) 105–39.
19. See Ian Donaldson, "Volpone: Quick and Dead," *Essays in Criticism* 21 (1971): 121–34.

READING LIST

Barton, Anne. *Ben Jonson, Dramatist.* Cambridge: Cambridge UP, 1984.

Bushnell, Rebecca W. *A Culture of Teaching: Early Modern Humanism in Theory and Practice.* Ithaca: Cornell UP, 1996.

Clarke, M. L. *Classical Education in England.* Cambridge: Cambridge UP, 1959.

Craig, D. H., ed. *Ben Jonson: The Critical Heritage 1599–1798.* London: Routledge, 1990.

Donaldson, Ian. "Volpone: Quick and Dead." *Essays in Criticism* 21 (1971): 121–34.

Duncan, Douglas. *Ben Jonson and the Lucianic Tradition.* Cambridge: Cambridge UP, 1979.

Dutton, Richard. *Ben Jonson: Authority: Criticism.* Houndmills: Macmillan, 1996.

Farley-Hills, David. "Jonson and the Neo-Classical Rules in *Sejanus* and *Volpone.*" *Review of English Studies* n.s. 46 (1995): 153–73.

Greene, Thomas M. *The Light in Troy: Imitation and Discovery in Renaissance Poetry.* New Haven: Yale UP, 1982.

Harp, Richard, and Stanley Stewart, eds. *The Cambridge Companion to Ben Jonson.* Cambridge: Cambridge UP, 2000.

Loewenstein, Joseph. "Humanism and Seventeenth-Century English Literature." *The Cambridge Companion to Renaissance Humanism.* Ed. Jill Kraye. Cambridge: Cambridge UP, 1996. 269–93.

Maus, Katharine Eisaman. *Ben Jonson and the Roman Frame of Mind.* Princeton: Princeton UP, 1984.

McPherson, David. "Ben Jonson's Library and Marginalia: An Annotated Catalogue." *Studies in Philology* 71 (1974): 1–106.

Pigman, George W. "Versions of Imitation in the Renaissance." *Renaissance Quarterly* 33 (1981): 1–32.

Riggs, David. *Ben Jonson: A Life.* Cambridge, M.: Harvard UP, 1989.

Warneke, Sara. *Images of the Educational Traveller in Early Modern England.* Leiden: E.J. Brill, 1995.

Wayne, Don E. "Mediation and Contestation: English Classicism from Sidney to Jonson." *Criticism* 25 (1983): 211–37.

17

The Knight of the Burning Pestle and Generic Experimentation

Lucy Munro

London, 1607. *The Knight of the Burning Pestle* receives its first performance at the Blackfriars Theater. Written by Francis Beaumont, it is commissioned and performed by the Children of the Revels, the most successful of the Jacobean children's companies—troupes in which all the roles, male and female, were performed by boys and young men. The theater itself is comparatively small, holding at the most around seven hundred spectators, and, unlike the big, open-air amphitheaters such as the Globe, it is located within an existing building (part of the old Blackfriars monastery precinct), where performances take place under candlelight. Seats and boxes crowd closely around the stage, and some of the audience—young, self-consciously fashionable gallants—are sitting on the stage itself, on display to the rest of the spectators even as they await the play. The boy who is to say the prologue enters and begins his speech:

> From all that's near the court, from all that's great
> Within the compass of the city-walls,
> We now have brought our scene— (Induction 1–3)[1]

Suddenly there is a disturbance in the audience, and a citizen appears, shouting at the nervous prologue: "Hold your peace, goodman boy" (Induction 4). Aware of the satiric plays that the Children of the Revels often performed, he is not impressed: "This seven years there hath been plays at this house, I have observed it, you have still girds at citizens; and now you call your play *The London Merchant*. Down with your title, boy, down with your title!" (Induction 6–9). Judging on the basis of the reputation of the company, the title of the play, and the first three lines of the prologue, the Citizen has concluded that *The London Merchant* is likely to make fun of London tradesmen and that it is his responsibility to prevent this from happening. Somehow, as the rest of the audience look on, the Citizen and his wife persuade the prologue—and the rest of the Children of the Revels—to follow their instructions for the play and to cast their apprentice, Rafe, as the hero. Eventually mollified by the prologue's promises, they take their seats with the gallants on the edge of the stage, and allow him to finish his speech.

The whole scene has, of course, been plotted in advance by the playwright and the company: the Citizen and his Wife are played by actors and the disturbance is part of the play. As *The Knight of the Burning Pestle* progresses the effect of the citizens' interruption becomes clear. In effect, two plays are performed simultaneously: the first is the satiric city comedy that the company set out to perform and for which the prologue was written; the second is a chivalric romance featuring Rafe as a heroic "grocer errant." Scenes from the two plays alternate, mingle, and separate again, interspersed with comments from the citizens and their arguments with the representatives of the company. *The Knight of the Burning Pestle* also incorporates innumerable references to other plays, to popular entertainments such as freak shows and puppet shows, and to ballads and popular songs. The play can seem impossibly postmodern: as Jeffrey Masten points out, Roland Barthes could be describing *The Knight of the Burning Pestle* when he asserts that a text is "a multi-dimensional space in which a variety of writings, none of them original, blend and clash."[2] The effect is that of a self-referential, witty, and parodic farrago, and an extreme example of a willingness to innovate and to play with different kinds of drama within the confines of one play. It is generic experimentation par excellence.

In fact, Beaumont and the Children of the Revels may have pushed their innovation too far, because the play was a failure in the theater. When it was printed in 1613, the publisher, Walter Burre, prefaced the text with a letter to Robert Keysar, a goldsmith who in 1607 had been a leading shareholder in the Children of the Revels. Burre describes the play as an "unfortunate child," "exposed to the wide world, who for want of judgement, or not understanding the privy mark of irony about it (which showed it was no offspring of any vulgar brain) utterly rejected it."[3] The audience, Burre suggests, didn't understand the play, and its humor went over their heads. It is likely that the first performance of *The Knight of the Burning Pestle* was the last for a number of years; the first performances that we know to have been successful took place nearly thirty years later, when the play was revived by Queen Henrietta Maria's Men. By the mid-1660s, it was still more in tune with dramatic sensibility. A new prologue, written specially for a revival in 1665–67 and spoken by the famous Restoration actress Nell Gywn, tells the audience that the author has "burlesqued all he himself had writ" and has "farcified a play," using generic terms ("farce" and "burlesque") that were not in use when *The Knight of the Burning Pestle* was first performed but that seem to capture something of its anarchic comic spirit.[4]

We can best understand what the play was trying to achieve, and why the audience may have been confused or hostile to its generic innovation, by focusing in the first place on what an early Jacobean writer, actor, or spectator might have understood by genre. We can then use some of that knowledge to think about how particular techniques in *The Knight of the Burning Pestle* might have been intended to affect the Blackfriars audience. Therefore, in the first part of this chapter I will focus on genre itself, and in the second part I will highlight some aspects of the play's generic experimentation, focusing on the way in which it combines the two different kinds of narrative: city comedy and chivalric romance.

Defining Genre

A theatrical genre is best understood as a set of conventions that were used by dramatists and playing companies and recognized (or, in the case of *The Knight of the Burning Pestle,* perhaps not recognized) by audiences. These conventions could affect different aspects of the play, such as its narrative, its subject matter, its characters, and its language. This way of defining genre would have been familiar to writers and readers in the late sixteenth and early seventeenth centuries. In addition, terms such as comedy and tragedy are still widely understood, as are romance, history, or pastoral, but interpretation of the terms can differ because their associations have shifted over time. In an early dictionary entitled *Glossographia,* Thomas Blount provides definitions of comedy and tragedy. He writes that

> a *Tragedy* treats of exilements, murders, matters of grief, &c. a *Comedy* of love-toyes, merry fictions and petty matters; In a *Tragedy* the greatest parts of the actors are Kings and Noble persons; In a *Com[e]dy,* private persons of meaner state and condition. The subject of a *Comedy* is often feigned, but of a *Tragedy* it is commonly true and once really performed[.] (2R4^{r})[5]

For Blount, comedies and tragedies have different subject matter: comedies deal with light-hearted material, tragedies with serious issues; comedies feature ordinary people, tragedies focus on those of high status; comedies are usually fictional, tragedies are often based on real events. Similarly, in another dictionary, *An English Expositor,* John Bullokar defines a comedy as a "play or interlude, the beginning whereof is euer full of troubles, and the end ioyfull" and a tragedy as "a play or Historie ending with great sorrow and bloodshed" (D7^{v}, O6^{v}).[6] Tragedies have one kind of plotline, beginning harmoniously and ending sorrowfully; comedies have the opposite trajectory.

Genres do not, however, stand still, and even in their own day many comedies and tragedies did not fit Blount or Bullokar's definitions. This is because each new comedy or tragedy is a negotiation between an inherited form and current ideas and fashions. When a new work is written the genres on which it draws are reconfigured and their ideological associations are adjusted. For instance, in the 1590s companies began to perform tragedies about middle-class citizens, rather than kings or nobles. These plays would not fit Blount's idea of tragedy in some respects, but they are recognizable as tragedies: they focus on murder and bloodshed, and their narratives progress from seeming harmony to explosive discord. Thus, a genre such as tragedy can seem fixed or even timeless, but its boundaries are in fact continually shifting and modulating.

Some of the more specific terms that we use to group particular kinds of plays—"revenge tragedy," for instance, or "city comedy"—would have been unfamiliar to a Jacobean playgoer, but the characteristics they encompass would have been recognizable. For example, the Induction to *A Warning for Fair Women* (c. 1588–90) features the feuding personifications of three genres: Comedy, Tragedy, and History. As they quarrel, Comedy satirically describes Tragedy's function in terms that encompass many of the features of what we would now call revenge tragedy, familiar to us from plays such as Thomas Kyd's *Spanish Tragedy,* William Shakespeare's *Hamlet,* and Thomas Middleton's *Revenger's Tragedy:*

> How some damnd tyrant, to obtaine a crowne,
> Stabs, hangs, impoysons, smothers, cutteth throats,
> And then a Chorus too comes howling in,
> And tels vs of the worrying of a cat,
> Then of a filthie whining ghost,
> Lapt in some fowle sheete, or a leather pelch,
> Comes skreaming like a pigge halfe stickt,
> And cries *Vindicta* reuenge, reuenge:
> With that a little Rosen flasheth forth,
> Like smoke out of a Tabacco pipe, or a boyes squib. (A2^{v}–A3^{r})[7]

Comedy criticizes the muddled and mundane techniques of contemporary tragedy. The Chorus, rather than describing lofty affairs, "tels us of the worrying of a cat." The ghost, familiar from tragedies of revenge, is not noble or awe-inspiring, but "filthie," "whining," ill costumed, and accompanied by a cheap theatrical effect, "like smoke out of a Tabacco pipe, or a boyes squib." Tragedy may try to embody a classical ideal, but in reality she is subject to theatrical fashion. This is demonstrated ironically in the fact that the play that follows Tragedy's eventual triumph over Comedy and History is one of the new breed of "domestic tragedies," which break generic decorum by focusing on the crimes of middle-class murderers. Genres, it seems, cannot remain static.

As these examples suggest, in order to recognize that a playwright is experimenting with a genre, we need to be able to identify that genre in the first place and to understand what its "normal" characteristics might be. Generic experimentation can therefore be risky, because members of the audience might fail to recognize the structures with which the dramatist is playing. For that reason a play might contain indications regarding its form. Sometimes these generic instructions are external to the work itself. The prologues of sixteenth and seventeenth century plays often specify that the following drama is a comedy or a tragedy: the prologue to Ben Jonson's *Volpone* (1605), for instance, claims that the play "presents quick *comedy,* refined, / As best critics have designed" (Prologue 29–30).[8] Addressing the readers of his "pastoral tragicomedy" *The Faithful Shepherdess* (1607–08), John Fletcher ruefully acknowledges that he should have written a prologue like that provided by Jonson, and that when he failed to do so his audience completely misinterpreted the play:

> the people seeing when it was plaid, having ever had a singuler guift in defining, concluded [it] to be a play of country hired Shepheards, in gray cloakes, with curtaild dogs in strings, sometimes laughing together, and sometimes killing one another: And missing whitsun ales, creame, wassel and morris dances, began to be angry. (497.4–8)[9]

As Fletcher implies, a playwright could be too clever or sophisticated with his generic experimentation: he made the mistake of omitting the rustic merriment that the audience associated with pastoral and confused them by using a term, tragicomedy, with which they were unfamiliar.

In other plays, indications of genre are internal. We still recognize some of the generic "markers" that were used by early modern playwrights: we expect comedies to end happily and tragedies to be marked by some bloodshed; comedies are more likely to make us laugh, tragedies to make us cry. Other generic markers have changed since the seventeenth century: we do not expect tragedy to feature only kings and nobles, or comedy to focus only on more plebeian matters. Identification of internal characteristics of genres requires that the audience pay close attention to what is taking place on stage. Watching *The Knight of the Burning Pestle, The Faithful Shepherdess,* or even *Volpone,* they cannot simply relax and expect events to follow a stereotypically comic or tragic course. They must instead catch particular generic indications and be alert to whether a genre is being played "straight" or is being parodied.

The confusions that genre could cause were not helped by the fact that dramatists were often ambivalent about genre and inconsistent in their attitudes toward it. In some contexts they insist that there are such things as genres, and that their dictates ought to be followed. In others, they insist—equally vehemently—that their works adhere to no generic pattern. A play such as *The Knight of the Burning Pestle* is an expression of deeply divided attitudes toward generic categorization. Its very composition indicates that its writer and performers were happy to mingle genres and to produce something that conformed to no individual generic pattern; on the other hand, however, without an awareness of the nature of the genres it mingles and parodies we would simply be confused by the play, unable to understand or interpret it.

Generic Experimentation

One of the most important aspects of generic play in *The Knight of the Burning Pestle* is the way in which it juxtaposes two particular kinds of drama. As I outlined earlier, the play contains two plotlines, one derived from city comedy, the other from chivalric romance. In the first, *The London Merchant,* Jasper is apprenticed to Venturewell, a rich merchant. When he informs his master that he has fallen in love with his daughter, Luce, Venturewell—who wants Luce to marry a rich gentleman, Humphrey—drives him away. The plot focuses on Jasper's attempts to elope with Luce, while a subsidiary narrative details the conflict between his father, Master Merrythought, and his step-mother, who is convinced that Jasper is out to disinherit her son Michael. The second plot in *The Knight of the Burning Pestle* features Rafe's heroic adventures and has little in the way of a narrative thread. Rafe encounters a giant, turns down marriage with Pomponia, daughter of the king of Moldavia, is chosen to be lord of the May, leads troops of citizens in their martial drilling at Mile End, and finally meets his death. This lack of narrative is partly dictated by the characteristics of romance, which tends to be episodic, but it also has a more local cause in the fact that all of Rafe's actions are subject to the whims of the watching Citizens.

Each kind of play has ideological implications. The subject matter of city comedy is usually the seedy underbelly of city life, a milieu in which usurers cozen foolish young men of their fortunes, apprentices disobey their masters, fortune-seekers chase heiresses or rich widows, and prostitution is rife. Those who succeed in city comedy tend to be the witty tricksters, those characters who plot their way out of financial or personal trouble. In Middleton's *A Trick to Catch the Old One* (c. 1605), for instance, the young prodigal Witgood teams up with his former lover, known only as the Courtesan, to cheat his fortune back from his usurious uncle Lucre. At the end of the play Witgood regains his fortune and marries Joyce, the niece of Hoard, Lucre's fellow usurer and desperate rival; the Courtesan, disguised as a rich widow, marries the unwitting Hoard. City comedy is unsentimental about love; in *A Trick to Catch the Old One,* Witgood welcomes the return of his mortgage bond thus:

> Thou soul of my estate I kiss thee,
> I miss life's comfort when I miss thee.
> Oh, never will we part again,
> Until I leave the sight of men. (4.2.87–90)[10]

This speech, addressed to a piece of paper, is far more "romantic" than anything Witgood says to Joyce in the course of the play. In city comedy, money and land are not just more important than romance; romance itself is inextricably tied up in the need to make and keep a fortune.

Chivalric romance, on the other hand, is a far more idealistic genre. It tends to ignore the practical realities of everyday life and to focus on stirring narratives about far-flung countries and heroic deeds: knights fight monsters and win the love of fair maidens, they protect the needy and vanquish tyrants. It usually has an epic scope, covering vast areas of the globe and equally vast periods of time. Romance is primarily a nondramatic genre, and was widely read throughout Europe. Popular texts in England in the late sixteenth and early seventeenth centuries included a number of translations—*Amadis de Gaul,* Ortuñez de Calahorra's *Espejo de Principes y Cavalleros* or *The Mirror of Knighthood, Palmerin D'Oliva* and its sequel *Palmerin of England*—and English romance encompassed chivalric tales such as *Bevis of Hampton* and *Guy of Warwick,* prose narratives including Robert Greene's *Pandosto* and Philip Sidney's *Arcadia,* and Edmund Spenser's epic poem *The Faerie Queene.* These English romances continued to be popular and influential at the time when *The Knight of the Burning Pestle* was written. *The Arcadia* was reprinted in 1605, *Pandosto* in 1607, and *The Faerie Queene* in 1609, and romance exercised a shaping influence on Jacobean plays including John Day's *The Isle of Gulls* (1606), Fletcher's *The Faithful Shepherdess,* Shakespeare and George Wilkins' *Pericles* (1607–08) and Shakespeare's *The Winter's Tale* (1611), which is based directly on *Pandosto.*

Ironically, Sidney himself condemned the kinds of excesses found in dramatic romance; he complains at length in his treatise *An Apology for Poetry* (published 1595) about improbable narratives in which neoclassical dictates about the unity of place and time are utterly neglected:

> you shall have Asia of the one side, and Afric of the other, and so many other under-kingdoms, that the player, when he cometh in, must ever begin with telling where he is, or else the tale will not be conceived. Now ye shall have three ladies walk to gather flowers and then we must believe the stage to be a garden. By and by we hear news of shipwreck in the same place, and then we are to blame if we accept it not for a rock. Upon the back of that comes out a hideous monster with fire and smoke, and then the miserable beholders are bound to take it for a cave. While in the meantime two armies fly in, represented with four swords and bucklers, and then what hard heart will not receive it for a pitched field?[11]

The conglomeration of events and characters described by Sidney are evoked and burlesqued in the romance narrative of *The Knight of the Burning Pestle.* Beaumont, like Sidney, is acutely aware of the difficulties associated with staging this kind of romance material but foregrounds and parodies those difficulties rather than attempting to conceal them.

Like city comedy, romance has ideological implications. It was associated with upper-class display—many of the entertainments performed for Elizabeth I and James I use chivalric motifs and romance narratives—but also with escapist middle- and lower-class enjoyment. Citizens are often portrayed as being enthusiasts for chivalric romance, and city comedy itself often plays with the disjunction between what people read and the way their lives are. In Ben Jonson, George Chapman, and John Marston's *Eastward Ho* (1605), Gertrude, the elder daughter of a goldsmith, has married a worthless specimen of Jacobean knighthood, Sir Petronel Flash. Abandoned by Sir Petronel, Gertrude bewails the fact that her knight is not like those in the stories:

> The knighthood nowadays are nothing like the knighthood of old time. They rid a-horseback; ours go afoot. They were attended by their squires; ours by their lackeys. They went buckled in their armour; ours muffled in their cloaks. They travelled wildernesses and deserts; ours dare scarce walk the streets. They were still prest to engage their honour; ours still ready to pawn their clothes. They would gallop on at sight of a monster; ours run away at the sight of a sergeant. They would help poor ladies; ours make poor ladies.[12]

The clash of reality and fantasy is used to show both the seductive attractions of fictional narratives and the ways in which contemporary knights fail to live up to those ideals.

The fondness of citizens for romance narratives also led to a different kind of fusion, plays in which citizen heroes or contemporary figures faced fabulous adventures: examples include Thomas Heywood's *The Four Prentices of London* (c. 1590) and John Day, William Rowley, and George Wilkins's *The Travels of the Three English Brothers* (1607). We can see some of the tension between different ideas of romance—romance as an elite genre and as a popular entertainment—in *The Knight of the Burning Pestle*. When the citizens demand a sequence showing the courtship of Rafe and Princess Pomponia, a boy from the theater company complains that "it will show ill-favouredly to have a grocer's prentice to court a king's daughter" (4.45–46). The Citizen reacts to this slur against his class and profession by citing textual authority: "You are well read in histories! I pray you, what was Sir Dagonet? Was he not prentice to a grocer in London? Read the play of *The Four Prentices of London,* where they toss their pikes so" (4.47–50). The boy remains unconvinced, telling the audience, "It is not our fault, gentlemen" (4.51).

In *The Knight of the Burning Pestle,* both the city comedy plot and the chivalric romance plot are parodied and burlesqued, and the differing ideologies lying behind each genre are brought into conflict. This can be seen from the moment that the Citizen takes the stage in the Induction. In place of the city comedy narrative, in which he fears that citizens will be portrayed as either foolish or villainous, the Citizen wants a city hero: "I will have a grocer, and he shall do admirable things" (Induction 33–34). The Wife proposes a classic romance narrative, but with a twist: "Let him kill a lion with a pestle, husband; let him kill a lion with a pestle" (Induction 42–43). *The Four Prentices of London* features an apprentice who claims to have killed a lion with his bare hands, but the suggestion that the grocer's pestle should be used as a weapon already suggests that the romance is not going to be taken particularly seriously. Similarly, the title proposed by the Citizen for his play, *The Grocer's Honour,* is undercut by the Prologue's alternative title, *The Knight of the Burning Pestle,* which picks up the Wife's reference to the pestle and parodies the Knight of the Burning Sword, a character in *Amadis de Gaul.* "Burning Pestle" also carries a suggestion of venereal disease, an unromantic issue to which the play will later return.

This kind of trifling with romance convention is continued in the first of Rafe's scenes, in which the "knight" studiously coaches Tim and George, the junior apprentices who must act as his squire and dwarf, in how to speak in a manner suited to romance:

> I charge you that henceforth you never call me by any other name but the "Right Courteous and Valiant Knight of the Burning Pestle," and that you never call any female by the name of

> a woman or wench, but "Fair Lady," if she have her desires, if not, "Distressed Damsel"; that you call all forests and hearths "deserts," and all horses "palfreys." (1.270–79)

Throughout *The Knight of the Burning Pestle,* fun is had with the laughable aspects of romance, including its archaic language, conventional characterization, and rigid gender roles.

The city comedy plot, on the other hand, begins in a deadpan manner: Venturewell's blank-verse speech to Jasper, and the exchanges between Jasper and Luce, could be part of any "normal" city comedy. As it progresses, however, *The London Merchant* becomes more eccentric, notably with the appearances of Humphrey and Master Merrythought. Humphrey is a splendidly ludicrous figure, exceeding even the stereotypical suitors found in many Jacobean comedies. Even his speech—absurdly stiff rhyming couplets—marks him out from the rest of the cast: "Father, it's true in arms I ne'er shall clasp her, / For she is stol'n away by your man Jasper" (2.396–97). It is a mark of the citizens' inability to "read" the city comedy genre that they are far more impressed with Humphrey than they are with Jasper, who embodies the rather ambivalent trickster hero of plays such as *A Trick to Catch the Old One.* As Lee Bliss remarks, "what they would censure in life, they reject in art."[13] In a similar manipulation of the stock characters of city comedy, Master Merrythought is portrayed as an elderly version of the spendthrift prodigal gallant who neglects his land and his family duties. He refuses to even speak in a conventional manner; instead his speech is composed of quotations from ballads and contemporary songs.

The progressively anarchic plot of *The London Merchant,* in which Jasper fakes his own death and appears as his own ghost, seems to become infected by the excesses of the romance plot. Simultaneously, however, the romance plot is infected by realities of city life. One particularly striking example is the sequence in which Rafe fights the giant Barbaroso. The fight with a giant is a romance staple, but in *The Knight of the Burning Pestle* the sequence is simultaneously a romance narrative and a satiric portrayal of contemporary London. Having spent the night at an inn, Rafe asks the Host if he knows of "any sad adventures [. . .] Where errant knight may through his prowess win / Eternal fame" (3.208–10). The Host whispers to the Tapster, "Sirrah, go to Nick the barber, and bid him prepare himself as I told you before, quickly" (212–13)—within the play's fiction, the Host, the Tapster, and "Nick the barber" are indulging the fantasy of Rafe, the Knight of the Burning Pestle, just as the theater company are indulging the whims of the citizens by writing Rafe into their play in the first place. Beaumont here draws on a strand of intertextual parody within the romance genre, of which the best-known example is Cervantes's *Don Quixote,* in which the hero has been driven mad by reading too many romances and thinks that he is a chivalric knight.

The Host speaks in colloquial prose to the Tapster, but moves into blank verse as he describes the "giant" to Rafe:

> Not far from hence, near to a craggy cliff,
> At the north end of this distressed town,
> There doth stand a lowly house
> Ruggedly builded, and in it a cave
> In which an ugly giant now doth won,
> Ycleped Barbaroso. (3.227–32)

That the giant is really the barber-surgeon becomes clear as the Host's description continues:

> In his hand
> He shakes a naked lance of purest steel,
> With sleeves turned up, and him before he wears
> A motley garment to preserve his clothes
> From blood of those knights which he massacres,
> And ladies gent. Without his door doth hang
> A copper basin on a prickant spear,
> At which no sooner gentle knights can knock
> But the shrill sound fierce Barbaroso hears,
> And rushing forth, brings in an enchanted chair. (3.232–42)

The "copper basin on a prickant spear" is the sign of the barber-surgeon, consisting of a red and white pole with a copper ball on top, which demonstrated that the barber carried out minor surgical procedures such as drawing teeth and letting blood. The Host's description of "Barbaroso"—complete with such romantic archaisms as "Ycleped," "won" (meaning "dwell"), and "gent" ("fair")—transforms mundane details of the barber-surgeon's appearance and trade into sinister indications of his barbarity.

Rafe encounters the giant, knocks him down, and rescues his prisoners. In another jarring fusion of everyday detail and romance narrative, the knights describe their ordeal at Barbaroso's hands. The first enters *"winking, with a basin under his chin"* (3.365 s.d.), the second has *"a patch o'er his nose"* (3.386 s.d.), and the third has *"a glass of lotion in his hand"*; his lady holds *"diet-bread and drink"* (3.427 s.d.). As these physical details suggest, the knights and lady are suffering from the symptoms of venereal disease, something that barber-surgeons were accustomed to treating, and the treatments are represented as outrages committed against them. The first complains that he has been lured to Barbaroso's cave "Under pretence of killing of the itch, / And all my body with a powder strewed" (3.374–75). The second introduces himself as "Sir Pockhole," saying although he is a Londoner,

> my ancestors
> Were Frenchmen all; and riding hard this way
> Upon a trotting horse, my bones did ache;
> And I, faint knight, to ease my weary limbs,
> Light at this cave, when straight this furious fiend,
> With sharpest instrument of purest steel
> Did cut the gristle of my nose away,
> And in the place this velvet plaster stands. (3.394–401)

Pockhole's name indicates that he suffers from syphilis, known as the "French pox"; his aching bones and the incisions to his nose (made by the barber-surgeon to relieve chancres), together with the Wife's comment that "his breath stinks" (3.404), are also indications of his disease. The third knight and his lady are also syphilitic, the lady having been stolen "from her friends in Turnbull Street" (3.437), a notorious location for brothels.

The play's treatment of chivalric romance is a more fully developed version of that in *Eastward Ho,* described earlier. Romance is used to satirize characters and habits common in city comedy and in contemporary society, notably young men and their sexual mores. Although *The Knight of the Burning Pestle* mocks certain aspects of romance narrative and its archaic style, Rafe's well-meaning attempts to help those in need are more endearing than the behavior of the exploitative Host and the pocky knights, or that of Jasper in the *London Merchant* plot, who risks his relationship with Luce by deciding to test her loyalty.

Toward the end of *The Knight of the Burning Pestle,* the *London Merchant* is heading toward happy reconciliation of all the major characters and the comic conclusion of a marriage. Unhappy that "Everybody's part is come to an end but Rafe's, and he's left out," the citizens decide that Rafe should have a grand tragic death scene, and order their apprentice to "come away quickly and die" (5.267–68, 273). One of the boy actors protests, "'Twill be very unfit he should die, sir, upon no occasion, and in a comedy too," but the Citizen, unabashed, replies, "Take you no care of that, sir boy, is not his part at an end, think you, when he's dead?" (5.274–77). In a sequence familiar from television comedy, Rafe enters *"with a forked arrow through his head"* (5.277 s.d.) and delivers a stirring death oration, closely modeled on speeches delivered by ghosts in Kyd's *Spanish Tragedy* and Shakespeare's *Richard III.* The Citizen's control over the play extends to altering its genre in order to supplement Rafe's role, with the company's representative complaining that not only is Rafe's death unnatural—"upon no occasion"—but that it is unsuited to the play as comedy. In this case, however, the introduction of a burlesqued tragic element into comedy is itself funny and, despite the boy's complaint, suited to a comedy. The play has paradoxically kept generic decorum in the very act of breaking it.

This is indicative of the technique displayed in *The Knight of the Burning Pestle.* Its elements are gathered together from a number of sources—dramatic and nondramatic romance, city comedy, tragedy, ballads, and songs, to name only a few—but they are put to the same purpose: to make an audience laugh. By inserting all of this material into their comedy, Beaumont and the Children of the Revels change the genre itself, molding it into something that is capable of both literary and social satire but is also surprisingly affectionate toward the characters and narratives on which they draw. It is perhaps a mark of this ambivalence toward generic stereotypes—a paradoxical combination of amused superiority and genuine affection—that the Children of the Revels' audience at the Blackfriars in 1607 did not appreciate its "privy irony" or its experiments with dramatic form.

NOTES

1. See Francis Beaumont, *The Knight of the Burning Pestle,* ed. Michael Hattaway (London: Ernest Benn, 1969).
2. Jeffrey Masten, *Textual Intercourse: Collaboration, Authorship and Sexualities in Renaissance Drama* (Cambridge: Cambridge UP, 1997) 25–26.
3. See Beaumont 3.3–6.
4. See Sheldon P. Zitner, ed., *The Knight of the Burning Pestle* (Manchester: Manchester UP, 1984) 163.
5. See Thomas Blount, *Glossographia* (London, 1656).

6. See John Bullokar, *An English Expositor* (London, 1616).
7. See *A Warning for Fair Women* (London, 1599).
8. See *Volpone,* ed. Philip Brockbank (London: Ernest Benn, 1968).
9. See John Fletcher, *The Faithful Shepherdess,* ed. Cyrus Hoy, *The Dramatic Works in the Beaumont and Fletcher Canon,* ed. Fredson Bowers. Vol. 4. (Cambridge: Cambridge UP, 1976) 483–612.
10. See Thomas Middleton, *A Trick to Catch the Old One,* ed. G. J. Watson (London: Ernest Benn, 1968).
11. See Sir Philip Sidney, *An Apology for Poetry (or The Defence of Poesy),* ed. Geoffrey Shepherd. Rev. R. W. Maslen (Manchester: Manchester UP, 2002) 110–11.
12. See George Chapman, Ben Jonson, and John Marston, *Eastward Ho,* ed. R. W. Van Fossen (Manchester: Manchester UP, 1979) 5.1.37–47.
13. See Lee Bliss, "'Plot Mee No Plots': The Life of Drama and the Drama of Life in *The Knight of the Burning Pestle.*" *Modern Language Quarterly* 45 (1984): 3–21, esp. 8.

READING LIST

Bliss, Lee. "'Plot Mee No Plots': The Life of Drama and the Drama of Life in *The Knight of the Burning Pestle.*" *Modern Language Quarterly* 45 (1984): 3–21.

Colie, Rosalie L. *The Resources of Kind.* Ed. Barbara K. Lewalski. Berkeley: U of California P, 1973.

Danson, Lawrence. *Shakespeare's Dramatic Genres.* Oxford: Oxford UP, 2000.

Dillon, Janette. "'Is Not All the World Mile End, Mother?': The Blackfriars Theater, the City of London and *The Knight of the Burning Pestle.*" *Medieval and Renaissance Drama in England* 9 (1997): 127–48.

Dubrow, Heather. *Genre.* London: Methuen, 1982.

Duff, David, ed. *Modern Genre Theory.* London: Longman, 2000.

Lesser, Zachary. "Walter Burre's *The Knight of the Burning Pestle.*" *English Literary Renaissance* 29 (1999): 22–43.

Masten, Jeffrey. *Textual Intercourse: Collaboration, Authorship and Sexualities in Renaissance Drama.* Cambridge: Cambridge UP, 1997.

Miller, Ronald F. "Dramatic Form and the Dramatic Imagination in Beaumont's *The Knight of the Burning Pestle.*" *English Literary Renaissance* 8 (1978): 67–84.

Osborne, Laurie E. "Female Audiences and Female Authority in *The Knight of the Burning Pestle.*" *Exemplaria* 3 (1991): 491–517.

Tigges, Wim. "Romance and Parody." *The Companion to Middle English Romance.* Ed. Henk Aertsen and Alisdair A. MacDonald. Amsterdam: VU UP, 1990. 129–51.

Wall, Wendy. "Tending to Bodies and Boys: Queer Physic in *Knight of the Burning Pestle.*" *Staging Domesticity: Household Work and English Identity in Early Modern Drama.* Cambridge: Cambridge UP, 2002. 161–88.

18

The Alchemist and Science

Katherine Eggert

Ben Jonson's *The Alchemist*[1] was probably first staged in the same year that a telescope first gave a scientist cause to find fault with the sun.[2] As far as historians are able to determine, spots on the surface of the sun were first observed, contemporaneously but independently, late in the year 1610 by Englishman Thomas Hariot—mathematician, navigator, and author of *A Brief and True Report of the Newfound Land of Virginia* (1588)—and Italian Galileo Galilei, who published his findings in 1613. Joining a lively debate initiated by other continental astronomers, Galileo famously proposed that the sun is not, as the tradition deriving from Aristotle's *Physics* had it, perfect. If one can see sunspots, then the Aristotelian doctrine, not the observation, must be in error: "So long as men were in fact obliged to call the sun 'most pure and most lucid,' no shadows or impurities whatever had been perceived in it; but now it shows itself to us as partly impure and spotty, why should we not call it 'spotty and not pure'?"[3] Here and in his other astronomical writings Galileo describes the earth and the heavens as one substance, equally knowable and equally measurable; he furthermore promotes the evidence of experimental data over the precepts of the ancients. These two radical principles—that unified laws govern all matter and that observation, not precedent textual authority, best accounts for natural phenomena—underpin extraordinary developments in seventeenth-century science, from Isaac Newton's laws of motion to Johannes Kepler's measurements of planetary orbits to Robert Boyle's air pump. As well, these principles eventually have the effect of diminishing scientists' attention to the divine. Though ordered ultimately by God, the universe is subject to ongoing and accretive acts of human rationality that cumulatively crack Nature's code.

One is tempted to make the most of historical coincidence and to discern in *The Alchemist* a proleptic triumph of experiment over textual authority and of human over divine authority. Despite the play's adherence to the Aristotelian unities, it largely eschews classical models.[4] Indeed, *The Alchemist* treats all predecessor texts, from Erasmus to Paracelsus to the religious belaborings of Hugh Broughton, as likely fodder for either the contrivances of the con artists or the ranting of their gulls. And once textual authority is debunked, only human ingenuity remains. *The Alchemist* reads as a tour de force of human invention, as Subtle, Face, and Dol improvise their way into every scheme and out of nearly every debacle imaginable. The result is a radical revision of hierarchical order. Even when the master returns, he does not exert his supreme and quasi-deific authority to rearrange the play-world in his own image. Rather, Lovewit joins in and profits by the scheme that his servant Face/Jeremy devises for him, winning the rich widow, Dame Pliant, who is paired with the philosopher's stone as the play's supreme object of desire.

The Alchemist's irreverence, in other words, encourages us to associate it with all manner of modernity, including scientific modernity. But this teleological account is adequate neither to a description of the state of European science in the early seventeenth century nor to a reading of the appeal of alchemy in Jonson's play. In recent decades, historians have quarreled with the notion of a seventeenth-century "Scientific Revolution": some have argued that the revolutionary ideas of seventeenth-century science derived from earlier natural philosophy; and others have demonstrated that premodern systems of scientific thought survived well into the late seventeenth century.[5] As opposed to rupture and revolution, these historians emphasize the continuity and coexistence of medieval and early modern science. Thus, for example, the Italian philosopher Giordano Bruno saw no contradiction between accepting Copernicus's concept of the heliocentric universe and adapting the Copernican diagram into a mystical, hermeticist-kabbalistic scheme of an infinite number of infinite worlds. Similarly, the founder of modern physics himself, Newton, was seriously engaged in alchemy, finding in alchemy's universalizing systems some of the same explanatory power that he found in his own laws of motion and optics.[6] Like Bruno and like Newton, *The Alchemist* balances its relentlessly iconoclastic debunking of science of the past—in this case, alchemy—with an undeniable attraction to the inventive patterns of thought that this "old-fashioned" science proffers.[7] *The Alchemist*'s ambivalent treatment of alchemy and of other branches of the natural sciences establishes Jonson not simply as an advance man for the Scientific Revolution but rather as a writer profoundly engaged with scientific practice as it existed in his time, which was a long period of both transition and overlap between old and new.

Systems of Knowledge: Science and the Dream of Perfection

European scientific knowledge before the seventeenth century understood the world through the resemblances of things. The cosmos was imagined as an intricately nested set of structures, each smaller structure the microcosm of a larger, the largest of which is the totality of divine creation, the sum of all goodness. (This schema, derived from Plato's *Republic* and *Timaeus* and modified by medieval Christian philosophers such as Thomas Aquinas, is described by Arthur Lovejoy in his classic study *The Great Chain of Being*.)[8] All matter and all beings exist in a gradation of forms, from simplest and least perfect to highest and most perfect; but their common participation in the plenitude of God's creation assures them an "interconnectedness of things (*connexio rerum*) by which nature passes only by steps from one kind to another."[9] Further, the interrelation of microcosm and macrocosm implies hidden affinities between the two, making it possible for bodies to "act on each other at a distance through occult powers of sympathy, attraction, or repulsion." These occult powers explained how, for example, the stars influenced human affairs or magnets attracted iron (Shapin, *Scientific* 42). The work of the scientist—in medieval terminology, the "natural philosopher," the student of nature's wisdom—was to discover and explicate that interconnectedness.

According to Michel Foucault, this scientific work amounted to decoding the great system of signs that constituted the Book of Nature, a term that medieval thinkers meant literally: "the space inhabited by immediate resemblances becomes like a vast open book; it bristles with written signs; every page is seen to be filled with strange figures that intertwine and in some places repeat themselves. All that remains is to decipher them."[10] The task of deciphering and recording nature's semiotic complexity gave rise to two related modes of medieval scientific writing: first, the encyclopedia, the book of all learning, modeled after Roman naturalist Pliny the Elder's *Natural History* (first century CE) and exemplified by such monumental works as French Dominican friar Vincent of Beauvais's *Speculum majus* (*The Great Mirror*, early thirteenth century); and second, *libri secretorum*, or books of secrets, which were "compilations of recipes, formulas, and 'experiments' of all kinds, including everything from medical prescriptions and technical formulas to magical procedures, cooking recipes, parlor tricks, and practical jokes."[11] In their medieval forms, the encyclopedia and the book of secrets share a fascination with nature's marvels rather than nature's norms. A reader who had access to both kinds of texts would take from both the lesson that all natural phenomena, no matter how odd—from Pliny's dog-headed people to what the Italian monk Heraclius described (in a tenth-century *liber secretorum* on artists' techniques) as the capacity of a billy goat's blood to engrave precious gems (Eamon 35)—hold equal part in the same perfectly ordered system of divinely created plenitude.

Books of secrets, however, assert far more emphatically than encyclopedias do that a full description of natural relationships is available only to the man of ultimate knowledge and skill, the magus. The magus's first qualification is his access to all human learning, from Plato and the Neoplatonists to patristic and medieval Christian theology to Hebrew Kabbalah and its Christian adaptations. His second qualification is his piety. As *The Alchemist*'s Surly cautions Sir Epicure Mammon, the manipulator of the essence of things "must be *homo frugi* [a man of temperance], / A pious, holy, and religious man, / One free from mortal sin" (2.2.97–99); and Subtle readily blames the taint of Mammon's lustful nature when the manufacture of the philosopher's stone "fails" (4.5.35–41). Part of the excusatory apparatus—and, perhaps, part of the joke—of books of magical knowledge is their obligatory admonition that the reader not reveal the book's contents to another living soul. "Know therefore that whoever betrays these secrets and reveals these mysteries to the unworthy shall not be safe from the misfortune that shall soon befall him": this is how the phenomenally popular *Secretum secretorum* (*Secret of Secrets*), an Arabic text falsely ascribed to Aristotle that reached Europe in the thirteenth century, put the warning (qtd. in Eamon 47).[12] In the wrong hands, magic might set the universe awry—as the "sorcerer's apprentice" comic subplots of late sixteenth-century plays like Robert Greene's *Friar Bacon and Friar Bungay* and Christopher Marlowe's *Doctor Faustus* attest. The right hands are those of the magus, who manipulates natural processes only to make them fulfill their divine essence.

As explicated by the widely influential early-sixteenth-century German magician and natural philosopher Heinrich Cornelius Agrippa, the magus's power extends to any plane he chooses, whether terrestrial (manipulating earthly elements and bodies), celestial (altering the influence of the stars), or supercelestial (summoning the aid of angelic spirits).[13] If the magus must be pure of soul, then, it is because he wishes not only to perceive the correspondences between the earthly, the celestial, and the divine but also to assist terrestrial elements in ascending the ladder toward higher modes of existence. Alchemy is the foremost premodern science in this regard, as it not only studies but also effects this ascent. As Lyndy Abraham succinctly puts it, alchemy is "the art of transmuting or perfecting everything in its own nature [. . .] including the mystic transformation of base man into a state of spiritual perfection, a process referred to by John

Donne in 'The First Anniversarie' as the 'true religious Alchimy.'"[14] Both Christian and Neoplatonic thought encouraged upward movement from earthly error to heavenly truth, but alchemy was devoted to this ascent in both tangible and esoteric ways: transmuting base metals into gold, putting humans in communication with angels, and possibly even transforming human society itself into a heaven on earth. The longed-for "golden age" was more than a metaphor, in other words: it expressed alchemists' hope that all terrestrial matter could aspire to the purity of the purest terrestrial element. As Subtle says of Sir Epicure Mammon, who hopes to use the philosopher's stone not only to enrich himself but also to cure the sick and reform the state, "If his dream last, he'll turn the age, to gold" (1.4.29). "So," remarks Francis Bacon in *The Advancement of Learning,* "have the alchemists made a philosophy out of a few experiments of the furnace."[15]

The resilience of the dream of perfection meant that alchemy remained a worthwhile study for many of the greatest of late-seventeenth-century scientists, including Newton and Boyle. Some still held out hopes for practical transmutation of baser substances into gold, as Boyle did, and others, like Newton, also hoped alchemy would demonstrate "the existence and means of divine activity in the world" (Principe, "Alchemies" 215). Adopting the newfangled scientific method—in which the scientist's empirical observation, guided not by a classical authority but by an intelligent hypothesis, inductively leads him or her to formulate a universal law—did not initially require abandoning thinking of the universe as a system of analogous, mysteriously interacting structures whose sum of perfection approaches divinity. Newton himself, reluctant to discard notions of "active powers" by which higher forms of matter purposefully influence lower, asserted that the existence of such powers is not contradicted by the discovery of such forces as gravitation (Shapin, *Scientific* 157). Similarly, the fact that the developers of modern chemistry retain alchemical goals of transmutation speaks to their continued desire not merely to account for natural processes but to alter them. This desire prompted protests that scientists' wild imaginations produced falsified results (as Boyle accused Blaise Pascal regarding Pascal's treatise on hydrostatics [Shapin, *Scientific* 83]) or that scientists contrived experimental apparatuses so elaborate that they hubristically overwent anything fashioned by nature.[16] While these two responses to the scientific experiment—either it's faked or it's so effective that it meddles in nature—seem mutually exclusive, a number of late-seventeenth-century critics of the scientific enterprise give equal voice to both kinds of reservations. Subtle anticipates their condemnation when he mocks Sir Epicure Mammon's ambitions: "He will make / Nature ashamed of her long sleep, when art, / Who's but a step-dame, shall do more than She / In her best love to mankind ever could" (1.4.26–28). The mockery cuts both ways: Mammon is a fool who cannot possibly convert his fantasies into observable reality, but his dreams correlate closely with those of the overreaching magus, who interferes improperly in matters beyond legitimate human provenance.

Scientific Language

Jonson's 1616 masque for the court of King James I, *Mercury Vindicated from the Alchemists at Court,* makes an even stronger case than Subtle's jesting does for the superiority of nature over the meddling scientist's art. Mercury, who is here both the Greek god and the element essential to many alchemical experiments, protests against being subjected to Vulcan's minions, who are both alchemists (the men they create wear "limbecks" or alembics, the upper part of a distilling apparatus, on their heads) and courtiers on the make. As Jonathan Goldberg points out, Mercury's complaint is in part about the corruption and misuse of language: the alchemists at court "talk of nothing; theirs is a creation *ex nihilo* that comes to nothing, too. What they call *business* and activity is merely motion, juggling, deception, wordplay."[17] In Goldberg's description we hear echoes of *The Alchemist,* whose entire action is "motion, juggling, deception, wordplay," and whose relentless debunking of alchemical cant is so overt as almost to require no commentary. Alvin Kernan, like many critics, believes that this debunking demonstrates Jonson's conservative preference of natural to artificial change.[18] If we were to combine Goldberg's and Kernan's readings, we would arrive at a Ben Jonson opposed not only to the aims of alchemy but also to the wordplay and the theatrical stratagems with which alchemy is equated, since quick-change artifice in any form pales in comparison to the slower but authentic transformations brought about by nature.

This amalgamated reading, however, would not take note of several salient aspects of premodern science that might contribute to Jonson's view of wordplay and of other transformative theatrical effects and that might contradict a sense of Jonson as so conservative on the supremacy of nature over art that he is, in effect, antiscientific. Remember that, as Foucault points out, science before the Scientific Revolution understood the universe as a vast semiotic system, in which the qualities and interconnectedness of things are evident in signs apparent to the discerning and adept interpreter (17–30). That interpreter's next step is often to draw up an intricate scheme—a diagram accompanied by words, a series of emblems accompanied by poetic texts, or the like—that expresses in both graphic and linguistic terms the complexity of the interrelated signs he has read. The drawing, however, is not merely a drawing: it is *equivalent* to and *constitutive* of the structures it describes, not merely *representative* of them. Books of premodern science are thus preternaturally devoted to the diagram. Lacking the mathematical or taxonomic systems that come to structure scientific discourse after the Scientific Revolution, premodern science relies on and revels in the picture, the table, the symbol, the accompanying code or caption. The advantages of these schemes for the scientific text are manifold. First, they paradoxically both invite and prevent the reader's understanding: their complexity promises transparency, but generally proves to be as obfuscatory as it is aesthetically appealing. As William Slights notes of Subtle's discussion of alchemy as written in "mystic symbols" (2.3.203), Subtle's "theory of language [. . .] is an essentially occlusive one [. . .] [but also] an invitation to interpret what he says, to find out his secret meanings."[19] Second, textual schemes display the scientist's ingenuity, in both intellectual and aesthetic terms: many of these schemes are, quite frankly, stunningly beautiful in their complexity and their inventiveness, and they reinforce the impression that the writer of the text is a graphic and verbal artist, a creator rather than simply a describer.

At their most ambitious, premodern scientific texts aspire to compose a very language that is transformative. In one of the many theologically oriented debates that occupied premodern science, Adam was claimed to be human history's best scientist, since before the Fall he could influence natural processes in quasi-divine fashion.[20] (Sir Epicure Mammon agrees: he offers to show Surly "a treatise penned by Adam [. . .]

O' the philosopher's stone" [2.1.83–84]). Because Adam was believed by many to have spoken Hebrew, the language of the Old Testament, Hebrew was thought to retain transformative properties. Thus scientists of the sixteenth and seventeenth centuries were fascinated by the Kabbalah, a body of medieval Jewish mystical texts that derived theological insight and sometimes magical utterances in part from manipulating the Tetragrammaton, the unpronounceable name of God that Christian translators of the Hebrew Bible rendered "Yahweh" or "Jehovah." The Kabbalah was just one approach, though, in what Umberto Eco calls "the search for the perfect language." In his utterly wacky *Monas hieroglyphica* (1564), John Dee, the English Renaissance mathematician, cartographer, antiquary, alchemist, and magus famous for conjuring spirits and mentioned in *The Alchemist* (2.6.20), concocts his very own language, kabbalistically derived but not Hebrew, that can generate all the truths in the universe, and all other human languages besides.[21]

The search for the perfect language was shared by nonscientists who hoped to return the world to its Edenic origins, and *The Alchemist* satirizes this aim in the Anabaptist Ananias's suspicions that "All's heathen, but the Hebrew" (2.5.17). Nevertheless, as Anne Barton has argued, *The Alchemist* evidences Jonson's increasing confidence in the notion that words could have the Edenic property of expressing the true natures of things, rather than arbitrarily signifying them.[22] Some of the nomenclatural correspondences in *The Alchemist* are unremarkable: names like Epicure Mammon and Kastrel (a small, fierce falcon) are merely comically apt for their bearers. With other characters, however, their names and their qualities seem to be mutually and progressively constitutive, especially Face, the former "Jeremy" who has been named by Subtle (1.1.81) and whose name seems both to connote and to confer his talent for falsehood and his capacity to "face" any challenge. ("Face" also meant the third quarter of a celestial astrological sign, a fact Jonson surely knew.) Similarly, Dol Common overgoes her stereotypical whore's moniker, as Barton points out, by either becoming or inventing a multitude of names and roles: "Dol Proper," "Dol Singular," "Claridiana," "Bradamante," and "Her Grace the Faery Queen," to name just a few (Barton 190). The more personae Dol assumes, the more she seems to personify Subtle's metaphorical description of Face as the philosopher's stone, a substance that is both the product and the agent of change (1.1.68–71).

The Alchemist's ready theatrical transformations constitute the most obvious instances of alchemy, metaphorical if not literal, in the play. A hastily donned costume and a convincing-enough voice make a faery queen of Dol Common and a captain of Face; a well-timed offstage explosion convinces everyone that an entire alchemical laboratory has gone up in smoke. Despite the moral condemnation critics have often heaped upon the conspirators' activities, it would be difficult to argue that the debunking of alchemy extends in this play to the debunking of theater itself. A play whose preface "To the Reader" (included in the 1613 quarto edition) derides the kind of art that "run[s] away from nature" must surely be promoting itself, in contrast, as dramatic art that works in tandem with nature, as premodern scientists, including alchemists, claimed to do (Jonson 4). *The Alchemist* also displays some allegiance to the premodern idea of scientific schemes—those tables, diagrams, and emblems—and scientific language as themselves transformative. What one notices most about language in *The Alchemist* is how delightful, and how essential to the play, is the very jargon the play purports to debunk. In the same way that Mercury in *Mercury Vindicated*[23] humorously flaunts alchemical lingo at the same time that he claims to be weary of it—"I am [the alchemists'] crude and sublimate, their precipitate and their unctuous; their male and their female; sometimes their hermaphrodite; what they list to style me" (ll. 32–35)—so too does *The Alchemist* deploy alchemical terminology for all it's worth. Moreover, the play makes clear that such language is worthwhile only if artfully designed. The sign Subtle plans for Abel Drugger's shop is humorous because its rebus is so ridiculously legible: a bell + [John] Dee + a rug + a dog who growls "er" = ABEL DRUGGER. In contrast, the "table, / With mathematical demonstrations, / Touching the art of quarrels" that Subtle makes for Kastrel (2.6.66–68) seems like a thing worth marveling at, and perhaps even worth mastering, if only for the fun of it.

Fun is, in fact, another way in which *The Alchemist* partakes in, rather than merely scoffs at, the scientific discourse of Jonson's day. Paula Findlen has demonstrated that the joke, or *lusus,* was an important element of scientific practice in the sixteenth and seventeenth centuries, one that grew from Renaissance humanists' fondness for dealing with serious topics ironically, as in Thomas More's *Utopia* or Erasmus's *Praise of Folly*. The fact that nature produces what scientists considered follies—from the small stature of African pygmies to oddly shaped seashells to a fantastically gigantic cabbage—only proves nature's infinite variety and capacity for invention.[24] Sixteenth- and seventeenth-century scientists and collectors in fact built jokes into their displays and experiments, hoping thereby to imitate nature, as well as simply to delight their audiences. Even Galileo, whose rationalism helped found a scientific practice that eventually lost interest in jokes of nature, emphasized "that pleasure was at the foundation of scientific pursuits."[25] In this light, *The Alchemist* looks like a premodern scientist's dream, an alchemical experiment in which jokes test the limits of how human ingenuity can shape a world.

The Experimental Space

The initial stage direction of *Mercury Vindicated* describes the setting as "a laboratory, or Alchemist's workhouse." The word "laboratory," denoting a separate room or building devoted entirely to scientific pursuits, was new enough to the English at the time of the masque's production that it required definition even for the masque's educated courtly audience. The popular conception, then and now, of an alchemist's study is not a "laboratory," but rather a chamber of secrets, where books and magic instruments hold equal pride of place with experimental equipment, and where the solitary magus carries on his art with the aid of only an assistant or two. While *The Alchemist*'s con artists exploit this preconception in evoking Subtle's mysterious offstage furnace chamber, which not even the skeptic Surly demands to see for himself, at times Subtle seems to possess the assemblage of equipment that belonged to the actual working alchemist and that served as a prototype for the laboratory of the late seventeenth century and beyond.

Alchemical equipment has a strange status in *The Alchemist:* both real and imaginary, both material in its breakability and evanescent in its sometimes purely linguistic existence. Face boasts that his aid has afforded Subtle an impressive array of both the raw matter of alchemy and the apparatus with which to manipulate it: "I ga' you count'nance, credit for your coals, / Your stills, your glasses, your materials, / Built you a furnace, drew you customers, / Advanced all your black arts" (1.1.43–46). Calling attention to the actuality of at least one of these items, Dol breaks up her confederates' initial quarrel by smashing Subtle's "glass," a generic term for an alchemical vessel (1.1.115). Subtle's accumulation of such expensive equipment puts him in rather elite scientific company. The magician, astrologer, and physician Simon Forman, Jonson's contemporary, had to practice ten years or more before he could afford the apparatus and materials to amalgamate metals, and his diary records his unhappiness at instances of breakage (Kassell 347). While Subtle's ongoing exchanges with his "assistant" Face (in his guise as Lungs) about the heat of the furnace or the condition of the vials in process are of course intended to gull the likes of Sir Epicure Mammon, they also display a certain pride of ownership, as well as delight at the sheer plethora and variety of alchemical gear that a successful practitioner might amass. We find ourselves rather disappointed when, at the end of the play, Lovewit finds the equipment left in his house to be in fact relatively minimal: "A few cracked pots, and glasses, and a furnace" (5.5.40).

Alchemy has generally sustained a rather poor reputation as a dead end on the way to modern chemistry; its practitioners have been characterized as interested more in occult spells than in reproducible experiments. Recently, however, Lawrence Principe has emphasized the care that medieval and early modern alchemists took to control their equipment, record their results, and produce, insofar as possible, a repeatable experimental protocol (Principe, "Apparatus"). Furthermore, practical alchemy did not really take place in secret, but rather in groups that included the alchemist's servants, friends, fellow adepts, and students. In this respect, too, alchemy was the forerunner of the great early experimental phase of the Scientific Revolution, during which the public "demonstration" of such new techniques as blood transfusion or the air pump became one of the central activities of London's Royal Society of scientists. Late-seventeenth-century experimentation was an intensely social act, and late-seventeenth-century science, as Lisa Jardine has argued, was a sociable profession, carried out in coffeehouse discussions more than it was in solitary thought. *The Alchemist*'s primary conceit—that alchemy gives an extraordinary collection of people occasion to visit an experimental space—anticipates the later age of scientists like Newton and Boyle, when experimental venues, like Subtle's, were most often located within the houses of gentlemen and were subject to unannounced social calls by the curious.[26] Boyle's attempts to get some time alone to work by posting a sign on his laboratory door, "Mr. Boyle cannot be spoken with to-day," were considered unusual (Shapin, "House" 287). Indeed, seventeenth-century science was more than just social: at times, it was an intensely *theatrical* enterprise: demonstrations, including anatomy lessons, were often held in an amphitheaterlike space, and critical spectators would declare themselves either impressed or disappointed. Science and theater are thus analogous not only because both depend on sham or because both are transformative, but because scientific demonstration, like theater, consisted of "performances" for an audience's "deliberation, instruction, and entertainment" (Shapin, "House" 301).

The Uses of Science

Science in the seventeenth century was a social activity partly out of necessity: a scientist who lacked independent means required a patron, someone who bankrolled his or her pursuits and thus maintained a legitimate interest in monitoring the results. Then as now, the patron was often more interested in lucrative discoveries than in the pursuit of knowledge for its own sake. Chief among these patrons were monarchs. Despite the fact that alchemy, having been associated with witchcraft and sorcery, was illegal by royal statute, English kings from Henry VI (ruled 1422–61) to Charles II (ruled 1660–85) counted alchemists among those they sponsored financially.[27] Despite alchemists' reputation for being intellectual mavericks and—especially if successful—potential social subversives, monarchs had great incentive to exploit alchemical research. As Dol Common puts it when Sir Epicure Mammon spins out his vision of unlimited wealth and power brought by the philosopher's stone, "But, in a monarchy, how will this be? / The Prince will soon take notice; and both seize / You, and your stone: it being a wealth unfit / For any private subject" (4.1.147–50).

Alchemy was thought to have—and, in some respects, did have—enormous practical and profitable use. Chief among these was the manufacture of medicines. Early-sixteenth-century German scientist and magician Paracelsus applied his important innovations in alchemy to medical science: rejecting the Galenic model of medicine as a matter of balancing bodily humours (blood, phlegm, black bile, and yellow bile), Paracelsus pioneered modern pharmacy by treating illness with inorganic compounds, including mercury, sulfur, and arsenic.[28] His treatments are among those that Abel Drugger, whose name suggests pharmaceutical expertise, carries in his shop (1.4.73–77). In the early 1660s, King Charles II commanded his court alchemist, Nicaise Le Fèvre, to produce a medicinal cordial based on a recipe by Sir Walter Raleigh, who was reputed to have spent his imprisonment in the Tower of London during the reign of King James I in alchemical experiment. The cordial, whose recipe was published by Le Fèvre in 1663, includes such exotic ingredients as hart's horn, viper's liver, and ground pearls; its claimed curative powers for everything from heart palpitations to impotence were attested to by many, including Robert Boyle, who also cooked up the cordial.[29] In comparison, Sir Epicure's alchemical hopes of "fright[ing] the plague / Out o' the kingdom, in three months" (2.1.70) with the help of the philosopher's stone do not sound so outlandish.

Alchemy's second arena of practical application was in metallurgy. Alchemical techniques had been used to assay, amalgamate, and purify metals since the later Middle Ages,[30] and these skills became profoundly important as Europeans sought to mine and transport the mineral riches of the New World. While many of their schemes to extract gold from obviously nonprecious New World ores have the aura of *The Alchemist*'s con games, alchemists' contributions to metallurgical advances were incalculable. George Starkey, the alchemist and physician who in the 1650s demonstrated in London the impossible extraction of silver from antimony and transmutation of iron into gold (Abraham 13), had also helped found the first large-scale ironworks in the Massachusetts Bay colony.[31] Sir Epicure dreams up a project similar to Starkey's aim of transmuting lesser English metal into gold and silver—bringing home the riches of the New World, without the bother of traveling abroad: "Yes, and I'll purchase Devonshire and Cornwall, / And make them perfect Indies!" (2.1.35–36).

The increasing associations between alchemy's pursuit of gold and New World moneymaking ventures attest to science's increasing ties to capitalism, and especially to the developing market economy's need for larger quantities of capital. As Peggy Knapp argues, alchemy takes on a new vocabulary in the sixteenth and seventeenth centuries, a vocabulary of *venture* and *commodity* that is also the vocabulary of Face, Subtle, and

Dol. In the world of *The Alchemist*'s "venture tripartite" (1.1.135), "[e]very kind of thing is for sale, from the secrets preserved from the time of Thoth to the simple marketing ploys Subtle confides to Drugger. [. . .] As in modern exchange, some of these commodities are real, although never what they are made out to be, some entirely illusory" (586).[32] Because nearly all strata of society are involved in capitalistic ventures, alchemical pursuits interest everyone from the monarch to the shopkeeper. Drugger's shop, with its enticing selection of useful remedies (including tobacco, which was thought to cure all kinds of health problems), is the forerunner of the later seventeenth-century retail outlet for scientific products, including instruments such as lenses and microscopes. Even those without shops or patrons could make money from their scientific endeavors through commercial exchange of their results, a practice that ultimately made it possible for nonaristocratic women to enter the scientific profession, even though women were barred from scientific organizations like the Royal Society. Zoologist Maria Sybilla Merian, after "she returned from her two-year stay in the South American colony of Surinam in September 1701, [. . .] supported herself and her daughters by advertising both watercolours and preserved specimens she had brought back with her for sale on the open market."[33]

To identify science's associations with nascent capitalism, however, is not to downplay the sheer pleasure and appeal of undertaking scientific activity or witnessing its results. In his influential discussion of how we respond to gorgeous or unusual objects (like those collected, tested, and displayed by early modern scientists), Stephen Greenblatt points out that the viewer's fantasy of owning such objects does not negate the wonder, the aesthetic appreciation, that he or she takes from the experience.[34] Sir Epicure's extravagant dreams of limitless wealth and power—"Now you set your foot on shore / In Novo Orbe; here's the rich Peru, / And there within, sir, are the golden mines, / Great Solomon's Ophir!" (2.1.1–4)—certainly register the colonialist dream of rapacious possession, and remind us, as Denise Albanese argues, that "[e]xpeditions to America and scientific programs both propagandize themselves as voyages out into uncharted territory, where the sense of excitement that attaches to new ventures covers over the work of domination to underwrite exploration of the globe and of nature."[35] But in their expansiveness, Sir Epicure's near-operatic fantasias also both register and occasion wonder at all there is to know and discover in the world. In *The New Atlantis,* published in 1627, Francis Bacon imagines the exchange of knowledge as a trade undertaken not for commerce's sake, but for knowledge's: in his utopia, voyages of discovery "maintain a trade, not for gold, silver, or jewels; nor for silks, nor for spices, nor any other commodity of matter; but only for God's first creature, which was *Light;* to have *light* (I say) of the growth of all parts of the world" (472). A shareholder in the Virginia Colony, Bacon of course knew better what trade truly meant; but here, he reimagines it as furthering science's horizon. The *Novum Orbis* or New World, for science of the early seventeenth century, was not only the newly encountered lands of the Western Hemisphere, but also the world of the heavens and the earth. Even if *The Alchemist* satirizes the pursuit of knowledge for mercenary ends, it shows us briefly—within the time specified by the unities, within the one scene of Lovewit's house, and within a fictional neighborhood that is also the actual neighborhood of Jonson's Blackfriars Theater—another version of that *Novum Orbis*: the world of the theater, where all people come for knowledge's sake, and from which those who, like Lovewit, "love a teeming wit as I love my nourishment" (5.1.16) can leave satisfied.

NOTES

1. See Ben Jonson, *The Alchemist,* ed. Elizabeth Cook (London: A & C Black, 1991). All citations from the play refer to this text.
2. I use the term "scientist" in this chapter for familiarity's and convenience's sake, even though it is anachronistic, dating only from the early nineteenth century. The closest catchall term available in the seventeenth century is "natural philosopher," but strictly speaking, natural philosophy excludes studies of mathematics, medicine, astronomy, and the occult, disciplines that contribute to the development of early modern science (Peter Dear, *Revolutionizing the Sciences* [Princeton: Princeton UP, 2001] 10–29). I also generally refer to the scientist as male, in accordance with the way he is imagined by sixteenth- and seventeenth-century thinkers. However, a number of women were significant contributors to alchemical and other scientific disciplines of the period, including such literary and philosophical figures as Margaret Cavendish, Anne Conway, Queen Christina of Sweden, and Princess Elizabeth of Bohemia (Dear 118–19). Space limitations in this chapter prohibit consideration of the important topic of gender and science.
3. Qtd. in Stephen Shapin, *The Scientific Revolution* (Chicago: U of Chicago P, 1990) 18.
4. *The Alchemist* relies distantly on only one significant classical source: Plautus's *Mostellaria,* with its theme of a servant abusing his absent master's trust.
5. See H. Floris Cohen, *The Scientific Revolution: A Historiographical Inquiry* (Chicago: U of Chicago P, 1994) 169–82, 239–307.
6. See Betty Jo Teeter Dobbs, *The Janus Face of Genius: The Role of Alchemy in Newton's Thought* (Cambridge: Cambridge UP, 1991), and Paula Findlen, "Athanasius Kircher and Isaac Newton," *Rethinking the Scientific Revolution,* ed. Margaret J. Osler (Cambridge: Cambridge UP, 2000) 221–46.
7. While I use "alchemy" as a general term in this chapter, it is important to recognize that alchemy has been in existence since the fourth century and is hardly a uniform set of beliefs or procedures. For a cogent discussion of alchemy's divergent practices in the later seventeenth century, see Lawrence M. Principe, "The Alchemies of Robert Boyle and Isaac Newton: Alternate Approaches and Divergent Deployments," *Rethinking the Scientific Revolution,* ed. Margaret J. Osler (Cambridge: Cambridge UP, 2000) 201–20.
8. See Arthur O. Lovejoy, *The Great Chain of Being,* 2nd ed. (New York: Harper & Row, 1960).
9. See Lia Formigari, "The Great Chain of Being," *Dictionary of the History of Ideas: Studies of Selected Pivotal Ideas,* ed. Philip P. Wiener (New York: Scribner, 1973) 1.325–35, esp. 326.
10. See Michel Foucault, *The Order of Things: An Archaeology of the Human Sciences* (1966; New York: Vintage Books, 1970) 27.
11. See William Eamon, *Science and the Secrets of Nature: Books of Secrets in Medieval and Early Modern Culture* (Princeton: Princeton UP, 1994) 16.
12. The fact that most *libri secretorum,* like most alchemical texts, circulated in manuscript, even after the invention of the printing press, reinforces their promise of membership in a secret club.
13. See Frances Yates, *The Occult Philosophy in the Elizabethan Age* (London: Routledge & Kegan Paul, 1979) 53.
14. See Lyndy Abraham, *Marvell and Alchemy* (Aldershot: Scolar Press, 1990) 1.
15. See Francis Bacon, *The Major Works,* ed. Brian Vickers (Oxford: Oxford UP, 1996) 146.
16. See Walter Cohen, *Drama of a Nation: Public Theater in Renaissance England and Spain* (Ithaca: Cornell UP, 1985) 183–84.
17. See Jonathan Goldberg, *James I and the Politics of Literature: Jonson, Shakespeare, Donne, and Their Contemporaries* (Stanford: Stanford UP, 1989) 60.
18. See Alvin B. Kernan, ed., *The Alchemist,* by Ben Jonson (New Haven: Yale UP, 1974) 15.
19. See William W. E. Slights, *Ben Jonson and the Art of Secrecy* (Toronto: U of Toronto P, 1994) 108.

20. See Lauren Kassell, "'The Food of Angels': Simon Forman's Alchemical Medicine," *Secrets of Nature: Astrology and Alchemy in Early Modern Europe,* ed. William R. Newman and Anthony Grafton (Cambridge: MIT P, 2001) 345–84.
21. See Umberto Eco, *The Search for the Perfect Language,* trans. James Fentress (Oxford: Blackwell, 1995) 185–90.
22. See Anne Barton, *Ben Jonson, Dramatist* (Cambridge: Cambridge UP, 1984) 170–93.
23. See Ben Jonson, *Mercury Vindicated from the Alchemists at Court, Ben Jonson's Plays and Masques,* ed. Robert M. Adams (New York: Norton, 1979) 356–63.
24. See Paula Findlen, "Jokes of Nature and Jokes of Knowledge: The Playfulness of Scientific Discourse in Early Modern Europe," *Renaissance Quarterly* 43 (1990): 292–331.
25. See Mary Baine Campbell, *Wonder and Science: Imagining Worlds in Early Modern Europe* (Ithaca: Cornell UP, 1999) 127.
26. See Steven Shapin, "The House of Experiment in Seventeenth-Century England," *The Scientific Enterprise in Early Modern Europe: Readings from Isis,* ed. Peter Dear (Chicago: U of Chicago P, 1997) 273–304.
27. Royal statutes prohibiting alchemy were passed in 1404, under King Henry IV (see William H. Sherman, "'Gold Is the Strength, the Sinnewes of the World': Thomas Dekker's *Old Fortunatus* and England's Golden Age," *Medieval and Renaissance Drama in England* 6 [1993]: 85–102, esp. 91), and in 1541, under King Henry VIII. The latter of these laws—referred to in *The Alchemist* as "The statute of sorcerie, *tricesimo tertio* / Of Harry the Eight" (1.1.112–13)—was reaffirmed under James I in 1604, and not repealed until 1689 (Kernan 205 n.112).
28. See Dear 49–52.
29. See Charles Nicholl, *The Chemical Theatre* (London: Routledge and Kegan Paul, 1980) 16–17.
30. See William R. Newman, "Alchemy, Assaying, and Experiment," *Instruments and Experimentation in the History of Chemistry,* ed. Frederic L. Holmes and Trevor H. Levere (Cambridge: MIT P, 2000) 35–54.
31. See William R. Newman and Lawrence M. Principe, *Alchemy Tried in the Fire: Starkey, Boyle, and the Fate of Helmontian Chemistry* (Chicago: U of Chicago P, 2002) 157–61.
32. See Peggy A. Knapp, "The Work of Alchemy," *Journal of Medieval and Early Modern Studies* 30 (2000): 575–99. For alchemy's association with the commodity, see also Cohen 192–200, and Eric Wilson, "Abel Drugger's Sign and the Fetishes of Material Culture," *Historicism, Psychoanalysis, and Early Modern Culture,* ed. Carla Mazzio and Douglas Trevor (New York: Routledge, 2000) 110–35.
33. See Lisa Jardine, *Ingenious Pursuits: Building the Scientific Revolution* (New York: Doubleday, 1999) 277.
34. See Stephen Greenblatt, *Learning to Curse: Essays in Early Modern Culture* (New York: Routledge, 1990) 161–83.
35. See Denise Albanese, *New Science, New World* (Durham: Duke UP, 1996) 97.

READING LIST

Campbell, Mary Baine. *Wonder and Science: Imagining Worlds in Early Modern Europe*. Ithaca: Cornell UP, 1999.

Cohen, Walter. *Drama of a Nation: Public Theater in Renaissance England and Spain*. Ithaca: Cornell UP, 1985.

Goldberg, Jonathan. *James I and the Politics of Literature: Jonson, Shakespeare, Donne, and Their Contemporaries*. Stanford: Stanford UP, 1989.

Greenblatt, Stephen. "Resonance and Wonder." *Learning to Curse: Essays in Early Modern Culture.* New York: Routledge, 1990. 161–83.

Holmes, Frederic L., and Trevor H. Levere, eds. *Instruments and Experimentation in the History of Chemistry.* Cambridge: MIT P, 2000.

Jardine, Lisa. *Ingenious Pursuits: Building the Scientific Revolution.* New York: Doubleday, 1999.

Principe, Lawrence M. "Apparatus and Reproducibility in Alchemy." *Instruments and Experimentation in the History of Chemistry.* Ed. Frederic L. Holmes and Trevor H. Levere. Cambridge: MIT P, 2000. 55–74.

Sherman, William H. "'Gold Is the Strength, the Sinnewes of the World': Thomas Dekker's *Old Fortunatus* and England's Golden Age." *Medieval and Renaissance Drama in England* 6 (1993): 85–102.

Wilson, Eric. "Abel Drugger's Sign and the Fetishes of Material Culture." *Historicism, Psychoanalysis, and Early Modern Culture.* Ed. Carla Mazzio and Douglas Trevor. New York: Routledge, 2000. 110–35.

19

The Roaring Girl and the London Underworld

Clare McManus

At London's Fortune Theater, during a performance of Thomas Middleton and Thomas Dekker's *The Roaring Girl* in late April or early May 1611, a remarkable spectacle unfolded. At the side of the stage sat a woman called Mary Frith, otherwise known as Moll Cutpurse, a notorious thief, fencer of stolen goods, and cross-dresser. Frith's antics formed the basis of Middleton and Dekker's drama and she herself turned up to watch and comment. The play's epilogue, in addition to pleading for applause, had acted as advance publicity, explaining to audiences a few days earlier that

> The Roaring Girl herself, some few days hence,
> Shall on this stage give larger recompense;
> Which mirth that you may share in, herself does woo you,
> And craves this sign: your hands to beckon her to you. (Epilogue 35–38)[1]

Such an appearance, even after the play's conclusion, was controversial. Women were not allowed to perform in the London city theaters, and Frith suffered for her boldness. Court records dating from January 27, 1612, describe her performance and its punishment. Noting that she was dressed "in mans apparell & in her boot*es* & w*i*th a sword by her side," it goes on to say that she

> told the company there pr*esent* *tha*t she thought many of them were of opinion *tha*t she was a man, but if any of them would come to her lodging they should finde that she is a woman & some other im*m*odest & lascivious speaches she also vsed at *tha*t time And also sat there vppon the stage in the publique viewe of all the people there p*rese*nte in mans apparrell & playd vppon her lute & sange a songe. (Mulholland 262)

Frith's punishment for her song and dance routine, among her other misdemeanors, was imprisonment in the city's Bridewell prison. Her crimes included associating with "Ruffinly swaggering & lewd company as namely w*i*th cut purses blasphemous drunkard*es* & others of bad note" and "most dissolute behavior [. . .] to the great shame of her sexe" (Mulholland 262). More than her cross-dressing, Frith's association with dissolute thieves and cutpurses of London's underworld ensured her punishment.

What, then, of this underworld that made Frith such a draw for the Fortune audiences? While the term "underworld" suggests a delineated subculture with readily identifiable inhabitants, critical opinion differs as to the extent to which seventeenth-century London's underworld was organized. There were certainly areas, like Alsatia and Southwark (the latter also the site of several theaters), in which criminals congregated.[2] There is also evidence to suggest an imaginative ranking of criminals, with distinct names assigned in the canting language of the rogue, such as the "ruffler" or rogue and the "doxy," the "sexually initiated female vagrant," both of which are found in *The Roaring Girl*

(Salgado 215, 210). Such naming imaginatively constructed an antisociety of sorts, fitting criminals and those on the edges of legitimacy (pawn-brokers, ballad sellers, and alehouse proprietors) into a structure that inversely mirrored the reassuring order of everyday society.[3] However, how much such ordering was actual, how much imaginative wish fulfillment is debatable. Prositution, women's main underworld "career," seems to have been more organized than most (Twyning 54), and the extent to which Moll Cutpurse can or should be read as a prostitute will be explored later. What is clear though, is that, as *The Roaring Girl* shows, in the hard world of early modern London the fall from security into an illicit scramble for survival was a constant threat.

As the role of cant in creating the rogues' society demonstrates, the language of the underworld was pivotal to its various identities, distinguishing citizen from aristocrat from cutpurse, forming bonds of community between its members and excluding the ignorant. It was also gobbled up by a fascinated public, as the sheer wealth of cheap "cony-catching" pamphlets by writers such as Robert Greene—which taught both the art of spotting and (indirectly) of being a cutpurse—shows. Thomas Dekker himself wrote such texts, including *Lanthorn and Candlelight, or the Bellman's Second Night's Walk* (1608). This contained "The Canter's Dictionary," which documented the rogues' language and was the basis for the canting scenes of *The Roaring Girl*.[4] Given the imaginative fascination with the underworld, Frith is an ideal figure for the investigation of its theatrical representation. Indeed, Frith's appearance in the Fortune and her transformation into a dramatic character demonstrate the proximity between early modern London's theater and its underworld.

Although to modern eyes Frith's cross-dressing seems her main transgression, the early modern codes surrounding social status and femininity that she contravened on the Fortune stage are legion. Firstly, although indeed dressed as a man, her impersonation of her "betters" also extended to the way that she sat at the side of the stage like a fashionable male gallant, to be seen and admired by less socially elevated audience members. Equally, the location of this personal appearance was unacceptable. The public and private theaters of Renaissance London banned women from their stages (although, as we shall see, not entirely from the court stage), and the sight of Frith on stage dressed as a man begged the audience to compare her to the transvestite boy actors and, in particular, to the boy who earlier in the evening had played the part of Moll herself. This moment reveals a great deal about the changes taking place on the all-male stage and will lead to a comparison between Frith and (of all people) Anna of Denmark, queen consort of James VI and I. More important at this point, though, is the fact that the playhouse is revealed as a place where London came to gaze at heightened versions of itself against the staged backdrop of what looked like its daily life (i.e., its locations, its shops, its slang), populated by fictionalized members of the underworld who, though feared in the streets, made for high theatrical entertainment. Staged in front of an audience consisting of gentry, citizens, prostitutes, and cutpurses, *The Roaring Girl* asks that audience to look back at itself in all its variety and indulges in a kind of vicarious cultural tourism, safely touring the various worlds that made up England's early modern metropolis.[5] If we set Frith's stay in the Bridewell alongside the performance it was partly designed to punish, the proximity of theater to the underworld becomes clear.

As the dual role of Southwark as a hideout and one of London's "theater districts" suggests, the location of Frith's stage debut added much to the resonances of the relationship between city and stage. The Fortune was situated in the north of London, beyond the city walls. This position, outside the direct control of the authorities (as were the Globe and the Rose in the Liberties south of the Thames and the Blackfriars in the heart of the city), gave a certain amount of protection from censorship and allowed the theater industry to develop from its roots in the early modern London underworld. Playhouses rubbed shoulders with bear-baitings, cock-fights, and brothels, and Londoners may well have considered these activities to be near neighbors conceptually as well as geographically (see Newman, Chapter 21 of this volume). What is more, the link between the theater and the other kinds of trades that went on in these areas, and that between the players and the masterless men who populated them, was further institutionalized in the famous Elizabethan proclamation of 1598 that declared actors to be "Rogues Vagabonds and Sturdy Beggars."[6] The links between the player, the playhouse, and the underworld were more than simply geographical; as Jean-Christophe Agnew writes, theater demonstrated "how precarious social identity was, how vulnerable to unexpected disruptions and disclosure it was, and therefore how deeply theatrical it was."[7] In several ways, therefore, Frith shared her status as an outcast with the players.

The playhouses were also, however, a place where the world of the "sturdy rogues" intersected with that of the elite. These were, after all, the same playing companies that found protection from royal or courtly patrons and were regularly called to give command performances in the Jacobean court at Whitehall. So, while the companies might have been legally identified with rogues, practice did not make it so. That said, there certainly was a conceptual link between the actor and the rogue; as both the servants of the great and as threatening vagabonds, the playing companies' position was liminal and shifting. Add to this the erotic appeal of the actor that so worried antitheatricalist writers like Philip Stubbes and Stephen Gosson and the heady combination that results perhaps explains why the theater was the right place to tell Frith's story. Early modern theater crossed the barriers between the tolerable and the intolerable, linking the world of the court directly to that of the vagabond and the beggar. As I will discuss later, this is made real in the play in the tour of underworld London that Moll conducts for members of the elite. The scene in which she gives Lord Noland and his companions safe passage to view the world of beggars and cutpurses (5.1) reveals much about the mutual relationships between London and its underworld.

Crime and Punishment in Early Modern London

The play that Frith watched from the sidelines offers a sanitized version of her life and the London underworld she inhabited, but it also gave the audience the illicit thrill of glimpsing the worlds that made up their city. As both an onstage spectacle and an audience for the boy actor who played her role, Frith watched a representation of herself as the comic, facilitating Moll of Dekker and Middleton's play. Their Moll walks with impunity with gentry and cutpurses, brings a thwarted love to a satisfying resolution in marriage, and—in sharp contrast to Frith's bold invitation to the audience—defends the chastity of her sex in a duel that proves her prowess over the impotent and impoverished aristocrat, Laxton. Dekker and Middleton's Moll is a charismatic and energetic protagonist. She is the roaring girl, a version of the roaring boys, a group of "noisy and riotous young [men] who terrorised decent people in the streets of London."[8] In their roaring girl, Dekker and Middleton stage an "underworld chic" (Knowles xix). So who was this woman who appeared on the Fortune stage, and how does her performance embody the connections between theater and the underworld?

City comedy relied on a heterogeneous audience, and the Fortune audience was predominantly "lower-class" (Knowles xxxviii). In a sense, Frith was presented to this rather mixed group of spectators as both a creature of their own lives and as a strange and monstrous spectacle, a thrilling glimpse of the exotic and threatening world of the roaring boy and cutpurse that was on their very doorstep. If we examine her life, the links between Frith's status as a social outcast and her access to the London city stage become clearer. Frith was the middle-class daughter of a shoemaker who was born in the Barbican area in 1584.[9] That date varies, however, from source to source and is cited as 1589 in the introduction to a prose tract called *The Life and Death of Mal Cutpurse* (published in 1662).[10] *The Life* purports to be Frith's autobiography, but it was in all probability not written, or not all written, by Frith herself (Todd and Spearing xi). Even though the roaring girl was perhaps not the author, *The Life* is testimony to the huge interest that her scandalous career generated. Of particular interest, then as now, is her everyday practice of dressing as a man. *The Life* has Frith as a tomboy who, as a young woman, could not abide the thought of being in service, but rejected respectability in favor of a life spent dressed in men's clothes, fencing stolen goods and frequenting taverns (Todd and Spearing 9–17). She is not, however, a woman disguised as a man; she makes no attempt to pass and her sex is no secret; indeed she announces it from the Fortune stage. Instead, Frith took on a masculine social role by looking and acting like a man. Such an upward move was frowned upon in the highly stratified social structure of early modern England; the preface to *The Life* describes Frith as resolving to "usurp and invade the Doublet" (Todd and Spearing 13). Such a move is also, however, a kind of impersonation that fitted Frith for the stage and that also further shows how the stage was a reflection of the performances that permeated an early modern society that read identity through appearance and action rather than inner essence.[11]

There is, of course, a great difference between what you can get away with in a playhouse and in the world. For both the character of Moll and the "real" Frith, cross-dressing emphasizes social marginalization and forms a visual link between the woman, the character, and the London underworld; her ostracism stands for that of all who live beyond "respectable" society. Moll herself is a mobile character, moving between the different worlds of the play, inhabiting both with apparent ease. This ability to move between seemingly firmly opposed positions, like Moll's linguistic skill of conversing with both aristocrats and cutpurses (5.1), hints at a doubleness that is encapsulated in the figure of the hermaphrodite. The image of the body that is both male and female shows how even apparently natural oppositions (male/female, aristocrat/cutpurse) can be broken down and also shows the extent to which the social could be represented through the sexual. And yet, as neither one thing nor the other either socially or sexually but defined above all by class, Moll is marginalized, a chorus rather than an accepted member of either elite society or the underworld (Orgel 13). As such, Moll is imagined as the hermaphrodite, her position demonstrating the intersections of early modern discourses of class and gender.

Dekker and Middleton's play is not the only narrative concerning Frith, nor was her turn at the Fortune her only public appearance. Another performance shows Frith's propensity for criminality, society's attempts to bring her and those like her back into line, and, following the work of the influential French theorist Michel Foucault, the theatricality both of the public forms of punishment used to enforce conformity and of the performance of early modern identity itself.[12] In a letter to Sir Dudley Carleton dated February 12, 1612 (about a year after the production of *The Roaring Girl*), the court writer Sir John Chamberlain describes an incident that took place at St. Paul's Cross, a place of public penance:

> this last Sonday Mall Cut-Purse a notorious bagage (that used to go in mans apparell and challenged the field of divers gallants) was brought to [St. Paul's Cross], where she wept bitterly and seemed very penitent, but yt is since doubted she was maudlin druncke, beeing discovered to have tipled of three quarts of sacke before she came to her penaunce: she had the daintiest preacher or ghostly father that ever I saw in pulpit, one Ratcliffe of Brazen Nose in Oxford [. . .] but the best is he did extreem badly, and so wearied the audience that the best part went away, and the rest tarried rather to heare Mall Cutpurse then him.[13]

This, along with the deposition against Frith, allows us a glimpse into crime, punishment, and their performance in early modern London. Indeed, the parenthetical section could easily describe the action of *The Roaring Girl*. At the Cross, Frith again appears in front of an "audience" (Chamberlain's term) that was to interpret her speech and gestures. In an echo of the dramatic duel with Laxton, her bravado outwits and humiliates the man who intends to test and punish her. Once again the dangerously mixed social space of the city theaters, in which cutpurse watched with aristocrat, is revealed to be closely affiliated to the world it represents.

Certainly, Frith's arraignments and her elaborate performance of penance are the penalty for membership of the underworld. However, Frith's drunken performance at St. Paul's Cross shows the extent to which such performances, although designed as spectacles of bodily humiliation to educate and discipline the watchers, could be appropriated by the individual being punished and used to state quite a different case. Frith's virtuoso disregard for the law that seeks to humiliate her—the glamour and bravado of the roaring boy enacted by a woman—suggests that the members of such cultural groups had their own social codes of behavior that certainly did not involve penitence before the law.

One way in which Frith turns her penance on its head is by playing against early modern expectations of femininity. Chamberlain is clearly captivated by the contrast between Frith's abnormal "manliness" and the delicate effeminacy of the churchman who was supposed to be in authority over her (Orgel 22). This reaction perhaps explains why the energetic, subversive Frith made such perfect material for Dekker and Middleton. Rejecting femininity, Frith acts as a particular kind of man—the roaring boy. First, though, come the tears. By crying, Frith lulls her audience into a false sense of security, seeming both contrite and feminine, incapable of emotional and physical containment. Not for long. Her tears turn out to be the result not of sincere penitence but the artificial product of drunkenness. It is as if Frith is crying not salt tears of the open and leaky female body, but alcoholic tears that are the product of her masculine drinking habit (Orgel 22).[14] With this bravura "cross-dressed" display of masculinity (Kastan 101–21),

Frith undermines the purpose of her public humiliation with a public drunkenness that should be shaming but here works to her advantage. In taking a shame of her own on herself and embracing the drunkenness of the roaring boy, Frith avoids the official shame the legislating powers sought to impose upon her.

How, then, does *The Roaring Girl* represent those involved in a life of crime and (occasional) punishment and the fascination of those like Chamberlain with the underworld? As suggested earlier, the play sanitizes the less palatable aspects of Frith's career, and I will return to this with regard to the play's depiction of female sexuality as a part of the London subculture. Certainly, the brash masculinity of the roaring boy that Moll takes on is reflected in much of the play. Indeed it horrifies the more conventional characters. Pretending to regale his party with a tale told to him by some other unfortunate father, Sir Alexander insults his son's supposed bride-to-be with words that soon become his own:

> "A creature," saith he, "nature hath brought forth
> To mock the sex of woman." It is a thing
> One knows not how to name: her birth began
> Ere she was all made. 'Tis woman more than man,
> Man more than woman, and—which to none can hap—
> The sun gives her two shadows to one shape;
> Nay, more, let this strange thing walk, stand, or sit,
> No blazing star draws more eyes after it. (1.2.127–34)

One of the dinner guests, Sir Davy, responds in kind, exclaiming that the woman is "A monster! 'Tis some monster!" (1.2.135), and Sebastian, in a moment of theatrical self-consciousness typical of the play, tells the audience "Now is my cue to bristle" (1.2.136). Sir Alexander's description betrays a fascination akin to Chamberlain's, but his words emphasize the threat to his family caused by Moll's position as social outcast. And, of course, Sebastian is banking on his father coming to this conclusion. Playing cleverly on Sir Alexander's role as the *senex* of *The Roaring Girl*'s conventional New Comedy plot (the foolish old man who stands in the way of true love and a comic resolution), in Moll Cutpurse Sebastian has found a woman who will make his first choice, Mary Fitzallard, seem eminently preferable.[15] However, the play makes clear that Moll and Mary share far more than their interchangeable names. When he rejected Mary Fitzallard as a suitable wife for his son, Sir Alexander did so mainly on economic grounds.[16] Despite appearances, Moll is rejected for similar reasons; as Sir Alexander's mention of the "blazing star that draws [. . .] eyes after it" suggests, social reputation and status are at stake in the threatened match (Miller 15–16). Female characters enter the motherless, all-male Wengrave household only as servants or as roaring girls, and, for the father of that household, they seem to sum up the threat of the social other emanating from those of a different class or gender.[17]

As the gull of the play, Sir Alexander's opinion of Moll is not to be trusted. A character of sheer energy and brash charm, Moll reveals the venality of both male and female characters, citizen, gentry, or rogue alike. For instance, in her first appearance at the row of shops (2.1), those who speak ill of her or who, like Mistress Openwork, try to bar her from her shop are revealed to be themselves weak and corruptible. Similarly, Moll's moral energy unveils Laxton's plotting and maneuvers Sir Alexander into a corner from which he cannot but agree to the initial marriage that he had so unfairly blocked. The codes that rule Sir Alexander's behavior are revealed to be flawed: it is Moll who is to be trusted. The glamorous figure of the rebel, outlaw, or rogue whose energies revitalize conformist society is the perennial stuff of theater and is the basic component of *The Roaring Girl*.

Above all, though, *The Roaring Girl* is a city comedy, a play about London for a London audience, which stages the shops, haunts, characters, and languages of the city. The fairly conventional trickster plot of the city comedy is in this case structured around the social ranks and spaces of the city, as are the interlocking sexual plots (Howard 176). For instance, Laxton the profligate aristocrat behaves according to predatory stereotype, as do the lustful shopkeepers' wives whose husbands cannot satisfy them economically or sexually. However, Dekker and Middleton's standard plot of tricksters and gulls differs from a play like Jonson's *Alchemist* (more of which later), in that the lively and charismatic trickster here explicitly fights for social order. In showing such a character and her haunts, *The Roaring Girl* stages a cultural tour of the parts of the city into which the audience might ordinarily fear to go.

The reality of London was rather less safe than its stage depiction and the reasons to fear it probably well-founded. As is already clear, we can learn about Frith's world from surviving court records and legal documents. Other sources include ballads, pamphlets, and prose tracts, including those by Dekker himself, which document the languages and activities of the city's underworld and influenced the play's canting scene. Such tracts, and the languages and practices that they record, reflect a world of taverns, brothels, bear-baitings, and cock-fights—a vivid, dynamic world of thieves, rogues, fencers, beggars, cony-catchers, balladeers, and pamphleteers. Early modern London gave birth to a very particular kind of theater, one it profoundly influenced not only in its subject matter but also in its perceptions and representations. The links between the London underworld and *The Roaring Girl* go far deeper than its subject matter: they cut to the heart of early modern English theater itself.

The Roaring Girl itself draws attention to the links between the stage spectacle and the theater in which it was performed. Take, for instance, the well-known metatheatrical moment early on in the play when Sir Alexander describes his "galleries":

> Stories of men and women, mixed together,
> Fair ones with foul, like sunshine in wet weather;
> Within one square a thousand heads are laid
> So close that all of heads the room seems made; [. . .]
> And here and there, whilst with obsequious ears,
> Thronged heaps do listen, a cutpurse thrusts and leers
> With hawk's eyes for his prey—(1.2.17–20, 25–27)

Men and women, cutpurse and playgoer, elite and "lower-class" all mingle together in the social space of the playhouse, and such mixing is also shown to a certain extent on the stage. As Knowles notes, "*The Roaring Girl* develops the City as a spectacle, full of dangers, pleasures, monsters, and prodigies" (xxxviii). *The Roaring Girl* also shows that its theater was just such another space of spectacle: a place where those who watched from the auditorium saw themselves reflected in the prodigious action of the stage; a place where the underworld became entertainment.

As part of the business of theater, Dekker and Middleton's play itself is a commodity that offers up a roaring girl and the underworld for the pleasurable consumption of its audience (Miller 14). At the same time the play also validates its audience by offering them in Moll a merry rogue with a heart of gold and a strict moral sensibility that just happens to conform to their own ideals. The canting scenes are central in indicating the intersecting worlds of the play and Moll's shifting position as both part and not part of the underworld. Near the end of the play, Moll leads Sir Beauteous Ganymede and several other characters, including the aristocrat Lord Noland, on a walking tour of rogues' London, toward Pimlico (5.1). There she deals with the fraudulent soldiers Trapdoor and Tearcat and, able to understand the beggars' cant, uses her skill to translate and order it for the "touring" gentry, censuring its sexual content when it seems inappropriate for her noble audience (Orgel 22).[18] Just as much as the cross-dressed body or the brands that marked the body of the criminal—think, for instance, of the thumb-brand that identified Ben Jonson as a murderer and that Sir Alexander sees on Trapdoor's hand (1.2.207–09)—language operates as another marker of criminality for the stage. Cant, the language of the dispossessed, "byzantine" in its complexity (Mikalachki 120) and bravura in style, is used by the playwrights as a sign of social and moral status (Knowles xx). Getting language right or wrong marks characters out as sincere or false, truly virtuous or foolishly aspirational. Language creates community, and the inhabitants of London's stage underworld are bound together by their shared language, called "pedlar's French" (5.1.179) in a neat encapsulation of the sense of a self-contained community—perhaps even a nation—within London. The onstage gentry, positioned as outsiders by their ignorance of cant, are abroad in a foreign world.

Despite Moll's apparently insurmountable charms, there are some characters in the play over whom her control is weaker. As her guided tour continues, she and her group encounter underworld inhabitants of an entirely different order from Trapdoor and Tearcat, namely a cutpurse disguised as an aristocrat and accompanied by four or five men. The cutpurse is a less amenable version of criminality from whom not even Moll can protect her companions; he must be dismissed from the stage rather than allowed to converse with them. Equally significantly, she cannot converse with Lord Noland. Careful to exclude Moll from the walking group (Mikalachki 127–29), he barely addresses her, merely wondering aloud "how [she] camest to the knowledge of these nasty villains" (5.1.311–12). Rather than an equal, Moll has become an employee, handing out Noland's money to the beggars at his demand (Mikalachki 124). Tainted by her knowledge of "pedlar's French" and its implications of low degree and sexuality, her skill makes her fascinating to the gentry and also means that they will never accept her as anything other than a servant. Moll's function, it transpires, is to take both her onstage and offstage audience on an orphic tour through the underworld as Virgil to their (and our) Dante.

Molls and Dolls: Women in the London Underworld

Mary Frith's life was the ideal material for playwrights looking for inspiration and a guaranteed audience. As I suggested earlier, however, in putting such a controversial figure on the stage Middleton and Dekker transform her from Bridewell inmate into an altogether safer character. Like her comic counterpart, Shakespeare's Falstaff, who (albeit unwittingly) educates the wild Prince Hal to become the Machiavellian but inspirational King Henry V (see *1* and *2 Henry IV* and *Henry V*) by showing him the sights, sounds, and experiences of the underworld, Moll is the means by which Sebastian and his father can be reconciled and Sebastian can marry Mary Fitzallard. Moll herself is rendered safe, the dangers of her drunken penance banished from the play and her outspoken sexual invitations kept until after its conclusion. Middleton himself admits to this process in an epistle to the play: "Worse things, I must needs confess, the world has taxed her for than has been written of her; but 'tis the excellency of a writer to leave things better than he finds 'em" ("Epistle" 19–22). Fittingly, Dekker and Middleton transform Frith into the stuff of theater and into Moll. She becomes a plot device to ensure that Sebastian and Mary Fitzallard can marry, an entertainment set piece in the duel with Laxton, and a charismatic central protagonist who leads the audience on a tour through a vision of the dangerous city in which they live.

The extent to which Dekker and Middleton do indeed defuse Moll's dangers and the differences between her representation and that of other comic female characters on the early-seventeenth-century stage are clear in a comparison between Moll and Doll Common of Ben Jonson's *Alchemist*.[19] Another city comedy, *The Alchemist* also stages a trickster subculture that dazzles its audience with intersecting con-schemes and satirizes the apparently respectable but venial citizens who are the dupes of the fraudsters' devices. Although one of the most forthright, versatile, and theatrical of Jonson's female roles, Doll's depiction is tainted by the early modern English theater's damning representation of female sexuality. As her name suggests, Doll Common is a prostitute, the common property of Face and Subtle, her partners in the "venture tripartite" (1.1.135) and a character whose performances as the Queen of Fairy and in a "fit of talking" (4.5) mark her as dangerously changeable and theatrical. At the end of the play she and Subtle are cast out into the city with no profit from their plots. In contrast, Moll, who despite her bawdy comments, tobacco smoking, and duelling is the only sexually unavailable female character in her play, achieves success of a sort at its conclusion.

Above and beyond simply remaining chaste, Moll is figured as the defender of her sex. In a rousing speech read by some as proto-feminist, she speaks out against women's sexual exploitation. Preparing to duel with Laxton at Gray's Inn Fields (itself associated with illicit assignations) she confronts his assumption that her cross-dressing determines her sexual availability:

> Thou'rt one of those
> That thinks each woman thy fond flexible whore: [. . .]
> In thee I defy all men, their worst hates
> And their best flatteries, all their golden witchcrafts
> With which they entangle the poor spirit of fools:
> Distresséd needlewomen and trade-fallen wives—
> Fish that must needs bite, or themselves be bitten— [. . .]
> But why, good fisherman,
> Am I thought meat for you, that never yet
> Had angling rod cast towards me?— [. . .]
> I scorn to prostitute myself to a man,
> I can that can prostitute a man to me!—(3.1.72–73, 92–96, 101–03, 111–12).

Though it may seem to defend women, this speech in fact distances Moll from her sex, portraying her as a unique observer rather than as someone who shares their circumstances.[20] For those looking to suggest that Moll is a feminist before her time, her final assertive declaration that she will never be a whore while she can hire male whores also causes problems. Most forceful of all, though, are the economic reasons that Moll declares lie at the root of women's sexual exploitation in Renaissance London. She describes a hard world in which women are prey to men who drive them to market their sexuality in order to ensure their survival or satisfaction. In this speech, Moll might almost be referring to characters such as Doll, and she works hard to distinguish herself from such figures. In so doing, she describes a London that trades on sex, a trade to which women have access. In this world, Moll differs from Doll in that she is depicted as having opted out of the commodification of her sexuality, declaring herself economically and sexually separate from other women by asserting her chastity.

In a world trading in sex, Moll paints a picture of herself as her own master, or, more accurately, as masterless. The masterless individual, moving unanchored through the world and answerable to no specific authority, was a threatening figure and a staple of pamphlets and ballads. Add to this Moll's illegal cross-dressing, and such masterlessness becomes ever more sexualized. The close proximity between such mobility and a threatening female sexuality are clear in the play. When he first sees Moll, Laxton declares that "She slips from one company to another like a fat eel between a Dutchman's fingers" (2.1.206–07). Such a rush of masturbatory imagery to describe Moll's movement between social ranks is telling in itself. To Laxton, Moll's adaptability and her mobility between groups of different social degree renders her sexual. As we have seen, Moll exploits this impression to revenge herself on Laxton, but such perceptions and her participation in Sebastian's marriage plot depend upon a definition of her as both socially mobile and sexually threatening.

Moll ends the play in triumph, having secured the marriage of Mary Fitzallard and Sebastian Wengrave, saved Jack Dapper from his father, ensured Laxton's humiliation, and avoided her own. This success is only possible, though, because the desires Moll acts on are not hers but rather the conventional heterosexual desires of Mary and Sebastian. In many ways, Moll remains a rather marginal figure, a fascinatingly monstrous incomer from the underworld made safe because she schemes on behalf of the seemingly stable order of the everyday world. Like the watching Frith herself, Moll comments from the sidelines and is never truly assimilated into the various societies of the play.

Conclusion: Theater and the Underworld

Both inside and outside the Fortune's stage picture, the real Frith is an apt image for the way in which the early modern theater connects London's different worlds. And, perhaps surprisingly, Frith herself can be connected (through theater) with the most exalted of that society. As an exception to the general rule, a few women could legitimately perform on the early modern English stage. Royal and courtly women regularly took part in the Jacobean court masque, and Frith, as an early female performer, is linked to Queen Anna of Denmark, who regularly commissioned and performed Jonson's masques. Silent spectacles of grace and luxury, the elite women of Anna's court performed alongside professional London players who provided the speaking parts of the masque and often cross-dressed in order to do so. On this stage, male cross-dresser and female performer came together just as they did when Frith appeared on the side of the Fortune stage. A great deal of the fun and titillation of *The Roaring Girl* depends on the fact that Moll was played by a boy. But in the jumbled theatrical world of London in 1611, women were beginning to edge their way onto the stage. The theatrical connection between the outcast Frith and the queen of Scotland and England reveals the presence and inevitable collapse of binary opposites. In more historical terms, the bond between these two apparently opposed women shows that degree or social order is a system of mutually dependent connections. Much as it might seem to deny it, Renaissance London needs its underworld. Likewise, much as it might seem to threaten it, the underworld needs the city. Theater and performance show the subtle interdependencies of the "high" and "low" worlds of early modern London. As Hamlet puts it, "a king may go a progress through the guts of a beggar" (*Ham.* 4.3.30–31).

NOTES

1. I am grateful to Victoria Price for her discussions during the writing of this chapter. All references are to Thomas Dekker and Thomas Middleton, *The Roaring Girl,* ed. Paul A. Mulholland (Manchester: Manchester UP, 1987). Further references appear in the text.
2. Gãmini Salgado, *The Elizabethan Underworld* (Gloucestershire: Allan Sutton, 1995) 7.
3. John Twyning, *London Dispossessed: Literature and Social Space in the Early Modern City* (Basingstoke: Macmillan, 1998) 89.
4. James Knowles, "Introduction," *The Roaring Girl and Other City Comedies,* ed. James Knowles with notes by Eugene Giddens (Oxford: Oxford World's Classics, 2001) vii–xlv, xxix.
5. Joseph Roach, "The Enchanted Island: Vicarious Tourism in Restoration Adaptations of *The Tempest,*" *"The Tempest" and Its Travels,* ed. Peter Hulme and William H. Sherman (London: Reaktion Books, 2000) 60–70, 62.
6. R. A. Foakes, "Playhouses and Players," *The Cambridge Companion to English Renaissance Drama,* ed. A. R. Braunmuller and Michael Hattaway (Cambridge: Cambridge UP, 1990) 1–52, 2.
7. Jean-Christophe Agnew, *The Market and the Theater in Anglo-American Thought, 1550–1750* (Cambridge: Cambridge UP, 1986) 112.
8. Janet Todd and Elizabeth Spearing, "Introduction," *Counterfeit Ladies: The Life and Death of Mary Frith, the Case of Mary Carleton* (London: William Pickering, 1994) 1–74, xiv.
9. Stephen Orgel, "The Subtexts of *The Roaring Girl,*" *Erotic Politics: Desire on the Renaissance Stage,* ed. Susan Zimmerman (New York: Routledge, 1992) 12–26, 20.
10. Anonymous, *The Life and Death of Mrs Mary Frith, Commonly Called Mal Cutpurse,* in Todd and Spearing.
11. David Scott Kastan, "Is There a Class in This (Shakespearean) Text?," *Renaissance Drama* 25 (1993): 101–21, 103–07.
12. Michel Foucault, *Discipline and Punish: The Birth of the Prison,* trans. Alan Sheridan (London: Penguin, 1991) 1–69.
13. Norman Egbert McClure, ed., *The Letters of John Chamberlain,* 2 vols. (Philadelphia: American Philosophical Society, 1939) 1.334.

14. Peter Stallybrass, "Patriarchal Territories: The Body Enclosed," *Rewriting the Renaissance: The Discourse of Sexual Difference in Early Modern Europe,* ed. Margaret W. Ferguson, Maureen Quilligan, and Nancy J. Vickers (Chicago: U of Chicago P, 1986) 123–42.
15. Mary Beth Rose, "Women in Men's Clothing: Apparel and Social Stability in *The Roaring Girl,*" *English Literary Renaissance* (1984): 367–91, 380.
16. Jo E. Miller, "Women and the Market in *The Roaring Girl,*" *Renaissance and Reformation* 26 (1990): 11–23, 13–14.
17. Jean E. Howard, "Sex and Social Conflict: The Erotics of *The Roaring Girl,*" *Erotic Politics: Desire on the Renaissance Stage,* ed. Susan Zimmerman (London: Routledge, 1992) 170–90, 176, 181–82.
18. Jodi Mikalachki, "Gender, Cant and Cross-Talking in *The Roaring Girl,*" *Renaissance Drama* (1994): 119–43, 123, 132.
19. Ben Jonson, *The Alchemist, "The Alchemist" and Other Plays,* ed. Gordon Campbell (Oxford: Oxford World's Classics, 1998) 211–326.
20. Susan E. Krantz, "The Sexual Identities of Moll Cutpurse in Dekker and Middleton's *The Roaring Girl* and in London," *Renaissance and Reformation* 19 (1995): 5–20, 9–10.

READING LIST

Ferris, Lesley, ed. *Crossing the Stage: Controversies on Cross-Dressing.* London: Routledge, 1993.

Findlay, Alison. *A Feminist Perspective on Renaissance Drama.* Oxford: Blackwell, 1999.

Garber, Marjorie. *Vested Interests: Cross-Dressing and Cultural Anxiety.* New York: Routledge, 1992.

Gurr, Andrew. *Playgoing in Shakespeare's London.* 2nd ed. Cambridge: Cambridge UP, 1996.

———. *The Shakespearean Stage, 1574–1642.* 3rd ed. Cambridge: Cambridge UP, 1992.

Howard, Jean E. "Sex and Social Conflict: The Erotics of *The Roaring Girl.*" *Erotic Politics: Desire on the Renaissance Stage.* Ed. Susan Zimmerman. New York: Routledge, 1992. 170–90.

Levine, Laura. *Men in Women's Clothing: Anti-Theatricality and Effeminization, 1579–1642.* Cambridge: Cambridge UP, 1994.

Miller, Jo E. "Women and the Market in *The Roaring Girl.*" *Renaissance and Reformation* 26 (1990): 11–23.

Mullaney, Steven. *Place of the Stage: License, Play, and Power in Renaissance England.* Chicago: U of Chicago P, 1988.

Orgel, Stephen. "The Subtexts of *The Roaring Girl.*" *Erotic Politics: Desire on the Renaissance Stage.* Ed. Susan Zimmerman. New York: Routledge, 1992. 12–26.

Rose, Mary Beth. "Women in Men's Clothing: Apparel and Social Stability in *The Roaring Girl.*" *English Literary Renaissance* (1984): 367–91.

20

The White Devil and the Law

Luke Wilson

Early in *The White Devil* we find Bracciano's wife Isabella taking matters into her own hands. Her husband, who is carrying on an affair with Vittoria, has brutally rejected her, declaring them divorced. Isabella knows that if her brother Francisco finds out, there will be war; and so she conceals Bracciano's marital treachery and publicly takes the blame by divorcing *him*.

> Sir, let me borrow of you but one kiss;
> Henceforth I'll never lie with you, by this,
> This wedding ring.
> [. . .]
> And this divorce shall be as truly kept,
> As if in throngèd court a thousand ears
> Had heard it, and a thousand lawyers' hands
> Sealed to the separation. (2.1.252–58)[1]

Throughout the scene, Isabella speaks publicly a parodic version of what Bracciano has said to her in private. Here, her lines imitate the words he has used in divorcing her sixty lines earlier:

> Your hand I'll kiss,
> This is the latest ceremony of my love;
> Henceforth I'll never lie with thee, by this,
> This wedding-ring; I'll ne'er more lie with thee.
> And this divorce shall be as truly kept,
> As if the judge had doomed it; fare you well,
> Our sleeps are severed. (2.1.192–98)

By repeating and revising her husband's words, Isabella seems to take control and appears to undercut, by outdoing, his rhetoric. Whether she really gains anything by doing so is open to debate; but in any case it is important to notice that neither she nor Bracciano have the authority to make such pronouncements with any legal force, and this helplessness—Bracciano cannot divorce his wife—indirectly results in the murders to follow. That they nevertheless play at having such authority raises a fundamental question about the law: since law is essentially only speech, how does speech come to have the authority of law? The power to speak the law is called jurisdiction—*juris* (of law) + *dictio* (speech)—and both Bracciano and Isabella assert a jurisdiction by analogy, one that borrows the authority of the law through counterfactual "as if" expressions: "as if the judge had doomed it" (Bracciano); "as if in throngèd court a thousand ears / Had heard it, and a thousand lawyers' hands / Sealed to the separation" (Isabella). But

Isabella's "as if" doesn't simply hyperbolize Bracciano's, for in amplifying one judge into a thousand lawyers she shifts the jurisdiction in which she imagines her divorce case being heard. No trial in England in the seventeenth century would have employed a thousand lawyers, and only one court had room for a thousand auditors (or even five hundred, figuring two ears to each auditor): Westminster Hall, where peers of the realm were sometimes brought to trial.[2] Webster may have had this venue in mind; but he was almost certainly thinking as well of the only other structures of comparable capacity (excepting St. Paul's church and Westminster Abbey) in early-seventeenth-century London, the great amphitheater playhouses, including the Red Bull in Clerkenwell, where *The White Devil* was first performed in 1612.[3]

Isabella thus appeals to and claims the authority of a jurisdiction in which the theater has taken the place of the courtroom and in which the theatrical audience, split in her conceit into auditors (ears) and judges (hands), possesses the authority to hear and determine; the lawyer's hands, which seal (sign and authorize) the divorce papers, become the hands with which an audience registers its judgment through applause. In this, Isabella invokes an analogy between law court and theater fundamental to the early modern period. Both examine human disputes in oral exchanges before spectators called upon to judge. Both are centrally concerned with the representation of past actions, both rely upon and interrogate evidence of those actions, and in both one person acts for, as, or on behalf of another: the actor playing the dramatic role assigned him, the lawyer representing the client. But how, within these similarities, do law and theater work differently? What is their relation?

Several approaches can be identified. First, rhetorically oriented scholars, arguing from the importance of forensic rhetoric in English humanist education and poetic practice, identify literature, and especially drama, with a particular division of the law called equity.[4] Equity is a form of legal interpretation that enables a principled adjustment of the letter of the law where a strict application would result in injustice. If a law whose implicit purpose is to prevent betrayal of the city to the enemy forbids any citizen from opening the gates of the city at night, and a citizen opens the gates to admit another citizen fleeing that enemy, equity might excuse the conduct as outside the intent of the law even if it violates its letter. Equitable interpretation considers the intentions of the lawmaker as well as the particulars of the case (the motives and circumstances of the accused); as part of its heuristic it also considers hypothetical cases, imaginative "what if" scenarios. This concern for intention, for motive, for the hypothetical, and generally for a wider frame of reference than the law, strictly construed, allows, scholars have identified with the theater, which enables ethically complex evaluations by presenting human actions in a richly explanatory context.

In early modern England, equity was a component of the common law—the law, established primarily by precedents rather than statutes, practiced in the central courts of King's Bench and Common Pleas, and in itinerant assize courts throughout the land. But it was also a branch of law in itself, practiced in the so-called equity courts, especially the Court of Chancery, which had originally functioned as a court of appeal for those who felt they could not get justice at common law, and which from the early sixteenth century became known as possessing an equitable jurisdiction.[5]

The equitable account of the relation between law and drama posits drama as a "humanization" of the law, a critique of its inflexibility, its ethical superficiality, and its positivism. But built into the equity model is an ambiguity that legal theorists were much concerned with. Is equity a principle within the law itself or supplemental to and separate from it? Applied to the drama, the corresponding question is whether it corrects the law from outside or confirms it from within, whether its equitable features do anything more than mystify and consolidate an alignment between the two. In the first alternative, theater is effectively absorbed into law. It does to law what law as equity does to law as law; the foundations on which legal reasoning is built are deployed rather than challenged. The second model implicitly favors the notion that equity is jurisdictionally distinct and that, in institutional terms, equity courts like Chancery offer real jurisdictional alternatives. It is also open to the idea that theater, as more remote from the letter of the law, can be a critique of both common law and institutionalized equity.

This sense that distance produces interpretive independence, an ability to see things from a truly alternative perspective, is even more pronounced in a view of literature's relation to law which abandons the equitable model and holds that the theater challenges not only the law's fairness (and its ability to self-correct through equity) but also its ethical coherence and philosophical value. In support of this view may be cited the prima facie irrelevance of the law in tragedy: there is no sense in *Hamlet* that Hamlet's problems might be solved by putting Claudius on trial. In an extension of this argument, the theater's critique of the law is a critique of the social, political, and ideological status quo that the law helps to reproduce.

These models are potentially valuable, but they run the risk of caricaturing the law, of underestimating its technical, ideological, and even imaginative complexity, as well as its mutability. Equitable interpretations of the drama relying on ancient rhetorical connections between legal and dramatic oration, for example, tend to underestimate discrepancies between this rhetorical foundation and more localized legal practices. It is crucial to distinguish between classical theories of equity found in Aristotle and the political work performed by the concept in particular early modern legal cases. Depending on the institutional context of its use, equity may mystify the operation of the law in the interests of the rich and powerful, or it may aid the disadvantaged. If we say that the theater functions equitably, what sort of equity do we mean? Claims that the theater is a radical critique of the law, on the other hand, tend to locate the powers of disruption exclusively in the theater and its language and to imagine that the language of the law can do no more than seek to preserve its own stability. The law is often described as structurally hostile to and even terrified of literary or figurative language.[6] But such language abounded in early modern legal discourse. Lawyers spoke quite confidently of persons who did not exist, without contradiction described remote foreign places as located in London, and happily committed themselves to many other fictions.[7] If the law is not to serve as a straw figure for unexamined assumptions about power against which we define the "more interesting" discourse of the literary, it must itself become the object of our study. In order to read the law in the drama we have to read the law.

The assumption that the law is ideologically monolithic, that law is Law, also underestimates the significance of its internal divisions. In early modern English legal practice the authority of the law was always potentially multiple. Jurisdiction gave authority to speak the law within a geographic or conceptual domain; but jurisdictions in England were numerous, distinctions between them uncertain, and disputes frequent. Legal authority might lodge almost anywhere: in lawmakers, in the king, in the judges of numerous courts, in bishops and other officials of the ecclesiastical courts, in lawyers, in the prosecutors who worked for the king, in juries, and in litigants themselves. When Law takes the place of law, the distinction between those administering the law and those subjected to it is drawn with unnecessary sharpness. Administrators of the law did not escape subjection to it; and those subjected to it were not *only* subjected to it.

Finally, it is often suggested that the theater offers in particular a critique of the law's systematic oppression of women. There is something to this; but when we seek evidence of the oppression upon which this claim is predicated, what we see depends on where we look. A review of the records of the central common law courts might suggest that women possessed virtually no legal standing and only rarely were litigants in their own right, that the law functioned primarily to disempower and silence them. Yet if we look beyond the common law, at petitions of war widows to county courts during the civil war period, at suits in the Court of Requests by widows using customary rather than common law to demand their widow's portion, at women suing women in the consistory courts, or at the litigation of marriage portions in the Court of Chancery, women emerge as significantly more empowered than one might expect.[8]

We can now begin to evaluate Webster's engagement with the law in *The White Devil*. Legal themes were common in early modern drama; it was a litigious society, and interest in and knowledge of the law was widespread. Webster's plays do suggest, however, that both his interest and his knowledge were unusually strong. To the Arraignment of Vittoria in *The White Devil* can be added trial scenes in his *Famous History of Sir Thomas Wyatt, The Devil's Law Case, A Cure for a Cuckold,* and *Appius and Virginia;* and incidental references to the law are scattered throughout his plays. Though it has not been demonstrated conclusively, the playwright was probably the "Magister Johannes Webster" admitted to the Middle Temple on August 1, 1598.[9] At this, one of the four London Inns of Court that trained the common lawyers of the realm, Webster not only would have learned the law but also would have made the acquaintance of future playwrights and poets, including John Marston, Sir Thomas Overbury, John Ford, and Sir John Davies.[10] Some practicing lawyers, and plenty of men who trained at the Inns of Court, were poets. The law and the theater were, in particular, closely interwoven institutions. Law students attended the theater, and playwrights, actors, and theatrical entrepreneurs pressed their claims against one another in the courts of law. The Inns of Court were themselves centers of literary activity; students organized elaborate revels in which they put on their own plays or had the professional players in to perform for them.[11]

There is no evidence that Webster ever practiced law. His earnings as a playwright were sporadic, and he probably had other employment, perhaps in the family's coachmaking business.[12] It was not unusual for law students to pursue other careers, and we cannot infer Webster's attitude toward the law from his apparent decision not to practice. Nor are his dramatic depictions of law invariably negative. And yet, having likely been trained in the law but remaining professionally outside it, Webster was well placed to identify and articulate its deficiencies, and he is often regarded as having done so in *The White Devil.* Dena Goldberg, for example, argues that the play is a progressive critique of the legal system, part of an emergent attack on the old order that was to culminate in the legal and political reforms of the Civil War period and interregnum.[13] In Flamineo's and Lodovico's complaints about injustice and judicial corruption, and especially in the scene of Vittoria's arraignment, the play calls attention to serious flaws in legal procedure, as if to advocate some fairly radical reforms—separation of prosecutorial and judicial roles, more systematic evaluation of evidence, equality under the law—that ran against deeply entrenched legal principles and practices (Goldberg 43–54).

In this view, Webster's play was part of a progressive movement whose end result was representative, parliamentary government; and its critique aligns the injustices of the law with its injustices against women. But here a problem appears. Seventeenth-century legal reform was pursued especially by those seeking the common law's ascendancy over competing jurisdictions, and one of its central accomplishments was the elimination or curtailment of the prerogative or conciliar courts—those courts that derived their authority directly from the king, including Chancery, Star Chamber, and Requests—in favor of the common law (Baker 213). A progressivist, "whig" account of the inevitable displacement of royal by parliamentary, common law authority can with some justification represent this as progress toward liberal ideals of representative government and the franchise. And yet it was through these courts, together with local, customary law courts also under fire from common law advocates, that women were able to overcome in some measure the profound limitations imposed on their agency in common law. Recent historical work has demonstrated that these courts were comparatively amenable to women as litigants, and afforded them rights unavailable to them elsewhere.[14] Seventeenth-century common law hostility toward the crown, despite expanding (modestly) the extent of the franchise among men, probably resulted on balance in a setback for women.

It may be correct to align *The White Devil* with emergent demands for legal reform. But if so, the play reveals an unexpected contradiction between its progressive politics and its implication that the predicament of women before the law, and their gestures toward alternative jurisdictions, are arguments for such reform. For if Isabella's performance hints at a jurisdictional shift, from law court to theater, the arraignment of her rival and double, Vittoria, repeats this gesture and complicates it. The scene (3.2) is central to the design of the play, and will repay close attention. In shaping the scene Webster had a free hand, for although he was working from one or more versions of the story of the historical Vittoria Corombona, an exhaustive study of the sources has concluded that none provides any details of her trial.[15]

As most recent discussions of act 3, scene 2 observe, Webster manages to present a woman who is guilty of adultery, and possibly complicit in the murders of her husband and her lover's wife, in such a way as to make it almost impossible (for modern audiences and readers at least) to withhold sympathy, while simultaneously complicating this response by repeatedly reminding us of her transgressions.[16] Whether a contemporary audience would have been equally sympathetic is unclear, though the play obviously presents her accusers' motives as compromised and seems to suggest that if Vittoria is bad Monticelso and Francisco are at best no better. As if to model the proper English response to this dispute among foreigners, it is the English ambassador who praises Vittoria's "brave spirit" (3.2.140) and remarks in her defense that Monticelso is "too bitter" (3.2.108). But the primary reason to side with Vittoria in this scene is her extraordinary skill in deflecting the charges against her. This rhetorical performance has been extensively analyzed, often with an eye to her destabilization of the masculine authority of the court or to the gendered condition of her agency and its limitations.[17]

Before examining this performance, we need to consider the structure of the scene. It presents, first of all, some basic jurisdictional ambiguities. Are we in a court, or a theater? Whose rules of judgment apply? Are we in Italy, or England? To which country's legal practices should we compare Vittoria's trial? This last question arises in general form in English Renaissance plays in which the setting is foreign but the concerns alluded to are local. Such plays often deliberately elicit the complications that result from this superimposition of locations, especially where scenes set in a Catholic country allude to life in England, a nation that virtually defined itself in opposition to continental Catholicism. Webster and his audience would probably have referred the scene primarily to English legal practice, since that is what they knew best; but the fictional foreign locale would have reminded them that English ecclesiastical courts were often associated with Catholicism.

On top of these uncertainties, the scene shows Monticelso's court undergoing a series of significant shifts: from Latin to English; from the Lawyer to Monticelso as judge and prosecutor; from the crime of murder to the crime of adultery; from Vittoria as defendant to Vittoria as (momentarily) plaintiff. These, again, raise jurisdictional questions: What is the language of authority? Who is authorized to judge? To what crimes does the authority of the court extend? Who is on trial here? The first question arises as a result of Vittoria's refusal to answer any charges brought against her in Latin. She herself knows the language, but "amongst this auditory / Which came to hear my cause, the half or more / May be ignorant in't. [. . .] I will not have my accusation clouded / In a strange tongue. All this assembly / Shall hear what you can charge me with" (3.2.14–20). The auditory Vittoria (or Webster) has in mind here is not her fellow Italians, or even the visiting ambassadors (Latin being the language of European diplomacy, an ambassador would be the last person not to know Latin), but rather the theater audience, who "came to hear my cause" (Luckyj, "Gender" 192). As Webster's utterance, this is a deferential nod to a difficult audience likely to find *The White Devil* hard going. As Vittoria's, it is a metatheatrical gesture in which she steps out of theatrical illusion and addresses the audience directly, effecting as she does so a jurisdictional shift: she's asking to be judged not by Monticelso's court but by the theater audience, just as Isabella solicited the judgment of the thousand auditors in her dispute with her husband.

Vittoria's demand is more than metatheater, however, since it echoes stories of Queen Catherine Parr's religious debates with her husband Henry VIII's advisers. Samuel Rowley's *When You See Me You Know Me* (2.254; performed 1604), and especially Shakespeare's *Henry VIII* (3.1.41–46; performed 1613) both depict similar situations: a woman addressed by churchmen in Latin and insisting on plain English on behalf of the auditors. In the context of English ecclesiastical law, this recollection of the doctrinal battles of the early days of the Reformation hints at the incomplete reform of the church courts and suggests that they have not escaped their tainted origins, a point reinforced by the Catholic (Italian) setting. The play here targets Catholicism itself (as it does elsewhere in mocking Catholic sacraments and rituals), and Monticelso's character of a whore may recall the whore of Babylon (identified by Protestants with the

Catholic church), so that he inadvertently condemns the source of his own authority (Franklin 41–42). The reference to Parr, however, together with the habit of reading local significance into foreign settings, suggests that the satire is also directed against the ecclesiastical law in England.

Hostility toward the church courts in early-seventeenth-century London came primarily from two sources. Puritans (nonconformists) insisted both that these courts were too lax on serious sins such as adultery and that, having originated as part of the transnational Catholic ecclesiastical apparatus, they were corrupt, reminiscent of Catholicism, and lacking jurisdictional authority. The common lawyers, locked in jurisdictional dispute with the ecclesiastical courts since before the Reformation, objected that these courts tried cases properly belonging before the common law. By the 1590s these two strains of hostility had begun to coalesce, and, along with the prerogative courts, the church courts were abolished temporarily in 1640 at the beginning of the Long Parliament.[18]

Until the mid-twentieth century, modern historians, relying on puritan and common law critiques, tended to accept the view that the ecclesiastical courts were inefficient, ineffectual, and corrupt. More recent regional studies of particular ecclesiastical jurisdictions suggest that this is incorrect, that there was less corruption, more popular support, and greater fairness and efficiency than had been supposed (Ingram 7–14).[19] It has been demonstrated, moreover, that London consistory courts (ecclesiastical courts under the authority of church bishops and presided over by Canon law chancellors) provided exceptional if ambiguous opportunities for women. In contrast to the common law courts, where the principle of coverture (the subsumption of the married woman's legal identity under that of her husband) could prevent married women from going to law and where female litigants were rare, in the consistory courts "married, single and widowed women sued cases in their own names over disputed wills, tithes, and, most often, sex and marriage" (Gowing 26). In short, the consistory courts did not silence or particularly oppress women. On the contrary, in them women had a legal identity and a verbal authority mostly unavailable at the common law.

Monticelso's court, then, less resembles early-seventeenth-century English ecclesiastical practice than it does prejudicial accounts of that practice circulated at the time by puritan and common law critics. As a London citizen with an Inns of Court education and family ties to the London business community, Webster lived in a milieu closely associated with both puritan and common law interests, and it makes sense to think of him as sympathetic to such accounts. To the extent that Webster's play reflects this sympathy, it is "progressive" only in a contradictory sense. If the arraignment scene mobilizes a critique of the ecclesiastical courts in order to produce a sympathetic (though ambivalent) engagement with Vittoria's plight as a woman brought before the law, it nevertheless locates the problem in one of the venues in which women were in fact unusually empowered. Webster's (admittedly limited) feminism is in conflict with his political commitments, a conflict built into the depiction of Monticelso's court, which shows Vittoria actively and to some extent effectively engaged in her defense, but which seems to imply that the jurisdiction itself is oppressive and tainted by its Catholic origin.

This does not mean, of course, that Webster was a whig historian or that he simply valorizes the common law. He is skeptical and ambivalent about all claims to authority, and in the arraignment scene he explores his relation to the common law point of view through a cagey mixing of features of ecclesiastical and common law. This exploration is most evident in the shift from the charge of murder to the charge of adultery. Though the proceedings have the sanction of the pope (3.2.3–4), Monticelso is uncertain from the start about his chances of getting a murder conviction. Vittoria dispenses easily with his one piece of evidence for her complicity in her husband's death (2.2.121–23), and when Francisco suggests they abandon this charge and pursue instead the "matter of incontinence" (3.2.190), Monticelso does not object.

Clearly, he doesn't have the evidence. Considered in relation to English ecclesiastical courts, however, the hasty abandonment of the murder charge further suggests, though no one says this, that the court has overstepped its jurisdiction. Certainly if this were an English ecclesiastical court it would have been perceived as doing so. In England the church had jurisdiction over homicide (but never murder) only when the accused was or claimed to be a member of the clergy and only when he had first been tried and convicted at common law. The privilege called "benefit of clergy" did not technically set free the man able to read Latin (and therefore deemed a churchman); rather it referred the case to the church courts for prosecution and punishment (Baker 513–15). By the seventeenth century benefit of clergy had become a common law fiction enabling judges to set free those whose crimes they considered excusable. This was hugely advantageous for the convicted criminal, since while the common law was able to punish most homicides by death if it chose to, the ecclesiastical courts could impose no punishment more severe than excommunication.[20]

Adultery, on the other hand, had been since 1286 the responsibility of the church; punishment was normally penance, for which payment of a fine was sometimes substituted.[21] Here again however the question of available punishments arose. Even before the Reformation there were complaints that the church's punishment for adultery was too lenient and demands that either these punishments be made more severe or that adultery be made a crime under the common law (Ingram 151). Puritan agitation for more severe punishments culminated in a 1650 statute making adultery a capital, common law offense (Baker 214–15). Since one rationale for prohibiting the church from trying murder was that it did not have available an adequate punishment, by floating the hypothesis that it did possess this authority, and then leaving unresolved what punishment it might impose upon conviction, the scene alludes to the limitations of remedy available to the church, and speculatively reimagines the relation between ecclesiastical and common law.

A similar testing of judicial boundaries seems implicit in Vittoria's cry, "A rape, a rape!" (3.2.274). She is responding directly to Monticelso's "Away with her. Take her hence" by describing this taking into custody as rape in its original sense, the abduction of a woman rather than her sexual penetration. But she immediately explains that "you have ravished justice / Forced her to do your pleasure" (3.2.273–74). Justice is ravished by being subordinated to private interests; she shifts the label of sexual criminal from herself onto Monticelso. She complains not of her own rape but of that of justice; but the clear implication is that she feels violated by the law, and that this violation is a gendered form of aggression (Finin-Farber 235–37). She also momentarily positions herself as a plaintiff, simultaneously appealing her sentence to another jurisdiction, since rape was a common law offense that the ecclesiastical courts had no authority to try.[22] If church law lacks the authority to resolve the question of Vittoria's complicity in

Camillo's death, or to punish her properly for it if it could, it also cannot offer a remedy for the violence it has done to Vittoria herself.

The common law, however, is no help either. Setting the court in the trial scene as one unable to impose the penalty—death—demanded by the law of tragedy instead positions revenge, with its generic ties to the theater rather than to the common law, as the authority necessary to brings things to a conclusion. But revenge too is thoroughly compromised. In a Christian culture increasingly alarmed by acts of private justice, the behavior of revengers must have elicited ambivalence. And in *The White Devil* the revenge Francisco and his accomplices exact has only the flimsiest claim to justice; they've already dispatched Bracciano when they learn from Zanche that he was responsible for Isabella's and Camillo's murders. If then revenge cannot here be considered just (see 5.3.264), where are we to look for justice? The usual answer is that we will look in vain; Webster is notorious for the bleakness of his worldview and his lack of confidence in human beings and their institutions. Insofar as we are able to recognize the inadequacy of the ecclesiastical law, or of revenge, it is because the play is enabling us to make judgments from within a different, if not necessarily superior, system of evaluation. But to what extent does the play in fact permit us such recognitions? How far is it willing to help us judge? It helps, I think, by refusing to help; and it refuses to help by refusing a supplemental relation to the law.

We have seen how both Isabella and Vittoria invoke the theater as an alternative place of judgment. If the theater is an equitable jurisdiction, as has been suggested, the shift from law to theater is also a shift from law to equity, the theater enacting an equitable adjustment of the letter of the law.[23] By examining context and probing motivations it enables a deeper and truer (but not necessarily more forgiving) judgment of the characters. Knowing more about Vittoria, Bracciano, and Flamineo than Monticelso or the revengers do does give our faculty of judgment more to work with. It may seem reasonable, too, that women are the ones to gesture toward this alternative. If law is—as it is—primarily the invention of men, it makes sense that women would point the way out. Moreover, in the context of seventeenth-century legal practice, the argument that women seek out the equitable in the play may appear to reflect women's recourse to the prerogative courts, especially the equitable jurisdiction of the Chancery.

Attractive as it is, however, an equitable reading of *The White Devil* is complicated in two ways. First, even if the superiority of equity courts for women can be traced to equitable principles in their classical form, in practice the advantages were technical rather than founded on any principled appeal to context or intention. Theatrical equity does not much resemble equity in its institutionalized forms. More significantly, Vittoria's arguments in the arraignment scene are not distinctly equitable at all. Though she plays successfully on the sympathy of the audience, she denies and evades rather than extenuating, and her reinterpretations of the evidence brought against her do not depend on alternative explanations of her state of mind. She focuses on the speech and behavior of others rather than on her own. Indeed, the revelation of interiority as exculpatory with which equity in its classical form is associated is almost entirely absent. This is partly because Vittoria is not exactly innocent; but it is striking that she does not attempt even a speciously equitable argument. Almost to the end she manages to avoid any direct lies, preferring to sidestep accusations rather than countering them with fictions of her own. She does not deploy the tools of theatrical authority, at least to the extent that those tools are equitable; despite her metatheatrical appeal to the Red Bull audience she is, in fact, "consistently anti-theatrical" (Luckyj, "Gender" 198) not only in her emphasis on words rather than spectacle but also in her refusal to make words revelatory of her identity.

Nor does she reveal much about herself elsewhere in the play. Like Bracciano, she never speaks in soliloquy; she has few asides, and in fact speaks fewer lines than either Flamineo or Bracciano. If the play nevertheless makes it difficult to condemn her (or entirely approve of her either), it does so otherwise than through equitable means. Information is never in itself, of course, necessarily exculpatory. Both Flamineo and Francisco soliloquize, thus expanding the field of data by which we evaluate them; but I wonder if this does not simplify rather than complicate our judgments, making it easier to condemn them. Similarly, I think, knowing more about Vittoria would make her behavior seem less understandable and less forgiveable. This means that *The White Devil* is an anti-equitable play, one that refuses to stand as a humanizing supplement to the law. It does elicit judgments more ethically complex than those the law, as depicted, is capable of. But it does so by withholding, rather than asserting, its jurisdiction, and in this sense the play is antitheatrical as well. As we have seen, Webster knew the law without being professionally committed to it. But if he was not a lawyer he was not a professional playwright either.[24] The coach maker standing with at least one foot outside both institutions may have been uniquely positioned to understand their relation, and to refuse to offer either as a remedy for the other. Perhaps this is a way of saying that *The White Devil* does not assert its own superiority over the dark and deeply compromised lives it presents to us.[25]

NOTES

1. References to *The White Devil* are to the text and act, scene, and line divisions of *The White Devil and Other Plays,* ed. René Weis (Oxford: Oxford UP, 1996).
2. Use of Westminster Hall for state trials involved removal of the partitioning that defined the courts of Chancery and King's Bench on either side of the rear of the hall, as was done for the trial of Charles I in 1649.
3. The Red Bull probably had a capacity of around two thousand. See Mark Bayer, "Moving Up Market: The Queen Anne's Men at the Cockpit in Drury Lane, 1617," *Early Theatre* 4 (2001): 138–48.
4. See Wesley Trimpi, *Muses of One Mind: The Literary Analysis of Experience and Its Continuity* (Princeton: Princeton UP, 1983); Joel Altman, *The Tudor Play of Mind: Rhetorical Inquiry and the Development of Elizabethan Drama* (Berkeley: U of California P, 1978); Kathy Eden, *Poetic Diction and Legal Fiction in the Aristotelian Tradition* (Princeton: Princeton UP, 1986).
5. On this distinction, and for a comprehensive contemporary account of equity in the late sixteenth century, see Edward Hake, *Epieikeia: A Dialogue of Equity in Three Parts,* ed. D. E. C. Yale (Yale Law Library Publications, no. 13; New Haven: Yale UP, 1953).
6. Kathryn R. Finin-Farber, "Framing (the) Woman: *The White Devil* and the Deployment of Law," *Renaissance Drama* n.s. 25 (1994): 230.
7. J. H. Baker, *An Introduction to English Legal History,* 4th ed. (London: Butterworths, 2002) 282, 122.
8. Geoffrey L. Hudson, "Negotiating for Blood Money: War Widows and the Courts in Seventeenth-Century England," *Women, Crime and the Courts in Early Modern England,* ed. Jenny Kermode and Garthine Walker (London: U College London P, 1994) 146–69;

Tim Stretton, "Women, Custom and Equity in the Court of Requests," in Kermode and Walker 170–89; Laura Gowing, "Language, Power and the Law: Women's Slander Litigation in Early Modern England," in Kermode and Walker 26–47; Amy Louise Erickson, "Common Law Versus Common Practice: The Use of Marriage Settlements in Early Modern England," *Economic History Review,* 2nd ser. 43 (1990): 21–39.

9. M. C. Bradbrook, *John Webster, Citizen and Dramatist* (New York: Columbia UP, 1980) 28; Antony Hammond, "John Webster," *Jacobean and Caroline Dramatists. Dictionary of Literary Biography,* vol. 58, ed. Fredson Bowers (Detroit: Gale, 1987) 286.
10. The likelihood that Webster attended the Middle Temple is strengthened by his involvement with several of these figures. He made additions to Overbury's popular *Characters* and collaborated with Marston on *The Malcontent;* Ford praised him in a poem prefixed to *The Duchess of Malfi* (Bradbrook 28–45).
11. See Philip J. Finkelpearl, *John Marston of the Middle Temple: An Elizabethan Dramatist in His Social Setting* (Cambridge: Harvard UP, 1969); Wilfrid R. Prest, *The Inns of Court Under Elizabeth I and the Early Stuarts, 1590–1640* (Totowa, NJ: Rowman and Littlefield, 1972); and A. Wigfall Green, *The Inns of Court and Early English Drama* (New York: B. Blom, 1931).
12. Webster was mocked by a contemporary as a "playwright-cartwright" and was admitted to the Merchant Taylors Guild (to which coachmakers belonged) following his father's death in 1614 (Bradbrook 17–18).
13. Dena Goldberg, *Between Worlds: A Study of the Plays of John Webster* (Waterloo, Ont.: Wilfrid Laurier UP, 1987).
14. Maria L. Cioni, *Women and Law in Elizabethan England with Particular Reference to the Court of Chancery* (New York: Garland, 1985); W. R. Prest, "Law and Women's Rights in Early Modern England," *Seventeenth Century* 6 (1991): 169–87; Erickson; and the essays in Kermode and Walker.
15. Gunnar Bokland, *The Sources of* The White Devil (Uppsala: A.-B. Lundequistska Bokhandeln, 1957) 111–12.
16. See especially Christina Luckyj, *A Winter's Snake: Dramatic Form in the Tragedies of John Webster* (Athens: U of Georgia P, 1989) 116.
17. H. Bruce Franklin, "The Trial Scene of Webster's *The White Devil* Examined in Terms of Renaissance Rhetoric," *Studies in English Literature* 1 (1961): 35–51; Finin-Farber 227–34; Goldberg 52–60; Christina Luckyj, "Gender, Rhetoric and Performance in *The White Devil,*" *Revenge Tragedy,* ed. Stevie Simkin (New York: Palgrave, 2001) 198–200.
18. Martin Ingram, *Church Courts, Sex and Marriage in England, 1570–1640* (Cambridge: Cambridge UP, 1987) 4–6.
19. Unlike common law criminal prosecutions, English ecclesiastical courts did not forbid criminal defendants legal representation; both plaintiffs and defendants not only were allowed such representation but also could call witnesses on their own behalf (Ingram 48–49). Ironically, in this respect Monticelso's court more closely resembles the common law.
20. On ecclesiastical punishments see Ingram 52–54.
21. Vittoria's own punishment, confinement in the house of convertites, was an unusual, though increasingly popular, alternative (Finin-Farber 235).
22. Compare 3.2.128–29.
23. For an engagement with these issues, see Ina Habermann, "'She Has That in Her Belly Will Dry up Your Ink': Femininity as Challenge in the 'Equitable Drama' of John Webster," *Literature, Politics and Law in Renaissance England,* ed. Erica Sheen and Lorna Hutson (Basingstoke: Palgrave, 2005) 100–120.
24. Between his collaboration with Marston on *The Malcontent* in 1604 and the performance of *The White Devil* in 1612, there is no conclusive record of Webster's writing for the theater, though a manuscript discovered in 1985 may contain a fragment of a play written in Webster's

hand and dating later than 1605. At least during this period, Webster cannot have supported himself as a playwright. See Hammond 289.

25. More satisfactory ways of understanding the relation between *The White Devil* and the law have begun to appear. See especially the discussion of the play in Subha Mukherji, *Law, Evidence and Representation in Early Modern Drama* (Cambridge: Cambridge UP, forthcoming).

READING LIST

Baker, J. H. *An Introduction to English Legal History.* 4th ed. London: Butterworths, 2002.

Dolan, Frances E., ed. *Renaissance Drama and the Law. Renaissance Drama* n.s. 25 (1994).

Goodrich, Peter. *Law in the Courts of Love : Literature and Other Minor Jurisprudences.* London: Routledge, 1996.

Green, A. Wigfall. *The Inns of Court and Early English Drama.* New York: B. Blom, 1931.

Greene, Gayle. "Women on Trial in Shakespeare and Webster: "The Mettle of [Their] Sex." *Topic* 36 (1982): 5–19.

Hake, Edward. *Epieikeia: A Dialogue of Equity in Three Parts.* Ed. D. E. C. Yale. Yale Law Library Publications, no. 13. New Haven: Yale UP, 1953.

Hutson, Lorna, and Erica Sheen, eds. *Literature, Politics and Law in Renaissance England.* Basingstoke: Palgrave, 2004.

Kahn, Victoria, and Lorna Hutson, eds. *Rhetoric and Law in Early Modern Europe.* New Haven: Yale UP, 2001.

Kermode, Jenny, and Garthine Walker, eds. *Women, Crime and the Courts in Early Modern England.* London: U College London P, 1994.

Kezar, Dennis, ed. *Solon and Thespis: Law and Theater in the English Renaissance.* South Bend: U of Notre Dame P, forthcoming.

Mendelson, Sara Heller. *Women in Early Modern England, 1550–1720.* Oxford: Clarendon, 1998.

Prest, Wilfrid R. *The Inns of Court Under Elizabeth I and the Early Stuarts, 1590–1640.* Totowa, N.J.: Rowman and Littlefield, 1972.

Stretton, Tim. *Women Waging Law in Elizabethan England.* Cambridge: Cambridge UP, 1998.

Wilson, Luke. *Theaters of Intention: Drama and the Law in Early Modern England.* Stanford: Stanford UP, 2000.

21

A Chaste Maid in Cheapside and London

Karen Newman

In the extended title of his *Londinopolis,* the seventeenth-century traveler James Howell dubs London the "chief Emporium of Great Britain." "London," he writes in his dedication, is "a most renowned Mart for multitude of Merchants, and Commerce."[1] Antiquarians like the chronicler of London, John Stow, to whom Howell himself was much indebted; travelers like Thomas Plater and Howell himself; city comedy dramatists like Middleton; and everyday inhabitants of the city all recognized London as a center of commerce and trade. The seat of monarchy, of government and of the courts, the principal manufacturing and financial center of England, and the country's major port, London was by far the largest and most important city in England. The late sixteenth and seventeenth centuries saw remarkable urbanization in western Europe,[2] but London grew prodigiously and may have quadrupled its population in the period 1550–1650, from 80,000 to some 400,000; by 1700 its population was well over half a million and it had become the largest city in Europe.[3]

Middleton sets *A Chaste Maid in Cheapside,* as its title indicates, in Cheapside, the commercial center of London. Cheapside was the old market street that extended from St. Paul's to the Poultry and that derived its name, as the editor of the New Mermaids edition of the play points out, from the Anglo-Saxon word "ceap," which meant *barter.*[4] Its side streets and lanes were named for the various commodities made and sold in them: Bread, Milk, and Wood Streets; Honey Lane; Friday Street (the fishmongers); and Ironmongers Lane (where, in fact, Middleton's father, a bricklayer and builder, owned a house in which the playwright spent his early years). In his study of medieval Cheap as Cheapside was called before 1600, Derek Keene estimates that the area had some four hundred shops and four thousand trading plots that employed enough people "to populate a market town of considerable size."[5] By 1600, Cheapside housed not only the provisions merchants but also a variety of trades, including the goldsmiths, who, as John Stow put it, "as they have found their best advantage," moved from Gutheron's Lane to Cheap. According to Stow,

> the most beautiful of houses and shops that be within the walls of London, or elsewhere in England, commonly called Goldsmith's Row, betwixt Bread street end and the cross in Cheape, [. . . are] within this Bread street ward; the same was built by Thomas Wood, one of the sheriffs of London, in the year 1491. It containeth in number ten fair dwelling-houses and fourteen shops, all in one frame, uniformly built four stories high, beautiful towards the street with the Goldsmiths arms and the likeness of woodmen, in memory of his name, riding on monstrous beasts, all which is cast in lead, richly painted over and gilt. [. . .] [6]

Middleton's play, then, is set in the center of commercial London and in perhaps its most prosperous street. Why does Middleton choose to make his merchant characters, the Yellowhammers, goldsmiths, and to situate the action of the play in Cheapside?

A Chaste Maid in Cheapside begins with mother/daughter bickering: Maudline chides Moll for her dullness and her "drossy spirits." *Dross* is a waste product, metallic in character, taken off molten metal during smelting and thus part of the play's network of metallurgical images. Maudline's reasons for chiding her daughter seem twofold. On one hand, like so many successful merchant families in early modern London, the Yellowhammers have social aspirations. They seek to marry their daughter to a knight, and with that goal in mind, they are bringing her up with the cultural capital of her social betters: Moll evidently studies music and has dancing lessons with a dancing master, for Maudline's opening line demands to know if her daughter has practiced "o'the virginals," and a few lines later she asks when "the dancer was last with you." On the other hand, the aptly named Maudline's (Magdalene's) speech, including her opening query about playing the virginals, is filled with sexual innuendo in which she reminisces about her own apparently less than chaste past and berates Moll for her "errors." To her husband's conventional wisdom concerning Moll, "there is no woman made without a flaw," Maudline replies bawdily with a metaphor appropriate to the goldsmith trade, "But 'tis a husband solders up all cracks" (1.1.31).

Moll, her mother laments, is dull; despite being the child of a well-off goldsmith, she dances "like a plumber's daughter." In the first of a series of equivalences that run throughout the play, Maudline asserts that Moll deserves "two thousand pound in lead to [her] marriage, and not in goldsmith's ware" (1.1.19–20). Dross instead of gold. Moll's "error" in hanging back and being neither "lightsome" nor "quick" gives the play a part of its title, for her mother's complaint against her is Moll's chaste behavior, which is apparently so unlike her own as a young woman growing up in the city. Moll's mother seems to view her daughter's chastity as undesirable and unlikely to win her a husband even with her dowry of goldsmith's ware. For Middleton's early modern audience, his title, with its pun on *chased,* adorned (metal or plate) with engraving or embossed work, also implied a contradiction since trade in Cheapside would have encompassed not only commercial, but also sexual, exchange: chaste maids are apparently unusual in Cheapside and thus the title is almost an oxymoron.

The goldsmiths were perhaps the wealthiest of the London guilds.[7] In many companies in the sixteenth and seventeenth centuries, small master craftsmen struggled against a ruling elite of merchants and middlemen (Unwin 254). During the second decade of the seventeenth century, the gold and silver wire drawers, then part of the goldsmiths' guild, sought an independent charter, and between 1614 and 1621, the goldsmiths and the crown fought over the monopoly for the manufacture of gold and silver thread (Glover 309; Unwin 315–17). Thus there may well have been topical interest in the goldsmiths at the time Middleton is believed to have written his play, now usually dated 1613. Middleton is also believed to have had personal reasons for targeting the goldsmiths for satire since a suit for debt had been brought against him in 1609 by a Cheapside goldsmith (Middleton xv). But whatever the topical resonance of goldsmiths for the playwright, gold occupies a special place in the cultural imaginary of both early modern England and the development of Western capitalism more generally. From the Golden Age of classical mythology to nineteenth-century economic and political theory, from the golden fleece and Midas's golden touch to Mammon's hoard of gold portrayed by Spenser in the *Faerie Queene,* from Dekker's *Old Fortunatus* in which "gold is the strength, the sinnewes of the world" to Volpone's paean to gold in the opening speech of Jonson's play in which gold turns the world upside down, "gold" was overdetermined in its meanings and functions. Volpone's well-known speech perhaps best represents the status of gold in early modern England:

Hail the world's soul, and mine.
[. . .]
O, thou son of Sol,
(But brighter than thy father) let me kiss,
With adoration, thee, and every relic
Of sacred treasure in this blessed room.
Well did wise poets, by thy glorious name,
Title that age, which they would have the best;
Thou being the best of things—and far transcending
All style of joy, in children, parents, friends,
[. . .]
Dear saint,
Riches, the dumb god, that giv'st all men tongues:
That canst do naught, and yet mak'st men do all things;
The price of souls; even hell with thee to boot,
Is made worth heaven! Thou art virtue, fame,
Honour, and all things else![8]

In this apostrophe to gold which begins Jonson's play, and in which the word itself remains unspoken, in which the signifier never appears, gold is everything, all things to all men, the universal equivalent: it outshines the sun, the divine, love, family, friends, virtue, fame, honor, all.

Not only Renaissance literary satire but also early modern economic treatises such as Gerard de Malynes's *The Maintenance of Free Trade* (1622) insist that gold was an uncommon commodity. Malynes, a commissioner of foreign trade under both Elizabeth and James who wrote widely on foreign exchange, insists on the distinction between money "coyned of the purest mettals of *silver* and *gold* and the commodities whose price they measure."[9] Both Elizabeth's and James's governments privileged gold and issued proclamations against removing the metal from the kingdom.[10] But gold's (and secondarily silver's) movement from being a commodity like any other to being a universal equivalent is crucial for our understanding of gold and its function culturally, economically, and dramatically in Middleton's play.[11]

In the first chapter of volume I of *Capital,* Marx writes powerfully of this process. He begins with "the simplest expression of value, x commodity A = y commodity B," famously, a coat equals 20 yards of linen.[12] Marx argues that value comes to seem to be lodged in the commodity as a "social property inherent in its nature," independent of the equivalence relation. But in fact, that "property" is a process whereby exchange value displaces use value, a process that is complete when "the universal equivalent form became identified with the natural form of a particular commodity, and thus crystalized into the money form" (187). That particular commodity is gold.[13] Gold, Marx argues, is a "purely ideal or notional form" (189). Though all commodities—iron, linen, corn, a coat, and so on—have value in and of themselves, that is, the value that inheres in the labor expended to produce them, that value "is signified through their equality with gold" even though "it does not require the tiniest particle of real gold to give a valuation in gold of millions of pounds' worth of commodities" (190). Gold has become the universal equivalent form of value.[14] "[F]rom the elementary value relationship between two commodities, to the complex relations among numerous commodities, a select few of which become privileged in the interplay of transactions [. . .] and finally to the monopoly of an exceptional commodity in which all value seems to find expression," Marx offers "an analysis not only of the exchange of commodities but also of the whole theatre of evaluations, substitutions, and *social supplementations*" in which the "'value relation between one commodity and another' is the starting point, the original equation."[15]

In his *Symbolic Economies, After Marx and Freud,* Jean-Joseph Goux considers how the exchange of equivalents and the development of a universal equivalent, described by Marx in the first chapter of *Capital* and outlined earlier, matters for language and literature. Value, he argues, "is implied in every replacement" and thus in every exchange, whether it "involves comparison, substitution, supplementation—or translation and representation—value enters into it" (9).[16] Language, particularly literary language, works via metaphor, signs, and representations, all of which involve replacements or substitutions, and thus produce and depend on value. Such values, "whether linguistic, commercial, sexual, or legal," may be seen in the interplay of any substitutive formation, "in the 'in the place of' structure that inheres in every sign in general" (10). The structural logic of the general equivalent leads Goux to extend and analyze that notion in other domains, to the formation of identity, to the workings of language, and to psychoanalysis: "the *Father* becomes the general equivalent of subjects, *Language* the general equivalent of signs, and the *Phallus* the general equivalent of objects" monopolizing the role of signifier of desire (2). Goux's project is part of a larger twentieth-century literary and theoretical transformation associated with the work of the Swiss linguist Ferdinand de Saussure, who challenged the mimetic paradigm in which words are imagined to refer to things. In its place is the theory of the differential sign in which the relation between words or "signifiers," and things or "signifieds," is arbitrary and language is understood as a system of contrasts and distinctions.[17] Signifiers never exist independently, in isolation, but always in relation to one another forming a system which is language. Or as Goux puts it, "Signs refer to other signs; meaning is determined by their relations" (1).

These reflections on symbolic economies, exchange, and equivalence enable us to understand *A Chaste Maid in Cheapside,* a play concerned with equivalence, circulation, and value. Already in the play's opening scene, as I've noted, values are topsy turvy—a mother, in effect, admonishes her daughter not to remain chaste if she wishes to get a husband, and lead, not gold, should be Moll's marriage portion. As the scene and the play progress, equivalences proliferate, succeed, and fail: values are upended, revised, inverted, subjected to irony. Young Tim's garbled Latin is mistranslated into English first by his mother and then by the porter; Sir Walter Whorehound claims he will turn his Welsh whore "into gold" by marrying her to the Yellowhammers' son Tim; a wedding ring that should symbolize fidelity and honesty is inscribed "Love that's wise, blinds parents' eyes" (1.1.199); and the cuckold Allwit claims cuckoldry as "the happiest state that ever man was born to" (1.2.22). Later in the action, Yellowhammer likens Moll to his gold: "I will lock up this baggage / As carefully as my gold" (3.1.43–44), and Sir Walter joins "two thousand pound in gold" by no more than the copula (and) to "a sweet maidenhead" (4.2.92–93).

Touchwood Junior's success in courting Moll and the ultimate failure of Sir Walter's plans to marry her are already foreshadowed in act 1, scene 1 when Touchwood Junior orders a golden wedding ring from his duped father-in-law-to-be. In a scene apparently set in Yellowhammer's Cheapside shop, he orders a ring "for a gentlewoman," which the play insists Moll is not. The two men discuss the specifics of the gold ring, its weight ("some half ounce"), and a diamond Touchwood Junior apparently brings with him to be set in the ring. The dialogue is filled with comic irony since we in the audience know of Touchwood Junior's courtship of Moll, but her father does not. Initially, Yellowhammer worries aloud in front of her suitor about Moll's being in love ("The girl is wondrous peevish; I fear nothing / But that she's taken with some other love," 169–70) just at the moment Touchwood Junior determines "'Twere a good mirth now to set him a-work / To make her wedding ring" (165–66). The mocking posy quoted earlier that he has inscribed in the ring, "Love that's wise, blinds parents' eyes" (199), emphasizes the New Comic opposition of the parents to the young lovers' plans.[18] Equivalences and ironies abound: when Yellowhammer views the diamond Touchwood Junior has brought along, he declares "'tis a pure one," to which the young man responds, "So is the mistress." When Yellowhammer asks about the ring's size, Touchwood Junior offers "Just such another gentlewoman that's your daughter, sir" (187), to which her father responds, "And therefore sir no gentlewoman." Yellowhammer's dogged insistence that Moll is *not* a gentlewoman betrays his motives for marrying his daughter to Sir Walter: social aspirations, status inadequacy, and, most importantly, his ambitions for land. Early modern England was status based and hierarchical, and elite identity remained rooted in land ownership. In seeking to marry Moll to Sir Walter, the Yellowhammers hope to make her a gentlewoman and to improve their social status. But Touchwood Junior replies in his turn, "I protest I never saw two maids handed more alike" (189), thus admitting Yellowhammer's distinction, yet qualifying it: he insists the putative two maids are alike while at the same time reminding the audience they are in fact one and the same.

The play offers up other, even more unexpected and, to some, discomfiting equivalences in the Allwit plot, which opens with the happy husband detailing the pleasures of his wife's adultery with Sir Walter: maintenance of his household "this ten years" (1.2.16), a good table, church duties, fire in winter, a nurse for his children, medical remedies, all the accoutrements necessary to childbirth among the elite such that his wife lays like a lady, as if "with all the gaudy shops / In Gresham's Burse about her" (1.2.34–35).[19] Though Allwit claims his wife enjoys the elite trappings of a lady at childbirth ("embossings, / Embroiderings, spanglings"), the Allwits come by these accoutrements commercially and thus appropriately to their middling origins in an early modern version of the shopping mall, the Royal Exchange.

Not only does Allwit boast that he is freed from the labor of supporting his household, he is also freed even from the labor of getting "his" children: "the knight / Hath took that labour all out of my hands; / I may sit still and play," he boasts. What he means by the ambiguous "play" may be suggested in the telling chorus with which Allwit's soliloquy ends:

La dildo, dildo la dildo, la dildo dildo de dildo. (1.2.57)

Though *dildo* was a nonsense word often used in the chorus of songs and ballads in the period, by the time of Middleton's play it had already come to mean a substitute penis.[20] Sir Walter is Allwit's dildo, the supplier of all his desires, the phallus par excellence, or as Allwit himself puts it, "in his gold I shine" (1.2.41). At this point in the action, Sir Walter seems to be in line to gain everything. He is the father of Allwit's children, the lover of his wife, young Moll's fiancée, in possession of Sir Touchwood Senior's fortune, and he is about to marry his cast off Welsh whore to the Yellowhammers' son. In short, Sir Walter is father, phallus, gold.

As Richard Levin has observed in his study of the play's four plots, Sir Walter is the "principal link" among them.[21] Though commentators have occasionally differed about the number of plots, most agree on four: the main plot involving Touchwood Junior's attempts to win Moll Yellowhammer over the objections of her parents; the second dealing with Sir Walter's cuckoldry and the Allwit household; the third concerning the Kixes' efforts to have a child and heir with the help of the fantastically potent Touchwood Senior; and the fourth dealing with Tim Yellowhammer's courtship and marriage to the supposed Welsh heiress. Though the plots are linked by family ties and neighborly proximity, Middleton expands on these "perfunctory, external relationships [. . .] to establish much more important causal connexions among the different plots" (Levin 16). The play contrasts two plots of young people marrying and two involving long-married couples, a sexual triangle, and the birth of a child (the play begins with the birth of Allwit's [Sir Walter's] child and ends with the impending birth of the Kix heir). Levin contrasts the pairs of plots—Moll and Touchwood Junior's marriage is seemingly based on love, is initially thwarted by her parents (the Yellowhammers), and according to him represents the play's "romantic" union, while Tim's and the Welsh whore's marriage is based on interest, is initially encouraged by his parents (also the Yellowhammers), and represents the play's "antiromantic" union. Though Levin makes much of these contrasts,[22] in fact these comfortable values and distinctions are undermined repeatedly by the equivalences Middleton sets up among the four plots, equivalences he presents in comically explicit economic terms: Moll's dowry, for example, is "two thousand pound in gold" and the Welsh whore's is imputed to be "two thousand runts."

Far from representing Tim's marriage to the whore as different from and devalued in comparison with the marriage of Touchwood Junior and Moll, the evidence contradicts such moralizing judgments. They deceive in order to marry and their marriage is treated perfunctorily, as is their "wondrous" resurrection (5.4.55). Though Middleton gives Moll the melodramatic diction of thwarted love ("O my heart dies," "O bring me death tonight, love pitying fates, / Let me not see tomorrow up upon the world" 4.2.59, 79–80), its seriousness is undermined by her parents' vulgar epithets ("Dissembling, cunning baggage," "Impudent Strumpet," 4.2.70, 71) and the comic effect of Moll's being hauled in from her attempted elopement, dripping wet, by her hair. Later when it seems she is ill and might not recover, even sympathetic description of her maidenly pallor is expressed in a mercantile equivalence: "Gold into white money was never so changed, / As is my sister's colour into paleness" (5.2.20–21). Finally, the young lovers whose plot is called upon to represent the romantic union in the play-world "rise from their coffins," as the stage direction indicates, and are summarily married and hustled off to bed with bawdy teasing exhorting them to use their winding sheets for their bridal bed.

It is worth noting that the play actually ends with Tim, not Touchwood Junior and Moll's union. Tim's marriage, which Levin claims marks "the lowest point in the play's scale of value" (18), is likened to his sister's. He resigns himself with little complaint to exploring his new wife's lower regions, and, at his mother Maudline's behest, symmetrical with her exhortations to Moll that open the play, proves a whore honest by logic as he has earlier boasted he can do. Though Tim is one of the play's fools and his Latin is execrable, Middleton plays with language and the equivalences of translation to make a whore a wife. Tim uses chop logic—*uxor non est meretrix, ergo falacis* (A wife is not a whore, therefore you are wrong)—to prove his wife honest. Maudline questions his logic with yet another sexual joke, "O there's a trick beyond your logic Tim," *trick* being common wordplay for the Latin *meretrix* or whore (5.4.118). Tim gamely offers nevertheless to love her for her wit, which also stands for her genitalia, and he swears he will "mount" her. The nuptials of both pairs of lovers issue in explicit, and conventional, sexual teasing and bawdy. The final lines of the play are spoken by Yellowhammer, the father, who asserts sententiously that fortune seldom "deals two marriages / With one hand, and both lucky" (123–24), lines that, even in their suggestion of difference, equate the two marriages linguistically (*two, both*). This equivalence is underlined by Yellowhammer himself when he declares "The best is / One feast will serve them both" (124–25). Pleased at the economy of his children's double matrimony, he invites the entire company to Goldsmith's Hall for the conventional comic feast. In short, Middleton seems bent on setting up equivalences that undermine traditional distinctions (maid and whore), status hierarchies (merchant and gentlewoman) and institutions, particularly patriarchal marriage (the Allwits, the Kixes), and sectarian religion (the Puritans in the christening scene).

Many critics have moralized Middleton's play by seeking to distinguish, as does Levin, between the sordidness and commercial values of the Yellowhammers and Allwits and the triumph of Moll and Touchwood's love and fidelity. Arthur Marotti, for example, despite his recognition of the play's "procreative vitality" and Middleton's affirmation of "some aspects of a basically unattractive situation" (70), nevertheless draws putative distinctions between the two sets of plots and insists that Middleton is intent on making moral judgments. Marotti claims Touchwood Senior's motives for his adultery with Lady Kix, for example, are "healthy" in contradistinction to Sir Walter's "brutalizing [relationship to the Allwits] that strikes at the very foundation of marriage and the family" (70). But as we have seen, Middleton seems at pains to draw equivalences among the various relationships and plots rather than moral distinctions among them.

In the scene in which Touchwood Senior is confronted by a country wench bearing his bastard child, and in the subsequent notorious promoters scene, Middleton uses a hilarious pun on "flesh" in which Touchwood Senior wonders to himself "What shift she'll make now with this piece of flesh / In this strict time of Lent" (2.1.106–07) thereby equating the child with meat (Marotti 70). The pun sets up the next scene with the promoters in which this equivalence is reiterated. Touchwood Senior is no loving husband estranged from his wife by their poverty, as is sometimes claimed. He insists on his own carnality, compares the country wench and her child to "mutton" (2.1.81), suggests the child might be syphilitic, which of course implicates him as well, and tries to buy her off with the contents of his purse saying crassly, "would I were rid of all the ware i' the shop so" (2.1.99). Women are "ware" in this play made up of commercial transactions, and Touchwood implies the country wench is one of many—in fact, the wench herself reveals he has seduced her cousin as well. In short, Touchwood is easily Sir Walter's sexual match.

Following Touchwood Senior's encounter with the country wench, she encounters the promoters, enforcers who prowl the parish in search of persons who break the Lenten stricture against the eating of meat. Their dialogue reveals their own corruption since they sell the meat they confiscate for profit. When they accost her and inquire what she carries in her basket, she dupes them by palming off her bastard child hiding under a leg of mutton. Middleton equates Touchwood Senior's and Sir Walter's sexual exploits rather than distinguishing between them by "quicken[ing] his audience's ethical awareness" (Marotti 67). Later when Allwit attempts to discredit Sir Walter by recounting his adultery to Yellowhammer, the goldsmith's response is "what serves marriage, but to call him back, / I have kept a whore myself, and had a bastard" (4.1.272–73). Keeping company with whores seems to be the business of all the men in the play, just as keeping sexual company with men is the business of the women. Though the young lovers, Touchwood Junior and Moll, are so far exempt from this generalization, far from emphasizing their difference from Tim and his Welsh whore, as we have seen, Middleton minimizes it. Sir Walter himself is repudiated not for his promiscuous behavior, but only when he is revealed to have lost his fortune. Though his fate remains unclear—the Allwits threaten to call officers because he has supposedly murdered Touchwood Junior—in fact he leaves with his servants, assuring us that his eyes have been opened (5.1.158) to the Allwits' mercenary motives.[23] His servant Davy denounces Allwit, and the only results of their repudiation of Sir Walter Whorehound, far from uplifting, are that the Allwits determine to establish a whorehouse.

Feminist readers of the play have similarly sought to make moral distinctions, not between the different marriages or male sexual exploits, but on the basis of gender. Gail Paster, for example, considers the play's important network of images of wetness and water in terms of sexual difference.[24] She reads the incontinent women of Middleton's play, from Moll's tears to the drunken incontinence of the Puritan women who bepiss themselves in the christening scene to Lady Kix's wet kisses, as "the thematizing of female uncontrol." Sir Walter, whose name plays on water since Walter was pronounced *water* in the period, and Touchwood Senior are both associated with water-as-semen, which, by contrast with the women in the play, represents "power, not leaking or loss of control": "Male water—unlike female leaking—has economic value and under the right circumstances can even be shared in order to preserve or enlarge dynastic claims" (59). What are the right circumstances? For as we have seen, male water renders marriages equivalent: sex and adultery for all. First Allwit is cuckolded by Sir Walter's water, then Touchwood Senior cuckolds Sir Oliver Kix. Like Allwit, Sir Oliver invites Touchwood Senior into the Kixes' household to continue his dissemination. As Paster herself points out, Touchwood Senior simply substitutes for Sir Walter: Sir Oliver Kix, "rather than Master Allwit, becomes the play's contented cuckold." Though male potency is so exaggerated in the play that it comes to resemble the female loss of self control (60–61), Paster explains away this resemblance by arguing that male authority reasserts itself to control "female appetite and reproduction." But as we have seen, Middleton insists on equivalences in the exercise of appetite, male and female alike. Female appetite is shown exercising itself voraciously, from Moll's stubborn refusal of her parents' marriage partner to the various female characters' sexual exploits (every female character in the play except Moll herself reveals that she has enthusiastically engaged in sexual relations before marriage). Middleton leaves the critique of the Puritan women's hypocritical alcoholic indulgence and its urinary aftermath to the play's primary fools, Allwit and Tim. Paster claims the "leaky vessels" are contained, but in the world of Middleton's play, the circulation of waters, not their containment, continues unabated.

Sir Walter is the one character Middleton banishes from the stage and the conventional comic feast that ends the play, but he is hardly a villain. Once the marriages he intends are enacted (his own to Moll and Tim's to the Welsh whore), he plans to apprentice one of his sons by Mrs. Allwit to his new father-in-law, the goldsmith, thus doing his part for his child's welfare and ensuring the reproduction of labor and the system of exchange on which the play's action turns. Sir Walter's plans are thwarted by the equally sexually active, but even more potent, Touchwood Senior, whose Machiavellian trick impregnates Lady Kix with the heir that leads in turn to the loss of Sir Walter's fortune.[25] Middleton wastes little moral outrage on Sir Walter. In fact, he seems at pains to refuse distinctions, to equate plots and situations, and, for all the play's at times caustic satire, to eschew moral judgments. For *A Chaste Maid in Cheapside* is more concerned with circulation itself than with supporting what we might now term "family values." Much has been written on the importance of patriarchal marriage in the early modern period, the investment of early modern culture in women's chastity to protect inheritance, and the like.[26] But in Middleton's play, men and women alike are sexually active; marriage to a whore is treated no differently from marriage to the play's chaste maid, the Kixes are saved, and Touchwood Senior's couple is rescued not by a child duly sired by its right father, but by a bastard. Patriarchal marriage is undermined at every turn and casually equated with adultery.

At the time Middleton wrote *A Chaste Maid in Cheapside,* the playwright had begun working for the city and its ruling merchant elite. He wrote pageants and entertainments for various London companies and for individual merchants and in 1620 was appointed City Chronologer.[27] Middleton was a Londoner and in *A Chaste Maid in Cheapside,* he pays tribute to the city by making it a "character itself in the action." London, with its wharves and stairs, but even more importantly, its commercial streets and shops, Goldsmiths' Row and the Royal Exchange, gives precision to the action and, as the editor of the New Mermaids edition argues, "persuade the audience to accept the inflated perversity of [Middleton's] characters" (Middleton xxvi). As the "chief Emporium of Great Britain" and "a most renowned Mart," London is a place of never-ending exchange and circulation symbolized in the play by gold and its various equivalents that mark *A Chaste Maid in Cheapside's* vision of social relations and institutions.

NOTES

1. See James Howell, *Londinopolis; an Historicall Discourse or Perlustration of the City of London, The Imperial Chamber, and Chief Emporium of Great Britain* (London, 1657).

2. See Jan de Vries, *European Urbanization 1500–1800* (Cambridge: Harvard UP, 1984); on the larger processes of urbanization and the importance of networks or systems of cities, see also H. J. Dyos, "Agenda for Urban Historians," *The Study of Urban History,* ed. H. J. Dyos (London: St. Martin's P, 1968).
3. See Vanessa Harding, "The Population of London, 1550–1700: A Review of the Published Evidence," *London Journal* 15 (1990): 111–28.
4. See Thomas Middleton, *A Chaste Maid in Cheapside,* 2nd ed., ed. Alan Brissenden (London: A & C Black, 2002) xi. All references to the play are to this edition and will be cited by act, scene, and line number in the text.
5. See Derek Keene, "Shops and Shopping in Medieval London," *Medieval Art, Architecture and Archaeology in London,* ed. L. Grant (London: British Archaeological Association, 1990) 29–46.
6. See John Stow, *Survey of London,* ed. H. B. Wheatley (London: Dent, 1987).
7. On goldsmiths in England, see Christopher Lever, *Goldsmiths and Silversmiths of England* (London: Hutchinson, 1975); Elizabeth Glover, *The Gold and Silver Wyre-Drawers* (London: Phillimore, 1979). Stella Kramer, *The English Craft Gilds [sic.]: Studies in Their Progress and Decline* (New York: Columbia UP, 1927); Hermann Schadt, *Goldsmith's Art: Five Thousand Years of Jewellry and Holloware* (Stuttgart: Arnoldsche, 1996); and George Unwin, *Gilds [sic] and Companies of London* (London, 1908; rpt. New York: Barnes and Noble, 1966). On the adaptation of guilds to change, see Joseph Ward, *Metropolitan Communities* (Stanford: Stanford UP, 1997).
8. See Ben Jonson, *The Alchemist and Other Plays,* ed. Gordon Campbell (Oxford: Clarendon P, 1995) 1.1.1–26.
9. Qtd. in Craig Muldrew, "Hard Food for Midas: Cash and Its Social Value in Early Modern Britain," *Past and Present* 170 (2001): 81.
10. The contemporary belief that the economy was based on gold led to a series of royal proclamations against its removal from the kingdom and against the manufacture of gold and silver thread and gold leaf. See Glover 10.
11. On gold in early modern drama, see William H. Sherman, "'Gold Is the Strength, the Sinnewes of the World': Thomas Dekker's *Old Fortunatus* and England's Golden Age," *Medieval and Renaissance Drama in England* 6 (1993): 85–102.
12. Karl Marx, *Capital. A Critique of Political Economy,* vol. 1, intro. Ernest Mandel, trans. Ben Fowkes (London: Penguin, 1976, rpt. 1990) 187.
13. Marx recognizes that other commodities also play this role, but he assumes "that gold is the money commodity, for the sake of simplicity" (188).
14. As universal equivalent, gold apparently played/s a crucial role in supporting Al Qaeda networks both before and after the September 11, 2001, attack on New York City and Washington, DC. See Douglas Farah, "Al Qaeda's Gold: Following Trail to Dubai," *International Herald Tribune,* February 18, 2002: 1, 7.
15. Jean-Joseph Goux, *Symbolic Economies, After Marx and Freud,* trans. Jennifer Curtiss Gage (Ithaca: Cornell UP, 1990) 13.
16. This volume is made up of selections from two books by Goux published in French, *Freud, Marx: Economie et symbolique* (Paris: Éditions de Seuil, 1973) and *Les iconolastes* (Paris: Éditions de Seuil, 1978).
17. Ferdinand de Saussure, "On the Nature of Language," *Introduction to Structuralism,* ed. Michael Lane (New York: Basic Books, 1970) 43.
18. On the play's relation to Old Comedy, phallic song, and fertility ritual, see Arthur Marotti, "Fertility and Comic Form in *A Chaste Maid in Cheapside,*" *Comparative Drama* 3 (1969): 65–74.
19. Gresham's Burse or the Royal Exchange was built in the mid-sixteenth century by Sir Thomas Gresham; myriad goods were offered for sale there to the public.

20. See Thomas Nashe's poem "A Choise of Valentines" or "Nashe His Dildo," *The Works of Thomas Nashe,* 5 vols, ed. Ronald B. McKerrow, rpt. from original 1904 edition with additions by F. P. Wilson (Oxford: Blackwell, 1966).
21. Richard Levin, "The Four Plots of *A Chaste Maid in Cheapside,*" *Review of English Studies* 16 (1965): 21.
22. "In all significant respects—emotional, intellectual, moral, and financial—the story of Tim and his bride is made to seem a kind of false imitation or parody of the main plot" (Levin 18).
23. In his introduction to the New Mermaids edition of the play, Alan Brissenden in fact claims that Sir Walter undergoes a moral change and has "a spiritual victory of sorts" (Middleton xviii–xix).
24. Wetness, and particularly water, is an important nexus of images in the play signifying fertility, potency, and also a lack of control. See Ruby Chatterje, "Theme, Imagery, and Unity in *A Chaste Maid in Cheapside,*" *Renaissance Drama* 8 (1965): 105–26; and Gail K. Paster, "Leaky Vessels: The Incontinent Women of City Comedy," *Renaissance Drama* 18 (1987): 43–65.
25. Touchwood Senior's trick owes much to Machiavelli's similar plot device in *La Mandrogola.*
26. The *locus classicus* is Lawrence Stone, *The Family, Sex and Marriage in England, 1500–1800* (New York: Harper & Row, 1977).
27. W. Power, "Thomas Middleton vs. King James I," *Notes & Queries* 202 (1957): 526–34.

READING LIST

Chatterje, Ruby. "Theme, Imagery, and Unity in *A Chaste Maid in Cheapside.*" *Renaissance Drama* 8 (1965): 105–26.

Levin, Richard. "The Four Plots of *A Chaste Maid in Cheapside.*" *Review of English Studies* 16 (1965): 14–24.

Marotti, Arthur. "Fertility and Comic Form in *A Chaste Maid in Cheapside.*" *Comparative Drama* 3 (1969): 65–74.

Paster, Gail Kern. "Leaky Vessels: The Incontinent Women of City Comedy." *Renaissance Drama* 18 (1987): 43–65.

Sherman, William H. "'Gold Is the Strength, the Sinnewes of the World': Thomas Dekker's *Old Fortunatus* and England's Golden Age." *Medieval and Renaissance Drama in England* 6 (1993): 85–102.

Ward, Joseph. *Metropolitan Communities.* Stanford: Stanford UP, 1997.

22

The Tragedy of Mariam and the Politics of Marriage

Danielle Clarke

Elizabeth Cary's closet drama, *The Tragedy of Mariam* (1613), is a paradoxical text. The virtuous are punished and killed, the wicked live and prosper, marriage begets conflict and discontent rather than harmony and happiness, and close blood ties are repeatedly sacrificed to personal ambition and political imperatives. Surfaces are suspect and deceptive, unable to disclose unequivocal meaning: Mariam herself is addressed as "painted devil / Thou white enchantress" (4.4.175–76), "fair fiend" (4.4.213), and "Foul pith contain'd in the fairest rind" (4.4.189).[1] Words carry power rather than truth: truth is frequently driven inward, out of sight, known only to the conscience of the individual, and the breach between words and the heart is alluded to repeatedly: "[t]he word dissented from the speaker's will" (2.2.164), ears are "prejudicate" (2.4.401), and Mariam herself "speaks a beauteous language, but within / Her heart is false as powder" (4.7.429–30).

The play is paradoxical in other ways too. On the one hand, it is exceptional in the Renaissance canon, and not only for being the first original play written by an Englishwoman, but also for its intense focus on marital relationships as microcosm (the contract between two individuals) and as macrocosm (as an image of the reciprocal duties of ruler and subject). On the other hand, it frequently draws upon the familiar conventions and clichés of Renaissance thought and dramatic style, adhering closely both to source materials and to generic expectations. The vexed relationship between convention and subversion underpins *Mariam* at every level, as Cary explores the discontinuities and dilemmas of female subjectivity and identity through the traditional framework of women's roles and status as wives and mothers. Like many other early modern plays, *Mariam* does not take unequivocal positions on questions relating to female identity and integrity, but seeks to explore such issues in all their instability and complexity. Whatever the reader may conclude about Cary's ambiguous feminism, the play demonstrates unequivocally that women are central politically, sexually, and ethically to questions that suffuse early modern culture.

One of the factors that makes the prospect of *Mariam* so appealing to modern readers is precisely that it is a *play*. So much of our sense of the Renaissance as a period that can continue to speak to us derives from our experience of drama, with its interest in political, sexual, ethical, and emotional dilemmas. *Mariam* does not disappoint: its primary concern is conflict, and the ways in which apparent oppositions collapse under pressure—husband/wife, ruler/subject, public/private, conscience/duty, inner/outer, speech/silence—a shading of distinctions gestured at by Cary's personal motto, "be and seem."[2] *Mariam* can certainly "speak" to us, but we have to establish the terms in which it can speak, to find our way in to *Mariam*'s specific modes of expression and its lexicon of cultural assumptions. It is primarily through the *language* of drama that we feel that we have access to early modern sensibilities, in particular through the dynamic and tensile use of the English language in a state of evolution. But in approaching a text like *Mariam,* it is important to think about the nature of dramatic language and to consider it as a *collective* medium, as an articulation of culture, as well as the specific expression of a singular individual; Cary's voice is simultaneously subjective and individual, *and* plural and social. Cary's text is inevitably shaped by the experience of marriage for an intellectually inclined woman, but it cannot be read straightforwardly as an autobiographical text.

Mariam is full of plots and intrigues, conspiracies and back-biting, threats, poisonings, curses, violence, and all the extremes of emotion of which human beings are capable. It is paradoxical that these "actions" are performed via the dynamism and verve of Cary's potentially static rhetoric; the play as such is not interested in dramatic action and does not use stage directions for any functions other than entrances and exits. It is also a profoundly serious text, indebted to its classical roots and concerned with weighty contemporary ethical matters. And while the question of how far the play is illuminated by reading it through an exclusively feminist framework will underlie this chapter, the fact remains that in *Mariam* we encounter a range of female characters that manage to step outside the parameters for womanhood dictated by early modern culture. Cary creates linguistically sophisticated representations of women that transcend stereotypes without taking refuge in fantasy; thus her women are complex, often torn between competing imperatives (dynastic ambition, for example, versus personal morality). They are not unequivocal paragons of virtue or embodiments of vice, but figures who struggle to reconcile what is expected of them with what they expect of themselves, who worry about what people—and not just men—think of them and recognize the uneasy combination of marginality and centrality that they occupy in early modern life. That is, women are central to the reproduction of power and culture, but are often invisible within it; Cary's female characters complicate this simplistic model. Apart from anything else, Cary gives an unprecedented amount of space in her play to female speakers; by and large they predominate, as is fitting in a play that uses a plot that hinges on the hereditary claim to power of a woman. I can't think of another Renaissance play in which the first male character speaks only in the fourth scene of act 1, the majority of scenes include at least one female speaker, and so many powerful soliloquies are delivered by women. This may reflect the gender of the play's author, but it also has a generic component. Yet, as we will see, Cary's play does not subscribe to a simplistic or idealized view of women; rather she attempts to explore the very real contradictions that structure the representation (and self-representation) of the female subject. As Alexandra Bennett argues, *Mariam* is "not simply a tale of one woman's unshakeable integrity in the face of oppression, but instead an exploration of duplicity, multiplicity, and their implications for women."[3]

Mariam: Plot, Genre and Context

Cary's play takes a complex historical situation and condenses it in order to conform to the demands of her chosen genre. The Elizabethan and Jacobean periods witnessed a significant indebtedness to the style and ideas of Seneca in drama, but Cary's engagement belongs to a specific and short-lived subgenre, that of closet drama, which was not specifically designed for public performance. This is characterized by the observation of the unities; the use of the *nuntius* or messenger; few characters; dramatic irony; long, highly stylized speeches; and an abiding concern with the relationship between private allegiance and public government. Closet dramas, however, are not in any sense marginal, but represent a specific kind of engagement with ethics and politics in the late Elizabethan period, a politics initially linked to the stoicism and Protestantism of the Sidney circle.[4] It is tempting to make a clear link between the prohibitions on female literary production and choice of genre, especially in the light of Mary Sidney Herbert's earlier deployment of the same form, via translation, in *The Tragedy of Antonie* (1592). Whilst it is true that this less public form paradoxically enabled a freer articulation of female character, not, for example, being constrained by the conventions surrounding women's speech in public, there are other aspects to closet drama in the Senecan style that may well have suited Cary's purposes. It is not the case that closet drama is per se interested in female subjectivity; rather, it is concerned with the intersection of private and public morality and the ways in which private actions map onto public ones. In addition, it encouraged an engagement with the kinds of issues that were frequently seen as off-limits for women writers in a medium defined by its attempted containment of the morally troubling aspects of drama. The antitheatrical controversialist Stephen Gosson explains that drama may, in certain circumstances, provide moral enlightenment in his discussion of the radical Protestant George Buchanan:

> Whatsoever such Plays as contain good matter are set out in print, may be read with profit, but cannot be played, without a manifest breach of Gods commandment. Let the Author of plays and pastimes, take heed how he read the action, pronunciation, agility of body [. . .] plays consisting of these cannot be evil.[5]

For Gosson, the aim of writing is moral and didactic, and the Senecan drama admirably fulfilled these functions without beguiling readers with dramatic dissimulation or display.

Mariam is set in Palestine, a relatively unusual dramatic setting in this period. The play examines the events that result from Herod's unexpected return from Rome and reveals the underlying feelings and motivations of several distinct but related groups of characters once they *think* that they have been fortuitously freed from Herod's tyranny. The background narrative to the play is complex, dependent upon several conflicting sources. Like many other dramatic pieces of the period, *Mariam* cannot be seen as "original" in any modern sense of that term; rather, it takes an existing narrative and tailors it to contemporary purposes. Cary's key source was the Jewish historian Josephus, not a mainstream choice, but one that conformed to Cary's intellectual interests in history and fit neatly with the kinds of questions that she clearly wished to explore. Josephus wrote in Greek, and his account of Herod the Great's marriage to Mariam is found both in his *Antiquities of the Jews* (ca. 93 CE) and in his *Jewish War* (69–79 CE). Despite the fact that the biographical account of Cary's life written by her daughter asserts Cary's prodigious linguistic talent, it seems likely that Cary used Thomas Lodge's 1602 translation of the *Antiquities,* just as Shakespeare had used North's translation of Plutarch as the source for his Roman plays.[6] Having said this, *Mariam* reveals Cary's wider reading in its repeated use of both classical and biblical reference, to the background story of Anthony and Cleopatra in particular. Although the play focuses on the narrative of

Herod the Great's marriage to Mariam, and its political and dynastic consequences, more familiar aspects of Roman history, the fall of the republic in particular, frame the play.[7] The figure of Cleopatra, for example, is frequently invoked as a foil to offset Mariam's superior beauty and virtue, but also to underline the ligatures of power that Mariam's heritage represents. As Mariam's deeply ambitious mother, Alexandra, suggests

> [. . .] if thy portraiture had only gone,
> His life from Herod, Anthony had taken:
> He would have lovèd thee, and thee alone,
> And left the brown Egyptian clean forsaken,
> [. . .]
> Then Mariam in a Roman's chariot set,
> In place of Cleopatra might have shown. (1.2.187–90, 195–96)

This series of "what ifs" is a response to the crisis prompted by Herod's rule and its consequences for the dynastic future not only of Mariam's family, but also for the various other groupings in the play that find themselves renegotiating their position in the absence of the tyrannical figure who represents the dynamic center of the play.

The context to *Mariam* is complex, based upon contradictory historical accounts, but it is used as deep background to highlight specific kinds of dilemmas in the play.[8] *Mariam* deals with several different but overlapping alliances of kinship and politics. Foremost amongst these is the relationship between Mariam and Herod, primarily a dynastic marriage, contracted to legitimate Herod's claim to the throne through Mariam's paternal line, but cemented by Herod's excessive love of Mariam, which fatally compromises his judgment. This marital and political alliance, however, necessitated Herod's divorce from his first wife, Doris, and his repudiation of his sons from that marriage in favor of his sons by Mariam. The various power struggles played out in *Mariam* all stem from Herod's usurpation of the throne; thus the sons of Babas, active opponents of Herod, were condemned to death. Constabarus, who through his marriage to Salome was Herod's brother-in-law, defied Herod's orders to kill Babas's sons in the expectation that they might be useful to him later on, and this group of characters represents a quite distinct and more traditionally political and masculine form of resistance to Herod's rule. Pheroras, Herod's brother, had been contracted to a child-bride, but on hearing news of Herod's supposed death, finds that he can pursue his desired love-match to the low-born Graphina. In this way, the various characters are locked into a set of dynastic relationships that they each attempt to manipulate. These variously repressed desires are unleashed upon hearing the false news that Herod has been put to death in Rome, where he had gone to make a strategic alliance with Caesar on the overthrow of his "great friend" Mark Anthony (*Mariam,* "Argument" 67). The device upon which the plot hinges is that of rumor, or false report, leading to inference and supposition, the attribution of false motives, and a good deal of power-brokering, as Herod's sister Salome suggests early in the play:

> More plotting yet? Why, now you have the thing
> For which so oft you spent your suppliant breath:
> And Mariam hopes to have another king.
> Her eyes do sparkle joy for Herod's death. (1.3.207–10)

Salome attempts to rewrite Mariam's reputation by suggesting that her tears are those of pleasure, that Herod's death fulfills her unspoken desires, and that Mariam's sexual/ political ambition will now be unchecked. It is this conflation of social, political, and sexual ambition that forms the bedrock of Cary's play.

Marriage as Metaphor

As Elaine Beilin has argued, "[m]arriage is the battlefield of the play."[9] It would be incorrect to dispute this; however, it is critical to see *Mariam*'s treatment of marriage in the broadest possible context. It not only attempts to dramatize the social and political effects of this most intimate of relationships but also asks searching questions about the limits of authority and jurisdiction, both within marriage itself and in the wider contexts in which it figures and adumbrates. In other words, marriage is more than a metaphor for tyranny and regiment; it is the *ground* on which these questions are played out. In addition, the topic of marriage also resonates biographically and topically. The *Life* of Cary makes it abundantly clear that her marriage was not happy and that Cary herself struggled to reconcile her duty and her desire. Questions relating to ideas of marriage were extensively debated in the Jacobean period, as writers and commentators sought to conceptualize marriage according to Protestant thinking. More specifically, debates on marriage and divorce were foregrounded around the time that *Mariam* was printed because of the marriage of King James's daughter Elizabeth to Frederick of Bohemia in February 1613 and the divorce of the countess of Essex in May of the same year.[10]

The very idea that *Mariam* explores, that marriage is a Januslike representation of political relationships and the complexities of the subject–ruler bond, can be found repeatedly in early modern political theory and in conduct literature. In such accounts, the family was the foundational unit of all other social and political structures, and the patriarchal basis of the family and of monarchy had repeatedly been underlined by James I, following as he did a long period of female regiment that had necessitated the careful realignment of gender, sexuality, and politics. Just as the husband was the head of the family unit, so the male monarch was the head of the nation or commonwealth. The married couple was "the first original match of all others. All other couples and pairs, as father and son, master and servant, king and subject come out this pair."[11] This analogy was repeatedly deployed to the end of asserting the rootedness of a series of overlapping relationships in the notion of obedience: "He the head, and she as part of the members, which so being, to be divided and at odds, were as the hand to lift up, or the foot to kick against the head, the King and Governor."[12] This is the assumption against which *Mariam*'s carefully calibrated questioning of the limits and responsibilities of patriarchal rule is played out. However, most early modern commentators stress the need for mutual affection and respect within the framework of obedience and stress that tyrannical rule negates or at least undermines authority: "See then (all ye husbands) that your words to your wives hold agreement with the Laws of God, and of your public governors not repugnant thereto, else you govern not, but tyrannize; and to disobey you, is the best obedience."[13]

That Herod is a tyrant and a usurper is hardly in doubt. His actions prior to the events of the play are clearly some way from legitimate succession. Having used the leverage of Roman rule to claim the throne, once there, Herod deploys his stolen authority to dispatch all opposition and all supposed enemies: Babas's sons, Mariam's grandfather Hircanus ("the rightful king and priest" [*Mariam,* "Argument" 67]), and her brother Aristobulus, the legitimate heir. Having disposed of all the male challengers, Herod proceeds to secure his position through marriage to Mariam, hence "Herod in his wife's right had the best title" (67). The action of the play is engineered by Alexandra, Mariam's mother, as she tips off Rome about Herod's actions, and he is summoned to answer her accusations. In addition, *Mariam* is full of insults asserting Herod's illegitimacy and tyranny, and thus raises direct questions about the extent to which he should be obeyed. These insults not only trade upon his lineage, ethnicity, and usurpation ("Base Edomite, the damnèd Esau's heir" [1.2.84]) but also concentrate notably upon his behavior: he is "cruel Herod" (1.1.37; 1.2.99), he is a "vile wretch' (1.2.86), he has "a cruel nature" (1.2.104) and "ever thirsts for blood" (1.2.106). Herod's actions throughout the play are driven by ambition, jealousy, and unchecked desire, the very characteristics of tyrants, who fail to temper their emotions with reason, and thus affect (and image) disorder in the body politic.[14] It is precisely this that Alexandra infers when she says, "I know by fits he show'd some signs of love, / And yet not love, but raging lunacy" (1.2.123–24).

If marriage is posited by early modern thinkers as the institution that orders all others, it is entirely fitting that *Mariam* should explore its fault-lines. The play shows a repeated concern with the point at which marriages break down, are dissolved, or simply cannot sustain the pressure of the ideological work that they are asked to do. This entails not only an engagement with the marital ideal but also a consideration of divorce. Unlike many other Protestant jurisdictions, early modern England adhered to a primarily Catholic view of divorce, viewing it as permissible only on the grounds of adultery and concluding that the innocent party was allowed to remarry. These principles are complicated in *Mariam* by the text's historical setting; in Judaic law a husband could separate from his wife if she failed to find favor with him (Deut. 24:1–4), which is the basis upon which Salome attempts to divorce Constabarus in favor of Silleus. This self-willed "divorce" is often read as a proto-feminist moment in the play, as Salome argues from analogy that what is a male legal right should also be extended to women:

> If he to me did bear as earnest hate,
> As I to him, for him there were an ease;
> A separating bill might free his fate
> From such a yoke that did so much displease.
> Why should such privilege to man be given?
> Or given to them, why barr'd from women then?
> Are men than we in greater grace with Heaven?
> Or cannot women hate as well as men?
> I'll be the custom-breaker: and begin
> To show my sex the way to freedom's door. (1.4.301–10)

Salome argues from a position based upon the rights enshrined in Jewish law for husbands, but one that finds no echo in English law. Unlike her former husband (also called, confusingly, Josephus) Constabarus is very much alive, and her desire to divorce is not based upon his adultery or desertion.[15] The point here is an articulation less of a doctrine of equality than of the dangers attendant upon the dissolution of the marital bond where this is based upon ambition and sexual desire, rather than on morality and law. Having said this, Cary's inclusion of it is a radical gesture, and it constitutes one of a series of competing voices in *Mariam* on the question of marriage and the rights of the female subject within it.

It is often difficult in *Mariam* to pinpoint arguments as representing Cary's own view, or even to isolate normative statements that we are supposed to take as indicative of the ideology of the play. Senecan drama, with its interest in teasing out multiplicity and rhetorical complexity, is the ideal vehicle for this kind of potentially subversive and contradictory exploration, and the relative conservatism of the chorus in relation to the roles of the sexes (act 3) or the discussion of the ethics of revenge (act 4) are instances of this. For example, it is clear that Salome's desire to divorce is to be condemned. As Constabarus suggests, echoing Niccholes's conventional statement about order:

Are Hebrew women now transformed to men?
Why do you not as well our battles fight,
And wear our armour? Suffer this, and then
Let all the world be topsy-turvèd quite. (1.6.421–24)

That Constabarus is a consistently moral and principled character in the play, despite what we would consider as his antifeminist stance, indicates the way in which *Mariam* interweaves moral and sexual questions in complex and sometimes contradictory ways.

Salome's position on the dissolubility of marriage is clearly intended to position her as the archetype of threatening femininity, but her circumstances are merely a more extreme and clear-cut articulation of the arguments presented about the limits to obedience in marriage and the way in which dissent can be figured as both sexual and political. Salome is by no means the only female character in the play whose marital situation challenges convention. Mariam, despite critical tendencies to view her as unequivocally virtuous and chaste, occupies an unstable position in relation to the question of remarriage. Mariam is a second wife, and the legitimacy of her position depends crucially on whether Herod's previous marriage to Doris is a divorce or not and whether Herod was permitted to remarry. Once again, Judaic and Christian ideologies of divorce cut across and destabilize one another. This equivocal situation reveals the paradox at the heart of the play; namely that the very thing that grants Mariam power (her role in securing the succession through marriage to Herod) is also the thing that makes her position precarious and open to question. It is vital, in this dynamic, that Mariam is chaste, and seen to be chaste, in order to guarantee that Herod's children by Mariam are in fact his:

He not a whit his first-born son esteem'd,
Because as well as his he was not mine:
My children only for his own he deem'd,
These boys that did descend from royal line. (1.2.135–38)

Alexandra, Doris, and Salome all challenge Mariam's position for their own ends. Doris seeks to impugn Mariam's virtue for both personal and dynastic reasons, as she tries to reinstate her son by Herod, Antipater, as the rightful heir. This maneuver suggests the way in which women's fortunes are bound up with patriarchal structures and the ways in which it is through these structures that female power is both expressed and mediated. Doris's approach is to challenge the validity of Herod's marriage to Mariam, although it is Mariam on whom her opprobrium falls, in a fascinating inversion of homosociality.[16] Here, because of Mariam's own patrilineal descent, power is exchanged between women, via husbands and sons. Doris claims that Mariam's "soul is black and spotted, full of sin: / You in adult'ry liv'd nine year together, / And Heav'n will never let adult'ry in" (4.8.576–78). Within Protestant concepts of marriage, Doris's marriage to Herod remains legitimate. As she asserts, she is "Herod's lawful wife" (4.8.584), and the grounds on which he divorced her find no sanction within English law. As Pheroras states, in support of his desire to marry Graphina for love, "He, for his passion, Doris did remove; / I needed not a *lawful* wife displace" (2.1.31–32, emphasis added).

The reference to "passion" is central, as it is clear that Herod's actions were motivated by desire, both sexual and political. In addition, Mariam's status—and thus the legitimacy of her children—is open to question, leading to Herod's policing of her fidelity and his obsessive concern with the question of adultery. This is closely linked to Herod's dependence upon Mariam as the guarantor of his image and of his rule. His need for legitimate heirs means that any whiff of adultery calls his paternity into question. Adultery is a central theme of *Mariam*. It refers not only to extramarital sexual activity but also to the idea of *political* resistance, as the idea of transferring allegiance (sexual, emotional, or political) is frequently troped as an adulterous act in the Renaissance. Herod's accusations of adultery map suspicions about Mariam's questioning of his authority, but they are expressed through normative early modern ideas regarding female speech as suspect, and women's bodies as unable to signify unequivocally. Herod's "passion" for Mariam also calls his authority into question; as Heale suggests, if a man cannot govern his wife, "how can he be thought fit to manage the affairs of a common wealth?"[17]

Mariam's resistance to Herod is simultaneously emotional (as in her opening soliloquy), sexual ("I have forsworn his bed" [3.3.134]), and political. Mariam's refusal to allow Herod sexual access is a clear breach of marriage ideology that stressed the importance of sexual relations "an essential duty of marriage,"[18] but it also suggests her resistance to the prevailing notion that women were subsumed into the husband's identity upon marriage.[19] Mariam herself also challenges much early modern marriage theory regarding the proper role of wives, although this is often contradicted by other key points in the play, for example, when the Chorus argues that for married women "their thoughts no more can be their own, / And therefore should to none but one be known" (3.3.237–38). By forcibly reminding him of the murder of her grandfather and brother—and thus Herod's illegitimacy as a ruler—Mariam breaches two central tenets of marriage: the necessity of obedience and the requirement that women curb their speech. She refuses to lie—"I cannot frame disguise, nor ever taught / My face a look dissenting from my thought" (4.3.145–46)—illustrating her resistance to the notion of subjection and her placement of conscience above duty. Mariam subtly exploits Herod's double dependency upon her, both as the legitimator of his rule and as the embodied image of that rule, as imagined through the alignment of private governance within marriage and public government. As she continues to refuse to confirm and reflect his image of her ("I will not speak, unless to be believ'd" [4.3.139]), Herod becomes more and more unstable; his speech becomes hysterical and self-contradictory, allying him with the archetypal imagery of tyranny—unstable, multiple, driven by passion rather than reason. As Rebecca Bushnell argues, the tyrant is marked by feminine attributes, threatened by what he cannot control.[20] His language becomes increasingly contradictory, and marked by an inability to make decisions or to turn words into deeds, a turn that Herod himself remarks upon:

> My wisdom long ago a-wand'ring fell,
> Thy face, encount'ring it, my wit did fetter,
> And made me for delight my freedom sell. (4.4.224–26)

This is a classic case of projection, in which the undoing of Herod's self is blamed on Mariam's failure to conform to early modern ideals of womanhood. Mariam insists upon integrity, rather than outward conformity.

Speech and Ethics

Mariam's refusal to conform to the image that Herod has of her is largely a question of image and speech. On Herod's return, he greets her, echoing the terminology of the marriage manuals as "[m]y best and dearest half" (4.3.88), but immediately chides her for her "dusky habits" (4.3.90). Her response is to assert a position outside of Herod's construction of her, "I suit my garment to my mind, / And there no cheerful colours can I find" (4.3.91–92). This is one example of a repeated trope in *Mariam,* the disjunction between inner and outer, Mariam's refusal to dissemble and to place proper wifely obedience above conscience. This key issue is addressed through the careful exploration of female speech and the terms on which it may signify. *Mariam* clearly reflects and confronts early modern cultural imperatives relating to female speech, but it also subtly considers the internal contradictions of the expectations that women's words will encode obedience, submission, and modesty.

Criticism of Cary's play has rightly been preoccupied with the ways in which *Mariam,* perhaps uniquely, explores the signification of female speech and suggests its crucial importance in the maintenance of patriarchal order. It is emphatically not the case that silence is seen as an unproblematic ideal; rather, the play confronts the ways in which silence may in fact undermine or challenge the key role that bonds of obedience play in the enforcement of order and additionally explores the central place of appropriate speech within those bonds. Mariam's opening speech, famously, addresses directly the problematics of the female speaking subject, less by questioning her *right* to speak, but by examining the limits to what she might say and the degree to which her speech is expected to reinforce cultural ideals rather than challenging them, even when the price of that reinforcement is conscience and integrity. While on the one hand circulating cultural prohibitions on female speech ("How oft have I with public voice run on" [1.1.1]) and suggesting the ways in which women's words do not signify straightforwardly ("Mistaking is with us but too too common" [1.1.8]), on the other hand this opening soliloquy represents the breach between public appearance and private feeling. The failure to conform to early modern prescriptions for decorum in speech is repeatedly identified as Mariam's downfall: "Unbridled speech is Mariam's worst disgrace, / And will endanger her without desert" (3.3.183–84). It is not so much that silence is required, but rather that a woman must show deference and obedience, particularly to her husband.

This requirement *necessitates* speech: "Silence, as it is opposed to speech, would imply stoutness of stomach, and stubbornness of heart."[21] Thus silence is not so much a sign of virtue, but of discontent, as Pheroras makes clear to his bride-to-be, Graphina: "Why speaks thou not, fair creature? Move thy tongue / For silence is a sign of discontent:" (2.1.41–42).

Although *Mariam* reveals a clear preoccupation with the limits and authority of female speech, the play betrays a broader concern with the relationship between power and who is permitted to speak. The play is repeatedly concerned with speech crimes (a preoccupation reinforced by Cary's choice of genre with its foregrounding of speech itself as the primary dramatic element) such as slander and the breaking of vows, as well as with the competition for the control of meaning. The plot itself turns on a speech-act, namely Sohemus's revelation to Mariam of Herod's plan to have her killed if he fails to return from Rome, an act that figures primarily dynastically, but also hints at the way in which this is bound up with issues of representation: Herod wishes to circulate *his* image of Mariam as underpinning his rule through her beauty and obedience, not to permit her to figure as her *self.* Various betrayals in the play are imaged through the breaking of vows: Pheroras betrays Constabarus; Salome, Constabarus; Salome, Mariam; Mariam, herself. These betrayals cumulatively serve as a questioning of the relationship between words and deeds, located primarily in the early modern concept of personal credit, the degree to which an individual's reputation underwrites the truth-value of their statements. This is exemplified neatly by Constabarus's reaction to Salome's announcement of her intention to divorce him:

> I was Silleus, and not long ago
> Josephus then was Constabarus now:
> When you became my friend you prov'd his foe,
> As now for him you break to me your vow. (1.6.461–64)

Such breaches of vow are set against the only solid tie of allegiance in the play, that between Constabarus and Babus's sons, in which an act of protection produces unconditional allegiance: "our lives and liberties belong to you" (2.2.90). Interestingly, this allegiance needs no explicit articulation, being based in "virtue," "'tis written in the heart, / And [needs] no amplifying with the tongue" (2.2.114, 115–16).

The question of the degree to which words and oaths are binding and the ways in which they might be dissembled, misread, or framed to suit political or emotional expediency is addressed repeatedly in *Mariam.* Sohemus is killed specifically for a speech-crime and for breaking his vow to the king: "I slighted so his breath" (3.3.191). Mariam herself is killed for refusing overt allegiance, as well as for breaking her marital vow of obedience. The validity of oaths is called into question by Herod's own behavior as monarch, as he refuses to acknowledge his murder of Mariam's brother and grandfather:

> Wilt thou believe no oaths to clear thy lord?
> How oft have I with execration sworn:
> Thou art by me belov'd, by me ador'd,
> Yet are my protestations heard with scorn. (4.3.117–20)

Here the idea of an oath is not predicated upon truth, but upon power. Mariam's "breach of vow" (4.4.184) is a breaking not simply of the vow of marriage but also of the attendant political relationships of allegiance and obedience. Herod repeatedly demands that Mariam show outward conformity in order to shore up his image: "let your look declare a milder thought" (4.3.153), "do but smile" (4.3.143). Mariam refuses to comply, taking refuge in circumlocution and equivocation: "Why didst thou love Sohemus? MARIAM. They can tell / That say I lov'd him, Mariam says not so" (4.4.193–94). Herod's response, that "denial / Makes of thy falsehood but a greater trial" (4.4.197–98), sees her answer as a refusal to reaffirm her allegiance to him and, ultimately, seals her fate.

Cary's *Mariam* is a rich and resonant text, which provides a fascinating counterpoint to the more familiar representations of femininity in Renaissance drama. While it shares many assumptions and preoccupations with texts like Shakespeare's *Othello* or Webster's *The Duchess of Malfi,* Cary's choice of closet drama alters perceptions of the female subject in important ways. Cary's heroine, for example, is continually subject to the construction of others, yet manages to negotiate a space—albeit a precarious and provisional one—within ideological constraints from which to articulate the paradoxes at the heart of Renaissance perceptions of woman. *Mariam*'s interest in female speech and rhetoric, for example, moves considerably beyond the either/or paradigms of silence or loquacity that so frequently structure early modern texts, allowing readers to excavate something of the complexities of conformity and obligation that demand, rather than excise, women's words.

NOTES

1. *The Tragedy of Mariam the Fair Queen of Jewry, with The Lady Falkland Her Life,* ed. Barry Weller and Margaret W. Ferguson (Berkeley: U of California P, 1994). All references will be to this edition and will be included parenthetically in the text.
2. This motto is found in the fullest—but not necessarily objective—account of Cary's life, written by her daughter, in Weller and Ferguson 195.
3. Alexandra G. Bennett, "Female Performativity in *The Tragedy of Mariam,*" *Studies in English Literature* 40 (2000): 293–309, 298.
4. See works by Kyd, Daniel, and Greville.
5. Stephen Gosson, *Playes Confuted in Five Actions* (London, 1582) sig. E6r–v.
6. See Weller and Ferguson 186–92.
7. Cary's Herod is not the same as the Herod of the New Testament, who massacred the innocents; rather, he is a conflation of several different Herods. For a full account, see Weller and Ferguson 20–22.
8. See the account given in Weller and Ferguson 63–64.
9. Elaine V. Beilin, *Redeeming Eve: Women Writers of the English Renaissance* (Princeton: Princeton UP, 1987) 167.
10. Weller and Ferguson argue that *Mariam* also alludes to Henry VIII's "divorce" from Catherine of Aragon (which was, technically, an annulment) 30–35.
11. John King, *Vitis Palatina* (London, 1614) 5.
12. Alexander Niccholes, *A Discourse of Marriage and Wiving* (London, 1615) sig. G2v.
13. William Whately, *A Bride-Bush: Or, A Direction for Married Persons* (London, 1619) 116.
14. See Rebecca W. Bushnell, *Tragedies of Tyrants: Political Thought and Theater in the English Renaissance* (Ithaca: Cornell UP, 1990).
15. For details on English Renaissance views of divorce, see Roderick Phillips, *Putting Asunder: A History of Divorce in Western Society* (Oxford: Oxford UP, 1988), ch. 2 and 3, and Lawrence Stone, *Road to Divorce: England 1530–1987* (Oxford: Oxford UP, 1990).

16. The term is Eve Kosovsky Sedgwick's, in *Between Men: English Literature and Male Homosocial Desire* (New York: Columbia UP, 1985).
17. William Heale, *An Apologie for Women* (Oxford, 1609) 17.
18. William Perkins, *Christian Oeconomie,* trans. Thomas Pickering (London, 1609) 111.
19. See the discussion of this question in the Chorus to act 3.
20. Bushnell 9–23.
21. William Gouge, *Of Domesticall Duties, Eight Treatises* (London, 1634) 284.

READING LIST

Belsey, Catherine. *The Subject of Tragedy: Identity and Difference in Renaissance Drama.* London: Routledge Kegan Paul, 1985.

Bennett, Alexandra G. "Female Performativity in *The Tragedy of Mariam.*" *Studies in English Literature* 40 (2000): 293–309.

Ferguson, Margaret W. *Dido's Daughters: Literacy, Gender and Empire in Early Modern England and France.* Chicago: U of Chicago P, 2003.

Goldberg, Jonathan. *Desiring Women Writing: English Renaissance Examples.* Stanford: Stanford UP, 1997.

Green, Reina. "'Ears Prejudicate' in *Mariam* and the *Duchess of Malfi.*" *Studies in English Literature* 43 (2003): 459–74.

Lewalski, Barbara. *Writing Women in Jacobean England.* Cambridge: Harvard UP, 1993.

Purkiss, Diane. "Blood, Sacrifice, Marriage: Why Iphigeneia and Mariam Have to Die." *Women's Writing* 6 (1999): 27–45.

Raber, Karen L. "Gender and the Political Subject in the *Tragedy of Mariam.*" *Studies in English Literature* 35 (1995): 321–43.

Shannon, Laurie, J. "*The Tragedie of Mariam:* Cary's Critique of the Terms of Founding Social Discourses." *English Literary Renaissance* 24 (1994): 135–53.

Straznicky, Marta. "'Profane Stoical Paradoxes': *The Tragedie of Mariam* and Sidneian Closet Drama." *English Literary Renaissance* 24 (1994): 104–34.

23

Bartholomew Fair and the Humoral Body

Gail Kern Paster

One of the Stage-keeper's complaints in the Induction to Ben Jonson's *Bartholomew Fair* is the author's inaccuracy in depicting the great annual London fair's denizens, visitors, and usual attractions. "He has not hit the humours, he does not know 'em," the Stage-keeper tells the audience waiting for the play to begin (Induction 11–12).[1] He then offers a long and sweeping list of the playwright's omissions—the play lacks "Bartholomew-birds," rowdies, a kindly toothdrawer, a juggler with his "well-educated ape to come over the chain, for the King of England, and back again for the Prince, and sit still on his arse for the Pope, and the King of Spain" (17–20).

Jonson's theater audience—in modern productions as in the original public performance at the brand-new Hope Theatre on October 31, 1614—understands that the Induction is a piece of stage business written by Jonson himself. It serves as a mock-impromptu prologue, part of an old theatrical in-joke that would-be drama critics lurk everywhere, perhaps especially backstage. But a modern audience will not understand why the Stage-keeper uses the word *humors* to signal those characters and traits of behavior—here odd or quaint ones (*OED* 6c)—that would make a theatrical representation of Bartholomew Fair lifelike or not. For speakers of contemporary English, the term *humors* refers almost exclusively to disembodied moods or states of mind. Our tendency is to distinguish sharply between mental and physical events, even to regard them as exclusive categories. Today, we might remark that someone is in a good or bad humor but we do not locate the source of a mood in a part of someone's body, or even in all of his body. Even though mood is expressed in and by means of bodily gestures and behaviors, we speak of mood as floating free of embodiment.[2]

The Stage-keeper's use of the term "humors" in this context then requires a bit of historical explanation about early modern notions of the relation of mind and body. For Jonson, like other speakers of early modern English, there was no conceptual separation between the categories that we now designate as the physical and the psychological. For them, the term "humors" had many meanings: in the most general sense, it referred to the liquids in plants and animals. As Jonson's character Asper explains in *Every Man out of His Humor,* humor is "a quality of air or water" so that whatever "hath fluxure and humidity, / As wanting power to contain itself, / Is humor" (Induction 89, 93–95). In the human body, there were the four humors of blood, phlegm, choler, and melancholy, which were "real bodily fluids to which largely hypothetical origins, sites and functions were ascribed."[3] The humoral body's internal organs produced these four fluids and sent them out into the bloodstream to deliver their qualities of cold, hot, moist, and dry to all the body's parts. From blood came the qualities of hot and moist; from phlegm, cold and moist; from choler, hot and dry; and from melancholy, cold and dry. Humors were what gave all living things—including the things and people belonging to a fair—their physical and behavioral distinctiveness. By introducing the term "humors" so early in *Bartholomew Fair,* Jonson signals his thematic interest in the relations between what we might call inner and outer worlds—between the inner world of an individual's impulses, appetites, and desire for personal expression and the outer physical world made up of objects, of other people and their own desires, and the physical environment that they inhabit together. But in the play itself, as we shall see later, the term "humors" is replaced by the synonymous term "vapors." What humors are to other Jonson comedies, vapors are to *Bartholomew Fair*—a term that subsumes all forms of meaningful difference into its own endless metamorphoses, both grammatical and material. That Jonson wishes us to understand the two terms as nearly interchangeable is signaled by Jordan Knockem's reliance on *vapors* as personal verbal signature and catchall phrase for things as they are—especially emotionally driven things as they are.

Thus, although the Stage-keeper's early reference to the "humors" is a narrow one, the humors themselves were an important building block of early modern cosmology. They formed part of the mental furniture of early modern men and women. The four qualities of hot/cold, wet/dry were the basis in nature for human behaviors and emotions because the physical model underlying ancient and early modern psychology was "a simple hydraulic one, based on a clear localization of psychological function by organ or system of organs."[4] At every moment in the course of a day, a month, a season, or a lifetime, the humors and the qualities residing in them were thought to calibrate a body's internal heat and moisture—what the Elizabethans called its temper or complexion. In the humoral interaction of the four qualities, the early moderns accounted for a person's thoughts and deeds in a way that did not distinguish between the psychological and the physiological. As Thomas Wright explains in his 1604 moral treatise *The Passions of the Mind in General,* "the Passions ingender Humours, and humours breed passions."[5]

The forces of cold, hot, wet, and dry comprised the material basis of any living creature's characteristic appraisals of and responses to its immediate environment; they altered the character of a body's substances and, by doing so, organized its ability to act or even to think. "The Minds inclination follows the Bodies Temperature," the jurist John Selden noted in *Titles of Honor,* repeating a medical commonplace of his age (Selden b4). Heat stimulated action, cold depressed it. Clear judgment and prudent action required the free flow of clear fluids in the brain, but melancholy or choler altered and darkened them. The young warrior's choler gave him impulsiveness and the capacity for rage. Phlegm helped to produce his cowardly opposite's lethargy and was responsible for the general inconstancy of women. Youth was hot and moist, age cold and dry; men as a sex were hotter and drier than women.[6]

But in the 1590s, a new meaning of the term "humor" came into vogue among the fashionable classes to designate a person's whim or impulse.[7] London gallants claimed to "have a humor" in order to describe, publicize, and ultimately excuse their affectations in food, dress, speech, and other social behaviors. In his 1609 pamphlet *The Gull's Hornbook*—a mock encomium to gallants—Thomas Dekker satirically describes the "true humorous gallant" as one who "desires to pour himself into all fashions" and in order "to excel even compliment itself must as well practise to diminish his walks"—that is, walk only in the places that fashionable men walk and adopt their proud gait while doing so—"as to be various in his salads, curious in his tobacco, or ingenious in the trussing up of a new Scotch hose."[8] Corporal Nym, an irascible minor character in

Shakespeare's *Henry V* and *The Merry Wives of Windsor,* defends his actions by citing his humor as that force within him that moves him to feel and do: "I have an humor to knock you indifferently well," he tells Pistol early in *Henry V,* "I would prick your guts a little in good terms, as I may, and that's the humor of it" (2.1.55–59). It is this new meaning for the term "humors" that becomes the basis for Elizabethan playwrights' attack on social pretension in the 1590s' comedy of manners known as humors comedy—of which Ben Jonson was a leading exponent. It is the unfortunate gap in meaning between the humors as a fundamental part of the natural order and the humors as the ridiculous manners of the would-be gallant (or soldier) that Jonson seeks to expose in his humors comedy. In using the term "humor" to claim social privilege based on individuality and the ability to satisfy his whims, the gallant radically misrecognizes his place in the universe. As Jonson's spokesman Asper exclaims in *Every Man out of His Humor,*

> But that a rook, in wearing a pied feather,
> The cable hatband, or the three-piled ruff,
> A yard of shoetie, or the Switzers' knot
> On his French garters, should affect a humour! (Induction, 110–13)

For Jonson, as for other playwrights in early modern England then, there are two separate but related discourses of the humors. One is a straightforward physiological discourse that borrows heavily from ancient medical theory in order to explain physical, behavioral, and cultural difference. The other is a fashionable discourse that presents the humors as an agreed-upon social fiction by which individuals—mostly men—promote their claims to individuality. The Stage-keeper's reference to "the humours" relies on both these discourses because the social power of the second discourse was very much a function of the explanatory power of the first. The humors were part of the fabric of the universe as it was then imagined. Characters who base their claims to social privilege by citing their humors do so emboldened by the "truths" of early modern physiology—by the four bodily fluids held responsible for traits of personality, behavior, status, gender, age, and ethnicity. In this respect, the humors become a perfect instance of what Judith Butler sees as bodily materiality's uncontested status in Western discourse as that which escapes signification.[9] As part of the natural order, the humors were used to justify the hierarchical differences embedded in the social order. The right to have a humor—especially an angry or otherwise aggressive humor—becomes part of the everyday adjustments in urban life that Jonson is eager to represent and satirize in comic actions.

In *Bartholomew Fair,* both humoral discourses are engaged in the representation of the various Londoners who visit the fair and those characters such as Ursula the pig-woman, Leatherhead, and Joan Trash who traveled from fair to fair selling their goods and services. The social collisions that are an inevitable part of fairgoing—then as now—become the source of comic action in the play and the theatrical occasion for a full-scale representation of the humors in action. Jonson presents the fair as a distinctly childlike environment. It is a holiday dedicated to the satisfaction of bodily appetites and responsive to the impulses and whims of the pleasure-seekers who flocked there. Jonson presents the fair as bewilderingly full of sights, sounds, smells, and physical movement, so that it functions to overload the senses not only of the characters themselves but also of the audience struggling to follow its multiple plots.[10] The play's action is almost a perfect example of the humoral maxim that "Passions ingender Humours, and humours breed passions." The fair's commitment to the satisfaction of bodily pleasures threatens to break down the emotional as well as physical self-control of its visitors. Perhaps, as Thomas Cartelli suggests, Jonson wishes to portray the fair as a kind of urban arcadia, a place apart (154). But in terms of hitting the humors, the real Bartholomew Fair's importance as a popular holiday destination allows Jonson to present his theatrical version of the fair as a social laboratory challenging the capacities for rational self-management both in the community and in the individual. That the fair's central authority—Justice Adam Overdo—spends most of the play in disguise as a madman in order to discover the fair's "enormities" suggests the fair's capacity to thwart rational calculation and straightforward dealing. Furthermore, the names for some of Jonson's male characters, such as Zeal-of-the-Land Busy, Overdo, Wasp, Quarlous, Knockem, and Trouble-All, suggest Jonson's preoccupation with the relation between individual temperament, the control of aggressive passions, and the governing conditions of a particular environment. Other characters' names—Littlewit, Mooncalf, Purecraft, Cokes, and Leatherhead—suggest a complementary preoccupation with innate mental capacities. ("Cokes" is Elizabethan slang for a dolt, the oxymoronic phrase "pure craft" suggests slyness, and "mooncalf" suggests physical deformity as well as mental retardation [*OED* 1b and c].) That Jonson means us to understand the fair as a challenge to rational and emotional self-management is especially clear in his portrayal of Bartholomew Cokes, who is both the play's most childlike, most impulsive character and the one most attuned to the fair's delights: "'twas all the end of my journey," he tells his disapproving tutor Wasp, "indeed, to shew Mistress Grace my Fair: I call't my Fair, because of Bartholomew: you know my name is Bartholomew, and Bartholomew Fair" (1.5.61–64).

The explanatory power of humoral discourse for representing a fair was that it explained the reciprocal relationship between an individual's state of mind and body, on the one hand, and the conditions of a particular environment, on the other. Jonson portrays the fair as full of things and people, more and less wonderful—but all functioning as objective causes for primary emotions such as pleasure and aversion, desire, fear, wonder, terror, and anger. In the main action, the fair's appeal to the bodily humors is immediately apparent when John Littlewit persuades his wife Win—who may or may not be newly pregnant—to counterfeit a longing to eat the roasted pig sold at the fair: "Win, long to eat of a pig, sweet Win, i' the Fair; do you see? I' the heart o' the Fair; not at Pie-corner. Your mother will do anything, Win, to satisfy your longing" (1.5.151–53). Win's sudden longing—recognizable as a bodily humor of pregnancy if not actually called one—introduces the idea of urgent bodily appetites being feigned in order to claim special privileges (here the privileges granted to pregnant women) and to evade social sanctions. We learn much later that Littlewit's real motive for visiting the heart of the fair is less to eat roast pork himself than it is to see the puppet show he has penned about the classical tragic lovers Hero and Leander. When Win's mother Dame Purecraft asks her preacher Rabbi Zeal-of-the-Land Busy if fair-going may be construed as lawful for godly Puritans, we watch the gluttonous and hypocritical Busy yield to the gustatory temptations of roasted pork by distinguishing between spiritually lawful and unlawful ways of eating it: "we may be religious in midst of the profane, so it be eaten with a reformed mouth, with sobriety, and humbleness" (1.6.71–73). He vows himself to "eat exceedingly" and "by the public eating of swine's flesh, to profess our hate and loathing of Judaism" (92, 93–95).

It is Busy's phrase, eating with "a reformed mouth," that suggests how brilliantly Jonson uses humoral discourse in *Bartholomew Fair*. Busy's phrase alludes first of all to the current religious controversies in England over the meaning and status of the Eucharist—the question of whether or not Christ's body was actually or only symbolically present in communion bread. The phrase also evokes the bitter struggle within English Protestantism over the extent and practices of the reformation. Part of this struggle was waged over traditional holiday celebrations such as saints' days and traditional customs such as fasting or fair-going.[11] These customs were promoted by King James I and his conservative bishops but strongly opposed by English Puritans who saw themselves as the godly elect and advocated the celebration only of sabbath days and then only in sober observance. On days traditionally set aside for religious fasting, for example, Puritans expressed their opposition by public feasting (Poole 51). Busy wants to pretend that eating at the fair might be part of this religious sanction. *Bartholomew Fair,* in exposing Busy's hypocritical self-righteousness, seems to intervene in the contest on the side of traditional holiday practices.

But Busy's phrase also contains traces of a related contemporary conflict over what we might call the social reformation of the body—sometimes called the reformation of manners. In this contest, the question was one of emotional and bodily self-regulation—what historians have influentially named "the civilizing process." According to their accounts, the sixteenth century saw a gradual transformation in the shame threshold thanks to a historically new set of demands placed on individuals to moderate their gestures, refine their manners, tame their emotions, and cultivate a high degree of self-consciousness about causing bodily offense to others.[12] New norms for table manners, for the private management of bodily evacuations, for controlling impulsiveness, and for inculcating emotional restraint had the effect of targeting certain emotions, certain behaviors, and certain groups—rustics, women, the lower classes generally—for subtle (and not so subtle) forms of social discipline.[13] Thus in addition to religious controversy, Rabbi Busy's notion of eating with "a reformed mouth" calls up the gradual struggles of the civilizing process over the management of appetites no less than the management of passions.

It is a fair's obvious appeal to bodily appetites that most clearly signals Jonson's thematic interest in the struggles of the civilizing process in *Bartholomew Fair*. Though fairs had arisen in medieval times as agricultural markets, by the early seventeenth century they were largely holiday occasions dedicated to the arousal and satisfaction of bodily appetites—from the desire for pork or gingerbread to one for toys, sheet music, or puppet shows (Laroque 165–67). In places such as London where parish feasting had largely disappeared, fairs served as a communal replacement (Hutton 243). But it is not surprising that fairs would also be associated with threats to order, since they attracted "a whole shady world of beggars, cutpurses, charlatans, 'cony-catchers,' prostitutes and pimps" who committed the offenses that Justice Overdo's Court of Pie Powders would have adjudicated and that he, in his disguise as Mad Arthur of Bradley, vows to root out (Laroque 165–67).

Bartholomew Fair's location offers an even more specific association with personal violence, since it was held in an open space outside the city walls where criminals were often executed and where men went to display their swordsmanship and resolve quarrels (Sugden 471–72). In the Induction, Jonson takes pains to reply to the Stage-keeper's charges against the play's realism by drawing up a contract identifying the two environments of fairgrounds and theater: "though the Fair be not kept in the same region that some here, perhaps, would have it, yet think that herein the author hath observ'd a special decorum, the place being as dirty as Smithfield, and as stinking every whit" (Induction, 158–62). Jonson *has* hit the humors of Bartholomew Fair, these Articles of Agreement tell us, in representing human appetites for activities and things to be found—perhaps especially—in dirty and smelly places.

It is not surprising—given the social and gender differences naturalized by early modern humoral theory—that the play's female characters find the fair a special challenge to their capacity for bodily self-possession. As I have argued elsewhere, they are presented in the action as vessels of bodily incontinence and subjected to a variety of physical embarrassments.[14] Both Win Littlewit and Dame Overdo find themselves needing to urinate in a public place lacking what we would call sanitary facilities. They end up competing for use of the chamber pot in Ursula the pig-woman's booth. The extent of their embarrassment is signaled by their reluctance even to name their bodily need. Win tells her husband John, "I know not what to do [. . .] For a thing, I am asham'd to tell you, i'faith and 'tis too far to go home" (3.6.113, 115–16). Alice Overdo, abandoned by the rest of her family, is obliged to reveal her need to a total stranger. Telling Captain Whit that she is "a little distemper'd with these enormities"—the arrest of tutor Wasp—she cannot go on to let him know that she needs a chamber pot: "I cannot with modesty speak of it out, but—" (4.4.184, 188). The play's satiric exposure of Justice Adam Overdo culminates when his wife, dressed in the gaudy clothes of a prostitute, vomits drunkenly onstage.

The play's huge central figure—the obese pig-woman Ursula—not only is explicitly named for a she-bear, but also takes on the lineaments of a raging and monstrous animal-mother.[15] Knockem exclaims on entering, "Urs'la! my she-bear! art thou alive yet? With thy litter of pigs" (2.3.1–2). Ursula's resemblance to her pigs is made reciprocal through an identification of hot emotions and hot temperatures. Mooncalf jokingly describes the pigs' roasting by telling Ursula that they are "very passionate, mistress, one on 'em has wept out an eye" (2.4.55–56). Yet it is Ursula herself who is *Bartholomew Fair*'s most passionate, hence most primal character. She laments, "I am all fire, and fat, Nightingale; I shall e'en melt away to the first woman, a rib, again, I am afraid. I do water the ground in knots as I go, like a great garden-pot; you may follow me by the S's I make" (2.2.49–53). Overheated by the fire she tends, she spends most of the play in a distemper of female choler, raging against her customers, her fellow fair denizens, and her terrified employee. Infuriated by the insults of Quarlous and Winwife, Ursula tries to scald them with a pan of cooking grease only to burn herself instead and become immobilized. "Thou shalt sit i'thy chair, and give directions," Knockem tells her consolingly, "and shine Ursa major" (2.5.177–79).

Critics have suggested that Jonson makes Ursula's booth resemble the hell-mouth toward which sinners are drawn in medieval morality plays.[16] More to the point for this chapter is that Jonson—by likening Ursula to Eve and by making her booth the play world's central source of heat, food, drink, sex, and evacuation—constitutes the fair as primordial, as an elemental image of the whole physical world. As such it offers a wonderful example of the reciprocity between body and world that the Russian critic Mikhail Bakhtin described as characteristic of "the grotesque body": the grotesque body is "not separated from the rest of the world. It is not a closed, completed unit: it is unfinished, outgrows itself, transgresses its own limits. The stress is laid on those parts of the body that are open to the outside world, that is, the part through which the world enters the body or emerges from it, or through which the body itself goes out to meet the world."[17] Rabelais, according to Bakhtin, was the primary exponent in the Renaissance of this celebratory idea of a collective human body, swallowing up individual bodies and individual appetites in its glorious excess and battling the forces of repression lined up against it. (One can see this symbolic battle clearly in Breughel's painting of *The Battle of Carnival Against Lent.*)

But Jonson, even as he relies on the symbolic characteristics of the grotesque body in order to depict the collective activities of the characters in *Bartholomew Fair,* is clearly more ambivalent about them than Rabelais.[18] The disorder that emanates from Ursula's booth and grows to encompass the whole fair is seen as both shaming and liberating to its various participants. It is thanks to a failing of husbandly and familial discipline that Win Littlewit and Alice Overdo end up in Ursula's booth, where they are approached by Jordan Knockem and persuaded to become "bird[s] o' the game" (4.5.17–18). Their moral yielding is excused at least in part because both women have been abandoned by their male keepers—the too-complaisant John Littlewit, the ineffectual tutor Humphrey Wasp, and the virtually absent Adam Overdo. But Jonson's satiric portrait of London wives yielding to sexual impulse is itself counterposed by his positive representation of the newly impulsive behavior of Grace Wellborn, who—desperate to avoid her arranged match to the doltish Cokes—decides to stage a whimsical wooing contest between the rival suitors Quarlous and Winwife. The revelation of her impending marriage to Winwife at the end of the play goes far to sanction the impulsiveness for which the fair itself is partly responsible and that has worked to shame the play's other respectable women.

In *Bartholomew Fair,* however, it is the language of vapors that most tellingly reveals the action of the humors and the release of disorderly emotions that the fair brings about. "Let's drink it out, good Urs, and no vapours!" (2.3.22–23), Knockem tells Ursula on first finding the irascible pig-woman at the fair and hoping to enter into a comfortable business relationship with her. Yet, as becomes clear in Knockem's endless playing with the word, the vapors are conceptually even more useful than the humors had been for expressing the deep reciprocity linking self to world in early modern cosmology. Humors and vapors are alike in being fluids, but vapor is liquid involved with heat and air—matter, says the *Oxford English Dictionary,* in "the form of a steamy or imperceptible exhalation," an "emanation of imperceptible particles, usually due to the effect of heat upon moisture" (*OED* 1 and 2a). The concoction of vapors was thus one of the basic physical activities of the humoral body and one way that the human body expressed its likeness to elemental forms of atmospheric action. Many of the constituent elements of human bodies in the period are described as vapors: thus sleep was caused by vapors rising into the brain from the concoctions of the lower body. Their release was fundamental to health. In *The Castel of Helth,* Sir Thomas Elyot distinguishes among the consistencies of humors: "Of humors some are more grosse and colde, some are subtyle and hot, and are called vapours."[19] Jonson's brilliance in *Bartholomew Fair* is first to establish the vapors as an idiosyncratic feature of one character's language—that is, a word used like the language of the humors to claim or prove individuality—and then to produce vapors theatrically in the redolent steam rising from the booth where Ursula roasts her pigs and serves her ale. The metamorphosis of pigs from animal to food to human self aligns with the fermentation of the ale to suggest the dynamism, causality, and endless transformability of the physical world and the human beings within it.[20]

In act 4 the vapors become the name of a word-and-drinking game structured around quarreling, created by an assortment of male characters including Wasp, the wrestler Puppy, Captain Whit, and Knockem's accomplice Val Cutting. Language and stage properties come together to make vapors virtually a dramatic emblem—of physical appetite and social reciprocity, of the metamorphosis of forms, of the human body as a threshold for the passage of air and other elements, and of language itself as an atmospheric social barometer. Here I want to concentrate on the game of vapors as Jonson's emblematic representation, in this play, of male humors in distilled form. As Jonson explains the game in a stage direction, the job of the game's players is *"to oppose the last man that spoke, whether it concern'd him, or no"* (4.4.28 s.d). The reason to call the game "vapors" has to do with Knockem's equation of humors and vapors—his reduction of vapors to moods (indeed to bad moods unless the word is otherwise modified). Thus, when he asks Ursula for "a bottle of fresh ale, and a pipe of tobacco; and no vapours" (2.3.56–57), it is the power of her rage that he fears. And it is to countervail her mood that he welcomes the arrival of Ezekiel Edgworth as bringing "a kind heart and good vapours" (60–61). By act 4, when Jonson introduces the game of vapors, its most important player Wasp has been exhausted by a day spent wandering more or less aimlessly around the fair with Cokes's marriage license in a box. As Edgworth explains it to Quarlous and Winwife,

> Yonder he is, your man with the box fall'n into the finest company, and so transported with vapours; they ha' got in a northern clothier, and one Puppy, a western man, that's come to wrestle before my Lord Mayor anon, and Captain Whit, and one Val Cutting, that helps Captain Jordan to roar, a circling boy: with whom your Numps is so taken, that you may strip him of his clothes, if you will. I'll undertake to geld him for you; if you had but a surgeon, ready, to sear him. (4.3.106–14)

Wasp is transported by vapors—carried away by emotion—in several senses: he is transported by his own choleric vapors as one of the play's grumpiest characters who, having spent the day looking for Cokes, is even grumpier than usual. And he is transported by the vaporish activity—human and gastronomic—that rises in the air around Ursula's booth. Finally, he is transported by the force of his new attraction to Val Cutting. It is the congregation of vapors—of physical steam, of quarreling language, of human moodiness—that reveals the production of emotion at the fair as a physical and social transaction between individuals rather than an experience within the body of the individual subject. As M. L. Lyon and J. M. Barbalet have pointed out with respect to emotion generally, "emotion is not only embodied but also essentially social in character."[21] The fair itself, as an ephemeral occasion supported by its satisfaction of appetite and the release from the everyday that its customers seek, helps to underscore this definition of emotion. That is, both the fair's attention to appetite and its ephemerality align it with the humors and the passions that they breed. Here the humors and passions float free of their ordinary social contexts, especially in the game of vapors in which the participants have only just come together at the booth as strangers. Within that context, the game of vapors considers biological life-functions to be both fundamentally pneumatic and fundamentally oppositional in nature, occurring in the public space of the air as the site and instrumentation of noise.[22] The vapors are a language game structured around contradiction, produced through the warming stimulation of drink and the exhalation of air. As a symbol for embodied emotions, the game changes constantly yet predictably. Most important, perhaps, the nature of the vapors game goes unrecognized by all the participants. In order to participate in the game at all, each man must take turns, cooperate, and perhaps above all listen to one another. Ordinary conversational strategies of give-and-take may be stretched here almost beyond recognition, yet the structure of the game insists on contradiction as an intimately social act, even among strangers. The result is a paradoxical set of speech acts—an improvised agreement to engage in contradiction—as the result:

> *Knockem:* To what do you say nay, sir?
> *Wasp:* To anything, whatsoever it is, so long as I do not like it.
> *Whit:* Pardon me, little man, but you musht like it a little.
> *Cutting:* No, he must not like it at all, sir; there you are i' the wrong. (4.4.28–32).

With its physical backdrop of the steam arising from Ursula's pig-booth (with its own fundamental concoctions of pig flesh), this occasion for playing a game of vapors shows emotionally embodied life as a difficult, fluid but rule-bound form of play with opposition itself as event, structure, and goal. The game, like the characters themselves, occurs in and through the vaporous air, with the thresholds of the players' bodies continually crossed and recrossed as characters take in the air (and sounds) of each other's contradictions—saying yea or nay in turn—and respond with their own. Yet the game holds its participants in social and emotional bonds as they negotiate the limits of disagreement, finding in their desire to disagree with one another an expression of social form and improvisatory rule making. Wasp is probably the essential exponent of the game, declaring the complete dichotomy between his appetitive and his rational selves: "I have no reason, nor I will hear of no reason, nor I will look for no reason, and he is an ass that either knows any, or looks for't from me" (38–40). But in the metamorphic logic of the vapors, no position—even a confession that "I have no reason" (45)—may long obtain. No sooner does Wasp relent on the question of whether or not he makes sense then the "vapor" of relenting is itself made the subject of debate—whether it is sufficient or not, sweet or stinking, and whether or not Wasp gives his vapor permission to stink. (Parsing nonsense, we soon discover, is as risky a proposition as nonsense itself.) Wasp's final paradoxical position—a Cretan liar's declaration that he was "not i'the right, nor never was i' the right, nor never will be i' the right, while I am in my right mind" (66–68)—is itself met by a paradoxical debate on whether or not anyone in the group is listening to what Wasp says.

The game's potential—the potential of language itself—to extend itself indefinitely as dialogic opposition is resolved by Quarlous and Winwife's desire to use Edgworth to steal the marriage license out of the box. But Quarlous's definition of the vapors as a "belching of quarrel" (73) expresses the nature of vapors—and the humors they stand in for—exactly. As Quarlous seems almost to recognize in watching the spectacle of strangers listening intently to one another only for the purposes of contradiction, a quarrel belched is the physical product of drink and the social product of urban fair-going. It is a use of the air that is both humoral self-expression and physiological event, both language and sound, both mental intention and bodily eruption. It signals control and loss of control, aggression and release.

At such moments and in such phrases, Jonson invokes humorality in order to represent the body and its products—even its affective products—as the endlessly renewable raw materials of social signification. Feeding one's humor, declaring one's humorality or lack of humorality is, as we have seen, a complex social performance. As a performance, it relies for its rhetorical persuasiveness and material power upon the stern facts of the body as resistant physical matter. But, in *Bartholomew Fair* as in social life generally, humoral strategies do not always carry the day in a contest between bodily obduracy and the social hierarchy. To be in one's humor or out of it is not always in a man or woman's power to decide. And it is with such a recognition of the complex interrelations of inside and outside, of self and many, of the force of appetite and the need to find socially harmonious ways of celebrating it that the play ends. Adam Overdo, defeated in his desire to control the fair's activities, recognizes the fair as a legitimate occasion for social release and in response to Quarlous's suggestion invites all the play's characters—visitor and denizen alike—home to his house for a feast. As Quarlous describes it, "get your wife out o'the air, it will make her worse else; and remember you are but Adam, flesh and blood! You will have your frailty, forget your other name of Overdo, and invite us all to supper. There you and I will compare our discoveries; and drown the memory of all enormity in your biggest bowl at home" (5.6.98–104). The invitation is a more or less symbolic one, a nostalgic image of social community in a play where quarreling, confusion, and roguery have been the norm. In the idea of an offstage feast, Jonson recognizes the human capacity for communal recreation, but it is in his brilliant invention of the game of vapors—in which contradiction is the outer expression of the inward self's most fundamental need to declare itself separate and unique—that Jonson hits the humors indeed.

NOTES

1. All quotations from Jonson's play come from *Bartholomew Fair*, ed. E. A. Horsman (Manchester: Manchester UP, 1960).
2. Such dualism is entirely characteristic of modern thought about the relation of mind and body. As the philosopher Charles Taylor points out, "Much modern philosophy has striven against this kind of dualism. But this is a mode of thought we easily fall into. The onus of argument, the effort, falls to those who want to overcome dualism" (*Sources of the Self: The Making of the Modern Identity* [Cambridge: Harvard UP, 1989] 189).
3. See Nancy G. Siraisi, *Medieval and Early Modern Medicine: An Introduction to Knowledge and Practice* (Chicago: U of Chicago P, 1990) 105.
4. See Katharine Park, "The Organic Soul," *The Cambridge History of Renaissance Philosophy*, ed. Charles B. Schmitt et al. (Cambridge: Cambridge UP, 1988) 469.

5. See Thomas Wright, *The Passions of the Mind in General* (1604), ed. William Webster Newbold (New York: Garland Publishing, 1986) 64.
6. See Zirka Z. Filipczak, *Hot Dry Men Cold Wet Women: The Theory of Humors in Western European Art 1575–1700* (New York: American Federation of Arts, 1997) 14–23; and Gail Kern Paster, "The Unbearable Coldness of Female Being: Women's Imperfection in the Humoral Economy," *English Literary Renaissance* 28 (1998): 416–40, esp. 416.
7. See J. B. Bamborough, *The Little World of Man* (London: Longmans, Green, 1952) 103.
8. See Thomas Dekker, *"The Gull's Hornbook," Thomas Dekker,* ed. E. D. Pendry (Cambridge: Harvard UP, 1968) 88.
9. See Judith Butler, *Bodies That Matter: On the Discursive Limits of Sex* (New York: Routledge, 1993) 28.
10. See Richard Levin, *The Multiple Plot in English Renaissance Drama* (Chicago: U of Chicago P, 1971) 202–14.
11. See Kristen Poole, *Radical Religion from Shakespeare to Milton: Figures of Nonconformity in Early Modern England* (Cambridge: Cambridge UP, 2000) 48–54.
12. See Norbert Elias, *The History of Manners,* vol. 1 of *The Civilizing Process,* trans. Edmund Jephcott (New York: Pantheon, 1978); and Barbara Correll, *The End of Conduct: "Grobianus" and the Renaissance Text of the Subject* (Ithaca: Cornell UP, 1996) 32–57.
13. See Gail Kern Paster, *The Body Embarrassed: Drama and the Disciplines of Shame in Early Modern England* (Ithaca: Cornell UP, 1993) 1–22.
14. See Paster, *The Body* 35–39.
15. See Mark Thornton Burnett, *Constructing "Monsters" in Shakespearean Drama and Early Modern Culture* (Basingstoke: Palgrave Macmillan, 2002).
16. See Eugene M. Waith, "Appendix II," *Ben Jonson: Bartholomew Fair,* ed. Eugene M. Waith, The Yale Ben Jonson (New Haven: Yale UP, 1963) 205–17.
17. See Mikhail Bakhtin, *Rabelais and His World,* trans. Helene Iswolsky (Bloomington: Indiana UP, 1984) 26.
18. See Peter Stallybrass and Allon White, *The Politics and Poetics of Transgression* (Ithaca: Cornell UP, 1986) 61–79.
19. Sir Thomas Elyot, *Castel of Helth* (London: 1541) 53.
20. In the early modern universe, James Bono points out, "Nature is fundamentally playful and creative; it is, in short, poetic [. . .] Nature can mimic; it can take natural forms and make them metamorphose into other shapes; it is inherently active, transformative, plastic [. . .] Such transformations and mirroring, then, display the analogical, metaphorical, and hierarchical structure of the divine system of nature." See James J. Bono, *The Word of God and the Languages of Man: Interpreting Nature in Early Modern Science and Medicine* (Madison: U of Wisconsin P, 1995) 184.
21. See M. L. Lyon and J. M. Barbalet, "Society's Body: Emotion and the 'Somatization' of Social Theory," *Embodiment and Experience: The Existential Ground of Culture and Self,* ed. Thomas J. Csordas (Cambridge: Cambridge UP, 1994) 57.
22. See Bruce Smith, *The Acoustic World of Early Modern England* (Chicago: U of Chicago P, 1999) 206–08.

READING LIST

Bakhtin, Mikhail. *Rabelais and His World.* Trans. Helene Iswolsky. Bloomington: Indiana UP, 1984.

Bamborough, J. B. *The Little World of Man.* London: Longmans, Green, 1952.

Burnett, Mark Thornton. *Constructing "Monsters" in Shakespearean Drama and Early Modern Culture.* Basingstoke: Palgrave Macmillan, 2002.

Cartelli, Thomas. "*Bartholomew Fair* as Urban Arcadia: Jonson Responds to Shakespeare." *Renaissance Drama* 14 (1983): 151–72.

Correll, Barbara. *The End of Conduct: "Grobianus" and the Renaissance Text of the Subject.* Ithaca: Cornell UP, 1996.

Dekker, Thomas. *The Gull's Hornbook. Thomas Dekker.* Ed. E.D. Pendry. Cambridge: Harvard UP, 1968.

Elias, Norbert. *The History of Manners.* Vol. 1 of *The Civilizing Process.* Trans. Edmund Jephcott. New York: Pantheon, 1978.

Filipczak, Zirka Z. *Hot Dry Men Cold Wet Women: The Theory of Humors in Western European Art 1575–1700.* New York: American Federation of Arts, 1997.

Hutton, Ronald. *The Rise and Fall of Merry England: The Ritual Year 1400–1700.* Oxford: Oxford UP, 1991.

Laroque, François. *Shakespeare's Festive World: Elizabethan Seasonal Entertainment and the Professional Stage.* Trans. Janet Lloyd. Cambridge: Cambridge UP, 1991.

Park, Katharine. "The Organic Soul." *The Cambridge History of Renaissance Philosophy.* Ed. Charles B. Schmitt et al. Cambridge: Cambridge UP, 1988.

Paster, Gail Kern. *The Body Embarrassed: Drama and the Disciplines of Shame in Early Modern England.* Ithaca: Cornell UP, 1993.

Poole, Kristen. *Radical Religion from Shakespeare to Milton: Figures of Nonconformity in Early Modern England.* Cambridge: Cambridge UP, 2000.

Stallybrass, Peter, and Allon White. *The Politics and Poetics of Transgression.* Ithaca: Cornell UP, 1986.

Sugden, Edward H. *A Topographical Dictionary to the Works of Shakespeare and His Fellow Dramatists.* Manchester: Manchester UP, 1925.

Wright, Thomas. *The Passions of the Mind in General.* 1604. Ed. William Webster Newbold. New York: Garland, 1986.

Waith, Eugene M, ed. *Ben Jonson: Bartholomew Fair.* The Yale Ben Jonson. New Haven: Yale UP, 1963.

24

The Duchess of Malfi and Early Modern Widows

Dympna Callaghan

Ferdinand: You are a Widowe:
You know already what man is; and therefore
Let not youth, high promotion, eloquence—
Cardinal: No, nor anything without the addition, honour,
Sway your high blood.
Ferdinand: Marry! They are most luxurious
Will wed twice. (1.1.293–98)[1]

In tracts, pamphlets, theological treatises, philosophical disputations, popular literature, and stage-plays, there persisted in early modern England a pervasive cultural ambivalence about widows who wed again. This manifested itself on a spectrum ranging from distrust and disapproval to outright moral censure. It did so alongside the social prevalence of remarriage because throughout the period such high proportions of women of reproductive age were widows. The axiom that "the world must be peopled" meant that widows must remarry and that patriarchal social and conceptual relations pertaining to female sexuality must, perforce, reconfigure themselves to accommodate the necessity of their doing so. Objections, like those voiced by the Cardinal and Ferdinand, about women of substance marrying beneath them and about remarriage as a sign of gross sexual appetite were standard components of cultural disapprobation.[2] In *The Duchess of Malfi,* however, Webster's literary rendition of the social reality of the remarrying widow is extraordinarily sympathetic. The Duchess is tortured and murdered for defying her brothers' prohibition against remarriage by wedding her servant, Antonio. But the scene of her onstage strangulation becomes a poignant reproof of the world of moral manipulation and political corruption that surrounds her.[3] That the remarriage of a widow is the motor of Ferdinand's demented reprisal, however, merits deeper scrutiny. This chapter asks precisely what was at stake in the cultural debate about widows' economic and sexual power into which Webster's *Duchess of Malfi* was such a macabre, compelling, and yet tolerant intervention.

The remarriage of widows was frequently the stuff of comedy on the Jacobean stage, where, as Jennifer Panek has argued, a "rich and powerful widow [. . .] makes the fortune of an obscure but deserving young man."[4] More punitive scenarios typically ensue for widows in tragedies and histories, however.[5] Shakespeare's remarrying widows, for example, do not fare well. Gertrude is poisoned in *Hamlet;* Anne Neville in

Richard III (notoriously seduced over the corpse of her dead husband by his murderer) is killed by her new husband; in *Anthony and Cleopatra,* before her untimely death, Octavia is abandoned by Anthony for the more sexually alluring Egyptian queen; Tamora, who in *Titus Andronicus* is widowed, remarried, and in an adulterous relationship with Aaron the Moor, lives to taste her Goth offspring baked in a pie before being killed. Insofar as she is a completely innocent victim, Webster's sympathetic Duchess is a marked contrast to such figures. *The Duchess of Malfi* is in many ways a reprise of his earlier and less successful play, *The White Devil,* which also struggled with the iconoclastic idea of a female tragic protagonist in the midst of corrupt power structures. *The Duchess,* like its predecessor, demonstrates Webster's interest in women at the center of the tragic predicament, a perspective that serves both to focus and to exacerbate issues about power, sexuality, and the transmission of property that that were being worked out in the everyday practices of households as well as in the political arena. Indeed, the debate about the sexual and social status of widows was itself but one spotlighted dimension of the ongoing cultural conversation about the troubled and contradictory status of women. Widowhood was simply an intensified condition of early modern femininity, just as female sovereignty might be said to be an exaggerated one—womanhood *in extremis,* so to speak. In *The Duchess of Malfi,* then, the melodramatic revenge scenario and particularly the figure of the remarried widowed sovereign as tragic protagonist artfully intensifies and magnifies pressing Jacobean cultural contradictions specifically about widowhood, but also about sexuality and power more generally.

Widowed and Remarried

A much higher proportion of women were widowed in early modern Europe than is the case today, often giving them a degree of financial and personal autonomy they could not hope to exercise as wives. Wealthy widows of all ages became objects of desire for aspiring young men who hoped to improve their financial and social status, and younger widows often sought protection and companionship for themselves and their children in a new match. Yet the culture was riven with contradictions about the remarriage of widows. On the one hand, there was a "deeply rooted, lingering prejudice against remarrying widows" (Kehler 400), but this existed alongside considerable social support for their remarriage, especially insofar as it led to improved prospects for men. For example, though eyebrows were raised when twenty-one-year-old equerry (or "master of the horse") Adrian Stokes married his employer, the widowed Frances Grey, duchess of Suffolk, who was almost forty, apparently within days of her first husband's execution,[6] consternation was directed not at the groom but at the bride. When Queen Elizabeth was informed of the match, she declared, "What! Has she married her horse-keeper?"[7] After a brief union (Frances died), Stokes was financially and socially rewarded with a knighthood and eventually election to the House of Commons.[8]

Webster himself was capable of writing on both sides of the question of the remarriage of widows. In 1615, he is believed to have added character sketches to *Characters, Drawn to the Life of Several Persons in Several Qualities* by the deceased Thomas Overbury in 1615,[9] including "An Ordinarie Widow" who remarries and "A Vertuous

Widow" who remains single. While these character sketches do give us some sense of the poles of prevailing discourse about widowhood, it must be cautioned that they are part of a discursive game, which can be played both ways, and as such, should not be taken as undistorted mirrors of prevailing social reality. An "Ordinarie Widdow"

> Is like the Heralds Hearse-cloath; shee serves to many funerals, with very little altering the colour. The end of her husband beginnes in teares; and the end of her teares beginnes in a husband. [. . .] Her chiefest pride is in the multitude of her suitors; and by them shee gaines: for one serves to draw on another, and with one at last she shootes out another, as Boies do Pellets in Elderne Gunnes . [. . .] Thus like a too ripe Apple, she falles of her selfe: but hee that hath her, is Lord but of a filthy purchase, for the title is crackt.[10]

For such a woman as this, the death of a husband only serves to permit her the pleasure of serial courtships. In marked contrast, "A Vertuous Widdow"

> Is the Palme-tree, that thrives not after the supplanting of her husband. For her Children's sake she first marries, for she married that she might have children, and for their sakes she marries no more. She is like the purest gold, only imployd for Princes meddals, she never receives but one mans impression; the large jointure moves her not, titles of honor cannot sway her [. . .] shee thinkes she hath traveled all the world in one man; the rest of her time therefore shee directs to heaven. No calamity can now come neere her, for in suffering the losse of her husband, she accounts all the rest trifles: she hath laid his dead body in the worthyest monument that can be: Shee hath buried it in her owne heart. To conclude, shee is a Relique, that without any susperstition in the world, though she will not be kist, yet may be reverenc'd. (Overbury, 373–74)[11]

This woman marries the first time only to become a mother, and her chastity, or more accurately her complete absence of sexual desire, is what defines and constitutes her virtue. Interestingly too, this woman becomes a relic, exactly the condition against which the Duchess of Malfi protests:

> Why should I,
> Of all the other princes of the world
> Be cas'd up, like a holy relic? (3.2.137–39)

Unlike the character sketches, the Duchess is a three-dimensional dramatic character whose sexuality is represented as an integral aspect of being alive in the world rather than being immured in a reliquary or, as she tells Antonio, in effigy at her husband's tomb.[12] However desirable widows might have been as marriage prospects for aspiring men in early-seventeenth-century London, they remained threatening figures in the cultural imaginary insofar as they brought together categories that, theoretically at least, were posited as mutually exclusive, namely femininity and power. It is not hard to see why a social system that placed rigid restrictions on married women would find widows threatening. In some parts of Europe the law tried to avert the threat posed by widows by barring women from inheriting property on which public offices were entailed. (For instance, in France, Salic law prevented women from inheriting the French crown.) [13]

The Italian setting of *The Duchess of Malfi* is significant in that some of the restrictions on women in Italy appear to have been greater than those elsewhere in Europe. One Italian text written by the Venetian Francesco Barbaro, *De re uxoria* (1416), which articulates Renaissance norms about the relation between the household and the state (ideas also recapitulated by Antonio at the beginning of *The Duchess of Malfi*), argued for controlling women's activities as a means of securing dynastic integrity. Barbaro, however, recognized the difficulty of control presented by widows: "We can scarce with great ingeny [*sic*], elaborate industry, and singular care reduce widows, formed both to their own and other humors, to our own customes" (qtd. in Jordan 46). Another Italian text, Giovanni Giorgio Trissino's *Epistola del Trissino de la vita che dee tenere una donna vedova* (1542), described a widow as "a free woman: [. . .] such may not be subject to a husband, or a father, or anyone else." Surprisingly, Trissino argued, widows should consider themselves men. And indeed, Italian widows, unlike Italian wives, were entitled to appear in court, do business, and deal in property. However, as Trissino pointed out, the widow's is "a bitter liberty." She may not, he specifically stipulated, interest herself in politics: "to speak of what the Turk is up to in Constantinople, or the sultan of Egypt, or of what may be decided at the Diet of Augustus [. . .] nothing is more inappropriate than to hear a woman speak of war and discuss statecraft" (Jordan 71, 72). This is indeed the Duchess's predicament. Despite her clear legal claim to power, she cannot exercise it free of the control of her brothers. The Cardinal seeks dynastic sway, while the Duchess's twin, Ferdinand, is deranged by incestuous desire to control his sister's sexuality. He instructs Bosola:

> observe the Duchess,
> To note all the particulars of her 'haviour:
> What suitors do solicit her for marriage
> And whom she best affects: she's a young widow,
> I would not have her marry again.
>
> *Bosola:* No, sir?
>
> *Ferdinand:* Do not you ask the reason: but be satisfied,
> I say I would not. (1.2.173–78)

In these extraordinary circumstances, the Duchess, a preeminently public figure, is compelled to marry—that is, to undertake what should be a solemn and public undertaking—in the secrecy of an informal arrangement:

> *Duchess:* If all my royal kindred
> Lay in my way into this marriage:
> I'll'd make them my low foot-steps. And even now,
> Even in this hate, as men in some great battles
> By apprehending danger, have achiev'd
> Almost impossible actions: I have heard soldiers say so,
> So I, through frights and threat'nings, will assay
> This dangerous venture. Let old wives report
> I winked, and chose a husband. (1.2.260–68)

Webster's play echoes, though it does not endorse, the cultural commonplaces about concupiscent widows in particular as well as about excesses of female sexual appetite in general.[14] Ferdinand reiterates these stereotypes by referring to his sister as "lusty widow" (1.2.259) and by claiming that "women like that part, which, like the lamprey, / Hath nev'r a bone in't" (1.2.255–56).[15] An an eel-like fish, the lamprey as a phallic image is simultaneously fascinating, repulsive, and comic. In this, Ferdinand's language captures something of the tenor of Joseph Swetnam's infamously misogynist tract, *The Arraignment of Lewde, idle, froward and unconstant women* (1615): "[I]t is more easie for a young man or maid to forbeare carnall acts then it is for a widow."[16] However, as Jennifer Panek has acutely observed, the lusty widow stereotype is not self-explanatory but is related to "another, less-known facet of early modern discourse about widows—a pervasive anxiety that they made domineering, emasculating wives."[17] Indeed, a central tenet of Swetnam's argument was that widows were simply more difficult to deal with than women who had never been married. Swetnam's diatribe enraged some of his female readers, and one, writing under the pseudonym Ester Sowernam, in a pamphlet entitled *Ester Hath Hang'd Haman; or, An answere to a lewd pamphlet entituled The Arraignment of Women* (London 1617), argued that if maids were malleable and widows stubborn, it must follow that it was the experience of marriage that made them so: "How cometh it then that this gentle and mild disposition [of the maid] is afterwards altered?" (Henderson and MacManus 239).

The status of the widow contrasted sharply with that of the married woman. A married woman was, to use the legal term for her condition, *feme covert*. That is, upon marriage all the woman's rights and property converted to her husband, and her very legal identity was subsumed into his. Once married, "coverture" (as the woman's status as *feme covert* was known) was a legal fiction that proposed that husband and wife were one person—on the biblical basis that in marriage the two become "one flesh." Furthermore, that one flesh belonged to the man. In practice, this meant that, as a wife, a woman could not, for example, sign a contract or obtain credit on her own behalf.[18] While such a system may seem at first glance to have women firmly in its rigid thrall, it is important to remember that, unlike today when most adult women in the population at any given time are married, most in early modern England were not—the majority were either unmarried or widowed (Erickson 9). Additionally, although in theory primogeniture (the common law right of eldest sons to inherit their father's wealth) militated against widows inheriting, in practice, there were other forms of law—ecclesiastical and civil—that allowed for community property in marriage and partiability of inheritance (i.e., the right to divide inheritance up among surviving family members rather than bestowing everything to the eldest son) (Erickson 6). Often as well, widows kept jointure lands and had a life interest in the primary domiciles. More basically, however, male rule floundered upon the fact that men often died early, that only sixty percent of marriages produced a son, and that, demographically, it was unlikely that a son would be of age at the time of his father's death. A son's inheritance thus often came, at least temporarily, into his mother's hands (Erickson 9).

Though set in Italy, this is precisely the Duchess's situation. Since Ferdinand is her twin brother, the Duchess must have inherited her sovereignty from her husband, their son being too young to inherit his father's dukedom. This seems to be corroborated by Ferdinand's outburst upon discovering that his sister has had children:

> Write to the Duke of Malfi, my young nephew
> She had by her first husband, and acquaint him
> With's mother's honesty. (3.3.67–69)

At the end of the play, however, it is specifically Antonio's son, and not her son by her first husband, who is presented by Delio as the new heir, despite the fact that his nativity horoscope predicted short life and violent death:[19]

> join all our force
> To establish this young hopeful gentleman
> In's mother's right. (5.5.111–12)

Whatever vagueness the play exhibits about the inheritance pattern by which the Duchess (and later, Antonio's son) inherits sovereignty, it is certainly the case that, as a widow, the Duchess has the potential she did not possess as a wife to wield power independently of a husband and to sever allegiances with other male kin.

While we in the twentieth century tend to connect widowhood with old age, this was far from being the case in Jacobean England, where it was quite possible for a woman both to become a widow at any age and to find herself widowed more than once in a lifetime. Women like the Duchess might well be in the prime of life, or even very young, when their husbands died. *The Law's Resolutions of Women's Rights: or, The Law's Provisions for Women* (1632), whose author is unknown, though an address to the reader was written by someone whose identity was indicated only by the letters T. E.,[20] was published some years after Webster's play. Nonetheless it is important for our consideration of remarrying widows in that it represents research on the laws of 1597–98, many years prior to its publication (Klein 27). Unlike the continental theorist Juan Luis Vives, who in *The Instruction of a Christian Woman,* translated by Richard Hyrde in 1529, urges widows to the precept of St. Paul—"I say to unmarried women and widows, it were good for them if they kept themselves as I am: but yet if they cannot suffer, let them marry. For it is better to marry than burn' (Klein 121)—the *Law's Resolutions* suggests, on purely material grounds, that women are better off remaining single:

> The widow married again to her own great liking, though not with applause of most friends and acquaintance. But, alas, what would they have her to have done? She was fair, young, rich, gracious in her carriage, and so well became her mourning apparel that when she went to church on Sundays, the casements opened of their own accord on both sides [of] the streets that bachelors and widowers might behold her [. . .] Her man[servant] at home kissed her pantables [slippers] and served diligently; her late husband's physician came and visited her often. The lawyer to whom she went for counsel took opportunity to advise for himself. [. . .] Therefore to set men's hearts and her own at rest, she chuse amongst them, one not of the long robe, nor a man macerate and dried up with study, but a gallant gulburd lad, that might well be worthy of her hand had he been as thrifty, as kindhearted, or half so wise as hardy and adventurous. [. . .] Within less than a year [. . .] the bags were all empty, the plate was all at pawn, all to keep the square bones in their amble and to relieve companions. (Klein 54)

Interestingly, the widow's servant is listed first among her suitors, none of whom are presented as suitable or desirable; all are potential financial liabilities, men-on-the-make, and the man she does choose brings about her financial ruin. This text urges women to rely on God for protection for themselves and their children rather than on a new husband, and in this it comports with Catholic writings, such as *The Treasure of Vowed Chastity* (1621), written for those "who have a true desire to imbrace the state of vowed chastity, and yet remaine in the world among secular persons."[21] However, *Laws* was not an attempt to constrict women's choices or contain their sexuality. The author acts more as an advocate for women, urging them to enjoy their liberty and to "Consider how long you have been in subjection under the predominance of parents, of your husbands; now you be free [. . .] at your own law" (Klein 50; see also 28).

Until recently, the prevailing wisdom among social historians was that "women who could afford to resisted all pressure to remarry and so retained their independence."[22] Despite these earlier estimations of women's remarriage, important new work by historians Jeremy Boulton and Vivien Brodsky, as well as literary critics Jennifer Panek and Kathryn Jacobs, has overturned long-standing assumptions about widows in England.[23] According to these studies, women in London remarried with considerable alacrity and they did so in droves: "In most parts of England, male remarriage was both more common and more rapid, but London widows remarried as often and as quickly as their male counterparts."[24]

Mavis E. Mate's study of women's remarriage in Sussex emphasizes the vulnerability of widows and argues that physical vulnerability provided a strong incentive to remarry:

> A woman who did not want her neighbours to gossip about her behaviour had to stay close to home, and eschew all social contact with men. Furthermore sons and male labourers might refuse to carry out her orders, and unable to punish them physically, she would be hard-pressed to maintain her authority. Her property of her person might be attacked. Henry Chesilbergh, for example, harassed his kinswoman, Agnes, after the death of her first husband, and took from her two quarters of oats, one parcel of straw, one parcel of hay, iron and other utensils. Shortly after this incident she remarried. [. . .] [M]ore importantly, the widow of a craftsman or labourer with limited resources was likely to face a drop in her standard of living in widowhood. Such widows would be likely to think that the benefits of marriage outweighed any loss of autonomy.[25]

The Duchess's susceptibility to threats and intimidation probably resonated all too clearly with Webster's audience. For many widows remarriage in either direction on the social ladder was part of the struggle to stabilize, protect, and maintain rather than necessarily improve their social status. The wills of husbands in England reflect, more often than we might anticipate, a desire to protect vulnerable survivors rather than a wish to prevent remarriage. In this, social practice and cultural prejudice seem to part company (see Jacobs 132–55). Richard Brathwaite's *The Description of a Good Wife: or, a rare one among Women* (1619) urged husbands to take fiscal control from beyond the grave:

> Lastly he may (for it is in his power)
> Now in his *Exit,* when he turnes to earth
> To make his *wife,* his sole *Executour*
> And by that meanes to *beggar* all his birth,
> But I should rather limit her a *dower*
> Which might her ranke and order well befit,
> For then so soone she will not *him forget.*[26]

On the competing relations between the discursive and social realities of widowhood, Kathryn Jacobs writes that the "widows of the stage, were probably not created with the intention of mimicking marital reality—though they may be more realistic than previously thought, if [Vivien] Brodsky's study of Elizabethan marriages in London is accurate.

More likely, they were influenced by the literary tradition that long preceded the remarriage patterns of Brodsky's study or the existence of the London Theatre" (133). In light of this insight, it is perhaps not so surprising that, Brathwaite's ditty not withstanding, Fenland yeoman John Pyne, in 1598, directed that "my wiefe and my sonne [. . .] shall remaine together with the encrease of their stockes and if my wief doe chaunce to mary then my will ys that my sons porcon [portion] shalbe putt inthe thandes [the hands] of [my overseer] [. . .] to be put forth," and "boundes [bonds] shalbe taken of the parties that shall have my childrens porcons" (Erickson 168). Another practice designed to evade the problem of coverture was that of granting a bequest for the lifetime of the widow. This gave widows maximum control over property while at the same time protecting it from any subsequent husband (Erickson 169). In Italy, the situation was somewhat different. As Thomas Kuehn has argued: "In their wills husbands commonly included clauses leaving their widows usufruct [use] on the house, furnishings, and other properties, as long as they lived there with their children in chaste widowhood. This testamentary device encouraged widows to stay in their husbands' homes." In Florence, however, Kuehn has discovered that brothers not infrequently gave financial support to their widowed sisters, and left bequests to make sure that support continued even after their deaths: "[T]he statutes of Florence guaranteed widows the right to return to live with their fathers or brothers; and these men too gave substance to these rights in their wills or other actions."[27]

Widowhood, then as now, presented both huge financial and emotional hurdles. Astrologer-physician Richard Napier treated women who continued to grieve deceased husbands even after remarriage (Todd 79). Although the Duchess is indeed "no longer in submissive mourning,"[28] neither does she conform to the stereotypes mouthed by the deranged Ferdinand about lecherous widows eager to remarry as soon as possible. *The Duchess of Malfi* offers a more compassionate view of its protagonist, and it does so in part by reminding the audience of the domestic reality and even the pathos of the lives of many women upon the death of their spouses. In one of the most poignant domestic scenes in the play, we see the Duchess at her toilette, brushing her graying hair in an apt confirmation of what she earlier tells Antonio: "Tis not the figure cut in Alabaster / Kneels at my husband's tomb" (1.1.444–45). She reminds the audience of the difference between representation—between the effigies of living women in wood and marble, depicted praying for the souls of their departed husbands, concrete versions of the discursive stereotypes about widows—and their continuing lived reality. Yet, this reminder in the figure of the kneeling Duchess also connotes the very reason widows were so troubling: they were no longer in the position of subservience. Rather in the play, this posture is echoed and inverted by Antonio's kneeling in a gesture of deference when the Duchess proposes marriage to him, and by her own gesture of stoic yet pious submission when she kneels for execution. Through the gesture of genuflection, the play meditates upon the power and autonomy that might fall to a woman upon her husband's death.

Pregnant and in Power

Though *The Duchess of Malfi* is often read as a valorization of marriage as a private phenomenon, separable from issues of state power, the Duchess's pregnancy offers a visual reminder of the patriarchal rationale that resisted female government and made explicit the link between fears of gynocracy, the rule of women, and a more culturally generalized "gynophobia," that is, a fear about the sexual and reproductive capacities of the female body. That dynasties needed male heirs but could not circumvent the women needed to produce them was, indeed, the central theme of the ongoing saga of the Tudor monarchy. Henry VIII married six times and dispatched two wives with the executioner's axe. Even though he succeeded in producing one legitimate son (Edward VI), Edward's untimely death brought his sister Mary Tudor to the English throne in 1553. This was an event that shook the very patriarchal foundations of English dynasticism. Mary, beset by gynecological problems, went into seclusion at the end of what was thought to be a pregnancy but proved instead to be a massively metastasized ovarian tumor. Elizabeth I turned her femininity to what advantage she could only by rejecting decisively and permanently the possibility of pregnancy. But she did so at great cost: she produced no heir, and her only possible successor was James, the son of her cousin, Mary Queen of Scots. Mary, who had been beheaded at Elizabeth's command, was a woman whose sexual history—widowed and remarried by conspiring to have her husband murdered—contributed in no small measure to her ruin.

Given this bloody history of the commingling of government and gynecology, what did it mean then, especially in a play that revels in the lurid and the macabre, for a pregnant body to be represented by the transvestite actor Richard Sharpe in a "loose-bodied gown"?[29] That Webster shows us the Duchess onstage and pregnant is a factor of the utmost significance, since woman's sexuality constituted in the Renaissance the single and most intransigent obstacle to any argument that countered the belief in innate female inferiority. Constance Jordan summarizes the case:

> Woman, it is generally agreed, is not as strong physically as man and, more important, is vulnerable sexually as he is not. Not only because pregnancy and lactation make her dependent on other persons, although this physical dependence is clearly important, but because her sexual activity, in contrast to his, can result in scandal and disgrace. Her body can and commonly does signify that she is sexually active whether or not she wishes the fact to be known. Maternity, unlike paternity, is not a discretionary matter, to be acknowledged or not, at will. These biological facts underlie arguments for restricting all women's activities, particularly those that take her into the public arena. Misogynists tend to perceive her inability to control the effects of her sexuality—pregnancy—as an indication of an inherent moral debility. (29)

The problem that presented itself, then, was that if women were innately, biologically, and ontologically inferior to men—always potentially pregnant—how could female government ever be justified? It could not—at least according to John Knox's *The First Blast of the Trumpet Against the Monstrous Regiment of Women* (1558):

> To promote a woman to bear rule, superiority, dominion or empire above any realm, nation, or city is repugnant to nature, contumely to God, a thing most contrarious to his revealed will and approved ordinance, and finally it is the subversion of good order, and all equity and justice [. . .] I affirm the empire of a woman to be a thing repugnant to nature, I mean not only that God by the order of his creation hath spoiled women of authority and dominion, but also that man hath seen, proved and pronounced just causes why that it so should be. Man, I say, in many other cases blind, doth in this behalf see very clearly. For the causes be so manifest

> that they cannot be hid. For who can deny that it repugneth to nature, that the blind shall be appointed to lead and conduct such as do see? That the weak, the sick and the impotent persons shall nourish and keep the whole and strong, and finally, that the foolish, mad and frenetic shall govern the discreet, and give counsel to such as be sober of mind? And such be all women compared unto man, in bearing of authority. For their sight in civil regiment is but a blindness: their strength weakness: their counsel foolishness: and judgement frenzy, if it be rightly considered.[30]

In response, John Aylmer wrote his *Harborow for Faithfull and Trewe Subjects* (1559). This tract urged obedience to the monarch regardless of sex and attributed to female monarchs the same authority as male sovereigns. Knox's treatise, Aylmer argued, "almost cracked the duty of true obedience" (Aughterson 140). Knox's diatribe was directed principally at the Catholic queens Mary Tudor and Mary Queen of Scots, but when the Protestant Elizabeth ascended the throne in the same year that Knox's tract was published, no amount of intricate ideological maneuvering could undo the prevailing notion that the government of women, whether at the national or domestic level, contravened the natural order. Even the ultra-Protestant John Calvin, in Geneva, when consulted by Elizabeth's chief advisor, William Cecil, struck an equivocal note:

> Two years ago John Knox asked of me, in a private conversation, what I thought about the Government of Women. I candidly replied, that as it was a deviation from the original and proper order of nature, it was to be ranked, no less than slavery, among the punishments consequent upon the fall of man: but that there were occasionally women so endowed, that the singular good qualities which shone forth in them made it evident that they were raised up by Divine authority.[31]

In response to such discourses, Elizabeth, as we have noted, presented herself as utterly impregnable and inviolable. To buttress the myth of the Virgin Queen, a barrage of classical iconography was used to rationalize what might otherwise be construed as her unnatural and monstrous reign. She was identified with Diana, the goddess of Chastity, and with Astrea, the virgin of Virgil's fourth Eclogue, who returns to reestablish the golden age. Paintings of Elizabeth sometimes depicted her with a sieve that holds water (a concept that was meant to represent her literally impenetrable virginity), but also with iconography that brings her a little closer to the values represented by Webster's Duchess, namely, ears of corn, which were associated with Ceres, the goddess of fertility. In remaining unmarried, Elizabeth avoided the problem of the conflict between the sovereign's duty to govern the realm and the necessity that a wife submit to a husband, though, as we have seen, she succumbed to another, namely, the failure to produce an heir. If a female sovereign married, there was always the danger of a foreign power threatening the autonomy of English government. In the Duchess's case, the realm may, upon her marriage, be effectively governed by her steward, who has from the very beginning of the play expressed very definite—and laudable—views about how the state should be run. On the other hand, the Duchess represents sovereignty not just in the state but also in the family household. Her class status could not make it otherwise. One of the problems Aylmer had been most concerned to address was the knotty question of a married female ruler: "Yea say you, God hath apoynted her to be subject to her husband. [. . .] [T]herefore she maye not be the heade. I graunte that, so farre as pertaineth to the bandes of marriage, and the office of a wife, she muste be a subjecte but as a magistrate she maye be her husband's head" (Aughterson 141). The problem with the sexually female body was that it was never fully autonomous—either conjoined in "one flesh" with a husband, or bearing the body of a fetus: "[W]hen God chooseth himself by sending to a king, whose succession is ruled by inheritance and lineal descent, no heirs male: it is a plain argument that for some secret purpose he mindeth the female should reign and govern" (Aughterson 141). A woman ruler, Aylmer claimed, was not a monstrosity but an anomaly, no more serious than those which occur in nature, such as twins or a man whose hair does not turn gray with age.

Certainly, misogynist arguments abound that the gross, leaky body of the pregnant woman is just another more exacerbated sign of female monstrosity. The Duchess's pregnancy, however, does not strike a note of sadistic voyeurism (although that perspective is represented by Ferdinand, and simultaneously disqualified as a viable perspective on the grounds that he believes himself to be a wolf with "hair on the inside") but as a reassuring sense of domestic health and harmonious connubiality. The sick world is that of the court, as the play warns us at the beginning: "death and diseases through the whole land spread." Played at the more exclusive venue of Blackfriars, a private theater, the play was necessarily a pointed glance at the corruption, favoritism, and the sexual intrigue of the Jacobean court.[32]

Although she positions her as a lover and not as a head of state, Celia Daileder makes the telling observation that the Duchess is a "female sexual martyr," one of those "women who literally die for love."[33] The connection with religious martyrdom is a telling one because like crypto-religiousity, the Duchess's family life is not just private; it is, of necessity, given the murderous propensities of her brothers, *secret*.[34] What finally betrays the Duchess's clandestine marriage to her subjects is of course her pregnant body—the somatic marker of her femininity. In the scheme of patriarchal dynasticism, a woman's fecundity, even more than her chastity, was not merely an abstract construct but a means of securing dynastic integrity: "it was the foundation upon which patriarchal society rested" (Jordan 29). The business of determining whether a woman—married or not—was pregnant, then, was invested with weighty public and social significance. Medical manuals and popular handbooks of the period detailed "the signs to know whether a woman be with child or no" and "the tokens and signs whereby ye may perceive whether the time of labour be near."[35] Some women were taken by surprise and gave birth without knowing they were pregnant, like Lady Anne Effingham in 1602, who went into labor during a game of shuttlecock and "was brought to bed of a child without a midwife, she never suspecting that she had been with child" (qtd. in Cressy 42). Unusual incidents such as this one suggested the alarming possibility that a woman might keep total control of her reproductive life. When the Duchess goes into premature labor, Antonio, like a good husband, follows the advice of William Gouge by providing "such things as are needful for (the woman's) travail and lying in childbed" (qtd. in Cressy 44). But in his case, what is most "needful" is that he maintain the secret of his wife's childbearing. The most famous instance of clandestine pregnancy in the Renaissance was that of Pope Joan, recorded in one of the most prominent books of the Italian Renaissance, Boccaccio's *De mulieribus claris* (c. 1380). Allegedly a book of famous women, it is essentially a catalog of notorious members of the sex, including Joan, who, in male disguise, advances in the church hierarchy until she is elected pope. God, however, intervenes:

> pitying his people from on high, did not permit a woman to occupy such a high place [as the papacy] [. . .] Advised by the devil [. . .] , elected to the supreme office of the papacy, [Joan] was overcome with a burning lust [*ardor libidinis*]. [. . .] She found one who mounted [*de fricere*] her in secret (she, the successor of Peter!) and thus allayed her flaming prurience. (qtd. in Jordan 39–40)

Joan becomes pregnant and gives birth ignominiously in public. Thus, the labor of Pope Joan exemplifies the scandal of commingling the otherwise discrete categories of private femininity and public power.

Although the apricots applied by Bosola to get proof of the Duchess's pregnancy were not commonly known to accelerate delivery, a number of herbs contained properties that were believed to do so: stinking gladdon (a variety of iris), dragonwort, and cyclamen were all known as purgatives which "scoureth and cleanseth [the womb] mightily" (Cressy 50). What endows Bosola's pregnancy test with an even more sinister cast is that its application could potentially operate as an abortifacient. The apricots thus fall into the category of those herbals about which the author of the period's definitive treatise on midwifery, Nicholas Culpeper, warned: "give not any of these to any that is with child, lest you turn murderers" (qtd. in Cressy 49). Bosola is, of course, finally transformed from murderous henchman to remorseful villain by the spectacle of the Duchess's sorrowful motherhood and stoic death, and after her demise, the focus of audience attention rests on him. Replacing the Duchess's tragic centrality, he becomes feminized himself, and, more specifically, he is linked imagistically with the maternal. As Lynn Enterline has remarked, "Bosola's tears seem feminine enough to provoke him into calling them 'manly'" (266):

> This is manly sorrow.
> These teares, I am very certaine, never grew
> In my Mother's Milke (4.2.389–91)

The tragedy of court life has, to a large extent, consisted of its inability to integrate femininity in a patriarchal system that remains, like it or not, entirely dependent on the reproductive powers of women.

Conclusion

There is, of course, no known or obvious external cause for the issue I proposed to inquire into at the start of this chapter, namely, Ferdinand's psychotic insistence that his widowed sister should not remarry. Ferdinand is beset by the itching perversity of an obsessive compulsion, by the hair that he believes is inside his skin. Having in this chapter drawn attention to the sometimes very considerable distance between literature and social history, it may seem as if the elaboration of contextual detail about widows and ideas about female sexuality to which social constructions of widowhood are necessarily attached does not much address this signally literary melodrama of revenge. However, while I have chosen to focus on one dimension of the play in great detail, it is my belief that such concentrated attention shows Webster's propensity to take social problems to their most extreme. A woman in crisis is rendered as symptomatic of cultural crises. Thus Ferdinand is a plausible caricature of prevailing ideas about widows who remarried in ways that were deemed to violate social decorum and moral decency. In this, Webster mocked social reality by illustrating its sometimes absurd endpoints.

NOTES

1. All play references are to John Webster, *The Duchess of Malfi,* ed. John Russell Brown (Cambridge: Harvard UP, 1964); on the complexity on the play's notion of tragedy, see also Dympna Callaghan, *Woman and Gender in Renaissance Tragedy* (Brighton: Harvester, 1989).
2. Additionally, there was a fear that widows might even "exploit sexuality in mourning," but as Patricia Philippy demonstrates, there was no parallel anxiety about widowers. See *Women, Death and Literature in Post-Reformation England* (Cambridge: Cambridge UP, 2002) 28.
3. R. S. White, "The Moral Design of the Duchess of Malfi," *The Duchess of Malfi,* ed. Dympna Callaghan (New York: Palgrave, 2001) 201–19.
4. Jennifer Panek, "'My Naked Weapon': Male Anxiety and the Violent Courtship of the Jacobean Stage Widow," *Comparative Drama* 34 (2000): 321–44, esp. 341.
5. Dorothea Kehler, "The First Quarto of *Hamlet:* Reforming Widow Gertred," *Shakespeare Quarterly* 46 (1995): 338–413.
6. In *An Apologie for Women* (Oxford, 1609), William Heale writes, "A widdow that remarrieth within her yeare of mourning, is by the law free from infamie, but by the lawe also adjudged unworthie of matrimonial dignity." Qtd. in Frank W. Wadsworth, "Webster's *Duchess of Malfi* in the Light of Some Contemporary Ideas on Marriage and Remarriage," *Philological Quarterly* 35 (1956): 1: 394–407, esp. 397. While Heale's remarks apply specifically to the time frame of remarriage, which is not much of an issue in Webster's play, they also powerfully speak to the complex, socially nuanced nature of the restrictions operating on widows as well as to the freedoms that were allowed them.
7. P. W. Hasler, *The House of Commons, 1558–1603,* vol. 3 (London: Her Majesty's Stationary Office for the History of Parliament Trust, 1981) 449.
8. Hasler 1. 6–7.
9. M. C. Bradbrook, *John Webster: Citizen and Dramatist* (New York: Columbia UP, 1980) 167.
10. Sir Thomas Overbury, *Characters,* 6th ed. (London, 1615) 375–76.
11. David Gunby observes that the *ideal* of Jacobean widowhood, whatever the reality, involved withdrawing "altogether from the marriage stakes." See David Carnegie Gunby and MacDonald Jackson, eds., *The Works of John Webster* (Cambridge: Cambridge UP, 2003) 2.22.
12. See Michael Neill for a brilliant account of the importance of death imagery relating to the Duchess. *Issues of Death: Mortality and Identity in English Renaissance Tragedy* (New York: Oxford UP, 1997) 328–35; and on the relic image, see 342.
13. Constance Jordan, *Renaissance Feminism: Literary Texts and Political Models* (Ithaca: Cornell UP, 1990) 95.
14. See Lisa Jardine, *Still Harping on Daughters: Women and Drama in the Age of Shakespeare* (New York: Columbia UP, 1983) 68–102.
15. This image occurs in the same passage in which Ferdinand refers to his father's poniard (1.1.331). Carol Hansen remarks that "The father's and brother's control meet in the image of the poniard—steely domination." *Woman as Individual in English Renaissance Drama: A Defiance of the Masculine Code* (New York: Peter Lang, 1993) 129.

16. K. Usher Henderson and B. MacManus, *Half Humankind: Contexts and Texts of the Controversy About Women in England, 1540–1640* (Urbana: U of Illinois P, 1985) 239.
17. Panek 323.
18. Amy Louise Erickson, *Women and Property in Early Modern England* (New York: Routledge, 1993) 3.
19. Jacobs argues that *The Duchess of Malfi* is unusual in mentioning a son by a previous marriage (139). *Marriage Contracts from Chaucer to the Renaissance Stage* (Gainesville: UP of Florida, 2001).
20. Quotations from this text refer to Joan Larsen Klein, *Daughters, Wives, and Widows: Writings by Men About Women and Marriage in England, 1500–1640* (Urbana: U of Illinois P, 1992).
21. On the relation between Catholic and Protestant views of widows, see Margaret Lael Mikesell, "Catholic and Protestant Widows in *The Duchess of Malfi*," *Renaissance and Reformation* 19 (1983): 265–79.
22. Merry E. Weisner, *Woman and Gender in Early Modern Europe* (Cambridge: Cambridge UP, 1993) 75. Barbara Todd writes, "Once it was economically viable to remain unmarried without great sacrifice, a complex mixture of other factors discouraging remarriage would come into play. Fear of losing legal rights was one of these." "The Remarrying Widow: A Stereotype Reconsidered," *Women in English Society 1500–1800*, ed. Mary Prior (London: Methuen, 1985) 54–83; 79. On the Duchess's exercise of power, see Alison Findlay, *A Feminist Perspective on Renaissance Drama* (Oxford: Blackwell 1999) 100–05.
23. Jeremy Boulton, "London Widowhood Revisited: The Decline of Female Remarriage in the Seventeenth and Early Eighteenth Centuries," *Continuity and Change* 5 (1990): 323–55; Vivien Brodsky, "Widows in Late Elizabethan London: Remarriage, Economic Opportunity and Family Orientations," *The World We Have Gained*, ed. L. Bonfield, R. M. Smith, and K. Wrightson (Oxford: Oxford UP, 1986) 122–54; Jacobs, esp. ch. 7, "Remarrying Widows on the Renaissance Stage" 132–55; and Panek 321–44.
24. I am deeply indebted to Jennifer Panek, who generously allowed me to read portions of her wonderful new book in advance of its publication, *Widows and Suitors in Early Modern English Comedy* (Cambridge: Cambridge UP, 2004). Panek argues that the remarrying widow of comedies accurately mirrored social reality in England in the sense that both before the Reformation and after it, there was social pressure on women to remarry rather than to refrain from doing so. Thus acceptance and even enthusiasm shown for remarriage in the comedies reflect the attitudes of the culture. However, representations of the widows themselves do not so much show what they were really like as the characterizations reflect male desires and anxieties about widows. This work is part of an ongoing discussion in early modern studies about the specificity of literature and its complex relation to social reality. See, for example, the introduction to Dympna Callaghan, ed., *Romeo and Juliet: The Text in Context* (New York: Bedford St. Martins, 2003).
25. Mavis E. Mate, *Daughters, Wives and Widows After the Black Death: Women in Sussex, 1350–1535* (Rochester: Boydell P, 1998) 130–31.
26. Qtd. in Pompa Banerjee, *Burning Women: Widows, Witches, and Early Modern European Travelers in India* (New York: Palgrave 2003) 132; on widows and property, see Mary Hodges, "Widows of the 'Middling Sort' and Their Assets in Two Seventeenth-Century Towns," *When Death Do Us Part: Understanding and Interpreting the Probate Records of Early Modern England*, ed. Tom Arkell, Nesta Evans, and Nigel Goose (Oxford: Leopard's Head P, 2000) 306–24.
27. Thomas Kuehn, "Daughters, Mothers, Wives, and Widows: Women as Legal Persons," *Time, Space, and Women's Lives in Early Modern Europe*, ed. Anne Jacobson Schutte, Thomas Kuehn, and Silvana Seidel Menchi, *Sixteenth Century Essays and Studies*, vol. 57 (Kirksville, MO: Truman State UP, 2001): 97–115; 111.

28. Brian Gibbons, ed., *John Webster: The Duchess of Malfi* (New York: Norton, 2001) xxi.
29. See Lynn Enterline, *The Tears of Narcissus: Melancholia and Masculinity in Early Modern Writing* (Stanford: Stanford UP, 1995) 266.
30. Kate Aughterson, ed., *Renaissance Woman: Constructions of Femininity in England* (New York: Routledge 1995) 138.
31. Philippa Berry, *Of Chastity and Power: Elizabethan Literature and the Unmarried Queen* (London: Routledge 1989) 69.
32. See Alastair Bellany, *The Politics of Court Scandal in Early Modern England: News Culture and the Overbury Affair, 1603–06* (Cambridge: Cambridge UP, 2002) 5. Bellany makes a connection between the play and the breaking Overbury scandal. Sir Thomas Overbury was poisoned because he stood in the way of the divorce of the countess of Essex and her remarriage to James's favorite, Robert Carr, earl of Somerset.
33. Celia Daileader, *Eroticism on the Renaissance Stage* (Cambridge: Cambridge UP, 1998) 131; see Linda Woodbridge, "Queen of Apricots: *The Duchess of Malfi,* Hero of Desire," *The Female Tragic Hero in English Renaissance Drama,* ed. Naomi Conn Liebler (New York: Palgrave 2002) 162.
34. See Lisa Hopkins's excellent study of interiority and secrecy in the play. *The Female Hero in English Renaissance Tragedy* (New York: Palgrave 2002).
35. David Cressy, *Birth, Marriage, and Death: Ritual, Religion, and the Life-Cycle in Tudor and Stuart England* (Oxford: Oxford UP, 1997) 41.

READING LIST

Berry, Philippa. *Of Chastity and Power: Elizabethan Literature and the Unmarried Queen*. London: Routledge 1989.

Callaghan, Dympna. *Woman and Gender in Renaissance Tragedy*. Brighton: Harvester, 1989.

Cressy, David. *Birth, Marriage, and Death: Ritual, Religion, and the Life-Cycle in Tudor and Stuart England*. Oxford: Oxford UP, 1997.

Enterline, Lynn. *The Tears of Narcissus: Melancholia and Masculinity in Early Modern Writing*. Stanford: Stanford UP, 1995.

Hopkins, Lisa. *The Female Hero in English Renaissance Tragedy*. New York: Palgrave 2002.

Jardine, Lisa. *Still Harping on Daughters: Women and Drama in the Age of Shakespeare.* New York: Columbia UP, 1983.

Jordan, Constance. *Renaissance Feminism: Literary Texts and Political Models*. Ithaca: Cornell UP, 1990.

Panek, Jennifer. *Widows and Suitors in Early Modern English Comedy*. Cambridge: Cambridge UP, 2004.

25

The Island Princess and Race

Claire Jowitt

The Island Princess is centrally concerned with human differences of nation and religion, of color and ethnicity. It is a play preoccupied by the "racial" markers that distinguish Europeans—specifically Portuguese colonialists—from the indigenous inhabitants of the Spice Islands. In what follows, I explore *The Island Princess* in relation to Renaissance understandings of human difference, focusing on the ways in which culturally constructed markers of color, ethnicity, religion, and nation are deployed. It is important to signal at this point how complex a term "race" is in this period. Hence, before embarking on a detailed analysis of the play's use of what a modern reader would term "racial" signs, it is important to establish the limits of the meanings for the term "race" in circulation at the time Fletcher was writing. According to the *Oxford English Dictionary* it was first used to mean "group" in 1508 by William Dunbar in a poem "The Dance of the Seven Deadly Sins," in which Envy's troupe were described as "bakbyttaris of sundry races." Other contemporary usages are more specific as the word comes to mean lineage (as in Antony's complaint to Cleopatra about his difficulties over "getting a lawful Race" on his wife [3.13.107]), and nation (Sir John Wynne, for instance, speaks of the "British race" in his 1600 text *History of the Gwydir Family*); it could refer to gender and sexuality (Edmund Spenser talked of a "bounteous race / Of woman kind" in *The Faerie Queene*) or to class, as "noble race" or "base race" were phrases employed frequently in early modern writing. It was applied in relation to blackness; Ben Jonson's *Masque of Blackness* of 1605 is a prime example since the masque opens with a song to "Fair Niger [. . .] / With all his beauteous race / Who, though but black in face, Yet they are bright" (79–83). Indeed Renaissance writing increasingly uses "race" to denote color particularly in relation to inhabitants of Africa or "the race of Ham" (Noah's disobedient son whom God made black in punishment).[1] Finally, another significant way that "race" operates in relation to *The Island Princess* is in terms of religion; as Ania Loomba remarks, "in Early Modern Europe the bitterest conflicts between European Christians and others had to do with religion."[2] This chapter will show in turn the ways in which Fletcher's play resonates with these understandings of "race," despite the text's lack of explicit usage of the term. In particular, it explores the play's colonial contexts, its dramatization of religious conversion (as native Tidoreans and Portuguese soldiers attempt to persuade each other to adopt their respective religions), and the fact that this text was written at the time when skin color started to be understood as a key marker of human difference. In terms of the taxonomy of "racial" categories emerging at the time *The Island Princess* is particularly significant in terms of its attitude to colonialism, religion, and color.

The plot of *The Island Princess* is concerned with the release of the abducted king of Tidore and the marriage of the non-Christian Princess Quisara of Tidore. More generally, *The Island Princess* describes the varying (sometimes harmonious, sometimes antagonistic) relations between native inhabitants of the Spice Islands of the Moluccas and colonialists, represented in the play by Portuguese soldiers and sailors. The play starts with the capture of the king of the island of Tidore—where the Portuguese have established a garrison and trading relations—by the "Governour" (described in the cast list as "[a]n ill man") of a neighboring island, Ternata.[3] The king's sister Quisara (who is besieged by eager suitors including the captain of the garrison, Ruy Dias) promises she will marry the man who rescues her brother. Quisara hopes that Ruy Dias will perform the honorable deed, but his prevarication results in the king being rescued by another Portuguese, the recently arrived Armusia, who has also fallen in love with the beautiful princess. Once restored, the king tries to hasten the nuptials between his sister and his rescuer, but Quisara stalls for time, simultaneously plotting—as does Ruy Dias separately—a scheme to get rid of Armusia. Both repent their dishonorable plans, but meanwhile the governor reappears in disguise and, wanting his revenge on the Tidoreans, tries to divide colonist and colonized over the issue of religion. He encourages Quisara to make Armusia's conversion to her religion a prerequisite for their marriage, and Armusia's horror at such a thought sufficiently angers the king for the latter to imprison him and threaten him with death. Quisara—who now loves Armusia—asserts that she will die with him in the Christian faith—and tragedy is only averted at the end by the Portuguese, now led by a once more honorable Ruy Dias, unmasking the duplicitous governor. This, superficially at least, restores good relations between the Tidoreans and the Portuguese.

Colonial Context

As we shall see, the colonial context for Fletcher's text impacts with the play's racial politics. In general terms the rise of European colonialism in Africa and the New World and the increased trade and diplomatic links with Asia and the East had lead to more contact between European and non-European peoples. Differences in the histories of these cultural meetings meant that the "race" of peoples encountered was variously understood. For instance, inhabitants of Persia, India, or Turkey were more easily seen by Europeans as in possession of a culture or history, while Native Americans were often seen as uncivilized.[4] European colonialism complicated the ways "race" was understood, and racial thinking developed and changed as a result of interrelation between ideologies of European superiority and colonial practices toward different kinds of outsiders.[5]

Clearly the colonial setting is important to our understanding of this play, but exactly what Fletcher is trying to tell his audience, or indeed which colonial spheres of operation he invokes in his representation, has been the subject of recent critical debate. According to the 1647 folio edition of Fletcher's works (printed by Humphrey Moseley) *The Island Princess* is set in "India," but the play itself refers more specifically to two islands, Ternata and Tidore, in the Bay of Bengal, which were better known as the Spice Islands at the time. This setting is extremely important since these islands had been at the center of a fierce colonial struggle for over a hundred years as Portugal, Holland, and to a lesser extent England had sought to control the valuable trade for rare spices.[6] Indeed Shankar Raman in an influential essay "Imaginary Islands: Staging the East" has argued that the ghostly presence of the English explorer and pirate/privateer Francis Drake—who arrived in the Portuguese-controlled Ternata on his circumnavigation of the globe on November 3, 1579—informs Fletcher's play.[7] Drake pretended to the Portuguese garrison that his voyage had been completed faster than any previous Portuguese expeditions, and then stole the trade from under his host's noses by negotiating a verbal agreement with the king of Ternata to traffic with England for spices. In the competition between the two Portuguese, Armusia and Ruy Dias, for the Princess Quisara, Raman detects textual traces of Drake. He argues that the bitter rivalry between Drake and the Portuguese for control of the islands is refigured when the brave newcomer Armusia (Drake) supercedes the garrison's commander Ruy Dias, "a near perfect representation of the real form taken by Portuguese authority in its India possessions: appointed master of the fort by the Portuguese king, he is a nobleman or *fidalgo* who bases his identity upon the honor of blood and social status."[8] According to this reading, then, Fletcher's play is an allegory of national competition between rival imperial, or aspiring imperial, powers.

But *The Island Princess* has also been seen as indebted to a different colonial context, the English experiences in Jamestown, owing to its depiction of the marriage between a Christian European and a native woman. Gordon McMullan suggests that John Rolfe's marriage to Pocahontas is "thoroughly rehearsed, though geographically transposed" as Fletcher's play "demonstrates through the metaphor of the native woman as object of desire the anxieties which seem characteristic of the colonial."[9] McMullan and Raman are united, then, in reading a play about Portuguese empire as a comment on English colonialism, though they suggest that the precise details of colonial context the play engages with vary. McMullan's analysis also usefully signals the central importance of gender to the play's racial politics. The rhetoric of colonial exploration in the Renaissance possessed a strongly gendered dynamic as new terrain is often described as a fertile female available for marriage with European male colonialists.[10] Certainly in the play's representation of Quisara as a desirable bride, we can see echoes of the kinds of descriptions commonplace in promotional colonial literature of the time. The aspiration to marry Quisara motivates her suitors' actions in the play. Even before the governor captures her brother, the opening scene describes how she is plagued by all the local nobles and kings as they compete for her hand in marriage ("all the neighbour Princes, are mad for her," 1.1.50). But it soon becomes clear that Quisara will not marry a native Spice Islander. These men are represented as unworthy of her; the king of Siana says little and is inactive in rescuing her brother, the king of Bakam says much but likewise fails to rescue him, and the governor of Ternata has kidnapped him in dastardly fashion. The play thus speedily establishes that her hand will be won by one of the Portuguese colonists, either Ruy Dias, who "stands in favour" with Quisara ("he is no Portugall else," 1.1.88–89), or the newly arrived Armusia, "a brave companion" and one that "dares fight any where" (1.1.121–23).

Fletcher's representation of Quisara is distinctly similar to colonial propaganda of the time, such as Samuel Purchas's descriptions of America in terms of a female body. Virginia, for instance, is represented to potential colonists as a virgin in need of husbandry:

> View her lovely looks (howsoever like a modest Virgin she is now vailed with wild Coverts and shadie Woods, expecting rather ravishment then marriage from her Native Savages) survey her Heavens, Elements, Situation; her divisions by armes of Bayes and Rivers into so

> goodly and well proportioned limmes and members; her Virgin portion nothing empaired, nay not yet improved, in Natures best Legacies; the neighbouring Regions and Seas so commodious and obsequious; [. . .] in all these you shall see, that she is worth the wooing and loves of the best Husband.[11]

This rhetoric establishes Virginia, like Quisara, as a prize to be won by the "best husband." Furthermore, the urgency of the project is emphasized since unless speedy action is undertaken by English colonists Virginia's sexual status may change. The language is designed to foster in colonial male readers a sense of chivalry normally associated with romance writing, since Virginia needs protection from rape by her indigenous inhabitants. "Virginia" will respond favorably to such chivalric protection and will be transformed into the bride every man wants—beautiful, rich, and subservient. Purchas, then, is arguing for Virginia's preference for a European husband to protect her from the advances of "Native Savages." In *The Island Princess* similar sentiments can be detected as Quisara's indigenous suitors are maligned, and she is described as a valuable prize or commodity to be won by her future (Portuguese) husband. Hence, when the Portuguese soldiers discuss her beauty it becomes clear that, for Pyniero at least, her good looks are indelibly associated with her royal status: "She is a Princesse, and she must be faire" (1.1.46). To Christopher's innocent question "Is she not faire then?," he cynically responds "But her hopes are fairer?" (1.1.51) The test that Quisara sets up to determine who shall marry her thus possesses a racial dynamic, since she expects that only a European will be able to perform the "brave thing" (1.2.57) she demands of her suitor, as white men "have a power beyond ours that preserves you" (1.2.60). Certainly Ruy Dias understands her in these terms since he describes any personal failure in terms of national identity: "When I grow so cold, and disgrace my nation, / that from their hardy nurses sucke adventures, / 'Twere fit I wore a Tombstone" (1.2.86–88).

These gendered descriptions of land did not operate solely in relation to Western colonization. The East Indies were also represented in terms of male sexual possession of female terrain. Purchas employed identical rhetorical tropes in his descriptions of the Dutch conquest of the English spice factory on the island of Banda in 1620, representing the attack in similar ways. Banda is "a rich and beautiful bride [who] was once envied to English arms, and seemeth by the cries on both sides, to have been lately ravished from her new husband, unwarned, unarmed, I know not whither by greater force or fraud."[12] The English traders are thus constructed sympathetically as grieving new husbands deprived of the caresses of their lawful wife. In *The Island Princess,* then, the colonial context is important in terms of the text's representations of human difference. Indigenous men are represented as inferior to their European counterparts and hence as a corollary of this, native women are imagined as sexual terrain to be conquered by European colonists. In other words, the opening of *The Island Princess* seeks to legitimize European men's access to indigenous women since they are superior to foolish, cowardly, or dastardly indigenous men. Fletcher's alteration of his source material, le Seigneur de Bellan's novel *L'Histoire de Ruis Dias, et de Quixaire, Princess des Moloques* (1615) and Bartolome Leonando de Argensola's *Conquista de las Islas Molucas* (1609), is relevant here. In de Bellan's text, the Portuguese suitors die and the hero is a young Tidorean aristocrat, Salama, who performs the roles allotted to Armusia in Fletcher's version (he also succeeds to the throne at the end of the novella). Salama's displacement by a European is significant, since it stresses the colonial and racial context of the events in the play.[13]

However, that Ruy Dias *does* fail to demonstrate any kind of "brave thing"—he prevaricates in the attempt to rescue Quisara's brother allowing Armusia to get there first—and also later plots Armusia's murder in dastardly fashion might complicate the distinction between Portuguese and native islander that the text originally set up. His nephew Pyniero views his uncle's behavior as rotten and diseased as he questions "to what scurvy things this love converts us? / What stinking things?" (3.1.92–93). Love is represented as causing Ruy Dias to behave without honor and this in turn results in a loss of Portuguese national identity. Pyniero's lines about "these Islanders" who are "false and desperate" "cruell, and crafty soules" (1.1.3–6), which opened the play, immediately established a hierarchy between honorable Portuguese and treacherous indigenous inhabitants. Thus when Dias repents his perfidious plan to have Armusia murdered, Pyniero sees it as a return, a "conversion" (4.2.57) to his former identity: "I am glad to see this mans conversion, / I was afraid honor had been bedrid, / Or beaten out o'th'Island" (4.2.57–59). The blurring of different identities is noticeable as "Island" identity is here yoked to a Portuguese colonist, Dias, because of his dishonorable conduct. Again it is island identity that is represented as without honor, as in Pyniero's view no native male islander could live up to European conceptions of gentlemanly conduct. In fact, noticeably, Pyniero does not refer to Dias as "Portuguese" in the passages in which he condemns him—his uncle has forfeited that right. Dias is referred to as Portuguese only at the beginning of the play ("he is no Portugall else" 1.1.88–89) and at its conclusion when he helps to unmask the governor. Once Dias becomes treacherous, Pyniero describes only Armusio as Portuguese, "an honest man, a brave man, / A valiant, and a virtuous man, my country-man" (3.1.226–27), whereas Dias tries to describe him as an alien "that Armusia, that new thing, that stranger" (4.2.43). What seems to be happening, then, in *The Island Princess* is that Fletcher, through Dias's treachery and abdication of Portuguese national identity, temporarily undermines the distinction set up at the play's outset between honorable Portuguese and underhand Islander. The distinction is reasserted fairly quickly when Dias's honor is reestablished, but the fact that the boundary between colonist and colonized broke down at all does suggest that this play is not completely confident of European superiority over native inhabitants.

Race and Religion

As has already been hinted through Pyniero's use of the word "conversion" in relation to changes in Dias's behavior, differences in religion are one of the key ways that *The Island Princess* distinguishes between human groups. The connection between "race" and "religion" in the early modern period was a complex one, something that is reflected by the attitudes to conversion and the exchange of religions in the play. The religious dynamic to conceptions of "race" emerged during the Crusades. These religious wars resulted in the settlement of some Christians in Muslim lands and lead, of course, to intermingling. However, as Loomba describes, "these cross-overs do not really erode religious difference" because religious hostility was the reason that the contact was originally established.[14] However, conversion—particularly of foreign women to Christianity—was an accepted part of Christian patriarchy from the Crusades onward as it was seen as one way of overpowering foes. Hence Quisara's conversion to Christianity in order to marry Armusia at the end of *The Island Princess* is an example of a literary staple as the beautiful infidel recognizes the errors of her religion and embraces Christianity: "I do embrace your faith sir, and your fortune" (5.2.121). It is also comically invoked in the romance between Pyniero and Panura, Quisara's waiting-woman: "*Panura,* / If thou wilt give me leave, Ile get thee with Christian, / The best way to convert thee" (5.4.13–15).

But, as with the text's doubts concerning European superiority over native inhabitants, Quisara's conversion is also represented in a subtly ambiguous manner. Her religious affiliation is consistently revealed to be subservient to her erotic desires. In the first act, she allows Ruy Dias to believe that she would be prepared to convert to Christianity in order to encourage him to undertake the love-test of rescuing her brother. Similarly, when in act 4, scene 2 the governor, in disguise as a Moorish priest, encourages Quisara to convert Armusia to Islam/Sun and Moon worship (the text implies both) as a condition of the marriage, he does so by appealing to her vanity concerning her beauty and the influence she believes it can exert on her suitors: "You are a Saint esteem'd here for your beauty, / And many a longing heart." (147–48): "Use it discreetly [. . .] fairely bring 'em home to our devotions, / Which will be blessed, and for which, you sainted" (153–66). The governor's repetition of the idea that Quisara's successful conversion of Armusia would accord her beatific status is designed to appeal to her sense of self-importance, and it is well aimed since Quisara is easily seduced by the notion that the Gods need her "helpe" (154) and the "miracle" that her "heavenly forme" must "worke" (160–61) on the Portuguese. It is status that Quisara seeks through religion rather than the possession of a stable faith, a fact that is soon revealed in *The Island Princess*. When Armusia expresses horror at the thought of conversion to her "devillish" religion (4.5.136), and she is in danger of losing her admirer, Quisara's faith collapses and she soon converts to Christianity. The audience is encouraged to have little faith in the integrity of her conversion since it soon becomes apparent that it is being used to provide yet another dramatic role for her, that of Virgin martyr: "Keepe on your way, a virgin will assist ye, / A virgin won by youre faire constancy, / And glorying that she is won so, will dye by ye" (5.2.105–10).

Though the tragedy of such martyrdom is avoided because the governor is unmasked and his machinations revealed, the cultural harmony that the prospective nuptials between Armusia and Quisara represent does not suggest a secure basis on which to build either a colony's or a nation's future. In the play, the Portuguese have triumphed only superficially, since the audience—aware of Quisara's vanity and autocratic behavior and Armusia's deep-seated hostility to her culture—can have small faith in a harmonious future for either their relationship or any dynastic and national alliances that are built upon it. Hence, when Quisara attempts to persuade Armusia to convert to her religion, his reaction is violent in the extreme:

> I hate and curse ye,
> Contemne your deities, spurne at their powers,
> And where I meet your maumet Gods, I'le swing 'em
> Thus o're my head, and kick 'em into puddles,
> Nay I will out of vengeance search your Temples,
> And with those hearts that serve my God, demolish
> Your shambles of wild worships. (4.5.112–18)

Under pressure, Armusia's knee-jerk reaction is to threaten violent vengeance and cultural annihilation. Furthermore, Quisara's apostasy is motivated solely by the strength of her erotic desires, which, given the superficiality of these feelings, hardly suggests that cultural harmony is secure. Quisara may assert that whichever way Armusia will go she "must follow necessary," sharing "One life, and one death" (5.5.41–42), and Armusia may apologize for his "rashnesse" to the king and the other indigenous rulers: "for I was agrie, / And out of that might utter some distemper, / Think not 'tis my nature" (5.5.72–75). Yet, in another crisis it is by no means clear that a peaceful understanding between colonizer and colonized would or could be maintained. Quisara, the island princess, as an unmarried woman/virgin territory/heir to a throne, is tempting bait for the Portuguese colonialists. But the audience is encouraged to see the "peace" that the king proclaims at the end of the play as more to be hoped for than certainly achieved, particularly as he himself remains only "half-converted" to Portuguese values.[15] In the relationship between colonizer and colonized there will be (potentially insuperable) barriers that put the dynastic and national alliance under severe strain. In other words, in Quisara's conversion, *The Island Princess* conforms to orthodox views of the superiority of the Christian religion over indigenous beliefs and practices. Indeed the precise nature of the Spice Islanders' religion appears of little concern. As previously described the governor of Ternata appears disguised as a "Moore Priest" (apparently a Muslim) (4.1 s.d.) and later as a worshiper of "the Sun and Moone" (4.5.70). This confusion may be indicative of the text's lack of interest in native practices, or it may represent a desire to undermine the standing and constancy of Moluccan religious beliefs. Hence the play seems rather uncertain over its prognosis for long-term religious harmony as continuing differences between the Portuguese and the Tidoreans mean that future conflict and misunderstanding must remain likely.

Color

The final section of this chapter focuses on the ways the racial marker of color is deployed in *The Island Princess*. In England, as Neill argues, the sixteenth-century dominant paradigm of human difference was cultural: dress, weapons, social organization, manners, custom, and religion were the key indicators in classifying otherness. This changed in the seventeenth century as increased trade and exploration resulted in greater contact with more sophisticated foreign cultures and definitions of alterity were refigured accordingly.[16] Instead of culture it is possible to see color becoming the dominant criteria for determining degrees of otherness as gradations of "phenotype" (observable characteristics determined by genotype and environment) begin to carry greater significance. At the turn of the century, the Dutch traveler Van Linschoten in *Iohn Huighen Van Linschoten His Discours of Voyages into ye Easte and West Indies* (1598) attempted to classify the differences between various Asian peoples. The people of Ormuz "are white like the Persians," those of Bengal "somewhat whiter than the Chingalas"; "The people of Aracan, Pegu and Sian are [. . .] much like those of China, onely one difference they have, which is, that they are somewhat whiter then the Bengalon, and somewhat browner then the men of China." In China itself, "Those that dwell on the Sea side [. . .] are a people of a *brownish* color, like the *white* Moores in Africa and Barabaria, and part of the Spaniards, but those that dwell within the land, *are for color like Netherlanders & high Dutches*." Yet "[t]here are many among them that are *cleane blacke*" while "[i]n the lande lying westward from China, they say there are white people, and the land called Cathaia, where (as it is thought) are many Christians."[17] Indeed, in the early decades of the seventeenth century there were competing understandings of human difference in terms of color.[18] Van Linschoten described complex taxonomic variations in hue between people—both non-European and, *crucially*, European—at the start of the seventeenth century. Yet, "[d]uring the first three decades of the seventeenth century, uncertainties about the nature of human difference are gradually flattened out in the literature of East Indian voyaging, as the people of the region begin to be categorized, according to the crudest distinction of color, as 'black'—a designation that serves solely to distinguish them from 'white' Europeans."[19] In other words, shared European "whiteness" was established as an identity distinct from that of people of varying hues of "blackness." As we shall see, *The Island Princess,* written in 1619, contains both these ideologies of race. In what follows I will concentrate on the ways in which these two competing ideologies of color—one about degrees of "blackness" and one about distinctions between "blackness" and "whiteness"—are important in establishing human difference in *The Island Princess*.

As already described, from the first Crusades onward the marriage of a *fair* infidel woman by a Christian man became a culturally accepted practice and one that was reflected in many literary texts. The woman's *fairness* is important here since, if the woman is white, or almost white, then "biological" ideas of race concerned with color difference, or phenotype, could be reduced or elided. In other words, as blackness was often associated with sin, rebellion, and the devil, the anxieties for white patriarchal culture about future offspring generated by miscegenation with foreign women could be allayed if the women concerned were almost white.[20] Thomas Cavendish's description of East Indians clearly possesses a gender dynamic as "although the men bee tawnie of color [. . .] yet their women be faire of complexion."[21] In *The Island Princess* Quisara's color is of signal concern to her European suitors. As previously described she is frequently represented as *fair* ("Is she not faire then?" 1.1.51), but the text then goes on to provide explanations for her whiteness. Christophero argues that "The very Sun I thinke, affects her sweetnesse, / And dares not as he does to all else, dye it / Into his tauny Livery" (1.1.60–62). In other words, Quisara's whiteness is a mark of her moral stature—"I hold her a compleate one" (1.1.59); "I guesse her stout and vertuous" (1.1.81)—which prevents the sun's tanning process. Furthermore, Quisara's whiteness is also linked to her class—her status as a princess—since it evades the servility associated with the wearing of a "Livery." But this positive reading of her whiteness is immediately undermined by the cynical Pyniero, who represents it as duplicitous since it is due to Quisara's unnatural and cowardly avoidance of the sun: "She dares not see him, / And keepes her selfe at distance from his kisses, / And weares her complexion in a case; let him but like it / A week or two, or three, she would looke like a Lion" (1.1.62–65). Likewise Pyniero refuses to believe in her honor, persistently representing her in sexual terms: it is the sun's "kisses" she refuses, and he represents the Governor's desires for her in graphic sexualized terms—"if he have the tricke [. . .] / To take her too, if he be but skil'd in bat-fowling, / And lime his bush right" (1.1.77–79). For Pyniero her honor is equated with her sexuality, and, like her whiteness, it is feigned and unnatural.

Gender and "race" are clearly linked here as Christophero argues that Quisara's whiteness reflects her sexual purity, whereas though Pyniero also sees her color in sexual terms, for him it is a mask, camouflaging a (literally) darker moral and physical reality: "Things of these natures have strange outsides *Pedro,* And cunning shadowes, set 'em far from us, / Draw 'em but neare, they are grosse, and they abuse us" (1.1.40–42). Pyniero's emphasis on her underlying blackness is reasserted later in the play when Quisara attempts to convert Armusia as he rages "Your painted sister I despise too" (4.5.135), and increasingly the Portuguese men align themselves against the polluted blackness and servility of the Spice Islanders. More insistently and with mounting frequency the Moluccans are described as "barbarous slaves" (5.1.19), "these Barbarians" (5.1.24), and "Devils" (5.1.34), as the Portuguese assert their own honorable European whiteness and national identity in contradistinction: "you are a Gentleman, / An honest man, and you dare love your Nation, / Dare stick to virtue though she be opprest, / And for her owne faire sake step to her Rescue" (5.1.59–62). But a rhetorical sleight of hand has been performed here, as it is the (female) Portuguese nation, not Quisara, that is now described as honorable and *faire*. Under pressure the Portuguese colonials start to invoke their superiority, and island inferiority, in terms of color, as fairness becomes solely associated with Europeans and blackness with islanders. The descriptions of Quisara's fairness are similar to the complexities of phenotype that Van Linschoten described, but Armusia's, Pyniero's, and the other Portuguese soldiers' descriptions of the islanders as black devils as opposed to their own white purity reveals at work the changing ways color was understood in this period as fairness becomes a contested term. Originally used to describe Quisara, as the play progresses it becomes a term used to signal Europeanness, and this change in deployment mirrors the larger change that Neill describes. Gradations of blackness were more frequently used by Europeans in contrast to their own shared whiteness. For instance, Purchas in 1613 used "European" to describe a shared color identity in opposition to other phenotypes when he compared "the tawney Moore, black negro, duskie Libyan, ash-colored Indian, oliue-colored American [. . .] with the whiter European."[22]

Fletcher's *The Island Princess* is an important cultural document as it reflects the complexities of early-seventeenth-century ideas about race. Overlapping markers of human difference are explored as the racial politics of the play engages with ideas of color, religion, colonialism, and gender. What this chapter reveals is the careful ambivalence of the play's racial politics in terms of religion, color, and colonialism. It is perfectly possible to read Fletcher's play as a celebration of "white" European colonial and Christian superiority over "black" idolatrous Spice Islanders. But as I have suggested, Fletcher's play is rather more complex, providing in each of these debates an alternative view that can be seen to question the merits of such an orthodox narrative. The "Portuguese" in the play are both Iberians and English, colonial rivals and simultaneously the bearers of English colonial ambition. On close inspection the cultural harmony apparently achieved at the end of the play between colonist and islander looks precarious. And the presence in the play of competing ideologies concerning the racial marker of color—the development of a taxonomy of "blackness" as both hue and an oppositional category to "whiteness"—mean that *The Island Princess*'s racial politics can be read in more than one way. The play is best seen, perhaps, as poised between contradictory positions as it can be equally read as a celebration of and a challenge to the superiority of the "white" Christian colonist.

NOTES

1. See Ania Loomba, *Shakespeare, Race and Colonialism* (Oxford: Oxford UP, 2002) 29–44.
2. See Loomba 2.
3. See John Fletcher, *The Island Princess, The Dramatic Works in the Beaumont and Fletcher Canon,* 10 vols., ed. George Walton Williams, gen. ed. Fredson Bowers (Cambridge: Cambridge UP, 1979) 5.539–651, esp. 552.
4. See Anthony Pagden, "Dispossessing the Barbarian: The Language of Spanish Thomism and the Debate over the Property Rights of the American Indians," *Theories of Empire 1450–1800,* ed. David Armitage (Aldershot: Ashgate, 1998) 79–98; and P. J. Marshall, "The English in Asia to 1700," *The Origins of Empire: British Overseas Enterprise to the Close of the Seventeenth Century,* ed. Nicholas Canny (Oxford: Oxford UP, 1998) 264–85.
5. See Loomba 39–44.
6. See Marshall 267–76; and Jerry Brotton, *Trading Territories: Mapping the Early Modern World* (London: Reaktion, 1997) 119–50.
7. See Shankar Raman, "Imaginary Islands: Staging the East," *Renaissance Drama* 26 (1995): 131–61.
8. See Raman 136.
9. See Gordon McMullan, *The Politics of Unease in the Plays of Beaumont and Fletcher* (Amherst: U of Massachusetts P, 1994) 224.
10. See Louis Montrose, "The Work of Gender in the Discourse of Discovery," *Representations* 33 (1991): 1–41; and Peter Hulme, *Colonial Encounters: Europe and the Native Caribbean* (London: Routledge, 1986) 159–60.
11. See Samuel Purchas, *Virginia's Verger; Or a Discourse Shewing the Benefits Which May Grow to This Kingdome from American English Plantations, and Specially Those of Virginia and Summer Ilands, Hakluytus Posthumus or Purchas His Pilgrimes,* 20 vols. (Glasgow: Maclehose, 1905–07) 19:242.
12. See Purchas 5.237; and Michael Neill, *Putting History to the Question: Power, Politics and Society in English Renaissance Drama* (New York: Columbia UP, 2000) 322–30.
13. See McMullan 224.
14. See Loomba 23.
15. See Andrew Hadfield, *Literature, Travel, and Colonial Writing in the English Renaissance 1545–1625* (Oxford: Clarendon P, 1998) 261–63; and Claire Jowitt, *Voyage Drama and Gender Politics 1589–1642* (Manchester: Manchester UP, 2002) 121–34.
16. See Michael Neill, "'Mulattos,' 'Blacks' and 'Indian Moors': Othello and Early Modern Constructions of Human Difference," *Shakespeare Quarterly* 49 (1998): 361–74, esp. 366–67.
17. See Neill, "'Mulattos'" 367.
18. Benjamin Braude, "The Sons of Noah and the Construction of Ethnic and Geographical Identities in the Medieval and Early Modern Periods," *William and Mary Quarterly* 54 (1997): 103–42.
19. See Neill, "'Mulattos'" 368.
20. See Dympna Callaghan, "Re-reading Elizabeth Cary's *The Tragedie of Mariam, Faire Queene of Jewry,*" *Women, Race and Writing in the Early Modern Period,* ed. Margo Hendricks and Patricia Parker (London: Routledge, 1994) 163–77, esp. 173–77.
21. See Purchas 2.181; and Neill, "'Mulattos'" 367.
22. See Neill, "'Mulattos'" 369; and Samuel Purchas, *Purchas His Pilgrimage or Relations of the World and the Religions Observed in All Ages* (London, 1613) 546.

READING LIST

Callaghan, Dympna. "Re-reading Elizabeth Cary's *The Tragedie of Mariam, Faire Queene of Jewry*." *Women, Race and Writing in the Early Modern Period.* Ed. Margo Hendricks and Patricia Parker. London: Routledge, 1994. 163–77.

Hadfield, Andrew. *Literature, Travel, and Colonial Writing in the English Renaissance 1545–1625.* Oxford: Clarendon P, 1998.

Hulme, Peter. *Colonial Encounters: Europe and the Native Caribbean.* London: Routledge, 1986.

Jowitt, Claire. *Voyage Drama and Gender Politics 1589–1642.* Manchester: Manchester UP, 2002.

Loomba, Ania. *Shakespeare, Race and Colonialism.* Oxford: Oxford UP, 2002.

McMullan, Gordon. *The Politics of Unease in the Plays of Beaumont and Fletcher.* Amherst: U of Massachusetts P, 1994.

Neill, Michael. "'Mulattos,' 'Blacks' and 'Indian Moors': Othello and Early Modern Constructions of Human Difference." *Shakespeare Quarterly* 49 (1998): 361–74.

Raman, Shankar. "Imaginary Islands: Staging the East." *Renaissance Drama* 26 (1995): 131–61.

26

The Changeling and Masters and Servants

Mark Thornton Burnett

In early modern England, service was a vital part of the contemporary economy. The majority of young people, of almost every social class, would have entered service at some stage, whether to serve as apprentices, domestic servants of the middling sort, or paid employees of the aristocracy. James Sharpe argues that, on the evidence of settlement papers, "perhaps 81 per cent of the laboring population had been in service at some time in their lives."[1] Given the importance of the institution, it is perhaps not surprising that the drama of the period engaged with and asked questions of relations between masters and servants, and Thomas Middleton and William Rowley's *The Changeling*[2] (1622) is no exception to this rule. The play concerns De Flores, the servant of Vermandero, an Alicant nobleman. Over the course of the play, he succeeds in seducing Beatrice Joanna, his master's daughter, wresting her from Alsemero, her husband. As this action unfolds, a number of other service-centered relations are affected, to the extent that the drama works most powerfully as an investigation of a mode of social organization in a state of acute disrepair. In particular, *The Changeling* privileges types of inversion as signs of the collapse of the institution, finding energy, as well, in discourses of carnival, the contemporary practice in which the lower orders were briefly allowed to take authority into their own hands. The play stands, finally, as a dramatization of a horrifying scenario—the abandonment by the servant of his role and his domination (and even reformation) of the society that has held him in thrall.

In moral and religious commentaries, at least, the early modern construction of material reality was that masters and servants occupied fixed places in the hierarchy, with their orderly relations functioning as salient indications of a healthy body politic. Over and over, the polemical literature of the time cultivated the duties of servants and stressed their ideal virtues. Wrote John Dod and Robert Cleaver in 1598: servants should "chearefully, and willingly, performe the labours and workes, that their maisters, and mistresses, or dames, shall command them" and should be "faithfull in things comitted to them [. . .] carefull to obserue the vprightnesse of manners."[3] Above all, the servant was expected to be obedient and to subordinate a sense of self to the superiority of the employing class. As Thomas Fosset wrote in 1613, the servant must "wholly [. . .] reseigne himselfe to the will of his Master, and this is to obey [. . .] [servants] must be obedient at a worde, at a call, and at a becke."[4] Briefly, *The Changeling* does acknowledge the pervasive influence of these and similar structures of authority, as when Beatrice Joanna informs Alsemero that "there's one above me, sir" (1.1.82): her statement, referring, as it does, to her father, encapsulates not only an idea of paternal discipline but also the concept that individuals are bound in highly organized and strictly gradated arrangements.

More often than not, however, *The Changeling* chooses not to honor such idealized notions, since servants are rarely envisioned in static capacities; rather, they are seen as mobile and inconsistent, and their roles fail to connote authentically proper behavior. Crucially, De Flores is par excellence the servant who is ultimately unfaithful and disobedient, so that service itself is unmoored from its traditional meanings. It comes to signify, for instance, social exploitation and sexual perversion more than it does honest dependency. Preparing for Beatrice Joanna's nuptials, Alibius, the doctor, describes the celebratory masque he has organized as a "wild, distracted measure [. . .] out of form and figure, breaking time's head" (3.4.264–65), and, in many ways, his summation operates as an apt representation of the state of service in the play—out-of-time, impassioned, disorderly, deformed, and antithetical to ideological norms. Already at the start some of these deviations are hinted at when Jasperino reflects upon Alsemero's predilection for "weigh[ing] the anchor" (1.1.31) and "hoist[ing] sails" (1.1.32) with his servants: the lines communicate a blurring of the demarcated responsibilities of master and servant and a potential breakdown of the framework that kept the two distinct. Emerging from the suggestion is a further social possibility—the compromising of authority itself. This is confirmed in the scene in which Alsemero, reflecting upon De Flores's inattendance, remarks: "He's out of his place" (1.1.135). Ostensibly, the comment insinuates that De Flores is insufficiently devoted to his actual master, Vermandero, but the subsidiary connotation is that the servant is shifting, self-interested, and placeless and that, in these capacities, he destabilizes the system that maintains his subjection. Indeed, *The Changeling* as a whole discovers De Flores working in precisely such a manner; in so doing, he becomes a dramatic embodiment of what was most feared by contemporary moralists. Thomas Fosset wrote in 1613 that *"when a seruant raigneth [. . .] despiseth his maisters gouernment, and followeth his owne will [. . .] it is a thing so disorderly, that maketh the earth to be mooued, the whole house, yea somtimes the whole [. . .] city to be disquieted"* (A4^r), and he was joined in 1627 by Thomas Carter, who stated: "often times one leawd seruant spoyles a whole family."[5] Because De Flores is possessed of an agency that infects the collective, and because he is constructed as posing a threat to the coherence and integrity of his community, the servant's significance resides not simply in his fractured relation with his employers; it simultaneously hinges upon his conduct's wider social and cultural reverberations.

A dominant characteristic of De Flores being "out of his place" is inversion, which, as *The Changeling* develops, is formulated into a central motif. The first scene harbors suggestions about the reversals in status that the rest of the play goes on to anatomize. In a powerful statement about the sexual desire that he entertains, De Flores fantasizes about the gloves that Beatrice Joanna has cast upon the ground: "She had rather wear my pelt tanned in a pair / Of dancing pumps than I should thrust my fingers / Into her sockets here" (1.1.230–232). A. A. Bromham and Zara Bruzzi write that Beatrice Joanna's "throwing down" of the "glove is a [. . .] gesture of challenge"[6] while Anthony B. Dawson argues that De Flores's retrieval of the glove represents a "sign of his [. . .] penetration of her virginity."[7] Certainly, both social and sexual meanings are encoded here; however, a closer look at the exchange reveals more nuanced suggestions. At once the metaphorical act of cross-dressing (the implication is that Beatrice Joanna and De Flores will assume each other's clothes) entails the prospect of a transgression of the sumptuary laws, the regulations whereby individuals were expected to observe codes of dress befitting their positions. Such a confrontation with contemporary prescriptions hints at the likelihood of gendered inversions and a switch in, or leveling of, class locations. Not only will De Flores become a quasi-transvestite (a partly dressed woman); he will simultaneously be transformed into a social anomaly (elevated and made equal at one and the same time). Moreover, fluctuating roles here mirror later instabilities. "Would creation [. . .] Had formed me man" (2.2.107–08), exclaims Beatrice Joanna in a subsequent reflection, her sentiment having already been prepared for via De Flores's allusion to his "dancing pumps." The unholy union between the two protagonists (which is quickly elaborated as inevitable) involves both of them changing place at a number of metaphorical levels.

Inversion in *The Changeling* goes hand-in-hand with broader expressions of the "carnivalesque." Taking place on holiday occasions and characterized by rituals in which the lower orders usurped traditional roles, "carnival" took a variety of forms in the early modern period in England. Usually subordinated youth groups could play important parts, such as over the twelve days of Christmas, when town and church corporations appointed a "lord of misrule," sometimes from the ranks of local servants, and sponsored the provision of meals for children as part of the so-called feast of fools. Inversion, gender reversal, and cross-dressing were familiar practices: at Hocktide, for instance, women were permitted to bind the men of the parish, only releasing them for a fee, while men disguised themselves as Maid Marian during the annual May games. In these and similar activities, gender demarcations were playfully upset, and tensions and anxieties freely ventilated. On occasions, such festive departures from quotidian realities assumed punitive dimensions: known in England as the "riding" or the "skimmington," the "charivari" involved cacophonous music and demonstrations against moral transgressors. The object of a community's mockery, normally a husband who had been humiliated or cuckolded by his wife, was obliged to ride backward on an ass as part of his punishment. Common to all expressions of "carnival" or folk humor were, in the terminology of Mikhail Bakhtin,[8] the "classic canon" (a single physical form that is closed, complete, and elevated), "grotesque realism" (lower bodily strata associated with reproduction, degradation, eating, and dismemberment), and "billingsgate" (vulgarized language and popular scurrility).

It should already be clear that *The Changeling* derives much of its imaginative impetus from "carnival" and "carnivalesque" energies. But the play goes deeper than mere rehearsals of these phenomena, deploying "carnival" as an interpretive modality with which to understand master and servant infractions. Before De Flores and Beatrice Joanna begin their relationship, their positions in the Alicant hierarchy are elaborated in some detail. Elevation and rectitude mark Beatrice Joanna at the start: she boasts about her "Virginity" (1.1.192), treats De Flores contemptuously, and scolds him for his neglect of social proprieties. By contrast, De Flores's lowly status is registered in the demeaning language with which he is invariably associated. He is, for instance, tied to "troughs," "deformity," and the "slimy and dishonest eye" (2.1.43, 45). To recall Bakhtin, social hierarchies in the play are read through the "classical" body, "grotesque" lower bodily strata, and "billingsgate" abuse. Once their relationship has commenced, however, and their roles threaten to become inverted, Beatrice Joanna and De Flores's language undergoes one of several transformations. It is as if their words as well as their roles are exchanged. The loss of her virginity means that Beatrice Joanna can no longer maintain her "classical" pretensions, and a reduction to the "grotesque" is implied when she alludes to the "common sewer" that has robbed her of "distinction" (5.3.153). As Beatrice Joanna begins to slip in the hierarchy, De Flores advances. It is perhaps not coincidental that Beatrice Joanna promises to make the increasingly commanding servant "master / Of all the wealth" (3.4.155–56) in her treasury.

"Carnivalesque" inversion, in fact, is not so much a characteristic of De Flores's conduct in the play as the strategy he exploits in his drive to secure dominion. At different points, De Flores compares his situation to that of an "ass" (2.1.77) and his features to those of a "swine" (2.1.43), and the associations that gather about these totemic creatures recall the importance of animals not only to inversive processional rituals but also to festivity in general. Peter Stallybrass and Allon White, for instance, understand the "symbolic importance" of the pig in terms of "carnival [. . .] 'low discourses,' the body and the fair."[9] The effect of these references is to suggest that De Flores is the animal victim of a court system that would punish him for his transgressions. This is further confirmed when, in an echo of the bull-baiting spectacles that marked church ales, De Flores sees himself as a "Garden-bull" that takes "breath to be lugged again" (2.1.80–81). But it becomes increasingly obvious that animals in the play have subtler symbolic functions. They betoken not so much the servant's powerlessness as his imagined appropriation of inversive forms to secure his own ends. A later allusion to the "stag's fall" and the "keeper who has his fees" (3.4.39–40) implies that, even as he is being envisaged as a minor employee, De Flores will cuckold Alsemero (the animal will yield place to a more powerful human overseer), and it is precisely such a scenario that is borne out by the succeeding narrative. The central stages of the play map Beatrice Joanna's infidelities and De Flores's growing sexual influence. Once secure in the inversion that he has devised for himself, De Flores can, with the confidence of a "charivari" crowd, humiliate Alsemero in public, as his boast to the court suggests: "I coupled with your mate [. . .] her honor's prize / Was my reward, I thank life for nothing / But that pleasure" (5.3.162, 168–70). As well as assuming a master's prerogatives through his inversions, De Flores manages to replace Beatrice Joanna's husband in his mistress's affections.

An essential accompaniment of the celebratory impulse was social critique. Inversion, in particular, could open spaces within which social abuses and government policy were questioned, such as during periodic deforestation and enclosure riots, when male leaders dressed as "Lady Skimmington" in order to highlight the perceived malfeasance of local landlords and infringements of public property rights. (The impersonation of alternative identities seems to have encouraged the articulation of outspoken opinions.) By the same token, growing out of De Flores's inversive actions in *The Changeling* is a critical assessment of the differences inherent in the categories of master and servant. In showing up difficulties in the ruling elite and dangerous possibilities in De Flores's role, the play undoes the distinctions that normalize service-centered mentalities and institutions. One aspect of the play's assessment is its representation of the limitations of mastery. Changeableness, prevarication, incomprehension, hypocrisy, and self-justification mark the elite, communicated neatly in Alsemero's recollection of his first sight of Beatrice Joanna: "'Twas in the temple where I first beheld her, / And now again the same. What omen yet / Follows of that? [. . .] The place is holy, so is my intent" (1.1.1–3, 5). Beyond Alsemero's vacillating efforts to justify his emotions lie suggestions about the fallibilities of the aristocratic order and an inability to distinguish between immediate impressions and material realities. If the aristocratic order is vulnerable, then it is in its most obvious manifestation, the castle, that these suggestions receive their clearest statement. Vermandero argues that he is loath to show "our chief strengths to strangers: our citadels / Are placed conspicuous to outward view / On promonts' tops, but within are secrets" (1.1.162–64), which points to a fear that his defenses are susceptible to leakage and exposure. At any moment, it seems, the stronghold may be penetrated, revealing the inadequacy of its claims to impregnability. Traditionally, of course, one of the prime responsibilities of the servant was to guard and maintain the master's secrets. The idea was rehearsed in a 1573 compendium of advice by Isabella Whitney directed at servants themselves: "See that you secrets seale,"[10] she recommended. But De Flores acts in such a manner as to betray the secrets with which he has been entrusted, becoming, in the process, an antitype of the perfect dependant. His knowing exploitation of chinks in the armor of the upper echelons exposes flaws and weaknesses and, by extension, gaps and inconsistencies in the dominant order's representational stratagems. The master class, as *The Changeling* imagines it, is by no means the ideal preserve of confident sensibility or stable authority.

More generally, mastery in *The Changeling* is seen to be remiss in that the employing classes are frequently associated with derelictions in traditional responsibilities. William Basse wrote in 1602 that "serving-men" had come to be "slightly reckoned,"[11] and his remark is arrestingly realized in *The Changeling*'s investigation of master and servant relations. For example, the parallels drawn between De Flores and beasts may connote "carnival," but they simultaneously register an economy in which the servant is reified into a creature of burden and perceived as a diverting spectacle. His body and labor are constructed as expendable, to the extent that there are no compunctions in imagining his being "discarded" (2.1.93); here, as elsewhere, the suggestion is that De Flores is not so much an individuated personality as an anonymous, unwanted object. The theme of abuse continues into De Flores's reaction to Beatrice-Joanna's attempt to offer him money for the murder of Alonzo. "Do you place me in the rank of verminous fellows, / To destroy things for wages?" (3.4.64–65), he asks, going on to distinguish himself from what he terms a "journeyman in murder" (3.4.69). Illustrated in abundance at this point is De Flores's conviction that he cannot be treated simply as a economic instrument, as a "thing" that is bought and sold; indeed, in a prickly appraisal of his own abilities, the servant concludes by implicitly describing himself as a fully fledged "master" in murder and not a senior "apprentice" who is still at the stage of learning a trade. By representing himself via other types of servant, De Flores speaks out against an ideology that understands service only at the level of market values and that fails to move beyond a demeaning cash transaction. According to *The Changeling*'s most outspoken servant representative, then, qualities of compunction and compassion among the dominant order are singularly lacking; even when Beatrice Joanna offers to cure De Flores's afflicted complexion, it is in a parody of the ministering mistress. "I'll make a water for you shall cleanse this / Within a fortnight" (2.2.83–84), she pledges, but her promise clearly emerges as a transparent means to a self-centered end. In this sense, Beatrice Joanna is envisaged as the satirized obverse of a caring employer; she is, in fact, more akin to the failing heads of household described by Dod and Cleaver in 1598 who treat servants not as "men [but] beasts" and who "as Tyrants [. . .] vse their seruants as their horses or Asses" (371–72). *The Changeling* provides no straightforward perspective on master and servant relations, for, in the same moment that the play discovers servants moving "out of [. . .] place," so does it trace a measure of accountability to the failings of an inadequate mastery.

Complicating the vision of mastery still further is the suggestion that the female servant is no less maltreated than her male counterpart. The ideal "maidseruant," wrote Robert Hill in 1610, must be "Carefull [. . .] Faithfull [. . .] Patient [. . .] Neate [. . .] Chearefull [. . .] Cleanly [. . .] Quicke [. . .] Honest [. . .] Skilfull. And last of all Dumbe."[12] Clearly, Diaphanta, the speaking, appetitive, and sexualized maidservant of Beatrice Joanna, does not answer to these requirements. It would be a mistake, however, to endorse Lisa Jardine's view that Diaphanta is characterized merely by a "state of uncontrolled foolishness."[13] Rather, what the play makes clear is that the maidservant is manufactured as an antitype by an erring mastery and, in particular, by masculinist assumptions. "Used" in comparable ways to De Flores, Diaphanta functions to illuminate the gendered dimensions of servant abuse and to point up the contrasting sorts of power to which male and female employees can aspire. At the start, Diaphanta is immediately described by Jasperino as a "vessel" (1.1.89). "I'll board her. If she be lawful prize, down goes her top-sail" (1.1.89–91), he observes. The language is resonant, since it connotes both objectification and a social attachment that legitimizes sexual confrontation. We are transported to mercantile territory in Jasperino's comments and alerted to the imminence of a conquest that is associated with piratical capture. Divestiture and submission consort in a multifaceted image of a "vessel" that will be filled in order to be owned and appropriated. On a later occasion, Diaphanta is linked to other serving-women described as "ladies' cabinets" (2.2.6). Once again, the idea is of the woman as a receptacle, as a locked-up object that can only be unlocked (made sexually open) via male intervention. But male perspectives do not remain constant; as befits a play in which social constructions and gendered arrangements are turned upside-down, the views of one constituency are elaborated and extended by another. It is an index of Beatrice Joanna's continuing impercipience, and of the institutional dislocations that she has in part precipitated, for instance, that she, too, is assured of Diaphanta's fallibility: "Seeing that wench now / A trick comes into my mind; 'tis a nice piece / Gold cannot purchase" (4.1.52–54), the mistress states. The recurrence of the equation between class affiliation and bodily availability suggests that, in the wake of other master–servant relations facing collapse, gendered hierarchies are just as affected, with Beatrice Joanna no longer able to preserve the appearance of a "modest" woman. Instead, she must assume the part of a man and speak through a masculine register. Moreover, it is when Beatrice Joanna's dismissive attitude toward Diaphanta is at its height that the parallels between the maidservant and De Flores come into their own. Commenting upon Diaphanta's assignation with Alsemero, Beatrice Joanna states: "This strumpet serves her own ends, 'tis apparent now, / Devours the pleasure with a greedy appetite, / And never minds my honor or my peace, / Makes havoc of my right. But she pays dearly for't" (5.1.2–5). In an echo of earlier inversions, the passage stresses the assumption of power by the maidservant: she is constructed as paying for her pleasure rather than being paid, and serving herself rather than others. There is a usurpation of "place" here, and a claim to "right"; however, since Beatrice Joanna has herself compromised these concepts and principles, the mistress's objections to her servant's transgressions take on an ironic cast. Ultimately, Diaphanta's fateful tryst with Alsemero (substituting for her mistress, the maidservant perishes in a fire that has been purposefully started to forestall the revelation of her dangerous knowledge) is counterpointed with De Flores's empowered alliance with Beatrice Joanna. Whereas the female servant is destroyed by the apocalyptic conflagration, the male servant emerges triumphant, an indication of a ruling system that both belittles on the basis of gender and seeks to reduce in the name of convention and propriety.

If mastery is interrogated and robbed of its contemporary allure, then service in *The Changeling,* by contrast, despite a tendency toward repression, is associated with emancipation and opportunity. Juxtaposed alongside the closed conditions of aristocratic Alicant, De Flores enjoys clear-sightedness and freedom of movement. His illegitimate impulses are particularly unsettling since they unfold within the framework of legitimate conduct; as De Flores states: "Some twenty times a day [. . .] Do I force errands [. . .] and excuses / To come into her [Beatrice Joanna's] sight" (2.1.29–31). James C. Scott argues that subaltern groups traditionally resisted the hegemony of their social superiors through "hidden transcripts," such as disguise, deception, indirection, and performative deference, which tested and exploited "all the loopholes, ambiguities, silences and lapses" available in "official" languages and behaviors.[14] De Flores, as the play understands him, is the arch exponent of the "hidden transcript," and nowhere more obviously than at the level of speech. He profits from the practical features of his office to say more than would usually be permissible and recognizes that his role as messenger can be linguistically utilized to his own advantage. The "words" of servants should, according to William Gouge in 1622, "be few, no more then must needs, euen when they haue occasion to speake";[15] De Flores, however, contravenes the recommendation, indulging in "unnecessary blabbing" (1.1.97), reveling in "dallying, trifling torment" (2.1.65), and parodically rehearsing irrelevant lists of titles. In so doing, he not only fills his linguistic space; he also stakes a claim to controlling the temporal economy. The net result is that the servant is linguistically empowered: placed in the self-elected role of a father confessor to Beatrice Joanna, De Flores is enabled to speak as a member of the master class and to leave behind the humility of earlier deliveries. Thus, when De Flores disposes of Alonzo's body in a hidden chamber, he states: "This vault serves to good use" (3.2.20). The vocables enlisted—"serve" and "use"—testify to the distance De Flores has traveled from his position as a domestic and point up the fact that he now conceives of himself through the expressions of his betters. A later speech crystallizes the transformation. Commenting upon waiting-women, De Flores is notably dismissive: " 'Push, they are termagents, / Especially when they fall upon their masters / And have their ladies' first-fruits; th'are mad whelps, / You cannot stave 'em off from game royal" (5.1.16–19). At once the reflection illuminates gendered gradations of degree among servants, with De Flores openly inserting the male servant into a superior category to the female servant. Because female servants are constructed as appetitively sexualized, the implicit assumption is that the male servant is free from such a taint. (Of course, the irony of the passage is that De Flores, too, sexually preys upon his employer). But there is the subsidiary suggestion that De Flores, having secured a new social dispensation, can manipulate a grammar of class from which he was previously excluded. Like a master, De Flores reifies the female dependant body, wields a familiar discourse of animalism, accepts unquestioningly an erring servant accountability, and locates his own lust elsewhere. Thanks to the "hidden transcript," De Flores accedes to a rhetorical method and an ideological persuasion entirely out-of-keeping with his nominated social identity.

In playing a commanding part in relation to language, De Flores also, it is implied, assumes a dominant influence over the narrative. That is, the servant is imaged as simultaneously in control of events and capable of determining actions still to come. In this sense, De Flores, in common with other servants in *The Changeling,* is visited with predictive functions and seen in quasi-supernatural terms as an eerily prescient presence. Already in the first scene such a species of empowerment is alluded to: reflecting upon Alsemero's changeable attitude, a nameless servant states: "We must not to sea today; this smoke will bring forth fire!" (1.1.50–51). It is a seemingly innocuous observation, yet, in the context of the play as a whole, it singles a servant out as uniquely prophetic, as guided by an authoritative and anticipatory wisdom. The idea is elaborated in De Flores, for he emerges not only as a voice of destiny but also, more arrestingly, as destiny itself. "[D]anger or ill luck [hangs] in my looks" (2.1.36), he exclaims, his comment forcefully functioning as a indication of the servant's fateful status. What is discovered at the level of De Flores's own fantasy of himself is taken up in Beatrice Joanna's conception of his preternatural dimensions. "[U]pon yon meteor / Ever hung my fate" (5.3.154–55), she states, gesturing to De Flores, echoing the language he earlier deployed and conjuring an uncanny, predetermined twinship. Of course, in the belief systems of early modern England, it was the master class rather than the servant fraternity that ideally commanded the unfolding course of events. In a variation of its representation of De Flores's relation to time, *The Changeling* plays fast and loose with contemporary expectations about service and figures a servant who simultaneously manipulates the temporal economy and incarnates the future forms of his world's operations.

Even as the categories of master and servant, and the structures of mastery and servitude, are being interrogated, so does the drama allude to the points of contact that bring them into unexpected conjunctions. The play's critique of the artificial divisions that separate masters and servants gains in intensity since it is conducted through De Flores, a servant whose status is ultimately ambiguous. De Flores is no stereotypical subversive. Instead, as Beatrice Joanna's assessment of him establishes, "he's a gentleman / In good respect with my father, and follows him" (1.1.133–34). (Lacking an inheritance, the younger sons of the gentry and aristocracy often entered service or trade in the period). One of the notable features of *The Changeling* is that the aristocratic world is not invaded from below or from without: it is penetrated from the inside. The ascription of gentility to De Flores has several implications. First, it establishes that the play goes beyond a simple conflict involving different class groupings; rather, the action focuses upon an insidious struggle between members of a similar social constituency who have roughly equivalent credentials. Second, it works to question the category of "gentleman," showing it up as multivalent. As De Flores himself argues in an exchange with Beatrice Joanna, "birth" (3.4.134) is not a reliable criterion, since, psychologically and behaviorly, the two of them are "equal" (3.4.133). In the same way that the play dismantles the conventions that dictate master and servant relations, then, so does it suggest that gentility, too, is an imperfect guarantee either of social standing or ideal behavior.

In the central stages of *The Changeling,* these interrogations are hinted at in the inversions that form so integral a part of De Flores's actions. But inversions themselves are dependent upon a complex of related factors and are sometimes achieved only through discussion and argument. In fact, inversion is one result of negotiation, and it would seem to be scenes involving the practice of negotiation that dominate the play most completely. In this respect, *The Changeling* takes energy from its contexts and finds an animating rationale in contemporary "carnivalesque" expressions that combined petitioning with festivity. Most obviously, it is De Flores's role as a negotiator upon which the play concentrates. At first, Beatrice Joanna assumes that De Flores will dispatch Alonso, her fiancé, unquestioningly, establishing himself as the obedient agent of her "employment" (2.2.94). What ensues, however, is the precise opposite—a pattern of petitions that De Flores inaugurates in order to "sue" for his mistress' "service" (2.2.117, 120). (The term, like so many others in this play, bristles with doubled social and sexual connotations). As a result, it dawns upon Beatrice Joanna that services are never rendered without a corresponding demand for payment, and, by the time Alonzo has been murdered, autocratic commands have given way to bargain-oriented exchanges—to a "process of reaction and counter-reaction" that, in Joost Daalder and Antony Telford Moore's words, demonstrate the extent to which the characters are "instrinsically joined."[16] These exchanges are initiated when De Flores shows his mistress the severed finger of her fiancé, still bearing its jewel. The move places Beatrice Joanna first in her servant's debt (she makes the fatal mistake warned against by Dod and Cleaver in 1598 and allows herself to become "too familiar with [. . .] seruants" who then "vnreuerently and vnmannerly [. . .] behaue themselues towards her" [384]) and later in his power. In a rejection of the "three thousand golden florins" (3.4.61) that Beatrice Joanna offers, De Flores threatens to abandon petitioning if his kisses are refused: "I will not stay so long to beg 'em shortly" (3.4.93), he states. The servant is now able to claim the full benefits of his mastery—"The last is not yet paid for" (3.4.106)—as he drives Beatrice Joanna to acknowledge their mutual responsibilities for the murders and joint status: "You must forget your parentage to me" (3.4.136). Distinctions of blood dissolve with this climactic declaration, and, in the act of kneeling (3.4.155), which amounts to a climactic moment of social leveling, Beatrice Joanna becomes the play's final petitioner and offers her most prized possession—the body of the aristocrat. No longer can it be assumed that lineage and rank ensure the servant's subjection.

The Changeling arguably assumes its most radical stance in relation to masters and servants by suggesting that De Flores can achieve power, not in acts of open revolt, but through a gradual and persistent weakening of aristocratic defenses. In this endeavor, negotiation becomes a vital weapon in his arsenal. It is difficult to see a match between a negotiation model and the play's final stages, however. Bent upon securing Beatrice Joanna for his own use, De Flores employs negotiation as a tactic, but the results hardly resemble a negotiated settlement—the servant has reduced the mistress to a form of sexual enslavement. Crucially, Beatrice Joanna is robbed of any sense of an individuated identity, since the terms she deploys in her self-descriptions hark back to those first enlisted by De Flores. This suggests that, when she appears on stage, with her body bearing, in Deborah G. Burks's formulation, "visible signs of [the servant's] violation,"[17] Beatrice Joanna functions as no more than echo of, or cipher for, the servant who is her master. But if, in the last scene, it seems as if society is in tatters, the characters are also pressed to own that it has undergone some productive transformations, highlighting the dependency of the aristocracy on those it would ostensibly dominate. De Flores might be a subversive, yet he is equally a force for the reassertion of order. Subversion, according to the play's paradoxical logic, promotes progress. The ramifications of the servant's relationship with Beatrice Joanna mean that Tomazo, Alonzo's brother, no longer requires revenge; that Antonio and Francisco, disguised in the madhouse, confess their follies; and that Alsemero speaks with a degree of insight absent from his early utterances. "Man and sorrow at the grave must part" (5.3.219), he states, assuming a new tone of confident authority. Ultimately, De Flores acts in such a way as to strip a pervasive blindness and to propel Alicant into a psychologically revitalized phase of its development. The social order has a servant to thank for its reformation.

Conjuring throughout with the types of master and servant delineated in conduct literature, *The Changeling* demonstrates its hankering for an idealized form of institutionalized relations. Even as it yearns for these "perfect" representatives, however, the play is pressed to acknowledge their impossible unavailability. For *The Changeling,* in many respects, adopts a demythologizing strategy, exploring the scenario the moralist wanted to repress and showing up both virtuous masters and servants as untenable projections. The institution of service, the play argues, cannot be supported by idealism alone, since master and servant are forever blurring into each other. Such a process suggests not only the inherent instability of these categories as organizational units but also the ways in which related institutional structures—including class and gender—are adversely affected by master–servant conflict. With idealism exposed as unworkable, the anxieties and fissures that underlie the world of *The Changeling* become abundantly apparent. In particular, the play uncovers pervasive concerns about dependency, the integrity of the status quo, and the fixity of hierarchical schemes. Through De Flores's mobilization of "hidden transcripts," and through his experience of mastery, fault lines in the fabric of authority are revealed, in such a way as to suggest that, in its deepest interstices, *The Changeling* is preoccupied with larger crises in service (such as falling rates of employment, newly disparaging attitudes, and alarming changes in the social complexion of the institution) that were overtaking early modern English society. *The Changeling* institutes a variety of solutions to these perceived crises, and even its investment in inversion and "carnival" might be seen as an attempt to arrive at a totalizing interpretive modality. Yet, by the close, the play is forced to admit that there can be no conclusive return to an unaffected social order. Instead, an audience is left with contradictory impressions, which invite us to reflect upon the locations of power, the political dimensions of misrule, and the potential for a servant to petition for a willful assertion of the self, thereby making an indelible mark, and claiming an unprecedented voice, in the historical process.

NOTES

1. See James Sharpe, *Early Modern England: A Social History 1550–1760,* 2nd ed. (London: Arnold, 1997) 218.
2. See Thomas Middleton and William Rowley, *The Changeling,* ed. Joost Daalder (London: Black, 1990). All quotations from the play reference this text.

3. See John Dod and Robert Cleaver, *A Godly Form of Householde Gouernement* (London, 1598) 385–86.
4. See Thomas Fosset, *The Servants Dutie* (London, 1613) 22.
5. See Thomas Carter, *Carters Christian Common Wealth* (London, 1627) 206.
6. See A. A. Bromham and Zara Bruzzi, *"The Changeling" and the Years of Crisis, 1619–1624* (London: Pinter, 1990) 29.
7. Anthony B. Dawson, "Giving the Finger: Puns and Transgression in *The Changeling,*" *The Elizabethan Theatre XII,* ed. A. L. Magnusson and C. E. McGee (Toronto: Meany, 1993) 93–112, esp. 99.
8. See Mikhail Bakhtin, *Rabelais and His World,* trans. Hélène Iswolsky (Cambridge: MIT P, 1968) 5, 19, 320.
9. See Peter Stallybrass and Allon White, *The Politics and Poetics of Transgression* (London: Methuen, 1986) 44.
10. See Isabella Whitney, *A Sweet Nosgay, or a Pleasant Posye* (London, 1573) Cviii^{v}.
11. See William Basse, *Sword and Buckler* (1602), *The Poetical Works of William Basse (1602–1653),* ed. R. Warwick Bond (London: Ellis and Elvey, 1893) 3–29, esp. 5.
12. See Robert Hill, *Christs Prayer Expounded* (London, 1610) 181.
13. See Lisa Jardine, *Reading Shakespeare Historically* (London: Routledge, 1996) 124.
14. See James C. Scott, *Domination and the Arts of Resistance: Hidden Transcripts* (New Haven: Yale UP, 1990) xii, 138.
15. See William Gouge, *Of Domesticall Duties* (London, 1622) 598.
16. See Joost Daalder and Antony Telford Moore, "'There's Scarce a Thing but Is Both Loved and Loathed': *The Changeling,*" *English Studies* 80 (1999): 499–508, esp. 501.
17. See Deborah G. Burks, "'I'll Want My Will Else': *The Changeling* and Women's Complicity with Their Rapists," *ELH* 62 (1995): 759–90, esp. 781.

READING LIST

Bromham, A. A., and Zara Bruzzi. *"The Changeling" and the Years of Crisis, 1619–1624.* London: Pinter, 1990.

Burks, Deborah G. "'I'll Want My Will Else': *The Changeling* and Women's Complicity with Their Rapists." *ELH* 62 (1995): 759–90.

Burnett, Mark Thornton. *Masters and Servants in English Renaissance Drama and Culture: Authority and Obedience.* Basingstoke: Macmillan, 1997.

Daalder, Joost, and Antony Telford Moore. "'There's Scarce a Thing but Is Both Loved and Loathed': *The Changeling.*" *English Studies* 80 (1999): 499–508.

Dawson, Anthony B. "Giving the Finger: Puns and Transgression in *The Changeling.*" *The Elizabethan Theatre XII.* Ed. A. L. Magnusson and C. E. McGee. Toronto: Meany, 1993. 93–112.

Jardine, Lisa. *Reading Shakespeare Historically.* London: Routledge, 1996.

27

'Tis Pity She's a Whore and Incest

Richard A. McCabe

The opening words of John Ford's *'Tis Pity She's a Whore,* "Dispute no more in this," serve to remind us that the play is concerned not so much with incest per se as with the social, moral, and political issues associated with it. By mounting an intellectual defense of incest the hero, Giovanni, has thrown down the gauntlet to received opinion and ultimately, as the friar recognises, to faith itself:

> for know, young man,
> These are no school-points; nice philosophy
> May tolerate unlikely arguments,
> But Heaven admits no jest: wits that presum'd
> On wit too much, by striving how to prove
> There was no God, with foolish grounds of art,
> Discover'd first the nearest way to hell,
> And fill'd the world with devilish atheism. (1.1.1–8)[1]

The link between incest and atheism had already been explored in such plays as Thomas Middleton's *The Atheist's Tragedy,* but Ford takes the matter into ever more disquieting areas.[2] Giovanni is characterized as a "young man," and his challenge to the established authority of the church reflects that of a new and more rationalistic age, an age of chronic disputation. In the fifteenth century the Italian philosopher Pomponazzi had asserted that he was content to believe as a Christian what he could not believe as a rationalist, and the friar demands that Giovanni do so also.[3] But the world had changed. The argument is taking place at a time of acute skepticism when, in the words of John Donne, "new Philosophy cals all in doubt" ("First Anniversary" 205).[4] The shock of discovering the New World, the divisive impact of the Reformation, and the disquieting implications of Galilean cosmology had eroded the very concept of "authority" to which the friar appeals. The incest topos supplied the perfect focus for an exploration of this situation.[5]

The preference that Aristotle displays in his *Poetics* for Sophocles's *Oedipus Tyrannus* helped to establish incest as a quintessentially tragic theme and, for English writers in particular, this emphasis was greatly reinforced by Henry VIII's attempt to divorce Catherine of Aragon on the grounds of forbidden relationship. In marrying his deceased brother's wife he had wed within the prohibited degrees as laid down in Leviticus (18:16), but the papacy had granted a dispensation, partly in accordance with the Law of Levirate, which stipulates that such a union *should* take place if the brother has died without issue—as Henry's had (Deut. 25:5–10). The contradiction appeared to be insoluble, and the inconclusiveness of the ensuing controversy, which preoccupied some of the foremost theologians and canon lawyers of the age, demonstrated the prevailing uncertainty in all such matters.[6] It is all the less surprising, therefore, that incest should supply the theme, or subtext, for plays as diverse as *Hamlet, King Lear, Pericles, A King and No King, The Fawn, The Duchess of Malfi,* and *The Unnatural Combat.* In all of them, albeit to varying degrees, it functions to unsettle established certainties and promote skeptical speculation.

According to received opinion incest was the worst species of sexual depravity. Bishop Arthur Lake explained why when he asserted that "incontinencie hath divers degrees,"

> *Fornication, Adulterie, Incest:* all communicate in *Incontinencie,* but so, that *Adulterie* is worse than *Fornication,* and *Incest* worse than *Adulterie. Fornication* violateth the good order that should be betweene single persons, through unruly Lusts; *Adulterie* addeth thereunto a confusion of Families, and taketh away the distinction of Heires, and Inheritance; but *Incest* moreover abolisheth the reverence which is ingraved by nature, to forbid that persons whom nature hath made so neere should one uncover the others shame.[7]

The circumstances of this declaration were themselves highly dramatic. Lake was delivering a sermon at St. Andrew's Church in Wells in the presence of a woman doing public penance for incest. Like Ford's friar he ends by assuring her of the value of such penitence (Lake 17). Lake preached a number of sermons on similar occasions and published them as a sequence in 1629 just four years prior to the first publication of *'Tis Pity* (1633). If the composition of the play may be dated to the years 1629–33 (as is commonly believed), the personal histories upon which the bishop comments may have helped to inspire it. Even if this is not the case, however, Lake's work remains important for the light it sheds upon contemporary attitudes.[8] As far as he is concerned, "God hath set downe certaine degrees both of Consanguinitie [blood relationship], and Affinitie [inlaw relationship], betweene which there may be no matches [. . .] because there is a reverence due unto these persons, and we passe the bownes of religious modestie if we match with them." "Had not God imprinted this reverence," he argues, "the necessarie cohabitation of Parents and Children, Brethern and Sisters would yeeld too much opportunitie, and be too strong an incentive unto this unlawfull coniunction" (21–22). The matter has direct relevance to Ford's methods of dramatization. It is often remarked as strange that Annabella seems not to recognize Giovanni on his first appearance in the play: "what blessed shape / Of some celestial creature now appears? / What man is he?" (1.2.126–28). But the apparent lack of recognition is precisely the emotional point. Annabella's ability to "see" Giovanni as an attractive "man," to separate the masculinity of his "figure" from the relationship of fraternity, suggests that the instinctive "reverence" credited with restraining incestuous desire is under severe threat. The phenomenon might well be familiar to a Renaissance audience since the common practice of fostering out male children often led to the estrangement of siblings and such estrangement has often been known to promote sexual attraction as, for example, in the case of adopted children reunited in later life.[9] The problem is even more aggravated in Giovanni's case since it is evident from his language that he loves Annabella *because* she is his sister rather than despite it:

> *Annabella:* You are my brother Giovanni.
> *Giovanni:* You
> My sister Annabella; I know this:
> And could afford you instance why to love
> So much the more for this. [. . .] (1.3.228–34)

There was no doubt in Bishop Lake's mind that those who engaged in the sort of "disputation" undertaken by Giovanni were primarily motivated by lust. The continued validity of the prohibitions, he claims, "is disputed [only] by those that favour licentiousnesse" (46). By observing the forbidden degrees recorded in Leviticus and codified in the Book of Common Prayer's "table of kindred and affinity," the faithful ensured the prevalence of rationality over passion, maintained a sense of "proprietie" in sexual relationships, and fulfilled God's plan for the production of "an holy seed" (20–21). Lake concedes, however, that not all of the relationships forbidden in Leviticus are unnatural in themselves. He distinguishes between actions that are intrinsically and extrinsically evil, those that are "prohibitum quia malum" [prohibited because evil] and "malum quia prohibitum" [evil because prohibited] (3). He holds it to be axiomatic that those in the direct line of descent (as, for example, between parents and children) are inherently unnatural, while those between siblings are evil because they contravene divine law. Technically speaking, the latter cannot be deemed unnatural because God has "dispensed" with the prohibition "of necessitie, when there were none but Adams children" (22).[10] Hence the point of the friar's concession to Giovanni that,

> Indeed, if we were sure there were no deity,
> Nor Heaven nor hell, then to be led alone
> By nature's light, as were philosophers
> Of elder times, might instance some defense.
> But 'tis not so; then, madman, thou wilt find
> That nature is in Heaven's positions blind. (2.5.29–34)

The sharp dichotomy hereby established between nature and grace demonstrates the considerable influence of Calvinism over Ford's play—despite its Roman Catholic setting.[11] Traditionally the "law of nature" had been regarded as morally normative. According to the celebrated lawyer Hugo Grotius, for example, "the law of nature is a dictate of right reason which points out that an act, according as it is or is not in conformity with rational and social nature, has in it a quality of moral baseness or moral necessity; and that, in consequence, such an act is either forbidden or enjoined by the author of nature, God."[12] Bishop Lake had no doubt that "the light of reason" led even Gentiles to "detest" incest as unnatural (23). The "nature" to which Giovanni appeals, however, leads reason in a very different direction:

> Say that we had one father, say one womb
> (Curse to my joys) gave both us life and birth;
> Are we not therefore each to other bound
> So much the more by nature, by the links
> Of blood, of reason—nay, if you will have't,
> Even of religion—to be ever one,
> One soul, one flesh, one love, one heart, one all? (1.1.28–34)[13]

The primeval origins of the "incest taboo" that Giovanni challenges here have been variously related to the attempted restraint of potentially disruptive "natural" desires (the equivalent of Lake's "lust"), to the expression of patterns of natural "aversion" or avoidance (akin to Lake's "reverence"), to the psychological pressures of evolution, to the biological need to diversify the gene pool, to the transition from "nature" to "culture," and to the emergence of complex systems of economic and sexual exchange.[14] The prohibitions themselves have been regarded both as products of nature and as constructions of society, as universal and localized, as obligatory and arbitrary. Although it is common to speak of the "universality" of the incest taboo, it is well to remember the diversity of conflicting codes and practices that this terminology embraces. Although all known societies recognize various degrees and categories of kinship (whether matrilineal, patrilineal, or both; whether by blood, affinity, fosterage, ritual, totem, etc.), the sexual consequences of such classification differ widely. The variability of the taboo arises from divergent interpretations of kinship.

Western practice developed under the influence of Hebraic, Roman, and Lombard law and has altered greatly over the centuries (Wolfram 21–51). During the late Middle Ages and the Renaissance the papacy frequently granted dispensations within the Levitical degrees but, as the Henrician divorce case demonstrated, the extent of its power in this area was greatly disputed. As Montaigne perceptively pointed out, the prohibition against incest—when regarded as a single phenomenon—is in no sense "universal." On the contrary there are countries "where not onely kindred and consanguinitie in the fourth degree, but in any furthest off, can by no meanes be tolerated in marriages" and others "where men may lawfully get their mothers with childe: where fathers may lie with their daughters, and with their sonnes." In effect, he concludes,

> The lawes of conscience, which we say to proceed from nature, rise and proceed of custome: every man holding in special regard, and inward veneration the opinions approved, and customes received about him [. . .] Whereupon it followeth, that whatsoever is beyond the compasse of custome, wee deeme likewise to bee beyond the compasse of reason; God knowes how for the most part, unreasonably.[15]

It is precisely the validity of "custome" that Giovanni challenges. "Shall a peevish sound," he asks, "a customary form, from man to man, / Of brother and of sister, be a bar / 'Twixt my perpetual happiness and me?" (1.1.24–27). For universalist theologians such as Thomas Aquinas the terms "brother" and "sister" were far more than merely "peevish sounds"; they signified real relationships of fraternity and sorority existing beyond the particular parties involved. For nominalists such as Duns Scotus, by contrast, "brother" and "sister" were no more than connotative terms. As Frederick Copleston explained, "a man is call'd a 'father' when he has generated a child; and there is no need to postulate the existence of a third entity, a relation of paternity, linking father to child [. . .] Relations are names or terms signifying absolutes; and a relation as such has no reality outside the mind."[16] It was the nominalist rather than the universalist position that informed seventeenth-century skepticism.[17]

In his discussion of the "idols of the mind" that formed part of the *Novum Organum* (1620), Lord Bacon observed how "men believe that their reason governs words; but it is also true that words react on the understanding [. . .] words being commonly fitted and applied according to the capacity of the vulgar, follow those lines of division which are most obvious to vulgar understanding. And whenever an understanding of greater acuteness or more diligent observation would alter those lines to suit the true divisions of nature, words stand in the way and resist the change."[18] "What's in a name?" Shakespeare's heroine asks in *Romeo and Juliet* (2.2.43), but Giovanni's question is far more unsettling because the "words" he challenges are central to the very concepts of kinship, inheritance, and familial association about which the whole of Christian society is constructed. Bishop Lake explained that "God would have a distinction kept between persons, he would not have the same person a Father and a Sonne, an Husband and a Brother [. . .] such perversenesse in matches can never be approved of reason, much lesse of God" (35). Because kinship terminology was held to define basic human relationships, to confound them was to risk the erosion of all moral value, a danger evident in Putana's assertion that "your brother's a man, I hope, and I say still, if a young wench feel the fit upon her, let her take anybody, father or brother, all is one." But for "the speech of the people" incest is "nothing" (2.1.51).[19] In Renaissance England the "common fame" of an incestuous relationship was sufficient to cause the suspected parties to be called before the ecclesiastical courts.

In effect, Ford has rewritten *Romeo and Juliet* for a more skeptical, uncertain age. Shakespeare's lovers are "star-crossed" because they are born into separate, feuding clans, because they are not "kin" in the wider sense of that term. His audience can feel assured that their sympathy for the lovers is deserved because the "ancient grudge" that impedes their union is senseless. By the end of the play they witness the two feuding factions belatedly united in grief. In forwarding the marriage of Romeo and Juliet, Friar Lawrence is seeking to promote one of the principle aims of matrimony, namely the promotion of social cohesion through the union of different families, the establishment of kinship between strangers. One of the traditional arguments against incest was its frustration of this social goal. According to St. Augustine, for example, exogamy (or marrying out) strengthened the fabric of society ("vinculum sociale") by creating new bonds of love or charity between ever greater numbers of people.[20] Drawing out the political implications of this attitude, Bishop Lake asserted that those who indulged in incest were "enemies to humane societie" because their sexual practices "abolisheth the greatest civill proprietie that is in a state; for wedlocke layeth the foundation of a state, and giveth the first beginning to societie" (21, 46). "If it might prevaile," he concluded, "Families must needs continue strangers each to the other, and they must confine their wealth and their love everie one to theire owne Howse" (35). The ideal, as far as Lake was concerned, was the extension of social "charitie" through matrimony. But the marriage between Annabella and Soranzo arranged by Ford's friar is not calculated to promote any form of social "charitie" and its ill-omened nature is made clear by the deadly masque, or rather antimasque, performed at the reception by Hippolyta.[21] The unhallowed "blessing" she pronounces upon the union exposes the friar's blessing for the travesty that it is.

In *Romeo and Juliet* the nurse's suggestion that Juliet enter a bigamous marriage with Count Paris is rejected with contempt (3.5.235–40). In *'Tis Pity,* however, the questionable union of Annabella and Soranzo is forwarded by the friar himself: "'tis thus agreed, / First, for your honor's safety, that you marry / The Lord Soranzo; next, to save your soul, / Leave off this life" (3.6.35–38). It is by no means clear that the dictates of "honour" and "salvation" are quite so easily reconciled as this suggests. When the subject of marriage is first broached by the friar, Giovanni replies "why, that's to damn her! that's to prove / Her greedy of variety of lust" (2.5.41–42)—and there is much force to the argument. What sort of "honour" does the friar promote? The Book of Common Prayer defines marriage as "an honourable estate [. . .] signifying unto us the mystical union that is betwixt Christ and the church." The union of Annabella, pregnant with her brother's child, and Soranzo, a known adulterer illicitly precontracted to Hippolyta, can hardly have the same signification. Given the level of deception being practiced, the marital "vow" that Annabella makes to Soranzo (3.6.54) is little better than the "vows" he had previously made to Hippolyta: "the vows I made [. . .] Were wicked and unlawful; 'twere more sin / To keep them than to break them" (2.2.84–87). Scene by scene the distinction between marriage, fornication, and adultery is being eroded.[22] It was one of the duties of an officiating priest to elicit the disclosure of any "impediment" that might render a marriage unlawful or inappropriate. By becoming a party to the deception practiced upon Soranzo the friar not only betrays his sacred function and violates the "holy rites perform'd" but also risks the incidence of future incest (4.1.1). Female chastity was valued in marital relationships because it guaranteed the purity of the blood-line and ensured the integrity of kinship. Without it, words such as "brother" and "sister" were worse than "peevish sounds," they were lies. "Now I must be the dad / To all that gallimaufry that's stuff'd / In thy corrupted bastard-bearing womb, / Say, must I?," asks Soranzo—and the answer implicit in the deceit that has been practiced upon him must be "yes." In seeking to oppose incest in the interests of kinship the friar has taken a course of action that threatens to render the concept of kinship meaningless.

Although the evolution of the laws relating to incest might seem to constitute a separate study from its psychology, Ford, as an avid reader of Burton's *Anatomy of Melancholy,* seems more interested in exploring their oddly symbiotic relationship.[23] One of the most ironic consequences of prohibition is the transformation of the prohibited object into an object of desire. In the present instance Giovanni's language leaves little doubt that his erotic feelings for Annabella are excited by their blood relationship: "nearness in birth or blood doth but persuade / A nearer nearness in affection" (1.3.235–36). The diction suggests the emotional claustrophobia that is developing between them at this point. In seeking to create a "nearer nearness" than blood relationship—something dangerously close to Hamlet's "little more than kin and less than kind" (1.2.65)—Giovanni risks confounding the relationship that already exists. The point was well understood by contemporary writers. "The love a man beareth to such a woman may be immoderate," observes Montaigne, "for, if the wedlocke, or husband-like affection be sound and perfect, as it ought to be, and also surcharged with that a man oweth to alliance and kindred, there is no doubt, but that surcrease may easily transport a husband beyond the bounds of reason" (*Essays* 1.211). These remarks accurately chart the course of Giovanni's growing obsession with Annabella. Even at the outset the immoderate nature of his feelings is signaled by the idolatrous language in which they are expressed. If he has turned to "atheism" to defend his passion, Giovanni has also created an alternative god:

> Must I not praise
> That beauty which, if fram's anew, the gods
> Would make a god of, if they had it there,
> And kneel to it, as I do kneel to them? (1.1.20–23)

That the lovers remain sympathetic despite such excesses is largely owing to the remarkable mutuality of their love and the repellent corruption of the surrounding community.[24] If they are, in Bishop Lake's terms, "enemies to humane societie" they are also its victims. Bruce Boehrer points to the obsession with secrecy that pervades the play and creates an impression of a society beyond all political or moral control, without a common code of behavior.[25] Of Annabella's three suitors one is an "idiot," one an adulterer, and one a murderer. The latter, Grimaldi, is shielded from civil justice by the Cardinal, the play's senior churchman who professes horror at incest but indulges homicide. It is from this state of affairs that the lovers attempt to insulate themselves in an alternative form of marriage sanctified by its own ceremonies and vows:

Annabella: On my knees,

[*She kneels.*]

Brother, even by our mother's dust, I charge you,
Do not betray me to your mirth or hate,
Love me or kill me, brother.

Giovanni: On my knees,

[*He kneels.*]

Sister, even by mother's dust, I charge you,
Do not betray me to your mirth or hate,
Love me or kill me, sister. (1.2.252–55)

In retrospect one can see that the seeds of destruction are present even within these rites of sexual passage. The familiar phrase "till death do us part" has been transformed into the potentially murderous "love me or kill me." Modern psychology has often associated incest with a death wish, but the association was keenly felt even in the Renaissance.[26] Lake explains that "the Civill Law calleth [incest] a *funestation* of a mans selfe, and indeed, the persons are dead in sinnes and trespasses that make such a coniunction" (37). All received values are inverted: in *The Broken Heart* (which Ford published along with *'Tis Pity* in 1633) a pathologically jealous husband accuses his wife of incest with her brother, whereas here a pathologically jealous brother accuses his sister of betraying him with her husband. When Annabella's murder finally occurs it is described in highly erotic terms as "a rape of life and beauty" (5.6.20). At the point at which mutuality of consent fails, Giovanni will "rape" Annabella by killing her in fulfilment of the vow he made to her in act 1. And it is easy to appreciate why. The vows initially taken by the lovers are equivalent in all respects but one: Annabella refers to "our mother," Giovanni to "my mother." Possessive pronouns dominate Giovanni's thinking: "my precious sister," "my Annabella's face," and even "my fate's my God." The role of the deceased mother is also significant. In one of the classical analogues upon which Ford may have drawn, the fifth story of Parthenius's *Erotica,* a young man named Leucippus falls in love with his sister "through the wrath of Aphrodite." He confides in his mother who, we are told, "summoned the maiden to her presence and united her to her brother and they consorted henceforward without fear of anybody"—at least until the sister's fiancée discovers the liaison. The active role of Leucippus's mother in promoting his incestuous desire appears to have informed the far more subtle, psychological influence of the absent mother over Ford's protagonists:

Florio: Where's the ring,
That which your mother in her will bequeath'd.
And charg'd you on her blessing not to give't
To any but your husband? Send back that.

Annabella: I have it not.

Florio: Ha! have it not? Where is't?

Annabella: My brother in the morning took it from me,
Said he would wear't today. (2.6.36–42)

Incest with a sibling can sometimes be interpreted as a sublimated form of incest with a parent and some suggestion of this may be implicit in such passages.[27] At the very least, it seems that the absent mother is a very powerful presence in Giovanni's psyche and that his feelings for his sister are deeply implicated in his memory of her. He is clearly in the power of forces he cannot control: "'tis not, I know, / My lust, but 'tis my fate that leads me on" (1.2.153–54). While at one level this might seem to be little more than an attempt to escape moral responsibility for his actions, at another it accurately articulates the tragic irony of Giovanni's situation. He frequently presents himself as an intellectual and emotional pioneer, a sort of Prometheus who will steal fire from heaven, and there is a distinctly Faustian tone to his language: "A life of pleasure is Elysium" (5.3.16). But the reality is quite different. Having tried all of the spiritual exercises suggested by the Friar he admits that "I am still the same" (1.2.152)—and it is a very different type of assertion from Webster's famous "I am Duchess of Malfi still." The Duchess asserts her self-identity, Giovanni confesses his self-entrapment. The truth of the matter is that he is nothing without the cooperation of Annabella, and it is often forgotten that hers is the titular role in the play:

> why, I hold fate,
> Clasp'd in my fist, and could command the course
> Of time's eternal motion, hadst thou been
> One thought more steady than an ebbing sea. (5.5.11–14)

Annabella's perception of the matter is quite different. What she asks "precious Time" to record is "a wretched, woeful woman's tragedy" and to some extent this is precisely what Ford has written (5.1.8).[28] The play's supreme object of desire is also its supreme object of denigration. It is not merely the Cardinal, but Soranzo, the friar, and ultimately Giovanni himself who judge Annabella to be a "whore." Yet the catastrophe is brought on not, as the Cardinal insinuates in the play's closing line, by Annabella's promiscuity but by her repentance, a repentance that, despite the intervention of the friar, is ultimately arrived at independently and declared in soliloquy: "my conscience now stands up against my lust" (5.1.9). In effect, Giovanni denies Annnabella the right to live in accordance with her conscience, preferring to attribute her change of heart to a sexual preference for Soranzo.[29] But Annabella is a far more complex character than her brother imagines. Though initially defiant when challenged by Soranzo, she is genuinely moved by his (feigned) professions of grief and attempts to kneel before him in a disturbing reprise of the scene in which she kneels to Giovanni (4.3.142). It is Giovanni's sexual attitudes, not Annabella's, that are degraded by the marriage to Soranzo:

> Busy opinion is an idle fool,
> That as a school-rod keeps a child in awe,
> Frights the unexperienc'd temper of the mind:
> So did it me; who, ere my precious sister
> Was married, thought all taste of love would die
> In such a contract; but I find no change
> Of pleasure in this formal law of sports. (5.3.1–7).[30]

Although he proceeds to speak of "the glory / Of two united hearts" (11–12), the prevailing sensuality of Giovanni's attitudes greatly undermine the high Platonic idealism in which the relationship is first couched—and may also cast a cynical light on the fashionable Neoplatonism of the Caroline court.[31] Annabella's pregnancy, described in almost scatological detail by Putana (3.3.10–16), emphasizes the physical nature of the incestuous relationship and draws even the friar into the ethos of intrigue and deception that dominates the play.[32] In the myth of Canace and Macareus, as recounted, for example, in Ovid's *Heroides* (XI), the birth of a child to the incestuous siblings prompts the murderous reaction of their father, Aeolus (McCabe 234). Here, however, it is Giovanni himself, rather than either Florio or Soranzo, who incongruously takes on the role of avenger. Contrary to all literary expectations, the incestuous avenge themselves upon the exogamous and feel justified in so doing. In declaring that "Revenge is mine"—a translation of the biblical "Vindicta mihi" (Rom. 12.19) and a clear echo of the first great revenge hero, Kyd's Hieronimo (*The Spanish Tragedy* 3.13.1)—Giovanni, who has previously compared himself to Jove, finally usurps the role of the god in whom he professes not to believe. The mingled echoes of Romeo *and* Othello throughout this speech attest to the confusion of his psyche. "What means this?" Annabella asks, and the answer is disconcerting: "to save thy fame, and kill thee in a kiss [. . .] honor doth love command" (5.5.83–86). It was a similar concern for "honor" that motivated the friar in arranging the match with Soranzo, and Giovanni's appeal to the same empty concept serves as an index to the corruption of his "love" and the "kiss" that first sealed it. Annabella's "Brother unkind, unkind" signals the first moment at which either of the lovers expressly deems their affection "unnatural." As the play opens an argumentative Giovanni is advised to "dispute no more" in the matter to hand, but he now finds himself inadequate to all such disputation:

When thou art dead
I'll give my reasons for't; for to dispute
With thy (even in thy death) most lovely beauty,
Would make me stagger to perform this act,
Which I most glory in. (5.5.87–91)

Such "reasons" are never supplied. Instead, the rhetoric of triumph (the ultimate expression of possessiveness) displaces that of disputation. If Annabella's love had made Giovanni a "god," her murder is necessary to offset its loss. Giovanni's emergence before the assembled company with his sister's heart on his dagger translates traditional erotic conceit into grim reality and reenacts Petrarch's "Triumph of Love": "The glory of my deed / Darken'd the midday sun, made noon as night" (5.6.22–23).[33] The oxymoron refutes itself and lends truth to Florio's assertion that "he's a frantic madmen" (5.6.43).

The contrast with the conclusion of *Romeo and Juliet* could scarcely be greater, but perhaps the most remarkable difference is the complete lack of moral or social affirmation. Not only is there no repentance on Giovanni's part (the only "grace" he desires is permission to enjoy Annabella's beauty in the next world), but there is no one present who is fit to grant absolution. The friar has abandoned his spiritual charge and the Cardinal, morally compromised by the Grimaldi incident, seems more intent on the seizure of property than the salvation of souls. Of the other survivors Vasques luxuriates in revenge for its own sake and Richardetto has become little more than a cipher. The sentencing of Putana to the stake does little to restore a sense of social balance.[34] Rather it seems that the incestuous lovers have become mere scapegoats for the collective guilt of a corrupt society, a society of which they were as much the products as the enemies:

> if ever after-times should hear
> Of our fast-knit affections, though perhaps
> The laws of conscience and of civil use
> May justly blame us, yet when they but know
> Our loves, that love will wipe away that rigor,
> Which would in other incests be abhorr'd. (5.3.68–73)

This is the last lucid contribution that Giovanni makes to the debate that opens the play, and it is noteworthy that what he presents is an argument from special circumstances rather than a defense of incest in general. Resolution of the great "dispute" is left to Ford's audience and thereafter to audiences down the centuries. The incest topos occurs, of course, in medieval literature, but its reinvention on the Renaissance stage, after "pagan" models and in an age of doubt and schism, lent it a renewed power to disturb and paved the way for such future treatments as, to name but a few, Shelley's *Cenci,* Miller's *A View from the Bridge,* and O'Neill's *A Moon for the Misbegotten*. Because it touches our most primary relationships, the incest taboo problematizes the very nature of "relationship" itself, the various ways in which we "make sense" of the world. It remains one of the most powerful themes of world drama and is likely to do so in perpetuity.

NOTES

1. All quotations are from N. A. Bawcutt, ed., *'Tis Pity She's a Whore* (Lincoln: U of Nebraska P, 1966).
2. See George T. Buckley, *Atheism in the English Renaissance* (Chicago: U of Chicago P, 1932) 13, 94–99.
3. See Herschel Baker, *The Wars of Truth: Studies in the Decay of Christian Humanism in the Earlier Seventeenth Century* (1952; Gloucester, MA: Peter Smith, 1969) 167.
4. See Mark Stavig, *John Ford and the Traditional Moral Order* (Madison: U of Wisconsin P, 1968) 20–35; John Donne, *The Complete English Poems,* ed. C. A. Patrides (London: Everyman, 1991) 335.
5. For a full account, see Richard A. McCabe, *Incest, Drama, and Nature's Law* (Cambridge: Cambridge UP, 1993).
6. See Henry Ansgar Kelly, *The Matrimonial Trials of Henry VIII* (Stanford: Stanford UP, 1976) 15–16, 47–48, 54–55, 89–131.
7. Arthur Lake, *Sermons with Some Religious Meditations* (London, 1629), part 2, 12.
8. For Ford's sources see Derek Roper, ed., *'Tis Pity She's a Whore* (London: Methuen, 1975) xxvi–xxxvii.
9. See Alan Macfarlane, *Marriage and Love in England: Modes of Reproduction 1300–1840* (Oxford: Blackwell, 1986) 82–88. For the problem of reuniting adopted children, see Karin C. Meiselman, *Incest: A Psychological Study of Cause and Effect with Treatment Recommendations* (San Francisco: Jossey-Bass, 1979) 269.
10. See R. S. White, *Natural Law in English Renaissance Literature* (Cambridge: Cambridge UP, 1996).
11. See Florence Ali, *Opposing Absolutes: Conviction and Convention in John Ford's Plays* (Salzburg: Institut für Englische Sprache und Literatur, Universität Salzburg, 1974) 21–25.

12. Qtd. in Heinrich A. Rommen, *The Natural Law,* trans. Thomas R. Hanley (1947; St. Louis: B. Herder, 1964) 71.
13. For Giovanni's mode of argumentation, see Albert R. Jonsen and Stephen Toulmin, *The Abuse of Casuistry: A History of Moral Reasoning* (Berkeley: U of California P, 1988) 125–27, 164–65.
14. The literature of incest is vast, but for a good overview of the conflicting theories and approaches, see James W. Twitchell, *Forbidden Partners: The Incest Taboo in Modern Culture* (New York: Columbia UP, 1987) 1–76; Sybil Wolfram, *In-Laws and Outlaws: Kinship and Marriage in England* (London: Croom Helm, 1987) 162–80.
15. Montaigne, *Essays,* trans. John Florio, ed. L. C. Harmer, 3 vols. (1910; London: Dent, 1965) 1.112, 114.
16. Frederick Copleston, *A History of Philosophy* (1953; Garden City: Image Books/Doubleday, 1963) 3.1.80–81.
17. See generally Richard H. Popkin, *The History of Scepticism from Erasmus to Descartes* (Berkeley: U of California P, 1960).
18. Bacon, *Works,* ed. J. Spedding, R. L. Ellis, and D. D. Heath. 14 vols. (London, 1857–74) 4.61.
19. See Ian Robson, *The Moral World of John Ford's Drama* (Salzburg: Institut für Anglistik und Amerikanistik, Universität Salzburg, 1983) 104–06.
20. *The City of God* (15.16), trans. George E. McCracken et al., Loeb Classical Library, 7 vols. (Cambridge: Harvard UP, 1957–72) 4.503–09.
21. Dorothy M. Farr, *John Ford and the Caroline Theatre* (London: Macmillan, 1979) 47–49.
22. Mary Beth Rose, *The Expense of Spirit: Love and Sexuality in English Renaissance Drama* (Ithaca: Cornell UP, 1988) 96.
23. See S. Blaine Ewing, *Burtonian Melancholy in the Plays of John Ford,* Princeton Studies in English 19 (Princeton: Princeton UP, 1940) passim.
24. See Alan Sinfield, *Literature in Protestant England 1560–1660* (London: Croom Helm, 1983) 90–91.
25. Bruce Thomas Boehrer, *Monarchy and Incest in Renaissance England: Literature, Culture, Kinship, and Kingship* (Philadelphia: U of Pennsylvania P, 1992) 121–27.
26. See Sigmund Freud, "The Theme of the Three Caskets," *The Standard Edition of the Complete Psychological Works of Sigmund Freud,* trans. James Strachey and Anna Freud, 24 vols. (London: Hogarth P and Institute of Psycho-analysis, 1953–73) 12.291–301.
27. See *Complete Psychological Works of Sigmund Freud* 16.335; Otto Rank, *The Incest Theme in Literature and Legend: Fundamentals of a Psychology of Literary Creation,* trans. Gregory C. Richter (1912; Baltimore: Johns Hopkins UP, 1992) 371, 462–65.
28. For a feminist approach, see Cheryl Black, "A Visible Oppression: Joanne Akalaitis's Staging of John Ford's *'Tis Pity She's a Whore,*" *Theatre Studies* 40 (1995): 5–16.
29. See John S. Wilks, *The Idea of Conscience in Renaissance Tragedy* (London: Routledge, 1990) 254–69.
30. See T. Orbison, *The Tragic Vision of John Ford* (Salzburg: Institut für Englische Sprache und Literatur, Universität Salzburg, 1974) 54–55.
31. For Caroline Neoplatonism, see Kevin Sharpe, *Criticism and Compliment: The Politics of Literature in the England of Charles I* (Cambridge: Cambridge UP, 1987) 22–25.
32. See Susan J. Wiseman, "*'Tis Pity She's a Whore:* Representing the Incestuous Body," *Renaissance Bodies: The Human Figure in English Culture c. 1540–1660,* ed. Lucy Gent and Nigel Llewellyn (London: Reaktion Books, 1990) 180–97.
33. For the heart imagery, see Ronald Huebert, *John Ford: Baroque English Dramatist* (Montreal: McGill-Queen's UP, 1977) 145–47.
34. This is assuming that the Cardinal refers to Putana (and not to Annabella's corpse) when he speaks of "this woman, chief in these effects" (5.6.133).

READING LIST

Boehrer, Bruce Thomas. *Monarchy and Incest in Renaissance England: Literature, Culture, Kinship, and Kingship*. Philadelphia: U of Pennsylvania P, 1992.

Huebert, Ronald. *John Ford: Baroque English Dramatist*. Montreal: McGill-Queen's UP, 1977.

Kelly, Henry Ansgar. *The Matrimonial Trials of Henry VIII*. Stanford: Stanford UP, 1976.

Lake, Arthur. *Sermons with Some Religious Meditations*. London, 1629. Part 2.

McCabe, Richard A. *Incest, Drama, and Nature's Law*. Cambridge: Cambridge UP, 1993.

Stavig, Mark. *John Ford and the Traditional Moral Order*. Madison: U of Wisconsin P, 1968.

Twitchell, James W. *Forbidden Partners: The Incest Taboo in Modern Culture*. New York: Columbia UP, 1987.

Wilks, John S. *The Idea of Conscience in Renaissance Tragedy*. London: Routledge, 1990.

Wolfram, Sybil. *In-Laws and Outlaws: Kinship and Marriage in England*. London: Croom Helm, 1987.

Biographical Notes on Authors

Paul D. Stegner

Francis Beaumont (1584–1616) matriculated to Broadgates Hall (Pembroke College), Oxford in 1597, though he left without taking a degree, and entered the Inner Temple, one of the Inns of Court, in 1600. While in London, he began writing poetry, beginning with verses prefaced to his brother John's *The Metamorphosis of Tobacco* (1602) and later the burlesque *Grammar Lecture* (c. 1600–05) and the erotic Ovidian epyllion *Salmacis and Hermaphroditus* (1602). He also became associated with Ben Jonson's circle at the Mermaid Tavern and affiliated with the Blackfriars Theatre as well as the King's Men. Around 1605, Beaumont began writing with his longtime collaborator John Fletcher, and in 1607 their names appeared together in the commendatory verses to the quarto edition of Ben Jonson's *Volpone, or The Fox*. Beaumont and Fletcher collaborated on at least six comedies and tragedies, such as *The Woman Hater* (c. 1605, published 1607), *The Knight of the Burning Pestle* (1607, published 1613), *Philaster or Love Lies a Bleeding* (c. 1609, published 1620), and *The Maid's Tragedy* (c. 1608–11, published 1619). In 1613, Beaumont married Ursula Isley, a Kentish heiress, and he retired from the stage shortly thereafter. On March 6, 1616, he died and was buried in the Poets' Corner Westminster Abbey. In 1647, a folio edition of thirty-five of Beaumont's and Fletcher's plays was published, and in 1679 a second folio was printed with an additional eighteen plays.

Elizabeth Cary, Lady Falkland (1585 or 1586–1639), was born in Oxfordshire and was the only child of Elizabeth Symondes and Lawrence Tanfield, a prosperous lawyer. Although she had no formal education, she taught herself French, Latin, Italian, and Hebrew. She would go on to translate Abraham Ortelius's *Le Miroir du Monde* as *The Mirror of World* and Cardinal Jacques Davy du Perron's *Réplique à la response du sérénissime roy a la Grand Bretagne* as *The Reply of the Most Illustrious Cardinal of Perron* (published in 1630 in Douay). In 1602, she married Sir Henry Cary, who became viscount of Falkland in 1620 and viceregent of Ireland in 1622. Between 1603 and about 1610, while Cary was separated from her husband, who was a soldier fighting and later captured in Holland, she composed several literary works, including a now lost verse life of Tamburlaine and *The Tragedy of Mariam* (published 1613). During her marriage, Cary gave birth to eleven children, nine of whom survived to adulthood, but her relationship with her husband was generally unhappy. Her longtime attraction and eventual conversion to Roman Catholicism (she publicly professed her new faith in 1626) only exacerbated their marital tensions. The couple separated in 1625 and she returned from Ireland to England, though they may have partially reconciled by his death in 1633. Toward the end of her life, she began translating some of the writings of the Flemish mystic Louis de Blois. In addition, Cary may be the author of two lives of Edward II (a folio version and a shorter octavo published in 1680). Four of Cary's daughters became nuns and entered a convent in Cambray, one of whom composed her biography, *The Lady Falkland: Her Life* (written c. 1643–50).

Thomas Dekker (1572?–1632) was a prolific author who composed several prose pamphlets, pageants, and plays. However, little information exists about his early life, family, or education. By January 1598, it is recorded that he was writing plays for Philip Henslowe and the Lord Admiral's Men. Throughout his life, he was imprisoned several times for debts, one occasion occurring on January 30, 1599, when he was imprisoned temporarily after a suit was brought against him by the Lord Chamberlain's Men. Typically, Dekker worked with collaborators: Henry Chettle; Michael Drayton; William Rowley; John Webster on *Westward Ho* (c. 1605, published 1607) and *Northward Ho* (c. 1606, published 1607); Thomas Middleton on *The Roaring Girl* (c. 1610, published 1611); and several other playwrights. He also composed unaided several plays, such as *The Shoemaker's Holiday* (1600), *Satiromastix* (1601), *The Whore of Babylon* (c. 1606), and *If It Be Not Good the Devil Is in It* (c. 1610). From *Old Fortunatus* and *The Shoemaker's Holiday,* he began publishing his plays in quarto editions. In addition, Dekker wrote several pamphlets, including *The Wonderful Year* (1603), a description of the plague in London; *Lanthorn and Candlelight* (1608); and the satire *The Gull's Hornbook* (1609). With Jonson, in 1603 Dekker wrote the pageant *The Magnificent Entertainment,* which marked King James's entrance into London that year. He continued writing through the 1620s and died sometime in 1632. He was buried on August 25, 1632, at St. James', Clerkenwell.

John Fletcher (1579–1625) was the son of Richard Fletcher, a minister who served as Bishop of London and later chaplain to Queen Elizabeth. He attended Bene't College (Corpus Christi), Cambridge, and possibly took his bachelor's degree in 1595 and his master's degree in 1598. However, he may have left the university before graduating for financial reasons after his father's death in 1596. No information exists about his activities between his father's death and 1607, when his name appeared along with that of Francis Beaumont, who would become his longtime collaborator, in the commendatory verses to the quarto edition of Ben Jonson's *Volpone, or The Fox*. Until Beaumont's retirement around 1613, they worked together on several comedies and tragedies, such as *The Woman Hater* (c. 1605, published 1607), *The Knight of the Burning Pestle* (1607, published 1613), *Philaster or Love Lies a Bleeding* (c. 1609, published 1620), and *The Maid's Tragedy* (c. 1608–11, published 1619). In addition, he almost certainly worked with Shakespeare on two plays: *Henry VIII or All Is True* and *Two Noble Kinsmen*. From the start of his career, Fletcher wrote for the King's Men and, after Shakespeare retired from the company around 1613, was their principal dramatist. He also wrote and published several works apparently without the aid of other playwrights, including *The Faithfull Shepheardesse* (c. 1608), *The Woman's Prize or The Tamer Tamed* (c. 1611), and *The Island Princess* (1621). At times throughout his career, Fletcher collaborated with many dramatists, including John Webster, Thomas Middleton, Ben Jonson, and John Ford, as well as with Philip Massinger on several plays. Although only nine of his plays were published during his lifetime, he contributed to or wrote unaided approximately forty-two plays. Fletcher apparently died of the plague in 1625 and was buried at St. Saviour's (now Southwark Cathedral) on August 29. In 1647, a folio edition of thirty-five of Beaumont and Fletcher's plays was published. A second folio followed in 1679 with an additional eighteen plays.

John Ford (1586–1639?), the son of a country gentleman, was baptized at Ilsington, Devonshire on April 17, 1586, and may have matriculated to Exeter College, Oxford, in 1601. In November 1602, he was admitted to the Middle Temple (part of the Inns of Court). Ford was expelled in 1605 for failing to pay his buttery or dining bill. In the period following his expulsion, Ford published *Fame's Memorial* (1606), a verse elegy on the death of the earl of Devonshire, and *Honor Triumphant: or the Peer's Challenge* (1606), a prose defense of courtly love. In 1608, Ford was reinstated to the Middle Temple and stayed in residence until at least 1617 and perhaps as late as 1638. Although Ford likely began composing plays around 1613, his early plays are lost and his first extant dramatic work is his collaboration with Thomas Dekker and William Rowley on *The Witch of Edmonton* (1621). From 1621 to about 1624, Ford collaborated with Dekker on several plays and the masque *The Sun's Darling* (1624). He also worked with Thomas Middleton and Rowley on *The Spanish Gypsy* (1623) and John Fletcher, John Webster, and Philip Massinger on *The Fair Maid of the Inn* (c. 1625). In the early 1630s, Ford wrote his most famous plays, including the tragedies *'Tis a Pity She's a Whore* (1633) and *The Broken Heart* (1633) and *The Chronicle Histories of Perkin Warbek* (1634). Ford published his last play, *The Lady's Trial,* in 1639 and nothing is known about his life after this date.

Ben Jonson (1572?–1637) attended Westminster School and studied under the classicist William Camden until he left school in 1588 or 1589. Instead of matriculating to university, he worked as bricklayer under his step-father and later served as soldier in the Low Countries (Netherlands). After his military service, he returned to England, probably in 1592, and married Anne Lewis on November 14, 1594. Over the next fourteen years, the couple had three sons and a daughter, but none of them survived. In 1597, Jonson was performing with the Lord Pembroke's Men at the Swan (a newly constructed theater) and was employed by Philip Henslowe as a playwright. In the same year, he was imprisoned for his involvement in the subversive satire *Isle of Dogs,* which he wrote with Thomas Nashe. On September 22, 1598, he was jailed for killing Gabriel Spencer, an actor in Henslowe's company, in a duel, but avoided execution by pleading benefit of clergy. While in prison, Jonson converted to Catholicism and remained a Catholic for twelve years before returning to the English Church. From the start of his dramatic career, Jonson composed a series of comedies, including *Every Man in His Humour* (c. 1598, published 1601), *Every Man out of His Humour* (1599, published 1600), *Cynthia's Revels* (1600, published 1601), *Poetaster* (1600, published 1601), *Eastward Ho* (1605, with George Chapman and John Marston), *Volpone, or The Fox* (1606, published 1607), *Epicoene, or the Silent Woman* (1609, published c. 1612), *The Alchemist* (1610, published 1612), and *The Devil Is an Ass* (1626, published 1631). He also wrote the Roman tragedy *Sejanus His Fall* (1603, published 1605). Throughout his career, Jonson also composed poetry, collected together and published in 1616. Beginning with *The Masque of Blackness,* which was written for Queen Anne and performed on January 6, 1605, he produced numerous masques, often with his collaborator and rival Inigo Jones. These include *The Masque of Beauty* (1608), *The Golden Age Restored* (1616), and *Pleasure Reconciled to Virtue* (1618). In 1616, Jonson published a folio edition of his plays, masques, and poems entitled *Works* and was awarded a pension by King James of one hundred marks. In 1628, Jonson was appointed City Chronologer of London and suffered a major stroke. Although he continued to write plays, such as *The*

New Inn, or the Light Heart (1629, published 1631) and *The Magnetic Lady, or Humours Reconciled* (1632, published 1640), his later works were largely unsuccessful in the commercial theater. Jonson was arranging his works for a planned second folio when he died on August 6, 1637, in Westminster; he is buried in Poets' Corner, Westminster Abby.

Thomas Kyd (1558–94) enrolled in the Merchant Taylors' School in London and afterward may have worked as a scrivener. Although little information is available about his life and works, he is author of the Senecan revenge play *The Spanish Tragedy* (c. 1587), and he translated Robert Garnier's Senecan drama *Cornélie* (1594). Several other dramatic works are attributed to Kyd, including the *Ur-Hamlet* (the lost predecessor to Shakespeare's *Hamlet* that was apparently written in the late 1580s) and the anonymously published *Soliman and Perseda* (1592). In the early 1590s, he may have shared a room with Christopher Marlowe, and both were in the employ of some "noble lord," probably Lord Strange or the earl of Sussex, from 1590 to 1593. In 1593, he was arrested and tortured on charges of atheism after some of his papers had been found by officers of the Star Chamber in their search of Marlowe's lodgings. Later that same year, Kyd died at the age of thirty-six and was buried on August 15 at St. Mary Colchurch.

Christopher Marlowe (1564–93) was educated at King's School, Canterbury, and matriculated on a Matthew Parker scholarship to Corpus Christi College, Cambridge, in 1580. He received his bachelor's degree in 1584, but was almost denied his master's degree because of suspicions arising from a visit to Rheims, France, a center for English Catholics. He seems to have been a government agent while still a student, and was awarded his master's in 1587 only after the intervention of the Privy Council. Following his graduation, he began his career in London as a playwright and a poet. Although his professional career only spanned six years, he obtained widespread popularity with the two parts of *Tamburlaine the Great* (published 1590, 1593), *Dido, Queen of Carthage* (published 1594), *The Jew of Malta* (published 1633), *Doctor Faustus* (published 1604, 1616), *Edward II* (published 1594), and *The Massacre at Paris* (publication date during the 1590s uncertain). He also composed the Ovidian minor epic *Hero and Leander* (published 1598) and translated Ovid's *Amores* as *Ovid's Elegies* (publication date during the 1590s or early 1600s uncertain) and the first book of Lucan's *Pharsalia* as *Lucan's First Book* (published 1600); he wrote two shorter poems: a pastoral lyric, "The Passionate Shepherd to His Love" (first published 1599) and "On the Death of Sir Roger Manwood," a Latin epitaph (found in manuscript). With the exception of the two parts of *Tamburlaine,* which were published anonymously, all of Marlowe's works were printed posthumously. In 1592, while in the Low Countries (Netherlands), he was accused of counterfeiting and was under house arrest on charges of sedition at the time of his death. On May 30, 1593, he was stabbed above the eye during a fight in Deptford, in an argument over the "reckoning," a bill for food and lodging, although modern theories speculate variously about political assassination.

Henry Medwall (1462?–1501?) was educated at Eton College and then matriculated to King's College, Cambridge, about 1480, where he was awarded his master's degree. Around 1487, he obtained a bachelor's of civil law in 1491. In 1490, he was ordained an acolyte and later received a benefice for Calais. In addition, Medwall received patronage from Cardinal John Morton, a papal legate, one of the most prominent members of the church in England in the 1490s, acting as his chaplain. Two of Medwall's household dramas, referred to as interludes in early printed editions, survive: *Nature* (published 1530), a morality play, and the earliest known secular play in England, *Fulgens and Lucrece* (published c. 1512–16), which might have been performed at Lambeth Palace during the Christmas season in 1497. Medwall is believed to have died about 1501.

Thomas Middleton (1580–1627) matriculated to Queen's College, Oxford, in 1598, but left without taking degree sometime between June 1600 and February 1601. While at Oxford, he published three books of verse: his inaugural work, *The Wisdom of Solomon Paraphrased* (1597); *Microcynicon: Six Snarling Satyres,* which was burned publicly in 1599; and *The Ghost of Lucrece* (1600), an Ovidian complaint. After moving to London, Middleton pursued the career of a professional writer and published several poems, almanacs, entertainments, and pamphlets, such as *The Penniless Parliament of Threadbare Poets* (1601) and *The Black Book* (1604). By May 1602, he was writing plays for the Admiral's Men as well as collaborating with several playwrights, including Thomas Dekker, Anthony Munday, John Webster, and perhaps Shakespeare. Around 1603, Middleton married Magdalen Marbecke, and their only son, Edward, was born between November 1603 and November 1604. Throughout his career, Middleton composed dramatic works in a variety of genres. His comedies include *A Trick to Catch the Old One* (c. 1605, published 1608), *The Roaring Girl* (c. 1610, published 1611), which he wrote with Dekker, and *A Chaste Maid in Cheapside* (c. 1613). He also wrote tragedies such as *Women Beware Women* (1621), *The Changeling* (1622), which he wrote with William Rowley, and perhaps *The Revenger's Tragedy* (1606, published 1607; attributed also to Cyril Tourneur). In 1613, he also produced a masque, *The Triumphs of Truth.* His final play, *A Game at Chess,* was a wildly popular anti-Catholic satire that was closed by the Privy Council in 1624 after nine days of sellout performances. From 1620 until his death in 1627, Middleton was employed as the city chronologer of London. Although many of his works were printed in quarto editions during his lifetime, his collected works were not published until 1840.

William Rowley (1585–1642?) was an actor in the Duke of York's company (which became the Prince's Men) and later the King's Men. Hardly anything is known about his life outside of his acting and writing career. He collaborated with Thomas Heywood on *Fortune by Land and Sea* (c. 1609), with Thomas Dekker and John Ford on *The Witch of Edmonton* (1621), and with Thomas Middleton on several plays, most notably *The Changeling* (1622). Rowley also acted in several of Middleton's plays, most famously perhaps as the Fat Bishop in *The Game at Chess* (1624). Although he likely wrote a number of plays unaided, only four are extant: three chronicle plays—*A Shoemaker, a Gentleman* (c. 1617–18), *All's Lost by Lust* (1619), and *A New Wonder, a Woman Never Vexed* (c. 1625)—and the city comedy, *A Match at Midnight* (c.1621). In addition, Rowley published a satiric pamphlet *A Search for Money; or, the Lamentable Complaint for the Loss of the Wandering Knight, Monsieur L'Argent* (1609).

William Shakespeare (1564–1616) was born in Stratford-on-Avon and most likely attended the grammar school at Stratford. In 1582 he married Anne Hathaway, who was eight years his senior, and the couple had three children: Susanna in 1583, and twins, Hamnet and Judith, in 1585. While Shakespeare's activities for the next seven years remain unclear, he was apparently an established actor and an emerging playwright in

London by 1592. He was a partner in the Lord Chamberlain's Men and, after King James ascended the throne in 1603, His Majesty's Servants or the King's Men. Shakespeare was probably composing plays as early as 1589, but his first published works were *Venus and Adonis* (1593) and *The Rape of Lucrece* (1594), two Ovidian epyllia dedicated to Henry Wriothesley, the earl of Southhampton. From *Titus Andronicus* in 1594, nineteen of Shakespeare's dramatic works were published in quarto editions. In the 1590s, Shakespeare mainly composed history plays—*Henry VI, Parts 1–3* (1589–91), *Richard III* (1592–93, published 1597), *Henry IV, Part 1* (1596–97, published 1598), *Henry IV, Part 2* (1598, published 1600), and *Henry V* (1599)—and comedies, such as *Comedy of Errors* (1592–94), *Midsummer Night's Dream* (1595–96, published 1600), *Much Ado About Nothing* (1598–99, published 1600), *As You Like It* (1599), and *Twelfth Night*. Although he wrote tragedies earlier in his career, such as *Titus Andronicus* and *Romeo and Juliet* (1595–96, published 1597 and 1599), Shakespeare produced a series of tragic dramas at the beginning of the seventeenth century: *Hamlet* (c. 1600–01, published 1603 and 1604), *Othello* (1604, published 1622), *King Lear* (1605, published 1608), *Macbeth* (1606), and *Antony and Cleopatra* (1606–07). During this period, he also wrote several problem comedies or dark comedies, including *Troilus and Cressida* (1601–02, published 1609), *All's Well That End's Well* (1602–03), and *Measure for Measure* (1604). In addition to his dramatic works, Shakespeare's sonnet sequence was published in 1609 as *Shake-speares Sonnets,* which included *A Lover's Complaint*. Toward the end of his career, he turned to the genre of romance and composed *Pericles* (1607–08, published 1609), *Cymbeline* (1609–10), *The Winter's Tale* (1610–11), and *The Tempest* (1611). His final plays, *Henry VIII* (1612–13) and *Two Noble Kinsmen* (1613), were almost certainly written in collaboration with John Fletcher. Shakespeare apparently retired to Stratford about 1612 or 1613 and died in 1616. In 1623, John Heminge and Henry Condell, two members of the King's Men, published a posthumous folio edition, *Mr. William Shakespeares Comedies, Histories, & Tragedies*.

John Webster (1580?–1625?) might have been educated at the Merchant Taylors' School and possibly matriculated to the Middle Temple, one of the Inns of Court, in 1598. Very little information exists about his early life. The earliest extant reference to his career as a writer occurs in Philip Henslowe's diary in 1602, where it is noted that he was collaborating on various plays with Anthony Munday, Thomas Dekker, Michael Drayton, Thomas Middleton, and others. In 1605 or 1606, Webster married Sara Penial and shortly thereafter a son, John, was born; the couple had four more children by 1617. In the first decade of the seventeenth century, he wrote the satires *Westward Ho* (1607) and *Northward Ho* (1607) with Dekker, as well as *The Malcontent* (1604) with John Marston. He also composed several well-known tragedies, including *The White Devil* (c. 1612), *The Duchess of Malfi* (c. 1614), and the posthumously published *Appius and Virginia*. In addition, he wrote a tragicomedy, *The Devil's Law Case* (1623); a funeral elegy on the death of Prince Henry, "A Monumental Column" (1613); a city pageant, *Monuments of Honour* (1624); and numerous collaborative plays. Webster is believed to have died after 1625, but no record of his death exists.

Notes on Contributors

Emily C. Bartels is associate professor of English at Rutgers University and associate director of the Bread Loaf School of English, Middlebury College. She is author of *Spectacles of Strangeness: Imperialism, Alienation, and Marlowe* (1993) and editor of *Critical Essays on Christopher Marlowe* (1997). She is currently completing a book entitled *Engaging "All the World": Moors in Early Modern English Drama.*

Mark Thornton Burnett is professor of Renaissance studies at Queen's University, Belfast. He is author of *Masters and Servants in English Renaissance Drama and Culture: Authority and Obedience* (1997) and *Constructing "Monsters" in Shakespearean Drama and Early Modern Culture* (2002).

Martin Butler is professor of English Renaissance drama at the University of Leeds. His most recent publication is an edition of *Cymbeline* (2005) for the New Cambridge Shakespeare series, and he is a general editor of the forthcoming *Cambridge Edition of the Works of Ben Jonson.*

Dympna Callaghan is Dean's Professor in the Humanities at Syracuse University. Her most recent recent books are *Shakespeare Without Women* (2000), *The Duchess of Malfi: Contemporary Critical Essays* (2000), *The Feminist Companion to Shakespeare* (2001), and *Romeo and Juliet: A Contextual Edition* (2003).

Patrick Cheney is professor of English and comparative literature at The Pennsylvania State University. Most recently, he is the author of *Shakespeare, National Poet-Playwright* (2004) and editor of *The Cambridge Companion to Christopher Marlowe* (2004).

Danielle Clarke is senior lecturer in the School of English at University College Dublin. Her publications include *The Politics of Early Modern Women's Writing* (2001), *Three Renaissance Women Poets: Isabella Whitney, Mary Sidney, Aemelia Lanyer* (2000), and essays and articles on Renaissance women's writing and sexuality. She is currently working on a book about language and gender in the early modern period.

Katherine Eggert is associate professor and chair of English at the University of Colorado, Boulder. She is the author of *Showing Like a Queen: Female Authority and Literary Experiment in Spenser, Shakespeare, and Milton* (2000).

John Gillies is professor in literature at The University of Essex. He is the author of *Shakespeare and the Geography of Difference* (1994), coeditor of *Performing Shakespeare in Japan* (2001) and *Playing the Globe: Genre and Geography in Early Modern Drama* (1998), and author of various essays on Shakespeare and early modern literature and drama.

Andrew Hadfield is professor of English at the University of Sussex and a fellow of the English Association. He is the author of several books, among the most recent of which are *Shakespeare, Spenser and the Matter of Britain* (2003) and *Shakespeare and Republicanism* (2005). He has also edited, with Raymond Gillespie, *The History of the Irish Book, Vol. III: The Irish Book in English, 1550–1800* (2005).

Constance Jordan is professor emerita of English at Claremont Graduate University. She is coeditor of the *Longman Anthology of British Literature* (2002). Her edition of *Hamlet* appeared in 2004.

Claire Jowitt is professor of English at Nottingham Trent University. Most recently, she is author of *Voyage Drama and Gender Politics 1589–1642* (2002) and coeditor of *The Arts of Seventeenth-Century Science* (2002).

Roslyn L. Knutson is professor of English at the University of Arkansas at Little Rock. In addition to numerous articles on theater history, she is the author of *Playing Companies and Commerce in Shakespeare's Time* (2001) and *The Repertory of Shakespeare's Company, 1594–1613* (1991).

Raphael Lyne is university lecturer in English at the University of Cambridge and a fellow of New Hall. He is the author of *Ovid's Changing Worlds: English Metamorphoses 1567–1632* (2001) and *Shakespeare's Late Work* (forthcoming, 2005).

R. W. Maslen is senior lecturer in the Department of English Literature at the University of Glasgow. He is the author of *Elizabethan Fictions: Espionage, Counter-espionage and the Duplicity of Fiction in Early Elizabethan Prose Narratives* (1997) and *Shakespeare and Comedy* (2005).

Richard A. McCabe is professor of English language and literature and fellow of Merton College Oxford. He is author of *Joseph Hall: A Study in Satire and Meditation* (1982), *The Pillars of Eternity: Time and Providence in "The Faerie Queene"* (1989), *Incest, Drama, and Nature's Law 1550–1700* (1993), and *Spenser's Monstrous Regiment: Elizabethan Ireland and the Poetics of Difference* (2004). He is also editor of *Edmund Spenser: The Shorter Poems* (1999).

Clare McManus is lecturer in English at Queen's University Belfast. She is the author of *Women on the Renaissance Stage: Anna of Denmark and Female Masquing in the Stuart Court (1590–1619)* (2002), editor of *Women and Culture at the Courts of the Stuart Queens* (2003), and coeditor of *Reconceiving the Renaissance: A Critical Reader* (2005).

Lucy Munro is lecturer in English at Keele University. She is the author of *Children of the Queen's Revels: A Jacobean Theatre Repertory* (2005) and editor of Edward Sharpham's *The Fleer* (2005).

Michael Neill is professor of English at the University of Auckland. He is the author of *Issues of Death* (1997) and *Putting History to the Question* (2000). He edited *Anthony and Cleopatra* (1994) for the Oxford Shakespeare and has recently completed *Othello* for the same series.

Karen Newman is university professor and professor of comparative literature and English at Brown University. Most recently she is the translator of Madeleine de Scudéry's *The Story of Sapho* (2003) and coeditor of *Time and the Literary* (2002). She is completing a book on the impact of urbanization on cultural production in early modern London and Paris.

Gail Kern Paster is director of the Folger Shakespeare Library in Washington, DC. Her books include *The Body Embarrassed: Drama and the Disciplines of Shame in Early Modern England* (1993) and *Humoring the Body: Emotions on the Shakespearean Stage* (2004). With Mary Floyd-Wilson and Katherine Rowe, she has edited *Reading the Early Modern Passions: Essays in the Cultural History of Emotions* (2004).

Kristen Poole is associate professor in the English Department at the University of Delaware. She is the author of *Radical Religion from Shakespeare to Milton: Figures of Nonconformity in Early Modern England* (2000).

Neil Rhodes is professor of English literature and cultural history at the University of St. Andrews. He is the author of *Shakespeare and the Origins of English* (2004) and editor (with Jennifer Richards and Joseph Marshall) of *James VI and I: Selected Writings* (2003).

Gregory M. Colón Semenza is assistant professor of English at the University of Connecticut. He is the author of two recent monographs: *Sport, Politics, and Literature in the English Renaissance* (2004) and *Graduate Study for the Twenty-first Century: How to Build a Career in the Humanities* (2005). He has just begun a book on pacifism in early modern England.

Paul D. Stegner is a doctoral candidate in English at The Pennsylvania State University. He is completing his dissertation, "Anxious Confessions: Penance, Desire, and Narrative in English Literature, 1385–1635." He also has a forthcoming article on *A Lover's Complaint* in a collection on Shakespeare's poem.

Alan Stewart is professor of English and comparative literature at Columbia University. He is the author of *Close Readers: Humanism and Sodomy in Early Modern England* (1997), *Hostage to Fortune: The Troubled Life of Francis Bacon* (with Lisa Jardine, 1998), *Philip Sidney: A Double Life* (2000), and *The Cradle King: A Life of James VI and I* (2003). With Heather Wolfe, he has curated the 2004 Folger Shakespeare Library exhibition, *Letterwriting in Renaissance England.*

Garrett A. Sullivan, Jr., is associate professor of English at The Pennsylvania State University. He is the author of *The Drama of Landscape: Land, Property and Social Relations on the Early Modern Stage* (1998) and *Memory and Forgetting in English Renaissance Drama: Shakespeare, Marlowe, Webster* (2005).

Daniel Vitkus is associate professor of English at Florida State University. He is the author of *Turning Turk: English Theater and the Multicultural Mediterranean, 1570–1620* (2004) and has edited *Three Turk Plays from Early Modern England* (2000) and *Piracy, Slavery, and Redemption: Barbary Captivity Narratives from Early Modern England* (2001).

Greg Walker is professor of early modern literature and culture at the University of Leicester. His most recent publications include *Medieval Drama: An Anthology* (2000), *The Private Life of Henry VIII* (2003), and *Writing Under Tyranny: English Literature and the Henrician Reformation* (2005).

Wendy Wall is professor of English at Northwestern University. She is the coeditor of *Renaissance Drama* as well as the author of *The Imprint of Gender: Authorship and Publication in the English Renaissance* (1993) and *Staging Domesticity: Household Work and English Identity in Early Modern Drama* (2002). She is currently at work on a book tentatively entitled *Reading Food: A Culinary History from Shakespeare to Martha Stewart.*

Luke Wilson is associate professor of English at the Ohio State University. He is the author of *Theaters of Intention: Drama and the Law in Early Modern England* (2000) and of articles on various aspects of early modern law and literature. He is currently writing a book on jurisdictional conflict and the origins of literary authority in the early modern period.

Index